Sir Henry Adolphus Byden Rattigan

The Law of Divorce Applicable to Christians in India

Sir Henry Adolphus Byden Rattigan

The Law of Divorce Applicable to Christians in India

ISBN/EAN: 9783744667050

Printed in Europe, USA, Canada, Australia, Japan

Cover: Foto ©Suzi / pixelio.de

More available books at **www.hansebooks.com**

THE
LAW OF DIVORCE

APPLICABLE TO

CHRISTIANS IN INDIA

(The Indian Divorce Act 1869)

BY

H. A. B. RATTIGAN, B.A. Oxon,

OF LINCOLN'S INN, BARRISTER-AT-LAW,
AND AN ADVOCATE OF THE HIGH COURT OF THE NORTH-WEST PROVINCES,
AND OF THE CHIEF COURT OF THE PUNJAB.

"It is the foremost duty of this Court, in dispensing the remedy of divorce, to uphold the institution of marriage. The possibility of freedom begets the desire to be set free, and the great evil of a marriage dissolved, that it loosens the bonds of so many others. The powers of this Court will be turned to good account if, while meting out justice to the parties, such order should be taken in the matter as to stay and quench this desire and repress this evil" (Sir J. P. WILDE, *Sidney v. Sidney*, 34 L. J., P. & M. 122).

WILDY & SONS,
LINCOLN'S INN ARCHWAY, LONDON,
Law Publishers.

THE "PIONEER" PRESS.
ALLAHABAD.

1897.

TO

My FATHER

THIS SMALL WORK, IN THE PREPARATION OF WHICH HE
HAS TAKEN SUCH KINDLY INTEREST, IS

𝔇𝔢𝔡𝔦𝔠𝔞𝔱𝔢𝔡

AS A SLIGHT TOKEN OF AFFECTIONATE

ADMIRATION AND RESPECT.

PREFACE.

SINCE the publication, in 1870, of Mr. Macrae's work on the Indian Divorce Act, 1869, no treatise dealing with that subject has appeared in the Indian press, although during this period a number of important decisions, both of the English Courts and the Indian High Courts, have elucidated difficult questions of Divorce Law applicable to Christians. In the present edition I have endeavoured to incorporate all these, as well as such of the earlier rulings of the Courts as have appeared to me to lay down general principles, or to be likely to prove useful to the legal practitioner. The principles of the Indian Act being to a large extent identical with those of the English Statutes, I have also considered it advisable to give under each section of the Act the corresponding sections of the Matrimonial

Acts of England. In this respect the present edition will (I trust) prove of some use not merely to the legal practitioner in India, but also, though necessarily to a less extent, to the legal profession in England, and not perhaps without value to the student of comparative legislation.

H. A. B. R.

October, 1897.

CONTENTS.

INDIAN DIVORCE ACT,   PAGE
    Act No. IV. of 1869   - - - - 1—322

APPENDIX—
- (A) Marriage   - - - - - 323—329
- (B) Identity of Parties   - - - 330, 331
- (C) Proof of Adultery   - - - - 332—336
- (D) *Res Judicature*—Estoppel - - - 337—341
- (E) Notes on Pleadings and Practice   - - 342—361
- (F) Costs   - - - - - 362—383
- (G) Rules and Regulations of the English Court of Divorce   - - - - - 384—412
-     Forms - - - - - 413—426

INDEX   - - - - - - - 427—460

TABLE OF CASES.

A.

A. v. A. 129, 297
— v. B. 129
— f.c. M. v. M. 250
Abbott v. Abbott 33, 281, 354
Adams v. Adams 378, 381
Adley v. Adley 79, 86, 88, 333
Administrator-General of Madras v. Ananduchari 5
Afford v. Afford 369
Agar-Ellis, In re 270, 272
Aldridge, Ex parte 58, 66
——— v. Aldridge 130, 357
Alexander v. Alexander .. 57, 86, 176, 299
——— v. Jones 21
Alexandre v. Alexandre 120
Ali Kadar v. Gobind Dass .. 345, 355, 358
Allen v. Allen 74, 103, 205, 273, 279, 296, 333, 334, 355, 360, 364, 370, 374, 375
Allumuddy v. Braham 159
Ambler v. Ambler 343
Amin Chund v. Collector of Sholapur 287, 290
Anderson v. Anderson 212
Andrews v. Ross 139
Anichini v. Anichini 95
Anon 15, 39, 132, 191
Anquez v. Anquez 180
Ansdall v. Ansdall 265
Anthony v. Anthony 51, 269
Appleyard v. Appleyard 347
Armitage v. Armitage 294
Ash v. Ash 373
Asirun Bibi v. Shariss Mundle 287
Astley v. Astley 334
Astrope v. Astrope 64
Atchley v. Sprigg 335
Att.-Gen. v. Parnther 141
Aubourg v. Aubourg 46, 51
Augustin v. Augustin 45
Austin v. Austin 345
Avila v. Avila 225

B.

B. v. B. 135
— v. C. 132, 295
— v. L. 132
Babbage v. Babbage 294
Bacon v. Bacon .. 86, 88, 245, 246, 359, 375
Badcock v. Badcock 378
Badham v. Badham 102
Bagot v. Bagot 72
Bai Tanku v. Shiva Toya.......... 91
Baily v. Baily 368
Baker v. Baker 284, 379
Bancroft v. Bancroft 153, 299
Banister v. Banister 299, 350
Baptist v. Baptist 46
Barber v. Barber 71
Barlee v. Barlee 177
Barnes v. Barnes 87, 94, 106, 117, 273, 278
Baroda Churn v. Govind Proshad .. 31
Bartlett v. Bartlett.............. 352
——— f.c. Rice v. Rice.......... 146
Basing v. Basing................. 63
Bates v. Bates 367
Baylis v. Baylis 105
Beanlands v. Beanlands 74, 89, 107
Beardman v. Beardman 48
Beauclerk v. Beauclerk 47, 101, 183
Beavan v. Beavan ..38, 63, 66, 211, 366
Beeby v. Beeby 79
Bell v. Bell 69, 74, 93, 107, 192
Beni Ram v. Ram Lall 286
Bennett v. Bennett 201

TABLE OF CASES.

Bent v. Bent 195, 219, 235, 239, 277, 280
Benyon v. Benyon....248, 252, 253, 256, 259, 264
Bernstein v. Bernstein....77, 78, 82, 83, 189, 190, 309, 378, 381
Besant v. Wood 156, 181, 357
Best v. Best 155
Bethell, *In re* 4
Bethune v. Bethune 47
Bikker v. Bikker.................. 193
Billingay v. Billingay..........196, 197
Binney v. Binney 100
Birch v. Birch 47, 51, 228, 237
Bird v. Bird 201, 363
Bishop v. Bishop..........237, 238, 252
Blackhall v. Blackhall 380, 381, 382
Blackman v. Brider 139
Blackmore v. Mills................ 201
Bland v. Bland 54, 338
Blandford v. Blandford......23, 80, 270
Boardman v. Boardman........296, 361
Boddington v. Boddington 378
Boddy v. Boddy 114, 115, 336
Bombay, &c. Navigation Co. v. S.S. Zuari..................... 31
Bonaparte v. Bonaparte 24
Bond v. Taylor 306
Bonsor v. Bonsor..............211, 239
Boreham v. Boreham 92, 102, 153
Borham v. Borham 345, 351
Bostock v. Bostock 53, 80
Bosvile v. Att.-Gen.............. 335
——— v. Bosvile..............257, 258
Boucher v. Boucher..............83, 96
Boulting v. Boulting 74, 77, 99
Boulton v. Boulton 122
Bowen v. Bowen 116, 383
Boynton v. Boynton 248, 259, 276
Bradley v. Bradley 215, 216
Bradshaw v. Bradshaw............ 59
Bray v. Bray...................43, 44
Bremner v. Bremner..206, 378, 379, 381
Briggs v. Briggs.................6, 15
Brinckley v. Att.-Gen............. 4
Broadhead v. Broadhead 363, 364
Brocas v. Brocas 38, 113
Bromfield v. Bromfield..........92, 151
Brook v. Brook ..17, 135, 137, 138, 298, 323, 346

Brown v. Brown.. 48, 75, 104, 105, 129, 157, 211, 294, 357
Bruce's Case 14
Buckmaster v. Buckmaster 62
Bullock v. Bullock................. 265
Burroughs v. Burroughs ..84, 178, 184, 185, 272, 359, 369
Burslem v. Burslem 295
Burt v. Burt..................... 24
Burton v. Sturgeon 247
Butler v. Butler ..86, 89, 120, 338, 370, 371, 376

C.

Callwell v. Callwell............194, 197
Campbell v. Campbell 299
Capstick v. Capstick 211
Carew v. Carew 117
Cargill v. Cargill 63, 169
Carryer v. Carryer................ 70
Carstairs v. Carstairs..245, 374, 377, 382
Carter v. Carter 213, 219
Cartlidge v. Cartlidge..272, 348, 350, 352
Castleden v. Castleden 134
Catterall v. Sweetman 326
Cavendish v. Cavendish 256
Chaldecott v. Chaldecott 370
Chalmers v. Chalmers 252
Chambers v. Chambers 269
Charles v. Charles 214, 215
Charter v. Charter................ 348
Chetwynd v. Chetwynd ..254, 260, 270, 278, 369
Chichester f.c. Mure v. Mure ..142, 143, 306
Chinta Monee v. Pearee Monee 30
Christian v. Christian 87
Chudley v. Chudley 60
Churchward v. Churchward 87
Clark v. Clark....156, 181, 196, 212, 357
Clarke v. Clarke 94, 145, 366
Clements v. Clements..........116, 117
Clifford v. Clifford 237, 252
Clout v. Clout 277, 280
Coates v. Coates 126, 189
Cock v. Cock 62, 156, 181
Cocksedge v. Cocksedge 180
Codrington v. Codrington......274, 378

TABLE OF CASES.

	PAGE
Coleman v. Coleman	97
Collett v. Collett	48, 335
Collins v. Collins	41, 81, 98
Comyn v. Comyn	193
Conradi v. Conradi	98, 338, 371, 379, 381
Constable v. Constable	211
Cooke v. Cooke	78, 224, 277, 370, 374
—— v. Fuller	172
Coombs v. Coombs	211
Cooper v. Cooper	82, 135, 367
—— v. Crane	146
—— v. Wane	84, 91
Corbett v. Corbett	220, 229
Cornish v. Cornish	69
Corrance v. Corrance	250, 265
Cotton v. Cotton	348
Coulthurst v. Coulthurst	66
Cousen v. Cousen	47, 51
Coward, In re	169
Cowing v. Cowing	193
Cox v. Cox	88, 105, 348, 357
Crabb v. Crabb	62, 157
Craignish, In re	13
Crampton v. Crampton	204, 207, 208
Crawford v. Crawford	117, 118, 382
Crisp v. Crisp	265
Crump v. Crump	201
Cubley v. Cubley	272
Culley v. Culley	82, 121, 126
Cunnington v. Cunnington	104, 106
Cuno v. Cuno	131, 135
Curling v. Curling	70, 108
Curtis v. Curtis	45, 48, 50, 53, 78, 80, 82, 353

D.

	PAGE
D. v. A.	130
— v. M.	127
Dagg v. Dagg	62, 65, 103, 181
D'Aguilar v. D'Aguilar	48, 79
Dale v. Dale	194
Dallas v. Dallas	65
D'Alton v. D'Alton	275, 276, 278
Darbishire v. Darbishire	192, 193
D'Arcy v. D'Arcy	53
Daryai Bibi v. Badri Prasad	31
Das Merces v. Cones	137

	PAGE
Davidson v. Davidson	333
Davies v. Davies	66, 238, 258
Davis, In re	161
—— v. Davis	272, 278
Dawes v. Crayke	160
Deane v. Deane	283
De Bretton v. De Bretton	113, 293
De Lossy v. De Lossy	237
Dempster v. Dempster	54, 78
De Niceville v. De Niceville	347
Dent v. Dent	80, 81, 92, 151, 351
Dera Kabai v. Jefferson	286
Dera Sayagam v. Naiyagam	99, 101
Dering v. Dering	104
Desmarest v. Desmarest	353
Dharm Singh v. Dewa Singh	31
Dickens v. Dickens	368, 374, 375
Dickenson v. Dickenson	56
Dixon v. Dixon	367, 369
Dolphin v. Robins	15
D'Oyley v. D'Oyley	204
Drevon v. Drevon	14
Drew v. Drew	56, 64
Drinkwater v. Drinkwater	70
Drummond v. Drummond	86, 94, 121, 153
Drysdale v. Drysdale	110
Dunn v. Dunn	203, 204
Duplany v. Duplany	109, 151, 154, 351, 356
Durand v. Durand	22, 27
Durant v. Durant	44, 45, 79
Durham v. Durham	140
Dysart v. Dysart	48

E.

	PAGE
Edwards v. Edwards	63, 102, 234, 239
Eldred v. Eldred	257
Ellam v. Ellam	24, 295
Elliott, In re	172
Ellis v. Ellis	79, 112, 201, 202, 203
Ellyatt v. Ellyatt	369
Elsley v. Elsley	348
Emery v. Emery	154
Empress v. Arshed Ali	328
—— v. Kallu	328
—— v. Pitamber Singh	328
—— v. Subbarayan	328

TABLE OF CASES.

	PAGE
Evans v. Evans	41, 72, 196, 197, 281, 370, 376, 379
Evered v. Evered	257
Ewens v. Tyterleigh	134
Ewin, In re	149
Ewing v. Wheatley	147

F.

	PAGE
F. v. D.	132, 133
— v. P.	133
Farmer v. Farmer	59, 61
Farrington v. Farrington	262
Faulkes v. Faulkes	66, 100
Fendall v. Goldsmid	123, 306
Fenton v. Livingstone	138, 323
Field v. Field	175, 374
Finlay v. Finlay	376
Finney v. Finney	37, 338
Firebrace v. Firebrace	8
Fisher v. Fisher	219, 225, 296
Fisk v. Fisk	238
Fitzgerald v. Chapman	247
——— v. Fitzgerald	39, 59, 60, 114, 345
Fletcher v. Fletcher	210
Flower v. Flower	82, 115, 120, 156, 371, 372
Flowers v. Flowers	180
Foden v. Foden	201, 202
Ford v. Ford	295
Forman v. Forman	343
Forster v. Forster	32, 94, 118, 153, 185, 195, 196, 198, 209, 381
Forsyth v. Forsyth	53, 265
Forth v. Forth	52, 163, 218
Foster v. Foster	344
Fowle v. Fowle	33, 55, 60, 219, 375
Fowler v. Fowler	115
Franks v. Franks	238
Frebout v. Frebout	368
Freegard v. Freegard	96, 185
Freke v. Lord Carberry	149
French-Brewster v. French-Brewster	63, 357
Frith v. Frith	331
Fry v. Fry	284
Fryer, In re	194
Furlonger v. Furlonger	51
Furness v. Furness	81

G.

	PAGE
G. v. G.	93, 130
— v. M.	131, 132
Gale v. Gale	44
Gandy v. Gandy	236, 237, 252
Garcia v. Garcia	61
Garstin v. Garstin	32
Gasper v. Gonsalvez	129, 187, 325
Gaston v. Gaston	355, 356
Gatehouse v. Gatehouse	60
Gaynor v. Gaynor	71, 210
George v. George	206
Gethin v. Gethin	86, 88
Gibbs v. Harding	180
Gibson v. Gibson	57
Gilham's Case	335
Gill v. Gill	69, 213, 265, 379
Gillis v. Gillis	14
Gilpin v. Gilpin	74
Ginger v. Ginger	336
Gipps v. Gipps	73, 74, 75, 78
Gladstone v. Gladstone	117, 118, 256, 260, 370, 371, 376
Glennie v. Glennie	74, 296
Goad v. Goad	275, 276, 277
Gobardhan Das v. Jasadamoni Das	6
Goldney v. Goldney	346
Goldsmith v. Goldsmith	376
Gomez v. Gomez	115
Gooch v. Gooch	83, 95, 153, 157, 181
Goode v. Goode	83, 95, 379, 381
Gooden v. Gooden	217
Goodheim v. Goodheim	206
Goodrich v. Goodrich	272, 274
Gopal Chunder v. Kurnodar	21
Gordon v. Gordon	102, 109, 205, 334, 358, 363
Gower v. Gower	74, 107
Grafton v. Grafton	209
Grant v. Grant	38, 113, 249, 333
Graves v. Graves	57
Gray v. Gray	86, 121, 350
Green v. Green	54, 184, 185, 350
Greenwood v. Greenwood	238
Grieve v. Grieve	117
Grossi v. Grossi	92
Grosvenor v. Grosvenor	94, 95
Groves v. Groves	105
Gurbakhsh Singh v. Shama Singh	24

TABLE OF CASES. xiii

Gurdyal Singh v. Raja of Faridkot.. 7
Gurney v. Gurney 335
Gyte v. Gyte 195

H.

H. v. P. 130, 133
Haigh v. Haigh 209, 223
Hakewell v. Hakewell 173, 206
Halfen v. Boddington 114
Hall, Ex parte 168, 171
—— v. Hall 37, 50, 79, 339, 371
Hamilton v. Hamilton 266
Hanbury v. Hanbury.........39, 50, 231
Hancock v. Peatty 140, 141, 284
Handley v. Handley 275, 280
Harding v. Harding 118, 368
Harford v. Morris 144
Har Nandan Sahai v. Behari Singh.. 31
Har Narain v. Bhagwant Kaur 32
Harris v. Harris..57, 63, 87, 209, 330, 331
Harrison v. Harrison 100, 133, 221, 222, 229
Harrod v. Harrod 141, 147
Harvie v. Farnie 8, 9, 15
Haswell v. Haswell 66, 93, 103, 107
Haviland v. Haviland 56, 211
Hawkins, In re 213, 223
—— —— v. Hawkins.............. 105
Hay v. Gordon................303, 304
Hayward v. Hayward 183, 206, 208
Heal v. Heal 373
Hechler v. Hechler............... 380
Henty v. Henty 58, 61
Hepworth v. Hepworth ..274, 299, 366, 367, 368, 375
Heyes v. Heyes 53, 65
Hick v. Hick 94
Hicks v. Hicks 115, 211
Higgs v. Higgs 344
Hill v. Cooper 160, 169
—— v. Hill 209, 357
Hilliard v. Mitchell..........135, 138
Hirabai v. Dhunjibhoy 204
Hobson, Ex parte 295
Hodges v. Hodges 78
Holloway v. Holloway............ 65
Holmes v. Holmes 177

Holmes v. Simmons 325
Holt v. Holt 203, 205
Hood v. Hood.................... 368
Hooper v. Hooper..............37, 155
Hope v. Hope 184, 185, 258
Horne v. Horne 23, 248, 249, 259, 269, 349
Hough v. Hough 373
Houliston v. Smyth 154
Howarth v. Howarth 82, 117, 119
Howe v. Howe 378
Hudson v. Hudson................. 49
Hughes v. Hughes................ 358
Hulse v. Hulse....82, 119, 121, 331, 380
Humphrey f.c., Williams v. Williams 128, 138
Hunt v. Hunt ...86, 156, 180, 195, 280
Hunter v. Hunter 70, 72, 115
Hutchinson v. Hutchinson 98
Hyde v. Hyde 5, 213, 219, 224, 276, 277, 279, 374

I.

Insole, In re 160
Irwin v. Irwin................... 379
Izard v. Izard.................... 193

J.

Jack v. Jack 9
Jackman v. Jackman 85, 360
Jadub Ram v. Ram Luchun 354
Jaffers v. Jaffers................. 71
Jardine v. Jardine 240
Jeffreys v. Jeffreys 103, 154
Jennings v. Jennings 212
Jessop v. Jessop 86, 118
Jewall v. Jewall 345
Jinkings v. Jinkings............67, 334
Johnson v. Johnson 259
—— v. Lander................ 160
Jolly v. Jolly 348
Jones v. Jones 69, 203, 371, 375
Jonnagadhu v. Thatiparthi 284
Jopp v. Wood 14
Joseph v. Joseph................. 96
Jowala v. Pirhbu 290

TABLE OF CASES.

	PAGE
Judkins v. Judkins	236
Jump v. Jump	252, 257

K.

Kanhya Lal v. Radha Charan	124, 339
Kanwal Ram v. Bhawani Ram	284
Kastolino v. Rastonji	283
Kaye v. Kaye	369
Keane v. Keane	366
Keats v. Keats	78, 79, 195, 219, 233, 239, 336, 366
Keech v. Keech	56, 63
Kelly v. Kelly	47, 202, 205, 218, 233, 277, 280, 297, 302, 333, 345, 363, 374
Kennedy v. Kennedy	67
Kenrick v. Kenrick	48
—— v. Wood	286
Kent v. Burgess	323
Keshar Lal v. Bai Parvati	177
Keyse v. Keyse	191
King v. Foxwell	14
—— v. King	112, 116, 117, 303, 344, 350, 353
Kingsley, In re	172
Knight v. Knight	46
Knox v. Bushell	163
Koolur Khansama v. Jan Khansama	176
Kumal Chunder v. Surbessur	286
Kyte v. Kyte	97, 120, 126, 189, 302, 329

L.

Ladmore v. Ladmore	241
Lambe v. Smythe	21
Lander v. Lander	106, 234, 240
Langworthy v. Langworthy	251, 280
Lapington v. Lapington	54, 158, 300, 351
Latham v. Latham	112, 113, 197, 201
Lautour v. Lautour	94
Lawrence v. Lawrence	58, 61, 249
Leader v. Leader	71
Learmouth v. Learmouth	377, 378
Ledlie v. Ledlie	269, 274, 329, 338, 349
Leeds v. Leeds	250
Leete v. Leete	346

	PAGE
Legard v. Bull	31
Lelim Tewarree v. Govindeer Gosain	21
Le Marchant v. Le Marchant	334
Le Mesurier v. Le Mesurier	7, 8, 9, 10
Lempriere v. Lempriere	153, 154, 356
Le Sueur v. Le Sueur	15
Lewis v. Hayward	131
—— v. Lewis	82, 114, 119, 121, 352
Lidstone v. Lidstone	344
Ling v. Ling	249, 278, 294
Linton v. Linton	223
Lisbey v. Lisbey	93, 98, 116, 338
Lister v. Lister	219, 229, 239
Lloyd v. Lloyd	86, 88
Lodge v. Lodge	55, 63, 357
Lolley's Case	8, 12
Long v. Long	194, 378
Lopez v. Lopez	25, 110, 128, 135, 137, 184, 326
Lord v. Colvin	13, 14
Louis v. Louis	224
Lovedon v. Lovedon	333
Lovering v. Lovering	78
Lutwyche v. Lutwyche	350
Lyne v. Lyne	194, 361

M.

M. f. c. C. v. C.	134, 374
— v. D.	135
— v. M.	356
Macarthur v. Macarthur	175
Macartney v. Macartney	295
Macdonald v. Macdonald	58, 65
MacKenzie v. MacKenzie	180
Macleod v. Macleod	276
Madan v. Madan	205, 206
Madge v. Adams	171
Maggs v. Maggs	99
Mahomed Shaffi v. Lal Din	22
Mallinson v. Mallinson	23, 270
Manning v. Manning	51, 52
Manton v. Manton	377
March v. March	24, 40, 254, 261, 272, 294, 295, 336, 339
Margetson v. Margetson	241
Marriott f. c. Burgess v. Burgess	134
Marris v. Marris	73, 74

TABLE OF CASES.

	PAGE
Marsh v. Marsh	50, 248, 261, 276, 277, 278
Marshall v. Hamilton	131
———— v. Marshall	156, 176, 181, 182, 357
Martin v. Lawrence	279
———— v. Martin	51, 276, 277, 345
Mason v. Mason	100, 175, 357
———— v. Mitchell	169
Masters v. Masters	118
Matthew v. Matthew	168
Matthews v. Matthews	100, 154
Maudslay v. Maudslay	253, 258, 277
Mawford v. Mawford	345, 356
Mayhew v. Mayhew	281, 363, 365
McCarthy v. De Caix	8
McCord v. McCord	83, 95
McCullock v. McCullock	334
McKechnie v. McKechnie	295
McKeever v. McKeever	45, 53
McLord v. McLord. *See* McCord v. McCord.	
McMullen v. McMullen	14
Meara v. Meara	56, 151, 182
Medley v. Medley	219, 228, 239, 240
Mela Ram v. Thanoo Ram	176
Meredyth v. Meredyth	263
Merryweather v. Jones	180
Mette v. Mette	17, 138
Meyern v. Meyern	199
Michell v. Michell	243, 244, 246
Midgeley *f. c.* Wood v. Wood	87
Midland Rail. Co. v. Pye	161, 172
Midwinter v. Midwinter	243, 244, 246
Miles v. Chilton	141, 201
Milford v. Milford	44, 277
Miller v. Adm.-Gen., Bengal	159, 167, 168
———— v. Miller	374
Millward, *In re*	5
———— v. Millward	374
Milner v. Milner	45
Moore v. Moore	32, 62, 80, 81, 97, 120, 156, 180, 185, 186, 225, 238, 251, 357
Moorsom v. Moorsom	74
Mordaunt v. Moncrieff	38, 93, 284
Morphett v. Morphett	49
Morrall v. Morrall	237, 252
Morris v. Morris	225, 366
Moss v. Moss	211, 238

	PAGE
Mucho v. Arzom Sahoo	183
Muhammad Kalu v. Saigulla	284
Muirhead, *In re*	194
Mullineaux v. Mullineaux	170
Mumby v. Mumby	212
Munroe v. Douglas	14
Munshi Buzloor v. Shumsoonim	44
Munt v. Glynes	160
Mycock v. Mycock	92, 151, 351
Mytton v. Mytton	47, 54, 80

N.

N. v. M.	131
—— v. N.	41
Narracott v. Narracott	197
Natall v. Natall	363, 365, 374
Nelson v. Nelson	377
Newman v. Newman	101
Newsome v. Newsome	81
Newton v. Newton	212, 220, 251
Niboyet v. Niboyet	9, 10
Nicholls v. Nicholls	206
Nicholson v. Drury Building Co.	169
———— v. Nicholson	99, 100, 202, 204
Nicol v. Nicol	181
Noakes v. Noakes	251
Noble v. Noble	96, 120, 143
Noel v. Noel	257, 264
Nokes v. Nokes	207, 208
Norman v. Villars	112, 201
Norris v. Norris	83, 243
Nott v. Nott	62, 156

O.

Odevaine v. Odevaine	202
Oldroyd v. Oldroyd	57, 65, 155, 179
Oliver v. Oliver	47, 48
Omrao Singh v. Prem Singh	286
Oppenheim v. Oppenheim	258
Ord v. Ord	219, 224
Orde v. Skinner	21
Ottaway v. Hamilton	164, 375
Otway v. Otway	95, 153, 186, 369, 370, 371, 376

xvi   TABLE OF CASES.

	PAGE		PAGE
Ousey v. Ousey and Atkinson	66, 114	Powell v. Powell	207
Oxford Guardians v. Barton	172	Power v. Power	49
		Priske v. Priske	378
		Pritchard v. Pritchard	52, 218
P.		Proby v. Proby	364, 365
		Proctor v. Proctor	67, 185
P. v. P.	367	Prole v. Soady	122
— v. S.	129	Pyne v. Pyne	347
Palmer v. Palmer	13, 76		
— v. —	54, 80, 114, 116		
Parker v. Parker	212		
Parkinson v. Parkinson	32, 62, 156, 181, 350, 357	**Q.**	
Parr v. Parr	241	Queen-Empress. *See* Empress.	
Parry v. Parry	104, 106	Quicke v. Quicke	71
Parsons, *In re*	244		
Patrickson v. Patrickson	328		
Patterson, *In re*	194	**R.**	
— v. Patterson	43, 113, 195, 208, 209	R. v. Kingston	335
Paul v. Paul	256, 261	— v. R.	205, 208, 209
Perianayakan v. Pottukani	5	Radford v. Radford	183
Payne v. Payne	69	Rahimbay v. Turner	304
Peacock v. Peacock	70, 72, 78, 369	Ram Paul Singh, *In re*	22
Pearce v. Pearce	263, 367	Ram Sahoy v. Rookhoo	369, 371
Pearman v. Pearman	52, 102, 360	Ramsden v. Brearley	172
Pearson v. Pearson	175	— v. Ramsden	189
Pellew v. Pellew	99	Ratcliffe v. Ratcliffe	88, 100, 228, 234
Penty v. Penty	70, 72	Rathnammal v. Manikkan	328
Percy v. Percy	302	Ravenscroft v. Ravenscroft	380
Pereira v. Pereira	81	Rawlins v. Rawlins	228
Phillip v. Phillip	273	Reasut v. Abdoolah	30
Phillips v. Phillips	74, 165, 347	Rebertest v. Rebertest	347
Pickard v. Pickard	52, 218	Redfern v. Redfern	359
Picken v. Picken	74, 106	Reeves v. Reeves	46
Piers v. Piers	326	Reg. v. Birmingham	326
Pimen v. Hindhaugh	138, 139	— v. Brawn	24
Pitt v. Pitt	69, 71	— v. Brighton	139
Pizzala v. Pizzala	57	— v. Chadwick	138, 149
Plowden v. Plowden	45	— v. Clarke	270
Plumer v. Plumer	299	— v. Hawes	23
Pollack v. Pollack	122	— v. Jackson	177
Pollard v. Pollard	258, 358	— v. Leresche	60
Pomero v. Pomero	83	— v. Mainwaring	326
Ponsonby v. Ponsonby	257, 260	— v. Penson	24
Poole v. Poole	116	— v. Robinson	139
Popkin v. Popkin	51, 335	— v. Saint Giles-in-the-Fields	139
Porter v. Porter	248, 343	— v. Twining	142
Potter v. Potter	96, 185	Regan v. Regan	327

TABLE OF CASES. xvii

	PAGE
Richardson v. Richardson	334, 380
Ricketts v. Ricketts	178
Ridgway v. Ridgway	81
Rippingall v. Rippingall	184
Robertson v. Robertson	216, 232, 369, 370
Robinson, In re	221
—— v. Robinson	334, 377, 382
Robotham v. Robotham	348
Roe v. Roe	71, 377
Rogers v. Halmshaw	306
—— v. Rogers	78, 81, 86, 89, 114, 119, 120, 207, 365
Rohilkand v. Kumaon Bank	285
Ronalds v. Ronalds	32, 205
Rooker v. Rooker	328, 329
Rose v. Rose	54, 80, 82, 83, 95
Ross v. Ross	75, 248
Round v. Round	353
Routh v. F.	284
Rowe v. Rowe	154, 356
Rowley v. Rowley	37, 39, 55, 82, 155, 345, 348, 351
Ruck v. Ruck	124, 336, 339
Russell v. Russell	41, 42, 43, 44, 47, 53, 57, 65, 67, 105, 151, 155, 179, 185, 345, 358
Ruxton v. Ruxton	49
Ryder v. Ryder	23, 270

S.

S. v. A.	131
— v. B.	133
St. Paul v. St. Paul	104, 106
Sansom v. Sansom	229
Saunders v. Saunders	48, 70, 72, 252, 264
Sayer v. Glossop	330
Schira v. Schira	108
Schofield v. Schofield	246
Scholey v. Goodman	63, 180, 181
Scott v. Att.-Gen.	15
—— v. Scott	49, 175, 187
—— v. Sebright	144, 145
Seatle v. Seatle	243, 244
Seaver v. Seaver	94, 185
Seddon v. Seddon	190, 274, 379, 381
Seller v. Seller	83, 95

	PAGE
Serrell v. Serrell	130, 359
Setanath Ghose v. Shama Sundari	30
Sewell, Ex parte	168
Sharpe, Ex parte	171
Shaw v. Gould	8, 9, 340
—— v. Shaw	357, 358
Shewell v. Shewell	274
Shilson v. Att.-Gen.	142
Shirley v. Shirley	210
Short v. Short	101
Sidney v. Sidney	212, 215, 220, 225, 239
Simonin v. Mallac	135
Sirdar Gurdyal Singh v. Raja of Faridkot (see Gurdyal Singh v. Raja of Faridkot).	
Skinner v. Skinner	92, 218, 294
Smallwood v. Smallwood	46, 154
Smith v. Morris	366
—— v. Smith	55, 61, 92, 151, 152, 175, 189, 204, 343, 349, 351, 381
Smithe v. Smithe	249, 379
Smythe v. Smythe	231
Snowdon v. Snowdon	211
Sopwith v. Sopwith	37, 185, 336, 337
Sottomayor v. De Barros	135, 136, 138
Southern v. Southern	115
Sowden v. Sowden	250
Spedding v. Spedding	188, 196, 347
Spering v. Spering	180, 357
Spilsbury v. Spilsbury	343
Spratt v. Spratt	272
Squires v. Squires	49, 345
Stacey v. Stacey	273
Stagg v. Edgecumbe	130, 132
Stanhope v. Stanhope	38, 112, 113, 249
Starbuck v. Starbuck	65
Starkey v. Starkey	369
Stephen v. Stephen	116, 117, 353
Sterbini v. Sterbini	37
Stern, In re	15
Stoate v. Stoate	117, 235, 375
Stoker v. Stoker	83, 95
Stone v. Stone	115, 194, 244, 265, 379
Story v. Story	82, 83, 95, 190
Strickland v. Strickland	60
Studdy v. Studdy	76
Styles v. Styles	95
Sudlow v. Sudlow	347
Sugg v. Sugg	86, 107

R.

b

TABLE OF CASES.

	PAGE
Suggate v. Suggate	51, 52, 82, 274, 276, 277, 343, 346, 374
Suresh Chunder v. Tugert Chunder	289
Sutton v. Sutton	73
——— v. Sutton and Peacock	38
Swatman v. Swatman	51
Swift v. Swift	177, 244, 246
Sykes v. Sykes	250, 263
Symington v. Symington	274, 276, 277
Symonds v. Symonds	255
Symons v. Symons	98, 368

T.

	PAGE
T. v. D.	133, 371
— v. M.	132
Taplen v. Taplen	380, 382
Taverner f. e. Ditchford v. Ditchford	110, 128, 358
Taylor v. Hailstone	364
——— v. Taylor	58, 196
Thapita Peter v. Thapita Lakhsmi	4, 5
The Indian Chief	14
Theobald v. Theobald	177
Thomas v. Head	172
——— v. Thomas	76, 202, 204, 265, 364
Thomasset v. Thomasset	23, 270, 272, 275
Thompson v. Thompson	55, 206, 210, 250, 253, 262, 273, 376
Thomson v. Thomson	250, 363, 364, 367
Thornton v. Thornton	6, 12, 184
Tietkins, In re	22
Todd v. Todd	76, 86
Tollemache v. Tollemache	71, 73, 101
Tomkins v. Tomkins	53
Tonge v. Tonge	212
Toofeah v. Jussundu	176
Townsend v. Townsend	64
Tress v. Tress	181, 357
Troward v. Troward	82, 121
Trubner v. Trubner	348
Tukaram v. Vithal	284
Tupper v. Tupper	254, 258
Turner v. Thompson	15
Turton v. Turton	77
Tuthill v. Tuthill	153, 356

U.

	PAGE
U. v. J.	133
Udny v. Udny	13, 14
Underwood v. Underwood	213, 221
Upendro Lal Bose, In re	283, 342

V.

Vanquelin v. Bonsard	340
Venkatramana v. Timappa	283
Vernall, Ex parte	163
Vicars v. Vicars	215
Virgo v. Virgo	40, 336, 339
Vivian v. Vivian	383

W.

Waddell v. Waddell	45, 48
Wadhawa v. Fatteh Muhammad	329
Waite v. Morland	160
Walker v. Walker	300, 350, 367
Wallace v. Wallace	273, 348
Wallis v. Wallis	225
Walmsley v. Walmsley	47
Walton v. Walton	75
Ward v. Ward	55, 59, 299, 367
Warden v. Warden	115
Warrender v. Warrender	4
Warter v. Warter	143, 306
Waterhouse v. Waterhouse	217, 220
Watton v. Watton	114
Watts v. Watts	251
Weber v. Weber	207, 363
Webster v. Webster	23, 248, 262, 270
Weir, In re	173
Welde v. Welde	131
Weldon v. Weldon	176
Weller v. Weller	239
Wells v. Cottam	286, 366
——— v. Malben	122, 160
——— v. Wells	203, 344, 345, 363
West v. West	376, 377
Westmeath v. Westmeath	180
Wheeler v. Wheeler	70, 71, 108
Whieldon v. Whieldon	224
White v. White	52

TABLE OF CASES.

	PAGE
Whithorne v. Thomas	21
Whitmore v. Whitmore	363, 370
Whittingham's Trusts, *In re*	170
Whitworth v. Whitworth	97
Wickham v. Wickham	120
Wigney v. Wigney	253, 255, 256, 260
Wilcocks v. Wilcocks	208, 224
Wildey v. Wildey	94
Wilkins v. Reynolds	134
Wilkinson v. Gibson	122
—— v. Wilkinson	237, 269, 349
Williams v. Dormer	15
—— v. Homfray	130, 132
—— v. Williams	58, 77, 99, 110, 156, 208, 333, 334, 348
Williamson v. Williamson	65
Willis v. Willis	115, 117
Wilson, *In re*	150
—— v. Wilson	10, 15, 32, 100, 129, 180, 212, 373, 383
Wing v. Taylor	139, 324, 326
Wingrove v. Wingrove	22, 27
Winscom v. Winscom	81, 377, 382
Winstone v. Winstone	215
Witt v. Witt	278, 335
Wodehouse v. Wodehouse	343

	PAGE
Wood v. Wood	54, 57, 60, 158, 195, 207, 228, 239, 263, 300, 351
Woodgate v. Taylor	284, 364
Woodsey v. Woodsey	179
Worman, *In re*	161, 173
Worsley v. Worsley	251, 264
Wyndham v. Wyndham	343

X.

X. v. Y.	132

Y.

Yarrow v. Yarrow	38
Yeatman v. Yeatman	57, 58, 65, 103, 155, 169, 178, 339, 356, 357, 367
Yelverton v. Yelverton	15
Young v. Young	364

Z.

Zaburdast Khan v. His Wife	5
Zyclinski v. Zyclinski	32

THE INDIAN DIVORCE ACT.
Act No. IV of 1869.

PASSED BY THE GOVERNOR-GENERAL OF INDIA IN COUNCIL.

(*Received the assent of the Governor-General on the 26th February,* 1869.)

An Act to amend the law relating to Divorce and Matrimonial Causes in India.

WHEREAS it is expedient to amend the law relating to the divorce of persons professing the Christian religion, and to confer upon certain Courts jurisdiction in matters matrimonial; It is hereby enacted as follows:— Preamble.

I.—*Preliminary.*

1. This Act may be called "The Indian Divorce Act," and shall come into operation on the first day of April, 1869. Short title. Commencement of Act.

NOTE.—The Bill, which was eventually passed as Act IV of 1869, was framed by Mr. Whitley Stokes, and was originally introduced by Mr. (afterwards Sir Henry) Maine on the 24th December, 1862. Mr. Maine, in moving for leave to introduce the Bill, stated that its object was to give effect to the policy embodied in the High Courts Act passed in 1861 (24 & 25 Vict. c. 104), and to the Letters Patent issued by her Majesty for constituting the High Courts. The object of the High Courts Act, he said, seemed to have been, not so much to create new branches of jurisdiction, as to constitute and re-distribute the power which already existed. The 9th clause gave power to her Majesty to confer on the High Courts such matrimonial jurisdiction as she thought fit; but, following the principle he had mentioned, her Majesty did not attempt to confer on the High Courts such a jurisdiction as was exercised by the Divorce Court in England. The Secretary of State had, therefore, requested the Governor-General to introduce a measure, conferring a jurisdiction on the High Courts here similar to that exercised by the Divorce Court sitting in London. (See "*Life and Speeches of Sir H. Maine,*" p. 95.) The Bill, after having been seven years before the Council of the Governor-General, received the assent of the Governor-General on the 26th February, 1869.

THE INDIAN DIVORCE ACT.

Extent of Act.

2. This Act shall extend to the whole of British India, and (so far only as regards British subjects within the dominions hereinafter mentioned) to the dominions of Princes and States in India in alliance with her Majesty.

Extent of power to grant relief generally.

Nothing hereinafter contained shall authorize any Court to grant any relief under this Act, except in cases where the petitioner professes the Christian religion and resides in India at the time of presenting the petition;

And to make decrees of dissolution.

or to make decrees of dissolution of marriage except in the following cases:—(a) where the marriage shall have been solemnized in India; or (b) where the adultery, rape or unnatural crime complained of shall have been committed in India; or (c) where the husband has, since the solemnization of the marriage, exchanged his profession of Christianity for the profession of some other form of religion;

Or of nullity.

or to make decrees of nullity of marriage except in cases where the marriage has been solemnized in India.

"British subjects":

(i) **"British subjects"**:

The provisions of the Indian Divorce Act, 1869, are applicable to suits between European British subjects resident in Native States, and sect. 2 of the Act, which extends those provisions to such persons, was not *ultra vires* of the Indian Legislature. (*Thornton* v. *Thornton*, I. L. R., x Bomb. 422.)

The Act has been declared to be in force in (1) *the Santhal Parganas* (Regs. iii of 1872 and iii of 1886); (2) *the Arakan Hill District* (Reg. ix of 1874); (3) *Upper Burma generally, except the Shan States* (Act XX of 1886); (4) *British Baluchistan* (Reg. i of 1890); (5) *Angul and the Khondmals* (Reg. i of 1894).

"Professes Christianity":

(ii) **"Professes the Christian religion"**:

(*a*) The Indian Divorce Act applies to all marriages contracted under Act III of 1872 ("*An Act to provide a form of marriage*

PRELIMINARY.

for persons who do not profess the Christian, Jewish, Hindu, Muhammadan, Parsi, Buddhist, Sikh or Jaina religion"), and any such marriage may be declared null or dissolved in the manner provided, and for the causes mentioned, in Act IV of 1869 (*Act III of* 1872, *sect.* 17). § 2.

(*b*) Unless his or her marriage was contracted under Act III of 1872, an atheist or infidel is not entitled to claim relief under the provisions of Act IV of 1869. The fact that the petitioner was married in accordance with the rites of the Christian religion, and professed that religion at the time of marriage, will not entitle him or her to relief under the Act unless he or she professes Christianity at the time of presenting the petition. Atheists, infidels.

(*c*) It is only necessary that *the petitioner* should profess Christianity at the time of presenting the petition; it is immaterial what religion (if any) *the respondent* professes at that time.

(*d*) Except as regards marriages contracted under Act III of 1872, the following conditions precedent must exist in order to entitle the petitioner to relief under the Indian Divorce Act:— (i) the petitioner must profess the Christian religion, *and* (ii) reside in India at the time of presenting the petition; (iii) *semble*, the marriage, in respect of which relief is sought, must be either one celebrated in accordance with the rites of the Christian religion, or one of a kind recognized as a marriage in Christian countries. Conditions precedent to grant of relief generally: (i) Profession of Christianity; (ii) Residence in India of petitioner; (iii) "Marriage in Christendom."

"The Act does not require in terms that the parties, or either of them, shall have been Christians at the time of the solemnization of marriage. There are provisions in the Act which presuppose Christianity as the religion of the parties at the time of the marriage, but it cannot be said that adherence to that religion at that time is made a condition precedent to the obtaining of relief under the Act. It by no means follows that the provisions of the Act can be made applicable to any marriage between non-Christians, although it may be a marriage which, according to the law governing them, is valid and legal. In applying the provisions of the Act, section 7 directs that the Court shall act and give relief on principles and rules on which the Court for Divorce and Matrimonial Causes in England for the time being acts and gives relief. In my opinion, the direction given in this section has to be kept in view by the Court in considering whether a given marriage should be recognized as such for the purposes of the Act. . . . . Now, in order to satisfy the English Divorce Court, while it is not necessary to prove that the marriage was celebrated with any specifically Christian

§ 2.

ceremonies, or even that both the parties were Christians, it is necessary to show that the union was *a union for life of one man with one woman to the exclusion of others*. This is what is meant by a Christian marriage, or·a marriage in Christendom" (*per* Shephard, J., *Thapita Peter* v. *Thapita Lakhsmi*, I. L. R., xvii Mad. 235);

"Marriage is substantially one and the same thing all the Christian world over; our whole law of marriage assumes this; and it is important to observe that we regard it as a wholly different thing, a different *status*, from Turkish or other marriages among infidel nations" (*per* Lord Brougham, *Warrender* v. *Warrender*, 2 Cl. & Fin. 532).

"Marriage in Christendom": Definition of.

A marriage, to be recognized as such by the Courts of a Christian country, must, therefore, be a voluntary union for life of one man with one woman to the exclusion of all others; but it need not necessarily have been celebrated in accordance with Christian rites or ceremonies. Thus a monogamous marriage contracted by a Christian with a non-Christian under the law of a non-Christian but monogamous country, such as Japan, was recognized as valid in England, the country of the Christian party's domicil (*Brinckley* v. *Att.-Gen.*, 15 P. D. 76; 59 L. J., P. & M. 54).

On the other hand, a union formed between a man and a woman, although it may under the law or custom, in accordance with which it was contracted, bear the name of marriage and the parties to it be designated husband and wife, is not a valid marriage according to the law of Christian countries unless it is formed on the same basis as marriages throughout Christendom.

Thus where a domiciled Englishman went through the form of marriage with a woman of the Baralong tribe, in Bechuanaland, according to the customs of the tribe, among whom polygamy is allowed, and the parties lived together thereafter as husband and wife, and the man refused to be married to the woman in a church on the ground that he had become a Baralong, it was held that the union was not a marriage in the Christian sense of the term (*Bethell, In re, Bethell* v. *Hildyard*, 38 Ch. D. 220; 57 L. J., Ch. 487).

So again, a marriage contracted in a country, where polygamy is lawful, between a man and a woman who profess a faith which allows polygamy, is not a marriage as understood in Christendom. In such a case the marriage, although it is valid by the *lex loci* and at the time it was contracted the parties were single and competent to contract marriage *inter se*, will not be

recognized as valid by the English Matrimonial Court in a suit § 2.
instituted by one of the parties against the other for the purpose
of enforcing matrimonial duties or obtaining relief for a breach
of matrimonial obligations (*Hyde* v. *Hyde and Woodmansee*,
L. R., 1 P. 130; 35 L. J., P. & M. 57).

Acting on this principle, the Indian Courts have held that
they have no jurisdiction under the Indian Divorce Act, 1869,
to dissolve the marriages of parties who, having been married
in accordance with Muhammadan Law, have since their marriage
become converts to Christianity (*Zaburdast Khan* v. *His Wife*,
2 N. W. P., H. C. R. 370).

Nor have the Courts jurisdiction under the Act to dissolve the
marriages of Hindus who, subsequently to their marriage, have
become converts to Christianity (*Perianayakan* v. *Pottukani*,
I. L. R., xiv Mad. 382; *Thapita Peter* v. *Thapita Lakhsmi*, I. L. R.,
xvii Mad. 235).

Nor in such cases does the mere fact that the husband has
married only one wife alter the character of the union, if under
the law, in accordance with which the marriage was contracted,
he was at liberty to marry several wives at the same time
(*Thapita Peter* v. *Thapita Lakhsmi, ubi supra*).

At the same time such "marriages," although not recognized
as such for the purposes of the Indian Divorce Act, are undoubtedly valid for other purposes. Thus, if a man and a
woman profess the Hindu religion, and as such contract a
marriage, their subsequent conversion to Christianity will entail
the penalties of bigamy upon that party to the marriage who,
during the lifetime of the other party, goes through a form of
marriage with a third person (*In re Millward*, I. L. R., x Mad.
218). And a Hindu woman who has been married to a Hindu
husband is entitled, upon the death of the latter intestate, to
succeed to her legal portion as his widow, although subsequently
to his marriage he had become a convert to Christianity (*Administrator-General of Madras* v. *Ananduchari*, I. L. R., ix Mad. 466).

The High Court of Calcutta, on the other hand, has held that, View of High
if a petitioner professes the Christian religion *at the time of* Court of
presenting the petition, he or she is entitled to relief under the Calcutta.
Indian Divorce Act, and this whether or not the "marriage,"
in respect of which relief is prayed, be recognized as such in
Christendom. Thus, in a case where the petitioner and respondent were married as Hindus, but subsequently became converts
to Christianity, it was held that the petitioner, who applied for
dissolution of his marriage, was entitled to relief under the Act,

§ 2.

inasmuch as he was a person professing the Christian religion at the time of presenting his petition (*Gobardhan Dass* v. *Jasadamoni Dass*, I. L. R., xviii Calc. 252).

(iii) " Resides in India " :

Matrimonial jurisdiction:
(a) for purposes of municipal law:

As regards *the power of granting relief generally*, the Indian Courts have, under this section and *for the purposes of municipal law*, jurisdiction to grant such relief provided that *the petitioner* professes Christianity and resides in India at the time of presenting the petition. The absence of the respondent from India at such time is immaterial (*Thornton* v. *Thornton*, I. L. R., x Bomb. 422).

But, although for the purposes of Indian municipal law, mere "residence" in India is sufficient, it is submitted that such residence must be at least *bonâ fide*, and not that of a mere casual traveller. Nor must it be a merely colourable residence for the purpose of obtaining relief under the Act.

(b) For purposes of international law.

For the purposes, and according to the principles, of *international law*, a jurisdiction in matrimonial causes, which is founded on *the residence* of the petitioner alone, is not sufficient. According to the principles of international law—

(a) The Courts of the husband's *domicil* have jurisdiction in all matrimonial suits, and the absence of the respondent (whether husband or wife) from the country of the domicil of the husband does not affect such jurisdiction;

(b) In every suit which involves the disruption of the matrimonial tie, the only Court of competent jurisdiction is the Court of the husband's *domicil;*

Provided (in both cases) that the *domicil* of the wife is not the *domicil* of the husband to such an extent as to compel her to become subject to the jurisdiction of the tribunals of any country in which the husband may choose to acquire a new *domicil* (*Briggs* v. *Briggs*, 5 P. D. 163; 49 L. J., P. & M. 38.)

(c) In matrimonial suits other than those which involve the disruption of the marriage tie, a Court, other than the Court of the husband's *domicil*, has jurisdiction to grant relief, *provided* that both the parties are resident within the jurisdiction of such Court at the time of suit, or that the respondent, if absent, has submitted to the jurisdiction of such Court. In suits such as those here referred to, a decree passed *in absentem* by a foreign Court (*i.e.* a Court other than the Court of the husband's domicil) to the jurisdiction of which the respondent has not in any way submitted himself or herself is by international law an absolute nullity. He or she is under no obligation of any kind to obey it, and it must be regarded as a mere nullity by the Courts of every nation, except (when authorized by special legislation) in the country of the *forum* by which it was pronounced (*Sirdar Gurdyal Singh* v. *Raja of Faridkot*, (1894) A. C. 670; I. L. R., xxii Calc. 222; No. 112, Punjab Record, 1894).

§ 2.

Jurisdiction in suits involving disruption of marriage tie.

In addition to the conditions precedent to the granting of *any relief* under the Indian Divorce Act, viz. the petitioner's profession of Christianity and residence in India at the time of presenting the petition, and also (it is submitted) "a marriage in the Christian sense," it is further necessary to give jurisdiction under the Act

(a) *In suits for dissolution of marriage*, that the marriage shall have been solemnized in India, *or* that the adultery, rape or unnatural crime complained of shall have been committed in India, *or* that the husband shall have, since the solemnization of the marriage, exchanged his profession of Christianity for the profession of some other form of religion;

(b) *In suits for nullity of marriage*, that the marriage shall have been solemnized in India.

If in any particular case the conditions precedent above set forth are found to exist, the Courts in British India have full jurisdiction, *for the purposes of municipal law*, to make a decree for dissolution or nullity of marriage, as the case may be, and any such decree will be valid for all purposes throughout British India.

But *for international purposes and according to international law*, the *domicil* for the time being of the married pair affords the only true test of jurisdiction to dissolve the marriage (*Le Mesurier* v. *Le Mesurier*, (1895) A. C. 517; 64 L. J., P. C. 97).

Where, therefore, the Courts of a country assume jurisdiction to decree a divorce between persons living in the country, the jurisdiction must be derived either from some recognized principle of the general law of nations, or from some rule of muni-

(a) Under Indian Divorce Act:

(b) For purposes of international law.

§ 2.

Indian Divorce Bill as originally framed.

Shaw v. Gould.

cipal law peculiar to its *forum* (*e.g.* under the Indian Divorce Act). Where the jurisdiction exercised is in accordance with the principles of international law, the decree ought to be respected by the tribunals of every civilized country; but where it is derived solely from some rule of the municipal law of the particular country, it cannot claim extra-territorial authority if it trenches upon the interests of any other country to whose tribunals the spouses are amenable (*ib.*).

In the Indian Divorce Bill, as originally framed, it was made a condition precedent to the exercise of jurisdiction in suits for dissolution of marriage that the marriage, in respect of which relief was sought, should have been solemnized in India, and that the domicil of the husband, both at the time of marriage and of the institution of the suit, should be in India, the reason being that *Lolley's Case* (Russ. & Ry. 237; 2 Cl. & Fin. 567) was at that time supposed to have decided that "a marriage solemnized in England was indissoluble by any foreign* Court" (*McCarthy* v. *Du Caix*, 3 Hagg. 642; 2 Russ. & Myl. 615). As a matter of fact, however, what was actually decided in that case was that "no sentence or act of any foreign country or state could dissolve an English marriage *a vinculo matrimonii* for grounds on which it was not liable to be dissolved *a vinculo matrimonii* in England" (*per* Hannen, P., *Harvey* v. *Farnie*, 5 P. D. 154). While, however, the Bill was still before the Select Committee, the House of Lords in the case of *Shaw* v. *Gould* (L. R., 3 E. & I. App. 55) explained the true theory of English law regarding the indissolubility of English marriages. According to that high authority, a competent foreign Court has jurisdiction to dissolve a marriage solemnized in England between English subjects, *provided* that the married pair are *domiciled* within the jurisdiction of such Court at the time of the institution of the suit. The decision in *Shaw* v. *Gould* was, therefore, sufficient authority for the omission from the provisions of the Bill of the condition precedent that the marriage to be dissolved should have been solemnized in India. For, irrespective of any question as to where the marriage ceremony was performed, the Courts of this country would be competent to dissolve the marriage of spouses *domiciled* in British India, and every such decree

---

* "Foreign" here means any Court other than the Courts in England. For the purposes of divorce jurisdiction, the British Colonies and Scotland and Ireland are deemed "foreign countries" (*Firebrace* v. *Firebrace*, 4 P. D. 63; 47 L. J., P. & M. 41).

of dissolution would be entitled to receive international recognition. It was felt, however, that a jurisdiction based on the *domicil* of the married pair would not suffice to meet the cases of those Europeans in India—and they form the majority of Europeans in this country—"who are *resident* in India, but whose residence falls somewhat short of *domicil*." Relying, therefore, on an *obiter dictum* in the judgment of Lord Colonsay (in *Shaw* v. *Gould*), which went the length of affirming that a domicil for all purposes might not be necessary, and that if both parties had been *bonâ fide* resident for a considerable time within the jurisdiction of the foreign Court which decreed a dissolution of marriage, such decree would be recognized as valid by the Courts of the domicil, the Select Committee decided to found the jurisdiction of the Indian Courts to grant a dissolution of marriage upon—not the *domicil* of the married pair, but—*the residence* of the petitioner in India at the time of presenting the petition (see the speech of Mr. (afterwards Sir Henry) Maine, in the Supplement to the *Gazette of India*, 1869, p. 293). In so deciding, it is obvious that the Select Committee went even further than the *dictum* of Lord Colonsay (a Scotch lawyer) warranted, and it was always a matter of grave doubt whether a jurisdiction based on so slender a foundation as that of the petitioner's residence in India at the time of instituting a suit for dissolution of marriage would receive international recognition. These doubts have now been completely removed by the decision of their Lordships of the Privy Council in the case of *Le Mesurier* v. *Le Mesurier* (*supra*), which, however, merely affirms the principle previously enunciated by the House of Lords in *Harvey* v. *Farnie* (8 App. Cas. 43; 52 L. J., P. & M. 33), that "the question of divorce is not an incident of the marriage contract to be governed by the *lex loci contractus*, but is an incident of *status* to be disposed of by the law of the domicil of the parties—that is, of the husband" (*cf.* Bishop, "Divorce," vol. 2, ch. x, § 136).

§ 2.

The majority of the English Court of Appeal (James and Cotton, L.JJ., Brett, L.J., dissenting) in 1878 decided, it is true, that a *bonâ fide* residence without domicil would suffice to give jurisdiction to the English Court to dissolve a marriage if the matrimonial offence had been committed in England (*Niboyet* v. *Niboyet*, 4 P. D. 1; 48 L. J., P. & M. 1). And in certain cases (*e.g.*, *Jack* v. *Jack*, 24 Sess. Cas., 2nd Ser. 467) the Scotch Courts developed a theory that a something which fell short of actual domicil, but which they termed "matrimonial domicil,"

Niboyet v. *Niboyet*.

§ 2.

explained as meaning "the home or seat of the marriage for the time being, the place where the spouses are actually resident if they be together, or, if from any cause they are separate, the place in which they are under an obligation to come and renew, or commence, their cohabitation as man and wife"—would be sufficient to give them jurisdiction in suits for dissolution of marriage. These decisions, however, were examined and severely criticized in *Le Mesurier's Case*, and their Lordships concluded by concurring, "without reservation, in the views expressed by Lord Penzance in *Wilson* v. *Wilson* (1 P. & D. 442), which were obviously meant to refer, *not* to questions arising in regard to the marital rights of married persons, but to jurisdiction in the matter of divorce:—'It is the strong inclination of my own opinion that the only fair and satisfactory rule to adopt in this matter of jurisdiction is to insist upon the parties in all cases referring their matrimonial differences to the Courts of the country in which they are domiciled. Different communities have different laws and views respecting matrimonial obligations, and a different estimate of the causes which should justify divorce. It is both just and reasonable, therefore, that the differences of married persons should be adjusted in accordance with the laws of the community to which they belong, and dealt with by the tribunals which alone can administer those laws. An honest adherence to this principle, moreover, will preclude the scandal which arises when a man and a woman are held to be man and wife in one country and strangers in another.'"

Le Mesurier v. Le Mesurier.

As remarked by the present Master of the Rolls, in his dissenting judgment in *Niboyet* v. *Niboyet* (4 P. D. at p. 13), if jurisdiction in suits involving the disruption of the married tie is founded on anything short of domicil, the relation or *status* of a married person will be one in the country of the Court making the decree, and another in all other countries. "That is to say, a man or a woman would be treated as married in one country, and not so in another; or married people might be enjoined to live together in one country and to live apart in another. *No Court ought to assume or presume to place people in so deplorable a position, unless forced to do so by the express law of the country whose law it is administering.*"

Possible solution of difficulty.

The question then arises, Are the Courts in India bound by the provisions of the Indian Divorce Act to place persons not domiciled in India in the deplorable position alluded to by Lord Justice Brett? A very learned American writer (Bishop,

"*Divorce*," vol. 2, §§ 114, 124) suggests a way out of the difficulty:—"The Courts of every country, both when they decree divorces and when they sit in judgment on foreign divorces, should do whatever they consistently can to establish rules preventive of a conflict of law. . . . . The international rule of jurisdiction is a part of our unwritten law. Hence, and because this law binds our Government in all its departments almost like our written constitutions, our statutes giving jurisdiction should be construed as mingled with and qualified by it; and never, except by such express words as admit of no other result, be permitted a meaning conflicting therewith. . . . . Any word employed in a statute may be modified, limited, or expanded in meaning by the connection in which it stands and the subject to which it is applied. Our divorce statutes, giving jurisdiction, commonly provide that the applicant shall have '*resided*' a given number of years in the state. The principles of international law, and the general principles of our own, requiring the residence for divorce to be *animo manendi*, the method of interpretation already pointed out indicates that the residence demanded shall be held to be permanent—the domicil."

§ 2.

Accepting this method of interpretation, the Courts of this country might construe the words "resides in India at the time of presenting the petition" as intended to mean "resides *animo manendi*, and must be actually present at the time of instituting the suit." If the petitioner is the husband, his residence *animo manendi*, that is to say, his domicil, is in law the residence *animo manendi* or domicil of his wife. If, on the other hand, the petitioner is the wife, her residence *animo manendi*, that is to say, her domicil, is in law (except in certain exceptional cases, referred to below) the domicil of her husband. In the latter event, the Court would refuse to entertain her suit, although she might be temporarily resident in India at the time, unless her husband's permanent home, or domicil, were in this country at the time when she presented her petition. This method of interpretation would, at least, preclude the "scandal" spoken of by Lord Penzance in *Wilson* v. *Wilson*, and would, of course, be necessary only in suits for dissolution of marriage. To refuse to entertain such a suit when instituted by a petitioner who is not domiciled in India at the time would very considerably limit the operation of the Indian Divorce Act. At the same time, to grant a decree in such a case would place the parties in the anomalous and "deplorable" position of being man and wife in the country of their permanent home,

§ 2.

and every other country except India, where they would be "strangers." And *Lolley's Case* (*supra*) is, at least, an authority to show that a decree of an Indian Court in such a case might not be considered a sufficient excuse for relieving from the penalties of bigamy a person who, in reliance upon such decree, and after his or her return to the country of domicil, went through a form of marriage with a third person during the lifetime of the other party.

Conclusion.

(i) For the purposes of municipal law, a decree of dissolution of marriage granted by a Court of competent jurisdiction is absolutely valid in the country of such Court, and none the less so, although the *domicil* of the spouses may be elsewhere, if the municipal law founds the jurisdiction of its Courts in such cases on mere *residence* as distinct from *domicil*.

(ii) For the purposes of international law, and to have extra-territorial validity, a decree of dissolution of marriage can only be granted by the Courts of the *domicil* of the parties.

(iii) For the purposes of international law as well as for those of municipal law, the decree of a Court of competent jurisdiction in all matrimonial suits other than those involving the disruption of the matrimonial tie is valid and binding; provided that both the parties were *resident* at the time within the jurisdiction of such Court, or that the respondent, if absent, submitted to such jurisdiction.

(iii A) For the purposes of international law, a decree of nullity of marriage to be valid must be the decree of a Court of the country in which the marriage was solemnized.

(iv) For the purposes of municipal law alone, the decree of a Court of competent jurisdiction in any matrimonial suit may be valid and binding, even if passed *in absentem* against a respondent who has in no way submitted to the jurisdiction of such Court, if the Court is authorized by its municipal law to grant a decree under such circumstances (*Thornton* v. *Thornton*, I. L. R., x Bomb. 422).

(v) But, although the decree of a Court dissolving a marriage between persons domiciled elsewhere is not entitled *per se* to extra-territorial recognition, the party at whose suit such marriage was so dissolved may be estopped, under certain circumstances, from disputing its validity. Thus, where a domiciled English subject went to America in 1850, and some six years thereafter his wife, who had followed him to that country, obtained a dissolution of the marriage in an American Court, it was held in a suit subsequently instituted by the wife in the

English Courts for dissolution of the same marriage, on the ground of her husband's adultery with a woman whom he had married after the American divorce, that the husband's cohabitation with the said woman, even if it amounted to adultery, was the natural consequence of the suit in America, and that the wife had, therefore, connived at such adultery and her petition must be dismissed (*Palmer* v. *Palmer*, 1 S. & T. 551; 29 L. J., P. & M. 26).

§ 2.

"Domicil":

As has been already pointed out, the question of the *domicil* of the parties is a matter of the greatest importance in all suits which involve the disruption of the marriage tie. It may be as well, therefore, to give a brief explanation of what constitutes "domicil" in the legal sense of the term.

"Domicil."

"Domicil" has been defined as "that place or country in which a person's habitation has been fixed without any present intention of removing therefrom" (*In re Craignish*, (1892) 3 Ch. 180); "that place in which a person has voluntarily fixed the habitation of himself and his family, not for a mere special or temporary purpose, but with a present intention of making it his permanent home, unless and until something (which is unexpected or uncertain) shall occur to induce him to adopt some other permanent home" (*Lord* v. *Colvin*, 28 L. J., Ch. 361).

Definition of domicil.

The domicil of a person is quite distinct from the *patria* or nationality to which he may belong (*Udny* v. *Udny*, L. R., 1 H. L. (Sc.) 460). Thus a person, who is by *nationality* an Englishman, may have his *domicil* in France.

Distinct from nationality.

It is a settled principle that no person shall be without a *domicil*, and to secure this end the law attributes to every individual, as soon as he is born, the *domicil* of his father, if the child be legitimate, and the *domicil* of his mother, if the child be illegitimate. This is called the "*domicil of origin*," and is involuntary. It is the creation of law—not of the party. It may be *extinguished* by act of law, as, for example, by sentence of death or exile for life, which puts an end to the *status civilis* of the criminal, but it cannot be destroyed by the will and act of the party.

"Domicil of origin."

But, although a person cannot by an act on his part absolutely extinguish or obliterate his domicil of origin, he is at liberty to create for himself a new domicil, called the "*domicil of choice*," and when a domicil of choice is acquired, the domicil of origin is in abeyance. If, however, the domicil of choice is at any time

"Domicil of choice."

§ 2. abandoned, the domicil of origin *ipso facto* revives, and no special intention to revert to it is necessary. If, therefore, a person abandons a domicil of choice and travels about in search of another domicil of choice, the domicil of origin comes instantly into action and continues until another domicil of choice is acquired (*Udny* v. *Udny, supra*).

A "domicil of choice" arises when a person having the power of changing his domicil (*i.e.*, a person *sui juris*, *Somerville* v. *Somerville*, 5 Ves. 786) voluntarily abandons his existing domicil and settles in another place or country with the intention of permanently residing there (*Lord* v. *Colvin, supra*).

No definite period of residence is necessary for the acquisition of a domicil of choice, but there must in all cases be a fixed present intention that the residence should be (so far as can be foreseen) permanent (*King* v. *Foxwell*, 3 Ch. D. 518).

Long residence raises a presumption in favour of the acquisition of a new domicil, but any such presumption may be rebutted by circumstances showing an absence of intention to acquire a new domicil (*Gillis* v. *Gillis*, 8 Ir. R., Eq. 597).

Englishmen coming out to India and residing in this country for a length of time, but with the fixed intention of returning to live in England, do not thereby lose their English domicil (*The Indian Chief*, 3 Rob. Adm. Rep. 28).

It was held, however, that persons who came out to enter the service of the East India Company acquired a new domicil in this country (*Jopp* v. *Wood*, 34 Beav. 88; on app., 34 L. J., Ch. 211; *Bruce's Case*, 2 Bosanquet & Puller's Reps. 230; *Munroe* v. *Douglas*, 5 Maddock's Reps. 379; *Drevon* v. *Drevon*, 34 L. J., Ch. 129). These cases, however, formed an exception to the general rule that persons who occupied an official position in a country were not to be regarded as domiciled therein merely by reason of their residing in such country for the purposes of their official duties. And it is now laid down in sect. 10 of the Indian Succession Act, 1865, that, although "a man acquires a new domicil by taking up his fixed habitation in a country which is not the country of his domicil of origin," yet " a man is not to be considered as having taken up his fixed habitation in British India merely by reason of his residing there in her Majesty's civil or military service, or in the exercise of any profession or calling" (cf. *In re Macreight*, 30 Ch. D. 165; 55 L. J., Ch. 28).

A domicil of choice is established by conduct, and not by mere assertion (*MacMullen* v. *Wadsworth*, 14 App. Cas. 631; 59

L. J., P. C. 7). The oath, therefore, of the person whose domicil is in question is not conclusive, and it is for the Court to decide whether, upon a review of all the circumstances, credit should be given to his evidence (*Wilson* v. *Wilson*, L. R., 2 P. 435; 41 L. J., P. & M. 74). So long as actual residence continues, the mere intention to change the domicil, or temporary absences, are not sufficient to destroy the domicil of choice (*In re Stern*, 28 L. J., Ex. 22).

§ 2.

A woman on her marriage acquires the domicil of her husband (Indian Succession Act, 1865, s. 15; *Yelverton* v. *Yelverton*, 1 S. & T. 574; *Turner* v. *Thompson*, 13 P. D. 37; *Harvey* v. *Furnie*, 5 P. D. 154; 8 App. Cas. 43).

Domicil of married woman.

But a wife who has been judicially separated, or has been deserted by her husband, may be entitled to acquire a distinct domicil for herself (Indian Succession Act, 1865, s. 16, exception; *Dolphin* v. *Robins*, 7 H. L. Cas. 390; *Williams* v. *Dormer*, 2 Rob. Eccl. 505; *Scott* v. *Att.-Gen.*, 11 P. D. 128). But such domicil is effective only for purposes affecting herself as apart from her husband, and she cannot in a suit for dissolution *a vinculo* make her husband amenable to the *lex fori* of her new domicil (*Le Sueur* v. *Le Sueur*, 1 P. D. 139).

On the other hand, the domicil of the wife is not the domicil of the husband to such an extent as to compel her to become subject to the jurisdiction of the tribunals of any country in which the husband may choose to acquire a new domicil (*Briggs* v. *Briggs*, 5 P. D. 163).

"Or where the husband has, since the solemnization of the marriage, exchanged his profession of Christianity for the profession of some other form of religion."

Perversion from Christianity on part of husband.

The object of this clause was to meet such cases as that in which the Madras High Court had held that a Hindu convert to Christianity who, after his conversion and his marriage as a Christian with a Christian woman, reverted to Hinduism, reacquired his rights of polygamy (*Anon.*, 3 Mad. App. 7). In such a case, although the mere reversion to Hinduism does not dissolve the marriage, section 10 of the Act provides that the wife is entitled to sue for dissolution of marriage if her husband, after the solemnization of the marriage, " exchanges his profession of Christianity for the profession of some other form of religion," *and* thereafter " goes through the form of marriage with some other woman."

That a wife should, under such circumstances, be entitled to

§ 2. a dissolution of the marriage, is only just and reasonable; but that a jurisdiction to grant a divorce should be founded (irrespective of the domicil of the parties, or of the place where the marriage was celebrated or the matrimonial offence committed), on the mere fact that a husband had, since the solemnization of his marriage, perverted from his profession of Christianity, is, at least, an anomaly. From the wording of the clause, curious (though, no doubt, unintended) results might follow. To give an extreme instance. A., a domiciled Englishman, marries B., an Englishwoman, in England. After the marriage A. is guilty of legal cruelty towards B., which is, however, condoned; and subsequently A., who has received an offer of a three years' employment at Bombay, comes out to India with B. They set up their home in Bombay and live together there for a few months, after the expiration of which A., with the full consent of B., returns to England, leaving B. at Bombay. On his return to England A. commits adultery, in consequence of which the previous condoned cruelty is revived. In such a case, although the matrimonial misconduct on the part of the husband would entitle the wife to a divorce, had the marriage been solemnized in India or the matrimonial offence been committed in India, the High Court of Bombay has, under the circumstances, no jurisdiction to dissolve B.'s marriage. If, however, A., being still in England, some ten years after the act of adultery exchanges his profession of Christianity for that of the Jewish religion, B. (if still resident in India and professing the Christian religion) will be entitled to apply to the High Court of Bombay for a dissolution of her marriage with A., and that Court will then have jurisdiction to grant the decree prayed for. In this instance, neither has the marriage been solemnized, nor have the matrimonial offences been committed, nor are the parties domiciled, in India, and the mere exchange by A. of Christianity for the Jewish religion is not *per se* a ground for dissolving the marriage. But the Bombay Court acquires, by reason of A.'s perversion, a jurisdiction, which, till then, it did not possess, to entertain B.'s suit for divorce.

It is also noticeable that it is *only the husband's* perversion from Christianity that gives jurisdiction to the Courts; if, therefore, it is the wife who has perverted, the Courts of this country will not have jurisdiction to grant a dissolution unless either the marriage has been solemnized in India or her adultery has been committed in India.

"Or to make decrees of nullity except in cases where the marriage has been solemnized in India."

§ 2.
Jurisdiction to grant decrees of nullity.

The jurisdiction thus conferred is in accordance with the principles of international law, for "jurisdiction to entertain a suit for the declaration of the nullity of a marriage depends, not on the domicil of the parties, but on the place where the marriage is celebrated. .... Domicil, indeed, cannot be the test of jurisdiction, for the domicil of the woman may depend on the very point demanding decision, viz., the validity of the marriage" (Dicey's Conflict of Laws, 1896, pp. 276, 277). But the jurisdiction of the Courts of the place where the marriage was celebrated is not exclusive if one or other of the parties is domiciled in some other country. "It is quite obvious that no civilized state can allow its domiciled subjects or citizens, by making a temporary visit to a foreign country, to enter into a contract to be performed in the place of domicil, if the contract is forbidden by the law of the place of domicil as contrary to religion or morality, or to any of its fundamental institutions" (*per* Lord Campbell, *Brook* v. *Brook*, 9 H. L. Cas. 193). Accordingly, a marriage, no matter where celebrated, between a domiciled English subject (possibly even between a person merely domiciled in England but not an English subject) and his deceased wife's sister will be declared null and void by the Courts in England, although it may be perfectly valid by the *lex loci celebrationis* (*Mette* v. *Mette*, 1 S. & T. 416; 28 L. J., P. & M. 117; *Brook* v. *Brook*, 9 H. L. Cas. 193). Under the Indian Divorce Act, however, the Courts of this country have no jurisdiction to declare a marriage between persons domiciled in India null and void *unless* such marriage was solemnized in India.

As regards the principles upon which the Courts in India act in deciding whether a particular marriage is or is not valid, see sect. 19, *post*, *s. t.* "*Prohibited degrees.*"

3. In this Act, unless there be something repugnant in the subject or context,—

Interpretation clause.

(1) "High Court" means, in any Regulation province,—the Court there established under the Act of the twenty-fourth and twenty-fifth of Victoria, chapter one hundred and four;

"High Court."

in the territories for the time being subject to

§ 3.

the government of the Lieutenant-Governor of the Punjab,—the Chief Court of the Punjab;

in Burma,—the special Court constituted under the Lower Burma Courts Act, 1889;

and in any other non-Regulation province and in any place in the dominions of the Princes and States in India in alliance with her Majesty,—the High Court or Chief Court to whose original criminal jurisdiction the petitioner is for the time being subject, or would be subject if he or she were an European British subject of her Majesty.

In the case of any petition under this Act, "High Court" is that one of the aforesaid Courts within the local limits of whose ordinary appellate jurisdiction, or of whose jurisdiction under this Act, the husband and wife reside or last resided together.

"District judge."

(2) "District Judge" means, in the Regulation provinces,—a Judge of a principal Civil Court of original jurisdiction;

in the non-Regulation provinces, other than Sindh and the areas for the time being comprised within the local limits of the ordinary civil jurisdiction of the Recorder of Rangoon and of the civil jurisdiction of the Court of the Judge of the town of Moulmain,—a Commissioner of a division;

in Sindh,—the Judicial Commissioner of that province;

in the areas aforesaid,—the Recorder of Rangoon and the Judge of the town of Moulmain, respectively;

and in any place in the dominions of the Princes

PRELIMINARY.

and States aforesaid, such officer as the Governor-General of India in Council shall from time to time appoint in this behalf by notification in the *Gazette of India*, and, in the absence of such officer, the High Court in the exercise of its original jurisdiction under this Act.

§ 3.

(3) "District Court" means, in the case of any petition under this Act, the Court of the District Judge within the local limits of whose ordinary jurisdiction, or of whose jurisdiction under this Act, the husband and wife reside, or last resided together.

"District Court."

(4) "Court" means the High Court or the District Court, as the case may be.

"Court."

(5) "Minor children" means, in the case of sons of native fathers, boys who have not completed the age of sixteen years, and, in the case of daughters of native fathers, girls who have not completed the age of thirteen years. In other cases it means unmarried children who have not completed the age of eighteen years.

"Minor children."

(6) "Incestuous adultery" means adultery committed by a husband with a woman, with whom, if his wife were dead, he could not lawfully contract marriage by reason of her being within the prohibited degrees of consanguinity (whether natural or legal) or affinity.

"Incestuous adultery."

(7) "Bigamy with adultery" means adultery with the same woman with whom the bigamy was committed.

"Bigamy with adultery."

(8) "Marriage with another woman" means marriage of any person, being married, to any

"Marriage with another woman."

§ 3.

other person during the life of the former wife, whether the second marriage shall have taken place within the dominions of her Majesty or elsewhere.

"Desertion."

(9) "Desertion" implies an abandonment against the wish of the person charging it; and

"Property."

(10) "Property" includes, in the case of a wife, any property to which she is entitled for an estate in remainder or reversion, or as trustee, executrix, or administratrix; and the date of the death of the testator or intestate shall be deemed to be the time at which any such wife becomes entitled as executrix or administratrix.

(i) Sect. 3 is as amended by Act XI of 1889 (the Lower Burma Courts Act).

The Punjab Courts Act, 1884, repealed so much of sect. 3 as defines "district judge" in the Punjab to mean "the commissioner of a division." For the definitions of "incestuous adultery" and "bigamy" given by sect. 27 of the Matrimonial Causes Act, 1857, see sect. 10, *post*.

"European British subject."

(ii) "European British subject":

As defined by the Criminal Procedure Code, 1882 (s. 4), "European British subject" means—

(a) Any subject of Her Majesty born, naturalized, or domiciled in the United Kingdom of Great Britain and Ireland, or in any of the European, American, or Australian colonies or possessions of Her Majesty, or in the colony of New Zealand, or in the colony of the Cape of Good Hope or Natal:

(b) Any child or grandchild of any such person by legitimate descent.

The criminal jurisdiction of the High Courts and of the Chief Court of the Punjab extends to European British subjects resident within the local limits of such Court's appellate criminal jurisdiction, and within such other territories as have been notified for that purpose by the Governor-General in Council under the provisions of 28 & 29 Vict. c. 15, s. 3. For a list of such territories, see Prinsep's "Criminal Procedure Code, 1882," under sect. 458.

§ 3.

(iii) "**Reside or last resided together**":

"Reside or last resided together."

In Webster's Dictionary the verb "to reside" is defined as meaning "to dwell permanently, or for a length of time; to have one's dwelling or home;" and in numerous cases the Courts have held that the words "dwelling," "place of abode," and "residence" are synonymous (see *Lambe* v. *Smythe*, 15 L. J., Ex. 287; *Alexander* v. *Jones*, L. R., 1 Ex. 133). A "dwelling" is the place where a man lives, and which he considers his home for the time being. It is constituted by an actual occupancy coupled with an intention to give the character of a certain permanency to such occupancy. If a man has a family dwelling in some place, but occasionally occupies a house and sleeps in another place, his "residence" will be in the former, and not the latter, place (cf. *Gopal Chunder Sircar* v. *Kurnodar Mooshee*, 7 Suth., W. R. 349).

Mere casual presence, or even "residence" for a temporary purpose with no intention of remaining, is not "dwelling," nor, where a party has a fixed "residence" out of the jurisdiction, will an occasional visit within the jurisdiction suffice to confer jurisdiction by reason of residency (*Lelim Tewarree* v. *Govingdeer Gosain*, Marsh. 64).

If a man has a dwelling in a certain place, a mere temporary absence, with the fixed intention of returning, will not alter the character of his residence in the former place (*Whithorne* v. *Thomas*, 7 Man. & Gr. 1).

A man who has a fixed dwelling in the plains does not the less "dwell" there, according to the proper and legal construction of the word, because for health or pleasure he passes the hot season on the hills (*Orde* v. *Skinner*, L. R., vii Ind. App. pp. 204, 205).

Where A., whose *zamindari* and dwelling-house in the district of D. had been sold, came to Calcutta in May, 1880, and there filed his petition under the Insolvents Act (11 & 12 Vict. c. 21), remaining in Calcutta in a hired house till September (when the Court rose for the vacation), and returning there shortly before the end of the vacation after a temporary absence for the purpose of raising funds for the insolvency proceedings, the High Court held that, although A. had no "residence" outside Calcutta, he did not "reside" there within the meaning of

§ 3. sect. 5 of the statute (*In re Ram Paul Singh*, 8 C. L. R. 14; cf. *In re Tietkins*, 1 B. L. R., O. C. 84).

Although the word "residence" or "reside" "may receive a larger or more restricted meaning, according to what the Court believes the intention of the Legislature to have been in framing the particular provision in which the word is used" (*per* Sargent, C.J., *Mahomed Shaffi* v. *Laldin*, I. L. R., iii Bomb. 227), the authorities, to which reference has been made above, tend to show that if a man has any kind of fixed home in a certain place, he must be regarded as "residing" there, although he may be temporarily absent for the purposes of health, pleasure, or business. If, therefore, during such absence from his home he and his wife have cohabited together for a time in another place, but have previously lived together at their "home," they will (it is submitted) have "last resided together" in the place where their home is situated, and not where they last cohabited together.

At the same time, if a man has no such fixed abode or home, he and his wife will have "last resided together" in the place where they last cohabited together. So, too, where a man has two homes or dwelling-houses in different places (as is possible, *Orde* v. *Skinner, supra*), he and his wife will have "last resided together" in that one of the two homes or dwelling-houses where they last cohabited together.

"District Court":

For the purposes of the Indian Divorce Act, the Divisional Court is, in the Punjab, deemed to be the District Court for all districts comprised in the division (Punjab Courts Act, 1884, s. 23 (*a*)).

As regards appeals from the decrees of the Judicial Commissioner of Oudh when exercising the powers of a district judge under Act XIII of 1879 and the Indian Divorce Act, and from the decrees of the District Court of Lucknow, see note to sect. 55, *post*.

"Reside or last resided together":

A district judge ought in all cases to inquire into, and set out in his judgment, the facts relied on as giving jurisdiction to the Court to pronounce a decree of dissolution (*Durand* v. *Durand*, 14 W. R. 416; *Wingrove* v. *Wingrove*, 14 W. R. 416).

"Minor children": §3.

"Minor children" is defined for the purposes of chap. xi. of the Act, which deals with the custody, education and maintenance of minor children, the marriage of whose parents is the subject of the particular suit.

In the case of children of other than native fathers, the age of minority, for the purposes of chap. xi., is extended by this Act to a period beyond that originally adopted by the English Divorce Court as the limit of its jurisdiction to deal with the custody, education and maintenance of the children of a marriage which was the subject of a suit before it. Following the decision of the Queen's Bench in *Reg.* v. *Hawes* (30 L. J., Mag. Cas. 47), that a father had the right to claim the custody of his children by legal process up to the age of sixteen, the English Divorce Court held that it had no power to deal with the custody, education and maintenance of children who were above that age (*Mallinson* v. *Mallinson*, L. R., 1 P. & D. 221; 35 L. J., P. & M. 84; *Ryder* v. *Ryder*, 2 S. & T. 225; 30 L. J., P. & M. 44; *Webster* v. *Webster*, 31 L. J., P. & M. 184). But in the recent case of *Thomasset* v. *Thomasset*, (1894) P. 295; 63 L. J., P. & M. 140, the Court of Appeal in England held (overruling *Blandford* v. *Blandford*, (1892) P. 148), that the Divorce Court has jurisdiction to make orders respecting these matters during the whole period of a child's infancy—that is to say, till the child attains the age of twenty-one years.

"Incestuous adultery":

As regards the question with whom a man, whose former wife is dead, may lawfully contract a marriage, see note to sect. 19 (*post*), where the question of capacity to marry and the validity of marriages in general will be found fully discussed.

"Bigamy with adultery":

The adultery must be with the same woman with whom the bigamy was committed (*Horne* v. *Horne*, 27 L. J., P. & M. 50).

It is not sufficient, to establish "bigamy with adultery," to prove that a ceremony of marriage has been gone through with a certain third person; substantive proof that adultery has also been committed with that person is absolutely necessary. Thus where all that was proved was that the respondent had gone through a form of marriage with another woman in America, and there was no evidence of any subsequent cohabitation between the parties to the bigamous marriage, the Court held that

§ 3. the mere proof of the ceremony of marriage was not sufficient to satisfy the words "bigamy with adultery" in sect. 27 of 20 & 21 Vict. c. 85 (*Ellam* v. *Ellam*, 58 L. J., P. & M. 56).

Nor will adultery be inferred from bigamy alone being charged in the petition (*Bonaparte* v. *Bonaparte*, 65 L. T. 795).

To establish "bigamy" as a ground for the sentence of the Divorce Court there must be proof of the performance of such a ceremony as, but for the former marriage, would constitute a valid marriage, and if the bigamy took place abroad or in a colony, proof of the marriage law of that country is necessary (*Burt* v. *Burt*, 2 S. & T. 88; 29 L. J., P. & M. 133).

But "bigamy with adultery" is established by proof of the subsequent marriage and cohabitation, although such subsequent marriage is null and void on the ground of consanguinity (*Reg.* v. *Penson*, 5 C. & P. 412; *Reg.* v. *Brawn*, 1 C. & K. 144; cf. *Gurbakhsh Singh* v. *Shama Singh*, No. 19, *Punjab Record*, 1876, crim. judgments). The bigamy must be proved; the mere proof of a conviction of bigamy not being sufficient (*March* v. *March*, 28 L. J., P. & M. 30).

"Marriage with another woman."

"Marriage with another woman":

Under the Indian Penal Code (sect. 494), a person "who contracts a marriage during the life of a former husband or wife" does not commit the offence of bigamy "if such husband or wife, at the time of the subsequent marriage, shall have been continually absent from such person for the space of seven years, and shall not have been heard of by such person as being alive within that time, providing that the person contracting such subsequent marriage shall, before such marriage takes place, inform the person with whom such marriage is contracted of the real state of the facts so far as the same are within his or her knowledge."

Under such circumstances a man who, during the life of his wife, marries another woman does not commit bigamy. But if, after such second marriage, he cohabits with such woman, or (apparently) commits adultery with any other woman, the wife is entitled, under sect. 10 of the Act, to apply for a dissolution of marriage just as she would have been entitled to apply had the husband been guilty of "bigamy with adultery."

II.—*Jurisdiction.*

4. The jurisdiction now exercised by the High Courts in respect of divorce *a mensâ et toro*, and in all other causes, suits and matters matrimonial, shall be exercised by such Courts and by the District Courts subject to the provisions in this Act contained, and not otherwise: except so far as relates to the granting of marriage licences, which may be granted as if this Act had not been passed.

Matrimonial jurisdiction of High Courts to be exercised subject to this Act. Exception.

Jurisdiction.—(1) The Select Committee purposely refrained from inserting in the Act a clause conferring on the High Courts the special jurisdiction which is vested in the Divorce Court in England by the Legitimacy Declaration Act, 1858 (21 & 22 Vict. c. 93). That statute enables the Court in England to make declarations of the validity or invalidity of a marriage, or of the legitimacy or illegitimacy of children; but the Select Committee, after carefully considering the matter, refused to confer such jurisdiction on the High Courts, out of deference to the authority of Sir Barnes Peacock, C. J., and Mr. Justice Norman, who gave weighty reasons against the insertion of any such clause.

Nor have the Courts in India jurisdiction to entertain suits in respect of "*jactitation of marriage,*" *i.e.*, suits to enforce perpetual silence on the person who falsely gives out that he or she is married to the complainant (see the Matrimonial Causes Act, 1857, sect. 6, for the jurisdiction of the English Divorce Court to entertain such suits).

(2) The jurisdiction in matrimonial causes exercised by the *High Courts* previously to the enactment of this Act was that conferred upon them (in virtue of 24 & 25 Vict. c. 104) by their respective charters, and extended to all Christian subjects of the Crown within the respective provinces, nothing being said, however, about the matrimonial law to be administered (see *Lopez* v. *Lopez*, I. L. R., xii Calc. at pp. 725, 726; see the note to sect. 1, *ante*).

"**Subject to the provisions in this Act contained**":

To give jurisdiction in matrimonial suits under this Act it is necessary *in all cases*—(i) that the petitioner profess the Christian

"Subject to the provisions in this Act."

§ 4.

religion and be residing in India at the time of presenting the petition; (ii) that the parties to the marriage have "last resided together" within the jurisdiction of the particular Court in which the suit is instituted; and (iii) *semble*, that the marriage between the parties to the suit is one of a kind recognized as such by the Courts of Christian countries (see note (*d*) to sect. 2).

In addition to the above requirements, it is further necessary— (a) *in suits for dissolution of marriage*, that the marriage shall have been solemnized in India, or that the adultery, rape, or unnatural crime complained of shall have been committed in India, or that the husband shall have, since the solemnization of the marriage, exchanged his profession of Christianity for that of some other form of religion; and (b) *in suits for nullity of marriage*, that the marriage shall have been solemnized in India.

The petitioner may present his petition either to the High Court or the District Court having original jurisdiction to try suits under this Act, within whose jurisdiction under the Act the husband and wife "last resided together."

Under sect. 8 of the Act, however, "the High Court may, whenever it thinks fit, remove and try and determine as a Court of original jurisdiction, any suit or proceeding instituted under this Act, in the Court of any district judge within the limits of its jurisdiction under this Act." And "the High Court may also withdraw any such suit or proceeding, and transfer it for trial or disposal to the Court of any other such district judge."

Moreover, under sect. 17 of the Act, "during the progress of the suit in the Court of the district judge, any person suspecting that any parties to the suit are or have been acting in collusion for the purpose of obtaining a divorce, shall be at liberty, in such manner as the High Court by general or special order from time to time directs, to apply to the High Court to remove the suit under sect. 8, and the High Court shall thereupon, if it think fit, remove such suit and try and determine the same as a Court of original jurisdiction, and the provisions contained in sect. 16 shall apply to every suit so removed; or it may direct the district judge to take such steps in respect of the alleged collusion as may be necessary to enable it to make a decree in accordance with the justice of the case."

A petition for dissolution or nullity of marriage may be presented to such District Court, but in such suits every decree made by the district judge dissolving or annulling the marriage is subject to confirmation by the High Court, and the provisions of sect. 17 (with the exception, in the case of a decree for nullity of marriage, of clause 5) apply to all such decrees.

§ 4.

If the district judge dismiss a petition for dissolution or nullity of marriage, the petitioner may appeal to the High Court, but there is no such appeal from a decree of a district judge dissolving or annulling the marriage, nor from the order of the High Court confirming, or refusing to confirm, such decree.

Except as above stated, all decrees and orders made by the district judge in any suit or proceeding under this Act may be appealed from in the like manner as the decrees and orders of such judge made in the exercise of his original civil jurisdiction may be appealed from under the laws, orders and rules for the time being in force (sect. 55 of the Act). But there is no appeal on the subject of costs alone.

In a suit for dissolution of marriage instituted in the District Court, any person may intervene, *during the progress of such suit*, as provided in sect. 17. There is, however, no provision made in the Act for such intervention during the interval between the decree of the district judge and the time (not less than six months thereafter) when the case comes on before the High Court for confirmation. If, on the other hand, the suit is instituted, in the High Court, any person is at liberty to intervene at any time after the pronouncing of the decree *nisi* and before such decree is made absolute. But in this case intervention is not allowable during the progress of the suit previous to the pronouncing of the decree *nisi*.

When a petition is presented to a district judge, the facts relied on as giving jurisdiction to the Court should appear on the face of the record, and the judge should in all cases inquire into such facts and set them out in his judgment (*Durand* v. *Durand*, 14 W. R. 416; *Wingrove* v. *Wingrove, ib.*).

As regards petitions for dissolution of marriage presented to a High Court, if the Court is satisfied on the evidence that the case of the petitioner is proved, and does not find that the petitioner has been guilty of conduct specified in sect. 14 as disentitling him or her to the relief prayed for, the Court shall pronounce a decree *nisi* declaring the marriage dissolved. After the expiration of such time, not less than six months from the pronouncing thereof, as the High Court, by general or special order, from time to time directs, the decree *nisi* may, on the motion of the petitioner, be made absolute. But unless the petitioner moves the Court within a reasonable time to have the

§ 4. decree *nisi* made absolute, the High Court may dismiss the suit (sect. 16).

If after a decree *nisi* has been pronounced, and before it has been made absolute, any person intervenes, the High Court may pass such order or decree thereon as justice demands, and may order the costs arising from such intervention to be paid by the parties, or such one or more of them, as it thinks fit. Every such order or decree is appealable in the like manner as the decrees and orders of the Court made in the exercise of its original civil jurisdiction are appealable, provided that there is no appeal on the subject of costs only.

A decree *nisi* or decree absolute made by the High Court, and all other decrees and orders made by such Court in any suit or proceeding under this Act, are appealable in the like manner (sect. 55). Moreover, by sect. 56, "any person may appeal to Her Majesty in Council from any decree (other than a decree *nisi*) or order under this Act of a High Court made on appeal or otherwise, and from any decree (other than a decree *nisi*) or order made in the exercise of original jurisdiction by judges of a High Court or of any Division Court from which an appeal shall not lie to the High Court, *when* the High Court declares that the case is a fit one for appeal to Her Majesty in Council."

Under that section an appeal lies (with the leave of the High Court) to Her Majesty in Council from the order of the High Court confirming, or refusing to confirm, the decree of a district judge for dissolution, or of nullity, of marriage.

Review of judgment.

Review of Judgment.

Neither the Indian Divorce Act nor the Civil Procedure Code (by which, subject to the provisions of the Act itself, all proceedings under the Act are to be regulated: sect. 45, Indian Divorce Act) makes any provision for the grant of new trials. But by sect. 623 of the Civil Procedure Code, 1882, "any person considering himself aggrieved" by a decree or order from which an appeal is allowed, but from which no appeal has been preferred, or by a decree or order from which no appeal is allowed, "and who, from the discovery of new and important matter or evidence, which, after the exercise of due diligence, was not within his knowledge, or could not be produced by him at the time when the decree was passed or the order made, or on account of some mistake or error apparent on the face of the record, *or for any other sufficient reason*, desires to obtain a review of the decree passed or order made against him, may apply for a review of judgment to the Court which passed the decree or made the order, or to the Court, if any, to which the business of the former Court has been transferred.

§ 4.

"A party who is not appealing from a decree may apply for a review of judgment, notwithstanding the pendency of an appeal by some other party, except when the ground of such appeal is common to the applicant and the appellant, or when, being the respondent, he can present to the Appellate Court the case on which he relies for the review." But sect. 624 provides that, "except upon the ground of the discovery of such new and important matter or evidence as aforesaid, or of some clerical error apparent on the face of the decree, no application for a review of judgment, *other than that of a High Court*, shall be made to any judge other than the judge who delivered it."

The rules laid down in the Civil Procedure Code as to the form of making appeals apply, *mutatis mutandis*, to applications for review (sect. 625).

An application for review of judgment must be filed within ninety days from the date of the decree or order, when such decree or order is that of a District Court or of the High Court, otherwise than in the exercise of its original jurisdiction, and within twenty days from the date of the decree or order when such decree or order is that of the High Court in the exercise of its original jurisdiction (*Limitation Act*, 1877, 2nd sch., arts. 162 and 173).

Limitation.

The Court fee on an application for review of judgment is the fee leviable on the plaint or memorandum of appeal, unless such application is presented before the ninetieth day from the date of the decree, when it is one-half of such fee (*Court Fees Act*, 1870, 1st sch., arts. 4, 5).

Court fee on application.

"If it appears to the Court that there is not sufficient ground for a review, it shall reject the application.

"If the Court be of opinion that the application for a review should be granted, it shall grant the same, and the judge shall record with his own hand his reasons for such opinion.

"*Provided* that (a) no such application shall be granted without previous notice to the opposite party, to enable him to appear and be heard in support of the decree, a review of which is applied for; and (b) no such application shall be granted on the ground of discovery of new matter or evidence which the applicant alleges was not within his knowledge, or could not be adduced by him when the decree or order was

THE INDIAN DIVORCE ACT.

§ 4. passed, without strict proof of such allegation; and (c) an application made under sect. 624 to the judge who delivered the judgment may, if that judge has ordered notice to issue under proviso (a) to this section, be disposed of by his successor" (sect. 626, Civil Procedure Code).

It is not sufficient for an applicant to merely state in his affidavit that he did not know of the existence of the new evidence; he must also state he had used due diligence and made all proper inquiries (*Seetanath Ghose* v. *Shama Sorndari*, 14 W. R. 26).

As to what constitutes "*other sufficient reason*" for granting an application for review—other than the grounds specified in sect. 623 of the Code—their Lordships of the Privy Council have held that it is not "an absolute defect of jurisdiction whenever the parties have failed to show that there was either positive error in law or new evidence to be brought forward which could not be brought forward on the first hearing. They do not consider the case cited in the *Indian Jurist* . . . . and the other cases cited, limit the discretion of the Court in saying what reason is good and sufficient, or what may be so far requisite to the ends of justice as to support an application for review. Upon an appeal, where an appeal lies, it may be open to the Court of Appeal to say that the judge ought not to have admitted a review; that is a different thing from ruling that he has acted wholly without jurisdiction" (*Reasut* v. *Abdoolah*, L. R., 3 Ind. App. 221; I. L. R., 2 Calc. 140).

"When an application for a review is granted, a note thereof shall be made in the register, and the Court may at once rehear the case or make such order in regard to the rehearing as it thinks fit" (sect. 630, Civil Procedure Code). When a review is granted, the Court possesses a discretion as to how far the whole case is to be reopened. In each case it must consider whether the review is necessary to correct any error or omission, or is otherwise requisite for the ends of justice, and there is no rule that no point can be raised on review which has already been decided at the original hearing, or that no new point which has not been raised at the hearing can be argued on review (*Chinta Monee* v. *Pearee Monee*, 15 W. R. (F. B.) 1).

"An order of the Court for rejecting the application shall be final; but whenever such application is admitted, the admission may be objected to on the ground that it was—(a) in contravention of the provisions of sect. 624; (b) in contravention of the provisions of sect. 626; or (c) after the expiration of the period of limitation prescribed therefor and without sufficient cause. § 4.

"Such objection may be made at once by an appeal against the order granting the application, or may be taken in any appeal against the final decree or order made in the suit.

"When the application has been rejected in consequence of the failure of the applicant to appear, he may apply for an order to have the rejected application restored to the file, and, if it be proved to the satisfaction of the Court that he was prevented by any sufficient cause from appearing when such application was called on for hearing, the Court may order it to be restored to the file upon such terms as to costs or otherwise as it thinks fit, and shall appoint a day for hearing the same.

"No order shall be made under this section unless the applicant has served the opposite party with notice in writing of the latter application.

"No application to review an order passed on review or on an application for review shall be entertained" (sect. 629, Civil Procedure Code).

Except as provided, and for the reasons specified in the above section, no appeal lies from an order granting a review (*Bombay and Persian Steam Navigation Co.* v. ss. "*Zuari,*" I. L. R., xii Bomb. 171; *Har Nandan Sahai* v. *Behari Sing*, I. L. R., xxii Calc. 3; *Baroda Churn* v. *Gorind Proshed*, I. L. R., xxii Calc. 984; *Duryai Bibi* v. *Badri Prasad*, I. L. R., xviii All. 44; *Dharm Singh* v. *Dewa Singh*, No. 62, *Punjab Record*, 1895).

"Objections to jurisdiction":

Objections to jurisdiction.

There is a distinction between cases in which a Court has no *inherent* jurisdiction in the suit and those in which the Court is competent to try the cause, but there are *irregularities in the initial procedure*. As regards the former class of cases, no consent or acquiescence on the part of the parties can convert the proceedings before the Court into a judicial process, whereas, in the latter case, if the parties join issue and go to trial upon the merits, neither party can afterwards dispute the jurisdiction of the Court on the ground of those irregularities which, if objected to at the time, would have led to the dismissal of the suit (*Ledgard* v. *Bull*, L. R., 13 Ind. App. 134; I. L. R., ix All. 191). If, however, a Court which has no *inherent* jurisdiction therein entertains and decides a suit, the decree will be set aside on that ground by the Appellate Court, although the point of juris-

§ 4. diction was not raised in the lower Court (*Har Narain* v. *Bhagwant Kaur*, I. L. R., xiii All. 300).

But, except in cases in which the Court has no inherent jurisdiction, it is a general rule that if the parties have put in an absolute appearance, it is too late to plead to the jurisdiction of the Court (*Zyclinski* v. *Zyclinski*, 2 S. & T. 420 ; 31 L. J., P. & M. 37). Nor can the respondent be permitted to withdraw such appearance in order to enter an appearance under protest to enable him to plead to the jurisdiction (*Moore* v. *Moore*, 5 Ir. R. Eq. 371). The respondent may, however, in his answer on the merits, allege facts raising the question of jurisdiction (*Wilson* v. *Wilson and Howell*, 2 L. R., P. 341 ; 41 L. J., P. & M. 1). So, it has been held that it is not absolutely necessary to raise the question of *domicil* in the pleadings, and that the Court can allow such question to be raised at the hearing if the evidence adduced points to a doubt as to the Court's jurisdiction (*Parkinson* v. *Parkinson*, 69 L. T. 53 ; cf. *Forster* v. *Forster and Berridge*, 3 S. & T. 144 ; 31 L. J., P. & M. 185). But, according to Rule 22 of the Rules and Regulations of the English Divorce Court, if a party wishes to raise any question as to the jurisdiction of the Court, he or she must enter an appearance under protest, and after the entry of an absolute appearance to the citation, a party cited cannot raise any objection to the jurisdiction of the Court (cf. *Garstin* v. *Garstin*, 34 L. J., P. & M. 45).

The Court is not debarred from ordering alimony *pendente lite* to be paid to a wife, because there is a plea to the jurisdiction of the Court (*Ronalds* v. *Ronalds*, L. R., 3 P. 259).

Enforcement of decrees or orders heretofore made by Supreme or High Court.

5. Any decree or order of the late Supreme Court of Judicature at Calcutta, Madras or Bombay sitting on the ecclesiastical side, or of any of the said High Courts sitting in the exercise of their matrimonial jurisdiction, respectively, in any cause or matter matrimonial, may be enforced and dealt with by the said High Courts, respectively, as hereinafter mentioned, in like manner as if such decree or order had been originally made under this Act by the Court so enforcing or dealing with the same.

Pending suits.

6. All suits and proceedings in causes and matters

matrimonial, which when this Act comes into operation are pending in any High Court, shall be dealt with and decided by such Court, so far as may be, as if they had been originally instituted therein under this Act.

§ 6.

7. Subject to the provisions contained in this Act, the High Courts and District Courts shall in all suits and proceedings hereunder, act and give relief on principles and rules which, in the opinion of the said Courts, are as nearly as may be conformable to the principles and rules on which the Court for Divorce and Matrimonial Causes in England for the time being acts and gives relief.

Court to act on principles of English Divorce Court.

"**Principles and Rules of English Divorce Court:**"

As regards matters of procedure, all proceedings under the Indian Divorce Act between party and party are to be regulated (subject to the express provisions of the Act itself) by the Code of Civil Procedure (sect. 45, *infra*). In all matters, therefore, which are provided for in the Code, the Courts must regulate their procedure in accordance with the provisions therein contained, and not with the Rules and Regulations of the Court for Divorce and Matrimonial Causes in England (*Abbott* v. *Abbott and Crump*, 4 B. L. R., O. C. 51). But, in the absence of any provision on the subject in the Code, sect. 7 enables the Courts of this country to follow, so far as is possible, the practice of the English Court, and it has therefore been thought convenient to append to this edition of the Act the Rules and Regulations of that Court (see Appendix (G)).

Principles and rules of English Divorce Court.

The decisions of the Probate and Divorce Court in England must be taken to be a guide to the Courts in India under the Indian Divorce Act, except when the facts of any particular case, arising out of the peculiar circumstances of Anglo-Indian life, constitute a situation such as the English Court is not likely to have had in view (*Fowle* v. *Fowle*, I. L. R., iv Calc. 260).

8. The High Court may, whenever it thinks fit, remove and try and determine, as a Court of original jurisdiction, any suit or proceeding instituted under this

Extraordinary jurisdiction of High Court.

§ 8.

Power to transfer suits.

Act in the Court of any district judge within the limits of its jurisdiction under this Act.

The High Court may also withdraw any such suit or proceeding, and transfer it for trial or disposal to the Court of any other such district judge.

> During the progress of a *suit for dissolution of marriage* in the Court of a district judge, any person suspecting that any parties to the suit are or have been acting in collusion for the purpose of obtaining a divorce, shall be at liberty, in such manner as the High Court by general or special order from time to time directs, to apply to the High Court to remove the suit under sect. 8, and the High Court shall thereupon, if it think fit, remove such suit, and try and determine the same as a Court of original jurisdiction, and the provisions contained in sect. 16 shall apply to every suit so removed; or it may direct the district judge to take such steps in respect of the alleged collusion as may be necessary to enable him to make a decree in accordance with the justice of the case (sect. 17, *post*).

Reference to High Court.

9. When any question of law or usage having the force of law arises at any point in the proceedings previous to the hearing of any suit under this Act by a District Court or at any subsequent stage of such suit, or in the execution of the decree therein or order thereon,

the Court may, either of its own motion or on the application of any of the parties, draw up a statement of the case and refer it, with the Court's own opinion thereon, to the decision of the High Court.

If the question has arisen previous to or in the hearing, the District Court may either stay such proceedings, or proceed in the case pending such reference, and pass a decree contingent upon the opinion of the High Court upon it.

If a decree or order has been made, its execution shall be stayed until the receipt of the order of the High Court upon such reference.

III.—*Dissolution of Marriage.*

10. Any husband may present a petition to the District Court or to the High Court, praying that his marriage may be dissolved, on the ground that his wife has, since the solemnization thereof, been guilty of adultery. *[When husband may petition for dissolution.]*

Any wife may present a petition to the District Court or to the High Court, praying that her marriage may be dissolved on the ground that, since the solemnization thereof, her husband has exchanged his profession of Christianity for the profession of some other religion, and gone through a form of marriage with another woman; *[When wife may petition for dissolution.]*

—or has been guilty of incestuous adultery,

—or of bigamy with adultery,

—or of marriage with another woman with adultery,

—or of rape, sodomy or bestiality,

—or of adultery coupled with such cruelty as without adultery would entitle her to a divorce *a mensâ et toro;*

—or of adultery coupled with desertion, without reasonable excuse, for two years or upwards.

Every such petition shall state, as distinctly as the nature of the case permits, the facts on which the claim to have such marriage dissolved is founded. *[Contents of petition.]*

The Matrimonial Causes Act, 1857 (20 & 21 Vict. c. 85), sect. 27, provides that :—

> "It shall be lawful for any husband to present a petition to the said Court praying that his marriage may be dissolved, on the ground that his wife has, since the celebration thereof, been guilty of adultery; and it shall be lawful for any wife to present a petition to the said Court, praying that her marriage may be dissolved, on the ground that, since the celebration thereof, her husband has been guilty of incestuous adultery, or of bigamy with adultery, or of rape, or of sodomy or bestiality, or of adultery coupled with such cruelty as would have entitled her to a divorce *a mensâ et thoro,* or of adultery coupled with desertion,

§ 10.

without reasonable excuse, for two years or upwards; and every such petition shall state, as distinctly as the nature of the case permits, the facts on which the claim to have such marriage dissolved is founded: provided that, for the purposes of this Act, incestuous adultery shall be taken to mean adultery committed by a husband with a woman with whom, if his wife were dead, he could not lawfully contract marriage by reason of her being within the prohibited degrees of consanguinity or affinity; and bigamy shall be taken to mean marriage of any person, being married, to any other person during the life of the former husband or wife, whether the second marriage shall have taken place within the dominions of Her Majesty or elsewhere."

(i) "**Any husband . . . . . Any wife :**"

Jurisdiction of Court.

In order to give jurisdiction to the Courts of British India to entertain a suit for dissolution of marriage, it is necessary that (a) the petitioner should profess the Christian religion and be residing in India at the time of presenting the petition; (b) that the marriage, of which dissolution is prayed, should be of a kind recognized as such by the Courts of Christian countries (see *ante*, p. 3); and (c) that *either* the marriage shall have been solemnized in India, *or* that the adultery, rape, or unnatural crime complained of, shall have been committed in India, *or* that the husband shall have, since the solemnization of the marriage, exchanged his profession of Christianity for that of some other religion.

In addition to the above requirements, it is necessary to give jurisdiction to the particular Court (whether District or High Court) that the parties to the marriage shall have last resided together within the limits of such Court's jurisdiction (section 3, *ante*, pp. 17, 18).

Husband or wife a lunatic, idiot, or minor.

When the husband or wife is a lunatic or idiot, a suit for dissolution of marriage may be brought on his or her behalf by the committee or other person entitled to his or her custody (sect. 48, *post*).

When the petitioner is a minor, he or she must sue by his or her next friend to be approved of by the Court; and no petition presented by a minor under this Act shall be filed until the next friend has undertaken in writing to be answerable for costs. Such undertaking must be filed in Court, and the next friend shall thereupon be liable in the same manner, and to the same extent, as if he were a plaintiff in an ordinary suit (sect. 49, *post*).

DISSOLUTION OF MARRIAGE.

(ii) "**May present a petition:**" § 10.

(a) *The Court Fee Stamp* on a petition for dissolution of marriage is one of Rs. 20 (Court Fees Act, 1870, 2nd Sch., Art. No. 20).

Court fee stamp.

(b) *Agreement in bar of Suit—Compromise of Suit.*
In England it has been held that a suit for dissolution of marriage may be compromised, and that if the husband or wife has agreed for good and valuable consideration, uninfluenced by fraud or mistake, to withdraw from a suit for dissolution, such party cannot afterwards, in violation of such agreement, sue in respect of the misconduct upon which the former suit was based, the right to complain in respect thereof having been bargained away (*Sterbini* v. *Sterbini*, 39 L. J., P. & M. 82; *Hooper* v. *Hooper*, 3 S. & T. 251; *Rowley* v. *Rowley*, L. R., 1 H. L. 63; 35 L. J., P. & M. 110).

Agreement in bar of suit.

But such agreement, unless followed by cohabitation, does not amount to condonation of the misconduct; and, by sect. 14 of the Act, if the Court does not find that the petitioner has been guilty of certain specified acts, it "shall" pronounce a decree *nisi* in his favour. At the same time it may be that sect. 7 gives the Courts a discretion in the matter, of which they will avail themselves, to follow the practice of the English Courts of Equity and Divorce.

(c) *Res judicata—Estoppel.*
The principles of estoppel and of *res judicata* applicable to ordinary civil suits apply equally to matrimonial suits; therefore a judgment of the Court upon a matter directly in issue is conclusive upon the same matter between the same parties in another suit. A party whose petition has been dismissed in a former suit, cannot in a subsequent suit set up matters previously found against him or her (*Sopwith* v. *Sopwith*, 2 S. & T. 160; 30 L. J., P. & M. 131; *Finney* v. *Finney*, L. R., 1 P. 483; 37 L. J., P. & M. 43).

Res judicata—estoppel.

But if the petition has been allowed to be withdrawn upon the application of the petitioner, the latter will not be estopped from setting up the same acts of adultery, upon which his first petition was based, in a suit subsequently instituted by him (*Hall* v. *Hall*, 48 L. J., P. & M. 57). [See further on this subject, Appendix (D).]

§ 10.

Abatement of suit:—
(a) death of petitioner:

(d) Abatement of Suit.

On the death of the petitioner at any time before decree absolute, a suit for dissolution of marriage will abate; and if the petitioner dies after a decree *nisi* has been pronounced, but before it has been made absolute, the legal representative of the petitioner cannot revive the suit for the purpose of applying to make the decree absolute (*Stanhope* v. *Stanhope*, 11 P. D. 103; 55 L. J., P. & M. 36; *Grant* v.*Grant and Bowles*, 2 S. & T. 522; 31 L. J., P. & M. 174; *Beavan* v. *Beavan*, 2 S. & T. 58; 28 L. J., P. & M. 127).

(b) death of respondent:

The suit will also abate on the death of the respondent at any time before the decree absolute; but in such an event the Court will not, on the application of the petitioner, order that the petition and affidavit in support be removed from the files of the Court (*Brocas* v. *Brocas*, 2 S. & T. 383; 30 L. J., P. & M. 172).

(c) death of co-respondent.

A suit for dissolution of marriage does not abate on the death of a co-respondent pending the suit, but application should be made by motion to strike out his name from the petition (*Sutton* v. *Sutton and Peacock*, 32 L. J., P. & M. 156).

Insanity of respondent.

(e) Insanity of Respondent.

The insanity of the respondent at the time of institution of the suit is no ground for staying proceedings therein (*Mordaunt* v. *Moncrieffe*, L. R., 2 H. L. (Sc.) 374; 43 L. J., P. & M. 49).

Nor is a mere plea of insanity a sufficient answer to a suit for dissolution. Accordingly, where in a suit by the husband for dissolution of marriage on the ground of his wife's adultery, the guardian *ad litem* of the wife,—the wife herself being insane at the time—pleaded that if she had committed adultery she was not of sound mind or responsible for her actions, and was incapable of either understanding the guilty nature of her acts or of legally consenting to them, it was held that although the wife might have been subject to insane delusions on some points, yet if at the time that she committed adultery she was capable of appreciating the nature of the act and its probable consequences, her insanity would afford no sufficient defence to the petition (*Yarrow* v. *Yarrow*, (1892) P. 92).

But "it may be that a person is so insane as to necessitate his or her confinement in an asylum or some other place of permanent detention, and the disease may be such that there is no hope of recovery or amelioration such as will allow of his or her discharge. When a disease of that sort seizes upon a person,

DISSOLUTION OF MARRIAGE.

and he or she has to be incarcerated or permanently to be placed in confinement, I should hesitate to say that, in regard to an act committed in such a state of insanity, a plea of insanity might not be an answer. But I think it is very different with regard to intermittent and recurrent insanity" (Butt, J., *Hanbury* v. *Hanbury*, (1892) P. 222).

§ 10.

"**Wife has, since the solemnization of the marriage, been guilty of adultery**":

In a suit for dissolution of marriage on the ground of the wife's adultery, the ante-nuptial incontinence of the wife cannot be pleaded, even though it and the adultery charged are alleged to have been committed with the same person (*Fitzgerald* v. *Fitzgerald*, 32 L. J., P. & M. 12).

As to *proof of adultery*, see Appendix (C).

Adultery on part of wife.

"**Wife's petition for divorce**":

In a suit by a wife for dissolution of marriage, if the facts proved are only sufficient to entitle her to a judicial separation, it is competent for the Court to grant the latter, although the petitioner only prays for dissolution (*Smith* v. *Smith*, 1 S. & T. 359). But if in such a case she refuses to amend her petition by praying for judicial separation, the petition will be dismissed (*Rowley* v. *Rowley*, 4 S. & T. 137; 12 L. T. 505).

Suit by wife, grounds for:

(a) "**Husband has, since the solemnization of the marriage, exchanged his profession of Christianity for that of some other religion, and gone through a form of marriage with some other woman**":

See p. 15, *ante*.

The mere fact that the husband has exchanged his profession of Christianity for that of some other form of religion is not a sufficient ground for dissolution of the marriage: it is also necessary that he should thereafter have gone through a form of marriage with another woman. But it is not necessary to prove that he has committed adultery either with such woman or any other woman.

This clause was inserted in consequence of the decision of the Madras Court to the effect that a Hindu who, after his conversion to Christianity and contraction of a Christian marriage, reverted to Hinduism, re-acquired his rights of polygamy (*Anon.*, 3 Mad. App. 7).

(a) Husband's perversion and marriage with another woman.

§ 10.

Incestuous adultery.

(b) **"Or has been guilty of incestuous adultery"**:

For the definition of "incestuous adultery," see sect. 3, *ante*, p. 19, and as to what is meant by the term "prohibited degrees," see sect. 19 (2), and note thereto, *post*.

Upon a wife's petition charging the respondent with incestuous adultery with his own child, a girl aged thirteen, it appeared that a jury in a criminal court had acquitted him of the more serious charge, but had convicted him of an attempt to carnally know the child. The Court, notwithstanding the certificate of conviction, allowed evidence to be given to prove that the incestuous adultery had in fact taken place (*Virgo* v. *Virgo*, 69 L. T. 460).

Bigamy with adultery.

(c) **"Or of bigamy with adultery"**:

As to this, see sect. 3, and note thereto, *ante*, p. 23.

Marriage with another woman with adultery.
Rape.

(d) **"Or of marriage with another woman with adultery"**:

As to this, see sect. 3, and note thereto, *ante*, p. 24.

(e) **"Or of rape"**:

"A man is said to commit 'rape,' who, except in the case hereinafter excepted, has sexual intercourse with a woman under circumstances falling under any of the five following descriptions:—

"*First*—against her will;

"*Secondly*—without her consent;

"*Thirdly*—with her consent, when her consent has been obtained by putting her in fear of death or of hurt;

"*Fourthly*—with her consent, when the man knows that he is not her husband, and that her consent is given because she believes that he is another man to whom she is, or believes herself to be, lawfully married;

"*Fifthly*—with or without her consent, when she is under twelve years of age.

"*Explanation.*—Penetration is sufficient to constitute the sexual intercourse necessary to the offence of rape.

"*Exception.*—Sexual intercourse by a man with his own wife, the wife not being under twelve years of age, is not rape" (*Indian Penal Code*, sect. 375).

Conviction in criminal court.

In a suit for dissolution of marriage on the ground that the husband has been guilty of rape, the rape must be duly proved, and a proof of a conviction for rape in a criminal court is not sufficient (*March* v. *March*, 28 L. J., P. & M. 30).

Although, as a general rule, a petitioner who has been found guilty of adultery will not be entitled to a decree for dissolution of marriage, the Court, in *Collins* v. *Collins* (9 P. D. 231; 53 L. J., P. & M. 116), granted a wife, who had in a previous suit been found guilty of adultery, a decree *nisi* for dissolution on the ground that her husband had been found guilty of rape subsequently to her own misconduct.

§ 10.

(f) "**Or of sodomy or bestiality**":

Sodomy or bestiality.

A man commits sodomy or bestiality who "voluntarily has carnal intercourse against the order of nature with any man, woman, or animal" (*Indian Penal Code*, sect. 377).

When a husband has carnal intercourse against the order of nature with his own wife, she not being a consenting party, he is guilty of sodomy within the meaning of sect. 10 of the Indian Divorce Act, and the wife is entitled to a decree of dissolution of marriage (No. 68, *Punjab Record*, 1882, civil judgments—full Bench). But the evidence in support of such a charge must be cogent and corroborated, and a wife's evidence of unnatural connection, had or attempted to be had with her by her husband, is not sufficient to establish the charge (*N——* v. *N——*, 3 S. & T. 234).

(g) "**Or of adultery coupled with such cruelty as without adultery would have entitled her to a divorce** *a mensâ et toro*":

Adultery and cruelty.

As to pleading cruelty, see Appendix (E), p. 345.

The question as to what constitutes *legal* cruelty has recently been elaborately discussed by the English Court of Appeal in the case of *Russell* v. *Russell*,* (1895) P. (C. A.) 315; 64 L. J., P. & M. 105). The following extract from the judgment of Lord Justice Lopes (Lindley, L.J., concurring, Rigby, L.J., diss.), will, it is hoped, prove of value in the elucidation of that difficult question:— .

Cruelty.

To constitute legal cruelty "there must be danger to life, limb or health, bodily or mental, or a reasonable apprehension of it. We propose to test this definition by some of the more important cases that have been decided on the subject. . . . . *Evans* v. *Evans* (1 Hagg. Cas. 38), decided by Lord Stowell in 1790, is the leading case on the subject. As we read that case, no husband could be found guilty of legal cruelty towards his wife unless he had either inflicted bodily injury upon her,

Russell v. *Russell*.

---

* The decision of the Court of Appeal in this case has been upheld by the House of Lords (see *Times* newspaper of July 17, 1897).

§ 10.
"cruelty."

or had so conducted himself towards her as to cause actual injury to her mental or bodily health, or so as to raise a reasonable apprehension that he would either inflict actual bodily injury upon her, or cause actual injury to her mental or bodily health. In a word, he must so have conducted himself towards her as to render future cohabitation more or less dangerous to her life or limb, or mental or bodily health. There are some expressions in that most admirable judgment of Lord Stowell to which we would wish to refer. At page 30, the learned judge says:—'What merely wounds the mental feelings is in few cases to be admitted, when they are not accompanied with bodily injury, either actual or menaced. Mere austerity of temper, petulance of manners, rudeness of language, a want of civil attention and accommodation, even occasional sallies of passion, if they do not threaten bodily harm, do not amount to legal cruelty; they are high moral offences in the marriage state undoubtedly, not innocent, surely, in any state of life, but they are not that cruelty against which the law can relieve.' At page 39, the learned judge sums up what he had previously said, thus:—'These are negative descriptions of cruelty; they show only what is not cruelty, and yet, perhaps, the safest definitions which can be given under the infinite variety of possible cases that may come before the Court. But if it were at all necessary to lay down an affirmative rule, I take it that the rule cited by Dr. Bever, from Clarke and the other books of practice, is a good general outline of the canon law, the law of this country, upon this subject. In the older cases of this sort, which I have had an opportunity of looking into, I have observed that the danger to life, limb or health is usually inserted as the ground upon which the Court has proceeded to a separation. This doctrine has been repeatedly applied by the Court in the cases that have been cited. The Court has never been driven off this ground. It has always been jealous of the inconvenience of departing from it, and I have heard no one case cited in which the Court has granted a divorce without proof of a reasonable apprehension of bodily hurt. I say an apprehension, because, assuredly, the Court is not to wait till the hurt is actually done; but the apprehension must be reasonable.' This was the state of the law in 1790, and we venture to say that the doctrine there enunciated as to what constituted legal cruelty has never been materially altered. At that time no amount of want of civility, rudeness, insult or abuse, however gross, which did not affect life, limb, or mental or bodily health, or where there was not a reasonable apprehension of its so doing, was considered by the ecclesiastical tribunals to amount to legal cruelty, and that though the parties were at the time cohabiting. So far as we can ascertain, the authority of the case of *Evans* v. *Evans* has never been questioned. . . . . Before the Divorce and Matrimonial Act, 1857, and since the passing of that Act, the same rule with regard to what constitutes legal cruelty has been followed by Sir Cresswell Cresswell, Lord Penzance and Sir James Hannen; and Sir Charles Butt in December, 1891, at the trial of the case of *Russell* v. *Russell,* when the present petitioner sued for a judicial separation on the ground of cruelty, said, in laying down the law to the jury, that cruelty had been very often defined as injury causing danger to life or limb or health, or causing reasonable apprehension of danger to life or limb or health; and it is, generally speaking, where the continuation of the conduct charged would be likely to produce injury, either bodily or mental, or injury to health without any physical violence, that this Court interposes to protect the wife. There is no case in the books where words alone, however violent, however galling, and even if imputing a crime of the most disgraceful kind, have been held *per se* to constitute legal cruelty, and this when the parties were cohabiting as husband and wife. The case of *Bray* v. *Bray* (1 Hagg. Eccl. 167) is a case which, so far as we can discover, has never been cited or followed as an authority, and is contrary to *Gale* v. *Gale,* subsequently referred to. *Bray* v. *Bray* was a decision only with regard to admitting an article."

The learned Lord Justice, after referring to some of the more important cases on the subject, proceeds to consider the observations of Lord Brougham in the case of *Patterson* v. *Patterson* (9 H. L. Cas. 308) :—" Lord Brougham, at page 328, says ' that if a man were continually charging his wife with every sort of immorality and criminal conduct, and there were not a shadow of foundation for the charges, made before her family, her friends, relatives and servants, and in the face of the world, there was little doubt that what then rested only upon opinions would ultimately assume the form of decisions, and that to such injurious treatment, making the marriage state impossible to be endured, and rendering life almost unbearable, the Courts of the country would extend the remedy of a divorce *a mensâ et thoro.*' These, however, were *obiter dicta,* and were not necessary for the decision. . . . . Again, at p. 318, Lord Brougham says this:— ' That the ground of the remedy is confined to personal violence is not the law of England and certainly not the law of Scotland.

§ 10.
"cruelty."

§ 10.
"*cruelty.*"

. . . . It is not true that the law of England either requires actual injury to the person or threat of such injury.' We presume that this means that a reasonable apprehension of danger to life, limb or health, bodily or mental, will suffice without any actual injury or threat of it" (cf. *Munshi Buzloor Rahim* v. *Shumsoonim Begam*, xi M. I. App. 551; and *Milford* v. *Milford*, L. R., 1 P. & D. 295; 36 L. J., P. & M. 30, and in app. 37 L. J., P. & M. 77). In the opinion of the majority of the Court, therefore, and upon the weight of authority, to constitute legal cruelty there must be danger to life, limb or health, bodily or mental, or a reasonable apprehension of such danger. Lord Justice Rigby, however, dissented from this statement of the law on the ground that personal danger was not in all cases absolutely necessary, and that, although what fell short of such danger or such apprehension of it was to be admitted with great caution, there might be exceptional cases in which, without bodily injury or threat of it, injury to the mental feelings might be sufficient to constitute legal cruelty.

Charge of unnatural offence:

In *Russell* v. *Russell* (*supra*) it was held (*per* Lindley and Lopes, L.JJ., Rigby, L.J., diss.) that for a wife, who had in a suit for judicial separation charged her husband with the commission of an unnatural offence, to persist in the charge after the husband had in such suit been acquitted thereof by the verdict of the jury, and to refuse to retract or apologize therefor, did not constitute legal cruelty, even though a jury found as a matter of fact that she had not a *bonâ fide* belief in the truth of such charge.

So, too, in *Gale* v. *Gale* (2 Robert. Eccl. Rep. 421), it was held that a charge of having committed incest was not *per se* sufficient to constitute legal cruelty, though, coupled with averments of a substantial character, it might form part of the libel. In *Bray* v. *Bray* (1 Hagg. Eccl. 167), however, Sir John Nicholl said that, in his opinion, it was not possible to conceive cruelty of a more grievous character (except, perhaps, great personal violence) than an accusation of incest made by a husband against his wife. But the decision in this case, though approved of by Lord Justice Rigby, did not commend itself to the majority of the Court of Appeal in the case of *Russell* v. *Russell* (*supra*).

or of immorality.

Nor does the bringing by the husband of malicious and groundless charges against his wife's chastity amount in itself to legal cruelty, though it will weigh with the Court in conjunction with other matters (*Durrant* v. *Durrant*, 1 Hagg. Eccl.

Rep. 752). But if a person has ill-treated his wife, and been guilty of acts of violence and words of menace, and finally has made a charge of misconduct and criminality which he has not attempted to prove or even to allege, and under that pretence has shut his door against her, it cannot be doubted that such conduct would be admissible matter in a suit for separation by reason of cruelty (*Ib.*). §10. "*cruelty.*"

A false charge by a husband against his wife of adultery, although such charge is made wilfully, maliciously, and without reasonable or probable cause, is not an act amounting at law to cruelty, so as to entitle the wife to a judicial separation (*Augustin* v. *Augustin*, I. L. R., iv All. 374). False charge of adultery.

Where, however, the acts of cruelty alleged are not of great violence, but evince a lack of self-control and of indignity, they may amount to legal cruelty (*Waddell* v. *Waddell*, 2 S. & T. 584; 31 L. J., P. & M. 123). So, where a man assaulted his wife in the public street without inflicting personal injury, but the assault was quite sufficient to show that the husband was unable to control himself, and could not be trusted not to break out into violence towards his wife, and he had by his conduct and filthy language led a passer-by to take her for a common prostitute and to insult her, it was held that he had been guilty of "the most abominable cruelty" (*Milner* v. *Milner*, 4 S. & T. 240; 31 L. J., P. & M. 159). Acts evincing lack of self-control.

Cruelty is in its character a cumulative charge. It must be sustained, and evince a continued want of self-control, and it must be referable to permanent causes so as to endanger the future safety of the wife's person or health, and therefore, where the charges were confined to three days alone of a cohabitation of three years, the Court held that the legal offence of cruelty had not been established (*Plowden* v. *Plowden*, 23 L. T. 266; 18 W. R. 902).

As regards acts of physical violence, the general rule is that to constitute legal cruelty they must be of such a nature as to show that further cohabitation is unsafe, and whatever may be the cause or motive of a husband's misconduct, the wife is entitled to the protection of the Court if cohabitation is rendered unsafe, unless she is herself greatly to blame (*Curtis* v. *Curtis*, 1 S. & T. 192; 27 L. J., P. & M. 73; in app., 28 L. J., P. & M. 55; *McKeever* v. *McKeever*, 11 Ir. R. Eq. 26).

A single act of violence by a husband towards his wife, not producing any considerable injury to the person, and not repeated, is not, although unwarrantable, sufficient to found Single act of violence.

§ 10.
"*cruelty.*"

a decree of judicial separation (*Smallwood* v. *Smallwood*, 2 S. & T. 397; 31 L. J., P. & M. 3). For it cannot be affirmed generally that every act of personal violence or that every combination of acts of personal violence voluntarily inflicted, and productive of hurt or alarm, constitutes legal cruelty; the extent of the injury, the causes conducing to the use of violence by the husband, the circumstances under which it occurred, the probability of the recurrence of similar or greater violence, are all matters requiring consideration (*Baptist* v. *Baptist*, No. 101, *Punjab Record*, 1882). But if the single act of violence is of such a character as to found a reasonable apprehension of further violence in case of cohabitation, the wife is entitled to the protection of the Court (*Reeves* v. *Reeves*, 3 S. & T. 139; 32 L. J., P. & M. 178); and even where the evidence of actual violence is not *per se* sufficient to warrant a decree on the ground of cruelty, the Court will take into consideration the general conduct of the husband towards the wife, and if this is of a character tending to degrade the wife, and subjecting her to a course of annoyance and indignity injurious to her health, will feel itself at liberty to pronounce the cruelty proved (*Swatman* v. *Swatman*, 4 S. & T. 135). Thus, where there were continual quarrels between the husband and the wife, caused by his acts of adultery, and such quarrels led to violence of demeanour and occasional acts of violence on his part, inducing mental and bodily suffering in the wife, it was held that his conduct amounted to legal cruelty (*Knight* v. *Knight*, 4 S. & T. 103; 34 L. J., P. & M. 112).

So, where subsequently to acts of physical violence, long since condoned, the wife had been deprived of her proper position in the household, neglected, degraded to the position, and made to do the work, of a menial servant, and had to take her meals and to sleep apart from the rest of the family, it was held that such treatment amounted to legal cruelty (Smith, L. J., *Aubourg* v. *Aubourg*, 72 L. T. 295).

But the husband's conduct, to amount to legal cruelty, must be such as to endanger or cause a reasonable apprehension of endangering the wife's personal health and safety. Therefore where a husband constantly swore at and abused his wife and refused to provide her with delicacies ordered by the doctor, used threats towards her and on several occasions wantonly beat the child in her presence, but it did not appear that the wife had suffered in health in consequence of such treatment or that she was apprehensive of her personal safety, it was held that the husband's conduct did not amount to legal cruelty (*Birch* v. *Birch*, 42 L. J., P. & M. 23).

On the other hand, if force, whether physical or moral, is systematically exerted by a husband to compel the submission of his wife, in such a manner and to such an extent as to break down her health and to render a serious malady imminent, it is legal cruelty (*Kelly* v. *Kelly*, L. R., 2 P. 31; in app., L. R., 2 P. 59; 39 L. J., P. & M. 28); and in *Bethune* v. *Bethune* ((1891) P. 205; 60 L. J., P. & M. 18), though the husband had not committed any act of physical violence upon the petitioner, yet throughout the married life had habitually insulted her and behaved towards her with neglect and studied unkindness, in consequence of which her health had been much impaired, it was held that she was entitled to a decree *nisi* for the dissolution of the marriage (cf. *Mytton* v. *Mytton*, per Butt, J., 11 P. D. 143).

§ 10. "*cruelty.*"

Indifference, neglect, aversion to wife's society, and cessation of matrimonial intercourse, without personal violence or words of menace, do not amount to legal cruelty, even though the husband be carrying on an adulterous intercourse with the servants of the house in which the wife is living (*Cousen* v. *Cousen*, 4 S. & T. 164; 34 L. J., P. & M. 139); and no general rule can be laid down as to what amount of mere insults and offensive conduct on the part of the husband towards the wife, in the absence of acts of physical violence, will amount to cruelty so as to entitle the wife to a decree of dissolution of marriage on the ground of adultery and cruelty (*Beauclerk* v. *Beauclerk*, (1891) P. 189; 60 L. J., P. & M. 20). But neglect, coldness and insult, whereby the petitioner's health was injured and entirely gave way, and a continuance of which would, according to the medical evidence, have produced melancholia, were held to constitute legal cruelty (*Walmesley* v. *Walmesley*, 1 R. 529; 69 L. T. 152).

Neglect of wife and adultery with servant in house where wife was living.

Words of menace importing the actual danger of bodily harm will justify the interposition of the Court, as the Court ought not to wait till the mischief is done. But the most innocent and deserving woman will sue in vain for the interference for words of mere insult, however galling (*Oliver* v. *Oliver*, 1 Hagg. Cons. Rep. 364).

Threats.

"There is no case in the books where words alone, however violent, however galling . . . . have been held *per se* to constitute legal cruelty" (*Russell* v. *Russell*, *ubi supra*). Thus, where the husband threatened to cut the wife's throat but did

§ 10.
"*cruelty.*"

not accompany the threat with any act of violence, it was held that the threat was merely an expression of passion and did not amount to legal cruelty (*Brown* v. *Brown*, 14 W. R. (Eng.) 318).

But where from the words of menace a malignant intention to do bodily harm, and a reasonable apprehension of such harm, may be inferred, the Court will interfere to prevent the actual mischief threatened (*D'Aguilar* v. *D'Aguilar*, 1 Hagg. 775; *Kenrick* v. *Kenrick*, 4 Hagg. 129; *Dysart* v. *Dysart*, 1 Robert. Eccl. Rep. 106; *Oliver* v. *Oliver*, *ubi supra*).

Spitting in wife's face.

Spitting in the wife's face has been held to amount to legal cruelty (*D'Aguilar* v. *D'Aguilar*, *ubi supra*; *Curtis* v. *Curtis*, 1 S. & T. 197; 27 L. J., P. & M. 173). But as regards such acts as spitting in the wife's face, the test is the sense in which they were received; if they were not resented at the time, less weight will be attached to the charge when brought (*Saunders* v. *Saunders*, 1 Robert. Eccl. Rep. 549; *Waddell* v. *Waddell*, 2 S. & T. 584; 31 L. J., P. & M. 123).

Whether, however, in any case such an act, though amounting to as gross an insult as can be imagined, would *per se* be held to amount to legal cruelty may be doubted. Combined with other acts of physical violence it will certainly weigh with the Court.

Communication of disease.

If a husband, knowing that he is in such a state of health that by having connection with his wife he will run the risk of communicating venereal disease to her, recklessly has connection with her and thereby communicates the disease to her, he is guilty of legal cruelty (*Beardman* v. *Beardman*, L. R., 1 P. 233).

But the husband's act must be wilful, and that it was so must be clearly and conclusively established (*Collett* v. *Collett*, 1 Curt. 678). Where, however, a husband is charged with having wilfully communicated a loathsome disease to his wife, and being a competent witness does not come forward to assert his ignorance, the Court will hold the charge of wilful intention proved (*Brown* v. *Brown*, L. R., 1 P. 46; 35 L. J., P. & M. 13).

Where there was no evidence beyond the presumption arising from the state of the wife—against whose character there was no imputation—that the husband had ever suffered from disease and he denied it, but the jury found that he had been guilty of cruelty in infecting his wife with syphilis, the Court (Willes, J., dissenting) granted a new trial on the ground that even if the husband had communicated the disease, there was no evidence to show that he had done so wilfully and knowingly (*Morphett*

v. *Morphett*, L. R., 1 P. 702; 38 L. J., P. & M. 23). In this §10. case it was held, *first*, that it devolved upon the wife to "*cruelty.*" establish affirmatively that her husband, having the disease himself, knew, either from medical advice or from the obvious character of the symptoms, that he had an infectious disease, and that it existed in such a stage and form that connection with his wife was at least distinctly dangerous; and *secondly*, that, in the absence of actual proof of the existence of disease in him, it was incumbent upon the wife, in the medical evidence adduced in support of her charge, to lay the foundation for a scientific conclusion which should take the place of such proof, and from which the jury could argue with reason, first, to the charge of knowledge, and through that to the charge of wilfulness.

But cruelty which consists in the communication of a venereal disease must be charged specifically, and in a case where there had been no allegation of such cruelty in the petition, although there was a general charge of cruelty, the Court refused to admit evidence on the point (*Squires* v. *Squires*, 3 S. & T. 541; 32 L. J., P. & M. 172).

Drunkenness, even when accompanied by acts of considerable Drunkenness. violence, is not *per se* a substantial ground for a decree of judicial separation (*Scott* v. *Scott*, 29 L. J., P. & M. 64).

Nor will the Court interfere to protect the wife from mere unhappiness resulting from an ill-assorted marriage, nor from the destruction of domestic comfort caused by drunkenness (*Hudson* v. *Hudson*, 3 S. & T. 314; 33 L. J., P. & M. 5). But the Court, on the question of cruelty, will consider the liability of danger which a wife would incur by returning to cohabitation with a husband subject to uncontrollable fits of drunkenness, such husband having used a certain amount of violence to the wife when under the influence of drink, and particular acts of violence will be viewed in connection with the cumulative misconduct of the husband (*Power* v. *Power*, 4 S. & T. 173; 34 L. J., P. & M. 137). But in such cases it is for the wife to show that a return to cohabitation would be unsafe (*Ruxton* v. *Ruxton*, 5 L. R. Ir. 19).

So, where a husband had for many years led a life of gross intemperance, and on various occasions, apparently while suffering from *delirium tremens*, had treated his wife with cruelty, it was held that as she could not return to cohabitation without incurring great peril of a renewal of the bodily injuries previously inflicted on her, she was entitled to a decree for judicial separation (*Marsh* v. *Marsh*, 1 S. & T. 312; 28 L. J., P. & M. 13).

§ 10.
"cruelty."

Cruelty by lunatic.

As a general rule, cruelty committed by an insane person is no ground for judicial separation; the remedy lies in the restraint of the lunatic, not in the release of the other party (*Hall* v. *Hall*, 3 S. & T. 348; 33 L. J., P. & M. 65).

Accordingly, acts of violence committed under the influence of an acute disorder, such as brain fever, where, the disorder having been subdued, there is no danger of their recurrence, are no ground for judicial separation. It is, however, otherwise if the result of such disease is a new condition of the brain rendering the person liable to such ungovernable fits of passion as would render future cohabitation unsafe (*Curtis* v. *Curtis*, 1 S. & T. 192; 27 L. J., P. & M. 74).

"If it can be shown that the insanity is of such a nature that it will produce violence on the part of the husband, and endanger the safety of the wife, though it need not entail the permanent incarceration of the man, but only his restraint from time to time,—if the mania is recurrent, and comes on suddenly from time to time, she may be placed in great jeopardy. In such a case I can well conceive that, although in some instances insanity may be one of those misfortunes which must be taken by a wife with her husband for better or for worse, and though it may assume the form of a disease, yet, if it is such as to imperil the wife's safety, she is entitled to the protection of this Court. Assuming for the moment that these attacks were not brought on the respondent by his own self-indulgence; assuming that they were the result of hereditary disease, I should still be disposed to hold that acts of cruelty committed in one of these fits of mania would entitle the wife to the remedy which she asks—separation from her husband. . . . . The ordinary protection which she is supposed to obtain by proceedings in lunacy is a delusion, because it does not protect her against the return home of her husband, who is liable at any moment to become a lunatic" (Butt, P., *Hanbury* v. *Hanbury*, (1892) P. 224, 225).

So, where acts of violence were proved, and at times a state of cerebral excitement, arising from the fatigues and anxieties of business, connected with some of the acts of violence, it was considered by the Court that renewed cohabitation would be attended with such liability to a recurrence of ungovernable passion and cerebral excitement as would make cohabitation unsafe to the wife, who was accordingly granted a decree of judicial separation (*Martin* v. *Martin*, 29 L. J., P. & M. 106).

An adulterous intercourse carried on by a husband with the female servants in the house in which his wife is living does not *per se* amount to legal cruelty (*Cousen* v. *Cousen*, 4 S. & T. 164; 34 L. J., P. & M. 139).

*But the attempts of a husband to debauch his own female servants "are a strong act of cruelty, perhaps not alone sufficient to divorce, but which might weigh, in conjunction with others, as an act of considerable indignity and outrage to his wife's feelings" (*Popkin* v. *Popkin*, 1 Hagg. 766). And the Court will take into consideration the position in which the wife is placed in the family by reason of any authority or control exercised over her by the servants by the direction of the husband, and the state of the wife's feelings arising from reasonable suspicion of undue familiarity between her husband and a maidservant (*Anthony* v. *Anthony*, 1 S. & T. 594). And even in the absence of any evidence of actual violence towards the wife, the Court will take into consideration his general conduct towards her, and if this be of a character tending to degrade her, and subjecting her to a course of annoyance and indignity injurious to her health, will feel itself at liberty to hold the cruelty proved (*Swatman* v. *Swatman*, 4 S. & T. 135; cf. *Aubourg* v. *Aubourg*, 72 L. T. 295).

§ 10.
"*cruelty.*"
Undue familiarities with female servants.

The essential element of constructive cruelty is that the acts should be done in the presence, and so directly shock the sensibility, of the wife; it is confined to cases of cruelty practised by a husband upon the children in the presence of their mother, and ought not to be applied to cases of mere neglect, nor where the wrong-doer is the wife (*Manning* v. *Manning*, 6 Ir. R. Eq. 417; and 7 Ir. R. Eq. 520). The wanton ill-treatment of a child in the presence of the mother and for the purpose of giving her pain may, *if carried to such an extent as to affect her health*, constitute legal cruelty towards her (*Birch* v. *Birch*, 42 L. J., P. & M. 23; *Suggate* v. *Suggate*, 1 S. & T. 489; 28 L. J., P. & M. 46).

Constructive cruelty.

In *Furlonger* v. *Furlonger* (5 Notes of Cases, 425) Dr. Lushington said:—"Generally speaking that would be cruelty if practised by a wife towards her husband which would be held to be cruelty if done by him towards her. I say generally speaking, for I think there must be some distinctions neces-

Cruelty on part of wife.

---

* According to Lord Herschell (*Russell* v. *Russell*, unreported at present) the word "cruelty" is here used by Lord Stowell in its *popular*, and not in its *legal* sense.

§ 10.
"cruelty."

sarily founded on the great difference between the sexes, and the power of the husband in ordinary circumstances to protect himself from the wife's violence; still, the same great rule of danger to life or limb must prevail; in these, as in all other cases of the same *genus*, necessary protection is the foundation of all separation." On this principle, the husband will be entitled to the protection of the Court where the wife's passions, from whatever cause, are so little under control that she is in the habit of using personal violence to her husband, from which habit he may be in danger of bodily injury, though no actual serious injury has been inflicted (*White* v. *White*, 1 S. & T. 591). For though the physical effects of a wife's violence may not generally be so serious to the personal safety of the husband as the effects of his violence towards her, yet the moral result of the wife's violence to all the proper relations of married life is so serious that the Court will interfere, and not drive the husband to the necessity of meeting force by force (*Pritchard* v. *Pritchard*, 3 S. & T. 523; *S.C. Pickard* v. *Pickard*, 33 L. J., P. & M. 158).

When cruelty on the part of the wife is charged, the sole question is not whether the husband's safety is endangered; the Court will also consider whether the conduct of the wife may not endanger her own safety by provoking the husband to retaliate and to meet force by force (*Forth* v. *Forth*, 36 L. J., P. & M. 122).

The doctrine of constructive cruelty is confined to cases of cruelty practised by the husband upon the children in the presence of their mother, and ought not to be applied where the wrongdoer is the wife (*Suggate* v. *Suggate*, 1 S. & T. 489; 28 L. J., P. & M. 48; *Manning* v. *Manning*, 6 Ir. R. Eq. 417, and 7 Ir. R. Eq. 520).

Drunken violence on the part of the wife only justifies such force on the part of the husband as may be necessary for her restraint (*Pearman* v. *Pearman*, 1 S. & T. 601; 29 L. J., P. & M. 54). But when, upon a husband's petition for dissolution of marriage on the ground of the wife's adultery, the adultery is fully proved against her, but she counter-charges cruelty on the part of her husband towards her, and it appears that the wife is a woman of drunken habits and that what she alleges as violence has been used upon her in consequence of her drunkenness, the Court requires a very strong case to be made out against the husband in order to bar his right to relief from the marriage tie. Unless it is proved that he has been guilty of such gross violence towards her as the Court cannot allow to be excused on the ground that he was provoked to it by her intemperance, the decree in his favour should not be withheld (*Forsyth* v. *Forsyth*, 63 L. T. 263).

§ 10. *"cruelty."*

So, too, violent and uncontrollable temper, habitual intemperance, violent conduct in the presence of the husband's guests, assaults on him, acts or threats of violence and offensive language and scandalous statements against his daughters by which he was obliged to remove them from his house, acts of violence towards his servants—all tending to affect his health and social position—constitute a legal defence to a suit by the wife for restitution of conjugal rights (*D'Arcy* v. *D'Arcy*, 19 L. R. Ir. 369—Mat.).

But intemperance, however gross and habitual, and violence of temper, however uncontrolled and persistent, are not in themselves sufficient reasons to justify a husband going away from his wife, leaving her to support herself and not troubling as to how she is living (*Heyes* v. *Heyes*, 13 P. D. 11; 51 J. P. 775).

Cruelty is a question of fact, and it is for the Court to "direct the jury, in cases which come before a jury, what acts constitute legal cruelty, and they will have to find whether the acts done are cruelty or not" (*Tomkins* v. *Tomkins*, 1 S. & T. 168).

Cruelty is a question of fact.

But the jury cannot found a verdict of cruelty on acts which do not amount in law to cruelty (*Russell* v. *Russell*, (1895) P. (C. A.) 315).

Condoned cruelty may be revived by acts of violence and threats calculated to revive a sense of insecurity and apprehension of danger (*Curtis* v. *Curtis*, 1 S. & T. 192; *M'Keever* v. *M'Keever*, 11 Ir. R. Eq. 26).

Condoned cruelty, how revived.

It may also be revived, even without actual violence, by threats of such a nature, and so expressed, as to satisfy the Court that future cohabitation would be attended with danger to the party threatened (*Bostock* v. *Bostock*, 1 S. & T. 221; 27 L. J., P. & M. 86).

Where a wife who had suffered such acts of cruelty from her husband as would probably have been sufficient to enable her to have then obtained a decree of judicial separation, returned to his house and lived with him for five years, during which time he treated her with continued unkindness, though he never struck her, but his conduct eventually so terrified his wife that she left him, it was held that, even if the latter acts did not amount to legal cruelty, they did nevertheless constitute such a revival of the earlier cruelty as to warrant the Court in granting

§ 10.
"cruelty."

the wife a decree of judicial separation (*Mytton* v. *Mytton*, 11 P. D. 141; 57 L. T. 92).

Cruelty once condoned may be so revived by subsequent adultery as to form, coupled with that cruelty, a ground for sentence of dissolution of marriage (*Palmer* v. *Palmer*, 2 S. & T. 61; 29 L. J., P. & M. 124; *Dempster* v. *Dempster*, 2 S. & T. 438; 31 L. J., P. & M. 20).

But if the wife has agreed for valuable consideration not to take any proceedings against her husband in respect of past cruelty, his subsequent adultery will not revive her right to complain of such cruelty (*Rose* v. *Rose*, 7 P. D. 225).

As regards "condonation," generally, see note to sect. 12, *post*.

Adultery by husband subsequently to decree of judicial separation on ground of his cruelty.

A wife who has obtained a decree of judicial separation on the ground of her husband's cruelty, if her husband subsequently commits adultery, is entitled, on proof of the former decree, and of the subsequent adultery, to a decree of dissolution of marriage (*Bland* v. *Bland*, L. R., 1 P. 237; 35 L. J., P. & M. 104; *Green* v. *Green*, L. R., 3 P. 121; 43 L. J., P. & M. 6).

Adultery and desertion.

(h) **"Or of adultery coupled with desertion without reasonable excuse for two years or upwards."**

"Desertion" implies an abandonment against the wish of the person charging it (sect. 3, *ante*, p. 20).

Desertion for two years or more.

"For two years or upwards."

When the statutory period of two years necessary to found a charge of desertion is not complete at the time when proceedings for divorce are commenced, such charge can only be pleaded and acted upon by being made the subject of a fresh petition when the period is completed (*Lapington* v. *Lapington*, 14 P. D. 21; 58 L. J., P. & M. 26).

But in another case where the adultery was proved, but the evidence of desertion fell short of the required period by several months, the hearing was adjourned; and twelve months afterwards—the respondent not having returned to cohabitation—the petitioner filed a supplemental petition charging desertion, on proof of which the Court granted a decree *nisi* (*Wood* v. *Wood*, 13 P. D. 22; 57 L. J., P. & M. 48; cf. sect. 54, *post*). And in such a case if the wife proves the adultery, but fails to prove desertion for two years, it is competent for the Court to decree judicial separation, although the petition only prays for a dissolution (*Smith* v. *Smith*, 1 S. & T. 359; 28 L. J., P. & M. 27). If, however, the petitioner refuses to amend the petition by praying for judicial separation, the petition will be dismissed (*Rowley* v. *Rowley*, 4 S. & T. 137; 12 L. T. 505).

§ 10. "*desertion.*"

A *bona fide* offer by the husband to return to or resume cohabitation will, if made before the two years have elapsed, deprive his absence of the character of desertion (*Lodge* v. *Lodge*, 15 P. D. 159; 59 L. J., P. & M. 84; and cases cited below, p. 63).

"*Abandonment.*"

There is no definition of "abandonment" in the Act, but the effect of the definition of "desertion," as implying "an abandonment against the wish of the person charging it," is to introduce into the Indian statute the view adopted by the Court in England in construing the English Act. Therefore the expression "against the wish of" must be construed as meaning "*contrary to an actively expressed wish of*" *the person charging abandonment, and notwithstanding the resistance or opposition of such person.* A wife, who seeks to prove desertion, must consequently give evidence of conduct on her part showing unmistakably that such desertion was against her wishes actively expressed (*Fowle* v. *Fowle*, I. L. R., iv Calc. 260; 3 C. L. R. 484).

Abandonment.

Absence, to constitute desertion, must be without the consent, direct or indirect, of the party alleging desertion and against such party's express wishes (*Ward* v. *Ward*, 1 S. & T. 185; 27 L. J., P. & M. 63).

So, where a husband, after residing with his wife for four years, went to London in search of employment and during the following sixteen years only once communicated with her, it was held that, as the wife had never applied to him for a renewal of cohabitation, the charge of desertion had not been established (*Thompson* v. *Thompson*, 1 S. & T. 231; 27 L. J., P. & M. 65).

And where a husband, after shamefully ill-treating his wife, left the house telling her that he was going to leave her, and the wife stayed in the house for some time and then, without making any inquiries about her husband, went to her sister's house and there remained, the full Court held that the husband had not "deserted" the wife, although it was proved that some six years after leaving her he had informed a friend of hers that he was living in adultery and would have nothing more to do with her (*Smith* v. *Smith*, 1 S. & T. 359; 28 L. J., P. & M. 27).

If, after the parties have separated by mutual consent, the

§ 10.
"desertion."

husband makes a *bonâ fide* offer to resume cohabitation, but his offer is unreasonably refused by the wife, his conduct in thereafter keeping away from her will not amount to "desertion," unless the wife has, subsequently to her refusal of his offer, herself made an offer to return to him (*Keech* v. *Keech*, L. R., 1 P. 641 ; 38 L. J., P. & M. 7).

But where a husband left his wife, and, after corresponding with her for some years, finally went abroad and started in another home with a woman, by whom he had children, and contributed nothing to his wife's support, it was held that he had "deserted" his wife, although the latter made no request to him to return to her or to take her back to live with him (*Drew* v. *Drew*, 64 L. T. 840).

Separation brought about by husband's misconduct.

But, although an abandonment to constitute desertion must be against the actively expressed wishes of the other party, a husband none the less "deserts" his wife because she uses expressions to the effect that she has no wish to see him again, when such expressions have been wrung from her by her husband's misconduct, if the desertion be otherwise proved (*Meara* v. *Meara*, 35 L. J., P. & M. 33).

Thus, where a wife reproached her husband for his connection with another woman, and, on his replying that he wished to go away and live with the woman in question, told him that he could go if he liked, but made him swear to return when he became tired of the other, it was held that the husband, who had never returned, had been guilty of desertion (*Haviland* v. *Haviland*, 32 L. J., P. & M. 65).

Nor does a husband any the less "desert" his wife because the wife has been compelled by his conduct to leave the house.

Where, therefore, a husband a few years after the marriage brought to his house a woman with whom he had immoral relations and insisted, despite his wife's protests, on keeping her in the house, and eventually informed his wife, when she told him that either the woman or she must leave the house, that she could please herself but that the woman would remain, and the wife went away and never afterwards resumed cohabitation, it was held that the husband had been guilty of desertion (*Dickenson* v. *Dickenson*, 62 L. T. 330).

So, where under the pressure of pecuniary difficulties, brought about by the husband's extravagance and dissolute habits, the husband and wife came to an arrangement by which she went to live with her friends, and he resided at his mother's house until they could again find means to provide a common house, and the husband subsequently left his mother's house and went to reside elsewhere, it was held that the separation, not being brought about by the act of the wife but by the husband's misconduct, amounted to desertion on his part (*Wood* v. *Wood*, I. L. R., iii Calc. 485; 1 C. L. R. 552).

§ 10. "*desertion.*"

And in a case where the intention of the husband clearly was not to live again with his wife, the Court held that he had been guilty of desertion, although it was the wife who, in consequence of his misconduct, had left the house in which they were residing, and despite her refusal, on hearing of an adulterous connection on his part, to return to cohabitation unless she was satisfied that such connection was at an end (*Graves* v. *Graves*, 3 S. & T. 350; 32 L. J., P. & M. 66; foll. in *Pizzala* v. *Pizzala*, Times Law Reps., vol. xii. p. 451).

In all such cases, if the husband offers to resume cohabitation, the wife is entitled to annex a reasonable condition to her acceptance of the offer, and her refusal to accept the offer except upon such condition will not deprive her of her right to sue on the ground of desertion (*Gibson* v. *Gibson*, 29 L. J., P. & M. 25; *Graves* v. *Graves*, *supra*). A condition that her husband gives up an adulterous connection is reasonable (*Alexander* v. *Alexander*, No. 51, *Punjab Record*, 1869).

But where a husband sent his wife back to her father's house three days after the marriage, saying that he could not afford to keep her, and eighteen months afterwards, during which time the wife had heard nothing of him, went to her father and asked to be allowed to see her, and the father refused to let him have any communication with her until he could support her, it was held that the husband's conduct in never afterwards returning to his wife, or asking her to return to him, did not amount to "desertion" (*Harris* v. *Harris*, 31 L. J., P. & M. 6).

If the wife's conduct has been such that the husband cannot reasonably be expected to live with her, he cannot be said to desert her without reasonable cause, although her conduct may not actually amount to a matrimonial offence (*Russell v. *Russell*, (1895) P. 315; 64 L. J., P. & M. 105; *Oldroyd* v. *Oldroyd*, 65 L. J., P. & M. 113). But "the cause should be grave and weighty which, in the judgment of the Court, should deprive a deserted wife of her remedy for that desertion, and her right to set it up as a bar to a divorce for adultery at her husband's suit" (Lord Penzance, *Yeatman* v. *Yeatman*, L. R., 1 P. 489; 37 L. J., P. & M. 37).

Separation brought about by wife's conduct.

---

* The decision of the Court of Appeal in this case has been upheld by the House of Lords (see *Times* newspaper of July 17, 1897).

§ 10.
"desertion."

Facts constituting desertion.

Facts constituting desertion.

The facts which constitute desertion vary with the circumstances and mode of life of the parties. So long, however, as a husband treats his wife as a wife by maintaining such degree and manner of intercourse with her as might naturally be expected from a husband of his calling and means, he cannot be said to have "deserted" her (*Williams* v. *Williams*, 3 S. & T. 547).

Absence on business.

The absence of a husband in his ordinary occupation as a mariner does not constitute desertion, nor in such a case can the Court take into consideration an actual desertion in past years which has been terminated by a return to cohabitation (*Ex parte Aldridge*, 1 S. & T. 88).

Mere absence on business does not amount to desertion, but the nature and extent of such absence and the conduct of the husband during the absence must be considered. Where a husband having fallen into difficulties, enlisted and went with his regiment to India, where he was subsequently discharged, and ceased to correspond with, or contribute to the support of, his wife, his conduct was held to amount to a desertion of his wife (*Henty* v. *Henty*, 33 L. T. 263).

So, where a husband left his wife in England and went to China to secure an appointment, and during his absence wrote her many affectionate letters, expressing regret for past misconduct and promising amendment in future, but in none suggesting a desire to return to his wife, and in one stating his intention not to return to England, and on his return to England three years afterwards gave her no address, and made no attempt to see her or her friends, although continually pressing her for money, the wife, on proof of his adultery, was granted a decree *nisi* for dissolution of the marriage (*Lawrence* v. *Lawrence*, 2 S. & T. 575 ; 31 L. J., P. & M. 145).

Husband making wife suitable allowance.

A wife is entitled to the society and protection of her husband: the mere fact, therefore, that he has made her a suitable allowance is no answer on his part to a charge of desertion (*Macdonald* v. *Macdonald*, 4 S. & T. 242; *Yeatman* v. *Yeatman*, L. R., 1 P. 489; 37 L. J., P. & M. 37).

But where a man left his wife in full possession of the family house, and subsequently, with her assent, visited his children there, but did not remain or return to cohabitation with his wife or hold any communication with her, it was held that his conduct was not evidence of desertion, but rather of separation by mutual consent (*Taylor* v. *Taylor*, 44 L. T. 31).

So, where a husband in 1880 ceased to reside with his wife on the pretence that his business compelled him to be absent, but supplied her with necessaries, corresponded with her and visited her occasionally, and a child was born in February, 1884, and in January, 1884, the wife discovered that he had been living for two years with another woman, it was held that the husband had not been guilty of desertion up to January, 1884. *Semble*, desertion commenced from the time when the wife discovered the adultery (*Farmer* v. *Farmer*, 9 P. D. 245; 53 L. J., P. & M. 113).

§ 10.
"*desertion.*"

On the other hand, the mere fact of a man leaving his wife to go and live with another woman does not *necessarily* constitute desertion (*Ward* v. *Ward*, 1 S. & T. 185; 27 L. J., P. & M. 63).

To constitute desertion there must be a withdrawal from existing cohabitation.

Withdrawal from existing cohabitation.

"No one can 'desert' who does not actively and wilfully bring to an end an existing state of cohabitation. Cohabitation may be put an end to by other acts besides that of actually quitting the common house. Advantage may be taken of temporary absence or separation to hold aloof from renewal of intercourse. This done wilfully, against the wish of the other party, and in execution of a design to cease cohabitation, would constitute desertion. *But if the state of cohabitation had already ceased to exist, whether by the adverse act of husband or wife, or even by the mutual consent of both, desertion, in my judgment, becomes from that moment impossible to either, at least until their common life and home has been resumed.* In the meantime, either party may have the right to call upon the other to resume their conjugal relations, and, if refused, to enforce their resumption; but such refusal cannot constitute the offence intended by the statute under the name of 'desertion without cause'" (*per* Lord Penzance, *Fitzgerald* v. *Fitzgerald*,* L. R., 1 P. 694; 38 L. J., P. & M. 14; followed in

---

* What *Fitzgerald* v. *Fitzgerald* decides is that a party cannot complain of desertion after voluntarily leaving his or her consort, and also that where the parties are living apart by mutual consent there is no desertion. It is clear that cohabitation often exists without the parties living under the same roof, as in the case of married persons in domestic service (*Bradshaw* v. *Bradshaw*, 66 L. J., P. & M. 31).

§ 10.
"desertion."

Wood v. *Wood*, I. L. R., iii Calc. 485; and *Fowle* v. *Fowle*, I. L. R., iv Calc. 260).

With every respect to the very learned judge whose words have been quoted above, it is not very easy to understand how, if the state of cohabitation has already ceased to exist *by the adverse act of one alone of the parties*, desertion becomes from that moment impossible to the other. Desertion can only become possible where the adverse act of one of the parties has already caused a cessation of the state of cohabitation. It is, of course, very different where both parties have already *mutually* consented to cease cohabitation, and the rule may, perhaps, be more accurately stated as laid down by the Court of Appeal (*Reg.* v. *Le Resche*, 65 L. T. 602), viz., that in order to constitute "desertion" there must be an active withdrawal from an existing cohabitation, and when once cohabitation has ceased to exist by mutual consent desertion is impossible—at least, until it has been resumed—even though the one party has called upon the other to resume cohabitation, and the other party has refused.

But a mere temporary separation between husband and wife for mutual convenience does not effect a cessation of cohabitation, or alter the marital relations (*Chudley* v. *Chudley*, 69 L. T. 617).

"There are cases in which the parties may have innocently ceased for a time to be actually living together, separated by the calls of everyday life or the exigencies of public duty, and the husband or the wife, taking advantage of the separation, may have purposely rejected all subsequent opportunities of coming together again, and this may constitute 'desertion.' For, in truth, in such cases, the state of cohabitation was not, in the first instance, wholly relinquished but only suspended till a fitting occasion for its resumption, and purposely to reject all such occasions is practically to abandon it" (*per* Lord Penzance, *Fitzgerald* v. *Fitzgerald*, *ubi supra*).

Separation may become desertion, though not so at first.

In such cases an intention to "desert" will be the more readily inferred when either party during an innocent separation forms an adulterous connection and breaks off all communications with the other party. Thus where a husband, while living apart from his wife under circumstances which did not constitute desertion, suddenly ceased to correspond with her, and formed an adulterous connection with another woman, and the facts showed that he had resolved to abandon his wife, his conduct was held to amount to desertion of the wife (*Gatehouse* v. *Gatehouse*, L. R., 1 P. 331; 36 L. J., P. & M. 121; cf. *Stickland* v.

Stickland, 35 L. T. 767; and *Lawrence* v. *Lawrence; Henty* v. *Henty; Farmer* v. *Farmer, supra*, pp. 58, 59).

§ 10.
"desertion."

So, where a husband and wife, four years after their marriage and in consequence of the pecuniary difficulties of the former, agreed that a house and shop should be taken for the wife, and that she should carry on business in a separate name, and the parties never lived together again, though the husband occasionally secretly visited the wife and made her an allowance, but refused in spite of her remonstrances to recommence open and avowed cohabitation, and the wife, having reason to suspect that he had formed an adulterous connection, subsequently refused to cohabit with him, and three years afterwards, when she received positive proof of his adultery, sued for a divorce on the ground of his adultery and desertion, it was held that there was sufficient evidence of desertion for two years and upwards without reasonable cause (*Garcia* v. *Garcia*, 13 P. D. 216; 57 L. J., P. & M. 101).

Again, a wife was granted a decree *nisi* for dissolution of marriage under the following circumstances:—the husband and wife agreed to separate owing to the husband's inability to maintain the wife, but they agreed to correspond, and numerous letters passed between them, in some of which the husband taunted the wife with not getting a divorce, and said it was cruel of her to "fetter" him. In answer to an offer made by the wife to return to him, he replied that he was ill, and eventually refused her offer. His letters ceased in July, 1885, and although the wife wrote four times in answer to his last letter, she received no reply from him, and eventually discovering that, while the correspondence was going on and afterwards, he had been keeping up an adulterous connection, and was at the time living under his mother's roof with another woman, she sued for a divorce on the ground of his adultery and desertion (*Smith* v. *Smith*, 58 L. T. 639).

Voluntary Separation under Separation Deed.

Where a husband and wife have voluntarily agreed to live separate, and have executed a deed of separation, and have thereafter lived apart from each other, desertion becomes impossible to either of them. In such a case each of the parties bargains away the right to claim relief on the ground of desertion. Nor does the fact that one of the parties has failed or refused to fulfil all the terms of the bargain convert such

Separation under deed of separation.

§ 10.
"*desertion.*"

separation into desertion (*Crabb* v. *Crabb*, L. R., 1 P. 601; 37 L. J., P. & M. 62).

So, where a husband deserted his wife, but a year afterwards agreed to a deed of separation whereby he covenanted to make her an allowance, and the deed was fully executed, but no part of the allowance was ever paid, it was held that the wife had bargained away her right to relief, and could not establish the charge of desertion (*Parkinson* v. *Parkinson*, L. R., 2 P. 25; 39 L. J., P. & M. 14).

But in another case, where the parties executed a deed of separation, and thereafter lived apart, and subsequently the husband sued for a divorce on the ground of his wife's adultery, and the wife counter-charged for desertion, and the deed of separation contained no covenant to sue or agreement to condone past offences, the jury having found all the issues in favour of the wife, the Court granted her a decree of judicial separation (*Moore* v. *Moore*, 12 P. D. 193; 56 L. J., P. & M. 104).

Where, however, a husband refused to live with his wife or to provide a home for her, but offered her 100*l.* on condition that she would not molest him in the future by insisting on her conjugal rights, and the wife agreed to the condition, and received the money, and cohabitation was never resumed, it was held that these facts did not constitute desertion (*Buckmaster* v. *Buckmaster*, L. R., 1 P. 713; 38 L. J., P. & M. 73).

But a deed of separation that has never been acted upon will not deprive a husband's subsequent separation from his wife against her will of the character of desertion (*Cock* v. *Cock*, 33 L. J., P. & M. 157).

And if a husband *without reasonable excuse* obtains from his wife an agreement that they shall live separate, and they live separate accordingly, he will be held guilty of such desertion of her as to disentitle him to a decree of dissolution of marriage on the ground of her subsequent adultery (*Dagg* v. *Dagg and Speke*, 7 P. D. 17; 51 L. J., P. & M. 19).

In a case in which it appeared that, subsequent to the husband's desertion, the parties had executed a deed of separation and the wife for three months thereafter continued to pay the husband a small allowance, the Court, being satisfied that the act of the wife was prompted wholly by affection and humanity, and that she never really assented to the desertion, granted her a decree *nisi* on the ground of her husband's adultery and desertion (*Nott* v. *Nott*, L. R., 1 P. 251; 36 L. J., P. & M. 10).

DISSOLUTION OF MARRIAGE.

In all cases a deed of separation is avoided by a resumption of cohabitation by the parties (*Scholey* v. *Goodman*, 1 C. & P. 36; 8 Moore, 350).

§ 10.
"*desertion.*"

Before the two years' absence is completed a *bonâ fide* offer to resume cohabitation will deprive a separation of the character of desertion (*Lodge* v. *Lodge*, 15 P. D. 159; 59 L. J., P. & M. 84; *Keech* v. *Keech*, L. R., 1 P. 641; 38 L. J., P. & M. 7). Such offer must be *bonâ fide*, and in order to judge whether it is so the Court will regard the whole conduct of the party making it (*Harris* v. *Harris*, 15 L. T. 448).

Offer by husband to return to cohabitation.

Where, therefore, the husband wrote letters to his wife professing his willingness to return, the Court directed the jury to consider whether the conduct of the husband was that of a man honestly intending to resume cohabitation, or whether the real and only object of his letters was to evade the consequences which might ensue, and to deprive the wife of the remedy to which she would be entitled on the completion of the two years' absence (*French-Brewster* v. *French-Brewster*, 62 L. T. 609).

On the other hand, when the desertion, without reasonable cause, for two years, is once completed, the deserted wife has a complete right to relief of which she cannot be deprived even by a *bonâ fide* offer to resume cohabitation made by the husband subsequently to the completion of the two years (*Cargill* v. *Cargill*, 1 S. & T. 235; 27 L. J., P. & M. 69).

Where, therefore, a husband has been guilty of adultery, and of desertion for two years and upwards, his offer to return to cohabitation, even if *bonâ fide*, will not disentitle the wife to sue for dissolution of marriage, for she is not, in any case, under any obligation to condone the adultery (*Basing* v. *Basing*, 3 S. & T. 516; 33 L. J., P. & M. 150).

And in any case a husband may be guilty of desertion, even though he is willing to return to cohabitation, if at the time he is so willing he is actually cohabiting with another woman (*Edwards* v. *Edwards*, 62 L. J., P. & M. 33).

To constitute Desertion, the withdrawal from Cohabitation must be Voluntary.

Separation must be voluntary.

To amount to desertion, the withdrawal from cohabitation must be voluntary (*Beavan* v. *Beavan*, 2 S. & T. 652; 32 L. J., P. & M. 36).

A separation which is the result of imprisonment does not, *per se*, constitute desertion.

§ 10.
"desertion."

A husband, who had committed several thefts, in order to evade arrest, separated from his wife with her consent. He was subsequently arrested and imprisoned, and, on his release, was again imprisoned for other offences. While in prison, and also in the intervals between his imprisonment, he kept up a correspondence with his wife, and made repeated requests to resume cohabitation, but she refused, and cohabitation was in fact never resumed. On the wife's petition for dissolution, on the ground of her husband's adultery and desertion, the Court held that the separation on the part of the husband, being involuntary, did not amount to desertion (*Townsend* v. *Townsend*, L. R., 3 P. 129; 42 L. J., P. & M. 71).

Where, however, the circumstances under which the separation commenced are such as to show an intention on the part of the husband to abandon his wife, the mere fact that he is subsequently prevented by imprisonment from returning to her will not deprive such separation of the character of desertion.

Thus, where it appeared that the husband when he left his wife told her that he was going to Ireland for a week's shooting, but in fact he went to Australia to evade arrest on a charge of embezzlement and up to the time of his flight was living in adultery with a woman with whom he had arranged to go away, and was afterwards found living with another woman at Sydney, and he was subsequently brought back to England in custody, tried and sentenced to ten years' penal servitude, it was held that the circumstances under which he left his wife constituted desertion, and that the desertion continued notwithstanding the fact that he was brought back in custody and prevented by his imprisonment from returning to his wife (*Drew* v. *Drew*, 13 P. D. 97; 57 L. J., P. & M. 64).

So, again, where a husband deserted his wife on the 4th October, 1854, and never returned to her afterwards, and on the 16th November, 1856, was arrested on a charge of felony and sentenced to four years' penal servitude, it was held in a suit by the wife for dissolution of marriage, instituted before the termination of the husband's imprisonment, that he had been guilty of desertion for two years and upwards, although between the two dates above given he had been twice imprisoned, on one occasion for seven days, and on another for nineteen days (*Astrope* v. *Astrope*, 29 L. J., P. & M. 27).

DISSOLUTION OF MARRIAGE.

§ 10.
"desertion."

"Without reasonable excuse":

Reasonable cause for separation.

A husband is bound to give his wife the security and comfort of his home so far as his position and business will admit, and the wife is entitled to the society and protection of her husband. He is only relieved of these duties when he can show that his wife's conduct was such as to justify him in leaving her. A "reasonable excuse" for a man leaving his wife does not necessarily mean a distinct matrimonial offence on which a decree for judicial separation or dissolution of marriage could be founded; it must, however, be grave and weighty. Mere frailty of temper and habits which are distasteful to the husband do not constitute reasonable cause for depriving a wife of the protection of his home and society (*Yeatman* v. *Yeatman*, L. R., 1 P. 489; 37 L. J., P. & M. 37; cf. *Russell* v. *Russell*, (1895) P. 315; *Oldroyd* v. *Oldroyd*, 65 L. J., P. & M. 113; (1896) P. 175). Intemperance, however gross and habitual, and violence of temper, however uncontrolled and persistent, are not sufficient reasons to justify a husband going away from his wife, leaving her to support herself and not troubling himself as to how she is living (*Heyes* v. *Heyes*, 13 P. D. 11; in app. 36 W. R. 527).

Nor is a husband justified in leaving his wife, who up to the time of such separation was a virtuous woman, because she has run him into debt (*Holloway* v. *Holloway and Campbell*, I. L. R., v All. 71; *Starbuck* v. *Starbuck*, 59 L. J., P. & M. 20).

Nor can a husband excuse his desertion by pleading an ample allowance made by him to his wife (*Yeatman* v. *Yeatman*, *ubi supra*; *Macdonald* v. *Macdonald*, 4 S. & T. 242).

Nor is the fact that the wife has agreed to a deed of separation, which the husband has obtained from her without reasonable cause, a sufficient excuse for the husband leaving the wife (*Dagg* v. *Dagg and Speke*, 7 P. D. 17; 51 L. J., P. & M. 19).

The conviction of either party of a criminal offence—unless it is also a matrimonial offence—is no sufficient reason for the other party refusing to resume cohabitation (*Williamson* v. *Williamson and Bates*, 7 P. D. 76; 51 L. J., P. & M. 54).

Where a man left his wife, and refused to return to cohabitation unless she wrote a letter exonerating a certain lady of whom she had reason to entertain suspicions, and she refused to write the letter, but offered to resume cohabitation, it was held that her refusal to write the letter did not constitute a reasonable cause for the husband leaving her (*Dallas* v. *Dallas*, 43 L. J., P. & M. 47).

§ 10.
"desertion."

A man married a woman whom he knew to be a prostitute, and, about six weeks after the marriage, went away to America, not on business, but because he lived on bad terms with his wife, who had also quarrelled with his family. He left her without subsistence, and supplied her with none during his absence of four years, but after his departure his family gave her a small pittance on one occasion, and had promised further assistance. In consequence, however, of her annoying them, they broke off all intercourse with her, and she returned to her former mode of life. In a suit by him for dissolution of marriage, it was held that there had been a wilful separation of the husband from the wife, and that it was without reasonable excuse (*Coulthurst* v. *Coulthurst and Gonthwaite*, 28 L. J., P. & M. 21).

Involuntary separation.

Reasonable Cause for Separation.

A separation which is purely involuntary cannot amount to desertion without reasonable excuse. (As regards imprisonment, see *ante*, p. 64.)

So, where a ward of Chancery, aged sixteen years, who had no means of his own, clandestinely married a prostitute, aged about thirty-five, and the Master of the Rolls, a month after marriage, ordered that the husband should be delivered into the custody of his guardian, and that the wife should be restrained from having any communication with him, it was held that, as the separation on his part was involuntary, and he had no means of contributing to his wife's support, he had not wilfully separated himself from her (*Beavan* v. *Beavan*, 2 S. & T. 652; 32 L. J., P. & M. 36).

A separation due to the exigencies of business or professional or public duties is not without reasonable cause (*Ex parte Aldridge*, 1 S. & T. 88; *Davies* v. *Davies and Hughes*, 3 S. & T. 221; 32 L. J., P. & M. 111).

Confession of adultery by wife.

A *bonâ fide* confession of adultery by a wife to her husband, believed in by him, is a reasonable cause for his leaving her (*Faulkes* v. *Faulkes*, 64 L. T. 834).

Wife allowing indecent liberties.

So is the fact that the wife has allowed indecent liberties to be taken with her (*Haswell* v. *Haswell*, 1 S. & T. 502; 29 L. J., P. & M. 21).

Refusal to consummate marriage.

So is the persistent and unreasonable refusal by the wife to consummate the marriage (*Ousey* v. *Ousey and Atkinson*, L. R., 3 P. 223; 43 L. J., P. & M. 35).

A wife's conduct in persisting in charging her husband with the commission of an unnatural offence, the charge not being true, nor believed by her to be true, justifies her husband in separating himself from her (*Russell* v. *Russell*, (1895) P. 315; 64 L. J., P. & M. 105).

§ 10. *"desertion."* Charging husband with unnatural offence.

A young man, who had just taken his degree at Cambridge, married a prostitute, but never afterwards cohabited with her. He had no means of providing her with a home or of contributing towards her support, and the very day after the marriage he separated from her and went to live with his father, who, on being informed of the marriage some months afterwards, caused a deed of separation to be executed by which an allowance of 1*l*. a week was secured to her, and was regularly paid by the husband's father. It was held that the separation, if wilful, was not without reasonable excuse (*Proctor* v. *Proctor and Smith*, 4 S. & T. 140; 34 L. J., P. & M. 99).

An officer of Marines, when only twenty years of age, married a woman, relying on certain statements made by her as to her having been entrapped into a ceremony of marriage with a man whom she subsequently found to have a wife living. After the marriage the husband discovered that the alleged bigamous marriage had never really taken place, but that the wife had been guilty of ante-nuptial incontinence, and was in an advanced stage of pregnancy. He thereupon left her, and the Court held that he had reasonable cause for doing so (*Kennedy* v. *Kennedy*, 62 L. T. 705).

"**Contents of petition**":

"Every petition under this Act for a decree of dissolution of marriage, or of nullity of marriage, or of judicial separation, shall state that there is not any collusion or connivance between the petitioner and the other party to the marriage.

"The statements contained in every petition under this Act shall be verified by the petitioner or some other competent person in manner required by law for the verification of plaints, and may at the hearing be referred to as evidence" (sect. 47, *infra*).

A petition for dissolution of marriage must bear a Court fee stamp of Rs. 20 (Court Fees Act, 1870, 2nd Sch., art. 20).

Contents of petition.

Court fee.

Service of petition.—See Appendix (E), pp. 347—349.

§ 10.
"*desertion.*"

"Shall state, as distinctly as the nature of the case permits, the facts on which the claim to have such marriage dissolved is founded":

As to this, see Appendix (E.); "Practice and Pleadings—Contents of Petition."

Adulterer to be made a co-respondent.

11. Upon any such petition presented by a husband, the petitioner shall make the alleged adulterer a co-respondent to the said petition, unless he is excused from doing so on one of the following grounds, to be allowed by the Court:—

(i) That the respondent is leading the life of a prostitute, and that the petitioner knows of no person with whom the adultery has been committed.

(ii) That the name of the alleged adulterer is unknown to the petitioner, although he has made due efforts to discover it.

(iii) That the alleged adulterer is dead.

The Matrimonial Causes Act, 1857 (20 & 21 Vict. c. 85), sect. 28, provides that:—

"Upon any such petition presented by a husband, the petitioner shall make the alleged adulterer a co-respondent to the said petition, unless on special grounds, to be allowed by the Court, he shall be excused from so doing; and on every petition presented by a wife for dissolution of marriage the Court, if it see fit, may direct that the person with whom the husband is alleged to have committed adultery be made a respondent; and the parties, or either of them, may insist on having the contested matters of fact tried by a jury as hereinafter mentioned."

See, also, Rules of the English Divorce Court, Nos. 4, 5, 6, 7 (Appendix (G)).

(i) Practice in England.

(i) "**Practice in England**":

It will be noticed that in England the husband, in a suit instituted by him for dissolution of marriage, must make the "alleged adulterer" a co-respondent, "unless, on special grounds to be allowed by the Court," he is excused from so doing. The Court in England has, therefore, a wider discretion in the matter than have the Courts of this country under the Indian Divorce Act;

DISSOLUTION OF MARRIAGE.

the latter can excuse the petitioner only on one or other of the three specified grounds. The English Court has, for instance, excused the petitioner from making the alleged adulterer a co-respondent when, although the name of the latter is known to the petitioner, the only evidence of the alleged adultery is the confession or admission of the wife (*Jinkings* v. *Jinkings*, L. R., 1 P. 330; 36 L. J., P. & M. 48). This, however, is not one of the grounds specified in sect. 11 of the Indian Divorce Act, and even in England the Court has in recent cases expressed dissatisfaction with the practice adopted in the above case (see *Gill* v. *Gill*, 60 L. T. 712; *Payne* v. *Payne*, 60 L. T. 238; *Cornish* v. *Cornish*, 15 P. D. 131; 59 L. J., P. & M. 84; *Jones* v. *Jones*, 65 L. J., P. & M. 101; (1896) P. 165).

§ 11.

It is further to be noticed that the English Court may, if it see fit, make the alleged adulteress a respondent to a suit by the wife for a dissolution of marriage. Although this is rarely done in practice (for an instance, see *Bell* v. *Bell*, 8 P. D. 217), the Court will make use of its discretionary power whenever it has reason to suspect collusion or connivance between the petitioner and her husband (*Jones* v. *Jones*, *ubi supra*).

(ii) "**The alleged Adulterer**":

(ii) "Alleged adulterer."

When a petition alleges adultery, there is an "alleged adulterer" within the meaning of the Act (*Pitt* v. *Pitt*, L. R., 1 P. 464).

The reason for making the alleged adulterer a co-respondent —and the same reasoning would justify a provision enabling the Court, when it saw fit, to make an alleged adulteress a respondent to a suit by a wife against her husband—is thus stated by Gorell Barnes, J., in a very recent case:—"The interests of the petitioner and the respondent are not all that the Court has to consider. The person or persons with whom the respondent is alleged to have contracted a guilty relationship require their interests to be watched over, *and, in the public interest*, collusion between the parties, connivance, and other matters, have to be carefully guarded against, and the presence of parties whose interests conflict with the petitioner's may assist the Court in dealing with these matters (*Jones* v. *Jones*, (1896) P. 165; 65 L. J., P. & M. 101). In this case the Court laid down a general rule that the mere fact that the petitioner is unable to obtain evidence against a man who is alleged to have committed the adultery charged with his wife, although he has evidence that she has committed the adultery with him, is not

§ 11.
"alleged adulterer."

of itself a sufficient special ground for exempting the petitioner from making that man a co-respondent. The majority of the Court of Appeal, however, has recently held that no hard-and-fast rule should be laid down in such cases, and that the Court is not bound to compel a petitioner, who knows the name of his wife's alleged paramour, to make such paramour a co-respondent. On the other hand, Smith, L.J., expressed approval of the rule laid down in *Jones* v. *Jones* (*Saunders* v. *Saunders*, (1897) P. 89).

The husband, therefore, while not compelled to charge adultery in the petition with every person with whom his wife may have committed adultery (*Hunter* v. *Hunter*, 28 L. J., P. & M. 3), must make *every person* whom his petition charges with such adultery a co-respondent, unless he is specially excused from doing so by the Court (*Carryer* v. *Carryer and Watson*, 4 S. & T. 94; 34 L. J., P. & M. 47). And if the petition charges adultery with persons unknown, the order of the Court must be obtained dispensing with making such persons co-respondents, although there are other known co-respondents who have been duly served with process (*Penty* v. *Penty*, 7 P. D. 19; 51 L. J., P. & M. 24).

In a recent case, where the petition in an undefended suit alleged adultery with two persons who were made co-respondents, and also with certain unknown persons, the Court ordered the paragraphs of the petition referring to the unknown persons to be struck out (*Peacock* v. *Peacock*, 6 R. 656).

Counter-charge by husband.

Counter-charge by husband.—Where, in a suit by the wife for a divorce, the husband in his answer made a counter-charge of adultery against his wife, by reason of which he also prayed for a divorce, and applied for leave to proceed without making a co-respondent, the Court granted the application, but reserved the question whether it had power in such a case to make the alleged adulterer a co-respondent (*Curling* v. *Curling*, 14 P. D. 13; 58 L. J., P. & M. 20).

But where the husband, while charging the wife, in his answer, with having committed adultery with a certain person, did not pray for a divorce, the Court allowed the alleged adulterer to intervene (*Wheeler* v. *Wheeler*, 14 P. D. 154; 58 L. J., P. & M. 65).

Affidavit of petitioner.

Affidavit of petitioner.—Upon a motion to dispense with making the alleged adulterer a co-respondent, an affidavit by the petitioner, stating the ground upon which the leave of the Court is asked, is indispensable (*Drinkwater* v. *Drinkwater*, 60 L. T. 398).

But, even in cases where the petition charges adultery with persons unknown, the Court will not act upon the affidavit of the petitioner alone: such affidavit must, in every case, be corroborated *aliunde* (*Leader* v. *Leader*, 32 L. J., P. & M. 136; *Pitt* v. *Pitt*, 37 L. J., P. & M. 24; *Barber* v. *Barber*, (1896) P. 73).

§ 11.

Application to dispense with co-respondent: when to be made.— An application to be excused from making the alleged adulterer a co-respondent should be made at an early stage of the suit, but, except under special circumstances, it will be allowed even after the respondent has filed her answer (*Jaffers* v. *Jaffers*, 2 P. D. 90; 46 L. J., P. & M. 80).

Application, when to be made.

If, however, the alleged adulterer is dead, the proper course is to apply at once for an order to be excused from making him a co-respondent (*Tollemache* v. *Tollemache*, 28 L. J., P. & M. 2).

Dismissal of co-respondent before hearing.—The Court has power to dismiss a co-respondent from the suit before the hearing, and this, too, irrespective of his consent (*Wheeler* v. *Wheeler and Howell*, L. R., 2 P. 353; 41 L. J., P. & M. 33).

Co-respondent dismissed from suit before hearing.

And if the co-respondent appears under protest and pleads to the jurisdiction of the Court, the Court may, on the application of the petitioner, and on payment of the co-respondent's costs, dismiss the latter from the suit (*Gaynor* v. *Gaynor and Dagliantoni*, 31 L. J., P. & M. 116).

"**Respondent leading the life of a prostitute**":

To dispense with the necessity of making an alleged adulterer a co-respondent upon this ground, it is not enough to show that the wife is leading the life of a prostitute: the petitioner in his affidavit must also state that he knows of no one with whom the adultery has been committed (*Quicke* v. *Quicke*, 2 S. & T. 419; 31 L. J., P. & M. 28). A woman who does not lead a life of promiscuous intercourse with all who seek her, but lives with separate persons in succession, and professes to be able to attribute her respective children to a father, does not lead "a life of prostitution" within the meaning of the Act (*Roe* v. *Roe*, 3 B. L. R., Ap. 9). In this case, inasmuch as the petitioner had neglected for fourteen years to take any steps to obtain a separation from his wife, whom he knew to be living in adultery, the Court refused to allow the petition to be amended by the addition of co-respondents.

Respondent leading life of a prostitute.

§ 11.
Name of alleged adulterer unknown to petitioner.

"The name of the alleged adulterer is unknown to the petitioner, although he has made due efforts to discover it":

In such a case, it is not enough to state that the petitioner has been unable to learn the name of the alleged adulterer; he must show that he has made due efforts to discover it (*Evans* v. *Evans*, 28 L. J., P. & M. 20).

But where the petitioner's affidavit stated facts showing that the respondent had committed adultery, and that the petitioner had no means of discovering with whom such adultery had been committed, it was held sufficient (*Hunter* v. *Hunter*, 28 L. J., P. & M. 3).

So, where no evidence was obtainable against the man whom the respondent had indicated as the father of one of her illegitimate children, and who was believed to be in America, the Court allowed the petitioner to proceed without citing the alleged adulterer as a co-respondent (*Bagot* v. *Bagot*, 62 L. T. 612).

If a husband decides that he will not charge adultery between his wife and the person named to him as guilty of adultery with his wife, whether because he does not believe in the truth of the accusation, or because he is convinced that he cannot prove such person's guilt, or for any other reason, the practice is to charge adultery with some person unknown and to apply to the Court for leave to dispense with a co-respondent upon a special affidavit stating the grounds on which the petitioner asks to be excused from making him a co-respondent (*Saunders* v. *Saunders*, (1897) P. 89; 13 T. L. R. 328, C. A.).

If the petition charges adultery with certain persons, of whom some are known but some are unknown to the petitioner, the petitioner must obtain an order from the Court to be excused from making the unknown persons co-respondents (*Penty* v. *Penty*, 7 P. D. 59; 51 L. J., P. & M. 24; but see *Peacock* v. *Peacock* and *Hunter* v. *Hunter*, *supra*, p. 70).

The mere fact that the petitioner knows the name of a person who, he is informed, was his wife's paramour, is not *per se* a ground for compelling him to make such person a co-respondent, when the petitioner is convinced that he cannot obtain evidence to prove the man's guilt[*] (*Saunders* v. *Saunders*, (1897) P. 89; 13 T. L. R. 328, C. A.).

---

[*] But as to this see *Edwards* v. *Edwards and Wilson*, where *Saunders* v. *Saunders* is explained by Jeune, J. (*Times* newspaper of 13th August, 1897).

"Alleged adulterer is dead":

§ 11. Alleged adulterer dead.

Where the alleged adulterer is dead, the petitioner should apply at once for an order to be excused from making him a co-respondent (*Tollemache* v. *Tollemache*, 28 L. J., P. & M. 2).

If a co-respondent dies pending suit, leave to strike out his name should be obtained by motion (*Sutton* v. *Sutton*, 32 L. J., P. & M. 156).

Costs of proceedings.—Unless the alleged adulterer is made co-respondent, he cannot be ordered to pay the whole or any of the costs of the proceedings (see sect. 35, *post*), but he may, apparently, be ordered to pay damages, provided the petition has been duly served on him (see sect. 34, *post*).

12. Upon any such petition for the dissolution of a marriage, the Court shall satisfy itself, so far as it reasonably can, not only as to the facts alleged, but also whether or not the petitioner has been in any manner accessory to, or conniving at, the going through of the said form of marriage or the adultery, or has condoned the same, and shall also inquire into any counter-charge which may be made against the petitioner.

Court to be satisfied of the absence of collusion.

The Matrimonial Causes Act, 1857 (20 & 21 Vict. c. 85), sect. 29:—

> "Upon any such petition for the dissolution of a marriage, it shall be the duty of the Court to satisfy itself, so far as it reasonably can, not only as to the facts alleged, but also whether or no the petitioner has been in any manner accessory to or conniving at the adultery, or has condoned the same, and shall also inquire into any counter-charge which may be made against the petitioner."

"Accessory to":

"Accessory to."

The words "accessory to the adultery" mean aiding in producing, or contributing to produce, the adultery (*Gipps* v. *Gipps and Hume*, 33 L. J., P. & M. 161). It is not necessary that the petitioner should be an accessory *before the fact* (*Marris* v. *Marris and Burke*, 2 S. & T. 530; 31 L. J., P. & M. 69).

The petitioner may be an accessory to the adultery if it has been directly brought about by agents employed by the petitioner to watch the other party, even though such agents in bringing

§ 12.

"Conniving at":
Connivance on part of husband.

about the adultery act without the knowledge or authority of the petitioner (*Gower* v. *Gower*, L. R., 2 P. 428; 41 L. J., P. & M. 49; *Picken* v. *Picken and Simmonds*, 34 L. J., P. & M. 22; *Bell* v. *Bell*, 58 L. J., P. & M. 54; *Beanlands* v. *Beanlands*, No. 45, *Punjab Record*, 1871).

See also note to sect. 14, *post, s.t.* "*Neglect or Misconduct.*"

"**Conniving at**":

Connivance on the part of the husband.—Connivance on the part of a husband means a knowledge of, or acquiescence in, his wife's adultery (*Boulting* v. *Boulting*, 3 S. & T. 329; 33 L. J., P. & M. 33).

To establish connivance on the part of the husband it must be clearly shown that he consented or acquiesced, either actively or passively, to or in the wife's adultery. It is not necessary to prove that he was an accessory before the fact, but it must appear that he was cognizant that adultery would follow from transactions of which he approved and to which he gave his consent. The term "connivance" means not merely a refusal to see an act of adultery, but also a wilful abstention from taking any step to prevent an adulterous intercourse which, from what passes before the husband's eyes, he must reasonably expect to occur. An intention that adultery should follow, or a reckless disregard whether it followed or not under circumstances showing that it was highly likely to follow, constitute "connivance" (*Gipps* v. *Gipps*, 11 H. L. Cas. 1; 33 L. J., P. & M. 161; *Phillips* v. *Phillips*, 1 Robert. 145; *Moorsom* v. *Moorsom*, 3 Hagg. E. R. 107; *Gilpin* v. *Gilpin*, 3 Hagg. E. R. 150; *Glennie* v. *Glennie and Bowles*, 31 L. J., P. & M. 171; *Marris* v. *Marris and Burke*, 2 S. & T. 530; 31 L. J., P. & M. 69).

But the presumption is against connivance, and if the acts are equivocal the Court will presume against connivance (*Phillips* v. *Phillips; Moorsom* v. *Moorsom, ubi supra*).

Mere dulness of apprehension or lack of foresight is not sufficient to constitute connivance (*Allen* v. *Allen and D'Arcy*, 30 L. J., P. & M. 2).

But if a man voluntarily blinds himself to the probable consequences of an intimacy between his wife and another man of which he is fully aware, and the acts and conduct of the wife and the third person are such as to make adultery between them highly likely, the husband will be held to have connived at the offence, even though he has taken no active steps to bring it about (*Gipps* v. *Gipps, ubi supra*).

So where a husband agreed to withdraw his suit for dissolution of marriage in consideration of a sum of money to be paid by the co-respondent in lieu of damages, but made no stipulations as to the wife's future conduct, and, on the failure of the co-respondent to fulfil his part of the agreement, filed another petition charging a different act of adultery between the same parties, it was held that his conduct amounted to connivance at or consent to the wife's intercourse with the co-respondent (*Gipps* v. *Gipps, ubi supra*).

§ 12.
"*connivance on part of husband.*"

Again, where a husband, who was at the time aware of an adulterous intercourse between his wife and the co-respondent, entered into an agreement with them whereby he covenanted to allow his wife to live separate from him as if unmarried, and to give her a certain maintenance, and the co-respondent covenanted that the wife should not molest her husband, that she should maintain a child of which the husband believed the co-respondent to be the father, and that the co-respondent should indemnify the husband against her debts, the Court held that the agreement was virtually an assignment of his wife by the husband to the co-respondent (*Walton* v. *Walton*, 28 L. J., P. & M. 97).

A husband allowed a man to visit frequently at his house in his absence, to send provisions there and to make his wife an allowance of 1*l.* a week. He also sent his wife to borrow money of the same person, and allowed the latter to escort her on a journey to London. The jury acquitted the husband of connivance, but found that he had been guilty of conduct conducing to the adultery (*Brown* v. *Brown and Robey*, 21 L. T. 181).

Connivance on part of wife.—To constitute connivance on the part of the wife, it is not necessary that there should be a willing consent to the husband's adultery. She may be unwilling to consent to his living with another woman, but if, under pressure of circumstances, short of force in the nature of duress, she should withdraw her scruples, that would amount to connivance on her part. Nor is it any the less connivance if she ultimately consents to his conduct in order to obtain an allowance from him (*Ross* v. *Ross*, L. R., 1 P. 734; 38 L. J., P. & M. 49).

Connivance on part of wife.

A deed of separation securing an allowance to the wife does not *per se* prove connivance on her part at the adultery of her husband, in the absence of evidence that she was at the time

§ 12.
"*connivance on part of wife.*"

aware of, and acquiesced in, her husband's misconduct with another woman (*Ross* v. *Ross*, L. R., 1 P. 374; 38 L. J., P. & M. 49).

But the case is very different when the wife is fully aware of her husband's adulterous intercourse. So, where a husband and wife executed a deed of separation which recited that the former had been living for some time with a Miss H., and referred to certain articles of agreement concerning trust moneys and other property to which Miss H. as well as the husband and wife had been parties, it was held that the execution of the deed by the wife, who knew at the time that her husband was cohabiting with Miss H., was virtually a consent to the continuance of the adulterous intercourse (*Thomas* v. *Thomas*, 2 S. & T. 113; 3 L. T. 180).

But equivocal conduct or words will not be presumed to constitute connivance, and will, if possible, receive an innocent interpretation. Where, therefore, a husband and wife executed a deed of separation which contained the expression "whatever his" (*i.e.*, the husband's) "way of living may be," and it was proved that before the execution of the deed the husband had been guilty of adultery, the Court held that, as the evidence was conflicting, it would presume in favour of an innocent meaning to the expression (*Studdy* v. *Studdy*, 1 S. & T. 321; 28 L. J., P. & M. 105).

An agreement between the husband and wife that the husband shall commit adultery, so as to enable the wife to obtain a divorce, constitutes connivance on her part at the adultery when committed (*Todd* v. *Todd*, L. R., 1 P. 121; 35 L. J., P. & M. 34).

The wife of a domiciled Englishman went out to join him in America, where he was living, and subsequently there obtained a decree dissolving the marriage, with liberty to either party to marry again. The husband afterwards married A., and it was held, in a suit instituted by the wife in England for a dissolution of the marriage on the ground of her husband's adultery with A., that her suit could not be maintained; either the decree of the American Court was valid, in which case the husband was at liberty to marry again, or, if it was invalid, the wife, at whose instance the decree had been made, could not complain of its probable consequences, and must be regarded as having connived at the adultery (*Palmer* v. *Palmer*, 1 S. & T. 551; 29 L. J., P. & M. 26).

Where a husband had committed incestuous adultery with his wife's sister, and that to the wife's knowledge, and yet the wife allowed the husband and her sister to travel out together to

India, the Court held that her conduct, though injudicious, was due to an anxiety to spare her family the disgrace of an exposure, and did not amount to connivance at the subsequent adultery between her husband and sister, especially as she had made the former swear to have no further intercourse with the latter (*Turton* v. *Turton*, 3 Hagg. 338).

§ 12. "*connivance on part of wife.*"

Connivance generally: delay in suing.—Whilst on the one hand there is no absolute limitation in the case of a petition for dissolution of marriage, yet, on the other hand, the first thing which the Court looks to when a charge of adultery is preferred is whether there has been such delay as to lead to the conclusion that the petitioner had either connived at the adultery or was wholly indifferent to it. But any presumption arising from apparent delay may always be rebutted by an explanation of the circumstances (*Williams* v. *Williams*, I. L. R., iii Calc. 688).

Delay in suing may be construed as connivance.

"The first thing which the Court looks to when a charge of adultery is preferred is the date of the charge relatively to the date of the criminal fact and knowledge of it by the party, because, if the interval be very long between the date and knowledge of the fact and the exhibition of them to this Court, it will be indisposed to relieve a party who appears to have slumbered in sufficient comfort over them, and it will be inclined to infer either an insincerity in the complaint, or an acquiescence in the injury, real or supposed, or a condonation of it. It therefore demands a full and satisfactory explanation in order to take it out of the reach of such interpretations" (*per* Lord Penzance, *Boulting* v. *Boulting*, 33 L. J., P. & M. 33).

Petitioner, who has connived at one act of adultery, suing in respect of another act of adultery.—As regards their consequences, there is a difference between condonation and connivance.

Condonation is forgiveness of the particular offence or offences known to and condoned by the party forgiving; it is not affected by the existence of, and does not operate as a forgiveness of, other unknown or subsequent adulteries (*Bernstein* v. *Bernstein*, (1893) P. 292; 63 L. J., P. & M. 3—C. A.).

Connivance, on the other hand, operates as a complete bar to a suit not only in respect of the particular adultery connived at, but also in respect of any other adulteries whether committed with the same person, adultery with whom was connived at, or with any other person. Therefore, a petitioner who has connived at a certain act of adultery with A. is thereafter debarred from suing either in respect of other subsequent acts of adultery with A., or in respect of any acts of adultery with Z. (*Lovering* v. *Lovering*, 3 Hagg. 85; *Gipps* v. *Gipps and Hume*, 3 S. & T. 116; 32 L. J., P. & M. 78). But if the adultery with Z. be committed long after the adultery with A., which was connived at, the petitioner may *possibly* be held entitled to relief (see *Hodges* v. *Hodges*, 3 Hagg. 118; *Rogers* v. *Rogers*, 3 Hagg. 57). This, however, is exceedingly doubtful.

§ 12.

"Condonation": a question of fact.

"**Condonation**":

Generally.—Condonation is a conclusion of fact and not of law, and means a full and absolute forgiveness of a conjugal offence with a knowledge of all that is forgiven; it is not affected by the existence, and does not operate as a forgiveness, of other unknown adulteries (*Bernstein* v. *Bernstein*, (1893) P. 292; 63 L. J., P. & M. 3; *Peacock* v. *Peacock*, 1 S. & T. 183; 27 L. J., P. & M. 71; *Dempster* v. *Dempster*, 2 S. & T. 438; 31 L. J., P. & M. 20).

To be perfect, condonation, especially on the part of the wife, must be voluntary and unconditional; therefore, a forced return to cohabitation is no condonation (*Cooke* v. *Cooke*, 3 S. & T. 26; 32 L. J., P. & M. 154; in app., 3 S. & T. 246).

But, although condonation is an absolute and unconditional forgiveness of the offence, there is in all condonation an *implied* condition that the misconduct condoned shall not be repeated, and a breach of such condition revives the original offence, even if the breach consists in misconduct which is not *ejusdem generis* with the offence condoned (*Curtis* v. *Curtis*, 1 S. & T. 192; 27 L. J., P. & M. 73; in app., 28 L. J., P. & M. 55).

Condonation amounts, therefore, to a blotting-out of the offence imputed so as to restore the offending party (so long as the implied condition is not broken) to the same position which he or she occupied before the offence was committed (*Keats* v. *Keats and Montezuma*, 1 S. & T. 334; 28 L. J., P. & M. 57).

Condonation of adultery.

As regards the offence of adultery, it is expressly provided in sect. 14 that such offence shall not be deemed to have been condoned unless conjugal cohabitation has been resumed or continued. And "conjugal cohabitation" means, generally speaking, conjugal intercourse and not the mere living together in the same house.

The fact that a husband continues to sleep in the same bed with his wife, after knowledge of her adultery, is not *conclusive proof* of condonation: it raises an exceedingly strong presumption of condonation, but such presumption is capable of being rebutted by evidence (*Hall* v. *Hall*, 60 L. J., P. & M. 73).

As regards other matrimonial offences, the rule is also that, to be perfect, condonation must be followed by cohabitation. Words alone, however strong, can at the highest be only regarded as imperfect forgiveness, and unless followed up by something which amounts to reconciliation and to a reinstatement of the offender in the condition in which he or she was before the transgression, such forgiveness must remain incomplete (*Keats* v. *Keats and Montezuma*, 1 S. & T. 334; 28 L. J., P. & M. 57).

It is not enough to show that the husband returned to conjugal cohabitation after receiving evidence of his wife's adultery; it must be proved that he gave credit to that evidence and received her back, believing her to be guilty and intending to forgive her. Where, therefore, in answer to an action for maintenance, the husband alleged his wife's adultery but failed to prove it, and thereafter cohabited with her, the Court refused to conclude that he had condoned the adultery (*Ellis* v. *Ellis and Smith*, 4 S. & T. 154; 34 L. J., P. & M. 100; cf. *Adley* v. *Adley*, No. 70, *Punjab Record*, 1873).

§ 12. "*condonation.*" Condonation of other matrimonial offences.

Condonation on the part of the wife.—There is even less presumption in favour of condonation on the part of the wife than on the part of the husband. It is a merit in her to bear, to be patient and to endeavour to reclaim, nor is it her duty, till compelled by the last necessity, to have recourse to legal remedy (*D'Aguilar* v. *D'Aguilar*, 1 Hagg. 786; *Beeby* v. *Beeby*, 1 Hagg. 793; *Durant* v. *Durant*, 1 Hagg. 752).

" A woman has not the same control over her husband, has not the same guard over his honour, has not the same means to enforce the observance of the matrimonial vow; his guilt is not of the same consequence to her; therefore, the rule of condonation is held more laxly against her" (*D'Aguilar* v. *D'Aguilar, ubi supra*).

" The effect of cohabitation is held less stringently on the wife; she is more *sub potestate*, more *inops consilii*, she may entertain more hopes of the recovery and reform of her husband" (*Beeby* v. *Beeby, ubi supra*).

Condonation on the part of the wife is not lightly to be presumed from a continuance of cohabitation after the commission of one or even of several acts of cruelty by the husband: in such cases the continuance of cohabitation may be due to the apprehension of some evil which is considered greater than personal

Condonation on part of wife.

§ 12.
"condona-tion."

injury, *e.g.*, the privation of children (*Curtis* v. *Curtis*, 1 S. & T. 192; 27 L. J., P. & M. 73).

Offence condoned may be revived.

Offence condoned may be revived by subsequent misconduct.

Although condonation means an absolute forgiveness of the offence condoned, there is, in all condonation, an implied condition that the misconduct shall not be repeated, and a breach of such condition, even if it consist in misconduct which is not *ejusdem generis* the condoned misconduct, revives the former offence (*Curtis* v. *Curtis*, 1 S. & T. 192; 27 L. J., P. & M. 73; in app., 28 L. J., P. & M. 55).

(a) Cruelty.

(a) *Condoned cruelty.*—Cruelty which has been condoned may be revived without actual violence by threats of such a nature as to satisfy the Court that future cohabitation would be attended with danger to the party so threatened (*Bostock* v. *Bostock*, 1 S. & T. 221; 27 L. J., P. & M. 86; *Mytton* v. *Mytton*, 11 P. D. 141).

Condoned cruelty may also be so revived by subsequent adultery as to form, coupled with that adultery, a ground for decree of dissolution of marriage (*Palmer* v. *Palmer*, 2 S. & T. 61; 29 L. J., P. & M. 124).

But a wife who has agreed for valuable consideration not to take any proceedings against her husband in respect of his past cruelty is not entitled, when he subsequently commits adultery, to complain of such cruelty (*Rose* v. *Rose*, 7 P. D. 225).

(b) Desertion.

(b) *Condoned desertion.*—Where a husband whose previous adultery and desertion had been condoned by a return to cohabitation on the part of the wife, subsequently again committed adultery, it was held that his misconduct revived the previously condoned offences (*Blundford* v. *Blundford*, 8 P. D. 19; 52 L. J., P. & M. 17).

(c) Adultery.

(c) *Condoned adultery.*—There is no question that subsequent adultery will revive previously condoned adultery, but it is not altogether free from doubt whether any misconduct other than adultery will revive adultery which has been previously condoned.

It has, on the one hand, been held that condoned adultery may be revived by subsequent cruelty (*Dent* v. *Dent*, 4 S. & T. 105; 34 L. J., P. & M. 100; *Moore* v. *Moore*, (1892) P. 382; 62 L. J., P. & M. 10), or even by improprieties of conduct tending to,

but falling short of, adultery (*Pereira* v. *Pereira and Bonnjour*, § 12.
I. L. R., v Mad. 118; *Winscom* v. *Winscom and Plowden*, 3 S.
& T. 380; 33 L. J., P. & M. 45; *Ridgway* v. *Ridgway*, 29 W. R.
(Eng.) 612).

On the other hand, the House of Lords has held that, in order to revive condoned adultery, the petitioner must prove adultery, and nothing less, subsequent to the condonation (*Collins* v. *Collins*, 9 App. Ca. 205; 32 W. R. (Eng.) 500).

Collins v. *Collins* was, it is true, a Scotch case, and, in the opinion both of Jeune, J. (*Rogers* v. *Rogers*, (1894) P. 161; 63 L. J., P. & M. 97), and of Gorell Barnes, J. (*Moore* v. *Moore*, *ubi supra*), was not intended to overrule *Dent* v. *Dent* (*ubi supra*). Lord Blackburn, however, in his judgment questioned *Dent* v. *Dent* on principle, and stated that even assuming it to be established English law that any matrimonial offence, though forgiven, may be revived by any other matrimonial offence of which the Courts take cognizance, it was very modern law and not so obviously just and expedient that it ought to be inferred that it either was or ought to have been introduced into the law of Scotland.

It has been held that condoned incestuous adultery may be revived by subsequent adultery which was not incestuous (*Newsome* v. *Newsome*, L. R., 2 P. 306; 40 L. J., P. & M. 71). It is, however, doubtful whether subsequent adultery will revive condoned bigamy (*Furness* v. *Furness*, 2 S. & T. 63; 29 L. J., P. & M. 133).

Condonation expressly conditional.—Of course if the party condoning grants forgiveness only on the express condition that there is to be no repetition of matrimonial misconduct, any subsequent misconduct will constitute a breach of such conditional forgiveness and revive the former offence. Thus, where the husband had been guilty of incestuous adultery, but the wife forgave him and agreed not to take any steps against him in respect of that offence provided that the husband remained true to her in love and duty, it was held that a subsequent act of adultery committed by him, although not incestuous, revived the previous incestuous adultery which had been condoned (*Newsome* v. *Newsome*, *ubi supra*).

Condonation is conditional.

Express agreement not to sue in respect of condoned offence.—If, however, the husband or wife has expressly and unconditionally agreed, with full knowledge of the facts, not to sue or to take

§ 12.

any proceedings in respect of a condoned offence, the subsequent misconduct of the party, whose previous offence was so condoned, will not revive the former offence so as to entitle the other party to sue in respect of it (*Rowley* v. *Rowley*, L. R., 1 P. 63; *Rose* v. *Rose*, 7 P. D. 225; in app., 8 P. D. 98; 52 L. J., P. & M. 25).

Condonation pendente lite or after decree *nisi*.

Condonation pending suit, or after decree nisi.—If the parties have become reconciled and returned to cohabitation pending the suit or after the decree *nisi*, the Court may, upon the application of an intervenor or of the respondent or petitioner, dismiss the petition (*Cooper* v. *Cooper*, 3 S. & T. 392; 33 L. J., P. & M. 71; *Troward* v. *Troward*, 32 W. R. (Eng.) 864; *Flower* v. *Flower*, (1893) P. 290; 63 L. J., P. & M. 22).

It was originally held that condonation subsequent to the decree *nisi* was not a ground upon which the Court could reverse such decree if otherwise properly obtained, the reason given being that the words (in sect. 16) "not brought before the Court" related to the period previous to the decree *nisi* being granted (*Lewis* v. *Lewis*, 30 L. J., P. & M. 199; 2 S. & T. 394; cf. *Culley* v. *Culley*, I. L. R., x All. 559).

But according to the more recent decisions the fact that condonation has taken place subsequently to the decree *nisi* does not prevent the Court from dismissing the petition and rescinding the decree *nisi* (see, in addition to the cases above cited, *Hulse* v. *Hulse and Tavernor*, L. R., 2 P. 357; 41 L. J., P. & M. 19; *Howarth* v. *Howarth*, 9 P. D. 218—C. A.).

Condonation not pleaded.

Condonation not pleaded.—Condonation, although not pleaded, will be noticed by the Court if proved at the hearing (*Curtis* v. *Curtis*, 4 S. & T. 234). But if, under such circumstances, the Court takes notice of condonation which has not been pleaded, it will also admit evidence of misconduct subsequent to the condonation, although such misconduct has not been pleaded (*Suggate* v. *Suggate*, 1 S. & T. 492; 29 L. J., P. & M. 167).

Condonation limited to offence condoned.

Condonation strictly limited to offence condoned.—Condonation means forgiveness of the particular offence or offences known to and condoned by the party forgiving; it is not affected by the existence, and does not operate as a forgiveness, of other adulteries unknown at the time to the party forgiving (*Bernstein* v. *Bernstein*, (1893) P. 292; 63 L. J., P. & M. 3—C. A.). In this case, the Court of Appeal (approving the earlier case of *Story* v. *Story*, 12 P. D. 196) held that a decree had rightly been granted to a petitioner who sued for a divorce on the ground of

DISSOLUTION OF MARRIAGE.

§ 12.

his wife's adultery with two co-respondents, although it was proved that he had condoned the adultery with one of the latter, but that at the time of such condonation he was not aware that she had also committed adultery with the other co-respondent.

Claim for damages after condonation.—It was formerly held that condonation of the wife's adultery was no bar to a claim by the husband for damages against the person with whom such adultery had been committed (*Pomero* v. *Pomero*, 10 P. D. 174).

The above case has, however, been recently overruled by the Court of Appeal, and it has been laid down that where, on a petition for divorce and for damages against the co-respondent, a divorce is refused on the ground that the adultery has been condoned, the petitioner is not entitled to a judgment, even for nominal damages, against the co-respondent, but the petition will be dismissed, and the claim for damages which is ancillary to, and dependent on, the petition, must be dismissed also, and the petitioner may be ordered to pay the co-respondent's costs (*Bernstein* v. *Bernstein*, (1893) P. 292; 63 L. J., P. & M. 3; cf. *Story* v. *Story*, 12 P. D. 196; *Norris* v. *Norris*, *Lawson and Mason*, 4 S. & T. 237).

Claim for damages after condonation.

Suit for divorce by party whose previous adultery has been condoned.—Although in *Seller* v. *Seller* (1 S. & T. 482; 28 L. J., P. & M. 99) it was held that the adultery of a wife, if condoned by the husband, is no bar to a suit by her for judicial separation on the ground of adultery subsequently committed by him; and in *Rose* v. *Rose* (8 P. D. 98; 52 L. J., P. & M. 25) Jessel, M. R., considered it an "open question" whether a husband's adultery which had been previously condoned would be a bar to a suit by him for divorce, it may now be taken as practically settled that condonation of the petitioner's previous adultery will not be regarded as a special circumstance to justify the Court in exercising its discretion in the petitioner's favour (*Goode* v. *Goode and Hansom*, 2 S. & T. 253; 30 L. J., P. & M. 105; *McCord* v. *McCord*, *Ogle and Caxon*, L. R., 3 P. 237; 44 L. J., P. & M. 38; *Story* v. *Story*, 12 P. D. 196; 57 L. J., P. & M. 15; *Stoker* v. *Stoker*, 14 P. D. 60; 58 L. J., P. & M. 40; *Boucher* v. *Boucher*, 67 L. T. 720).

Suit for dissolution by petitioner whose own adultery has been condoned.

In a suit for judicial separation, however, the Court has, apparently, a wider discretion, and may grant the petitioner, whose own adultery has been condoned, the relief prayed for (*Gooch* v. *Gooch*, (1893) P., at p. 105).

§ 12.
Counter-charge.

"**Counter-charge against petitioner**":

As to what may be pleaded by way of counter-charge, see Appendix (E.), "Practice—Answer."

As regards costs of counter-charges, see Appendix (F.), "Costs."

The inquiry into any counter-charge here referred to is limited to counter-charges duly made by a party to the proceedings, in accordance with the rules of procedure and practice applicable to such party. Therefore, in an undefended suit for dissolution of marriage, where it appeared that after service of summons a letter purporting to be from the respondent was received by the judge by post, which letter imputed gross misconduct to the petitioner, such as if the respondent had appeared and put in a formal answer would have amounted to counter-charges within the meaning of this section, and the letter announced that the writer was unable to appear to defend for want of means, it was held by the Chief Court of the Punjab, that the Court was not bound on this communication to inquire into the imputations so made (*Burroughs* v. *Burroughs*, No. 62, *Punjab Record*, 1887).

Where the respondent appears and makes counter-charges against the petitioner, which the latter denies, the Court is bound to make proper inquiry into the truth or otherwise of such counter-charges. Where, therefore, in a suit for dissolution of marriage instituted in a district court, the court recorded the statements of the petitioner and respondent, caused the documentary evidence produced by both to be filed, and thereupon proceeded at once to pronounce a decree *nisi*, without fixing issues upon the statements of the parties or causing any further inquiry to be made, although the respondent alleged acts of cruelty and adultery against the petitioner subsequent to the marriage, which allegations were denied by the petitioner, the Chief Court of the Punjab refused to confirm the decree *nisi*, on the ground that the investigation had been defective to a substantial extent with reference to sects. 12 and 14 of the Act (*Cooper* v. *Wane*, No. 130, *Punjab Record*, 1879).

Where, at the hearing of a petition by the husband for dissolution of marriage on the ground of his wife's adultery, the wife makes a counter-charge of adultery against the petitioner, the latter may, as part of his case, give his own evidence and call his witnesses in answer to the respondent's charge, or he may, in the alternative, reserve his answer to the charge until the respondent's witnesses in support of it have been examined; but he is not entitled to divide his case by giving his own evidence in the opening, and afterwards calling his witnesses in reply to the respondent's charge (*Jackman* v. *Jackman,* 14 P. D. 62; 58 L. J., P. & M. 72).

§ 12. "*counter-charge.*"

13. In case the Court, on the evidence in relation to any such petition, is satisfied that the petitioner's case has not been proved, or is not satisfied that the alleged adultery has been committed,

> or finds that the petitioner has, during the marriage, been accessory to, or conniving at, the going through of the said form of marriage, or the adultery of the other party to the marriage, or has condoned the adultery complained of,
>
> or that the petition is presented or prosecuted in collusion with either of the respondents,

then and in any of the said cases the Court shall dismiss the petition.

When a petition is dismissed by a District Court under this section, the petitioner may, nevertheless, present a similar petition to the High Court.

Dismissal of petition.

The Matrimonial Causes Act, 1857 (20 & 21 Vict. c. 85), sect. 30, provides that:—

> "In case the Court, on the evidence in relation to any such petition, shall not be satisfied that the alleged adultery has been committed, or shall find that the petitioner has during the marriage been accessory to, or conniving at, the adultery of the other party to the marriage, or has condoned the adultery complained of, or that the petition is presented or prosecuted in collusion with either of the respondents, then and in any of the said cases the Court shall dismiss the said petition."

"**Satisfied on the evidence**":

Evidence.

As regards evidence of adultery, see Appendix (C.), "Proof of Adultery."

§ 13.
"Collusion."

"**Petition presented or prosecuted in collusion with either of the respondents**":

The word "collusion" has at times been loosely used as including "connivance," or agreements between the parties to commit an offence (see *Todd* v. *Todd, ante,* p. 76), or even conduct conducing to adultery (see *Sugg* v. *Sugg and Moore,* 31 L. J., P. & M. 41).

But, as used in the Indian Divorce Act, the term is limited to any agreement or understanding between the petitioner and either or both of the respondents, or agents acting on their behalf and with their knowledge, as to the presentation of the petition or the conduct and prosecution of the suit (*Lloyd* v. *Lloyd,* 1 S. & T. 567; 30 L. J., P. & M. 97).

To establish collusion, therefore, there must be some kind of understanding, or an express agreement, between the parties or agents acting on their behalf and with their knowledge, either to put forward a false case or to stifle a defence (*Gethin* v. *Gethin,* 31 L. J., P. & M. 43; *Adley* v. *Adley,* No. 70, *Punjab Record,* 1873).

Collusion may consist in the keeping back evidence of what would be a good answer to the petition (*Jessop* v. *Jessop,* 2 S. & T. 302; *Bacon* v. *Bacon and Ashby,* 25 W. R. 560; *Drummond* v. *Drummond,* 30 L. J., P. & M. 177).

So, where both parties, being equally guilty, agree to put forward the guilt of one party alone, it amounts to collusion (*Gray* v. *Gray,* 2 S. & T. 559).

And it is equally collusion if the parties agree *inter se* to keep back pertinent and material facts which might be adduced against the petitioner in support of a counter-charge by the respondent or co-respondent, even though the suppressed facts might not have been sufficient to establish the counter-charge (*Hunt* v. *Hunt and Wright,* 47 L. J., P. & M. 22).

It has, indeed, been held that, if the petitioner is otherwise entitled to a decree, the suppression of material facts which might have been adduced is not necessarily a ground for refusing a decree (*Alexander* v. *Alexander,* L. R., 2 P. 164; 39 L. J., P. & M. 84, approved in *Rogers* v. *Rogers,* (1894) P. 161; 63 L. J., P. & M. 97, by Jeune, J.). But this principle has been doubted by the Court of Appeal in *Butler* v. *Butler* (15 P. D. 66; 59 L. J., P. & M. 25), where the law was stated to be as laid down in *Hunt* v. *Hunt and Wright* (*supra*). For, in the words of Lopes, L.J., in *Butler* v. *Butler,* "the object of this special provision with regard to collusion is to compel the parties to come into the Court of Divorce with clean hands. It is to oblige them to bring *all material and pertinent facts* to the notice of the Court; to prevent their blinding the eyes of the Court in any respect; to oblige them so to act as to enable the Court to be in a position to do justice between the parties."

§ 13. "*collusion.*"

It amounts to collusion if the parties concur in getting up the evidence of the case, even if it be a true case (*Midgeley f. c. Wood* v. *Wood*, 30 L. J., P. & M. 57).

And there may be collusion, even though no facts have been falsely dealt with or withheld (*Churchward* v. *Churchward*, (1895) P. 7; 64 L. J., P. & M. 18).

But where, in an undefended suit, it appeared at the hearing that the wife had given the petitioner's solicitor a photograph of herself, and attended at the hearing to aid in her identification, and for so doing received money from the said solicitor, the Court, notwithstanding, was satisfied that there was no collusion between her and the petitioner, and pronounced a decree *nisi* (*Harris* v. *Harris and Lambert*, 31 L. J., P. & M. 160).

Where, however, subsequently to the institution of a suit for divorce, and on the same day that it came on for hearing, the petitioner and respondent each filed petitions setting out an agreement between them that from that date their marriage should be dissolved, that neither of them should have any claim against the other, and that each should be at liberty to marry again, and praying that dissolution might be granted on these terms, each party bearing his or her own costs, it was held that such an agreement amounted to collusion within the meaning of sect. 13 (*Christian* v. *Christian*, I. L. R., xi Calc. 651).

The mere fact of the husband making his wife an allowance in lieu of alimony while the suit is pending is not *per se* proof of collusion.

But where a husband both before and after presenting his petition had several interviews with his wife, and at such interviews gave her sums of money, urging her not to oppose the petition, and promising her that, if she complied with his request, he would do no harm to the co-respondent, and would be a friend to her when the decree was passed, and the respondent and co-respondent did not appear at the trial, and material facts showing that the petitioner's conduct had conduced to the adultery were withheld, the Court held that these facts proved collusion between the parties (*Barnes* v. *Barnes and Grimwade*, L. R., 1 P.

§ 13.
"collusion."

505; 37 L. J., P. & M. 4; cf. *Bacon* v. *Bacon and Ashby*, 25 W. R. 560).

On the other hand, where, on the termination of an adulterer's intercourse, an agreement was entered into between the husband and the adulterer that the latter should pay the expenses of the wife's return to England and allow her 100*l.* per annum, and the husband on his part undertook that the adulterer should be put to no expense by any proceedings to be taken for the purpose of obtaining a divorce, it was held that as the agreement was made for the purpose of restoring the wife to her friends and not with a view to the continuation of the adultery, it was no bar to a divorce (*Ratcliffe* v. *Ratcliffe and Anderson*, 1 S. & T. 467; 29 L. J., P. & M. 171).

Collusion between agents of parties.

Collusion between the parties' agents.—Any agreement or understanding as to the conduct of the suit between the agents of the parties, acting on their behalf and with their knowledge, constitutes collusion. If, however, the parties themselves are ignorant of the irregularities committed by their agents, the suit will not be dismissed on that ground (*Cox* v. *Cox*, 30 L. J., P. & M. 255; 2 S. & T. 306; *Lloyd* v. *Lloyd and Chichester*, 1 S. & T. 567; 30 L. J., P. & M. 97).

Expression of desire for divorce.

Expression of desire for divorce.—It does not amount to collusion for a party to express a wish for divorce. The respondent and co-respondent might wish it, but the mere expression of a desire on their part to obtain a divorce where the petitioner accepts no assistance from them nor enters into any agreement or understanding that they shall facilitate it by evidence or otherwise, will not amount to collusion (*Adley* v. *Adley and Campion*, No. 70, *Punjab Record*, 1873, citing *Cox* v. *Cox; Gethin* v. *Gethin;* and *Lloyd* v. *Lloyd and Chichester, ubi supra*).

Collusion subsequent to decree *nisi*.

Collusion subsequent to decree nisi.—The decree *nisi* may have been properly obtained, but if it is proved that, subsequently to such decree, there has been collusion between the parties with a view to concealing material facts from the Court and thus inducing the Court to make the decree absolute, which, if it had the suppressed facts before it, it would not do, the Court will rescind the decree *nisi*.

Thus, where a wife, who had obtained a decree *nisi* for dissolution of marriage, was subsequently visited by the respondent, and there was an agreement between them to keep the visits from the knowledge of the Court, and the respondent, after so cohabiting with his wife, committed adultery with another woman, the Court held that the respondent's subsequent adultery revived the condoned offences, but that the agreement to conceal the condonation amounted to collusion, and, therefore, the decree *nisi* must be rescinded (*Rogers* v. *Rogers*, (1894) P. 161; 63 L. J., P. & M. 97).

§ 13.

Collusion means collusion in the suit pending.—Collusion in this section means, and is confined to, collusion in the suit pending before the Court.

Must be in the pending suit.

Where, therefore, the Queen's Proctor moved to dismiss a husband's petition for divorce on the ground that in a former suit he had been found guilty of adultery and collusion, the Court held that, although the fact of the petitioner's adultery could not be again disputed, yet it would be open to him to show such circumstances as would get rid of its effect, and that, if he could do so, the fact that he had in a previous suit been guilty of collusion would not disentitle him to relief in the present suit (*Butler* v. *Butler*, No. 1, (1893) P. 185; 62 L. J., P. & M. 105).

"**The Court shall dismiss the petition**":

Court shall dismiss.

These are not, of course, the only grounds upon which a petition may be dismissed.

As regards the abatement of suits, see *ante*, p. 38, and as regards the dismissal or withdrawal of petitions upon grounds other than those stated in sects. 12 and 13 of the Act, see Appendix (E.), "Practice"; "Dismissal and Withdrawal of Petitions."

"**May present a similar petition to the High Court**":

Similar petition.

This means a petition based on the same allegations as were contained in the petition which was dismissed; it is not competent to the petitioner in such an event to put forward, in his petition to the High Court, a fresh case compounded of new acts of adultery and of acts previously in litigation (*Beanlands* v. *Beanlands*, No. 45 *Punjab Record*, 1871).

There is no similar provision made in the Act in respect of suits for judicial separation, nullity of marriage, or restitution of conjugal rights.

§ 13.

If, instead of presenting "a similar petition" to the High Court, the petitioner prefers to appeal, it is open to him or her to do so under sect. 55, *post*.

Power to Court to pronounce decree for dissolving marriage.

14. In case the Court is satisfied on the evidence that the case of the petitioner has been proved,

> and does not find that the petitioner has been in any manner accessory to, or conniving at, the going through of the said form of marriage, or the adultery of the other party to the marriage, or has condoned the adultery complained of,
>
> or that the petition is presented or prosecuted in collusion with either of the respondents,

the Court shall pronounce a decree declaring such marriage to be dissolved in the manner and subject to all the provisions and limitations in sections sixteen and seventeen made and declared:

Provided that the Court shall not be bound to pronounce such decree if it finds that the petitioner has, during the marriage, been guilty of adultery,

> or if the petitioner has, in the opinion of the Court, been guilty of unreasonable delay in presenting or prosecuting such petition,
>
> or of cruelty towards the other party to the marriage,
>
> or of having deserted or wilfully separated himself or herself from the other party before the adultery complained of, and without reasonable excuse,
>
> or of such wilful neglect or misconduct of or towards the other party as has conduced to the adultery.

Condonation.

No adultery shall be deemed to have been condoned

§ 14.

within the meaning of this Act unless where conjugal cohabitation has been resumed or continued.

The Matrimonial Causes Act, 1857 (20 & 21 Vict. c. 85), sect. 31, provides that:—
"In case the Court shall be satisfied on the evidence that the case of the petitioner has been proved, and shall not find that the petitioner has been in any manner accessory to or conniving at the adultery of the other party to the marriage, or has condoned the adultery complained of, or that the petition is presented or prosecuted in collusion with either of the respondents, then the Court shall pronounce a decree declaring such marriage to be dissolved: Provided always, that the Court shall not be bound to pronounce such decree if it shall find that the petitioner has during the marriage been guilty of adultery, or if the petitioner shall, in the opinion of the Court, have been guilty of unreasonable delay in presenting or prosecuting such petition, or of cruelty towards the other party to the marriage, or of having deserted or wilfully separated himself or herself from the other party before the adultery complained of, and without reasonable excuse, or of such wilful neglect or misconduct as has conduced to the adultery."

"**In case the Court is satisfied on the evidence that the case of the petitioner has been proved**":

On the subject of Evidence of Adultery, see Appendix (C.), "Proof of Adultery."

A decree for dissolution of marriage cannot be made merely on admissions and without recording evidence (*Bai Kanku* v. *Shiva Toya*, I. L. R., xvii Bom. 624). Admissions by the parties.

So where, in a suit for dissolution of marriage, the District Court recorded the statements of the petitioner and respondent, and caused the documentary evidence produced by both to be filed, and thereupon proceeded at once to pronounce judgment granting a decree *nisi*, without fixing issues upon the statements of the parties or causing any further inquiry to be made, although the respondent made counter-charges against the petitioner which were denied by him, the Chief Court of the Punjab refused to confirm the decree *nisi* on the ground that the investigation was defective to a substantial extent with reference to sects. 12 and 14 of the Act (*Cooper* v. *Wane*, No. 130 *Punjab Record*, 1879).

And although sect. 51, *Proviso*, gives liberty to the parties, under certain specified conditions, "to verify their respective Affidavits.

§ 14.

cases in whole or in part by affidavit," it is only in very special circumstances that the Court will allow this to be done (see note to sect. 51, *post*). Nor is the petitioner entitled as of right to give evidence by affidavit (*Skinner* v. *Skinner*, No. 13 *Punjab Record*, 1891).

As regards affidavits generally, see Chapter XVI. of the Civil Procedure Code.

Court to pronounce a decree of dissolution.

" **The Court shall pronounce a decree declaring such marriage to be dissolved** " :

The Court is not bound to pass a decree of dissolution, and the petitioner may, under certain circumstances and irrespective of the respondent's consent, be permitted to amend the petition to one for judicial separation, even after proof of facts entitling the petitioner to a decree of dissolution (*Dent* v. *Dent*, 4 S. & T. 105; 34 L. J., P. & M. 118).

In a suit by the wife for dissolution of marriage, she proved both charges against the respondent, and the decree *nisi* was suspended at her request; she subsequently applied to amend the petition by substituting a prayer for judicial separation, but as the respondent opposed the alteration, and alleged that the wife had herself been guilty of adultery, the Court granted liberty to the respondent to file affidavits in support of his charge, and, on no affidavits being so filed within the period fixed, allowed the petition to be amended as prayed (*Mycock* v. *Mycock*, L. R., 2 P. 98; 39 L. J., P. & M. 56).

If, however, the petitioner has been proved guilty of any such conduct as is hereinafter specified, the Court will not allow the petition to be amended to one for judicial separation (*Boreham* v. *Boreham*, L. R., 1 P. 77).

Decree of judicial separation at prayer of petitioner.

Further, it is competent to the Court, irrespective of the respondent's consent, to grant a decree of judicial separation, although the petition prays for dissolution of marriage, if the facts proved entitle the petitioner to the former but not to the latter relief (*Smith* v. *Smith*, 1 S. & T. 359; 28 L. J., P. & M. 27; *Bromfield* v. *Bromfield*, 41 L. J., P. & M. 17; *Grossi* v. *Grossi*, L. R., 3 P. 111; 42 L. J., P. & M. 69).

Where a decree *nisi* had been obtained by the wife on the grounds of her husband's adultery and cruelty, but it afterwards appeared, on the intervention of the Queen's Proctor, that the adultery had been brought about, without her knowledge, by her solicitor's clerk, the Court rescinded the decree *nisi*, but

DISSOLUTION OF MARRIAGE.

refused to dismiss the wife's petition in order to give her an opportunity of applying for judicial separation (*Bell* v. *Bell*, 58 L. J., P. & M. 54).

§ 14.

"**Provided that the Court shall not be bound**":

Discretion of Court.

In granting or refusing a decree of dissolution of marriage, the Courts in India will adopt, as a guide in the exercise of their judicial discretion given by this section, the principles laid down in the English decisions with regard to the corresponding section in the English Act (20 & 21 Vict. c. 85, s. 31). Such discretion must be a regulated discretion, and the Court cannot grant or withhold a decree on the mere footing that the petitioner's adultery is more or less pardonable, or that it has been more or less frequent. There must be special circumstances attending the commission of such adultery, or special features placing it in some category capable of distinct statement and recognition, in order that the discretion may be fitly exercised in favour of a petitioner (*G.* v. *G.*, 8 Bom. H. C., O. C. 48; cf. *Morgan* v. *Morgan and Porter*, L. R., 1 P. 644; 38 L. J., P. & M. 41).

And in India, where there is no public officer corresponding to the Queen's Proctor, a judge, exercising jurisdiction under this Act, ought to make a large use of his powers to look into any matters which may come under his notice, affecting the proper exercise of the discretionary powers of the Court to grant or withhold a divorce under specified circumstances, even though such matters are not brought to his notice by a party to the proceedings or an intervener (*Lisbey* v. *Lisbey*, No. 6 *Punjab Record*, 1888).

But when the case of a petitioner has been duly proved, and the Court does not find that he has been accessory to, or conniving at, the adultery, or that there has been any condonation, or collusion, or connivance, the Court is bound to grant him a decree of dissolution unless it is established affirmatively that the petitioner has been guilty of one of the acts which gives the Court a discretionary power to refuse to dissolve the marriage (*Haswell* v. *Haswell and Sanderson*, 1 S. & T. 502; 29 L. J., P. & M. 21; cf. *Mordaunt* v. *Mordaunt and Moncrieffe*, L. R., 2 H. L. (Sc.) 374; 43 L. J., P. & M. 49).

"**Petitioner has during the marriage been guilty of adultery**":

Petitioner's adultery.

The cases are very few indeed in which a petitioner, who has during the marriage been guilty of adultery, will be granted a

§ 14. decree of dissolution of marriage (*Wildey* v. *Wildey and Ryder*, 26 W. R. (Eng.) 239; *Hick* v. *Hick and Kitchen*, 34 L. J., P. & M. 11; *Drummond* v. *Drummond*, 30 L. J., P. & M. 177; *Lautour* v. *Lautour*, 10 H. L. Ca. 685). Nor, as a general rule, does the Court feel justified in visiting with the penalty of adultery a wife whose husband has also been found guilty of that offence (*Barnes* v. *Barnes and Beaumont*, L. R., 1 P. 572; 38 L. J., P. & M. 101).

Therefore where, in a suit by the husband for dissolution of marriage, the jury found that the husband as well as the wife had been guilty of adultery, but it appeared that the husband's misconduct was long antecedent to that of the wife, who apparently did not know of it until the filing of the petition, the Court refused to grant him a decree, on the ground that mere lapse of time would not justify the exercise of the Court's discretion in his favour (*Morgan* v. *Morgan and Porter*, L. R., 1 P. 644; 38 L. J., P. & M. 41).

So, where the petitioner in a suit for dissolution of marriage, after his case had been proved, tendered himself for examination, and confessed that on a single occasion, during a separation from his wife, he had committed an act of adultery, the Court refused to grant him a decree (*Clarke* v. *Clarke and Clarke*, 34 L. J., P. & M. 94).

Nor was the Court more indulgent to a petitioner whose single act of adultery had been committed under the influence of drink and had been subsequently condoned by the wife (*Grosvenor* v. *Grosvenor*, 34 W. R. (Eng.) 140).

The Ecclesiastical Courts in England, in refusing relief to a petitioner under such circumstances, adopted the rule of the canon law, *mutuâ compensatione ambo adulteria abolentur*, and held that the adultery of the one party to the marriage acted as a sort of compensation for the adultery of the other (*Seaver* v. *Seaver*, 2 S. & T. 665; *Forster* v. *Forster*, 1 Hag. Cons. 148). That is to say, that the adultery of the petitioner wiped out the adultery of the respondent, and thus both parties were regarded as innocent of any matrimonial offence. But the Divorce Court, in refusing a petitioner, who has been guilty of adultery, a decree of dissolution or even of judicial separation, acts on the principle that the party who prays for relief must come into the Court with clean hands. In the words of Cotton, L. J., "A wife having been guilty of adultery has put herself in such a position that she cannot be considered as an innocent party in any proceedings which might have been taken in the old Ecclesiastical Courts, or which might now be taken in the Court of Divorce; and therefore, *on that ground*, she is not in a position to come to that Court to give her any relief as to any matrimonial offence which the husband may have committed, or to put it on the ground of compensation for a crime of the same nature" (*Otway* v. *Otway*, 13 P. D. 141; 57 L. J., P. & M. 81).

In this case the wife (petitioner) and the husband had been both guilty of adultery, but the wife claimed to set off her husband's adultery as compensation for her own, and to be entitled to a decree for judicial separation on the ground of his aggravated cruelty. The Court of Appeal, however, refused to accede to the argument based on the doctrine of *compensatio criminis*, and dismissed her petition on the broad ground that she did not come into Court with clean hands.

But to act as a bar to the petitioner's suit, the adultery must have been committed during the marriage of which a dissolution is sought. Adultery committed prior to the marriage will not disentitle the petitioner to relief (*Styles* v. *Styles*, 62 L. T. 613).

Adultery prior to marriage sought to be dissolved.

Condonation of the Petitioner's Adultery.

Condonation of petitioner's adultery.

The older decisions were to the effect that the petitioner's adultery, if condoned, was no bar to a suit for dissolution of marriage, or for judicial separation (*Anichini* v. *Anichini*, 2 Curt. 210; *Seller* v. *Seller*, 28 L. J., P. & M. 99).

And in a comparatively recent case, Jessel, M. R., stated that, though the question remained open, it was his impression that adultery by a husband which had been condoned was not necessarily a bar disentitling him to a decree for dissolution on the ground of the wife's subsequent adultery (*Rose* v. *Rose*, 8 P. D. 98; 52 L. J., P. & M. 25). So, too, the present President of the English Divorce Court stated in the case of *Gooch* v. *Gooch* ((1893) P. at p. 105) that "in cases of judicial separation, condonation gives to the Court a discretion to grant the relief notwithstanding the adultery of the petitioner."

But there can be no doubt that the later decisions all point to a reluctance on the part of the Court to grant relief to a petitioner who has been guilty of adultery, and to a refusal to regard the condonation of such adultery as a sufficient justification of the exercise of its discretion in favour of such a petitioner (*Goode* v. *Goode and Hansom*, 2 S. & T. 253; 32 L. J., P. & M. 105; *McCord* v. *McCord and Ogle*, L. R., 3 P. 237; 44 L. J., P. & M. 38; *Grosvenor* v. *Grosvenor*, 34 W. R. (Eng.) 140; *Story* v. *Story*,

§ 14. 12 P. D. 196; 57 L. J., P. & M. 15; *Stoker* v. *Stoker*, 14 P. D. 60; 58 L. J., P. & M. 40; *Boucher* v. *Boucher*, 67 L. T. 720).

Exceptions to general rule.

Exceptions to General Rule.

In certain exceptional cases the Court may exercise its discretion in favour of a petitioner despite the fact that he or she has also been guilty of adultery. These cases may be thus classified— (1) where the adultery has been committed in ignorance of (a) fact, or (b) law; (2) where the wife is the petitioner, and her adultery was due to compulsion exercised over her by the husband in order to force her to commit adultery; and—though this is exceedingly doubtful—(3) where the petitioner's adultery consisted of but a slight lapse, was long antecedent to, and disconnected with that of the respondent, was condoned and was never afterwards repeated.

(a) Adultery committed in ignorance of fact.

(i) *Adultery by petitioner committed in ignorance of fact.*—Where a husband, in the *bonâ fide* belief that his wife was dead, married again and discovered that his wife was alive and had committed adultery, the Court granted him a decree *nisi* notwithstanding his own bigamy with adultery (*Freegard* v. *Freegard*, 8 P. D. 186; 52 L. J., P. & M. 100).

So where a wife, who had been deserted by her husband for over sixteen years and who believed that her husband was dead, married another man and subsequently discovered that her husband was alive and had committed adultery, it was held that, notwithstanding her bigamy, she was entitled to a decree (*Potter* v. *Potter*, 67 L. T. 721).

But the Court must be satisfied that the petitioner at the time of the second marriage had a *bonâ fide* belief that the other party was dead (*Joseph* v. *Joseph and Wenzel*, 34 L. J., P. & M. 96).

(b) Adultery committed in ignorance of law.

(b) *Adultery by petitioner committed in ignorance of law.*—" It has been said that ignorance of law is no excuse. But when the Court has a discretion, the petitioner's ignorance of the law may be properly excused" (*Noble* v. *Noble and Goodman*, 38 L. J., P. & M. 52).

So, where a husband, in ignorance of the law, went through a form of marriage two weeks after he had obtained a decree *nisi* for the dissolution of his first marriage, his adultery was held to be excusable (*Noble* v. *Noble and Goodman*, *supra*). So, where a petitioner married another woman after the decree *nisi* of the District Court but before it had been confirmed, the Court, under the circumstances of the case, confirmed the decree despite the petitioner's adultery (*Kyte* v. *Kyte and Cooke*, I. L. R., xx Bomb. 362).

§ 14.

A wife, who had obtained a decree *nisi* for the dissolution of her marriage, more than six months thereafter went through the form of marriage with another man in the honest belief that her marriage had been dissolved by the decree *nisi*, but that she could not marry until the expiration of six months. After the death of the man with whom she had gone through the form of second marriage, she resumed cohabitation with her husband, but left him again on account of his cruelty. It was held that the condonation by resumption of cohabitation was conditional, and that the subsequent cruelty put the petitioner in a position to ask to have the decree *nisi* made absolute, and that as the petitioner in going through the form of second marriage *bonâ fide* believed that she had a legal right to do so, the Court ought to make the decree absolute as prayed for (*Moore* v. *Moore*, (1892) P. 382; 62 L. J., P. & M. 10).

A husband and wife signed a document to the effect that they had agreed to live separate, and that each was at liberty to marry again. The husband, who was of humble rank, believed this document to be legal and binding, and went through a form of marriage with another woman, from whom, however, he at once separated on hearing that the second marriage was not legal. He subsequently petitioned for dissolution of marriage, and it was held that, as he had acted in ignorance of the law and in the *bonâ fide* belief that the second marriage was legal, the case was a proper one for the exercise of the Court's discretion in his favour (*Whitworth* v. *Whitworth*, (1893) P. 85; 62 L. J., P. & M. 71).

(ii) *Adultery of wife (petitioner) due to her husband's compulsion.* —Where, in a suit for dissolution of marriage, the petitioner satisfied the Court that she had been terrified by the threats and ill-treatment of her husband into leading a life of immorality, contrary to her own will and desires, the Court considered that it was a fit case to exercise its discretion in her favour, notwithstanding her admitted prostitution during the marriage (*Coleman* v. *Coleman*, L. R., 1 P. 81; 35 L. J., P. & M. 37).

(c) Adultery due to compulsion.

In exercising its discretion as to granting a decree in favour of a petitioner who has been guilty of adultery, the circumstances which should be considered by the Court include the case of a

Respondent's misconduct conducing to petitioner's adultery.

§ 14.　husband causing or conducing to his wife's adultery by his own wilful neglect or misconduct. In such cases the Court may properly grant the wife a decree despite her own adultery (*Symons* v. *Symons*, (1897) P. 167; xiii T. L. R., p. 353).

(d) Isolated act of adultery long since condoned.

(iii) *Petitioner's isolated act of adultery long since condoned and never repeated.*—In a few cases, the authority of which, in view of later decisions, is at least questionable, it was held that an isolated act of adultery on the part of the petitioner, which was committed long previously to the respondent's misconduct and in no way conduced thereto, and had been condoned by the respondent, would not necessarily disentitle the petitioner to a decree of dissolution if the petitioner could satisfy the Court that, but for the one lapse proved, he had been a good and faithful husband (*Hutchinson* v. *Hutchinson and Barker*, 14 L. T. 338; *Conradi* v. *Conradi and Worral*, L. R., 1 P. 514; 37 L. J., P. & M. 55).

And the Chief Court of the Punjab held, following *Conradi* v. *Conradi and Worral*, that the circumstance that in a former suit for dissolution of marriage the Court decided to refuse the petitioner a decree, on the ground that he also had been guilty of adultery, was no bar to the exercise of its discretion in his favour in a subsequent suit by him, where it appeared that, assuming he had committed adultery since his marriage, such adultery had been condoned by the respondent and had no connection with the separation of the wife from her husband since the decision in the former suit, and in no way conduced to her subsequent life of open prostitution (*Lisbey* v. *Lisbey*, No. 6, *Punjab Record*, 1888).

The case of *Collins* v. *Collins* (9 P. D. 231; 53 L. J., P. & M. 116) was a very exceptional one. In that case it appeared that after the husband had obtained a decree *nisi* by reason of his wife's adultery, which was subsequently rescinded on the ground of his own adultery and cruelty, the parties lived together again. The husband thereafter committed other acts of cruelty and was subsequently convicted of rape, whereupon the wife filed a petition for dissolution of marriage. The Court, notwithstanding her adultery, decided, under the circumstances of the case, to grant her a decree.

But, despite the cases above cited, it is very doubtful whether the Court will, at the present day, exercise its discretion in favour of the petitioner simply on the ground that his act of adultery was long previous to that of the respondent, was condoned by her, and in no way conduced to her misconduct (see cases cited at pp. 94, 95). For, in the words of the present president of the English Divorce Court, "the Court's discretion in granting a decree to a petitioner guilty of adultery was only exercised in cases where it might be said that the petitioner might be absolved from *moral guilt*, as where a husband, believing that his wife was dead, went through a form of marriage with another woman" (*Maggs* v. *Maggs and Creedy*, xii T. L. R. 509).

§ 14.

"Petitioner guilty of unreasonable delay in presenting or prosecuting such petition":

Unreasonable delay.

The provisions of the Indian Limitation Act (XV of 1877) do not apply to suits or proceedings under the Indian Divorce Act of 1869 (sect. 1, cl. (a) of the Indian Limitation Act, 1877).

But while, on the one hand, there is no absolute limitation in the case of a petition for dissolution of marriage, yet the first thing which the Court looks to when a charge of adultery is preferred is whether there has been such delay as to lead to the conclusion that the petitioner had either connived at the adultery or was wholly indifferent to it; but any presumption arising from apparent delay may always be rebutted by an explanation of the circumstances (*Williams* v. *Williams*, I. L. R., iii Calc. 688).

"The first thing which the Court looks to when a charge of adultery is preferred is the date of the charge relatively to the date of the criminal fact and knowledge of it by the party, because if the interval be very long between the date and knowledge of the fact and the exhibition of them to the Court, it will be indisposed to relieve a party who appears to have slumbered in sufficient comfort over them, and it will be inclined to infer either an insincerity in the complaint, or an acquiescence in the injury, whether real or supposed, or a condonation of it. It therefore demands a full and satisfactory explanation in order to take it out of the reach of such interpretation" (*per* Sir J. P. Wilde, *Boulting* v. *Boulting*, 33 L. J., P. & M. 33; cf. *Nicholson* v. *Nicholson*, L. R., 3 P. 53; 29 L. T. 108).

The "unreasonable delay in presenting or prosecuting a petition for dissolution of marriage" is delay from which it would appear that the petitioner is insensible to the injury of which he complains (*Pellew* v. *Pellew and Berkeley*, 1 S. & T. 553; 29 L. J., P. & M. 44; cf. *Dera Sayagam* v. *Naiyagam*, 7 Mad. 284).

What is.

§ 14.

And where a suit is instituted by the wife on account of her husband's adultery and cruelty, a long delay may show that the suit is not instituted for the protection of the wife, but for some collateral purpose, and if the Court is satisfied that such is the case, the petition will be dismissed (*Matthews* v. *Matthews*, 1 S. & T. 499; 29 L. J., P. & M. 118; in app. 3 S. & T. 161).

Generally speaking, if a petitioner, with full knowledge of the facts, refrains from taking proceedings for two years, his petition will be dismissed unless the delay is satisfactorily explained (*Nicholson* v. *Nicholson*, L. R., 3 P. 53; 29 L. T. 108).

Excusable delay:
(a) Want of means.

Excusable delay.—A petitioner is not guilty of unreasonable delay in presenting his petition, although a long period may have elapsed since the adultery was committed, if he has been prevented by poverty from taking steps earlier to obtain a divorce (*Ratcliffe* v. *Ratcliffe and Anderson*, 1 S. & T. 467; 29 L. J., P. & M. 171; *Wilson* v. *Wilson*, L. R., 2 P. 435; *Faulkes* v. *Faulkes*, 64 L. T. 834; *Binney* v. *Binney*, 69 L. T. 498).

So, where a wife left her husband in 1844 on account of his cruelty and adultery, but had not the means of suing till shortly before the suit was instituted in 1863, and the husband had been leading a wandering life without employment, the Court held that the wife had not been guilty of unreasonable delay (*Harrison* v. *Harrison*, 3 S. & T. 362; 33 L. J., P. & M. 44).

In 1878 a husband obtained a judicial separation from his wife, and 80*l*. damages against the co-respondent, but took no steps to recover the latter. The wife continued to cohabit with the co-respondent, and in 1882 the husband petitioned for a divorce. The reason he gave for the delay and for not enforcing his claim for damages was that he had no money, being only in receipt of weekly wages, and that he hoped that his wife would return to him. The Court of Appeal held, reversing the decision of the lower Court, that the delay was not unreasonable under the circumstances (*Mason* v. *Mason*, 8 P. D. 21; 52 L. J., P. & M. 27; reversing 7 P. D. 233; 51 L. J., P. & M. 88).

(b) Ignorance of law.

A domiciled Englishman intermarried with a Scotch woman, and in 1841 obtained a divorce in the Scotch Courts, which divorce he believed to be of universal application, being confirmed in that belief by opinion of counsel. In 1854, however, he was informed that the divorce was of no validity in England, and he thereupon petitioned for leave to bring in a bill into the House of Lords declaring his marriage absolutely void since 1841. This petition was rejected, and in 1858 he sued for a dissolution of marriage on the ground of his wife's adultery in 1841 and at other times. The Court held that there had been no such lapse of time as to constitute unreasonable delay (*Tollemache* v. *Tollemache*, 1 S. & T. 557; 30 L. J., P. & M. 113).

§ 14.

A petitioner excused his delay in suing on the ground that he believed that after seven years he could legally contract a second marriage. The Court held that under the circumstances the delay was not unreasonable (*Dera Sayagam* v. *Naiyagam*, 7 Mad. 284).

A husband committed incestuous adultery with his wife's sister, but the wife delayed proceedings for eighteen years, giving, as an explanation of the delay, her mother's anxiety to avoid a public exposure of the scandal and her mother's urgent entreaties (to which she had yielded) to forbear from taking any proceedings. Upon her mother's death she instituted a suit for dissolution, and it was held that she had been guilty of unreasonable delay, but not of such a character as to disentitle her to a decree (*Newman* v. *Newman*, L. R., 2 P. 57; 39 L. J., P. & M. 36).

(c) Desire to avoid family scandal.

Unreasonable delay.—A husband presented his petition for divorce about fourteen years after he had discovered the fact of his wife's adultery. His excuse for the delay was that he had no means, but he admitted that he was a coal-hauler, and at the time of suit possessed stock-in-trade of the value of 600*l*. and nine horses, besides some cottages which he had purchased through a building society. The Court refused to accept his plea of want of means as a sufficient explanation of the delay (*Short* v. *Short and Bolwall*, L. R., 3 P. 193).

Unreasonable delay.

A wife, who had lived separately from her husband for twenty years, sued for a dissolution of marriage on the ground of his adultery, which was of recent date, and cruelty, which had been committed before the separation. Her explanation of the delay was that at first she hoped her husband would repent, and latterly she wished to wait till her son, the only child of the marriage, was grown up. The Court held that the delay was so unreasonable as to disentitle her to a decree (*Beauclerk* v. *Beauclerk*, (1891) P. 189; 60 L. J., P. & M. 20).

"**Or of cruelty towards the other party to the marriage**": "Cruelty."

As regards "cruelty" generally, see *ante*, note to sect. 10.

For the purposes of this section, it would seem that the

§ 14.

cruelty must be such as to have led or conduced to the respondent's misconduct (*Pearman* v. *Pearman and Burgess*, 29 L. J., P. & M. 54; *Edwards* v. *Edwards*, (1894) P. 33).

The fact that the petitioner's cruelty has been condoned by the respondent will not necessarily debar the Court from exercising its discretion against the petitioner (*Gordon* v. *Gordon and Saran*, 3 B. L. R., O. C. 136).

But it may be different where the respondent has executed a deed for valuable consideration, voluntarily relinquishing all right to complain of such cruelty. Thus, where a wife obtained a judicial separation from her husband on the ground of his cruelty, and was given the custody of her child, and subsequently the husband and wife executed a deed of agreement whereby the latter relinquished the custody of the child and her rights to alimony in consideration of a lump sum then paid to her by her husband, and shortly after the execution of the deed the husband discovered she was committing adultery and sued for a divorce, the Court held that the cruelty on his part was not such as would induce it to withhold a decree from the husband, especially as the deed of release had been executed by the wife with her eyes open (*Badham* v. *Badham*, 62 L. T. 663).

Where a husband was proved to have been guilty of adultery, but the wife (who was the petitioner) was also proved to have been guilty of cruelty and of wilful separation from the respondent before his adultery, and of wilful neglect and misconduct conducing to his adultery, the Court refused to grant her a decree of judicial separation (*Boreham* v. *Boreham*, L. R., 1 P. 77; 35 L. J., P. & M. 49).

"Or of having deserted or wilfully separated himself or herself from the other party before the adultery complained of and without reasonable excuse":

Desertion.

For "desertion" generally, see note to sect. 10, *ante*.

In order to found a suit for judicial separation, or, coupled with adultery, a suit by a wife for dissolution of marriage, the desertion complained of must have been for two years or upwards; but for the purposes of this section, it need not have been for any definite period.

It has been held that, for the purposes of this section, a desertion or wilful separation may be justified on grounds which would not justify a desertion sufficient to found a decree for judicial separation, and that, whereas in the latter case "a reasonable excuse" must be a distinct matrimonial offence, in the former case, conduct falling short of such matrimonial offence may afford a sufficient justification for separation (*Haswell* v. *Haswell and Sanderson*, 1 S. & T. 502; 29 L. J., P. & M. 21). Inasmuch, however, as in each case the words "*a reasonable excuse*" are used (see sects. 10, 14, and 22), it is difficult to see the reason for drawing such a distinction.

§ 14.

It is only in very exceptional cases indeed that the Court will grant a decree of dissolution in favour of a petitioner who has been guilty of desertion or wilful separation without reasonable excuse (*Yeatman* v. *Yeatman*, L. R., 2 P. 187; 39 L. J., P. & M. 77). Especially is this the case where the husband is the petitioner. For, "if chastity be the duty of the wife, protection is no less that of the husband. The wife has a right to the comfort and support of the husband's society, the security of his home and name, and the just protection of his presence, so far as his position and avocations will admit. Whoever falls short in this regard, if not the author of his own misfortune, is not wholly blameless in the issue, and though he may not have justified his wife, he has so far compromised himself as to forfeit his claim for a divorce" (*Jeffreys* v. *Jeffreys and Smith*, 3 S. & T. 495; 33 L. J., P. & M. 66).

It has been seen (see *ante*, p. 61) that a separation by mutual agreement does not constitute desertion; but if there was no reasonable excuse for such separation, it may be held to have been "wilful" within the meaning of this section, and to disentitle the petitioner to a decree of dissolution of marriage (*Dagg* v. *Dagg and Speke*, 7 P. D. 17; 51 L. J., P. & M. 19).

"**Or of such wilful neglect or misconduct of or towards the other party as has conduced to the adultery**":

Neglect or misconduct.

The neglect or misconduct here referred to means neglect or misconduct after the marriage (*Allen* v. *Allen and D'Arcy*, 28 L. J., P. & M. 81).

Wilful neglect necessarily includes wilful separation without reasonable excuse when the adultery is the result of such separation.

Mere carelessness does not constitute misconduct within the meaning of this section. Therefore, before a husband can be refused a decree on the ground of such misconduct, it must be found as a fact that there was an intimacy between the respondent and co-respondent of such a character as to be distinctly

§ 14.

dangerous, that he actually knew of so much of this intimacy as to perceive the danger, and that he either purposely or recklessly disregarded it and forbore to interfere (*Dering* v. *Dering and Blakeley*, L. R., 1 P. 531; 37 L. J., P. & M. 52).

Must amount to breach of marital duty.

The misconduct must be such as amounts to a breach of marital duty (*Cunnington* v. *Cunnington and Noble*, 1 S. & T. 475; 28 L. J., P. & M. 101; *Brown* v. *Brown and Robey*, 21 L. T. 181).

And must have conduced to the adultery.

And in order to disentitle the petitioner to relief the misconduct must have directly conduced to the adultery (*St. Paul* v. *St. Paul and Farquhar*, L. R., 1 P. 739). So, where in a suit by the husband for a divorce on the ground of his wife's adultery, which was admitted, the jury found that the petitioner had been guilty of "wilful neglect and misconduct conducing to the adultery," and it appeared that the parties were domestic servants and that the respondent had had an illegitimate child by the petitioner before marriage, and that during the marriage the petitioner was frequently away, for long intervals, from his wife on his duties but regularly made her an adequate allowance, the Court, notwithstanding the verdict of the jury, granted the petitioner a decree of dissolution. In this case, Gorell Barnes, J., said: "It is obvious that, if a husband is guilty of conduct conducing to his wife's adultery, the Court would not be readily disposed to pronounce a decree in his favour. But conduct conducing to adultery may vary greatly in degree. There may be such conduct as would lead necessarily and proximately to adultery; and, on the other hand, there may be conduct which so remotely conduces to adultery that, while it may be said there is some slight evidence that it did conduce to adultery, the conduct may yet be rather a *causa sine quâ non* than a *causa causans*. In cases at the first extreme, the Court could not reasonably be asked to pronounce a decree in the petitioner's favour, unless perhaps there were some very exceptional circumstances; but in cases approaching the other extreme, there may not be sufficient in the petitioner's conduct to cause the Court to refuse to exercise its discretion in his favour" (*Parry* v. *Parry*, (1896) P. 37; 65 L. J., P. & M. 35).

A man married a woman of loose character with whom he had previously cohabited, and shortly after the marriage separated from her against her will and sent her to live by herself in a place where she could be accessible to temptation and where she was as a matter of fact guilty of adultery. No reasonable excuse for the separation having been proved, it was held that the husband had been guilty of conduct conducing to the adultery on the part of the wife (*Baylis* v. *Baylis*, *Treavan and Cooper*, L. R., 1 P. 395; 36 L. J., P. & M. 89; cf. *Hawkins* v. *Hawkins*, 10 P. D. 177; 54 L. J., P. & M. 94). In the latter case Sir James Hannen said: " Every husband is bound to give his wife that protection which the society of a husband affords, and the fact that the respondent had been familiar with the petitioner before marriage made that duty more incumbent upon him, she being a person who might be more likely to yield to temptation."

§ 14.

A husband allowed his wife to live separately from him in lodgings where he occasionally visited her, and made her a small weekly allowance. On calling at her lodgings he frequently found her out so late as eleven and twelve o'clock at night, although she had no occupation which necessitated her absence from the lodgings at such hours. She committed adultery while so living apart, but the Court refused to grant the husband the decree prayed for, on the ground that his conduct had conduced to her adultery (*Groves* v. *Groves and Thompson*, 28 L. J., P. & M. 108).

Where the petitioner had permitted the co-respondent to visit frequently at his house, in his absence, and to make his wife an allowance of 1*l*. a week, and had sent his wife to borrow money from the co-respondent, and had allowed her to be escorted by the latter on a journey to London, the jury acquitted the petitioner of connivance at his wife's adultery with the co-respondent, but found that he had been guilty of wilful neglect and conduct conducing to her adultery (*Brown* v. *Brown and Robey*, 21 L. T. 181).

Where, in answer to a husband's suit for dissolution of marriage on the ground of his wife's adultery, the wife pleaded, as misconduct on the part of the husband conducing to her adultery, if any, a flirtation which he had carried on for some time with an unmarried lady and certain acts of familiarity (*e.g.*, putting his arm round her waist whilst she sat on his knees) with the same lady, despite the remonstrances of the respondent, the Court held that, as it was not impossible, if the facts alleged by the respondent were proved, that the judge might come to the conclusion that the husband's neglect had conduced to the wife's adultery, the facts so alleged ought not to be struck out of the answer (*Cox* v. *Cox*, 70 L. T. 200).

But the wilful neglect or misconduct here spoken of is not that neglect or misconduct which may have led to any particular

§ 14. act of adultery *after* the wife's lapse from virtue, *it must have directly conduced to her fall* (*St. Paul* v. *St. Paul and Farquhar, ubi supra*).

Where a husband, shortly after marriage, was convicted of felony and sentenced to transportation, and during such time as he was undergoing penal servitude his wife committed adultery, it was held, in a suit subsequently instituted by him for dissolution of marriage, that, although from the circumstances of the case there was no reason to doubt that but for the husband's absence caused by his own misconduct the wife would have remained faithful to him, yet the felony committed by him was not a violation of marital duty, and could not, therefore, be regarded as such misconduct as to disentitle him to the relief sought (*Cunnington* v. *Cunnington and Noble*, 1 S. & T. 475; 28 L. J., P. & M. 101). In this case the misconduct of the husband, though apparently a *causa sine quâ non*, was not a *causa causans* such as would necessarily and proximately lead to the adultery (see *Parry* v. *Parry, supra*).

Where, however, a husband went with his wife to dancing places and left his wife and the co-respondent together there, his conduct was held to have conduced to the adultery committed by them (*Barnes* v. *Barnes and Grimwade*, 37 L. J., P. & M. 4).

A husband was advised by his wife's doctor that further cohabitation with his wife, if it resulted in pregnancy, would probably prove dangerous to her, as her mind had become temporarily unhinged on the birth of her first child. He, therefore, refused ever after to resume cohabitation or even to see her, informing her that she was not to inquire into his mode of life and he would not interfere with hers, but he made her a regular allowance. It was held that the husband's conduct had not disentitled him to a decree on the ground of her adultery (*Lander* v. *Lander*, (1891) P. 161; 63 L. T. 237).

Act of adultery brought about by petitioner's agents.

Act of adultery brought about by petitioner's agent.—If persons, acting on behalf of the petitioner, bring about the adultery committed by the respondent, the Court will refuse to grant the petitioner a decree of dissolution, even though the petitioner had no knowledge of what such persons were doing (*Picken* v. *Picken and Symonds*, 34 L. J., P. & M. 22).

If, therefore, a person who is employed by the petitioner to watch the respondent for the purpose of obtaining evidence of adultery, brings about an act of adultery by the respondent, the petitioner will not be granted a decree of dissolution on the ground of such adultery, although such act on the part of the agent may have been wholly unauthorized by the petitioner (*Gower* v. *Gower and Pearson*, L. R., 2 P. 428; 41 L. J., P. & M. 49; *Bell* v. *Bell*, 58 L. J., P. & M. 54; *Beanlands* v. *Beanlands*, No. 45, *Punjab Record*, 1871).

§ 14.

Where a husband whose wife was leading a life of prostitution paid, or caused to be paid, money to a person to commit an act of adultery with her in order to obtain evidence to enable him to institute a suit for dissolution of marriage, the Court refused to grant him a decree on the ground of such adultery (*Sugg* v. *Sugg and Moore*, 31 L. J., P. & M. 41).

Discretionary bars to grant of relief to petitioner.—As regards the discretionary bars under this section to a petitioner's right to a decree, it must be remembered that, as soon as the petitioner's case is proved, and the Court does not find that the petitioner has been accessory to, or conniving at, the adultery complained of, or that there has been any condonation or collusion, the Court is *bound*, if the petitioner so wishes, to pronounce a decree of dissolution of marriage unless it is established *affirmatively* that the petitioner has been guilty of such conduct as, by virtue of the proviso in sect. 14, gives the Court a discretionary power to refuse to dissolve the marriage (*Haswell* v. *Haswell and Sanderson*, 1 S. & T. 502; 29 L. J., P. & M. 21).

Discretionary bars to relief.

" **No adultery shall be deemed to have been condoned** ":

As to what constitutes "condonation," see note to sect. 12, *ante*, p. 78.

15. In any suit instituted for dissolution of marriage, if the respondent opposes the relief sought on the ground, in case of such a suit instituted by a husband, of his adultery, cruelty, or desertion without reasonable excuse, or, in case of such a suit instituted by a wife, on the ground of her adultery and cruelty, the Court may in such suit give to the respondent, on his or her application, the same relief to which he or she would have been entitled in case he or she had presented a petition seeking such relief, and the respondent shall be

Relief in case of opposition on certain grounds.

§ 15.   competent to give evidence of or relating to such cruelty or desertion.

The Matrimonial Causes Act, 1866 (29 & 30 Vict. c. 32), sect. 2, provides that—

"In any suit instituted for dissolution of marriage, if the respondent shall oppose the relief sought on the ground in case of such a suit instituted by a husband of his adultery, cruelty, or desertion, or in case of such a suit instituted by a wife on the ground of her adultery or cruelty, the Court may in such suit give to the respondent, on his or her application, the same relief to which he or she would have been entitled in case he or she had filed a petition seeking such relief."

"Relief in case of opposition on certain grounds":

The object of this section is to do away with the necessity of cross-suits, and to enable the Court to deal fully and finally with the matters in issue between the parties. The practice in England, previously to the enactment of the Matrimonial Causes Act, 1866, was to stay one suit until the determination of the other. The present practice is, in the case of cross-petitions, to save a double hearing by consolidating the two suits, the conduct of the case being generally given to the first petitioner (see Browne and Powles' Divorce, 5th ed., p. 322).

Right of alleged adulterer to intervene.

Where the respondent in a suit for dissolution opposes the relief sought and applies for relief on the ground of the petitioner's misconduct, the petitioner will not be allowed to terminate the suit by having the petition dismissed, if the respondent opposes such proceedings (*Schira* v. *Schira*, L. R., 1 P. 466). In such cases the Court will allow the person charged by the respondent with having committed adultery with the petitioner, to intervene, and this whether or not the respondent claims dissolution (*Curling* v. *Curling*, 14 P. D. 13; 58 L. J., P. & M. 20; *Wheeler* v. *Wheeler*, 14 P. D. 154; 58 L. J., P. & M. 65).

Discretionary bars to relief.—The discretionary bars to relief under sect. 14 apply equally to the case of a respondent praying for relief under this section. Therefore, where the respondent was at the time of suit living in adultery with the co-respondent, and in opposition to her husband's suit for a divorce proved that he had been guilty of various acts of cruelty towards her, and prayed for a judicial separation on that ground, the Court held that her adultery disentitled her to relief (*Gordon* v. *Gordon and Saran*, 3 B. L. R., O. C. 136).

§ 15.

"In case of a suit instituted by the wife, on the ground of her adultery and cruelty":

"Adultery and cruelty."

* Despite the use of the word "*and*," it cannot be intended that the husband-respondent should have to prove both adultery *and* cruelty on the part of the wife. The corresponding section of the English Act reads "adultery *or* cruelty," and, no doubt, the word "*and*" in sect. 15 of the Indian Act must be construed disjunctively as meaning "*or*." If the intention was that the wife's cruelty alone was to be no bar to her suit, the words "and cruelty" might have been omitted altogether.

Inasmuch as under sect. 22 a husband is entitled to a judicial separation on the ground of his wife's "desertion without reasonable excuse," it is at least strange that no provision is made in this section enabling the husband, in a suit for dissolution instituted by the wife, to plead her desertion by way of answer, and to apply for a judicial separation on that ground. In such a case the husband must apparently bring a separate suit. From the omission of "desertion" in this part of the section, it would appear that desertion on the part of the wife is no positive bar to her suit for dissolution of marriage, as it has been held not to be to her suit for judicial separation (*Duplany* v. *Duplany*, (1892) P. 53; 66 L. T. 267). It is, however, a ground upon which the Court may refuse to grant her a decree under sect. 14 of the Act.

"The same relief to which he or she would have been entitled":

A decree for restitution of conjugal rights is not the relief in respect of desertion contemplated by this section. Therefore, a wife who filed an answer to a petition for dissolution of marriage wherein she denied the adultery charged, and alleged desertion and wilful separation on the part of the husband, was not allowed to add a prayer for restitution of conjugal rights to

---

* The husband can oppose his wife's suit for dissolution on the ground of her adultery alone, for such adultery, if proved, would certainly disentitle her to a decree, except under very exceptional circumstances.

§ 15.

her answer (*Drysdale* v. *Drysdale*, L. R., 1 P. 365; 36 L. J., P. & M. 39).

It is to be noticed that sect. 15 only applies to suits for dissolution of marriage. It is not permissible, therefore, to a respondent in a suit for nullity of marriage to plead the adultery, cruelty, or desertion on the part of the petitioner and to pray for relief in respect thereof (*Williams* v. *Williams*, 6 Jur. N. S. 151; *S. C.*, 29 L. J., P. & M. 62; *Taverner f. c. Ditchford* v. *Ditchford*, 33 L. J., P. & M. 105). But in a suit for nullity of marriage, the respondent can, in the answer to such suit, pray for restitution of conjugal rights (*Lopez* v. *Lopez*, I. L. R., xii Calc. 706).

Decrees for dissolution to be *nisi*.

16. Every decree for a dissolution of marriage made by a High Court not being a confirmation of a decree of a District Court, shall, in the first instance, be a decree *nisi*, not to be made absolute till after the expiration of such time, not less than six months from the pronouncing thereof, as the High Court, by general or special order from time to time, directs.

Collusion.

During that period any person shall be at liberty, in such manner as the High Court by general or special order from time to time directs, to show cause why the said decree should not be made absolute by reason of the same having been obtained by collusion or by reason of material facts not being brought before the Court.

On cause being so shown, the Court shall deal with the case by making the decree absolute, or by reversing the decree *nisi*, or by requiring further inquiry, or otherwise as justice may demand.

The High Court may order the costs of counsel and witnesses and otherwise arising from such cause being shown to be paid by the parties or such one or more of them as it thinks fit, including a wife if she have separate property.

DISSOLUTION OF MARRIAGE.

Whenever a decree *nisi* has been made, and the petitioner fails, within a reasonable time, to move to have such decree made absolute, the High Court may dismiss the suit.

§ 16.

The Matrimonial Causes Act, 1860 (23 & 24 Vict. c. 144), sect. 7, provides that :—

"Every decree for a divorce shall in the first instance be a decree *nisi*, not to be made absolute till after the expiration of such time, not less than three months* from the pronouncing thereof, as the Court shall by general or special order from time to time direct; and during that period any person shall be at liberty, in such manner as the Court shall by general or special order in that behalf from time to time direct, to show cause why the said decree should not be made absolute by reason of the same having been obtained by collusion or by reason of material facts not brought before the Court; and, on cause being so shown, the Court shall deal with the case by making the decree absolute, or by reversing the decree *nisi*, or by requiring further inquiry, or otherwise as justice may require; and at any time during the progress of the cause or before the decree is made absolute any person may give information to her Majesty's proctor of any matter material to the due decision of the case, who may thereupon take such steps as the Attorney-General may deem necessary or expedient; and if from any such information or otherwise the said proctor shall suspect that any parties to the suit are or have been acting in collusion for the purpose of obtaining a divorce contrary to the justice of the case, he may, under the direction of the Attorney-General, and by leave of the Court, intervene in the suit, alleging such case of collusion, and retain counsel and subpœna witnesses to prove it; and it shall be lawful for the Court to order the costs of such counsel and witnesses, and otherwise, arising from such intervention, to be paid by the parties or such of them as it shall see fit, including a wife if she have separate property; and in case the said proctor shall not thereby be fully satisfied his reasonable costs, he shall be entitled to charge and be reimbursed the difference as part of the expense of his office."

---

* Subsequently extended to six months, unless the Court fixes a shorter period (see sect. 3 of the Matrimonial Causes Act, 1866 (29 & 30 Vict. c. 32)). Sect. 7 of the Matrimonial Causes Act, 1860, and sect. 3 of the Matrimonial Causes Act, 1866, have been extended to decrees and suits for nullity of marriage (Matrimonial Causes Act, 1873 (36 Vict. c. 31), sect. 1).

§ 16.

By sect. 2 of the Matrimonial Causes Act, 1878 (41 Vict. c. 19), it is further provided that :—

> "Where the Queen's Proctor or any other person shall intervene or show cause against a decree *nisi* in any suit or proceeding for nullity of marriage, the Court may make such order as to the costs of the Queen's Proctor, or of any other person who shall intervene or show cause as aforesaid, or of all and every party or parties thereto occasioned by such intervention or showing cause as aforesaid as may seem just; and the Queen's Proctor, any other person as aforesaid, and such party or parties shall be entitled to recover such costs in like manner as in other cases: Provided that the Treasury may if it shall think fit order any costs which the Queen's Proctor shall, by any order of the Court made under this section, pay to the said party or parties to be deemed to be part of the expenses of his office."

Decree nisi does not terminate lis.

"**Shall be a decree nisi**":

After a decree *nisi* for dissolution of the marriage, the suit between the parties is not at an end, and the *lis* remains pending (*Ellis* v. *Ellis*, 8 P. D. 188; 52 L. J., P. & M. 99, overruling *Lathom* v. *Lathom*, 2 S. & T. 299; 30 L. J., P. & M. 103).

Consequently the *status* of a married woman is not affected by the pronouncing of a decree *nisi* for dissolution of her marriage. She continues to be subject to all the disabilities of coverture until the decree is made absolute (*Norman* v. *Villars*, 2 Ex. D. 359; 46 L. J., Ex. 579).

"The decree *nisi* does not dissolve the marriage. Sir W. Phillimore and Mr. Deane . . . endeavoured to show that after the decree *nisi* the *status* of the parties was a peculiar one—that they were in a sort of suspended condition, neither husband and wife nor divorced, and it is said there was authority for saying that if under such circumstances the man cohabited with the woman he would be committing adultery. But the authority has not been produced, and the idea appears to me full of absurdities" (Bowen, L.J., *Stanhope* v. *Stanhope*, 11 P. D. 103; 55 L. J., P. & M. 36).

Nor is it a decree within meaning of C. P. C. s. 1.

Inasmuch, therefore, as a decree *nisi* does not "decide" the suit, it is not, apparently, a "decree" within the meaning of sect. 1 of the Civil Procedure Code (*King* v. *King*, I. L. R., vi Bomb. 416).

Once a decree *nisi* has been pronounced neither the husband nor the wife can take any active step in the suit except to get the decree made absolute, but they may so act as to prevent the

DISSOLUTION OF MARRIAGE.

decree being made absolute (*Stanhope* v. *Stanhope, ubi supra*). A decree *nisi* is, however, appealable under sect. 55 of the Indian Divorce Act.

§ 16.

But is appealable.

If either the petitioner or the respondent dies at any time after the decree *nisi* has been pronounced, but before it has been made absolute, the suit abates *ipso facto* (*Grant* v. *Grant and Bowles*, 2 S. & T. 522; 31 L. J., P. & M. 174; *Brocas* v. *Brocas*, 2 S. & T. 383; 30 L. J., P. & M. 172).

Death of petitioner or respondent before decree is made absolute.

Nor can the legal representative of the petitioner apply to have the decree made absolute. "A man can no more be divorced after his death than he can be married or condemned to death. Marriage is a union for two lives; it can be dissolved either by death or by process of law. After it has been dissolved in one of those ways it cannot be dissolved again—a knot which has already been untied cannot be untied again" (Bowen, L.J., *Stanhope* v. *Stanhope, ubi supra*).

The Matrimonial Causes Act, 1873, provides that a decree for nullity of marriage shall also, in the first instance, be a decree *nisi*, and that any person may in the case of such a decree intervene in the same manner as in the case of a decree *nisi* for dissolution of marriage. This, however, is not the case in India: under the Indian Divorce Act, a decree of nullity when made by a High Court is a decree absolute; a decree of nullity when made by a District Court is, however, subject to the confirmation of the High Court (see sects. 19 and 20). But in neither case is there any provision made for intervention.

"Not to be made absolute":

A decree *nisi* will not be made absolute at the instance of the husband, when there are arrears of alimony *pendente lite*, until such arrears have been paid (*Lathom* v. *Lathom*, 2 S. & T. 299; 30 L. J., P. & M. 233; *De Bretton* v. *De Bretton*, I. L. R., iv All. 295).

Will not be made absolute if arrears of alimony *pendente lite*.

The Court cannot, however, after the time limited by statute, suspend a decree absolute on the ground that the petitioner has not paid his proctor's taxed costs (*Patterson* v. *Patterson and Graham*, L. R., 2 P. 192; 40 L. J., P. & M. 4).

"Not less than six months":

This means calendar months.

The petitioner has no absolute right to have the decree made absolute immediately on the expiration of the six months, for the

Right of petitioner to have decree made absolute.

§ 16.

High Court has power to fix such time, not *less* than six months, as it considers fit (*Watton* v. *Watton*, L. R., 1 P. 227; 35 L. J., P. & M. 95; *Palmer* v. *Palmer*, 4 S. & T. 143; 34 L. J., P. & M. 110).

The English Divorce Court may, if it thinks fit, make a decree absolute within a less period than six months, but this power is exercised only under very special circumstances (*Rogers* v. *Rogers*, 6 R. 589; *Fitzgerald* v. *Fitzgerald*, L. R., 3 P. 136; 43 L. J., P. & M. 13).

Application to make Decree absolute.

<small>Who may apply to make decree absolute.</small>

(a) It is *only the innocent party* who can apply to the Court to make the decree *nisi* absolute. Where, therefore, in a suit by the husband for dissolution of marriage on the ground of his wife's adultery, a decree *nisi* had been pronounced, but the husband failed within a reasonable time to apply to the Court to have such decree made absolute, the Court refused to entertain an application to that effect presented by the wife (*Ousey* v. *Ousey and Atkinson*, 1 P. D. 56; 45 L. J., P. & M. 56; cf. *Lewis* v. *Lewis*, 2 S. & T. 394; 30 L. J., P. & M. 199). If, however, the petitioner fails to make such application within a reasonable time, the respondent may call upon him or her to do so or show cause why the decree *nisi* should not be revoked and the petition be dismissed for want of prosecution; in such a case the respondent is entitled to have the petition dismissed for want of prosecution, and is also entitled to put an end to any obligation imposed upon him in the course of the suit, *e.g.*, an order for alimony (*Ousey* v. *Ousey and Atkinson, supra; Halfen* v. *Boddington*, 6 P. D. 13; and *Lewis* v. *Lewis*, (1892) P. 212). In England, where a decree of nullity is in the first instance a decree *nisi*, a decree *nisi* of nullity by reason of the respondent's impotence will not be made absolute upon the application of such respondent (*Halfen* v. *Boddington*, 6 P. D. 13).

<small>Application to be supported by affidavits.</small>

(b) The application by the petitioner to make absolute a decree *nisi* must be supported by affidavits of search for appearance by any person, and of non-appearance; and if an appearance has been entered, that no affidavits in opposition to the decree have been filed (*Boddy* v. *Boddy and Grover*, 30 L. J., P. & M. 95). See also Nos. 80, 194, and 207 of the Rules and Regulations of the English Divorce Court.

The affidavits must further show that the search was recent

(*Stone* v. *Stone and Brownrigg*, 2 S. & T. 113; 32 L. J., P. & M. 7).

A copy of the decree *nisi* must also be filed with the application (*Fowler* v. *Fowler*, 31 L. J., P. & M. 31).

§ 16.

Copy of decree *nisi* to be filed.

(c) As a rule notice of the motion should be served on the respondent and co-respondent (*Boddy* v. *Boddy and Grover*, 30 L. J., P. & M. 95).

Notice to respondent and co-respondent.

It has, however, been held that inasmuch as a respondent or co-respondent cannot come in to show cause why a decree *nisi* should not be made absolute, it is immaterial, in an application to make the decree absolute, that the respondent has had no notice of the application (*Willis* v. *Willis*, 4 B. L. R., O. C. 52; *Hicks* v. *Hicks*, I. L. R., viii Calc. 756).

And where a copy of the decree *nisi* has been served upon the respondent, it is not necessary to give him notice of the application to make it absolute (*Gomez* v. *Gomez*, I. L. R., xviii Calc. 443).

And even where the copy of the decree *nisi* has not been served upon the respondent or co-respondent owing to the fact that they have been keeping out of the way in order to elude service, the Court will make the decree absolute although neither the respondent nor the co-respondent has been served with notice of the application (*Warden* v. *Warden*, 9 B. L. R., Ap. 39). So, where, on an application to make a decree *nisi* absolute, it appeared that the decree had been passed *ex parte*, after the original summons had been personally served upon the respondent, and that the petitioner had been unable to serve the respondent with a copy of the decree owing to the latter having left Calcutta immediately after the decree was passed and having left no trace of his whereabouts, the Court made the decree absolute, although no notice of the application or copy of the decree *nisi* had been served on the respondent (*Hunter* v. *Hunter*, I. L. R., xviii Calc. 539).

(d) *Reasonable time for application.*—As to what is a reasonable time within which a petitioner should apply to make a decree absolute must depend upon the circumstances of each particular case.

When application should be made.

Where a wife, who had obtained a decree *nisi*, afterwards petitioned for permanent maintenance, and that petition was still pending, the Court held that the pendency of the proceedings for maintenance was a sufficient excuse for the delay on her part in applying to have the decree made absolute (*Southern* v. *Southern*, 62 L. T. 688).

§ 16.

Right of intervention.

"During that period any person shall be at liberty to show cause":

As regards intervention, there is a noticeable difference between suits for dissolution of marriage instituted in a High Court and those instituted in a District Court. In the former, a person can intervene only *after* a decree *nisi* has been made; in the latter, a person may intervene at any time *during the progress of the suit* in the District Court (sect. 17), but once the District Court has made its decree, no further intervention is allowed even for the purpose of showing cause against such decree being confirmed by the High Court.

Duty of judge.

"In India, where there is no public officer corresponding to the Queen's Proctor, a judge exercising jurisdiction under Act IV of 1869 ought to make a large use of his power to look into any matters which may come under his notice, affecting the proper exercise of the discretionary power of the Court to grant, or withhold a divorce under specified circumstances, even though such matters are not brought to his notice by a party to the proceedings or an intervenor" (*Lisbey* v. *Lisbey*, No. 6, *Punjab Record*, 1888).

The Courts in India will, therefore, take notice of any matters affecting the proper exercise of their discretionary power under this section, even though such matters have come to the knowledge of the Court in an informal and indirect manner (*King* v. *King*, I. L. R., vi Bomb. 416; *Stephen* v. *Stephen*, I. L. R., xvii Calc. 570).

In order to satisfy itself on this point, the Court will not hesitate to avail itself of the powers given to it by sect. 165 of the Indian Evidence Act, and sect. 171 of the Code of Civil Procedure, 1882.

During such period.

"*During such period.*"

At any time before a decree *nisi* is made absolute it is competent for any person to intervene, whether the minimum time required to elapse before a decree *nisi* can be made absolute has or has not elapsed (*Bowen* v. *Bowen*, 3 S. & T. 530; *Palmer* v. *Palmer*, 34 L. J., P. & M. 110; *Clements* v. *Clements*, 3 S. & T. 394; 33 L. J., P. & M. 74; *Poole* v. *Poole*, Times Law Reps., vol. xii. p. 509).

Who can intervene.

Who may intervene.

Any person may intervene for the purpose of showing cause

DISSOLUTION OF MARRIAGE.

why a decree *nisi* should not be made absolute, *except* the following persons:— §16.

(i) the respondent (*Stoate* v. *Stoate*, 30 L. J., P. & M. 173; 2 S. & T. 384; *Willis* v. *Willis*, 4 B. L. R., O. C. 52; *King* v. *King*, I. L. R., vi Bomb. 416; *Stephen* v. *Stephen*, I. L. R., xvii Calc. 570):

(ii) the co-respondent (*Clements* v. *Clements, ubi supra; Stoate* v. *Stoate, ubi supra*):

(iii) any third person acting at the instance, or on behalf, of the respondent or the co-respondent (*Clements* v. *Clements; King* v. *King, ubi supra*). But the mere fact that the intervenor happens to be a near relative of the respondent or co-respondent is not *per se* a ground for refusing to allow him to intervene (*Howarth* v. *Howarth*, 9 P. D. 218).

A third person, charged by an intervenor with having committed adultery with the petitioner will not be allowed to appear on such intervention (*Grieve* v. *Grieve*, (1893) P. 288; 63 L. J., P. & M. 29; *Carew* v. *Carew*, (1894) P. 31; 63 L. J., P. & M. 74). {Person charged by intervenor with adultery with petitioner.}

But though it is not open to the respondent or co-respondent to intervene for the purpose of showing cause against the decree *nisi* being made absolute, either of them is at liberty to apply for a *review* of the decree *nisi*, on the grounds specified in sect. 623 of the Civil Procedure Code. And in any case, if any person who is not entitled to intervene has come forward for that purpose and filed affidavits in support of his intervention, the Court will give notice to the petitioner that the decree *nisi* will not be made absolute until the matters set out in the affidavits, as regards collusion, &c., have been satisfactorily cleared up (*King* v. *King; Stephen* v. *Stephen, ubi supra*). Nor will the Court order such affidavits to be taken off the file. {But respondent or co-respondent can apply for review of judgment.}

Grounds of Intervention.

{Grounds of intervention.}

It is sufficient for an intervenor to allege in his plea that the decree was pronounced contrary to the justice of the case by reason of material facts not being brought to the knowledge of the Court (*Crawford* v. *Crawford*, 11 P. D. 150).

The petitioner is, however, entitled to particulars of such facts, and the intervenor will be ordered to furnish them (*Gladstone* v. *Gladstone*, L. R., 3 P. 260; 44 L. J., P. & M. 46; *Barnes* v. *Barnes and Grimwade*, 37 L. J., P. & M. 4).

And if the intervenor pleads that the decree was obtained by

§ 16.

collusion between the parties, he will be ordered to specify the nature of the collusion charged, but not to state the facts which he intends to prove (*Jessop* v. *Jessop*, 2 S. & T. 301; 30 L. J., P. & M. 193).

An intervenor is not barred from setting up an issue of fact which has already been pleaded by, but found against, the respondent (*Harding* v. *Harding and Lance*, 34 L. J., P. & M. 9).

It has, however, been held that an intervenor cannot rely on, as material facts, charges which had been pleaded in answer to the petition, but abandoned at the hearing (*Forster* v. *Forster and Berridge*, 32 L. J., P. & M. 206).

And where specific charges have been investigated and decided in favour of the petitioner, an intervenor is entitled to show that the finding ought to have been the other way in consequence of material facts not having been brought to the knowledge of the Court (*Crawford* v. *Crawford*, 55 L. J., P. & M. 42; 55 L. T. 304).

But unless the intervenor can show that the issue, which was previously decided in favour of the petitioner, was improperly decided in consequence of the suppression of material facts or by reason of collusion between the parties, he cannot set up such issue again, for " he has no right to obtain in an indirect manner a new trial of an issue which has already been tried and determined" (*Gladstone* v. *Gladstone*, L. R., 3 P. 260).

An intervenor is not, therefore, entitled to show cause against the decree being made absolute simply on the ground that he *suspects* that the verdict on the issues previously tried was an improper one, or was contrary to the weight of evidence.

It is not competent to a person who has intervened for the purpose of showing cause against the decree *nisi* being made absolute, to object that the Court had no jurisdiction over the parties to the suit, nor to support his opposition by matters which would only be ground for a motion by the parties for a new trial (*Forster* v. *Forster and Berridge*, 3 S. & T. 151; 32 L. J., P. & M. 206).

"Material facts not brought before the Court."

" **Material facts not being brought before the Court** " :

A respondent, by pleading, in answer to a petition for dissolution of marriage, material facts, of which no evidence is given at the hearing, does not bring them before the Court within the meaning of this section (*Masters* v. *Masters*, 34 L. J.,

P. & M. 7). And such facts may, after a decree *nisi* has been pronounced, be set up by an intervenor as a ground for not making the decree absolute.

§ 16.

The words "*not being brought before the Court*" mean "not brought before the Court at any time up to the date of intervention." It was, indeed, held in an early case that condonation subsequent to the decree *nisi* was not a ground upon which the Court could reverse such decree if properly obtained, the reason given being that the words "not brought before the Court" related to the period before the decree *nisi* was pronounced (*Lewis* v. *Lewis*, 30 L. J., P. & M. 199). This decision, however, has not been followed, and in a more recent case Lord Penzance held that the adultery of the petitioner subsequent to the decree *nisi* was a ground for reversing such decree. "When the Act empowers cause to be shown why the decree should not be made absolute by reason of material facts not being brought before the Court, I consider that the Court is bound to take notice of any material facts not previously brought before the Court, and it is not confined to the reception of facts occurring before the decree *nisi*. . . . I see no reason so to narrow the meaning of the words '*not brought before the Court.*' Adultery since the decree *nisi* is not the less a fact not brought before the Court because from the date of its occurrence it was impossible that it should have been so brought before the Court. If, indeed, the words necessarily implied any shortcoming or default on the part of the petitioner, they would be confined in their application as contended. But there are no expressions in the statute from which such an implication can properly be drawn, and the Court is therefore bound to give them their natural and full interpretation" (*Hulse* v. *Hulse and Tavernor*, L. R., 2 P. 357; 41 L. J., P. & M. 19; cf. *Rogers* v. *Rogers*, (1894) P. 161; 63 L. J., P. & M. 97).

Adultery, &c. subsequent to decree *nisi*.

This was also the conclusion arrived at by the Court of Appeal in *Howarth* v. *Howarth* (9 P. D. 218), in which case Lord Justice Cotton remarked: "I am not satisfied that subsequent adultery does not come within the words 'facts not brought before the Court.' Though it was a fact that could not be brought before the Court at the trial, it comes within the description of 'facts not brought before the Court.' I see no reason why it may not be held that power is given to anyone to intervene when, although there is no ground for saying that the decree *nisi* was wrong, it can be shown that the party applying for the divorce has so misconducted himself or herself before the decree was

§ 16.

Material facts suppressed, but petitioner otherwise entitled to decree.

made absolute as, on the ground of public policy, not to be entitled to have it made absolute."

The words "not brought before the fact" mean, therefore, not brought before the Court by accident or force of circumstances, as well as by intention.

It is doubtful whether the suppression of material facts will disentitle the petitioner to relief if, upon the whole case, he is otherwise entitled to a decree. On the one hand, the Court granted a decree to a petitioner who charged his wife with having committed adultery with two persons but suppressed the fact that he had condoned one of the said acts of adultery (*Alexandre* v. *Alexandre*, L. R., 2 P. 164; 39 L. J., P. & M. 84; see, too, *Rogers* v. *Rogers*, (1894) P. 161; 63 L. J., P. & M. 97). On the other hand, the Court of Appeal, while not expressly deciding the point, has expressed the opinion that in such a case the Court should refuse to grant relief to the petitioner (*Butler* v. *Butler*, 15 P. D. 66; 59 L. J., P. & M. 25). In this case Lord Justice Lopes said: "In my opinion an agreement between the parties to a divorce suit to withhold from the Court pertinent and material facts which might have been adduced on the trial in evidence in support of a counter-charge against the respondent and co-respondent amounts to collusion, even though the suppressed fact might not have been sufficient to have established the counter-charge."

As has been already stated, adultery committed by the petitioner subsequently to the decree *nisi* is a fact which may be set up by an intervenor as a ground for not making the decree absolute, and, if such adultery be proved, the Court will rescind the decree *nisi* and dismiss the petition. If, however, the petitioner has acted in ignorance of law, and has gone through a form of marriage after the decree *nisi* but before it has been made absolute, in the belief that he or she was legally entitled to do so, the Court will not, merely on the ground of such adultery, refuse to make the decree absolute (*Noble* v. *Noble and Goodman*, L. R., 1 P. 691; 38 L. J., P. & M. 52; *Wickham* v. *Wickham*, 6 P. D. 11; 49 L. J., P. & M. 70; *Moore* v. *Moore*, (1892) P. 382; 62 L. J., P. & M. 10; *Kyte* v. *Kyte and Cooke*, I. L. R., xx Bomb. 362).

Reconciliation of parties after decree nisi.

If, after a decree *nisi*, the parties become reconciled and resume cohabitation, the Court, on the motion of an intervenor, and upon being satisfied of the facts, will rescind the decree *nisi* and dismiss the petition (*Flower* v. *Flower*, (1893) P. 290; 63 L. J., P. & M. 28). So, too, if in such a case the petitioner applies to the Court to rescind the decree *nisi*, the Court will accede to the application, provided due notice thereof has been given to the respondent (*Troward* v. *Troward*, 32 W. R. (Eng.) 864).

§ 16.

But where, after a decree *nisi* had been pronounced at the suit of the wife, the parties resumed cohabitation, and the wife informed her attorney that she did not wish any further steps to be taken in the suit, the Court refused to grant an application by the husband to dismiss the petition, but stated that, if both parties consented, it would order all further proceedings in the suit to be stayed (*Lewis* v. *Lewis*, 2 S. & T. 394; 30 L. J., P. & M. 199).

In India the parties cannot prevent a decree *nisi passed by a District Court* from being made absolute, nor can the High Court set aside such a decree solely on the ground that the parties wish that it should be rescinded. But the High Court will, if both parties consent, stay all further proceedings in the suit (*Culley* v. *Culley*, I. L. R., x All. 559).

Decree *nisi* passed by District Court.

Evidence of Adultery pleaded by Intervenor.

Evidence of identity.

Upon the trial of an issue of adultery raised by an intervenor who shows cause against a decree being made absolute, the Court does not require such strict proof of the identity of the person charged with adultery as upon the trial of such an issue in a suit between husband and wife (*Hulse* v. *Hulse and Tavernor*, L. R., 2 P. 357; 41 L. J., P. & M, 19). The reason for this is, that in such cases collusion between the parties cannot be suspected, nor can it be doubted that the petitioner will do all he can to contest the intervenor's allegations and refute them if possible.

Withdrawal of Petition after Intervention.

Withdrawal of petition after intervention;

Once a person has duly intervened to show cause why a decree should not be made absolute, the petitioner will not be allowed to withdraw the petition (*Gray* v. *Gray*, 2 S. & T. 266; 4 L. T. 478). Nor can an intervenor be stopped from proving his case by the substitution (after the intervenor has come forward) of a prayer for judicial separation in place of that for dissolution of marriage (*Drummond* v. *Drummond*, 2 S. & T. 269; 30 L. J., P. & M. 177).

or substitution of prayer for judicial separation.

§ 16.

Admissions by, and non-appearance of, petitioner.

Intervention: Admissions by, or Non-appearance of, Petitioner.

If the intervenor alleges matters which would be ground for reversing the decree *nisi*, and the petitioner in his replication admits the truth of the allegations, the Court will rescind the decree without further proof of the facts admitted (*Boulton* v. *Boulton*, 31 L. J., P. & M. 115).

And the Court will reverse the decree *nisi*, without further proof of the intervenor's allegations, if upon the day fixed for the hearing of the issue the petitioner fails to appear, although ordered to do so (*Pollack* v. *Pollack and Deane*, 34 L. J., P. & M. 49).

Intervention: Costs.—See Appendix (F.), "Costs."

Effect of decree absolute.

Decree absolute for Dissolution of Marriage, effect of.

"A woman divorced is no longer a wife; she has not the rights, nor has she the duties, of a married woman. She is at liberty to marry again. The equitable doctrines of separate use and restraint against anticipation have no application to her until she does marry again. Whatever property she may have or acquire is her own; her former husband has no interest in it. He, on the other hand, is not bound to support her; she has no implied authority to pledge his credit, even for necessaries. She is free from him and he from her" (*per* Lindley, L. J., *Watkins* v. *Watkins*, (1896) P. 222).

It follows, therefore, that, after a decree of divorce has been made absolute, the whole of the wife's property, including such *choses in action* as have not been previously reduced into possession, belongs to her absolutely (*Wells* v. *Malban*, 31 L. J., Ch. 344; 31 Beav. 48; *Wilkinson* v. *Gibson*, L. R., 4 Eq. 162; 36 L. J., Ch. 646).

And when the decree *nisi* is made absolute, it takes effect for the above purpose from the date of the decree *nisi* (*Prole* v. *Soady*, L. R., 3 Ch. 220; 37 L. J., Ch. 246).

Right of woman to retain former name.

Right of divorced Wife to retain her former Husband's Name.

Marriage confers a name upon a woman. The name so conferred becomes an actual name and continues to be so even after a decree of divorce until she has acquired by repute some other name, which, so to speak, obliterates it (*Fendall, otherwise Goldsmid* v. *Goldsmid*, 2 P. D. 263; 46 L. J., P. & M. 70).

§ 16.

Decree absolute is a Decree in rem.

Decree absolute is decree *in rem*.

"A final judgment, order, or decree of a competent Court, in the exercise of probate, matrimonial . . . . jurisdiction which confers upon or takes away from any person any legal character, or which declares any person to be entitled to any such character, or to be entitled to any specific thing, not as against any specified person, but absolutely, is relevant when the existence of any such legal character or the title of any such person to any such thing is relevant.

"Such judgment, order, or decree is conclusive proof—

"that any legal character which it confers accrued at the time when such judgment, order, or decree came into operation;

"that any legal character, to which it declares any such person to be entitled, accrued to that person at the time when such judgment, order, or decree declares it to have accrued to that person;

"that any legal character which it takes away from any such person ceased at the time when such judgment, order, or decree declared that it had ceased or should cease;

"and that anything to which it declares any person to be so entitled was the property of that person at the time from which such judgment, order, or decree declares that it had been or should be his property" (sect. 41, Indian Evidence Act, 1872).

"The record of a decree in a suit for divorce, or of any other decree, is evidence that such a decree was pronounced, and the effect of a decree in a suit for a divorce *à vinculo matrimonii* is to cause the relationship of husband and wife to cease. It is conclusive upon all persons that the parties have been divorced, and that the parties are no longer husband and wife; *but it is not conclusive, nor even* primâ facie, *evidence against strangers that the cause for which the decree was pronounced existed.* For instance, if a divorce between A. and B. were granted, upon the ground of the adultery of B. with C., it would be conclusive as to the divorce, but it would not be even *primâ facie* evidence against C. that he was guilty of adultery with B., unless he

As regards strangers decree only conclusive that marriage is dissolved.

§ 16. were a party to the suit" (*per* Sir Barnes Peacock, *Kanhya Lal* v. *Radha Charan*, 7 W. R. (Ind.) 339).

So where in a suit by a husband for divorce on the ground of his wife's adultery with R., R. did not appear, but the decree stated that the wife had been guilty of adultery with R., and that R. had been condemned in costs, but did not contain a finding that R. had been guilty of adultery with the respondent, it was held, in a subsequent suit by R.'s wife for divorce, that the decree in the former suit was not *per se* sufficient evidence that R. had committed adultery (*Ruck* v. *Ruck*, (1896) P. 152; 65 L. J., P. & M. 87).

Confirmation of decree for dissolution by district judge.

17. Every decree for a dissolution of marriage made by a district judge shall be subject to confirmation by the High Court.

Cases for confirmation of a decree for dissolution of marriage shall be heard (where the number of the judges of the High Court is three or upwards) by a Court composed of three such judges, and in case of difference the opinion of the majority shall prevail, or (where the number of the judges of the High Court is two) by a Court composed of such two judges, and in case of difference the opinion of the senior judge shall prevail.

The High Court, if it think further enquiry or additional evidence to be necessary, may direct such enquiry to be made, or such evidence to be taken.

The result of such enquiry and the additional evidence shall be certified to the High Court by the district judge, and the High Court shall thereupon make an order confirming the decree for dissolution of marriage, or such other order as to the Court seems fit.

Provided that no decree shall be confirmed under this section till after the expiration of such time, not less than six months from the pronouncing thereof, as the High Court by general or special order from time to time directs.

During the progress of the suit in the Court of the district judge, any person suspecting that any parties to the suit are or have been acting in collusion for the purpose of obtaining a divorce, shall be at liberty, in such manner as the High Court by general or special order from time to time directs, to apply to the High Court to remove the suit under section eight, and the High Court shall thereupon, if it think fit, remove such suit and try and determine the same as a Court of original jurisdiction, and the provisions contained in section 16 shall apply to every suit so removed; or it may direct the district judge to take such steps in respect of the alleged collusion as may be necessary to enable him to make a decree in accordance with the justice of the case.

§ 17.

"**Every decree . . . made by a district judge**":

It is further provided by sect. 20 that every decree of nullity of marriage made by a district judge shall be subject to confirmation by the High Court, and that the provisions of sect. 17, clauses (1), (2), (3), and (4), shall *mutatis mutandis* apply to such decrees. It follows, therefore, that (i) a decree of nullity of marriage made by a district judge must be confirmed by the High Court, but may be confirmed at any time after the pronouncing thereof, whereas a decree of dissolution of marriage cannot be confirmed till after the expiration of at least six months; and (ii) that no provision is made for intervention in the case of a suit for nullity of marriage.

Decree of district judge.

There is no appeal from the decree of a district judge for dissolution of marriage or of nullity of marriage; nor from the order of a High Court confirming or refusing to confirm such decree (sect. 55, *post*).

No appeal in certain cases.

But a petitioner whose suit for dissolution or nullity of marriage has been dismissed may appeal to the High Court; or (in the case of a suit for dissolution) may present "a similar petition to the High Court" (sect. 13, *ante*).

"**Confirmation of decree by High Court**":

Inasmuch as a suit for divorce is to be dealt with (so far as is

Confirmation of decree by High Court.

§ 17.

possible) like all other cases between private litigants, the High Court ought not to make a decree *nisi*, passed by a district judge, absolute without a motion being made to it to that effect (*Culley* v. *Culley*, I. L. R., x All. 559).

As to award of damages;

When, however, the Court is moved under this section to confirm the decree *nisi* of a district judge, it has the fullest power to deal with the case as justice may require. And even if, in such a case, the co-respondent has not appealed against the award of damages by the lower Court, the High Court can deal with that part of the decree as well as the part dissolving the marriage (*Kyte* v. *Kyte and Cooke*, I. L. R., xx Bomb. 362).

and as to costs.

The decree of a District Court dissolving a marriage is a final decree as far as that Court is concerned, and, when costs are awarded, the order as to costs is not a separate order and cannot be treated as distinct from the decree for dissolution. The whole decree, including the order as to costs, is subject to confirmation by the High Court, and no portion of it can, until so confirmed, be capable of execution (*Coates* v. *Coates*, No. 35, *Punjab Record*, 1887).

Reconciliation of parties after decree of District Court.

Reconciliation of parties after decree nisi *made by district judge.*
—The Indian Divorce Act gives no express power to the parties to a suit for dissolution of marriage to prevent a decree *nisi* passed in it by the district judge from being made absolute, but the High Court will, in such a case, follow the principles of the practice of the English Divorce Court, and, if both parties so desire, will make an order staying all proceedings in the cause. The High Court cannot, however, set aside the decree *nisi* (*Culley* v. *Culley*, I. L. R., x All. 559).

Intervention: when to be made.

"**During the progress of the suit in the Court of the district judge**":

It is only in suits for dissolution of marriage that a person may apply to the High Court under this section, and it is only during the progress of the suit in the District Court that such application can be made. Apparently, it is not permissible to intervene after the district judge has made his decree; the fact, however, that the decree of a district judge cannot be confirmed till after the expiration of not less than six months from the pronouncing thereof would seem to show that the meaning of the Legislature was not that a person could intervene, by application to the High Court, only "during the progress of the suit" in the District Court.

Apparently, the sole ground upon which a person may apply to the High Court under this section is that the parties are, or have been, acting in *collusion* for the purpose of obtaining a divorce. But it could not have been intended to preclude the intervenor from bringing before the Court matters which would be good grounds for rescinding a decree *nisi* under sect. 16 of the Act.

§ 17. Ground of intervention.

IV.—*Nullity of Marriage.*

18. Any husband or wife may present a petition to the District Court or to the High Court, praying that his or her marriage may be declared null and void.

Petition for decree of nullity.

"**Any husband or wife**":

Under the Indian Divorce Act, apparently, only the husband or the wife (or if the petitioner is a lunatic or idiot, his or her committee or custodian, sect. 48; or if he or she is a minor, his or her next friend, sect. 49) can sue for a decree of nullity of marriage. But in England any person having a sufficient interest in annulling a marriage, or persons interested in property, the succession to which depends upon the validity or invalidity of the marriage, may sue for a declaration of nullity, unless the validity of the marriage be disputed on the ground of impotency, in which case only the person who suffers an injury from it may sue" (Browne and Powles' Divorce, 5th ed., p. 157).

Husband or wife.

Every petition for a declaration of nullity of marriage must state the absence of any collusion or connivance between the petitioner and the respondent (sect. 47). But if the marriage is absolutely void *ab initio*, no amount of collusion or connivance between the parties will disentitle the petitioner to a decree of nullity. Nor can any person intervene for the purpose of showing the existence of collusion between the parties (cf. *D.* v. *M. f. c. D.*, 28 L. T. 73). In England express provision is made by 36 Vict. c. 31 for intervention in such cases.

Absence of collusion or connivance to be stated in petition.

Every petition for nullity of marriage must bear a Court fee stamp of Rs. 20 (Court Fees Act, 1870, 2nd Sched., Art. 20).

Court fee stamp.

"**Marriage may be declared null and void**":

In a suit for nullity of marriage, the only question to be decided is, marriage or no marriage, and it is not open to the respondent in such a suit to counter-charge the petitioner with having been guilty of adultery or of cruelty, and to pray for a

Nullity of marriage.

Counter-charge of adultery against petitioner.

§ 18.

decree of dissolution or of judicial separation on those grounds (*Humphrey* v. *Williams f.c. Humphrey*, 2 S. & T. 30; 29 L. J., P. & M. 62; *Tavernor f.c. Ditchford* v. *Ditchford*, 33 L. J., P. & M. 105).

Jurisdiction of Courts to declare marriage null and void.

It must be remembered that in no case have the Courts in India jurisdiction under this Act to make decrees of nullity of marriage, unless the marriage has been solemnized in India (sect. 2, *ante*).

Ceremony of marriage must be proved.

Before a suit for nullity of marriage can be entertained, it must be proved that a ceremony of marriage was actually performed between the parties by a person competent to perform such ceremony (see Appendix (A.), "Proof of Marriage"). When this fact has been duly proved, the Court will presume that every *formality* has been duly complied with (*Lopez* v. *Lopez*, I. L. R., xii Calc. 706).

Grounds of decree.

19. Such decree may be made on any of the following grounds:—

(1.) That the respondent was impotent at the time of the marriage and at the time of the institution of the suit;

(2.) That the parties are within the prohibited degrees of consanguinity (whether natural or legal) or affinity;

(3.) That either party was a lunatic or idiot at the time of the marriage;

(4.) That the former husband or wife of either party was living at the time of the marriage, and the marriage with such former husband or wife was then in force.

Nothing in this section shall affect the jurisdiction of the High Court to make decrees of nullity of marriage on the ground that the consent of either party was obtained by force or fraud.

Decree of nullity.

"Such decree":

By 36 Vict. c. 31, every decree of nullity of marriage must, in the first instance, be a decree *nisi*, not to be made absolute

NULLITY OF MARRIAGE.

till after the expiration of six calendar months from the pronouncing thereof, unless the Court shall fix a shorter time. Under the Indian Divorce Act, a decree of nullity, when made by a High Court, is a decree absolute, but when made by a District Court must be confirmed by the High Court (sect. 20).

§ 19.

"**Any of the following grounds**":

No Court in India can entertain a suit of a matrimonial nature otherwise than as provided by the Indian Divorce Act, nor has it jurisdiction to make a decree of nullity on the ground that the marriage was invalid for some reason other than one of those specified in this section (*Gasper* v. *Gonsalez*, 13 B. L. R. 109).

Ground for.

(i) "**That the respondent was impotent at the time of the marriage and at the time of the institution of the suit**":

(i) Impotency of respondent.

In a suit for nullity of marriage *causâ impotentiæ*, the petitioner must prove that the *respondent* was impotent at the time of the marriage, as well as at the time of the institution of the suit: an impediment supervening *after* marriage is no ground for a decree of nullity (*Brown* v. *Brown*, 1 Hagg. Cons. 524).

It is not open to a husband or wife to sue for nullity of marriage on the ground of his or her own impotency. It has, however, been held in Ireland that, if the respondent altogether repudiates the marital relation, the impotent petitioner may show that there is no *verum matrimonium*, and maintain a suit for nullity on that ground (*A.* v. *A.*, sued as *B.*, 19 L. R., Ir. 403, Matr.).

Impotency of petitioner.

A marriage is not void, but voidable only, on the ground of impotency (*P.* v. *S.*, 37 L. J., P. & M. 80).

And the validity of a marriage can be impeached on this ground only by the party who suffers the injury and during the lifetime of both parties to such marriage (*A.* v. *B.*, L. R., 1 P. 559; *P.* v. *S.*, 37 L. J., P. & M. 80).

Marriage merely voidable, and only at instance of injured party.

A suit for nullity of marriage *causâ impotentiæ* may be compromised (*Wilson* v. *Wilson*, 1 H. L. Cas. 538).

And an agreement not to sue for nullity of marriage on the ground of impotency is a bar to a suit subsequently instituted on that ground. So, where in answer to the petition by the husband for a decree of nullity on the ground of the wife's incapacity, the wife pleaded that she and her husband, after a

Suit for nullity on such ground may be compromised.

§ 19.

year's cohabitation, had agreed to live apart and not to make any claim against each other in a Court of law or equity, it was held that the respondent's agreement not to sue was sufficient consideration for the husband's engagement not to sue, and that such an agreement was a bar to his petition (*Aldridge* v. *Aldridge*, 13 P. D. 210; 58 L. J., P. & M. 8).

Age of parties.

There is no rule as to any particular age constituting a bar to a petition for nullity of marriage by reason of malformation (*Williams* v. *Homfray f. c. Williams*, 2 S. & T. 240; 30 L. J., P. & M. 73).

What amounts to impotency.

Impotency: what constitutes.—The impotency of the respondent must be such that consummation of the marriage is practically impossible. If such be the case, it is not necessary to prove that there is any malformation or structural defect rendering consummation physically impossible (*G.* v. *G.*, L. R., 2 P. 287; 40 L. J., P. & M. 83).

So, where it appeared from the husband's evidence that whenever he attempted to have intercourse with his wife the act produced hysteria on her part, and that the marriage had not been consummated after a cohabitation of three years, and the wife refused to submit to inspection, the Court granted the petitioner a decree of nullity (*H.* v. *P. f. c. H.*, L. R., 3 P. 126).

Must be permanent.

But to be a ground for a decree of nullity, an incapacity to consummate marriage must be permanent and incurable. If, therefore, there is a possibility that the incapacity may be cured, even though such cure may be highly improbable, the Court will not pronounce a decree of nullity (*Stagg* v. *Edgecumbe*, 3 S. & T. 240; 32 L. J., P. & M. 153.)

A malformation, however, which might possibly be cured, but at great risk to life and with doubtful success as to the end desired, is equivalent to a permanent and irremovable malformation (*Serrell* v. *Serrell and Bamford*, 2 S. & T. 422; 31 L. J., P. & M. 55).

And where, after a partial cohabitation of two years and eight months' duration, it appeared that the woman was impotent, but that she might probably be cured if she would submit to an operation involving no great risk to life, and she refused to do so, the Court granted a decree of nullity (*L.* v. *L.*, 7 P. D. 16; 51 L. J., P. & M. 23).

The old ecclesiastical Courts granted a decree of nullity if, owing to a natural incurable malformation of the female, a partial connection only was possible (*D.* v. *A.*, 1 Roberts. Eccl. R. 279).

NULLITY OF MARRIAGE.

Impotency quoad hunc vel hanc.—A decree of nullity will be granted if the respondent, though generally capable of performing the act of coition, is yet incapable of performing it with the petitioner (*N.* v. *M.*, 2 Roberts. Eccl. R. 625; *G.* v. *M.*, L. R., 10 A. C. 171; and cf. *S.* v. *B.*, I. L. R., xvi Bomb. 639, a case under the Parsi Marriage Act, 1865). And although the general rule is that if a respondent, whose marriage has been declared null and void on the ground of his or her impotency, marries again and has children by the second marriage, the latter marriage must be set aside and the former marriage declared valid (*Welde* v. *Welde*, 1 Roberts. Eccl. R. 578), the rule cannot apply where the first marriage has been declared void merely on the ground of the respondent's impotency *quoad* the petitioner.

§ 19.

Quoad hunc vel hanc.

Impotency of respondent: burden of proof.—As a general rule, the burden of proof in suits for nullity *causâ impotentiæ* lies on the petitioner (*Cuno* v. *Cuno*, L. R., 2 H. L. (Sc.) 300).

Burden of proof.

But where, after a cohabitation of three years, the marriage remains non-consummated, the *onus* is shifted, and a presumption arises as to the impotency of the respondent (*Marshall f. c. Hamilton* v. *Hamilton*, 33 L. J., P. & M. 159).

Triennial cohabitation.

So where, after a cohabitation of fourteen years, the woman presented a petition for nullity on the ground of the man's impotency, and the medical evidence showed that she was a *virgo intacta et apta viro*, the House of Lords held that she was entitled to a decree on the ground that the cohabitation had been for a much more lengthened period than was required to raise the presumption against the man, and that the *onus* was thrown upon the respondent of either disproving the facts, or of showing by clear and satisfactory evidence that the result was due to causes other than his own impotency (*Lewis f. c. Hayward* v. *Hayward*, 35 L. J., P. & M. 105).

This rule of "triennial cohabitation" is derived from the canon law, but it has not been recognized in England beyond this point, that where a husband or a wife seeks a decree of nullity *propter impotentiam*, if there is no more evidence than that they have lived together in the same house for a period of three years and with ordinary opportunities of conjugal intercourse, and it has been clearly proved that there has been no consummation, then, if that is the whole state of the evidence, inability on the part of one or the other will be presumed. On the other hand, the presumption to be drawn from the fact of non-consummation after three years' cohabitation is capable of

§ 19.

being rebutted. Nor need every case be fortified with the presumption; for, although no *presumption* can arise from the absence of consummation within a less period than three years, yet *positive evidence* may be given from which the same inference of inability may be drawn (*G.* v. *M.*, 10 App. Ca. 171).

So the rule of triennial cohabitation is relaxed where the impotency is due to a malformation that is congenital or manifest and incurable. But even in such cases a cohabitation of a few months only will not suffice (*Stugg f. c. Edgecumbe* v. *Edgecumbe*, 3 S. & T. 240; 32 L. J., P. & M. 153; *F. f. c. D.* v. *D.*, 4 S. & T. 86; 34 L. J., P. & M. 66).

Proof of impotency.

Impotency of respondent: evidence.—As a general rule, a decree of nullity on the ground of the respondent's malformation will not be granted unless the existence of incurable malformation is proved by a medical man who has examined the respondent (*T.* v. *M. f. c. T.*, L. R., 1 P. 31; 35 L. J., P. & M. 10).

And where a question of impotency is raised medical inspectors are usually appointed to examine the parties. Each party has the right to nominate two such inspectors to examine him or her, and it is not necessary that the parties should be examined by the same inspectors (*B. f. c. C.* v. *C.*, 32 L. J., P. & M. 135).

The petitioner, when moving for the appointment of inspectors, should also move for an order that the respondent submit to inspection (*Anon.*, 31 L. J., P. & M. 164). It is not, however, the practice of the Court, in a suit for nullity by reason of the wife's malformation, to make an order for the inspection of the husband (*B.* v. *L.*, 16 W. R. (Eng.) 943).

The report of the inspectors is not conclusive, and the inspectors themselves and other medical men may be examined (*Williams* v. *Homfray f. c. Williams*, 2 S. & T. 240; 30 L. J., P. & M. 73).

In a suit for nullity on the ground of the respondent's impotency, any evidence is admissible which tends to throw light upon the case set up by the petitioner or the respondent. The parties may, therefore, give evidence as to disputes between them during the cohabitation, although the only issues raised by the pleadings are the respondent's impotency and consummation of the marriage (*X. f. c. Y.* v. *Y.*, 34 L. J., P. & M. 81).

As a general rule, the Court will not grant a decree of nullity on the unsupported oath of the party seeking to be relieved from its obligation (*U. f. c. J.* v. *J.*, 37 L. J., P. & M. 7).

So, where in a suit for nullity by the wife, her evidence was wholly unsupported, the physical appearances being consistent with consummation, and the parties had lived together for eight years without complaint by the woman, the Court dismissed her petition (*T. f. c. D.* v. *D.*, L. R., 1 P. 127; 35 L. J., P. & M. 51).

§ 19.

In certain cases, however, where the respondent confesses non-consummation of the marriage and refuses to undergo a medical inspection, the Court will grant the petitioner a decree of nullity *propter impotentiam* (*Harrison* v. *Harrison*, 4 Moore, P. C. C. 96; *L.* v. *L.*, 7 P. D. 16).

Where, therefore, in a suit for nullity by the wife, the man did not appear and did not submit to inspection, the Court, although the medical evidence was not conclusive as to the woman's virginity, took it as proved, on her evidence on affidavit, that (1) the marriage was never consummated; (2) that this was owing to the impotence of the respondent; and (3) that the physical appearance of the woman was to be accounted for otherwise than by consummation, and pronounced a decree in her favour (*F. f. c. D.* v. *D.*, 34 L. J., P. & M. 86).

So, again, where the evidence of the husband showed that, whenever he attempted to have intercourse with his wife, the act produced hysteria on her part, and that the marriage had not been consummated after a cohabitation of three years, and the wife refused to submit to inspection, the Court, on the husband's evidence, pronounced a decree of nullity (*H.* v. *P. f. c. H.*, L. R., 3 P. 126).

A wilful, wrongful refusal of marital intercourse is not *per se* sufficient to justify the Court in declaring a marriage null and void by reason of the respondent's impotency. But when after a reasonable time it is shown that there has been no sexual intercourse, and that the wife had resisted all attempts on the part of the husband, the Court, if satisfied of the *bona fides* of the suit, will infer that the refusal arises from incapacity, and will pronounce a decree of nullity (*S.* v. *A. f. c. S.*, 3 P. D. 72; 47 L. J., P. & M. 75). And from the fact of non-consummation of a *de facto* marriage after a period of cohabitation, during which one party made repeated attempts and was always willing and anxious to bring about consummation of the marriage, the Court, *notwithstanding the apparent competence of both parties*, may draw the inference that something more than seemingly mere wilful refusal must have animated the party who has, in fact, persistently refused to allow consummation (*F.* v. *P. f.c. F.*, 75 L. T. 192).

Wilful refusal of marital intercourse.

Delay in suing for a decree of nullity causâ impotentiæ.—Relief in suits for nullity on the ground of the respondent's impotency

Delay on part of petitioner.

§ 19.

Suggests want of sincerity.

will not, as a general rule, be granted unless the petitioner is prompt in seeking it and sincere in the motive for doing so (*M. f. c. C.* v. *C.*, L. R., 2 P. 414; 41 L. J., P. & M. 37).

But delay in instituting a suit for nullity on this ground is not an absolute bar; it suggests a want of sincerity on the part of the petitioner and ulterior motives for instituting the suit, and, when it exists, renders it necessary that the suit should be supported by evidence of the clearest and most satisfactory kind (*Ewens* v. *Tytherleigh f. c. Ewens*, 3 S. & T. 312; 33 L. J., P. & M. 37; *M. f. c. D.* v. *D.*, 10 P. D. 75; 54 L. J., P. & M. 68).

Where, therefore, a woman who had married in 1834 a man with whom she lived till 1838, when she separated from him, and in 1853 caused him to be sued for her debts, and obtained an allowance from him which was continued till October, 1858, and in November, 1858, sued for a decree of nullity of marriage on the ground of his impotency, it was held that she must give clear and unequivocal proof of the truth of her allegations (*Castleden* v. *Castleden*, 9 H. L. Cas. 186; 4 Macq. H. L. Cas. 159; 31 L. J., P. & M. 103).

And where the petitioner has been guilty of delay, it is necessary to show that the motive in suing is "sincere," that is to say, that the petitioner is suffering from a sense of injury due to the incapacity of the respondent to fulfil the duties of husband or wife, and that there is no other subsidiary motive (*Wilkins* v. *Reynolds*, 1 P. D. 405; 45 L. J., P. & M. 89).

So, where M. married B. in August, 1853, slept in the same bed with him for about two years, when, at his request, she occupied a separate room but lived in his house till June, 1863, when she left, and in 1864 sued for a decree of nullity of marriage on the ground of B.'s impotence and the medical evidence showed that she was a *virgo intacta*, the Court held that lapse of time, coupled with indirect motives in bringing the suit, disentitled her to the relief sought (*Marriott f. c. Burgess* v. *Burgess*, 3 S. & T. 550; 33 L. J., P. & M. 203).

A wife lived with her husband for twenty-one months after the marriage, when they separated for nine months, at the end of which time they again cohabited for five and a half years. She then left her husband in consequence of his cruelty, and twenty-seven years after the marriage and when she was forty-eight years of age, she sued for a decree of nullity on the ground of her husband's impotence, but the Court refused to grant her the relief prayed for (*Wilkins* v. *Reynolds*, *ubi supra*).

The doctrine of "want of sincerity" has, however, not been regarded with favour in the more recent decisions of the English

Court (see *G. v. M.*, 10 App. Cas. 171), and, in any case, where the impotence of the respondent is undoubted and complete, mere delay on the part of the petitioner will not disentitle him or her to relief (*Cuno* v. *Cuno*, L. R., 2 H. L. (Sc.) 300; *L. f. c. B.* v. *B.*, (1895) P. 274; 64 L. J., P. & M. 121).

§ 19.

Suit for nullity causâ impotentiæ: *adultery of petitioner.*—In a suit for nullity of marriage, matrimonial misconduct on the part of the petitioner is no bar to the grant of relief. Where, therefore, in a suit by the wife for nullity of marriage on the ground of her husband's impotence (which was fully proved), it was shown that she had been cohabiting with another man and only brought the suit when her misconduct was discovered, the Court nevertheless granted her a decree of nullity. In such cases the conduct of the petitioner must be judged with a knowledge of the fact that the respondent was incapable of marital duties (*M.* v. *D.*, 10 P. D. 75; 54 L. J., P. & M. 68).

Adultery of petitioner no bar to relief.

"**Prohibited degrees**":

"Prohibited degrees."

The "prohibited degrees" here referred to do not *necessarily* mean the degrees prohibited by the law of England (*Lopez* v. *Lopez*, I. L. R., xii Calc. 706; *Hilliard* v. *Mitchell*, I. L. R., xvii Calc. 324).

Nor is there any enactment in force in British India which expressly defines the term for the purposes of the Indian Divorce Act or for the various classes of Christians who are entitled to apply for relief thereunder. Accordingly, each case will have to be decided in accordance with general principles.

(i) According to the decided weight of authority, at least in England, the capacity to contract a valid marriage depends upon the law of a person's domicil * (Dicey's Conflict of Law, 1896, pp. 642, 643; *Brook* v. *Brook*, 9 H. L. Cas. 193; Lord Macnaghten, *Cooper v. Cooper*, 13 App. Cas. 88).

(i) Capacity to contract marriage depends on *lex domicilii*.

" It is a well-recognized principle of law that the question of

---

* See, however, *Simonin f. c. Mallac* v. *Mallac* (2 S. & T. 67; 29 L. J., P. & M. 97; and the observations of Hannen, P., in *Sottomayor* v. *De Barros*, 5 P. D. 100; Story's Conflict of Law, para. 103). According to these authorities, capacity to contract marriage depends upon the *lex loci celebrationis*. Inasmuch, however, as marriage, though a contract, is something more than a contract, as it is also a *status* arising out of contract, it would certainly seem more expedient to refer the question of capacity to the law of the domicil.

§ 19.

personal capacity to enter into any contract is to be decided by the law of domicil. It is, however, urged that this does not apply to the contract of marriage, and that a marriage valid according to the law of the country where it is solemnized is valid everywhere. This, in our opinion, is not a correct statement of the law. The law of a country where marriage is solemnized must alone decide all questions relating to the validity of the ceremony by which the marriage is alleged to have been constituted; but, as in other contracts, so in that of marriage, personal capacity must depend on the law of domicil; and if the laws of any country prohibit its subjects within certain degrees of consanguinity from contracting marriage and stamp a marriage between persons within the prohibited degrees as incestuous, this, in our opinion, imposes on the subjects of that country a personal incapacity which continues to affect them so long as they are domiciled in the country where this law prevails, and renders invalid a marriage between persons both, at the time of their marriage, subjects of and domiciled in the country which imposes this restriction, wherever such marriage may have been solemnized" (*Sottomayor* v. *De Barros*, 3 P. D. 1—C. A.).

(ii) If domicils different, depends on domicil of the man.

(ii) Personal capacity to contract marriage depends, when the domicils of the man and woman are different, upon the law of the man's domicil. If, therefore, the marriage is valid by the law of the man's domicil, it is valid, although it may be invalid by the law of the woman's domicil (*Sottomayor* v. *De Barros*, 5 P. D. 94; Dicey's Conflict of Law, 1896, p. 626).

This limitation of the general rule is, as Professor Dicey says, illogical, but must be "assumed to be good law" (Conflict of Law, p. 647).

Applying, then, these general principles, the following propositions may be laid down as to the conditions under which a marriage solemnized in India will be held valid or invalid:—

(a) IF BOTH PARTIES ARE DOMICILED IN INDIA.

(a) Both parties domiciled in British India.

There being no express law in British India which defines "the prohibited degrees of consanguinity or affinity," each case must be decided by reference to the personal law of the parties to the marriage, *i.e.*, to the customary law of the class to which such persons belong. If both parties are subject to the same personal law, the marriage will be invalid if forbidden, valid if allowed, by that law. If, on the other hand, they are not subject to the same personal law, the marriage, if allowed by the personal law of the husband, will (presumably) not be invalid by the law of British India simply because it may happen to be forbidden by the personal law of the woman. (Whether, however, this would be the case if the woman were a British subject, domiciled in India but of British birth, is, at least, questionable.)

§ 19.

If, then, the parties are domiciled in India and are not forbidden by their personal law to marry *inter se*, their marriage will be valid by the law of British India, although they may stand towards each other within the degrees prohibited by the law of England (*Das Merces* v. *Cones*, 2 Hyde, 65; *Lopez* v. *Lopez*, I. L. R., xii Calc. 706). Thus, the marriage of an East Indian Christian with his deceased wife's sister, also an East Indian, was held valid (*ib.*).

As regards *British subjects domiciled in India*, the personal law to which they are subject, as regards capacity to contract marriage, is the law of England as enacted by 32 Hen. VIII. c. 38, for the later statute (5 & 6 Will. IV. c. 54) is not, unless specially extended thereto, applicable to any conquered colony (*Brook* v. *Brook*, 9 H. L. Cas. 193), and in no way applies to any part of British India (*Das Merces* v. *Cones, ubi supra*).

Such British subjects, therefore, are, irrespective of the church to which they belong, prohibited from marrying *inter se*, if they are within the prohibited degrees set forth in Chapter 18 of Leviticus. Whether a marriage between British subjects, domiciled in India, who are within such prohibited degrees, is merely voidable at the option of either party during the lifetime of both, or is absolutely null and void (as it would be under 5 & 6 Will. IV. c. 54), is, for the purposes of the Indian Divorce Act, quite immaterial. In either event, it is open to the man or the woman to apply for a decree of nullity on the ground that the parties to the marriage were within the "prohibited degrees."

(*b*) IF ONE ONLY OF THE PARTIES IS DOMICILED IN INDIA.

(b) If one party alone domiciled in British India.

The question whether the parties were capable of marrying *inter se* will (presumably) depend upon either the personal law or the law of the domicil of the man,—the personal law, if it is he who is domiciled in India, the law of his domicil, if it is the woman who is domiciled in India. (But it is questionable whether the marriage of a woman, who is a British subject and of British birth, with a man whom she is prohibited from marrying by the law of England, will be held valid, although such a marriage may be allowed by the personal law or the law of the domicil, as the case may be, of the man.)

§ 19.

(c) Both parties domiciled abroad.

(c) IF BOTH PARTIES ARE DOMICILED ABROAD.

(i) *If their domicil is the same*, their capacity to marry *inter se* will depend upon the law of that domicil.

(ii) *If their domicils are different.*—*When the man's domicil is English, the marriage, if valid by English law, will (presumably) be valid by the law of British India, although the marriage may be prohibited by the law of the woman's domicil.

*When the domicil of the man is not English, the marriage, if valid by the law of his domicil, will (presumably) be valid by the law of British India, although the marriage may be invalid by the law of the woman's domicil. (It is, however, questionable if this would be so held if the woman happened to be a British subject of British birth.)

*In either case, if the marriage is invalid by the law of the man's domicil, it will be invalid by the law of British India, although it may be valid by the law of the woman's domicil, whether the latter be English or not.

As regards persons, both of whom are domiciled in England, "the prohibited degrees" are the degrees prohibited by the law of England, viz., those referred to in the Church of England prayer book (*Reg.* v. *Chadwick*, 11 Q. B. 173). If such persons, being within the said prohibited degrees, intermarry in India, the marriage will be absolutely null and void (*Brook* v. *Brook*, 9 H. L. Cas. 193; *Fenton* v. *Livingstone*, 3 Macq. H. L. Cas. 497). For, although the statute of William IV. has not been extended to this country, persons *domiciled in England*, whether British subjects or aliens, are bound by its provisions wherever they may contract a marriage (*Brook* v. *Brook, ubi supra; Mette* v. *Mette*, 1 S. & T. 416; 28 L. J., P. & M. 117). Such marriages, when solemnized in India, will, therefore, be declared null and void (*Hilliard* v. *Mitchell*,† I. L. R., xvii Calc. 324; *Pimen* v.

---

* The propositions here laid down are, it is submitted, justified by the decision in *Sottomayor* v. *De Barres* (5 P. D. 94), and the provisions of sect. 7 of the Indian Divorce Act. It would, perhaps, be better to insist on the marriage being valid by the law of the domicil of the woman as well as by that of the man.

† In this case it is curious that the Court should have felt any doubt as to the domicil of the petitioner. Admittedly his domicil of origin was English, and as there was no proof that he had acquired any other domicil, he must, in law, be considered to have still retained that domicil (*Udny* v. *Udny*, and cases cited under "Domicil," note to sect. 2, *ante*).

Hindhaugh, unreported but referred to in *Reg.* v. *Robinson*, I. L. R., xvi. All. 212).

In no case, however, whatever may be the law of the parties' domicil, will the Courts of this country recognize as a valid marriage that which is held to be incestuous by the whole Christian world, *e.g.*, a marriage between a brother and sister (Dicey's Conflict of Law, 1896, p. 640).

§ 19.

Incestuous union.

"**Consanguinity (whether natural or legal) or affinity**":

Consanguinity or affinity.

This prohibition applies as well to illegitimate as to legitimate relations. Thus, not only is marriage with a deceased wife's sister void by the law of England (*Andrews f. c. Ross* v. *Ross*, 14 P. D. 15; 58 L. J., P. & M. 14), but also a marriage with a deceased wife's illegitimate sister (*Reg.* v. *Brighton*, 30 L. J., P. & M. 197; cf. *Reg.* v. *St. Giles-in-the-Fields*, 11 Q. B. 173; 17 L. J., Q. B. 81).

So, again, a marriage between a man and the daughter by a former marriage of his deceased wife is by the law of England absolutely null and void (*Blackman* v. *Brider*, 2 Phil. 360).

Nor, in such cases, does the fact that both parties went through the form of marriage with full knowledge of the impediment affect the matter (*Andrews f. c. Ross* v. *Ross*, *ubi supra*).

On the other hand, affinity is not constituted by mere carnal intercourse apart from marriage. Where, therefore, a man avowed that he had had intercourse with his wife's mother previously to his marriage with his wife, it was held that affinity could not be so established by the law of England (*Wing* v. *Taylor f. c. Wing*, 2 S. & T. 278; 30 L. J., P. & M. 258).

"**Either party was a lunatic or idiot at the time of the marriage**":

Lunacy or idiocy.

A marriage may be declared null and void on the ground that either the petitioner or the respondent was a lunatic or idiot *at the time when the ceremony of marriage was performed*. In the former case, unless the petitioner has recovered sanity, the suit may be brought by his or her committee or custodian (sect. 48). As to the course to be adopted when the respondent is of unsound mind at the time of suit, see the notes to sect. 48 (*infra*).

Marriage being a civil contract, it is necessary for its validity that the parties to it are capable of giving a true consent to its

§ 19.

performance. Inasmuch, therefore, as a lunatic or an idiot is, in law, incapable of giving a consent to the performance of any act, such person cannot contract a valid marriage. "Marriage is a contract as well as a religious vow, and, like all other contracts, will be invalidated by the want of consent of capable persons. And it may surely be added that if any contract more than another is capable of being invalidated on the ground of the insanity of either of the contracting parties, it should be the contract of marriage, an act by which the parties bind their property and their persons for the rest of their lives" (*per* Lord Penzance, *Hancock* v. *Peatty*, L. R., 1 P. 341).

Party subject to delusions.

Provided that the party was, in point of fact, incapable, at the time of marriage, of giving a true consent to the performance of the contract, it is not necessary that he or she should have been found a lunatic by inquisition. Accordingly, the marriage of a person who is subject to delusions, but is otherwise sane, may be invalidated. For "a mere comprehension of the words of the promises (of the marriage ceremony) exchanged is not sufficient; the mind of one of the parties may be capable of understanding the language used, but may yet be affected by such delusions or other symptoms of insanity as may satisfy the tribunal that there was not a real appreciation of the engagement apparently entered into" (*per* Hannen, J., *Durham* v. *Durham*, 10 P. D. 80).

Consideration for Court.

The consideration for the Court in each case is merely whether there was health or disease of the mind at the time when the marriage was solemnized. If disease is shown to have then existed, the marriage will be declared null and void, for the Court has no means of gauging the extent of the derangement consequent upon that disease, or of affirming the limits within which the disease might operate to obscure or divert the mental power (*Hancock* v. *Peatty*, L. R., 1 P. 335; 36 L. J., P. & M. 57).

Burden of proof.

In every case the burden of proving that there was insanity or idiocy on the part of one of the parties to a marriage at the time it was celebrated rests upon the party asserting it (*Durham* v. *Durham*, 10 P. D. 80).

Supervening lunacy.

It is only insanity or idiocy *at the time of marriage* that invalidates the contract. Therefore, a marriage contracted in a lucid interval by a person who was previously insane, and who subsequently to the marriage ceremony again relapses into insanity, is valid. But in such a case the *onus* of establishing the fact that the marriage was contracted in a lucid interval rests

NULLITY OF MARRIAGE.

§ 19.

upon the party who alleges it, and such party must show sanity and competence on the part of the other party at the period when the act was done, and to which the lucid interval refers (*Att.-Gen.* v. *Paruther*, 3 Br. C. C. 444).

If, therefore, both parties were capable of giving a legal consent to the celebration of the marriage at the time when it was actually performed, the supervening lunacy or idiocy of either of them will not affect the validity of the marriage.

Deaf and dumb persons can enter into the contract of marriage, and the presumption in such cases is in favour of the validity of the marriage, and of the capacity of the parties to it. The *onus* of proof is, therefore, upon the party who impeaches its validity (*Harrod* v. *Harrod*, 1 K. & J. 4; 18 Jur. 853). — Deaf and dumb persons.

Where a suit for nullity of marriage on the ground of the petitioner's lunacy at the time of marriage is instituted by the guardian of a lunatic, and, though the fact alleged has been duly proved, there is reason to believe that the respondent can establish the fact of the petitioner's recovery, the Court will give the latter an opportunity of doing so, and, if it is thereafter satisfied of the fact of such recovery, will refuse to pronounce a decree of nullity, except at the personal instance of the petitioner (*Hancock* v. *Peatty, ubi supra*). — Suit by committee.

"The former husband or wife of either party was living at the time of the marriage, and the marriage with such former husband or wife was then in force": — Former husband or wife of party alive at time of subsequent marriage.

If the former husband or wife of either party was living at the time of the marriage sought to be annulled, *and* the marriage with such former husband or wife was then in force, the subsequent marriage is absolutely null and void. Therefore, no matter how gross has been the misconduct of the petitioner for a decree of nullity on this ground, the Court is bound to grant, and has no discretion to refuse, the decree prayed for (*Miles* v. *Chilton*, 1 Robert. 684).

It must be remembered, however, that the Courts in India have no jurisdiction under the Indian Divorce Act to grant any decree of nullity except in such cases in which it can be proved that the marriage, in respect of which relief is prayed, was solemnized in India.

A person does not commit the offence of bigamy when he or she, not having heard for seven years anything of his or her — "Bigamy."

§ 19.

wife or husband and believing her or him to be dead, goes through a form of marriage with another person; but if it subsequently appears that the former wife or husband was alive and the former marriage was in force at the time of the second marriage, the latter will be absolutely null and void. And this will be the case even if such former wife or husband dies immediately after the celebration of the second marriage between the other party to such former marriage and a third person.

Burden of proof.

But, as it is a criminal offence for a person, being already married, to go through a form of marriage with another person unless he or she has not heard of the former wife or husband for seven years, and as the law always presumes against the commission of a criminal offence, it is incumbent on the person impeaching the second marriage to give proof that at the time of its performance the former wife or husband was alive, even though the full period of seven years had not then elapsed (*Reg.* v. *Twyning,* 2 B. & A. 386). Of course, if at the time of the second marriage such former wife or husband had not been heard of by the other party for seven years, the burden of proving that she or he was actually then alive will rest on the person asserting the fact (see Evidence Act of 1872, s. 108).

Former marriage must be subsisting and legal.

In order to render the subsequent marriage null and void, it must be shown not only that the former marriage was subsisting at the time, but also that it was in force or legal. If, therefore, the alleged first marriage was one between persons who stood towards each other within the prohibited degrees, it, being a mere nullity under 5 & 6 Will. IV. c. 54, will not invalidate the second marriage (*Reg.* v. *Chadwick,* 11 Q. B. 173; 17 L. J., Q. B. 71).

So, again, where a man and a woman were married in 1874, but it appeared that the woman had previously gone through a form of marriage with another man, B., who was still alive, but that B. himself, at the time of his alleged marriage with the woman in question, had a wife living, the Court held (under the provisions of 21 & 22 Vict. c. 93) that the marriage of 1874 was valid and legal (*Shilson* v. *Att.-Gen.,* 22 W. R. (Eng.) 831).

Re-marriage of party to divorce before expiry of appointed time.

If one of the parties to a divorce marries again after the decree *nisi* has been pronounced, but before it has been made absolute, or (in this country) even after it has been made absolute but before the expiry of the further period of six months from the date of the decree absolute (see sect. 57), the marriage so contracted is null and void (*Chichester* v. *Mure f. c.*

Chichester, 3 S. & T. 223; *Noble* v. *Noble and Goodman*, L. R., 1 P. 691; 38 L. J., P. & M. 52; *Warter* v. *Warter*, 15 P. D. 152; 59 L. J., P. & M. 87).

§ 19.

For the prohibition contained in sect. 57 of the Indian Divorce Act against the marriage of either party within six months of the *final* decree, that is, the decree absolute, is an integral part of the proceedings, and a condition which must be fulfilled before the parties can contract a fresh marriage, and they cannot evade it by obtaining a domicil in another country (*Warter* v. *Warter, ubi supra*).

As regards the jurisdiction of a Court to grant a decree of nullity of marriage, which shall be effective to annul such marriage not only for the purposes of its own municipal law, but for the purposes of international law generally, see the notes to sect. 2, *ante*. For the purposes of international law, as well as for the purposes of the municipal law of British India, the Courts of this country have jurisdiction to annul a marriage only when such marriage was solemnized in India (sect. 2).

Jurisdiction of Court.

"**Jurisdiction of High Court to make decree of nullity of marriage**":

Force or fraud.

It will be noticed that it is only the "High Court," presumably as defined in sect. 3, which has jurisdiction to grant a decree of nullity on the ground that the consent of either party was obtained by force or fraud.

"**Consent was obtained by force or fraud**":

Are contracts of marriage if induced by force or fraud void or voidable?

Ordinary contracts, if induced by force or fraud, are voidable at the option of the party coerced or defrauded (see sect. 19, Indian Contract Act, 1872). But with regard to the contract of marriage a difficulty arises. If, like other contracts, it is, in such cases, merely voidable, can it be declared null and void after it has been consummated? If so, what would be the position of any offspring of such marriage? Would it be legitimate or illegitimate? If, on the other hand, it is absolutely null and void, even though consummated, then the party in fault is, equally with the other party, at liberty to apply to the Court for its annulment. In other words, a man who has, for a mere temporary purpose, coerced or defrauded a woman into marrying him, can take advantage of his own fraud and be relieved from a bond which he subsequently finds irksome or unpleasant. "The least inconvenient view" does indeed seem to be that

§ 19.

suggested by a learned writer in the *Law Quarterly Review* (1887, pp. 252, 253), viz., "that in such cases the marriage is void, but that the party in fault is estopped from denying its validity." That the marriage is not merely voidable but void is clear, for *consensus non concubitus facit matrimonium*, and consent there can, in truth, be none when the acquiescence of one of the parties has been obtained by force or fraud (cf. *Harford* v. *Morris*, 2 Hagg. Cons. 427).

Force.—As to the amount of force or pressure which, when exercised by the one party to induce the other to go through a ceremony of marriage, each case must be decided by its own circumstances. "It has sometimes been said that, in order to avoid a contract entered into through fear, the fear must be such as would impel a person of ordinary courage and resolution to yield to it. I do not think that this is an accurate statement of the law. Wherever, from natural weakness of intellect or from fear—*whether reasonably entertained or not*—either party is in a state of mental incompetence to resist pressure improperly brought to bear, there is no more consent than in the case of a person of stronger intellect and more robust courage yielding to a more serious danger" (Butt, J., *Scott* v. *Sebright*, 12 P. D. at p. 24).

Instances.

The most recent cases on this subject are the following :—

(a) The petitioner, a young woman of twenty-two years of age and entitled to a sum of 2,600*l.* in actual possession and a considerable sum in reversion, became engaged to the respondent, and, shortly after coming of age, was induced by him to accept bills to the amount of 3,325*l.* The persons who had discounted these bills subsequently issued writs against her, and threatened to make her a bankrupt. The distress caused by these threats seriously affected her health, and reduced her to a state of mental and bodily prostration in which she was incapable of resisting coercion and threats. Being assured by the respondent that the only method of evading bankruptcy proceedings and exposure was to marry him, she reluctantly went through a form of marriage with him at a registrar's office. In addition to threats of ruining her, the respondent, immediately before the ceremony, threatened to shoot her if she evinced any signs of not acting voluntarily. The marriage, *which was not consummated*, the parties leaving each other immediately after the ceremony, was declared null and void on the ground that there was no such consent on the part of the petitioner as the law requires (*Scott* v. *Sebright*, 12 P. D. 21; 56 L. J., P. & M. 11).

(b) Petitioner, who at the time was only seventeen years of age and of a weak and nervous temperament, was induced *by her mother*, acting in concert with the respondent, to go through a ceremony of marriage with the latter. At the time of the marriage, the mother, who was shown to have exercised an abnormal amount of control over her daughter, persuaded her that the ceremony she had gone through was merely one of betrothal. The marriage, *which was never consummated*, the parties leaving one another at the doors of the church and never meeting thereafter, was declared null and void, on the ground that the petitioner had acted *under the duress of her mother*, and was not a consenting party to the marriage (*Clarke* v. *Clarke*, (1896) P. 1; 65 L. J., P. & M. 13).

In this case the noticeable fact is that the duress was not so much that of the respondent as of the petitioner's own mother. Inasmuch, however, as the mother was acting in connivance with the respondent, the latter was as responsible for it as if he had himself been guilty of the wrong. Under the Indian Contract Act (sect. 19) he would, apparently, have been responsible for the mother's wrongful conduct, although he was unaware of it and in no way authorized it (cf. sects. 15, 16, 18, and 19 of that Act with sect. 17). Whether this be so or not as regards ordinary contracts, it may be a question whether in this respect the contract of marriage does not differ from other contracts. Assuming that, to render voidable an ordinary contract, the coercion or undue influence must, as in the case of fraud, be that of the other party to the contract or of someone acting with his connivance, or of his agent, will a marriage which has been induced by the coercion or undue influence of a stranger, acting without the knowledge or authority of the respondent, be regarded as valid or be set aside as a mere nullity? Presumably, it will be declared null and void, for the petitioner's consent is as much wanting in the one case as in the other, and the contract of marriage is in many respects dissimilar to ordinary contracts.

(c) A man, after paying attentions to a young girl of sixteen years of age, which she rejected, produced a pistol and threatened to blow out her brains. She, thereupon, consented to marry him if he put away the pistol, which he did. Shortly afterwards, she in the meantime having returned to her home, he intercepted her at a railway station and took her to the office of a marriage registrar, saying that they were going to see his mother.

§ 19.

During the ceremony she fainted, and immediately on its conclusion she left him. *The marriage was never consummated*, and the man never insisted on marital rights. Upon these facts the Court declared the marriage to be null and void (*Bartlett f. c. Rice* v. *Rice*, 72 L. T. 122).

(d) The respondent had made the petitioner an offer of marriage, which she had refused, and on a Sunday in July, 1888, under the pretence of going to the afternoon service at St. Paul's Cathedral, he took her to St. Bride's Church, Fleet Street, and outside the church suddenly said to her, " You must come into the church and marry me, or I will blow out my brains and you will be responsible." According to her own statement, she became so alarmed that she did not know what she was doing, and went into the church, where the ceremony was performed, and signed the register. The respondent had previously obtained a licence on a false declaration as to his own age and the petitioner's residence, and had made arrangements for the ceremony to be performed on that day. The vicar of St. Bride's, who performed the ceremony, stated that the petitioner went through it without showing any signs of unwillingness, repeated the responses in an audible tone, and signed the register in a clear, firm hand. After the ceremony the respondent took the petitioner home and left her at the door of the house. The marriage was never consummated, and the parties never saw each other again, though they corresponded, but on the footing of cousins, and not as husband and wife. The petitioner did not mention the marriage to her parents, because, as she explained, she did not regard it as binding on her. The respondent, who did not appear at the hearing, admitted that he did not care for the petitioner and only married her for her money. The evidence showed that the petitioner was of a weak, impressionable character, with not much power of resistance to a stronger will, but that she was not particularly disposed to fall into a hysterical state in the medical sense of the term. The Court held that the facts above set forth were insufficient to rebut the presumption of consent, that the marriage was valid, and that the petition must be dismissed (*Cooper f. c. Crane* v. *Crane*, (1891) P. 369). In arriving at this conclusion, Collins, J., was undoubtedly influenced by the evidence as to the conduct of the petitioner during the ceremony. "When," he remarks, "a person of full age and of sound mind has gone through the ceremony of marriage publicly in the presence of witnesses who discovered nothing in her demeanour to suggest constraint, and has herself

NULLITY OF MARRIAGE.

§ 19.

complied with the formality of signing her name and answering questions without apparent difficulty or confusion, very clear and cogent evidence must be given before the presumption of consent can be rebutted and the marriage annulled. . . . In order to hold that the ceremony so performed was not binding, I think I should have to infer as a fact one of two things—either that she was so perturbed by terror that her mind was unhinged, and she did not understand what she was doing—and this, I think, is what is meant by the words 'not know what she is about,' in the passage from Bishop, cited in the argument and which is based on *Fulwood's Case* (Cro. Car. 482, 488, 489)—or that, though she understood what she was doing, her powers of volition were so paralyzed that, by her words and acts, she merely gave expression to the will of the respondent, and not her own." After consideration the learned judge found that neither alternative was supported by the evidence.

Apart from any question of mental capacity, an objection that a deaf and dumb person did not understand the nature of the contract of marriage, which he or she had been induced to enter into, is an objection on the ground of fraud (*Harrod* v. *Harrod*, 1 K. & J. 4 ; 18 Jur. 853). *As regards deaf and dumb person.*

Mere deceit as to the position or circumstances of one of the parties is not a sufficient ground for a decree of nullity (*Templeton* v. *Tyree*, L. R., 2 P. 420; 41 L. J., P. & M. 86; *Ewing* v. *Wheatley*, 2 Hagg. Cons. 175). *Deceit as to position of one of the parties.*

Although nothing is said in this section as to *mistake*, it can hardly be doubted that the High Court has jurisdiction to declare null and void a marriage contracted by one of the parties under a *bonâ fide* mistake as to the *person* of the other party. For instance, A., a person who is both deaf and blind, goes through a ceremony of marriage with B., thinking that B. is C. In such a case there would be no consent whatever on the part of A. to marriage with B. *"Mistake."*

20. Every decree of nullity of marriage made by a district judge shall be subject to confirmation by the High Court, and the provisions of section seventeen, clauses one, two, three and four, shall *mutatis mutandis* apply to such decrees. *Confirmation of district judge's decree.*

In England, a decree of nullity of marriage is in the first instance a decree *nisi*, not to be made absolute (unless the Court

§ 20. expressly shortens the time) till the expiration of six months from the date of the decree *nisi*. During this interval any person may intervene, as in suits for dissolution of marriage (Matrimonial Causes Act, 1873, s. 1).

Under the Indian Divorce, no provision is made for intervention in a suit for nullity, whether instituted in the District Court or the High Court, and, except in the case of a decree made by a district judge, a decree of nullity is a final decree as soon as it is made. It is also to be noticed that, unlike a decree of dissolution, a decree of nullity made by a district judge may be confirmed by the High Court immediately after it has been made (see sect. 17).

Children of annulled marriage.

21. Where a marriage is annulled on the ground that a former husband or wife was living, and it is adjudged that the subsequent marriage was contracted in good faith and with the full belief of the parties that the former husband or wife was dead, or when a marriage is annulled on the ground of insanity, children begotten before the decree is made shall be specified in the decree, and shall be entitled to succeed, in the same manner as legitimate children, to the estate of the parent who at the time of the marriage was competent to contract.

Children of annulled marriage: right of succession.

"This section, which is taken textually from the New York Code, and resembles the provisions of the French Code and the numerous systems descended from Roman law, permits the children to succeed as legitimate to the property of the parent competent to marry, and thus relieves them *pro tanto* from the stigma of illegitimacy" (speech of Sir H. Maine, *Gazette of India*, February, 1869).

There are several observations to be made regarding the provisions of this section:—

(a) Only in certain cases.

(1) It is only in certain specified cases that the children of an annulled marriage are entitled to succeed as here laid down. Accordingly, no child born of a marriage which has been annulled on the ground that the parties were within the prohibited degrees, or on the ground that the consent of one of the parties

NULLITY OF MARRIAGE.

to the marriage was obtained by force or fraud, can succeed under this section to property as legitimate.

(2) The children of an annulled marriage are not hereby declared legitimate. The Select Committee, out of deference to the authority of Sir Barnes Peacock and Mr. Justice Norman, purposely refrained from giving jurisdiction to the Courts to make declarations of legitimacy, principally because such declarations would have no extra-territorial effect.

(3) It is only to the property of that parent who was at the time of the marriage competent to contract marriage that the child is entitled to succeed, as though legitimate; to the property of the other parent he or she has no claim whatever.

(4) "Children begotten before the decree is made," that is to say, any child either born before the decree is made or within 280 days from the date when the parties last had access to each other previously to the making of the decree (Indian Evidence Act, 1872, s. 112).

(5) The principle embodied in this section is not recognized in all systems of law. For instance, by the law of England, the children of a void marriage are illegitimate for all purposes. Inasmuch, therefore, as succession to immoveable property is governed by the *lex loci situs*, and to personal property by the *lex domicilii* of the late owner (see Indian Succession Act, 1865, ss. 5, 19; *Ewin, In re*, 5 B. & C. 451; *Freke* v. *Lord Carbery*, L. R., 16 Eq. 466; Westlake's Private International Law, 2nd ed., p. 168; Rattigan's Private International Law, pp. 80—87; Dicey's Conflict of Law, 1896, pp. 516, 682), if the estate of the parent who was competent to contract consists of immoveable property in, *e.g.*, England, or if it consists of moveable property (even though such moveable property be in India), but the late owner's domicil at the time of death was, *e.g.*, England, the claim of the child to succeed thereto would not be recognized by the English Courts. In such cases no difficulty can arise so far as immoveable property, situate out of British India, is concerned, for no decree of the Indian Courts can give the child a right to succeed to such property. But if the estate of the parent competent to contract marriage consists of moveables, and such parent's domicil at the time of death was English, the right of the child to succeed thereto would not ordinarily be recognized by the Courts of this country, even if the moveables were situate in British India. Sect. 21 of the Indian Divorce Act, however, engrafts an exception on to the ordinary law as laid down in the Indian Succession Act, and gives the child,

§ 21.

(b) Children not declared legitimate.

(c) Succeed only to property of parent competent to marry.

(d) If begotten before decree.

(e) Principle not universally recognized.

§ 21.

under the specified circumstances, a right which he or she would not otherwise have had in this country, and which would still be unenforceable in the English Courts.

If, however, the estate of the parent consists of immoveable property situate in, or of moveable property and such parent's domicil at the time of death was, British India or some other country, the law of which gives such child a right to succeed as legitimate (*e.g.*, that of Scotland, *Wilson, In re*, L. R., 1 Eq. 247; 35 L. J., Ch. 243), the right of such child to succeed will be recognized and enforced not only by the *lex loci situs* or *lex domicilii* of the late owner, as the case may be, but also will receive international recognition.

V.—*Judicial Separation.*

No decree for divorce *a mensâ et toro* to be made. Decree of judicial separation obtainable by husband or wife.

22. No decree shall hereafter be made for a divorce *a mensâ et toro*, but the husband or wife may obtain a decree of judicial separation, on the ground of adultery, or cruelty, or desertion without reasonable excuse for two years or upwards, and such decree shall have the effect of a divorce *a mensâ et toro* under the existing law, and such other legal effect as hereinafter mentioned.

The Matrimonial Causes Act (20 & 21 Vict. c. 85) of 1857, sect. 7 :—

"No decree shall hereafter be made for a divorce *a mensâ et thoro*, but in all cases in which a decree for a divorce *a mensâ et thoro* might now be pronounced, the Court may pronounce a decree for judicial separation, which shall have the same force and the same consequences as a divorce *a mensâ et thoro* now has."

Sect. 16 :—

"A sentence of judicial separation (which shall have the effect of a divorce *a mensâ et thoro* under the existing law and such other legal effect as herein mentioned) may be obtained, either by the husband or the wife, on the ground of adultery, or cruelty, or desertion without cause for two years and upwards."

"**Adultery, or cruelty, or desertion**" :

As to these, see the notes to sect. 10, *ante*.

JUDICIAL SEPARATION.

"May obtain a decree of judicial separation": § 22.

(1) Every petition for a decree of judicial separation must bear a Court fee stamp of Rs. 20 (Court Fees Act, 1870, 2nd Sch., Art. 20), and must state that there is no collusion or connivance between the petitioner and the other party to the marriage, and must be duly verified by the petitioner or some other competent person (sect. 47, *post*). — Court fee stamp.

(2) If the petitioner is the husband, and the ground of the suit is the adultery of the wife, damages can be claimed from the alleged adulterer. In such case the petition must be served on the latter, but apparently he need not be made a co-respondent, as he must be (except under certain circumstances) in suits for dissolution of marriage (see sect. 34, *post*). Unless, however, he is made co-respondent, he cannot be ordered to pay the whole or any part of the costs of the proceedings (sect. 35, *post*). — Claim by husband for damages.

(3) Although the petition only prays for a dissolution of marriage, it is competent to the Court to grant a decree for judicial separation if the facts proved entitle the petitioner to the latter and not to the former relief (*Smith* v. *Smith*, 1 S. & T. 359; 28 L. J., P. & M. 27; *Bromfield* v. *Bromfield*, 41 L. J., P. & M. 17; *Duplany* v. *Duplany*, (1892) P. 53). — Decree of judicial separation in suit for dissolution of marriage.

And the Court will, at the hearing, if the petitioner so prays, make a decree of judicial separation instead of a decree *nisi* for dissolution of marriage, although the petition prays for a dissolution and the facts proved warrant a decree for dissolution, and although the respondent objects to the alteration of the prayer (*Mycock* v. *Mycock*, 39 L. J., P. & M. 56; *Dent* v. *Dent*, 4 S. & T. 105; 34 L. J., P. & M. 118).

(4) Inasmuch as a petitioner for restitution of conjugal rights can fail to obtain a decree only on some ground which would be a ground for judicial separation or for nullity of marriage, the respondent in a suit for restitution of conjugal rights is entitled to add a prayer to his or her answer to such suit for a decree of judicial separation or for nullity of marriage, and, on the failure of the petitioner to obtain a decree for restitution, the Court may grant the respondent a decree for judicial separation or for nullity of marriage, as the case may be (see sect. 33, *post*, and cf. *Meara* v. *Meara*, 13 W. R. (Eng.) 50; *Russell* v. *Russell*, (1895) P. 315—C. A.). — At prayer of respondent in suit for restitution of conjugal rights.

(5) Sect. 5 of the Matrimonial Causes Act, 1884 (47 & 48 Vict. c. 68), provides that a respondent in a suit for restitution of conjugal rights, who fails to comply with a decree passed against him or her, is to be deemed to be guilty of desertion without reasonable cause sufficient to justify a decree for judicial separa-

THE INDIAN DIVORCE ACT.

§ 22.

tion being passed against him or her. But in India a refusal to obey a decree for restitution of conjugal rights, though it might render the respondent liable to attachment for contempt, does not constitute *per se* such desertion as would be a ground for judicial separation.

Respondent molesting petitioner after decree.

(6) If, after one of the parties has obtained a decree for judicial separation, the other party insists on molesting the decree-holder, the Court has no jurisdiction to attach him or her for contempt (*Smith* v. *Smith*, 59 L. J., P. & M. 15).

Application for separation made by petition.

23. Application for judicial separation on any one of the grounds aforesaid may be made by either husband or wife by petition to the District Court or the High Court; and the Court, on being satisfied of the truth of the statements made in such petition, and that there is no legal ground why the application should not be granted, may decree judicial separation accordingly.

Matrimonial Causes Act (20 & 21 Vict. c. 85), s. 17, as amended by Matrimonial Causes Act, 1858 (21 & 22 Vict. c. 108), s. 19:—

"Application for restitution of conjugal rights, or for judicial separation on any one of the grounds aforesaid, may be made by either husband or wife by petition to the Court; and the Court, on being satisfied of the truth of the allegations therein contained, and that there is no legal ground why the same should not be granted, may decree such restitution of conjugal rights or judicial separation accordingly, and, where the application is by the wife, may make any order for alimony which shall be deemed just."

"Petition to the District Court":

In cases of judicial separation, the decree of the district judge does not require to be confirmed by the High Court.

"Legal ground."

"No legal ground why the application should not be granted":

The Act does not expressly define the legal grounds which justify the Court in refusing to grant a decree to a petitioner for judicial separation. It is, however, clear that condonation of the offence charged, and collusion or connivance between the parties, will act as an absolute bar to relief. But it is scarcely necessary to observe that suits for judicial separation must, from the nature of things, be generally untainted with either collusion or connivance between the parties.

§ 23.

As regards the discretionary bars to relief, it may be stated that, as a general rule, the Court will not grant a decree for judicial separation in a case where, if the suit had been for dissolution of marriage, it would have refused to grant relief to the petitioner, although the case against the respondent had been duly established (see notes to sect. 14, *ante*).

A petitioner, therefore, will, ordinarily, be refused a decree for judicial separation who has been guilty of—

Discretionary bars to grant of relief:

(a) *Adultery*.—Thus where a wife who had herself committed adultery sued for a decree of judicial separation on the ground of her husband's cruelty and adultery, both of which were proved, she was refused a decree, notwithstanding that the cruelty of the husband had been very aggravated (*Otway* v. *Otway*, 13 P. D. 141; 57 L. J., P. & M. 81—C. A.; cf. *Drummond* v. *Drummond*, 30 L. J., P. & M. 177).

(a) Petitioner guilty of adultery.

And less is required to prove the adultery for this purpose than is required for the purpose of founding a decree for dissolution or judicial separation (*Forster* v. *Forster*, 1 Hagg. Cons. 144).

But the mere fact that the husband has instituted a suit for dissolution of marriage on the ground of his wife's adultery will not prevent the Court from granting her a decree for judicial separation on the ground of his cruelty (*Bancroft* v. *Bancroft*, 4 S. & T. 84; 34 L. J., P. & M. 70).

Under certain exceptional circumstances, the Court will grant a decree of judicial separation to a petitioner who has been guilty of adultery (see notes to sect. 14, *ante*).

And, possibly, in cases of judicial separation, condonation of the adultery gives the Court a discretion to grant the relief, notwithstanding the petitioner's adultery (*Gooch* v. *Gooch*, (1893) P., at p. 105).

(b) *Cruelty*.—Although cruelty on the part of the petitioner is ordinarily no bar to a suit for judicial separation on the ground of the respondent's adultery (*Tuthill* v. *Tuthill*, 31 L. J., P. & M. 214), such cruelty will probably disentitle the petitioner to relief if it can be shown to have conduced to the adultery (*Lempriere* v. *Lempriere*, L. R., 1 P. 569; 37 L. J., P. & M. 78; *Boreham* v. *Boreham*, L. R., 1 P. 77; 35 L. J., P. & M. 49).

(b) Petitioner guilty of cruelty.

And if the ground of the suit for judicial separation is the respondent's desertion, cruelty on the part of the petitioner

§ 23.

(c) Desertion on part of petitioner.

which has caused the withdrawal from cohabitation will probably act as a bar to relief (*Emery* v. *Emery*, 1 Y. & J. 501; 6 Price, 336; *Houliston* v. *Smyth*, 10 Moore, 582; 2 C. & P. 222).

(c) *Desertion without reasonable excuse.*—Possibly, however, it is only in cases where the desertion amounts to such wilful neglect or misconduct as has conduced to the adultery of the respondent that the petitioner will be disentitled to relief, especially if the petitioner is the wife. Thus it has been held that the fact that the wife has wilfully and without reasonable excuse deserted the husband will not disentitle her to a decree for judicial separation on the ground of the husband's adultery (*Duplany* v. *Duplany*, (1892) P. 53; 66 L. T. 267) or cruelty (*Rowe* v. *Rowe*, 4 S. & T. 162; 34 L. J., P. & M. 111).

Whether, however, a husband who has wilfully and without reasonable excuse deserted his wife would be granted a decree for judicial separation on the ground of her adultery is, at least, questionable. For, "if chastity be the duty of the wife, protection is no less that of the husband. The wife has a right to the comfort and support of the husband's society, the security of his home and name, and the just protection of his presence, so far as his avocations will admit. Whoever falls short in this regard, if not the author of his own misfortune, is not wholly blameless in the issue" (*Jeffreys* v. *Jeffreys and Smith*, 3 S. & T. 495; 33 L. J., P. & M. 66). The case cited was one for dissolution of marriage, but the principle of the decision would appear to apply equally to a suit for judicial separation (see especially, *Lempriere* v. *Lempriere and Roebel*, 37 L. J., P. & M. 78).

(d) Inexcusable delay in suing.

(d) *Inexcusable delay in suing.*—Mere delay in instituting a suit for judicial separation is no bar to the granting of relief to the petitioner. It is, however, a material fact for the consideration of the Court and requires explanation, for, if unexplained, it may suggest, in the case of adultery, an insensibility on the part of the petitioner to the injury suffered; in the case of cruelty, a lack of any serious apprehension of future violence; and, in the case of desertion, a callous indifference as to the presence or absence of the respondent. Unexplained delay in suing being thus suggestive of collateral motives, the petitioner will, as a general rule, have only himself or herself to blame if the suit is dismissed on this ground (*Smallwood* v. *Smallwood*, 2 S. & T. 397; 31 L. J., P. & M. 3; *Matthews* v. *Matthews*, 1 S. & T. 499; 29 L. J., P. & M. 118; in app., 3 S. & T. 161).

(e) *Wilful neglect or misconduct on the part of the petitioner conducing to the matrimonial offence on the part of the respondent.*— If the petitioner has not actually deserted the respondent, but the matrimonial offence on the part of the latter is directly traceable to the wilful neglect or misconduct of the petitioner, it is probable that the Court will refuse to grant a decree of judicial separation. If, for instance, the wife, by her own ill-temper, has drawn upon herself ill-treatment from her husband, she cannot reasonably urge his cruelty, unless wholly unjustified by the provocation, as a ground for judicial separation (*Best* v. *Best*, 1 Add. 411). And, generally, on this subject, see the notes to sect. 14, *ante*.

§ 23.

(e) Misconduct of petitioner conducing to offence.

(f) *Misconduct on part of petitioner falling short of matrimonial offence.*—In a suit for judicial separation on the ground of the respondent's "desertion," conduct on the part of the petitioner which, though it falls short of any matrimonial offence, has led to that desertion, will disentitle the petitioner to relief. Thus, the bringing of an infamous and totally unfounded charge against the respondent, though it may not amount to cruelty in the legal sense, will justify the respondent in withdrawing from the society of the petitioner, and will disentitle the latter to a decree of judicial separation on the ground of desertion. The reason, however, in such cases is, that there is, in truth, no desertion without reasonable excuse (see *Russell* v. *Russell*, (1895) P. 315; *Yeatman* v. *Yeatman*, L. R., 1 P. at p. 491; *Oldroyd* v. *Oldroyd*, 65 L. J., P. & M. 113; 12 T. L. R. 442).

(f) Misconduct of petitioner falling short of matrimonial offence.

Nor will a petitioner be entitled to sue for a judicial separation who—

(g) Has covenanted with the respondent not to sue in respect of the offence which is charged as the ground for judicial separation.

(g) Covenant not to sue.

If, therefore, by the terms of a separation deed the parties have voluntarily agreed to live separate, and either the husband or the wife has expressly covenanted not to sue in respect of misconduct on the part of the other committed prior to the execution of the deed, he or she will be held to have surrendered any right to relief in respect of such misconduct and will not be allowed to repudiate the agreement except on the ground of fraud or of such mistake in the terms of the agreement that it ought not to be held binding (*Rowley* v. *Rowley*, 34 L. J., P. & M. 97; *Hooper* v. *Hooper*, 3 S. & T. 251).

So, where a husband covenanted with the trustee of the deed

§ 23. to make his wife an allowance, and the trustee covenanted on behalf of the wife neither to sue for restitution of conjugal rights or alimony, nor to molest, trouble, or disturb the husband, and the wife shortly afterwards (although she had duly received her allowance) commenced proceedings in the Divorce Court for a judicial separation and alimony, it was held by the Court of Chancery that the husband was entitled to a perpetual injunction restraining such proceedings (*Flower* v. *Flower*, 25 L. T. 902; 20 W. R. (Eng.) 231; cf. *Hunt* v. *Hunt*, 31 L. J., Ch. 161).

Although, since the Judicature Act, such injunction cannot now be granted, a covenant not to sue affords a good defence to a suit brought in contravention of its terms (*Marshall* v. *Marshall*, 5 P. D. 19; 48 L. J., P. & M. 49; *Clark* v. *Clark*, 10 P. D. 188; 54 L. J., P. & M. 57).

Nor will mere trifling breaches of the covenant on the part of one of the parties justify the other in instituting a suit in violation of the agreement (*Besant* v. *Wood*, 12 Ch. D. 605).

And if the wife has absolutely bargained away her right to relief on the ground of desertion, the husband's failure to pay the allowance which he covenanted to pay will not revive her right to sue in respect of such desertion (*Parkinson* v. *Parkinson*, L. R., 2 P. 25; 39 L. J., P. & M. 14).

On the other hand, a mere agreement, whether embodied in a deed or not, between the parties that they will henceforth live apart, will not, in the absence of any express covenant not to sue, be a bar to a suit for judicial separation in respect of the other party's previous misconduct (*Moore* v. *Moore*, 12 P. D. 193; 56 L. J., P. & M. 104). But an allegation in the respondent's answer that the parties were living separate under a deed of separation will not be ordered to be struck out, even though no express covenant not to sue is alleged, as such deed of separation may, if proved, show that the suit was not instituted *bonâ fide*, but for the purpose of securing an increased allowance (*Williams* v. *Williams*, L. R., 1 P. 178; 35 L. J., P. & M. 85).

It is, of course, hardly necessary to add that proof that the parties were living apart under a separation deed would bar a suit for judicial separation on the ground of desertion, even though it contained no covenant not to sue. On the other hand, a deed of separation, which had never been acted on, will not disentitle either of the parties to it to sue for judicial separation on the ground of the other's desertion (*Cock* v. *Cock*, 3 S. & T. 514; 33 L. J., P. & M. 157; *Nott* v. *Nott*, L. R., 1 P. 251; 36 L. J., P. & M. 10).

Nor will a deed of separation which has been fraudulently obtained (*Crabb* v. *Crabb*, L. R., 1 P. 601; 37 L. J., P. & M. 42).

§ 23.

But a covenant not to sue in respect of previous misconduct will not debar the covenantor from pleading such misconduct *by way of answer* to a suit by the other party for judicial separation on account of the misconduct of the covenantor subsequently to the execution of the deed. "The view of the law in the present day, no doubt, is that, as the parties can compromise and agree to compromise a suit, so they can agree not to bring it, or can agree not to put forward specified matters as foundation for it. But it is altogether another thing to say, and I do not think that any of the last-mentioned cases show, that the parties can by any arrangement between themselves dictate to the Court on what principle relief sought is to be granted. If it is a rule that an adulterous spouse cannot obtain a judicial separation or dissolution except under certain special circumstances recognized by judicial authority, the parties, surely, cannot by any agreement relax or modify that rule. They may contract themselves out of their rights, but they cannot contract the Court out of its duty. That would be to make a law for themselves" (Jeune, P., *Gooch* v. *Gooch*, (1893) P. at pp. 106, 107). It was, therefore, held that a covenant by the husband not to sue in respect of his wife's previous adultery did not debar him, in a subsequent suit by the wife for judicial separation, from setting up her previous adultery as a defence to the suit, and as disentitling her to the relief sought.

So, where the parties had been living apart under a deed of separation, and the husband sued for dissolution of marriage on the ground of the wife's adultery, and the jury found all the issues in favour of the wife, who had counter-charged for cruelty and prayed for a judicial separation, it was held that the institution of the suit by the husband remitted the wife to the position which she held before the deed of separation, and that being the successful party, she was entitled to the full remedy allowed by law, viz., a decree of judicial separation (*Brown* v. *Brown and Shelton*, L. R., 3 P. 202; 43 L. J., P. & M. 47).

A covenant not to sue in respect of future adultery, that is to say, a covenant which practically amounts to a full licence to the other party to commit or live in adultery, would, no doubt, be held void *per se*, as being opposed to principles of social morality (Indian Contract Act, 1872, sect. 23). But though the covenant itself might not debar the covenantor from suing in respect of such future adultery, it would probably be held

§ 23.

that the conduct of the covenantor amounted to either connivance at the adultery, or to such wilful neglect and misconduct as conduced to the offence, and, therefore, disentitled the husband or wife from claiming relief.

(h) *Res judicata.*

(h) A plea of *res judicata*, if established, is an absolute bar to any suit. As to what amounts to *res judicata* or to an estoppel, see Appendix (D.), " *Res Judicata.*"

In this connection, however, it may be added that if in a suit for judicial separation on the ground of desertion for two years or upwards, the actual fact of an abandonment is proved, but it is not proved that the desertion has been for the full statutory period of two years, the Court may either adjourn the case until the time when the statutory period has elapsed (sect. 54, *post;* cf. *Wood* v. *Wood*, 13 P. D. 22 ; 57 L. J., P. & M. 48), or may allow the suit to be withdrawn with liberty to bring another suit when the period is complete (Civil Procedure Code, 1882, sect. 373; cf. *Lapington* v. *Lapington*, 14 P. D. 21 ; 58 L. J., P. & M. 26).

Separated wife to be deemed a spinster with respect to after-acquired property.

24. In every case of a judicial separation under this Act the wife shall, from the date of the sentence, and whilst the separation continues, be considered as unmarried with respect to property of every description which she may acquire, or which may come to or devolve upon her.

Such property may be disposed of by her in all respects as an unmarried woman, and on her decease the same shall, in case she dies intestate, go as the same would have gone if her husband had been then dead:

Provided that, if any such wife again cohabits with her husband, all such property as she may be entitled to when such cohabitation takes place shall be held to her separate use, subject, however, to any agreement in writing made between herself and her husband whilst separate.

The Matrimonial Causes Act (20 & 21 Vict. c. 85), sect. 25, provides as follows :—

"In every case of a judicial separation the wife shall, from the date of the sentence and whilst the separation shall continue, be considered as a *feme sole* with respect to property of every description which she may acquire or which may come to or devolve upon her; and such property may be disposed of by her in all respects as a *feme sole*, and on her decease the same shall, in case she shall die intestate, go as the same would have gone if her husband had been then dead: provided, that if any such wife should again cohabit with her husband, all such property as she may be entitled to when such cohabitation shall take place shall be held to her separate use, subject, however, to any agreement in writing made between herself and her husband whilst separate."

§ 24.

These provisions extend to property vested in a wife as executrix, administratrix, or trustee since the sentence of separation or the commencement of the desertion (Matrimonial Causes Act, 1858 (21 & 22 Vict. c. 108), sect. 7).

" Property of every description ":

By sect. 4 of the Indian Succession Act, 1865, "no person shall, by marriage, acquire any interest in the property of the person whom he or she marries, nor become incapable of doing any act in respect of his or her own property which he or she could have done if unmarried."

Property belonging to married woman.

This section, however, does not apply to (1) any marriage previous to 1st January, 1866, or to (2) any marriage, one or both of the parties to which professed, at the time of marriage, the Hindu, Muhammadan, Buddhist, Sikh, or Jaina religion (Act III of 1874, s. 2), or to (3) marriages between persons neither of whom is at the time of marriage domiciled in British India (sect. 44 of the Indian Succession Act, 1865; cf. *Miller* v. *Administrator-General of Bengal*, I. L. R., i Calc. 412).

Under the Married Women's Property Act of India, 1874, the wages and earnings of a married woman are her separate property, and she can be sued and sue in her own name in respect of any property which, under that Act or the Indian Succession Act, is her separate property. Act III of 1874 applies even to persons whose domicil is not British India (*Allumuddy* v. *Braham*, I. L. R., iv Calc. 140). But, except in the cases provided for by the Indian Succession Act, and the Married Women's Property Act of India, the property of a married woman, acquired by her after a decree of judicial separation, would continue to be at the mercy of her husband, and, even in cases provided for by the said Acts, he would be entitled to succeed to such property on her death intestate in the same

§ 24.

manner and to the same extent as if there had been no judicial separation. Sect. 24 of the Indian Divorce Act, however, provides that, after the date of the decree for judicial separation, the husband has no right or interest of any kind in any property which the wife may thereafter acquire or which may thereafter come to or devolve upon her, and that upon her death intestate all such property shall devolve as though her husband had been then dead.

To what property sect. 24 applies.

It is to be noticed that it is only to property which the wife may acquire or which may come to or devolve upon her *after the date of the decree* that sect. 24 applies. It has no application to such property as the wife is entitled to *in possession* at the date of the decree (*Waite* v. *Morland*, 38 Ch. D. 135; 57 L. J., Ch. 655—C. A.; *Hill* v. *Cooper*, (1893) 2 Q. B. 85; 62 L. J., Q. B. 423).

Wife's choses in action.

But the wife's *choses in action*, not reduced into possession at the date of the decree (*Wells* v. *Malben*, 31 Beav. 48; 31 L. J., Ch. 344; *Johnson* v. *Lander*, L. R., 7 Eq. 228; 38 L. J., Ch. 229), and all property to which she is entitled *in reversion* at the said date and which subsequently falls into possession (*Insole, In re*, L. R., 1 Eq. 470; 35 L. J., Ch. 177), become under this section her absolute property as if she were a *feme sole*.

After a decree of judicial separation, a wife, who had covenanted in her marriage settlement to settle whatever property she might acquire during the intended coverture, became entitled to certain stocks, and it was held that they belonged to her absolutely and that the covenant to settle had become inoperative (*Dawes* v. *Crayke*, 30 Ch. D. 500; 54 L. J., Ch. 1096).

Effect of decree on restraint against anticipation.

A decree of judicial separation has the effect of removing a restraint on anticipation imposed on property settled to the separate use of a married woman (*Munt* v. *Glynes*, 41 L. J., Ch. 639). But the restraint will revive immediately on the cessation of the separation, unless in the interval she has altered the form of investment effected by the original trust (see Eversley's Domestic Relations, p. 419).

There is a noticeable difference in the wording of sect. 24 and of sect. 27 (as to protection orders). Under the former it is "*from the date of the sentence*" that the woman is to be regarded as a *feme sole*, whereas under the latter it is *from the date of the desertion* that the protection order has effect. That is to say, the protection order has retrospective effect, and protects property which she may have acquired or become possessed of prior to the date of the order but after the desertion commenced. But a protection order will not enable the wife to maintain an action for damage to the property so protected, which was commenced before the order was passed (*Midland Rail. Co.* v. *Pye*, 10 C. B., N. S. 179).

§ 24.

The definition of "property" in sect. 3 of the Indian Divorce Act effects the object of sect. 7 of the Matrimonial Causes Act, 1858, which extends the provisions respecting the property of a wife who has been judicially separated or deserted, to "property to which such wife has become, or shall become, entitled as executrix, administratrix, or trustee, since the separation or the commencement of the desertion, as the case may be."

" **As the same would have gone if her husband had been then dead** ":

Husband loses all interest in or right to wife's property.

The husband of a wife who has been judicially separated from him is thus deprived of all rights to, or interests in, such property as the wife may have acquired or which may have come to or devolved upon her after the date of the decree. If, therefore, the wife dies intestate, letters of administration as to such property will be granted to her next of kin, and not to her husband (*Re the goods of Worman*, 29 L. J., P. & M. 164; 1 S. & T. 513). And this, too, though the decree had been made at the instance of the husband, though on what ground an innocent husband should be deprived of all right of succession to the wife's property of the kind specified it is difficult to understand. It certainly seems anomalous that a man who has become compelled by (*e.g.*) his wife's cruelty to seek for, and obtain, a decree of judicial separation, should for that reason alone lose any right which he might otherwise have had to succeed to her after-acquired property. Moreover, it would seem only fair that, if during such separation the husband were to die, the widow's claim to administration should be refused; but, apparently, the decree of judicial separation will not affect her rights of succession to, or administration of, her husband's property (*Re the goods of Davis*, 2 Cust. 628; see Lush's Husband and Wife, p. 97).

25. In every case of a judicial separation under this Act, the wife shall, whilst so separated, be considered as an unmarried woman for the purposes of contract, and wrongs and injuries, and suing and being sued in any civil proceeding; and her husband shall not be

Separated wife to be deemed a spinster for purposes of contract and suing.

R. M

§ 25. liable in respect of any contract, act or costs entered into, done, omitted or incurred by her during the separation:

Provided that where, upon any such judicial separation, alimony has been decreed or ordered to be paid to the wife, and the same is not duly paid by the husband, he shall be liable for necessaries supplied for her use.

Provided also that nothing shall prevent the wife from joining, at any time during such separation, in the exercise of any joint power given to herself and her husband.

Section 26 of the Matrimonial Causes Act, 1857 (20 & 21 Vict. c. 85), provides that :—

"In every case of a judicial separation the wife shall, whilst so separated, be considered as a *feme sole* for the purposes of contract, and wrongs and injuries, and suing and being sued in any civil proceeding ; and her husband shall not be liable in respect of any engagement or contract she may have entered into, or for any wrongful act or omission by her, or for any costs she may incur as plaintiff or defendant ; provided, that where upon any such judicial separation alimony has been decreed or ordered to be paid to the wife, and the same shall not be duly paid by the husband, he shall be liable for necessaries supplied for her use; provided also, that nothing shall prevent the wife from joining, at any time during such separation, in the exercise of any joint power given to herself and her husband."

Whilst so separated.

"**The wife shall, whilst so separated, be considered as an unmarried woman**":

Apart from the provisions of the Married Women's Property Act of India (III of 1874), it is only whilst the wife is so separated and in respect of causes of action accruing *during such separation* that the husband is freed from all liability. He would remain liable in respect of any contract, act, or costs done, omitted or incurred by her previous to the decree for judicial separation, nor could she be sued or sue in respect thereof.

Power of Court to grant wife an allowance.

"**Alimony has been decreed or ordered**":

In England, as a general rule, the Court will refuse to grant the husband a decree of judicial separation on the ground of the wife's cruelty unless he makes a suitable provision for her maintenance (*Forth* v. *Forth*, 36 L. J., P. & M. 122). But, apparently, under sect. 37 of the Indian Divorce Act, the Court has power to order permanent alimony to be paid to the wife only in cases where the decree of judicial separation has been obtained by her (see sect. 37, *post*).

§ 25.

"Necessaries":

"Necessaries."

It is only where the husband has been ordered, but has failed, to pay alimony to his wife that he is liable, after a decree of judicial separation, for "necessaries supplied for her use."

As to what are, and are not, "necessaries" no fixed rule can be laid down. "Necessaries is a relative word, varying with the rank, profession, position, and fortune of the parties; that which might be necessary for a peeress would be extravagant and wasteful luxury for the wife of a village apothecary. In order to protect creditors, the Court will permit the test of the position which the parties have chosen to assume and parade, and not their real pecuniary means and resources, for the purpose of ascertaining whether the articles supplied are, or are not, necessaries. Necessaries are things which cannot well be dispensed with, and, as applied to a wife, things which it is reasonable she should enjoy, and not merely articles which she is compelled to purchase. That which is a necessary at one time may not be so at another.... It is, however, an elastic term, and many things are described by it which, in popular language, could hardly be termed necessaries, but have been brought within the category in order to further the ends of justice" (Eversley's Domestic Relations, p. 281).

But, though in ordinary cases the Court will, in considering whether anything is or is not a necessary, regard rather the position which the parties have chosen to assume or parade than their actual position, it would hardly be fair to adopt this test when the question is with reference to articles purchased by a wife who has been judicially separated from her husband. In the latter case, the Court would probably hold the husband liable only for such things as are reasonably necessary for a person of the actual position of the wife.

Money borrowed to pay for necessaries may itself be a necessary (*Ex parte Vernall*, 10 M. B. R. 8; but see *Knox* v. *Bushell*, 3 C. B., N. S. 334).

A wife is entitled to pledge her husband's credit for all the costs, as between solicitor and client, reasonably incurred by

§ 25. her in respect of the institution of a divorce suit against her husband (*Ottaway* v. *Hamilton*, 3 C. P. D. 393).

Reversal of Decree of Separation.

Decree of separation obtained during the absence of husband or wife may be reversed.

26. Any husband or wife, upon the application of whose wife or husband, as the case may be, a decree of judicial separation has been pronounced, may, at any time thereafter, present a petition to the Court by which the decree was pronounced, praying for a reversal of such decree, on the ground that it was obtained in his or her absence, and that there was reasonable excuse for the alleged desertion, where desertion was the ground of such decree.

The Court may, on being satisfied of the truth of the allegations of such petition, reverse the decree accordingly; but such reversal shall not prejudice or affect the rights or remedies which any other person would have had, in case it had not been decreed, in respect of any debts, contracts, or acts of the wife incurred, entered into, or done between the times of the sentence of separation and of the reversal thereof.

Matrimonial Causes Act, 1857 (20 & 21 Vict. c. 85), sect. 23, is similarly worded. See Rules of the English Divorce Court, Nos. 63, 64, 65, 66; see also Form, No. 10. Sects. 8 and 10 of the Matrimonial Causes Act, 1858 (21 & 22 Vict. c. 108), protect and indemnify all persons in respect of rights and remedies which they would have had if such decree had not been reversed, and as regards payments, &c. made to the wife after reversal of the decree, provided they had not at the time notice of such reversal.

Reversal of decree.

"**Reversal of decree of separation**":

If, after a decree of judicial separation, the husband and wife resume cohabitation, the decree is *ipso facto* annulled (see Thicknesse's Husband and Wife, p. 175).

§ 26.

"In his or her absence":

"Absence."

This means non-appearance in the suit, and not absence without knowledge or notice of the suit. But in a petition for reversal of a decree of judicial separation it is not sufficient to allege the non-appearance of the respondent in the former suit; the causes of such non-appearance and circumstances tending to show that the decree was wrong on the merits must be set out in the petition (*Phillips* v. *Phillips*, L. R., 1 P. 169; 35 L. J., P. & M. 70).

"Such reversal shall not prejudice":

See also sect. 60, *post*.

VI.—*Protection Orders.*

27. Any wife to whom the fourth section of the Indian Succession Act, 1865, does not apply, may, when deserted by her husband, present a petition to the District Court or the High Court, at any time after such desertion, for an order to protect any property which she may have acquired or may acquire, and any property of which she may have become possessed or may become possessed after such desertion, against her husband or his creditors, or any person claiming under him.

Deserted wife may apply to the Court for protection.

The Matrimonial Causes Act, 1858 (21 & 22 Vict. c. 108), s. 6, provides that—

> "Every wife deserted by her husband, wheresoever resident in England, may, at any time after such desertion, apply to the said judge ordinary for an order to protect any money or property in England she may have acquired or may acquire by her own lawful industry, and any property she may have become possessed of or may become possessed of after such desertion, against her husband and his creditors, and any person claiming under him; and the judge ordinary shall exercise in respect of every such application all the powers conferred upon the Court for Divorce and Matrimonial Causes under the twentieth and twenty-first Victoria, chapter eighty-five, section twenty-one."

§ 27. Under sect. 21 of the Matrimonial Causes Act, 1857 (20 & 21 Vict. c. 85)—

"A wife deserted by her husband may, at any time after such desertion, if resident within the metropolitan district, apply to a police magistrate, or, if resident in the country, to justices in petty sessions, or in either case to the Court for an order to protect any money or property she may acquire by her own lawful industry, and property which she may become possessed of, after such desertion, against her husband or his creditors, or any person claiming under him; and such magistrate or justices or Court, if satisfied of the fact of such desertion, and that the same was without reasonable cause, and that the wife is maintaining herself by her own industry or property, may make and give to the wife an order protecting her earnings and property acquired since the commencement of such desertion, from her husband and all creditors and persons claiming under him, and such earnings and property shall belong to the wife as if she were a *feme sole:* Provided always, that every such order, if made by a police magistrate or justices at petty sessions, shall, within ten days after the making thereof, be entered with the registrar of the county court within whose jurisdiction the wife is resident; and that it shall be lawful for the husband, and any creditor or other person claiming under him, to apply to the Court, or to the magistrate or justices by whom such order was made, for the discharge thereof: Provided also, that if the husband or any creditor of or person claiming under the husband shall seize or continue to hold any property of the wife after notice of any such order, he shall be liable, at the suit of the wife (which she is hereby empowered to bring), to restore the specific property, and also for a sum equal to double the value of the property so seized or held after such notice as aforesaid: If any such order of protection be made, the wife shall during the continuance thereof be and be deemed to have been, during such desertion of her, in the like position in all respects, with regard to property and contracts, and suing and being sued, as she would be under this Act if she obtained a decree of judicial separation."

By sect. 1 of the Matrimonial Causes Act, 1864 (27 & 28 Vict. c. 44), it is provided that if any such magistrate shall have died or been removed or become incapable of acting, the successor in office of such magistrate may discharge the order of protection; and that an order for discharge or any order for protection may be applied for to and be granted by the Court, although the order for protection was not made by the Court; and that an order for protection made at one petty sessions may be discharged by the justices of any later petty sessions or by the Court.

See Rules of the English Divorce Court, Nos. 124, 125, and 197.

PROTECTION ORDERS.

"Any wife to whom the fourth section of the Indian Succession Act, 1865, does not apply":

The reason for this is that a wife to whom the fourth section of the Indian Succession Act, 1865, *does* apply, is sufficiently protected as regards her property by the provisions of that section, which are as follows:—" No person shall by marriage acquire any interest in the property of the person whom he or she marries, or become incapable of doing any act in respect of his or her own property which he or she could have done if unmarried."

The said section does not apply, *as regards moveable property*, to the following (cf. *sect.* 44 *of the Indian Succession Act*, 1865; and see *Miller* v. *Administrator-General of Bengal, I. L. R.,* i *Calc.* 412):—

(a) A wife who was married before 1st January, 1866; or

(b) A wife who, together with her husband, was at the time of marriage domiciled out of British India; or

(c) A wife who was married out of British India, whether the domicil of herself alone *or* of her husband alone at the time of marriage was in British India; or (*as regards all property*)

* (d) A wife who, or whose husband, at the time of marriage, professed the Hindu, Muhammadan, Buddhist, Sikh or Jaina religion (Married Women's Property Act of India, 1874, s. 2).

Accordingly, *as regards moveable property*, sect. 4 of the Indian Succession Act, 1865, will apply (apart from the provisions of sect. 2 of the Married Women's Property Act of India, 1874) to any wife who, being married after the 31st December, 1865, (a) was at the time of marriage domiciled in British India, *provided* that, if the marriage was not solemnized in British India, her husband was also at the time of marriage domiciled in British India; (b) was at the time of marriage domiciled out of British India, but was married in British India to a husband

§ 27.
Sect. 4 of Indian Succession Act, 1865.

To whom not applicable.

To whom applicable.

---

* As to whether the Courts can give relief, *under the Indian Divorce Act*, to a petitioner in respect of a marriage contracted under a system of law which permits polygamy, see *ante*, pp. 4, 5. In such cases, though the Courts might refuse to grant a decree of dissolution or nullity of marriage, or of judicial separation, or of restitution of conjugal rights, they might possibly grant a wife who, at the time of presenting her petition, professed Christianity, an order of protection under this section. This is, however, doubtful.

§ 27.

who at the time of marriage was domiciled in British India; (c) was at the time of marriage domiciled in British India and was married in British India to a husband who, at the time of marriage, was domiciled out of British India.

As regards the immoveable property of the wife.—Sect. 4 of the Indian Succession Act, 1865, enunciates the *lex loci* of British India, and will therefore apply in every case to immoveable property, situate in British India, and belonging to a wife who was married after the 31st December, 1865, and did not at the time of marriage herself profess, or marry a man who at the time of marriage professed, the Hindu, Muhammadan, Buddhist, Sikh, or Jaina religion (see *Miller* v. *Administrator-General of Bengal, ubi supra*).

Married Women's Property Act of India, 1874.

It is further provided by the Married Women's Property Act of India (III of 1874) that the wages and earnings of any married woman, acquired or gained by her after the passing of the Act (*i.e.*, the 24th of February, 1874), in any employment, occupation, or trade, carried on by her, and not by her husband, and also any money or other property acquired by her through the exercise of any literary, artistic, or scientific skill, and all savings from and investments of such wages, earnings, and property, shall be deemed to be her separate property, and her receipts alone shall be good discharges for such wages, earnings, and property, and that she may sue and be sued in respect of all property which is her separate property under Act III of 1874 or the Indian Succession Act of 1865.

"Petition."

"Present a petition":

Court fee stamp.

Such petition must bear a Court fee stamp of Rs. 20 (Court Fees Act, 1870, 2nd Sch., Art. 20).

As regards the practice of the English Court in these matters, see rules of the English Divorce Court, Nos. 124, 125, and 197.

The petition (see Form No. XI) must be supported by an affidavit on the part of the wife (*Ex parte Hall*, 27 L. J., P. & M. 19), and must state facts to satisfy the Court of the fact of the desertion; it is not enough merely to state that the husband has deserted the wife (*Ex parte Sewell*, 28 L. J., P. & M. 8). And if the husband's whereabouts are known the petition should be served on him (*Matthew* v. *Matthew*, 19 L. T. 662). See also sect. 50, *post*.

"After such desertion":

§ 27.

As to "Desertion," generally, see note to sect. 10, *ante*.

"Desertion." Not necessarily for two years.

The desertion here spoken of need not have been for two years, but it must be continuous, and a *bonâ fide* offer on the part of the husband to return and provide for the wife will, even if made at the time when she claims the order, deprive her of her right to it (*Cargill* v. *Cargill*, 1 S. & T. 235).

The desertion must have been "without reasonable excuse" (sect. 28). Such excuse need not necessarily be the commission of a matrimonial offence by the wife, but it must be grave and weighty (see cases cited under sect. 10, *ante*).

The mere fact that the husband makes the wife an allowance does not alter the character of an inexcusable withdrawal from cohabitation on his part (*Yeatman* v. *Yeatman*, L. R., 1 P. 489; 37 L. J., P. & M. 37).

"Property which she may have acquired," &c.:

Property acquired by wife.

Sect. 21 of the Matrimonial Causes Act, 1857, and sect. 6 of the Matrimonial Causes Act, 1858, speak of property which "she may have acquired or may acquire *by her own lawful industry*." It has accordingly been held in England that property acquired by keeping a brothel is not protected (*Mason* v. *Mitchell*, 3 H. & C. 528; 34 L. Ex. 68).

A protection order obtained by a married woman who has been deserted by her husband constitutes her a *feme sole* in respect only of such property as she may have acquired or may acquire, or of which she may have become or may become possessed after such desertion; it has no effect on property which she may have acquired or become possessed of previously to the desertion (*Hill* v. *Cooper*, (1893) 2 Q. B. 85; 62 L. J., Q. B. 423).

Protection only extends to property acquired after desertion.

But where a wife is, before such desertion, entitled to *choses in action* which are not reduced into possession till after the desertion, such property will be protected by an order under sect. 28 (*In re Coward*, L. R., 20 Eq. 179; 44 L. J., Ch. 384; *Nicholson* v. *Drury Building Co.*, 7 Ch. D. 48; 47 L. J., Ch. 192).

Choses in action.

The definition of "property" in sect. 3 of the Indian Divorce Act effects the object of sect. 7 of the Matrimonial Causes Act, 1858, which extends the operation of orders of protection to property which becomes vested in a married woman as executrix, administratrix, or trustee, after the date of the commencement of the desertion.

28. The Court, if satisfied of the fact of such desertion, and that the same was without reasonable excuse, and that the wife is maintaining herself by her own industry or property, may make and give to the wife an order protecting her earnings and other property from her husband and all creditors and persons claiming under him. Every such order shall state the time at which the desertion commenced, and shall, as regards all persons dealing with the wife in reliance thereon, be conclusive as to such time.

Court may grant protection order.

For the corresponding provisions of the English statutes, see under sect. 27, *ante;* sect. 9 of the Matrimonial Causes Act, 1858 (21 & 22 Vict. c. 108), further provides that "*every order . . . shall state the time at which the desertion in consequence whereof the order is made commenced; and the order shall, as regards all persons dealing with such wife in reliance thereon, be conclusive as to the time when such desertion commenced.*" Sect. 7 of the said Act extends the operation of such orders to property "*to which such wife has become or shall become entitled as executrix, administratrix, or trustee, since . . . the commencement of the desertion; and the death of the testator or intestate shall be deemed to be the time when such wife became entitled as executrix or administratrix.*" Sect. 8 of the said Act enacts that an order for protection of earnings or property shall be deemed valid until reversed or discharged, and that no right or remedies prior to reversal or discharge shall be prejudiced by such reversal or discharge, and sect. 10 protects and indemnifies all persons acting on faith of the order without notice of its discharge, reversal or variation.

Form of order.

"**An order**":

The order should be in general terms, as the Court has no power to decide what title the wife may have to specific property (*Ex parte Mullineaux,* 1 S. & T. 77; 27 L. J., P. & M. 19).

But the mere fact that such order is limited in its terms will not exclude from its operation property, not therein specified, which falls into her possession after the desertion (cf. *In re Whittingham's Trusts,* 10 L. T. 368).

29. The husband or any creditor of, or person claiming under, him may apply to the Court by which such order was made for the discharge or variation thereof, and the Court, if the desertion has ceased, or if for any other reason it think fit so to do, may discharge or vary the order accordingly.

<small>Discharge or variation of orders.</small>

For the corresponding provision of the English statute, see under sect. 27, *ante*.

For the practice of the English Court, see Rule, No. 125, of the Rules of the English Divorce Court.

"**May apply to the Court**":

It is only the Court which granted the order that can discharge or vary it (cf. *Ex parte Sharpe*, 43 L. J., M. C. 152).

<small>"Apply to the Court."</small>

It is open to the husband or creditor, or person claiming under the husband, to apply at any time for the discharge of the order of protection (*Ex parte Hall*, 27 L. J., P. & M. 19).

<small>Application may be made at any time.</small>

Nor need the application be made during the lifetime of the wife. Therefore, a claim to pronounce against the validity of the will of a married woman who had obtained a protection order, and a counter-claim to discharge the said order, may be included in the same action (*Madge* v. *Adams*, 6 P. D. 54; 50 L. J., P. & M. 49).

30. If the husband or any creditor of, or person claiming under, the husband seizes or continues to hold any property of the wife after notice of any such order, he shall be liable, at the suit of the wife (which she is hereby empowered to bring), to return or deliver to her the specific property, and also to pay her a sum equal to double its value.

<small>Liability of husband seizing his wife's property after notice of order.</small>

For the corresponding provision in the English statute, see under sect. 27, *ante*.

31. So long as any such order of protection remains in force, the wife shall be and be deemed to have been, during such desertion of her, in the like position in all

<small>Wife's legal position during continuance of order.</small>

§ 31.

respects, with regard to property and contracts and suing and being sued, as she would be under this Act if she obtained a decree of judicial separation.

For the corresponding provision in the English statute, see under sect. 27, *ante*.

Protection order, effect of.

"**So long as any such order of protection remains in force**":

A protection order has a retrospective effect and dates back to the commencement of the desertion. Therefore, where a married woman, after being deserted by her husband, acquired certain property by her own exertions, which she disposed of by will, and, subsequently to the making of the will, obtained an order of protection, it was held that the will was a valid instrument to pass the said property (*In re the goods of Elliott*, L. R., 2 P. 274; 40 L. J., P. & M. 76).

A married woman, who has obtained an order of protection, can maintain an action for libel in her own name (*Ramsden* v. *Brearley*, L. R., 10 Q. B. 147; 44 L. J., Q. B. 46). And she can maintain an action in respect of her earnings, although she has been living in adultery ever since the desertion (*Thomas* v. *Head*, 2 F. & F. 88).

But, apparently, an order of protection of a married woman's property will not enable her to maintain an action for injuries to such property which was commenced before the date of the order (*Midland Rail. Co.* v. *Pye*, 10 C. B., N. S. 179).

A woman, who has obtained an order of protection, is entitled to payment of a fund in Court representing a legacy bequeathed to her after the desertion but previous to the order (*In re Kingsley*, 26 Beav. 84; cf. also *Cooke* v. *Fuller*, 26 Beav. 99).

Continuing liability of husband.

Continuing liability of husband.—It is to be noticed that, whereas, in the case of a judicial separation, the husband is not liable "in respect of any contract, act, or costs entered into, done, omitted or incurred" by the wife during such separation, unless he has been ordered to pay her alimony and has failed to do so, when he is liable for "necessaries" supplied to her use (sect. 25), the husband of a woman who has obtained a protection order is not thereby freed from liability to contribute towards her maintenance (*Oxford Guardians* v. *Barton*, 33 L. T.

375). It appears, however, that a wife, who has obtained such order, has no longer any authority to pledge her husband's credit (*Hakewell* v. *Hakewell*, 30 L. J., P. & M. 255), but she does not thereby deprive herself of her right to alimony *pendente lite* in a suit subsequently instituted by her for dissolution of marriage (*ibid.*, and sect. 36, *post*).

§ 31.

Death of wife intestate.—Where a wife, who had obtained an order of protection, died intestate during her husband's lifetime, the Court granted letters of administration limited to such property as she had acquired or become possessed of since the desertion, without specifying of what that property consisted, to one of her next-of-kin and not to her husband (*In re goods of Worman*, 1 S. & T. 513; 29 L. J., P. & M. 164; cf. *In re goods of Weir*, 2 S. & T. 451; 31 L. J., P. & M. 88).

Death of wife intestate.

VII.—*Restitution of Conjugal Rights.*

32. When either the husband or the wife has, without reasonable excuse, withdrawn from the society of the other, either wife or husband may apply, by petition to the District Court or the High Court, for restitution of conjugal rights, and the Court, on being satisfied of the truth of the statements made in such petition, and that there is no legal ground why the application should not be granted, may decree restitution of conjugal rights accordingly.

Petition for restitution of conjugal rights.

For the corresponding provision in the English statute, see under sect. 23, *ante*.

The Matrimonial Causes Act, 1884 (47 & 48 Vict. c. 68), sect. 5, further provides that—

"If the respondent shall fail to comply with a decree of the Court for restitution of conjugal rights, such respondent shall thereupon be deemed to have been guilty of desertion without reasonable cause, and a suit for judicial separation may forthwith be instituted, and a sentence of judicial separation may be pronounced although the period of two years may not have elapsed since the failure to comply with the decree for restitution of conjugal rights; and when any husband who has been guilty of desertion by failure on his part to comply with a decree for restitution of conjugal

§ 32.

rights has also been guilty of adultery, the wife may forthwith present a petition for dissolution of her marriage, and the Court may pronounce a decree *nisi* for the dissolution of the marriage on the grounds of adultery coupled with desertion. Such decree *nisi* shall not be made absolute until after the expiration of six calendar months from the pronouncing thereof, unless the Court shall fix a shorter time."

By sect. 5 of the said Act the English Court has power—

"At any time before final decree on any application for restitution of conjugal rights, or after final decree, if the respondent shall fail to comply therewith, upon application for that purpose," to "make from time to time all such orders and provisions with respect to the custody, maintenance, and education of the children of the petitioner and respondent as might have been made by interim orders during the pendency of a trial for judicial separation between the same parties."

See also Rules of the English Divorce Court, Nos. 175 and 176.

Petition.

Court fee stamp.

Written demand for cohabitation.

"May apply by petition":

Every petition for restitution of conjugal rights must bear a Court fee stamp of Rs. 20 (Court Fees Act, 1870, 2nd Sch., Art. 20), must be duly verified by the petitioner or some other competent person (sect. 47, *post*), and must be served on the respondent, unless the Court dispenses with such service (sect. 50, *post*).

According to the practice of the English Court it is also necessary that the petition should be accompanied by an affidavit made by the petitioner verifying the facts of which he or she has personal cognizance and deposing as to belief in the truth of the other facts alleged in the petition (rule 2). Such affidavit must further state sufficient facts to satisfy one of the registrars that a written demand for cohabitation and restitution of conjugal rights has been made by the petitioner upon the party to be cited, and that after a reasonable opportunity of compliance therewith such cohabitation and restitution of conjugal rights have been withheld (rule 175). It is probable that the Courts of this country will adopt these rules. It may, therefore, be pointed out that such written demand need not be made by the petitioner, but may be made by a solicitor on his or her behalf. No particular form is necessary, but the demand must be of a *conciliatory* character. Where, therefore, without any previous friendly communication between the parties, the wife's solicitor wrote demanding restitution of conjugal rights on her behalf, and threatened legal proceedings in default, it was held that such a letter did not sufficiently comply with the rule (*Field* v. *Field*, 14 P. D. 26; 58 L. J., P. & M. 21; cf. *Mason* v. *Mason*, 61 L. T. 304; *Smith* v. *Smith*, 15 P. D. 47; 59 L. J., P. & M. 9).

§ 32.

If the whereabouts of the respondent are not known and cannot be discovered, the demand may be served on his or her solicitor (*Macarthur* v. *Macarthur*, 58 L. J., P. & M. 70).

"**Restitution of conjugal rights**":

In a suit for restitution of conjugal rights, the Court has no jurisdiction to make a decree in the petitioner's favour until the marriage has been duly proved, even though the respondent may have filed an answer not taking issue on the marriage (*Scott* v. *Scott*, 4 S. & T. 113; 34 L. J., P. & M. 23; as to proof of marriage, see Appendix (A.), "*Proof of Marriage*").

Marriage must be proved.

But in an undefended suit the Court will not make a decree merely upon proof of the marriage; evidence must be given of the other facts, *e.g.*, the withdrawal from cohabitation without reasonable excuse (*Pearson* v. *Pearson*, 33 L. J., P. & M. 156).

Alimony pendente lite.

Alimony pending suit.

In a suit for restitution of conjugal rights, whether instituted by the husband or the wife, the wife is, as a general rule, entitled to alimony pending the suit (see sect. 36, and notes thereto).

"**No legal ground**":

"Legal ground."

As to this, see sect. 33, *post*, and notes thereto.

Under rule 176 of the English Divorce Court Rules the respondent may, at any time after commencement of the proceedings, apply for a stay of proceedings by reason that he or she is willing to resume or return to cohabitation.

"**May decree**":

In a defended case, once the marriage has been duly proved, the petitioner will be entitled to a decree unless the respondent can establish a legal defence to the petition. The motives of the petitioner are quite immaterial, and the Court has no discretion to inquire into his or her sincerity in bringing the suit (*Scott* v. *Scott*, 4 S. & T. 113; 34 L. J., P. & M. 23). And, as a matter of fact, suits for restitution of conjugal rights are but rarely brought for the purpose of recovering the society of the

Motives of petitioner

§ 32.

respondent. "I must further observe," remarked a learned judge of very great experience, "that so far are suits for restitution of conjugal rights from being in truth or in fact what theoretically they purport to be, proceedings for the purpose of insisting on the fulfilment of the obligation of married persons to live together, I have never known an instance in which it has appeared that the suit was instituted for any other purpose than to enforce a money demand" (*per* Hannen, P., *Marshall* v. *Marshall*, 5 P. D. at p. 23).

A husband who has been served with a decree in a suit for restitution of conjugal rights, ordering him to take his wife back, is bound to take the initiative by inviting her to return (*Alexander* v. *Alexander*, 2 S. & T. 385; 30 L. J., P. & M. 73).

Allowance by husband not sufficient compliance with decree.

And it is no sufficient compliance on his part with such decree to merely supply his wife with a suitable establishment and sufficient income (*Weldon* v. *Weldon*, 9 P. D. 52; 53 L. J., P. & M. 9).

Form of decree.

Form of Decree for restitution of Conjugal Rights.

If the respondent is the husband, the proper form of decree is that the husband "do take the petitioner home and receive her as his wife, and render her conjugal rights" (see *Weldon* v. *Weldon*, 9 P. D. at p. 53).

If the respondent is the wife, the proper form is simply that the wife do return "and live with the husband, and render him conjugal rights."

The Court has no power to direct that the wife be bodily handed over to her husband (*Mela Ram* v. *Thanooram*, 9 W. R. 552; *Koolur Khansama* v. *Jan Khansama*, 8 W. R. 467; *Toofeah* v. *Jussundu*, 2 Agra, 337).

Satisfaction of decree.

Satisfaction of decree.—A decree for restitution of conjugal rights must necessarily be limited as to time, and it is satisfied and incapable of further execution when once the respondent has complied with it with the *bonâ fide* intention of resuming cohabitation. The Court "cannot direct permanent cohabitation without regard to the possibilities of occurrences which might render it dangerous," or without regard to the possibilities of occurrences which might justify the respondent in refusing further cohabitation. But if, after duly complying with and satisfying the decree, the respondent refuses to render conjugal rights, and again leaves the petitioner's society, a fresh cause of action will arise, unless the respondent can prove a reasonable excuse for such subsequent withdrawal (cf. *Keshar Lal* v. *Bai Parvati*, I. L. R., xviii Bomb. 327).

§ 32.

In the event, therefore, of such subsequent withdrawal by the respondent from the petitioner's society, the proper course for the petitioner is not to apply for execution of the former decree (which has been duly satisfied), but to present a fresh petition for restitution of conjugal rights. But a decree is not satisfied by a merely colourable compliance with its terms, with the full intention of breaking off cohabitation at the very first opportunity.

Subsequent withdrawal from cohabitation.

Enforcement of decree for restitution of conjugal rights.— "When the party against whom a decree . . . . for restitution of conjugal rights . . . . has had an opportunity of obeying the decree, ... and has wilfully failed to obey it, the decree may be enforced by his" (or her) "imprisonment, or by the attachment of his" (or her) "property, or by both" (Civil Procedure Code, 1882, s. 260, *q. v.*).

Enforcement of decree.

The husband cannot take his wife by force and restrain her of her liberty until she is willing to render him conjugal rights (*Reg.* v. *Jackson*, (1891) 1 Q. B. 671; 60 L. J., Q. B. 346).

As to the effect of not complying with a decree for restitution of conjugal rights in England, see sect. 5 of the Matrimonial Causes Act, 1884 (*ante*, p. 173). Under that statute the English Court has also power to order the respondent, who fails to comply with such decree, to make a settlement on the petitioner (*Theobald* v. *Theobald*, 15 P. D. 26; 59 L. J., P. & M. 21). And this, too, even if the respondent is the wife, provided she possesses separate property of her own (*Swift* v. *Swift*, 15 P. D. 118; 59 L. J., P. & M. 61). But the English Court has no longer the power to enforce such decree by attachment (sect. 2 of the said statute).

33. Nothing shall be pleaded in answer to a petition for restitution of conjugal rights which would not be a ground for a suit for judicial separation or for a decree of nullity of marriage.

Answer to petition.

"**Nothing shall be pleaded in answer**":
This was the general rule of the old Ecclesiastical Courts (*Holmes* v. *Holmes*, 2 Lee 116; *Barlee* v. *Barlee*, 1 Add. 305), and

Answer to suit.

§ 33.

Sect. 33 subject to sect. 32.

is, with certain exceptions, the rule of the English Court of Divorce of the present day (*Burroughs* v. *Burroughs*, 2 S. & T. 303; 30 L. J., P. & M. 186; *Ricketts* v. *Ricketts*, 35 L. J., P. & M. 52; *Yeatman* v. *Yeatman*, L. R., 1 P. 489).

Despite the explicitness of its terms, sect. 33 is, it is submitted, subject to sect. 32, and presupposes that the petitioner has duly fulfilled the conditions therein laid down, namely, that it has been duly proved to the satisfaction of the Court (1) that the petitioner is at the time of suit the husband or wife of the respondent; in other words, that there is between the petitioner and respondent a valid and subsisting marriage tie; and (2) that the respondent has withdrawn from the petitioner's society "without reasonable excuse."

That the respondent is competent to traverse each of these allegations can scarcely admit of doubt. For instance, it must be open to the respondent to dispute the *factum* of the marriage —to deny that the parties were ever legally married, or to prove that, though once legally married, they have since been divorced by a Court of competent jurisdiction. And it would seem to be equally clear that he or she can put the petitioner to the proof that (a) a withdrawal from petitioner's society has actually taken place, and (b) that such withdrawal, if proved, was without reasonable excuse. Even if the respondent is debarred from pleading, in answer to the petition and as an excuse for the withdrawal, anything which would not be a ground for judicial separation or for a decree of nullity of marriage, there is nothing, it seems, to prevent him or her from cross-examining the petitioner as to the matters which led to such withdrawal, or from giving evidence himself or herself on the point. Whether or not, when once a valid subsisting marriage has been duly proved and the respondent's withdrawal has also been proved or admitted, the Court will regard anything short of a distinct matrimonial offence on the part of the petitioner as a sufficient "*legal ground*" why the application should not be granted, is a question which awaits solution.

In England,* under peculiar circumstances, which do not exist in India, the Court will refuse to grant restitution of conjugal rights to a petitioner whose "conduct has led to desertion by the respondent and has amounted to sufficient cause to disentitle the petitioner to maintain a suit for judicial separation

---

* *I.e.* to say that a respondent who fails to comply with a decree of restitution of conjugal rights is deemed to have been guilty of such desertion as will entitle the petitioner to a decree of judicial separation.

on the ground of desertion" (Gorell Barnes, J., *Oldroyd* v. *Oldroyd*, (1896) P. 175). Accordingly, though it does not amount to legal cruelty for a wife to bring, and persist in making, the most infamous charges against her husband, well knowing the same to be absolutely untrue, the Court will allow the husband, in a suit by such wife for restitution of conjugal rights, to plead such conduct on her part as a bar to her suit (*Russell v. *Russell*, (1895) P. (A. C.) 315; 64 L. J., P. & M. 105).

§ 33.

And a husband has also been allowed to plead by way of answer that the wife has made his home uncomfortable; that she has systematically aggravated him in the hope that he would retaliate with some act of violence which would entitle her to a judicial separation, and that they had separated by mutual consent (*Woodsey* v. *Woodsey*, 31 L. T. 647; cf. *Stace* v. *Stace*, 37 L. J., P. & M. 51).

But under English law (Matrimonial Causes Act, 1884, s. 5), a respondent who fails to comply with a decree for restitution is at once guilty of such desertion as will enable the other party to obtain a judicial separation by reason thereof. Inasmuch, therefore, as a petitioner whose conduct would have disentitled him or her to a decree of judicial separation, cannot obtain the latter relief directly, the Court bases its refusal to grant him or her a decree for restitution on the ground that it will not grant relief indirectly which it would not grant directly. At the same time it does not seem to be in accordance with the principles of ordinary justice to compel a respondent, whose conduct in withdrawing from the petitioner's society the Court admits to be only natural and reasonable, to resume a cohabitation which is likely to be fraught with the greatest misery to a perfectly innocent party. As remarked by Lord Herschell, C., in a recent Scotch case in the House of Lords, "it is certain that a spouse may, without having committed an offence which would justify a decree of separation, have so acted as to deserve the reprobation of all right-minded members of the community. Take the case of a husband who has heaped insults upon his wife, but has just stopped short at that which the law regards as *sævitia* or cruelty; can he, when his own misconduct has led his wife to separate herself from him, come into Court, and, avowing his misdeeds,

---

* The decision of the Court of Appeal has very recently been upheld by a majority of the House of Lords (Lords Herschell, Watson, Macnaghten, Shand and Davey; Lords Halsbury, Hobhouse, Ashbourne and Morris *dissentientibus*).

§ 33.

insist that it is bound to give him a decree of adherence ? . . . Might not the Court refuse its aid to one who has so acted and regard his conduct as a bar to his claim to relief ? " (*Mackenzie* v. *Mackenzie*, (1895) A. C. at p. 389).

Possibly, therefore, the Courts of this country will hold that it is a condition precedent to the grant of relief that the petitioner's own conduct shall have been, not only free from the commission of any distinct matrimonial offence, but also of such a character that the respondent was in nowise reasonably justified in withdrawing from the society of the other. If so, then it will be open to the respondent to prove, either by the cross-examination of the petitioner or by his or her own evidence, that the withdrawal was with reasonable excuse, and, if the Court is satisfied that there was a reasonable excuse, it will refuse to grant a decree to the petitioner.

In England it is also competent to the respondent to plead in bar to the petitioner's suit—

Covenant not to sue for restitution of conjugal rights.

(b) *An agreement by the petitioner, for valuable consideration, not to sue for restitution of conjugal rights.*—Although an agreement between husband and wife which contemplates a *future* separation between them is contrary to public policy and illegal (*Westmeath* v. *Westmeath*, 1 Dow. & Clarke, 519; *Cocksedge* v. *Cocksedge*, 13 L. J., Ch. 384; *Merryweather* v. *Jones*, 10 L. T. 62), an agreement providing for the *immediate* separation of husband and wife is perfectly valid and binding (*Wilson* v. *Wilson*, 1 H. L. (Sc.) 538; *Gibbs* v. *Harding*, L. R., 8 Eq. 490; 38 L. J., Ch. 604; *Scholey* v. *Goodman*, 8 Moore, 350).

But though a deed of separation of the latter kind is valid, it is no bar or answer to a suit for restitution of conjugal rights, unless it contains an express covenant, for valuable consideration, on the part of the petitioner not to sue for the same (*Spering* v. *Spering*, 3 S. & T. 211; 32 L. J., P. & M. 116; *Moore* v. *Moore*, 12 P. D. 193; 56 L. J., P. & M. 104).

Previous to the Judicature Act of 1873 a covenant, for valuable consideration, not to sue for restitution of conjugal rights, was not regarded by the Divorce Court as a bar to such suit when subsequently instituted (*Hunt* v. *Hunt*, 32 L. J., P. & M. 168; *Anquez* v. *Anquez*, L. R., 1 P. 176; 35 L. J., P. & M. 93). But in such a case the respondent could apply to the Court of Chancery for a perpetual injunction to the extent of restraining the proceedings in the Divorce Court (*Flowers* v. *Flowers*, 25 L. T. 902).

Since the Judicature Act above referred to, the Divorce Court is part of the High Court of Justice, and consequently no cause

§ 33.

or proceeding pending in it can be restrained by prohibition or injunction. Inasmuch, however, as "matter of equity on which an injunction against the prosecution of any cause or proceeding might have been obtained if this Act had not been passed, either unconditionally or on any terms or conditions, may be relied on by way of defence (Judicature Act, 1873, s. 24), the respondent may now plead, by way of answer to a suit for restitution of conjugal rights, a covenant for valuable consideration by the petitioner not to sue for the same, and the plea, if proved, is a complete bar to the suit (*Marshall* v. *Marshall*, 5 P. D. 19; 48 L. J., P. & M. 49; *Clark* v. *Clark*, 10 P. D. 188; 54 L. J., P. & M. 57). But, although mere trifling breaches by the respondent of the covenants contained in the deed will not enable the petitioner to sue in spite of the covenant not to sue (*Besant* v. *Wood*, 12 Ch. D. 605), a total failure on the part of the respondent to carry out his or her part of the agreement will restore the petitioner to the same position which he or she would have been in, and to the rights which he or she would have had, if no such deed of separation had been executed (*Tress* v. *Tress*, 12 P. D. 128; 56 L. J., P. & M. 93; but, *contra*, *Parkinson* v. *Parkinson*, L. R., 2 P. 25; 39 L. J., P. & M. 14). Nor will a deed of separation, containing a covenant not to sue, act as a bar to a suit subsequently instituted, if such deed has never been acted upon by the parties (*Cock* v. *Cock*, 3 S. & T. 514; 33 L. J., P. & M. 57), or if it has been obtained by improper means or without reasonable excuse (*Dagg* v. *Dagg and Speke*, 7 P. D. 17; 51 L. J., P. & M. 19). Nor will a covenant not to sue in respect of previous misconduct prevent the covenantor from relying upon such misconduct as a bar to relief in a suit subsequently instituted by the covenantee (*Gooch* v. *Gooch*, (1893) P. 99). A deed of separation is completely put an end to by the reconciliation of the parties and resumption of cohabitation (*Scholey* v. *Goodman*, 8 Moore, 350; *Nicol* v. *Nicol*, 31 Ch. D. 524; 55 L. J., Ch. 437).

As regards suits for restitution of conjugal rights, instituted under the provisions of the Indian Divorce Act, a covenant not to sue cannot be pleaded by the respondent under sect. 33, as it is, of course, in no sense a ground for judicial separation. It is, also, to be remarked that sect. 32 does not speak of "desertion," but of a withdrawal without reasonable excuse from the society of the other party. Consequently, although the petitioner may have expressly agreed to live separate and not to sue for restitution of conjugal rights, such consent cannot *per se* make a withdrawal

§ 33.

reasonable which would otherwise be unreasonable. In other words, in suits for restitution of conjugal rights there is no question of "an abandonment against the wishes of the party complaining of it": there is, on the other hand, a loss of the other party's society, and though at one time the petitioner may have consented to be deprived of that society, that is no reason why he or she should thereafter and for ever be debarred from seeking a resumption of married life. The Courts of this country cannot, therefore, under the Indian Divorce Act, refuse a petitioner a decree for restitution of conjugal rights simply on the ground that he or she may have expressly covenanted not to sue for such restitution. But, although the respondent cannot plead such covenant as an answer to the suit, it may be that, when once such covenant is brought to its knowledge, the Court, *as a Court of Equity*, will refuse to permit a suit, brought in violation of a perfectly valid agreement, to proceed. For, as remarked by Mr. Justice Hannen, "it is in the highest degree desirable, for the preservation of the peace and reputation of families, that such agreements should be encouraged rather than that the parties should be forced to expose their matrimonial differences in a Court of Justice. And I must further observe that so far are suits for restitution from being in truth, and in fact, what theoretically they purport to be, proceedings for the purpose of insisting on the fulfilment of the obligation of married persons to live together, *I have never known an instance in which it has appeared that the suit was instituted for any other purpose than to enforce a money demand*" (*Marshall* v. *Marshall*, 5 P. D. at p. 23).

Poverty of husband petitioner.

(c) *Poverty of the husband-petitioner.*—It may be that a husband who sues *in formâ pauperis* for restitution of conjugal rights, and alleges in his petition that he has no means or home of his own, will be estopped from prosecuting his suit, especially if the wife is also not possessed of property (*Meara* v. *Meara*, 13 W. R. (Eng.) 50).

Change of religion.

(d) If a "marriage" contracted by a Hindu or Muhammadan, who subsequently becomes a convert to Christianity, is to be recognized as a marriage for the purposes of the Indian Divorce Act, provided only that the petitioner professes Christianity at the time of presenting the petition (see as to this, *ante*, pp. 4, 5), a difficulty of the following kind may arise: a Hindu marries a Hindu woman, and subsequently becomes a convert to Christianity; his wife remains a Hindu and repudiates her husband on his conversion. If, subsequently, the husband applies for restitution of conjugal rights, the wife, apparently, cannot plead his conversion in answer to his suit. And yet, as pointed out in a case decided previously to the Indian Divorce Act (*Mucho* v. *Arzom Sahoo*, 5 W. R. 535), a plea that "the husband by change of religion has placed himself in that position that she cannot live with him without doing extreme violence to her religious opinions and the social feelings in which she has been brought up, and in the enjoyment of which she married," would (apart from sect. 33 of the Indian Divorce Act) be a good plea in answer.

§ 33.

(e) *Delay in suing.*—The Court will not dismiss a petition for restitution of conjugal rights solely on account of the delay in instituting the suit (*Beauclerk* v. *Beauclerk*, 71 L. T. 376). And, of course, it is not open to the respondent to plead such delay in bar.

Delay in suing.

(f) *Insanity of petitioner.*—The insanity of the petitioner, supervening after marriage, is no ground for a decree of nullity of marriage, or, *per se*, for a decree of judicial separation; it cannot, therefore, be pleaded in answer to a suit for restitution of conjugal rights (*Hayward* v. *Hayward*, 1 S. & T. 81).

Insanity of petitioner.

If, however, the insanity is such as to render cohabitation unsafe, it can scarcely be contended that the respondent's withdrawal from the society of a dangerous lunatic was "without reasonable excuse" within the meaning of sect. 32. It would, therefore, be strange if the respondent were to be debarred from proving the dangerous character of the petitioner's insanity as a reason why the application for restitution should not be granted (cf. *Radford* v. *Radford*, 20 L. T. 279).

(g) *Lis pendens.*—A husband or wife who has withdrawn from the society of the other party in order to institute a suit for dissolution or nullity of marriage or judicial separation cannot be said to have acted "without reasonable excuse," provided that such suit has been duly instituted and is *bonâ fide*. In such a case the withdrawal is absolutely necessary, for continued cohabitation would amount either to condonation, or, in the case of a suit for nullity, a confirmation of the marriage, if such marriage were merely voidable, or a continuance in incest or fornication if such alleged marriage were absolutely void *ab initio*.

Suit for restitution of conjugal rights pending suit by respondent for dissolution or nullity.

If, therefore, a suit for restitution of conjugal rights is

§ 33.

instituted pending a suit by the other party for dissolution of marriage (whether instituted in the same or another Court), or for nullity of marriage or judicial separation, instituted in another Court, the suit for restitution should be stayed pending the determination of the respondent's suit (but see *Thornton* v. *Thornton*, I. L. R., x Bomb. 422). If, however, the suit for restitution of conjugal rights and the suit for nullity of marriage or for judicial separation are both instituted in the same Court, they can be consolidated and heard together. It is, however, only in suits for nullity of marriage or judicial separation that the respondent can, in answer to such suit, pray for restitution of conjugal rights (see *Lopez* v. *Lopez*, I. L. R., xii Calc. 706; and see note (4) to sect. 22, *ante*). It is not permissible to do so in suits for dissolution of marriage (see sect. 15, *ante*).

It follows that a respondent in a suit for restitution of conjugal rights can, in the answer, pray for judicial separation or nullity of marriage, as the case may be, but not for a dissolution of marriage.

Right to begin.

It may be here pointed out that, as a general rule, the petitioner in a suit for restitution of conjugal rights has the right to begin, although the substantive issue may be upon the respondent (*Burroughs* v. *Burroughs*, 2 S. & T. 544; 31 L. J., P. & M. 56).

What may be pleaded in answer to suit for restitution of conjugal rights.

"**Ground for a suit for judicial separation**":

The grounds for a suit for judicial separation are (1) *adultery*, or (2) *cruelty*, or (3) *desertion without reasonable excuse for two years or upwards*.

The respondent in a suit for restitution of conjugal rights may, therefore, plead in answer to such suit—

Petitioner's adultery.

(1.) *The petitioner's adultery.*—The general rule is that a husband or wife who has been guilty of adultery is not entitled to a decree for restitution of conjugal rights (*Hope* v. *Hope*, 27 L. J., P. & M. 43; *Green* v. *Green*, 21 L. T. 401).

But nothing short of actual adultery will suffice to disentitle the petitioner.

So, a wife's suit for restitution will not be dismissed merely on the ground of her impropriety of behaviour not amounting to a matrimonial offence, nor on the ground of her wilful refusal to permit conjugal intercourse (*Rippingall* v. *Rippingall*, 24 W. R. (Eng.) 967).

Accordingly, a plea by the respondent that the petitioner had given him cause for a strong and reasonable suspicion that she had committed adultery (*Burroughs* v. *Burroughs*, 2 S. & T. 303; 30 L. J., P. & M. 186), or that he had been induced to marry her on a false representation that she was pregnant by him (*Green* v. *Green*, 21 L. T. 401), is bad and should be struck out.

§ 33.

It has been held that if the respondent has connived at or condoned the petitioner's adultery, it cannot be pleaded in bar of the suit (*Moore* v. *Moore*, 3 Moore P. C. 86). But as to this see *infra, Compensatio criminis.*

Adultery committed by the petitioner under a *bonâ fide* belief, reasonably entertained, that the respondent was dead, is probably no bar to a suit for restitution of conjugal rights (cf. *Freegard* v. *Freegard*, 8 P. D. 186; 52 L. J., P. & M. 100; *Potter* v. *Potter*, 67 L. T. 721).

Nor can a husband or wife, whose own suit for dissolution of marriage or judicial separation on the ground of the other party's adultery has already been dismissed, rely upon these identical charges as an answer to a suit subsequently instituted by such other party for restitution of conjugal rights (*Sopwith* v. *Sopwith*, 2 S. & T. 160).

Compensatio criminis.—Can a husband or wife who has himself or herself been guilty of adultery sue for restitution of conjugal rights as against a respondent who has also been guilty of the same offence? According to the canon law and the earlier decisions of the Ecclesiastical Court, *mutuâ compensatione ambo adulteria abolentur,* that is to say, that the petitioner can set off the respondent's adultery as against his or her own, and thereafter claim restitution of conjugal rights as though wholly innocent of any matrimonial offence (*Eldred* v. *Eldred*, 2 Cust. 381; *Forster* v. *Forster*, 1 Hagg. Cons. 148; *Procter* v. *Procter*, 2 Hagg. Cons. 292). And, more recently, the Irish Court of Delegates granted a decree of restitution in a case where both petitioner and respondent had been equally guilty of adultery (*Seaver* v. *Seaver*, 2 S. & T. 665; cf. *per* Lopes, L. J., *Russell* v. *Russell*, (1895) P. 315; 64 L. J., P. & M. 105).

Compensatio criminis.

On the other hand, the judge ordinary (Sir Cresswell Cresswell), in *Hope* v. *Hope*, stated that this doctrine of *compensatio criminis* is no part of the law of England, and held that, where both parties had been guilty of adultery, a decree for restitution of conjugal rights could not be granted at the suit of either of them.

§ 33.

The modern tendency is undoubtedly in favour of the principle that relief in matrimonial cases should only be granted to a petitioner who comes into Court with a pure character and clean hands (see *Otway* v. *Otway*, 13 P. D. 141). As Cotton, L. J., remarked in the case last quoted, "a wife having been guilty of adultery has put herself in such a position that she cannot be considered as an innocent party in any proceedings which might have been taken in the old Ecclesiastical Courts, or which might now be taken in the Court of Divorce; and, therefore, on that ground, she is not in a position to come to that Court to give her any relief as to any matrimonial offence which the husband may have committed, or to put it on the ground of compensation for a crime of the same nature."

This being the general rule, it is doubtful how far the doctrine laid down in *Moore* v. *Moore* (*supra*), that adultery which has been connived at or condoned cannot be pleaded by the respondent in bar of a suit for restitution, will be accepted at the present day. That a respondent who has connived at or condoned the petitioner's adultery is not justified in subsequently pleading that offence as an answer to a suit for resumption of conjugal life may be admitted. But in granting relief the Court of Divorce regards the petitioner's conduct quite as carefully as that of the respondent, and is slow to relieve those who come to it with a past character which is not pure and blameless.

Petitioner's cruelty.

(2.) *Petitioner's cruelty.*—As to what constitutes such cruelty as would be a ground for judicial separation, see notes to sect. 10, *ante*.

Whether conduct on the part of the petitioner which, though falling short of legal cruelty, renders conjugal life almost impossible, will disentitle the petitioner to relief, is, at least, doubtful (see *ante*, p. 179).

Desertion by petitioner.

(3.) *Desertion by petitioner for statutory period.*—As to what constitutes desertion in the legal sense, see notes to sect. 10, *ante*.

It is to be remembered that it is only when the respondent has without reasonable excuse withdrawn from the society of the petitioner that the petitioner is entitled to sue for restitution of conjugal rights. If, however, the petitioner, though originally the party who separated from the other, makes a *bonâ fide* offer to resume cohabitation, and such offer is refused, the suit for restitution will not be barred unless the petitioner has "deserted" the respondent for two years or upwards.

§ 33.

"**Ground for a decree of nullity of marriage**":

(4.) It is obvious that, if the alleged marriage is absolutely null and void, no decree for restitution of conjugal rights in respect of it can be made. If it is merely voidable at the option of the respondent, the latter can elect to repudiate it when sued by the petitioner for restitution of conjugal rights. A respondent cannot plead his or her own impotency as a bar to a suit for restitution of conjugal rights.

But it is only on one or other of the grounds mentioned in sect. 19 that a decree of nullity can be made, and, therefore, it is only one or other of such grounds that can be pleaded by way of answer to a suit for restitution of conjugal rights. Mere informality of marriage is not such a ground (*Gasper* v. *Gonsalvez*, 13 B. L. R. 109).

But, before any decree of restitution can be made, it is essential (quite apart from the respondent's pleas) that a valid subsisting marriage between the petitioner and respondent should be proved (*Scott* v. *Scott*, 4 S. & T. 113; 34 L. J., P. & M. 23).

VIII.—*Damages and Costs.*

34. Any husband may, either in a petition for dissolution of marriage or for judicial separation, or in a petition to the District Court or the High Court limited to such object only, claim damages from any person on the ground of his having committed adultery with the wife of such petitioner.

Husband may claim damages from adulterer.

Such petition shall be served on the alleged adulterer and the wife, unless the Court dispenses with such service, or directs some other service to be substituted.

The damages to be recovered on any such petition shall be ascertained by the said Court, although the respondents or either of them may not appear.

After the decision has been given, the Court may

§ 34.

direct in what manner such damages shall be paid or applied.

The Matrimonial Causes Act, 1857 (20 & 21 Vict. c. 85), sect. 33, provides that:—

"Any husband may, either in a petition for dissolution of marriage or for judicial separation or in a petition limited to such object only, claim damages from any person on the ground of having committed adultery with the wife of such petitioner, and such petition shall be served on the alleged adulterer and the wife, unless the Court shall dispense with such service or direct some other service to be substituted; and the claim made by every such petition shall be heard and tried on the same principles, in the same manner and subject to the same or the like rules and regulations as actions for criminal conversation are now tried and decided in Courts of Common Law; and all the enactments herein contained with reference to the hearing and decision of petitions to the Court shall, so far as may be necessary, be deemed applicable to the hearing and decision of petitions presented under this enactment; and the damages to be recovered on any such petition shall in all cases be ascertained by the verdict of a jury, although the respondents or either of them may not appear; and after the verdict has been given, the Court shall have power to direct in what manner such damages shall be paid or applied, and to direct that the whole or any part thereof shall be settled for the benefit of the children (if any) of the marriage, or as a provision for the maintenance of the wife."

Husband's claim for damages.

"**Any husband may claim**":

(i) The petition must specify the amount which the husband claims (*Spedding* v. *Spedding*, 31 L. J., P. & M. 96).

Court fee stamp.

But no matter what the amount claimed may be, the petition, though limited to a claim for damages against the alleged adulterer, need only bear a Court fee stamp of Rs. 20 (Court Fees Act, 1870, 2nd Sch., Art. 20).

(ii) The petition, if it also prays for dissolution of marriage or for judicial separation, must state that there is no collusion or connivance between the husband and the wife, but, apparently, this is not necessary if the petition is limited to a claim for damages. It is, however, open to the alleged adulterer in all cases to prove in bar of any claim collusion or connivance between the husband and the wife (sect. 47, *post*).

(iii) Every petition must be verified as required by sect. 47 of the Act.

(iv) In a suit for dissolution of marriage instituted by the

§ 34.

wife, the husband may oppose the relief sought on the ground of the wife's adultery, pray for a dissolution of marriage or judicial separation, and claim damages against the alleged adulterer (sect. 15, *ante*).

(v) A husband whose wife has committed adultery is not bound to sue for dissolution of marriage. He can, if he prefers it, (a) sue merely for a judicial separation, with or without the addition of a prayer for damages against the adulterer; (b) bring a criminal complaint against the alleged adulterer under sect. 497 of the Indian Penal Code; or (c) sue merely for damages against the alleged adulterer.

(vi) The High Court, on a motion to confirm the decree of the District Court dissolving a marriage, has the fullest power to deal with the case as justice may require, including the award of damages by the lower Court, even though the co-respondent has not appealed (*Kyte* v. *Kyte and Cooke*, I. L. R., xx Bomb. 362; *Coates* v. *Coates*, No. 35, *Punjab Record*, 1887).

(vii) Where the husband is an uncertificated bankrupt he will be ordered to give security for the costs of the person against whom he claims damages (*Smith* v. *Smith*, 7 P. D. 227).

" Limited to such object only " :   *Claim only for damages.*

The mere fact that the husband has not sued, and does not intend to sue, for a dissolution of marriage or for judicial separation does not debar him from claiming damages against the adulterer. But a petition by the husband limited to damages alone is of very rare occurrence (but see *Ramsden* v. *Ramsden and Luck*, Times Law Reps., vol. ii. p. 867).

Although the husband does not claim relief against the wife, the petition for damages must be served on her, unless the Court otherwise orders.

But, although a husband is not bound to sue for dissolution of marriage or judicial separation if he wishes to claim damages against the adulterer, it must be remembered that a husband who has condoned his wife's adultery cannot claim damages from the man who committed the adultery so condoned (*Bernstein* v. *Bernstein*, (1893) P. 292; 63 L. J., P. & M. 3).

It does not, of course, follow that a man, who refrains from suing for dissolution of marriage or judicial separation on the ground of his wife's adultery, and merely sues the adulterer for damages, must be presumed to have condoned such adultery so far as the wife is concerned. But, in such a case, the Court

§ 34.

will not require such strict proof of the fact of condonation as might otherwise be necessary.

Answer to claim.

"**Adultery with the wife of the petitioner**":

In defence the alleged adulterer may urge the following pleas:—

(i) *As absolute bars to the claim.*—(a) That the alleged adultery was, in fact, never committed; *or* (b) that the adultery was committed, but that the petitioner connived at such adultery or has condoned the same; *or* (c) *that the petitioner's own conduct has been such as would give the Court a discretionary power to refuse a decree in his favour for dissolution of marriage in respect of the same adultery (*Seddon* v. *Seddon and Boyle*, 30 L. J., P. & M. 12; *Bernstein* v. *Bernstein*, (1893) P. 292; 63 L. J., P. & M. 3; *Story* v. *Story and O'Conor*, 12 P. D. 196; 57 L. J., P. & M. 15); *or* (d) that the petitioner and the woman were not husband and wife at the time of the alleged adultery.

Plea in mitigation of damages.

(ii) *In mitigation of damages.*—(a) That he did not know or have reason to believe that the woman was married at the time of the adultery. Inasmuch as damages are given not as a punishment to the adulterer, but as compensation to the husband for the loss of his wife, it is clear that the fact that the adulterer was in ignorance of the woman's true position cannot affect the question of damages, except so far as to go in mitigation. In such cases the woman would necessarily be the chief offender, for she must have deceived her paramour into believing her to be unmarried, and the loss of such wife to the husband would not be very great; (b) that it was not he who seduced the woman from her husband, but that the overtures came from her; (c) *that the woman's character and antecedents showed her to be a degraded and abandoned woman, whose loss to her husband was next to nothing; (d) that, previously to any act of the

---

* Ordinarily, in civil cases, evidence may only be given of a person's general character, and not of particular acts by which such character was shown (sect. 55 of the Indian Evidence Act, 1872). It is submitted, however, that in cases where a husband claims damages, it is open to the alleged adulterer to show that such petitioner ought not to receive damages at all, or, at any rate, merely nominal damages, by giving evidence as to such acts as show either what his character is, or what the character of his wife is (see sect. 12 of the Indian Evidence Act, and Field's Evidence Act, p. 356).

adulterer, the husband and wife had lived unhappily together, and that, consequently, the adulterer was in no way responsible for the breaking up of a happy home.

A co-respondent who had not at the time of adultery any reason to believe the respondent to be a married woman will not be made to pay the petitioner's costs (see sect. 35, *post*).

"**Such petition shall be served**":

In the old action of "Criminal Conversation" (now abolished, see sect. 61) the wife was not a party to the suit. But now she must be made a party even in cases where the petition is limited to damages against the alleged adulterer, and the petition must in all cases be served upon her as well as upon such alleged adulterer, except where the Court otherwise directs.

Petition, even if confined to damages, must be served on wife as well as alleged adulterer.

"**The damages to be recovered shall be ascertained by the said Court**":

Court to assess damages.

In England, when damages are claimed, the amount, if any, to be recovered must be ascertained by the verdict of a jury (Matrimonial Causes Act, 1857, s. 33).

If the adultery has been proved and the Court does not find any facts proved disentitling the petitioner to recover damages, the damages must be assessed at some sum, no matter how small, and the claim cannot be dismissed *in toto* simply on the ground that in point of fact the petitioner has suffered no damage (*Anon.*, 31 L. J., P. & M. 96, note).

Measure of Damages.

Measure of damages.

"In suits in which damages are claimed, any fact which will enable the Court to determine the amount of damages which ought to be awarded is relevant" (Indian Evidence Act, 1872, s. 12).

A claim for damages in a divorce case is founded by the hypothesis that the husband has suffered injury by being deprived of his wife's society through the wrongful act of the co-respondent. In order to award any damages, it is necessary to find (i) that the husband has in fact been damnified, (ii) that such damage has been brought about by the wrongful act of the co-respondent *without any fault on the part of the husband*. It is no part of the functions of a jury to punish the adulterer for his immorality. Their *sole duty is to compensate the husband for the*

Compensation to husband;

§ 34.
not punishment to adulterer.

injury (if any) which he has suffered through the wrongful act of the co-respondent. If a husband has a virtuous wife taken from him by the contrivance of another man, he is entitled to damages commensurate with the loss of such a wife; but if she has led a loose life before marriage, her value is not the same as that of a virtuous woman. In estimating the amount of damages to be awarded, the fact that the wife was earning money, of a portion of which the husband had the advantage, may properly be taken into account* (*Darbishire* v. *Darbishire,* 62 L. T. 664). "If it is proved that a man has led a happy life with his wife, that she has taken care of his children, that she has assisted in his business, and then some man appears upon the scene and seduces the wife away from her husband, then the jury will take these facts into consideration. But the question in this case, as in so many others, is whether or not these losses have been cast upon the petitioner by the act of the co-respondent. If he did not seduce her away from her husband, that makes a very material difference in considering the amount of damages to be given.

Conduct of husband to be considered.

In considering these questions, undoubtedly the conduct of the husband must be looked to. Here the husband and wife had been leading an unhappy life before they parted, and he knew that she had no means of living. . . . . What can any husband expect who has separated from his wife who he knows has no means? What will follow? Why, that in the ordinary course of things she may yield to the temptation of securing support from some other man" (*Keyse* v. *Keyse,* 11 P. D. at pp. 101, 102).

In assessing damages, according to Sir Cresswell Cresswell, "the first question is, How has the husband demeaned himself? Has he shown carelessness or want of caution, indicating a want of due value for his wife's chastity? The next question is, Did they live happily together? Because, if they lived unhappily, his loss in his wife is not so great. The next topic that is generally considered is the position of the defendant. How came he to be introduced? Under what circumstances did he become intimate with the family? Was there anything like treachery in his conduct? That is a legitimate consideration; not that you are to punish the man, but the conduct of the defendant, the mode in which he proceeds to obtain the affection of the lady, is important for your consideration. If a woman

---

* So also may the position of the husband as regards the marriage settlements (*Bell* v. *Bell and Anglesey,* 1 S. & T. 565; 29 L. J., P. & M. 149).

surrenders herself very readily to a man who takes no pains to obtain her affections, or if you have reason to suppose that she has made the first advances, you are to estimate, as far as you can form an estimate in money, the loss the husband has sustained" (*Comyn* v. *Comyn and Humphreys*, 32 L. J., P. & M. 210).

§ 34.

"The means of the co-respondent have nothing to do with the question. The only question is what damage the petitioner has sustained, and the damage that he has sustained is the same whether the co-respondent is a rich man or a poor man" (*Keyse* v. *Keyse*, 11 P. D. 102; *Darbishire* v. *Darbishire*, 62 L. T. 664; *Bikker* v. *Bikker and Whitewood*, 67 L. T. 141).

Means of co-respondent.

The fact that the adulterer is a poor man should not debar the Court from giving heavy damages against him if his conduct has entailed a heavy loss on the husband, for "if he cannot pay in purse he must pay in person" (*Cowing* v. *Cowing and Woolen*, 33 L. J., P. & M. 149).

Where a husband and wife were living apart under a deed of separation which had been executed in consequence of the wife's intimacy with the co-respondent, with whom the wife subsequently committed adultery, it was held that the husband was entitled to the same amount of damages as he would have been had no deed of separation been executed. But if the separation was in no way due to any conduct on the part of the co-respondent, the fact that the husband and wife were living apart under a deed of separation might be held to amount to an absolute bar to the recovery of damages by the husband, or, at all events, to reduce the damages to the smallest amount. "It must be obvious to anyone that if a husband and wife have consented to live separately, and have, in fact, lived separately for a number of years, the injury to the husband would be compensated in the smallest amount of damages. But each case varies with the different circumstances of life, and I have no hesitation in telling you that if a man makes the acquaintance of another man's wife, engages her affections, and is the cause of her separation from her husband, and then, after such separation, commits adultery with her, the husband is entitled to the same amount of damages as he would have been entitled to if no separation deed had been executed between them, and that even if no adultery had been committed before the separation" (Butt, J., *Izard* v. *Izard*, 14 P. D. 45; 58 L. J., P. & M. 83).

Husband and wife living apart under deed of separation.

Under sect. 33 of the Matrimonial Causes Act, 1857, the Court is bound by the assessment of the damages by the jury,

§ 34.

and is not at liberty to recognize any agreement between the petitioner and the co-respondent as to the amount to be paid by the latter (*Callwell* v. *Callwell and Kennedy*, 3 S. & T. 259).

This, however, is not the case in India under the Indian Divorce Act, and in any case, after the damages have been assessed, there is nothing to prevent the petitioner accepting a smaller sum than that awarded, if he so wishes (cf. *Dale* v. *Dale*, 15 L. T. 595).

Non-appearance of adulterer.

"**Although the respondents or either of them may not appear**":

If a co-respondent against whom a claim for damages is made does not appear, the Court must assume his guilt and assess damages against him, and this, too, though the respondent be acquitted of the offence charged (*Stone* v. *Stone and Appleton*, 3 S. & T. 608; 34 L. J., P. & M. 33; cf. *Long* v. *Long*, 15 P. D. 218; 60 L. J., P. & M. 27).

But on an issue of adultery raised between the husband and wife in a suit in which damages are asked for against a co-respondent who has not appeared, no evidence which is not admissible against the wife can be given to show that the co-respondent committed adultery. Any evidence, however, in aggravation of damages is admissible (*Stone* v. *Stone and Appleton, supra*).

A co-respondent who appears but puts in no answer is not entitled to address the jury in mitigation of damages or to cross-examine with that view (*Lyne* v. *Lyne and Blackney*, L. R., 1 P. 508; 37 L. J., P. & M. 9).

Bankruptcy of adulterer.

Bankruptcy of co-respondent.—When damages are awarded in the Divorce Court against a co-respondent, and are ordered to be paid to the petitioner, he undertaking to pay the same immediately into Court, such damages will not constitute a good petitioning creditor's debt on which to found an adjudication in bankruptcy (*In re Muirhead*, 2 Ch. D. 22; 45 L. J., Bk. 65). In such a case the petitioner is a mere receiver or collector for the Court of money which is not to be applied for his own benefit and is not a "judgment creditor" within the meaning of sect. 103 (5) of the Bankruptcy Act, 1883 (*In re Fryer*, 17 Q. B. D. 718; 55 L. J., Q. B. 478).

Accordingly, in order to avoid this difficulty, the Court may order the damages to be paid direct to the petitioner (*Patterson* v. *Patterson*, L. R., 2 P. 189; 40 L. J., P. & M. 5). It is, however,

§ 34.

doubtful whether the Court of Divorce has power to make such an order, and also whether in such an event the petitioner can prove for the amount under the co-respondent's bankruptcy (*ib.*; cf. *Wood* v. *Wood and Stanger*, L. R., 3 P. 467; 37 L. J., P. & M. 25).

Assignee of damages.—When a petitioner has assigned his damages, the assignee has no right to intervene in any way in the suit (*Hunt* v. *Hunt*, (1894) P. 247; 63 L. J., P. & M. 136). — Assignee of damages.

"**Court may direct in what manner such damages shall be paid or applied**": — Apportionment of damages.

Sect. 39 (*post*) provides that "the Court may direct that the whole or any part of the damages recovered under sect. 34 shall be settled for the benefit of the children of the marriage, or as a provision for the maintenance of the wife."

The usual order is that the co-respondent must pay the damages into the registry or to the petitioner, the latter undertaking to pay the same into Court. But if there is any fear of the damages being lost by such a procedure, *e.g.*, by the co-respondent's bankruptcy, the Court may make an order of speedy payment direct to the petitioner, he undertaking to apply the money under the orders of the Court (see *Bent* v. *Bent*, 30 L. J., P. & M. 189; *Patterson* v. *Patterson*, L. R., 2 P. 189; 40 L. J., P. & M. 5; *Gyte* v. *Gyte*, 10 P. D. 185). The Court, it was formerly held, had no jurisdiction to order that the damages be paid into Court (*Forster* v. *Forster and Berridge*, 32 L. J., P. & M. 133; but see *Gyte* v. *Gyte*, *supra*). When the damages have been paid into Court or to the petitioner, as the case may be, the Court will make an order as to the manner in which such damages shall be applied, and thereafter a regular deed of settlement, to be approved by the Court, will have to be drawn up.

Apportionment of damages.—It must be remembered that "the right of the husband is not, as the law now is, to have damages for his own pocket" (*Keats* v. *Keats and Montezuma*, 28 L. J., P. & M. at p. 61). The interests of the child or children of the marriage are to be first considered, nor are those even of the guilty wife to be ignored. And when the Court has made an order that the damages shall be applied in a certain manner for the benefit of the children and of the respondent, it — Damages not for husband's own pocket.

§ 34.

Costs of petitioner to be first paid out of damages.

will not countenance any private agreement between the petitioner and the co-respondent whereby the interests of the children are injuriously affected (*Forster* v. *Forster and Berridge*, 34 L. J., P. & M. 88).

But ordinarily the costs of the petitioner, over and above the amount he may have recovered from the co-respondent, will, when taxed, be paid out of the damages before any other payments are made (*Forster* v. *Forster and Berridge, supra; Billingay* v. *Billingay and Thomas*, 35 L. J., P. & M. 84; *Taylor* v. *Taylor and Walters*, 39 L. J., P. & M. 23).

After the petitioner's taxed costs have been duly satisfied, the Court has an absolute discretion to make any order it thinks fit as to the application of the damages, and the Court may make an order for the settlement of such damages either a part of the decree *nisi* (*Evans* v. *Evans and Bird*, L. R., 1 P. 36), or after the decree *nisi* has been made absolute (*Billingay* v. *Billingay and Thomas*, L. R., 1 P. 168). No general rules can, under the circumstances, be laid down, but the following may be taken as illustrations:—

(i) *Damages ordered to be applied for benefit of the Children of the Marriage.*

(a) Damages assessed at 250*l.*; the Court directed all the husband's interests in the damages to be assigned by him to a trustee for the use of the only child of the marriage, and in the event of the child's death under the age of twenty-one, and unmarried, for the use of the husband; the assignment to be settled by one of the conveyancing counsel of the Court of Chancery, and the decree absolute to be suspended until the assignment had been executed (*Clark* v. *Clark and Donck*, 2 S. & T. 520; 31 L. J., P. & M. 61).

(b) Damages 1,000*l.*; the Court ordered the damages to be paid to the husband in trust to pay thereout his own surplus costs, and as to the residue for the children of the marriage in equal shares, to be paid to them on attaining the age of twenty-one (*Spedding* v. *Spedding*, 32 L. J., P. & M. 31).

(c) The jury having recommended that the damages, which they assessed at 300*l.*, against the co-respondent should be settled entirely on the children of the marriage, the Court ordered that the petitioner's surplus costs having been taxed should be first paid out of the fund, and that the residue should be invested in the name of a trustee, the income to be expended for the maintenance and education of the children until they were of age, when the principal would be divided among them (*Billingay* v. *Billingay and Thomas*, 35 L. J., P. & M. 84).

§ 34.

(d) The whole of the damages, after payment of petitioner's costs, were ordered to be paid to a trustee for the benefit of a child which had been born after the separation between husband and wife, and which was suspected of being the child of the co-respondent (*Cullwell* v. *Cullwell*, 3 S. & T. 259).

(ii) *Damages ordered to be applied for the benefit of the Wife.*

Damages applied for benefit of wife.

(a) Damages, assessed at 150*l.*, ordered to be expended in purchasing a government annuity for the wife; the Court, at the same time, refused to make a settlement out of the earnings of the husband, who was a civil engineer in India with a yearly salary of 850*l.*; there were three children, the issue of the marriage (*Latham* v. *Latham and Gethin*, 30 L. J., P. & M. 43).

(b) Damages assessed at 2,500*l.*; "the undoubted conduct of the petitioner towards his wife, as disclosed at the trial, could hardly have commended itself to any who heard it"; the Court ordered that the damages, after payment of the surplus costs of the petitioner, should be settled on the respondent for life, *dum casta vixerit*; after her death or breach of the said condition, the fund to devolve on the two children of the marriage (*Narracott* v. *Narracott and Hesketh*, 33 L. J., P. & M. 132). The Court subsequently refused to vary this order by making the wife's interest continue only *dum casta et inupta vixerit* (*Narracott* v. *Narracott and Hesketh*, 34 L. J., P. & M. 54).

(iii) *Damages ordered to be applied for benefit of Husband.*

Damages applied for benefit of husband.

In a case where it was proved on the hearing of a petition that there had been no issue of the marriage, and that at the time of the hearing the respondent and the co-respondent were living together, the Court ordered that the damages assessed against the co-respondent should be paid to the petitioner and made its order part of the decree *nisi*, instead of postponing it till the decree absolute (*Evans* v. *Evans and Bird*, L. R., 1 P. 36).

(iv) *Damages apportioned between Husband, Children and Wife.*

Damages apportioned between husband, wife, and children.

(a) Damages, assessed at 5,000*l.*, ordered to be paid to the petitioner's solicitor and to be applied by him as follows:—1,000*l.*

§ 34.

to be paid by him to the petitioner, and out of the residue an annuity of 120*l.* to be purchased for the respondent's life to be paid to her *dum casta vixerit*, with remainder to two of her daughters; and the balance to be invested in an annuity for these two daughters (*Forster* v. *Forster and Berridge*, 3 S. & T. 158; 32 L. J., P. & M. 206). It was further ordered that a deed should be prepared and settled by one of the conveyancing counsel of the Court of Chancery whereby the order should be effectually carried out through the intervention of trustees and that anticipation of the annuities should be restrained.

(b) Damages, assessed at 5,000*l.*, were apportioned as follows:— 1,500*l.*, in addition to his surplus taxed costs, to be paid to the husband; 1,500*l.* to be settled on the youngest child of the marriage, aged five, the only one remaining with the petitioner, the three other children, all of whom were of full age, having left their father and cast in their lot with their mother; the balance to be invested in an annuity for the respondent's life, to be paid to her as long as she lived chastely and did not become the wife of the co-respondent, and in the event of her breaking any of these conditions, to be paid to the petitioner. In making this apportionment the learned judge said: "It appears that the co-respondent is a married man, and it is said that since her separation from the petitioner the respondent has been supported and visited by the co-respondent. Indeed, I am asked to come to the conclusion that their guilty intercourse has been carried on since the pronouncing of the decree in the suit. My object, then, in making the annuity payable to the respondent, so long as she lives a chaste life, is that she shall have the strongest possible motive to abstain from troubling the married life of the co-respondent and his wife. I do not impose as a condition that the respondent shall not marry again; that, perhaps, would be the best thing that could happen. But, in the event of the co-respondent's wife dying, and his marrying the respondent, then, as she would have to be supported by him, there would be no reason for her continuing to receive the annuity, and in that event it ought to go to the petitioner. I pass over the children, save the youngest, but not because I think they might not be entitled to some share in the damages by reason of their being of full age. I do not think that would be a sufficient reason for passing them over. There might be circumstances under which I should have allowed some portion of the damages to be paid to them, but two of these three children have cast in their lot with their mother, and in putting her in possession of this annuity I leave it to her to apply such portion of it to their maintenance as she may think fit, and also furnish another and additional motive for her observance of the conditions which I have named" (*Meyern* v. *Meyern and Myers*, 2 P. D. 254; 46 L. J., P. & M. 5). In this case the petitioner was a banker's clerk with a yearly salary of between 400*l*. and 500*l*., and the respondent had no means of support or provision for her maintenance; and of the three children of the marriage who were of full age two were sons and one a daughter.

35. Whenever in any petition presented by a husband the alleged adulterer has been made a co-respondent, and the adultery has been established, the Court may order the co-respondent to pay the whole or any part of the costs of the proceedings:

Provided that the co-respondent shall not be ordered to pay the petitioner's costs

(1) if the respondent was at the time of the adultery living apart from her husband and leading the life of a prostitute, or

(2) if the co-respondent had not at the time of the adultery reason to believe the respondent to be a married woman.

Whenever any application is made under section seventeen, the Court, if it thinks that the applicant had no grounds or no sufficient grounds for intervening, may order him to pay the whole or any part of the costs occasioned by the application.

The Matrimonial Causes Act, 1857 (20 & 21 Vict. c. 85), sects. 34 and 51, respectively provide as follows:—

"Whenever in any petition presented by a husband the alleged adulterer shall have been made a co-respondent and the adultery shall have been established, it shall be lawful for the Court to order the adulterer to pay the whole or any part of the costs of the proceedings" (sect. 34).

"The Court on the hearing of any suit, proceeding, or petition under this Act, and the House of Lords on the hearing of any appeal under this Act, may make such order as to costs as to such Court or House respectively may seem

§ 35.

just: Provided always, that there shall be no appeal on the subject of costs only" (sect. 51; contrast with this provision sect. 55 of the Indian Divorce Act, *post*).

As regards the English Divorce Court's power to regulate fees payable upon all proceedings before it, see sect. 54 of the Matrimonial Causes Act, 1857.

On the subject of costs, generally, see Rules 27, 50, 103, 110, 111, 116, 137, 151—159, 177—179, 193, 198, 200—203, 216—218, of the English Divorce Court Rules.

"**The Court may order the co-respondent to pay the whole or any part of the costs of the proceedings**":

The subject of costs will be found discussed generally in Appendix (F.), *post*.

IX.—*Alimony*.

Alimony *pendente lite*.

36. In any suit under this Act, whether it be instituted by a husband or a wife, and whether or not she has obtained an order of protection, the wife may present a petition for alimony pending the suit.

Such petition shall be served on the husband; and the Court, on being satisfied of the truth of the statements therein contained, may make such order on the husband for payment to the wife of alimony pending the suit as it may deem just:

Provided that alimony pending the suit shall in no case exceed one-fifth of the husband's average nett income for the three years next preceding the date of the order, and shall continue, in case of a decree for dissolution of marriage or of nullity of marriage, until the decree is made absolute or is confirmed, as the case may be.

The Matrimonial Causes Acts of England do not deal expressly with the subject of alimony pending the suit; the English Court, therefore, follows the practice of the Ecclesiastical Courts in this matter.

See Nos. 81—94, and 189—192, of the Rules of the English Divorce Court.

ALIMONY.

"In any suit under this Act":   **§ 36.**

(a) *Suit for nullity of marriage.*—In a suit for nullity of marriage, although it is apparent on the face of the petition and answer taken together that there was no valid marriage, the Court has jurisdiction to grant alimony *pendente lite*, on the principle that the *factum* of the marriage being admitted, costs and alimony *pendente lite* follow (*Miles* v. *Chilton*, 1 Robert. 684; *Bird* v. *Bird*, 1 Lee, 209, 418; *Foden* v. *Foden*, (1894) P. 307; 63 L. J., P. & M. 163—C. A.). In the case last cited the English Court of Appeal expressly dissented from the view of Lord Penzance (*Blackmore* v. *Mills*, 18 L. T., N. S. 586), to the effect that when the invalidity of the so-called marriage was apparent on the face of things, the Court had no power to grant alimony pending the suit.

Accordingly, an application for alimony pending a suit for nullity need only state that a ceremony of marriage was performed between the parties which might be a valid marriage; an affidavit to that effect is apparently unnecessary (*Crump* v. *Crump and Abbott*, 3 B. L. R., O. C. 101). In this case alimony *pendente lite* was granted to the applicant, although it was shown that she was the sister of the respondent's deceased wife.

Alimony pending suit. In suits for nullity of marriage.

(b) *Suit for dissolution of marriage.*—The Act expressly declares that alimony *pendente lite* is, when granted, to *continue* until the decree has been made absolute. But, if such alimony had not been granted before the making of the decree *nisi*, it was formerly held that the Court could not grant it in the interval between the decree *nisi* and the decree absolute (*Latham* v. *Latham*, 2 S.* & T. 299). This case has, however, been expressly overruled by the Court of Appeal on the ground that as the legal *status* of a married woman is not altered by the decree *nisi*, and as until the decree absolute the Court can make no permanent provision for the wife, it is only reasonable that it should have power to make some temporary provision for her during the interval between the two decrees (*Ellis* v. *Ellis*, 8 P. D. 188; 52 L. J., P. & M. 99).

In *Bennett* v. *Bennett* (I. L. R., xi Calc. 354), Norris, J., following *Latham* v. *Latham*, refused to grant alimony *pendente lite* after the decree *nisi*, on the ground that such decree puts an end to the *lis* between the parties. But it has now been definitely held that the *lis* is not put an end to by the decree *nisi*, and that the suit between the parties remains pending until the decree absolute (*Norman* v. *Villars*, 2 Ex. D. 359;

Suits for dissolution of marriage. Application for alimony pendente lite after decree nisi.

§ 36.   *Ellis* v. *Ellis, supra; Foden* v. *Foden,* (1894) P. 307; 63 L. J., P. & M. 163—C. A.).

And in the very recent case of *Thomas* v. *Thomas* (I. L. R., xxiii Calc. 913), Ameer Ali, J., held, on the authority of the above cases, that the Court had jurisdiction to entertain an application, made by the wife after the decree *nisi,* for alimony *pendente lite* for the time previous to such decree. In this case the decree *nisi* had been made at the instance of the husband, and on the ground of the wife's adultery.

Suits for judicial separation.

(c) *Suit for judicial separation.*—In a suit for judicial separation, the Court may grant alimony *pendente lite* to the wife, whether she is the petitioner or the respondent. But as regards the grant of *permanent* alimony, it is doubtful whether the Court has power to make an order under sect. 37 in favour of a wife whose husband has obtained a decree for judicial separation (see as to this, sect. 37, note " *Obtained by the Wife*").

Suits for restitution of conjugal rights.

(d) *Suit for restitution of conjugal rights.*—Although the Court has, under this section, power to grant alimony pending a suit for restitution of conjugal rights, it cannot, after decree in such suit, grant the wife permanent alimony under sect. 37 (see sect. 37, *post,* note).

Service of petition.

"**Petition shall be served on the husband**":

Under sect. 50 of the Act, the Court may, if it thinks fit, dispense with personal service of any petition under the Act. Where substituted service of the petition for dissolution had previously been permitted upon the respondent's agents, the Court allowed substituted service of the petition for alimony by registered letter addressed to the respondent's agent (*Odevaine* v. *Odevaine,* 58 L. T. 564).

"**Statements therein contained**":

See Form No. 12.

Payment to wife of alimony pending suit.

"**Payment to the wife of alimony pending the suit**":

As a general rule, alimony *pendente lite,* when granted, is payable from the date of the service, not of the return, of the citation (*Kelly* v. *Kelly and Saunders,* 3 B. L. R., App. 4; *Nicholson* v. *Nicholson and Ratcliffe,* 31 L. J., P. & M. 165; *Thomas* v. *Thomas,* I. L. R., xxiii Calc. 913).

But where the wife had for some time after the filing of the

suit and service of the citation continued to cohabit with the § 36.
co-respondent, the Court, in allotting alimony *pendente lite*,
directed that it should be payable from the date at which she
ceased to so cohabit, and not from the date of service of the
citation (*Holt* v. *Holt and Davies*, L. R., 1 P. 610; 38 L. J.,
P. & M. 33).

Alimony *pendente lite*, when granted, continues to be payable Payable till
to the wife until the final decree in the suit on the original final decree.
hearing, that is to say, in suits for dissolution or nullity of
marriage, when the decree is made absolute or confirmed, as the
case may be, and in suits for restitution of conjugal rights or
for judicial separation, when the Court in which such suit was
instituted has passed its decree thereon.

In a suit for dissolution of marriage, a wife to whom alimony
pending the suit is granted is entitled to have such alimony
continued until the decree *nisi* is made absolute or confirmed,
although such decree *nisi* has been made on the ground that
she has been proved guilty of adultery. In England the law is
different. Although there the Court has jurisdiction to grant
alimony *pendente lite* even after the decree *nisi* and to make such
alimony payable until the decree absolute (*Ellis* v. *Ellis*, 8 P. D.
188), yet a wife who has been found guilty of adultery forfeits
her *right* to alimony *pendente lite* immediately the adultery is
established, that is to say, when the case has been tried by a
jury as soon as the verdict is given, and when the case is tried
by the Court itself as soon as the decree *nisi* is pronounced (*Dunn*
v. *Dunn*, 13 P. D. 91; *Wells* v. *Wells and Hudson*, 3 S. & T.
542). But in cases tried by a jury the Court has power to continue the alimony *pendente lite* even after an adverse verdict if
it thinks "it not improbable that the wife will obtain a new
trial and succeed ultimately in establishing her innocence"
(Cotton, L. J., *Dunn* v. *Dunn*).

Alimony pending an appeal.—Alimony *pendente lite* only con- Alimony
tinues until the final decree on the original hearing, but if an pending
appeal be preferred, it is competent to the Appellate Court, if appeal.
so moved, to grant alimony pending the appeal to the wife.
Such alimony will usually be granted as a matter of course,
but the Court will refuse to grant it if satisfied that the appeal
is vexatious or frivolous or that the wife has been guilty of
laches (*Jones* v. *Jones*, L. R., 2 P. 333; 41 L. J., P. & M. 53).

Alimony pendente lite: *application for review of judgment.*—It Alimony
has been held in England that the Court has power to continue pending

§ 36.
application for review.

alimony *pendente lite* even after a final decree passed against the wife if she has applied for a new trial and the Court thinks it not improbable that she will succeed in such new trial (*Nicholson* v. *Nicholson*, 3 S. & T. 214; cf. *Dunn* v. *Dunn*, 13 P. D. 91).

In India there is no provision made for new trials, but the wife may apply, under sect. 623 of the Civil Procedure Code, for a review of judgment—a proceeding which is, in many respects, similar to an application for a new trial. If such application is made by the wife and she further prays that alimony *pendente lite* may be continued pending the petition for review, the Court (it is submitted) has jurisdiction to continue the alimony, and will, probably, do so if satisfied that it is not unlikely that the petition for review will succeed (*Hirabai* v. *Dhunjibhoy*, I. L. R., xvii Bomb. 148, *per* Jardine, J.).

Wife to be considered innocent.

Alimony pendente lite : *general principles.*—As a general rule, every wife is entitled to receive alimony pending the suit, and she will be considered, for the purpose of allotting such alimony, innocent of any charge or counter-charge preferred against her by her husband, even though by not answering to such charge or counter-charge she may have impliedly admitted her guilt (*Smith* v. *Smith and Tremeaux*, 4 S. & T. 228; 32 L. J., P. & M. 91).

Nor is her adultery, admitted or proved,* any ground for allotting her less than the usual amount; therefore, an averment in the answer to a petition for alimony that the wife has been guilty of adultery is irrelevant (*Crampton* v. *Crampton and Armstrong*, 32 L. J., P. & M. 142; *D'Oyley* v. *D'Oyley*, 4 S. & T. 226; 29 L. J., P. & M. 165).

So, where a wife, against whom a decree *nisi* for dissolution of marriage on the ground of her adultery had been passed, applied thereafter for alimony *pendente lite*, Ameer Ali, J., held that she was entitled to alimony *pendente lite* from the date of service of the citation, but referred it to the registrar to inquire into the facts alleged by the parties, and to report what, if any, alimony under the circumstances that might be established should, in his opinion, be given to the wife prior to the decree *nisi* * (*Thomas* v. *Thomas*, I. L. R., xxiii Calc. 913).

---

* In England, however, the rule is different, for when once the wife's adultery is proved, though she is still a wife, she loses her *right* to alimony *pendente lite* immediately the order of the Court is passed adversely to her (*Dunn* v. *Dunn*, 13 P. D. 91).

ALIMONY.

If, however, it is shown that the wife is at the time when she applies for alimony *pendente lite* continuing to cohabit with the co-respondent and is being provided for by him, the Court will refuse to grant her alimony so long as such cohabitation and maintenance continues. But the ground for this refusal is not the adultery on the part of the wife, but the fact that she has means of support independent of her husband. If, therefore, she leaves the co-respondent, or if the latter refuses to maintain her any longer, she is entitled to receive alimony pending the suit from the date when she leaves him or is no longer supported by him (*Holt* v. *Holt and Davies*, L. R., 1 P. 610; 38 L. J., P. & M. 33; *Madan* v. *Madan and Thoren*, 37 L. J., P. & M. 10).

§ 36. Wife supported by co-respondent.

It has also been held that a wife who is living apart from her husband under such circumstances that she cannot, in law, pledge his credit, is disentitled to alimony *pendente lite* (*Gordon* v. *Gordon*, 3 B. L. R. Ap. 13).

But the fact that the wife is at the time undergoing a sentence of imprisonment for felony is no ground for refusing to grant her alimony pending the suit (*Kelly* v. *Kelly*, 4 S. & T. 227; 32 L. J., P. & M. 181).

Wife undergoing sentence of imprisonment.

In a suit for dissolution of marriage by the wife the husband appeared under protest and pleaded that the Court had no jurisdiction in the suit on the ground that he had never been domiciled in England. The wife having thereafter filed a petition for alimony *pendente lite*, the husband moved for an order to stay all proceedings as to alimony until the question of jurisdiction should be determined, but the Court, though holding that it was a matter of discretion whether alimony should be granted pending the determination of such question, granted the wife's petition on the ground that the question of jurisdiction could not be determined for several months (*Ronalds* v. *Ronalds*, L. R., 3 P. 259).

Plea by husband to jurisdiction of Court.

The object of granting alimony *pendente lite* is to enable a wife during such time as there is litigation between her and her husband to live in the comfort appropriate to a woman of her rank and position. Accordingly, in allotting her such maintenance, the Court should take into consideration a comparison of the respective incomes of the husband and the wife, for "the wife of a man with 4,000*l*. a year is entitled to spend more on her maintenance than the wife of a poorer man" (*Allen* v. *Allen*, (1894) P. 134; 63 L. J., P. & M. 78—C. A.; cf. *R.* v. *R.*, I. L. R., xiv Mad., at p. 95).

Considerations for Court in allotting alimony *pendente lite*.

§ 36.

Wife having means of support independent of her husband.

Ordinarily, a wife who is in no need of support from her husband, either because she has separate property of her own or else because previously to the institution of the suit she has been supporting herself by her own earnings, will not be granted alimony *pendente lite* (*George* v. *George*, L. R., 1 P. 554; 37 L. J., P. & M. 17; *Thompson* v. *Thompson and Johnson*, L. R., 1 P. 553; *Goodheim* v. *Goodheim and Frankinson*, 2 S. & T. 250; 30 L. J., P. & M. 162).

Means derived from co-respondent.

If she has, independently of her husband, ample means of support, even if such means are derived from the co-respondent, she will be disentitled to alimony pending the suit (*Holt* v. *Holt and Davies*, L. R., 1 P. 610; *Madan* v. *Madan and De Thoren*, 37 L. J., P. & M. 10).

Both parties almost penniless.

And in cases where both parties are almost penniless the power of the wife to maintain herself should especially be considered (*Nicholls* v. *Nicholls*, 30 L. J., P. & M. 163, note).

Vexatious suits brought by wife against husband.

The institution of a number of vexatious suits, all ending unsuccessfully, by the wife against her husband is a ground for allotting her alimony at less than the ordinary rate (*Hakewell* v. *Hakewell*, 30 L. J., P. & M. 254).

Wife removing furniture from husband's house.

And where it was shown that the wife had removed furniture of very considerable value from her husband's house the Court refused to grant her alimony *pendente lite* so long as she retained possession of such furniture (*Bremner* v. *Bremner and Brett*, 3 S. & T. 249; 32 L. J., P. & M. 119).

Wife contracting extravagant debts.

But the mere fact that the wife has previously to the order for alimony contracted debts to an extravagant amount will not entitle the husband to claim a diminution of the usual amount allowed as alimony *pendente lite*; "because the husband is, legally, liable only for a reasonable amount, with reference to the position of the wife; and if she should have contracted debts to an unreasonable amount, I cannot assume that he will have to pay more. It may be that, by his own conduct in paying debts of a similar description before, he has encouraged persons to give credit to a larger amount than they would otherwise have done. If so, he must suffer; but I cannot take into consideration the large amount of the debts contracted in estimating the amount of alimony. I must assume that he is liable only for a reasonable sum for her support" (*Hayward* v. *Hayward*, 28 L. J., P. & M. 9; 1 S. & T. 85).

Postponement of suit at instance of wife.

If the trial of a suit by the wife is postponed at her instance, the Court may, under the circumstances, direct that the alimony *pendente lite* which has been allotted shall be suspended from the date of postponement until the cause is tried (*Rogers* v. *Rogers*, 34 L. J., P. & M. 87).

§ 36.

An allowance made to the wife under a deed of separation is not necessarily a bar to a petition by her for alimony *pendente lite;* but, in order to succeed, she must show reasonable grounds for an increase of allowance, *e.g.*, that she has been residing abroad or living cheaply in the country and requires more money in order to maintain or defend the suit (*Powell* v. *Powell and Jones*, L. R., 3 P. 186; 43 L. J., P. & M. 9).

Wife receiving allowance under separation deed.

Where a husband, who had agreed in a deed of separation to make his wife an allowance determinable on her molesting him, subsequently discontinued such allowance on the ground that she had broken her covenant, the wife in a suit for judicial separation instituted by her applied for, and obtained, alimony *pendente lite* (*Wood* v. *Wood*, 57 L. J., P. & M. 31). In such a case the Court would probably allot alimony at the same rate as the husband had covenanted to pay the wife in the deed of separation (*Weber* v. *Weber*, 1 S. & T. 219). The mere fact that since the execution of the deed the husband's income has increased is no ground for granting the wife alimony at a higher rate than that stipulated in such deed (*Powell* v. *Powell and Jones*, L. R., 3 P. 186; 43 L. J., P. & M. 9).

All payments made by the husband to the wife after the service of the citation will be deducted from alimony *pendente lite* (*Crampton* v. *Crampton and Armstrong*, 32 L. J., P. & M. 142).

Payments made to wife after service of citation.

"**Husband's average nett income**":

Husband's average nett income.

The husband in his answer to a petition for alimony *pendente lite* must state the amount of his *gross* income for the three years next preceding the date of the petition, and then specify what, if any, deductions he claims; it is not sufficient for him to merely state the amount of his *nett* income for that period (*Nokes* v. *Nokes*, 3 S. & T. 529; 33 L. J., P. & M. 24).

But, though the husband is bound to state his gross average income for the last three years, "he will still be at liberty to state what his income has been during the whole of the last nine"—or any other number of—"years, and also any other circumstances which may tend to account for his income being larger than ordinary in any particular year. He may state any facts from which the Court can properly draw a conclusion as to what his faculties now are; and for the purpose of determining that, the more facts before the Court the better. But to

What husband's answer may state.

§ 36.

state the average of his income for the last nine years is not sufficient" (*Williams* v. *Williams*, L. R., 1 P. 370; 36 L. J., P. & M. 39).

"It is an entire mistake to suppose that the phrase '*nett income*' in the Act has any other meaning than that which it ordinarily bears. . . . . Ordinarily, with an official drawing a fixed salary and having no other means, that expression would be taken to mean the amount of his salary *minus* deductions on account of income tax, charges for a pension fund and the like; and, in our judgment, that is the sense in which nett income is to be understood in dealing with a case under the Divorce Act" (*R.* v. *R.*, I. L. R., xiv Mad. 88).

All valuable property to be taken into consideration.

In the allotment of alimony, the whole of the husband's valuable property will be taken into account, whether or not he derives any income from it. Accordingly, the value of shares in a company, although no dividend is payable thereon, and the annual value of houses occupied by himself or belonging to him but occupied by others rent free, must be stated in his answer (*Crampton* v. *Crampton and Armstrong*, 32 L. J., P. & M. 142).

If property is mortgaged.

If the husband's property is mortgaged, the answer must state the date of the mortgage, the name of the mortgagee and the amount of the mortgage debt (*ibid.*), and in stating his income derived from land, the husband in his answer must state the *gross* rental and specify all outgoings (*Nokes* v. *Nokes*, 3 S. & T. 529; 33 L. J., P. & M. 24).

Income derived from land.

Allowable deductions.

Deductions claimable by husband.—After stating his average *gross* income for the last three years, the husband is at liberty to specify any deductions which he claims.

As regards income derived from real property, the husband is entitled to deduct the expenses of ordinary current repairs, but not of extraordinary and permanent improvements which ought to be charged on the *corpus* of the property (*Hayward* v. *Hayward*, 1 S. & T. 85; 28 L. J., P. & M. 9).

Deductions are allowable on account of income tax and charges made for a pension fund to which the husband subscribes on behalf of his family (*R.* v. *R.*, I. L. R., xiv Mad. 88).

But deductions are not, as a rule, allowable on account of sums paid by way of *premia* to maintain a policy of insurance on the husband's life (*Wilcocks* v. *Wilcocks*, 32 L. J., P. & M. 205; *Patterson* v. *Patterson and Curtis*, 33 L. J., P. & M. 36). But in a case where the policy was under settlement for the benefit of the wife and family, and the *premium* was deducted and paid over to the insurance office by the husband's employers, the Court allowed the amount of such *premium* to be deducted in the calculation of the income (*Forster* v. *Forster*, 2 S. & T. 553; 31 L. J., P. & M. 84).

§ 36.

The Court will take into consideration any arrangement which the husband has made for liquidating his debts, and if he has contracted to pay off a debt by annual instalments, he will be entitled to deduct the amount of each instalment from his income (*Patterson* v. *Patterson and Curtis*, 33 L. J., P. & M. 36; *R.* v. *R.*, I. L. R., xiv Mad. 88).

As a general rule, the expense of maintaining and educating his children *by a former marriage* does not form a legitimate deduction from a husband's income in the allotment of alimony, nor, apparently, is the fact that there are several such children any ground for allotting less than one-fifth of his income as alimony *pendente lite* (*Grafton* v. *Grafton*, 27 L. T. 768; *Hill* v. *Hill*, 33 L. J., P. & M. 104).

Expenses connected with maintenance of children.

The Court will, however, take into consideration expenses incurred by the husband in maintaining and educating children the issue of the marriage between him and the petitioner for alimony (*Harris* v. *Harris*, 1 Hagg. Eccl. 351; *R.* v. *R.*, I. L. R., xiv Mad. 88).

Joint income of husband and wife.—Although the wife may have brought a large sum to the husband, and although the cohabitation contemplated at the time of marriage may have become impossible owing to the husband's misconduct, the Court is not competent to grant as alimony *pendente lite* more than one-fifth of the joint income, or, in England, more than one moiety of such joint income (*Haigh* v. *Haigh*, L. R., 1 P. 709; 38 L. J., P. & M. 37).

Joint income of husband and wife.

Power to increase or reduce alimony pending the suit.—The High Court of Madras in a recent case (*R.* v. *R.*, I. L. R., xiv Mad. 88) doubted whether the Court has power to increase or diminish an allotment once made of alimony *pendente lite* on account of a change in the husband's position and means. The Court in England has the power to do so under Rule 92, and possibly sect. 7 of the Act may be held to authorize the Courts of this country to adopt the practice of the English Court.

Increase or reduction of alimony *pendente lite*.

If the husband applies to the Court to reduce the amount payable by him on the ground that since the date of the order his income has been materially diminished, he must explain

§ 36. the cause of such reduction and satisfy the Court that it was not due to extravagance on his own part (*Shirley* v. *Shirley and Wardropp*, 1 S. & T. 317).

Husband excused from paying alimony pendente lite.

Husband excused from paying Alimony pendente lite.

In the following cases the Court refused to order the husband to pay alimony *pendente lite*:

(a) The husband in his answer stated that he was an officer of the Bengal Army on sick leave in England, and that he had no means of his own; the wife, however, was granted her costs for moving for an allotment (*Gaynor* v. *Gaynor*, 31 L. J., P. & M. 144).

(b) The husband was a master pilot of the Bengal pilotage service on six months' leave of absence without pay, and was in receipt of no income and possessed of no property whatever, being dependent upon his friends for his living (*Fletcher* v. *Fletcher*, 2 S. & T. 434; 31 L. J., P. & M. 82).

But the mere fact that the husband is temporarily out of employment at the moment when his answer to the petition for alimony is sworn will not relieve him from the liability to pay alimony *pendente lite*. For "the Court looks to the average earnings of the husband for the last few years, and it assumes that in the current year his earnings will be about the same rate. It may happen that a man's income may not be derived from identically the same sources in the current year or in future years as in past years; but in ordinary life an income of about the same amount is generally derived from similar sources. In the case, for instance, of a professional income, a medical man may be presumed to derive as large an income in future years as in past, although not from the same patients. In a case like the present, a master mariner may be able to swear that he was not at the date of his answer in command of any vessel, but the Court may reasonably presume that in the ordinary course of events he will soon obtain a command" (*Thompson* v. *Thompson and Johnson*, L. R., 1 P. 553; 37 L. J., P. & M. 33).

(c) The husband was a minor, and his only source of income was that on the death or second marriage of his mother he would be entitled to a share in the residuary estate of his father, provided that he attained the age of twenty-one (*Beavan* v. *Beavan*, 2 S. & T. 652; 31 L. J., P. & M. 166).

(d) The husband had no income, and his only property was a legacy of 500*l*., which was not payable till nearly a year after the date of the petition for alimony (*Brown* v. *Brown and Simpson*, 3 S. & T. 217; 32 L. J., P. & M. 144).

(e) The husband was in insolvent circumstances, and his only means were weekly wages of meat, drink, lodging and washing, and four shillings (*Capstick* v. *Capstick, Furness, and Winder*, 33 L. J., P. & M. 105).

(f) The husband had an income of only 60*l*. per annum, and on separating from his wife had returned her the 70*l*. which was the amount of her fortune (*Coombs* v. *Coombs*, L. R., 1 P. 218).

(g) As a general rule, a wife cannot include in her husband's income any purely voluntary allowance made to him by his father or other person; but there may possibly be circumstances under which the wife may be entitled to alimony out of income to which the husband has no strictly legal right (*Haviland* v. *Haviland*, 3 S. & T. 114; 32 L. J., P. & M. 67; cf. *Moss* v. *Moss and Bushe*, 15 W. R. (Eng.) 532; cf. *Bonsor* v. *Bonsor*, (1897) P. 77; xiii Times L. R., p. 184).

§ 36.

Alimony pendente lite : *practice of the Courts.*

Practice of the Court.

See Rules of the English Divorce Court, Nos. 81—94, and 189—192.

If the husband wishes to controvert the allegations in the wife's petition for alimony, he is bound, under Rule 84, to file an answer thereto on oath; unless he does this, he cannot cross-examine or contradict the witnesses produced in support of the petition either on the application for alimony *pendente lite*, or on the hearing of the cause as to an allotment of permanent alimony (*Constable* v. *Constable*, L. R., 2 P. 17; 39 L. J., P. & M. 17; *Hicks* v. *Hicks*, 9 Ir. R. Eq. 175).

And if the husband fails or refuses to make such answer, the Court may by peremptory order direct him to file an answer within a week (*Snowdon* v. *Snowdon*, L. R., 2 P. 200; 40 L. J., P. & M. 29).

In order to save expense, the Court has allowed the wife to prove by affidavits the income of the respondent, who had filed

Affidavit by wife.

§ 36.

no answer to her petition for alimony, but it directed that notice should be given to the respondent of the filing of the said affidavits and of the wife's intention to apply for alimony upon the income proved therein (*Mumby* v. *Mumby*, L. R., 1 P. 701; 38 L. J., P. & M. 72).

A wife who has presented a petition for alimony has a right to subpœna her husband in order to examine him as a witness in support of her petition (*Jennings* v. *Jennings*, L. R., 1 P. 35; 35 L. J., P. & M. 12; *Anderson* v. *Anderson*, L. R., 1 P. 512; 37 L. J., P. & M. 64).

In such a case the husband is adopted by the wife as her witness and she cannot cross-examine him. It is only when the husband has filed an answer which is evasive or which does not satisfy the wife that the latter is entitled to apply to the Court for an order directing the husband to attend on the hearing of the petition, when he may be cross-examined by her (*Anderson* v. *Anderson, ubi supra*; *Parker* v. *Parker*, 26 L. T. 108; *Clark* v. *Clark*, 31 L. J., P. & M. 32; Rule No. 86).

"In an application for alimony pending suit, the wife is entitled to have the clear oath of the husband as to the net profits of his business, but it must be a very strong case to justify the Court in calling for documents which would disclose partnership accounts" (Jeune, J., *Tonge* v. *Tonge*, (1892) P. 51).

When on the application of the wife the Court allows a commission to issue to examine witnesses abroad as to the husband's means, it will not order the husband to give security for the wife's costs of the commission (*Wilson* v. *Wilson and Haswell*, 26 L. T. 107).

Injunction to restrain husband from dissipating property.

The Court will not, in order to protect a wife's right to alimony, grant an injunction to restrain the husband from removing his property out of the jurisdiction of the Court *before* an order for alimony has been made* (*Newton* v. *Newton*, 11 P. D. 11; 55 L. J., P. & M. 13). Nor in a case of judicial separation has the Court power, even after an order for alimony *pendente lite* has been passed, to restrain the husband by injunction from dealing with his property as he pleases (*Carter*

---

* In suits for dissolution of marriage, if there is a subsisting order for payment of alimony *pendente lite*, the Court may possibly grant an injunction to restrain the husband from dissipating or getting rid of his property (*Newton* v. *Newton, ubi supra*; *Sidney* v. *Sidney*, 17 L. T., N. S. 9; *Newton* v. *Newton*, (1896) P. 36; 65 L. J., P. & M. 15).

ALIMONY.

v. *Carter*, (1896) P. 35; 65 L. J., P. & M. 48; *Hyde* v. *Hyde*, 34 L. J., P. & M. 63).

Arrears of alimony payable under an order of the Divorce Court, which have accrued due after the date of the receiving order and before proof, are not provable in bankruptcy; possibly they are not so provable even when they have accrued due before the receiving order (*In re Hawkins*, (1894) 2 B. 25).

§ 36.

Arrears of alimony: proof of, in bankruptcy.

A promise to release arrears and future instalments of alimony for a sum less than the arrears is invalid for want of consideration; but if the husband has also promised to take no steps in the future to vacate the order for alimony, there would be sufficient consideration to support the promise to release such arrears and future instalments (*Underwood* v. *Underwood*, (1894) P. 204—C. A.).

Promise to release arrears and future instalments of alimony.

A co-respondent who has been condemned in costs is liable for the costs of proceedings to obtain alimony (*Gill* v. *Gill and Hogg*, 33 L. J., P. & M. 43).

Costs of petition for alimony.

37. The High Court may, if it think fit, on any decree absolute declaring a marriage to be dissolved, or on any decree of judicial separation obtained by the wife,

> and the district judge may, if he thinks fit, on the confirmation of any decree of his declaring a marriage to be dissolved, or on any decree of judicial separation obtained by the wife,

order that the husband shall, to the satisfaction of the Court, secure to the wife such gross sum of money, or such annual sum of money for any term not exceeding her own life, as, having regard to her fortune (if any), to the ability of the husband, and to the conduct of the parties, it thinks reasonable; and for that purpose may cause a proper instrument to be executed by all necessary parties.

Power to order permanent alimony.

In every such case the Court may make an order on the husband for payment to the wife of such monthly or weekly sums for her maintenance and support as the Court may think reasonable:

Power to order monthly or weekly payments.

§ 37.

Provided that if the husband afterwards from any cause becomes unable to make such payments, it shall be lawful for the Court to discharge or modify the order, or temporarily to suspend the same as to the whole or any part of the money so ordered to be paid, and again to revive the same order wholly or in part, as to the Court seems fit.

By sect. 17 of the Matrimonial Causes Act, 1857 (20 & 21 Vict. c. 85), the Court may upon an application for restitution of conjugal rights or for judicial separation decree such restitution of conjugal rights or judicial separation, "*and where the application is by the wife, may make any order for alimony which shall be deemed just.*"

And sect. 32 of the said Act provides that :

" The Court may, if it shall think fit, on any such* decree, order that the husband shall to the satisfaction of the Court secure to the wife such gross sum of money, or such annual sum of money for any term not exceeding her own life as, having regard to her fortune (if any), to the ability of the husband, and to the conduct of the parties, it shall deem reasonable, and for that purpose may refer it to any one of the conveyancing counsel of the Court of Chancery to settle and approve of a proper deed or instrument to be executed by all necessary parties ; and the said Court may in such case, if it shall see fit, suspend the pronouncing of its decree until such deed shall have been duly executed ; and upon any petition for dissolution of marriage the Court shall have the same power to make interim orders for payment of money, by way of alimony or otherwise, to the wife, as it would have in a suit instituted for judicial separation."

And the Matrimonial Causes Act, 1866 (29 & 30 Vict. c. 32), preamble and sect. 1, provides as follows :—

" And whereas it sometimes happens that a decree for a dissolution of marriage is obtained against a husband who has no property on which the payment of any such gross or annual sum can be secured, but nevertheless he would be able to make a monthly or weekly payment to the wife during their joint lives :

" Be it therefore enacted, &c.

" 1. In every such case it shall be lawful for the Court to make an order on the husband for payment to the wife

---

* "*Such decree*" means here a decree absolute for dissolution of marriage (sect. 31 of the Act ; *Charles* v. *Charles*, 36 L. J., P. & M. 17).

during their joint lives of such monthly or weekly sums for her maintenance and support as the Court may think reasonable: Provided always, that if the husband shall afterwards from any cause become unable to make such payments it shall be lawful for the Court to discharge or modify the order, or temporarily to suspend the same as to the whole or any part of the money so ordered to be paid, and again to revive the same order, wholly or in part, as to the Court may seem fit."

§ 37.

As regards the power of the English Court to order a respondent-husband, who fails to comply with a decree for restitution of conjugal rights, to pay periodical sums of money to the wife, and its power to vary such orders, see the Matrimonial Causes Act, 1884 (47 & 48 Vict. c. 68), sects. 2, 4, and Rules 214—218 of the English Divorce Court Rules.

For the practice of the English Court, see Rules 84—88, 91—103, 189—192, 214—218.

"**On any decree absolute**":

Permanent alimony: order for, after decree absolute.

According to the earlier decisions of the English Court, the order for permanent alimony under sect. 32 of the Matrimonial Causes Act, 1857 (which applies only to suits for dissolution of marriage), must be embodied in the decree absolute, and any petition by the wife for permanent alimony in such suits must be made before the decree *nisi* has been registered, for if once such decree has been registered, the Court has no further jurisdiction to entertain a petition for such alimony (*Vicars* v. *Vicars*, 29 L. J., P. & M. 20; *Charles* v. *Charles*, 36 L. J., P. & M. 17; *Winstone* v. *Winstone and Dyne*, 2 S. & T. 246; 30 L. J., P. & M. 109).

These were decisions upon the proper construction of sect. 32 of the Matrimonial Causes Act, 1857, which, as has been stated, applies only to suits for dissolution of marriage. Sect. 37 of the Indian Act applies also to decrees for judicial separation, and, according to the *ratio decidendi* of the above cases, the order for permanent alimony under this section must, in decrees for judicial separation, be incorporated in such decrees; if not, the Court has no jurisdiction to make a supplementary order for such alimony.

Apparently, however, the previous leading case on this subject, *Vicars* v. *Vicars*, has been overruled (*Bradley* v. *Bradley*, 3 P. D. 47; 47 L. J., P. & M. 53). In the case last cited it was held, on the strength of the decision of the House of Lords in *Sidney* v. *Sidney* (36 L. J., P. & M. 73), that the Court has power,

§ 37.

under sect. 32 of the Matrimonial Causes Act, 1857, to make an order for the permanent maintenance of a wife *after* a decree absolute has been pronounced. Indeed, the learned judge who decided the case was of opinion that, though the order for permanent alimony may be embodied in the judgment pronouncing the decree of dissolution, "there is nothing in the Act which requires it to be so, and that it is, in fact, *more regular* for the Court to pronounce a separate decree for maintenance, *after* it has made absolute the decree *nisi* for dissolution. If I had not the decision of the House of Lords to guide me, I should arrive at the same conclusion. The word 'on' is an elastic expression, which, so far from excluding the idea of its meaning after, is more consistent with that signification than any other. In some cases the expression 'on' may undoubtedly mean contemporaneously or immediately after, and the question now before the Court is, whether there is anything from which it can be seen that the legislature used the word in the 32nd section in this restricted sense? In some instances, as in questions of costs, it may be inferred that the legislature intended the Court to act at the time, that is, on the occasion of the facts being brought to its knowledge, and while these facts are fresh in its recollection; but no such reasons apply to the order for maintenance. That is to be the result of a separate investigation of facts, not necessarily before it when the decree of dissolution is pronounced. The investigation of the husband's means may be protracted, he may throw difficulties in the way of the Court obtaining the materials upon which to pronounce a just decision, or ordering a proper deed for the security of the wife being prepared. Where the husband is the petitioner, the decree which he asks may be suspended until he does what is right; but where the wife is the petitioner, to suspend the decree until the husband does something would delay the wife in obtaining redress as to the main object of the suit, because the respondent refuses to give her the means of obtaining a decision on a totally distinct and incidental question" (Hannen, J., *Bradley* v. *Bradley, ubi supra*). At the same time, "whatever meaning may be given to the word 'on' in the Act of Parliament, it is very difficult to extend it to above a year. . . . . 'On,' if not confined to the time of making the decree, must mean shortly after" (Jessel, M. R., *Robertson* v. *Robertson*, 8 P. D. at p. 96).

It would appear, therefore, that the more regular course is for the Court to make an independent order for permanent alimony, after it has pronounced the final decree as to the main object of

the suit. But, in suits for dissolution of marriage, the Court § 37.
has power, before the decree *nisi* has been made absolute, to
order the husband to secure maintenance to the wife upon the
decree being made absolute, and in the meantime to restrain him
from dealing with his property so as not to leave sufficient
security (*Waterhouse* v. *Waterhouse*, (1893) P. 284; 62 L. J.,
P. & M. 115—C. A.).

"**On any decree absolute or on any decree of judicial separation obtained by the wife**":

It is to be noticed that the Court has no power, under the Indian Divorce Act, to grant permanent maintenance to a wife who has obtained a decree for restitution of conjugal rights, with which the husband has refused to comply. The English Court has such power (see sect. 17 of the Matrimonial Causes Act, 1857, and the Matrimonial Causes Act, 1884, ss. 2, 4).

This section refers in terms only to a decree of judicial separation *obtained by the wife*. Can the Court grant permanent maintenance to a wife when it is the husband who has obtained the decree of judicial separation? According to sect. 17 of the Matrimonial Causes Act, 1857, any husband or wife may apply for judicial separation, and the Court may decree such judicial separation accordingly, "and, *where the application is by the wife, may make any order for alimony which shall be deemed just.*" In a recent case before the English Court of Appeal it was argued that these words only enable the Court to grant the wife permanent maintenance when the decree of judicial separation has been obtained by her; but it was held that they do not take away, or even negative, the jurisdiction which the English Divorce Court has inherited from the Ecclesiastical Courts of granting permanent alimony in a case where she is the respondent in a suit for judicial separation. For, as the English Divorce Court is, in all suits and proceedings other than proceedings to dissolve any marriage, to act and give relief on principles and rules which, in the opinion of such Court, shall be as nearly as may be conformable to the principles and rules on which the Ecclesiastical Courts acted and gave relief, subject to the express provisions of the Act, and as the Ecclesiastical Courts had jurisdiction to grant permanent maintenance to a wife whose husband had obtained a decree of divorce *a mensâ et thoro*, the English Divorce Court has the like jurisdiction in the absence of any express provision in the Act to the contrary (*Gooden* v. *Gooden*, (1892) P. 1). In fact, the English Court

Decree of judicial separation obtained by the wife.

§ 37.

will refuse, as a general rule, to grant a decree of judicial separation to the husband, unless he makes a suitable provision for the wife (*Prichard* v. *Prichard*, 3 S. & T. 523; 33 L. J., P. & M. 158; *Forth* v. *Forth*, 36 L. J., P. & M. 122).

"Although the Court, by a decree of judicial separation, gives a legal warranty to a husband and wife to live apart, still they remain husband and wife, and while they remain so the obligation also remains on the husband of contributing to the support of the wife" (*Forth* v. *Forth, ubi supra*). Nor does the Court, as a rule, refuse to grant permanent alimony to a guilty wife whose husband has obtained a decree of dissolution of marriage (*Kelly* v. *Kelly and Saunders*, 3 B. L. R. 71).

There is, therefore, no valid reason why a wife, whose husband has obtained a judicial separation, should not be granted permanent alimony, and possibly the Courts may, when the question arises, see their way to construing sect. 37 in the same way in which sect. 17 of the English statute of 1857 was construed by the Court of Appeal. They may hold that, in the absence of any words in the Act directly negativing such jurisdiction, sect. 7 of the Act enables the Court to make the same provision for a wife, who is respondent in a suit for judicial separation, that the English Court would make under the like circumstances.

Permanent alimony granted by district judge.

"**And the district judge .... on the confirmation of any decree of his declaring a marriage to be dissolved**":

In suits for dissolution of marriage an order for permanent alimony under this section cannot be made by a district judge until his decree in the suit has been confirmed by the High Court; after such confirmation, the wife can apply to the district judge for an order for permanent alimony, but, before her petition is granted, due notice thereof should be given to the husband (*Skinner* v. *Skinner*, No. 13, *Punjab Record*, 1891).

Permanent alimony, how secured.

"**Order that the husband shall, to the satisfaction of the Court, secure to the wife**":

"The word '*secure*' appears to be used in a particular way. It is contrasted with *payment*. . . . Therefore I think that the intention of the legislature was that the gross or annual sum should not be ordered at once to be paid over to the wife, but should be secured, and being secured should be paid to her from time to time; that would give a meaning to the word

ALIMONY.

'*secure*' as contrasted with '*pay*'" (Jessel, M. R., *Medley* v. *Medley*, 7 P. D. 122).

§ 37.

The usual way in which such gross or annual sum is secured is by the personal bond of the husband, with or without sureties, or by deed of settlement (*Keats* v. *Keats and Montezuma*, 28 L. J., P. & M. 57; *Bent* v. *Bent and Footman*, 30 L. J., P. & M. 175; *Lister* v. *Lister*, 15 P. D. 4).

Charging order on husband's property.—As a general rule, the Court will not make an order charging the husband's property with the payment of permanent alimony or maintenance.

Charging order on husband's property.

The order passed by the Ecclesiastical Courts in such cases was "that the husband, regard being had to his circumstances at the time of making the order, should make his wife a certain allowance. Those Courts dealt with the question as if the husband and wife were living together, and they considered what proportion of the income would fall to the lot of the wife. If the husband's property was afterwards increased, the Court exercised the power of increasing the alimony, and if it was diminished, of diminishing the alimony, so that the fortunes of the wife followed those of the husband. If this Court directly or indirectly charged the fortune of the husband with the payment of the alimony, it would tie his hands and prevent him from entering into trade or using it in any way for the improvement of his income, and such an order would have a totally different effect from any of the orders made by the Ecclesiastical Courts" (*Hyde* v. *Hyde*, 34 L. J., P. & M. 63; 4 S. & T. 80; followed in *Fowle* v. *Fowle*, I. L. R., iv Calc. 260; *Carter* v. *Carter*, (1896) P. 35; 65 L. J., P. & M. 48).

But the Court has the power of charging the husband's property with the payment of permanent alimony, and has occasionally exercised such power. Thus, the Court directed a deed to be executed by the husband whereby the payment of the annuity ordered to be paid as permanent alimony was secured on such fixed property as he possessed, and by his personal covenant (*Fisher* v. *Fisher*, 31 L. J., P. & M. 1; 2 S. & T. 414). And in another case the husband was ordered to execute a deed charging the goodwill and stock-in-trade of his business with the payment of Rs. 250 *per mensem* by way of permanent alimony (*Ord* v. *Ord*, 5 B. L. R., App. 34).

Where, under the terms of an instrument in the form of a settlement but proved as a will, real and personal estate was given to trustees upon trust for the sole use and benefit of the

§ 37.

respondent (son of the settlor), his heirs, executors and administrators, to be assigned and transferred to him as soon as conveniently might be after the settlor's death, subject to a proviso that if the respondent should die unmarried and without issue his share should go over, and also that the property assigned in trust for the respondent was to be held by the trustees upon the express condition that he should not, during his life, have power to mortgage, sell, alien, charge or encumber any part of the property, and that in that event the trustees should stand possessed of such property in trust for other persons, it was held by the Court of Appeal that the respondent took an absolute interest in fee simple under the instrument, that the condition of forfeiture in case of charge or alienation was therefore void as repugnant, and that, accordingly, he could be ordered to secure to his divorced wife an annual sum for maintenance by a charge on his interest under the instrument (*Corbett* v. *Corbett*, 14 P. D. 7).

Injunction to restrain husband from dealing with his property.
Injunction to restrain husband from dealing with his property.—Where the Court orders a husband to secure a gross or annual sum of money to his wife by way of permanent maintenance, it may also by injunction restrain him in the meantime from dealing with his property so as not to leave sufficient security (*Sidney* v. *Sidney*, 17 L. T., N. S. 9; *Waterhouse* v. *Waterhouse*, (1893) P. 284; 62 L. J., P. & M. 115; *Newton* v. *Newton*, (1896) P. 36; 65 L. J., P. & M. 15).

But such injunction will not be made before an order for alimony has been passed, merely *quia timet*, to restrain a respondent from dealing with his property (*Newton* v. *Newton*, 11 P. D. 11).

" **Such gross sum or such annual sum** " :

Nature of allowance.
"Under the procedure in the Divorce Court there are four distinct sums of money which may be ordered to be paid, and which are very different the one from the other in some of their qualities. First, there is the well-known alimony *pendente lite*. There is, secondly, alimony of a permanent character, which is directed to be paid upon a judicial separation being pronounced. Thirdly, there is the gross or annual sum which, upon the dissolution of the marriage, the Court is authorized by the Act of 1857, if it thinks fit, to direct to be paid by the husband to the wife; and, lastly, there are the monthly or weekly payments, which, under the Act of 1866, the Court may order

upon a dissolution of the marriage, in the event of its not finding the husband to be capable of paying either the gross sum or the annual sum under the statute of 1857" (Fry, L. J., *Harrison* v. *Harrison*, 13 P. D. 180).

§ 37.

As regards these different provisions for the wife, it has been held that permanent alimony granted to a wife upon a judicial separation is inalienable by her. "The Court which ordered it never lost control over it, and she could not by assignment or otherwise deprive herself of her right to it so long as she and her husband lived separate and apart from each other. This doctrine is based on the old ecclesiastical law, and was recognized and acted upon in *In re Robinson*, 27 Ch. D. 160" (Lindley, L. J., *Watkins* v. *Watkins*, (1896) P. 222; 65 L. J., P. & M. 175).

Permanent alimony is inalienable when granted after decree of judicial separation.

The same doctrine applies to the permanent allowance ordered to be paid to a divorced wife under sect. 1 of the Act of 1866, which is personal to herself and cannot be assigned or released by her without the sanction of the Court. "A divorced wife need not enforce an order for her own maintenance unless she pleases, and she may release and perhaps assign her right to arrears.* But it does not follow that she can bind herself not to enforce payment in future, nor that she can assign her right to future payments. I do not say that an order under sect. 1 of the Act of 1866 for permanent maintenance cannot be discharged by the Court with the consent of the divorced husband and wife, even if the man is able to pay it; but until such an order is discharged the divorced wife cannot, in my opinion, prospectively deprive herself or be deprived of the benefit of the maintenance which the Court has ordered to be paid to her" (Lindley, L. J., *Watkins* v. *Watkins, ubi supra*).

On the other hand, a gross or annual sum of money secured to a wife upon the dissolution of her marriage becomes to all intents and purposes her own permanent property subject to any restrictions which may be imposed upon it by the deed to be executed under the order of the Court and approved by the Court. Such deed may contain a provision against alienation or anticipation by the wife, but in the absence of any such pro-

Not so after decree absolute for dissolution of marriage unless so expressly provided.

---

* But in the recent case of *Underwood* v. *Underwood* ((1894) P. at p. 213), A. L. Smith, L. J., suggests that a wife can for proper consideration bind herself not to insist upon the monthly or weekly payment ordered to be made to her.

§ 37.

Distinction between permanent allowance after—
(i) judicial separation;
(ii) dissolution of marriage.

vision she would be at liberty to alienate or assign, and the Court would have no further control over such property (*Harrison* v. *Harrison*, 13 P. D. 186).

The Indian Divorce Act makes no distinction between the kinds of permanent provision which may be made for a wife upon judicial separation and upon dissolution of marriage; in either case the Court may order a gross or annual sum to be secured to her, or it may direct payment to her of monthly or weekly sums of money. But "there is a substantial difference between permanent alimony which is ordered after a judicial separation, and maintenance which is ordered after a divorce. There is, too, a substantial difference between the position of a wife who is judicially separated from her husband and a wife who is divorced. In the former case the relations of husband and wife continue and cohabitation may at any time be resumed. In the latter case the woman is no longer the wife. She cannot again become the wife unless, after the decree is made absolute, she re-marries her former husband. She may marry again. He is not bound to support her. She cannot pledge her husband's credit, even for necessaries. In point of fact, she becomes in every respect in the eye of the law a *feme sole* with all the liabilities and all the privileges of a *feme sole*" (Lopes, L. J., *Watkins* v. *Watkins, ubi supra*). And, for similar reasons, a permanent provision in the form of monthly or weekly payments of money is inalienable by the wife. For "the Court keeps its hands upon the maintenance, because if the husband is unable to make the payments the Court can discharge or modify the order or temporarily suspend the same as to the whole or any part of the money ordered to be paid, and again revive the same order wholly or in part. Why should the Court reserve to itself a power to revive a modified or suspended order if the wife might have alienated her interest? The Court would not be concerned to restore an order made in favour of a wife to assist an assignee who could have no claim on the husband; nor do I think that the Court would be justified in enforcing an order for maintenance against the husband on the application of the assignee" (Lopes, L. J., *Watkins* v. *Watkins, ubi supra*). Although, therefore, no distinction of the kind referred to above is made in the Indian Divorce Act between permanent alimony after judicial separation and permanent maintenance after dissolution of marriage, the principle enunciated in the decisions cited would still apply, and, consequently, here, as in England, the only alienable or assignable permanent provision would be the gross or annual sum secured to a wife upon the dissolution of marriage.

§ 37.

Bankruptcy of husband.

The bankruptcy of the husband does not discharge him from his obligation to pay his wife alimony under the order of the Divorce Court, and no proof can be had in respect of instalments of alimony, whether such instalments accrued due before or after the receiving order (*In re Hawkins*, (1894) 1 Q. B. D. 25; *Linton* v. *Linton*, 15 Q. B. D. 239).

"**As, having regard to her fortune (if any), to the ability of the husband and to the conduct of the parties, it thinks reasonable**":

Considerations for Court.

When, therefore, the Court orders the husband to secure to the wife a gross or annual sum of money for her permanent maintenance, the amount of such gross or annual sum will depend on the circumstances of the particular case, regard being had to (1) the fortune, if any, of the wife; (2) the ability of the husband, and (3) the conduct of the parties.

The English Court has laid down the following general principles:—

A. *In Cases of Judicial Separation.*

The Court must follow the rule laid down by the Ecclesiastical Courts and cannot allot as permanent alimony, after a decree for judicial separation, more than one-half of the joint income of the husband and wife, although the wife may have brought more than a moiety of the joint income into settlement, nor is a wife, who has brought a sum of money, large or small, to the husband in contemplation of a cohabitation which the husband's subsequent misconduct has rendered impossible, entitled to receive back the money which she has brought to the common fund (*Haigh* v. *Haigh*, L. R., 1 P. 709; 38 L. J., P. & M. 37).

This rule, however, is based on the ground that the powers given to the Court by sect. 32 of the Matrimonial Causes Act, 1857, only apply to suits for dissolution of marriage and have not been extended to suits for judicial separation. Consequently, the rule has no application to suits brought under the provisions of the Indian Divorce Act, for by sect. 37 the Courts of this country, both in suits for dissolution and for judicial separation, are given powers of allotting permanent alimony which, under the English statute, are given to the Court only in suits for dissolution.

§ 37.

It is not only the largeness of the husband's income, but also his conduct and other circumstances which have to be taken into consideration, and a husband who has for years been living in adultery is not entitled to much favour. In such a case, where the income of the husband was 1,650*l.*, the Court allotted 500*l. per annum* to the wife as permanent alimony (*Wilcocks* v. *Wilcocks*, 32 L. J., P. & M. 205).

If a husband receives a larger salary by reason of the increased expenses of his position, the wife will not be entitled to the usual proportion of his income,—that is to say, she will be granted less than the one-third of such larger salary. Accordingly, where the husband was promoted to a captaincy in Her Majesty's Indian Army and was about to proceed to India, where he would be entitled to pay at the rate of 480*l. per annum*, the Court refused to grant more than 120*l. per annum* to the wife as permanent alimony (*Louis* v. *Louis*, L. R., 1 P. 230; 35 L. J., P. & M. 92). Nor, again, where the husband is gaining his income by his own personal exertions will the Court, as a general rule, give the wife more than one-third of such income, no matter how gross the misconduct of the husband may have been (*Cooke* v. *Cooke*, 2 Phill. 44, 45; followed in *Ord* v. *Ord*, 5 B. L. R., App. 34). In the latter case, Norman, J., granted the wife Rs. 250 a month out of the husband's income of Rs. 1,000 a month, and directed that the sum allotted should be made a first charge on the stock-in-trade and goodwill of his business as an undertaker.

Wife providing for children.

The fact that the wife has to provide for the child of the marriage is no ground for allotting her more than the usual proportion, viz., one-third of the husband's income; the proper course in such a case is for the wife to ask the Court to make provision for its maintenance under sect. 35 of the Matrimonial Causes Act, 1857 (sect. 41 of the Indian Divorce Act) (*Hyde* v. *Hyde*, 29 L. J., P. & M. p. 151, note). But, in a later case, where the husband's income was 400*l.*, the Court allotted the wife, who had been given the custody of the three children of the marriage, 160*l.* as permanent alimony, of which 100*l.* was to be for herself, and 20*l.* for each of the children (*Whieldon* v. *Whieldon*, 30 L. J., P. & M. 174; 2 S. & T. 388). In allotting alimony, the husband's income in respect of an annuity payable to him for a term of years must be taken during the term to be the amount of the annuity and not a percentage on the present value of the annuity, on the ground that the husband can, in the event of his income being diminished, apply for a reduction of the amount of such alimony (*Moore* v. *Moore*, 34 L. J., P. & M. 146).

§ 37.

As a general rule, a moiety of the husband's income is only allotted in those cases where the wife has, on marriage, brought the husband a considerable sum of money or other property (*Wallis* v. *Wallis*, 29 L. J., P. & M. 151, note). But, if the husband's misconduct has been very gross, the Court will grant the wife a moiety of his income even though she may have brought him no property or money at all. So, where the husband, whose income was 60*l.* a year, derived from money invested in a pawnbroking business, had brought the woman with whom he had committed adultery into the house where he was living with his wife, who had, thereupon, been obliged to go elsewhere, the Court allotted the wife 30*l.* a year as permanent alimony (*Avila* v. *Avila*, 31 L. J., P. & M. 176).

B. *In Suits for Dissolution of Marriage.*

In an early case it was held by Sir Cresswell Cresswell that a wife who had obtained a dissolution of her marriage on the ground of her husband's misconduct was entitled to receive from him, by way of permanent provision for herself, merely such a sum as would suffice for her bare maintenance, on the ground that "it would not be politic to give to wives any great pecuniary interest in obtaining a dissolution of the marriage tie" (*Fisher* v. *Fisher*, 31 L. J., P. & M. 1).

But in a subsequent case the same learned judge, while adhering to the general principle laid down in the case last cited, animadverted upon the "cruel and heartless conduct" of the husband, whose income was 500*l.*, and granted the wife an order to the effect that the husband should give a warrant of attorney for 2,000*l.*, with defeasance, making it payable in two or three months (*Morris* v. *Morris*, 31 L. J., P. & M. 33).

And it is now settled that, in granting permanent maintenance after a dissolution of marriage, the Court "will not deal with the subject in any more niggard spirit than that in which the Ecclesiastical Court regarded the question of permanent alimony" (*Sidney* v. *Sidney*, 34 L. J., P. & M. 122). In this case the learned judge, referring to *Fisher* v. *Fisher*, gave his reasons for refusing to follow that case: "If a man, before the Divorce Act, treated his wife with cruelty and was also guilty of adultery, she could only obtain a divorce *a mensâ et thoro*, and an allowance, called permanent alimony, was made to her,

§ 37. which was generally calculated at the rate of one-third of the husband's income. Since the Divorce Act the same conduct on the part of the husband entitles the wife to a dissolution of her marriage; but it is hard to say that she was intended by the legislature to purchase that remedy by a surrender to which she would otherwise have been entitled. The needs of the wife and the wrongs of the husband are the same in both cases. In both cases the husband has of his own wrong and wickedness thrust forth his wife from the position of participator in his station and means. Obliged in both cases to withdraw from his home, she is, without any fault of her own, deprived of her fair and reasonable share of such necessaries and comforts as lay at his command. Why should not the husband's purse be called upon to meet both cases alike? It has been said that in one case she remains a wife, and in the other she does not. This remark would carry great weight with it, if the provision were intended to continue in the event of her second marriage. But it can hardly affect the rate of an allowance made and continued so long only as the wife remains chaste and unmarried. Again, it has been said that it is not desirable that the wife should have a pecuniary interest in preferring divorce to judicial separation. But it should be borne in mind that it is still less desirable that an adulterous husband should have a pecuniary interest in adding cruelty or desertion to his adultery, and thus evading the permanent alimony allowed on judicial separation. And this he would have if the amount of the maintenance to be accorded varied, not with his misconduct, but with the form of her remedy. . . . To such a man the Court may surely say with propriety, 'According to your ability you must still support the woman you have first chosen and then discarded. If you are relieved from your matrimonial vows, it is for the protection of the woman you have injured and not for your own sake, and so much of the duty of the husband as consists in the maintenance of his wife may be justly kept alive and enforced upon you in favour of her whom you have driven to relinquish your name and home.' If this be to give the wife a pecuniary interest in obtaining a divorce, it is also to hold a pecuniary penalty over the head of the husband for the observance of married duty; and if it be wise to repress divorce, it is wiser still to go a step higher and repress that conduct which makes divorce possible. It is the foremost duty of this Court in dispensing the remedy of divorce to uphold the institution of marriage." In this case the income of the husband was estimated at 715*l*. net, from his property, and 400*l*. from his profession, while that of the wife was estimated at 155*l*., making a total joint income of 1,270*l*. Out of this the Court allotted the wife 400*l*., being the 155*l*. of her own and 245*l*. to be paid to her by her husband.

§ 37.

In a recent case the Court of Appeal stated that, in estimating what would be a reasonable amount for the wife's maintenance and support during the joint lives of the husband and wife, the circumstances which should be taken into account are—(1) the conduct of the parties; (2) their position in life; (3) their ages and respective means; (4) the amount of the provision actually made; (5) the existence or non-existence of children, and who is to have the care and custody of them; (6) any other circumstances which may be important in any particular case. Lord Justice Lindley then proceeded to refer to the circumstances of the case before the Court: "As regards the conduct of the parties, the wife here was the petitioner, and nothing is, or can be, said against her. The misconduct of her husband drove her to seek a divorce. This is very material in considering whether the words *dum casta* should be inserted; for although, on the one hand, as forcibly pointed out by Jeune, J., it is unjust to make an allowance cease on marriage, and not on illicit intercourse, yet, on the other hand, it is an insult to any woman of spotless character to provide against the contingency of her sinking so low as to render such a provision necessary. This view of the question is quite as important as the other. As regards the position of the parties and their respective means, much must turn on these matters. The least that a man ought to do for the maintenance and support of his wife, when he so disregards his own duties to his wife as to drive her from her home without any fault on her part, and practically force her to obtain a divorce, is to do what he can, consistently with his means, to maintain her in reasonable comfort, having regard to her age, health, and position in society. Both the amount he ought to allow her, and the duration of such allowance, ought to be fixed with reference to this consideration. The amount of her property, if any, ought obviously to be taken into consideration. If, as in this case, the husband's means are such that he can only allow his wife a bare subsistence, and she has nothing, it seems to us unjust to her that even this subsistence money should cease merely because she may marry again. The continuance of the allowance may conduce very materially to her marrying, and to her future comfort and happiness. On the other hand, justice to him does not, in our opinion, require the

What Court should take into account.

§ 37.

cessation of so small an allowance on her marrying again" (*Wood* v. *Wood*, (1891) P. 272).

But the Court will not order a husband, who has obtained a decree of dissolution of marriage, to secure his wife a gross or annual sum of money under this section unless proof of the husband's ability to pay it is given (*Ratcliffe* v. *Ratcliffe and Anderson*, 29 L. J., P. & M. 171).

Power order gross or annual sum to be secured must be exercised once for all.

The power which the Court has of ordering the husband, on a dissolution of marriage, to secure the wife a gross or annual sum of money is one that must be exercised once and for all, and in such a case the Court cannot, as in the case of permanent alimony, "adjust the burthen to the altered fortunes of the husband." Where, therefore, it appeared in a case (previous to the passing of the Matrimonial Causes Act, 1866), that the husband had an income of 300*l*. from his profession, and that the wife, in addition to an income of 12*l*., was entitled in reversion, on the death of a person aged eighty, to property which would produce 70*l*. a year, the Court refused to grant permanent maintenance to the wife, who had obtained a dissolution of her marriage (*Rawlins* v. *Rawlins*, 34 L. J., P. & M. 147).

Instances.

Although the amount to be allotted as a permanent provision for a wife who has obtained a decree of dissolution of her marriage will depend upon the circumstances of the particular case, the following cases may be referred to in connection with this subject:—

(a) Where it appeared that the husband's income was 1,660*l*., derived almost exclusively from shares and mortgages in foreign countries, the husband himself living in considerable style in an expensive house in Paris, the order of the Court, as modified by the Court of Appeal, was that the husband should secure to the wife the gross sum of 7,500*l*. within one month, or that within the same time he should secure to her the sum of 500*l*. *per annum* for her life (*Medley* v. *Medley*, 7 P. D. 122; 51 L. J., P. & M. 74).

(b) The husband, a lieutenant-colonel in Her Majesty's Indian Army, had been allowed to retire on a pension of 359*l*. 12*s*. 6*d*. a year, and to commute one-third of such pension; the Court, on dissolving the marriage at the suit of the wife, allotted her maintenance at the rate of 11*l*. 9*s*. 6*d*. a month (*Birch* v. *Birch*, 8 P. D. 163; 52 L. J., P. & M. 88). In this case the sum of 148*l*. 9*s*. 1*d*. being due for costs and arrears of maintenance, a writ of sequestration was issued, and the wife moved the Court to restrain the husband or his agents from receiving the pension, or any part thereof, or any moneys arising from a commutation, and the sequestrators be authorized to receive the same until the said sum had been paid. The Court, however, held that a military pension of this kind was on the same footing as half-pay or as an allowance for maintenance to a public civil officer, and that the Court ought not by its order indirectly to make a pension assignable which the legislature had declared should not be so. The Court has, on the other hand, authorized sequestrators to receive portions of a civil service pension (*Sansom* v. *Sansom*, 4 P. D. 69).

(c) The only property brought into settlement belonged to the wife, who was petitioner in the suit, and consisted of 1,000*l.* invested on mortgage, and producing an income of 40*l.* a year. The wife was also entitled to the fifth part of a sum of 5,074*l.* 4*s.* 2*d.*, subject to the life interest of a lady seventy-five years of age. The husband had an income of 400*l.* a year, and had also a reversionary interest, dependent on the life of a lady of ninety years of age, in a sum which produced an income of from 400*l.* to 450*l.* The Court directed that the husband should secure to the petitioner, during their lives, the annual sum of 130*l.*, being about one-third of his income, leaving the petitioner, over and above that amount, in possession of the 40*l.* a year, the respondent's interest in which was to be extinguished, and leaving the reversionary interests of both husband and wife untouched (*Harrison* v. *Harrison*, 12 P. D. 130; 56 L. J., P. & M. 76).

(d) The wife had obtained a decree of dissolution of marriage, and on her petition for permanent maintenance it appeared that the husband, in addition to his pay and allowances as a surgeon in Her Majesty's Navy, amounting to 228*l.* 2*s.* 6*d.*, was also entitled under the will of his father to an income amounting to 109*l.* 4*s.* 6*d.* arising from certain houses and shares vested in trustees upon trust for the sole use and benefit of the respondent, and to be assigned, transferred, and handed over to him as soon as conveniently might be after the death of his father, subject to a proviso that if the respondent should die unmarried and without issue his share should go over,

§ 37.

and also that the property assigned in trust for the respondent was to be held by the trustees upon the express condition that he should not during his life have power to sell, alien, charge or encumber any part of the property, and that in that event the trustees should stand possessed of such property in trust for other persons. There was no issue of the marriage, and the wife was without means and wholly dependent upon her father. It was contended for the respondent that the property devised to him was not property on which a sum for the wife's maintenance could be secured, because, by the very act of charging the property in question with such sum, he would forfeit all his interest therein; but the Court held that the respondent took an absolute interest in fee simple under the instrument, and that the condition of forfeiture in case of charge or alienation was therefore void, and that he must be ordered to secure to his wife an annual sum of 84*l*. for her life (*Corbett* v. *Corbett*, 13 P. D. 136; affirmed on appeal, 14 P. D. 7).

(e) The wife, who had married the petitioner at the age of seventeen, thirteen years after the marriage sued for and obtained a decree of dissolution on the ground of the petitioner's adultery and cruelty; there was no issue of the marriage. The Court allotted the wife as permanent maintenance an annual sum of 195*l*., being one-third of the husband's income from securities and investments, for her life, and refused to make the maintenance dependent on her not marrying again (*Lister* v. *Lister*, 14 P. D. 175).

(f) The wife had obtained a decree of dissolution, and upon her application for permanent maintenance under sect. 32 of the Matrimonial Causes Act, 1857, it appeared that the husband was partner in a brewery, and was entitled to receive 200*l*. a month in respect of his share of the profits, but could not draw anything more without the consent of his partners. His share of the profits had for several years past amounted to 3,300*l*. a year, but he had received only the monthly allowance amounting to 2,400*l*. a year, the rest being carried to his account in the partnership books. The President of the Divorce Court (Mr. Justice Jeune) ordered the husband to secure permanent maintenance to his wife upon the basis of one-third of the whole of his share of the average profits to which he had been entitled during the three preceding years, but the Court of Appeal, reversing the order of the President, held that, for the purpose of determining the amount of the annual payment to be secured to the wife, the husband must be treated as having only an income of 2,400*l.*, and ordered that the sum of 300*l.* a year should be secured to her, leaving " the conveyancing counsel of the Court to exercise his ingenuity to devise the best security which he can, having regard, of course, to the terms of the partnership articles " (*Hanbury* v. *Hanbury*, (1894) P. 102; in app., p. 315).

§ 37.

(g) A wife, who had been deserted by her husband twenty-four years before suit, obtained a decree of dissolution on the ground of the desertion and adultery of her husband; in the two years previous to the date of the decree the husband's income had been Rs. 42,000, and Rs. 28,000 respectively, but the Court, in determining the suitable amount to award as permanent maintenance, took into consideration the circumstances of the husband at the time of the separation, and refused to grant maintenance in proportion to the improved circumstances of the husband, on the ground that the separation between the parties had continued for such a lengthy period (*Smythe* v. *Smythe*, 6 B. L. R., App. 153).

Permanent provision for guilty Wife.

Provision made for guilty wife.

As to whether the Court has jurisdiction to grant permanent alimony to a wife whose husband has obtained a decree for judicial separation on the ground of her misconduct, see *ante*, p. 217.

In a case which came before the Court of Appeal in 1883 it was contended on behalf of the husband, who had obtained a decree *nisi* for dissolution of the marriage, that up to that time permanent alimony for a guilty wife had not been ordered except with the consent of the husband, or under special circumstances. Jessel, M. R., thereupon remarked: "I am sorry to hear it. I am not giving a final opinion, but it appears to me that sect. 32 was intended to give the Court a discretion which was to be exercised according to the circumstances of each case, and that it was not intended that a guilty wife should be turned out into the streets to starve." And, subsequently,

§ 37.

in the course of his judgment, the same learned judge observed: "Now, under the thirty-second section, the practice seems to have grown up of not allowing maintenance to the guilty wife unless a special case is shown. I am not prepared to say on the present occasion that this is the correct rule. I am not going to lay it down that it is not. I should require further consideration and argument before doing so, but it appears to me that the thirty-second section of the Act has left an absolute discretion in the Court. I think that there was a good reason for doing so. When a divorce could only be obtained by Act of Parliament, it was in practice only obtained by wealthy persons, because it was very expensive, and it might well be considered right that where a wealthy man obtained a divorce from a wife who had no means of subsistence, he should, as a condition of his being granted that divorce, be compelled to make some provision for her, so that she should not be allowed to starve. But the Divorce Act was meant to apply not only to wealthy people but to all people, and, indeed, one of the strong grounds for passing it was that under the then system the wealthy alone could obtain a divorce. It was thought that this was not a right state of things, and consequently the remedy was made less expensive, so that all classes might be able to resort to it. Now in the case of people of small means very different considerations arise. When a working man who has married a washerwoman obtains a divorce, she can very well go to washing again. That is quite a different case from that of a gentleman of large means who obtains a special privilege by Act of Parliament. I should be inclined to say that where a wealthy gentleman obtains a divorce, the Court, in acting under sect. 32, ought to act on a rule somewhat similar to that established in the House of Lords under the old practice, for the reason of the thing appears to be the same; but we are not to be considered as finally deciding the point, or as laying down any rule for the guidance of the Divorce Court. I am only stating my present impression that the Court, under sect. 32, has full discretion, and is under no obligation to require special circumstances to be shown to entitle the guilty wife to some provision" (Jessel, M. R., *Robertson* v. *Robertson*, 8 P. D. 94).

Instances.

As a general rule, the Court will order some provision to be made for a guilty wife who has no means of her own, and is not in a position to earn her own living and support herself. In the following cases the husband, who had obtained a decree of dissolution of marriage, was ordered to make provision for the wife's maintenance :—

(a) The wife had no means of her own, but under the marriage settlement she was entitled to the dividends of 10,000*l.* consols for her life in the event of her surviving her husband, and also to a power of appointment by will of one-fifth part of that sum. The Court refused to interfere with the settlement, but ordered that a deed should be prepared by conveyancing counsel securing, during the husband's life, an annuity to his wife *quamdiu casta vixerit*, on condition that she gave up her right under the settlement to dispose of the 2,000*l.* consols (*Keats* v. *Keats and Montezuma*, 28 L. J., P. & M. at pp. 79, 80).

(b) The husband had obtained a decree of dissolution of marriage, but in the opinion of the Court he " did not take that care of his wife which he ought to have done, for it appears from the evidence that he allowed her to go out to parties alone without accompanying her, and that he allowed her, on these occasions, to remain out until late hours of the night. The co-respondent has absconded, and there appears to be no hope that he will make any provision for Mrs. Kelly. Under the circumstances the question is whether a small sum should be allowed to her for maintenance and support, or whether she should be left in a state of destitution." It appeared that the husband's pay amounted to Rs. 519 8 0 a month, and that his marriage expenses were Rs. 443 12 0. He had two daughters living, one by the respondent and one by a former wife, and he swore in his affidavit that he would be obliged to retire on his pension at the end of the year, when his income would be reduced to Rs. 220. He offered to settle on his wife the damages which he might recover in the suit, but there appeared to be very little prospect that those damages would ever be realized. The Court, under these circumstances, ordered the husband to pay his wife Rs. 50 a month for her maintenance so long as she continued chaste and unmarried, and also to settle on her any part of the damages which might be realized for her benefit so long as she continued chaste and unmarried; and after her death, or on forfeiture of that amount on account of any misconduct, the amount to be settled for the benefit of the child by her (*Kelly* v. *Kelly and Saunders*, 5 B. L. R. 71).

§ 37.

(c) The parties were married in 1873, and shortly after the birth of a son—the only issue of the marriage—the wife became temporarily insane and had to be confined in an asylum, from which, however, she was discharged in the same year. The husband was advised that, if cohabitation were resumed and his wife became pregnant, it would be dangerous to the health of the mother and child, and it was accordingly arranged, with the concurrence of the families of both parties, that they should live apart, and that the husband should allow his wife 1*l.* a week for the maintenance of herself and the child, which was regularly paid until the middle of 1889, but in May, 1879, the husband had taken the child away from the mother and assumed charge of it himself. The parties had not communicated with each other since 1880, and in 1889 the husband sued for, and obtained, a decree of dissolution of marriage on the ground of his wife's adultery with three co-respondents, resulting in the birth of four illegitimate children. The Court having intimated that it would not make the decree absolute until a provision had been made for the wife's maintenance, the husband agreed to allow her fifteen shillings a week, but asked that the payment should be ordered to her only so long as she remained chaste and unmarried. The Court, however, refused to order the insertion of a *dum casta et sola* clause, on the ground that it was a question, not of a large income, but of a bare allowance for the wife's support and maintenance (*Lander* v. *Lander*, (1891) P. 161).

(d) The husband's income was 126*l.* 14*s.* 5*d. per annum*, and at the trial the jury found that the wife and co-respondent had committed adultery, but that the petitioner had been guilty of cruelty towards his wife. Gorell Barnes, J., came to the conclusion that, as there was no finding that the petitioner's cruelty conduced in any way to the wife's adultery, a decree *nisi* might be pronounced, but stated that it would not be made absolute unless and until the petitioner had secured to the respondent, by a proper deed, the sum of 36*l. per annum, dum sola et casta vixerit* (*Edwards* v. *Edwards*, (1894) P. 33).

But where the marriage has been dissolved on account of the wife's misconduct the Court will not make an order under this section until proof of the husband's ability to provide permanent maintenance has been given (*Ratcliffe* v. *Ratcliffe and Anderson*, 29 L. J., P. & M. at p. 176).

And where damages have been awarded against the co-respondent the Court may order such damages to be settled upon the wife in lieu of ordering a settlement out of the husband's earnings (*Latham* v. *Latham and Gethin*, 30 L. J., P. & M. 43). So, in a case where 1,678*l.* had belonged to the wife, and on the marriage had been received by the husband, the Court, upon the dissolution of the marriage at the suit of the husband, ordered him to settle 1,000*l.* upon trust that the interest be applied for the benefit of the wife so long as she conducted herself properly and remained unmarried, and that, upon her interest ceasing, the fund should be held in trust for the children of the marriage in equal shares; and, further, that the 1,000*l.*, damages awarded against the co-respondent, should be paid to the husband in lieu of the sum which he would have to settle, and that the decree should be suspended until the settlement should be made (*Bent* v. *Bent and Footman*, 30 L. J., P. & M. 175).

§ 37.
Damages ordered to be settled on guilty wife.

If permanent alimony has been awarded to a wife upon her obtaining a judicial separation, and the husband afterwards obtains a decree *nisi* for dissolution of marriage on the ground of her adultery, the Court will not, before the decree has been made absolute, discharge the order for payment of alimony (*Stoate* v. *Stoate*, 30 L. J., P. & M. 108).

Allowance under Deed of Separation: Permanent Alimony or Maintenance.

Allowance under deed of separation, effect of upon question of permanent maintenance.

The question whether a wife who has been in receipt of an allowance under a deed of separation can, upon a decree of dissolution of marriage or of judicial separation, apply for an increased allowance by way of permanent maintenance depends upon the circumstances of the case.

In the first place, it is only in cases of dissolution of marriage that the Court "can inquire into the existence of ante-nuptial or post-nuptial settlements" and "make such orders with reference to the application of the whole or a portion of the property settled" as to the Court seems fit (sect. 40, Indian Divorce Act). This power is not given to the Court in cases of judicial separation. Where, therefore, the parties have separated owing to the adultery and cruelty of the husband and a deed of separation has been executed wherein the husband has covenanted to allow the wife a certain sum *per annum*, and the wife has, on her part, covenanted not to take any proceedings to compel her husband to allow her a larger amount of alimony, she is bound by such covenant, and cannot, upon a decree of judicial separation

(a) Upon decree of judicial separation.

§ 37.   subsequently obtained by her, apply for alimony at an increased rate, unless the misconduct of the husband has been such as to disentitle him to claim the benefit of the deed. "The wife is entitled to the annuity secured her by the deed, the husband is liable to pay the annuity. It is impossible, therefore, for the Court to allot such alimony as it may think just, because in the case of its thinking that the amount of alimony should be less than the annuity secured by the deed, it has no power of setting aside the deed and no power to stop an action brought under the covenants of the deed against the husband. It is, therefore, a case where the ordinary powers of the Court cannot be exercised, except in one direction, viz., by increasing the amount of alimony. That being so, we must consider whether in such a case of contract the Court can interfere except when one of the parties to the contract has so acted as to disentitle him to rely upon the contract at all. I am not saying that there may not be such a case; on the contrary, I can quite conceive such a case. But, unless there is such a case, why should the Court interfere with the contract? I see that the learned judge put it on the ground of public policy. I have explained more than once, and especially in a case which has been referred to by the learned judge himself, of *Besant* v. *Wood*, 12 Ch. D. 605, that there is no reason more dangerous to give, and no reason on which such difference of opinion exists, as public policy" (Jessel, M. R., *Gandy* v. *Gandy*, 7 P. D. 168; 51 L. J., P. & M. 41).

But, even in case of judicial separation, "it may well be that such gross misconduct, misconduct of a nature so entirely different from that which the parties were providing for when they entered into the deed of separation, might prevent the husband from in any way relying on that deed, and might render it just that the bargain made by the wife for maintenance should be disregarded on an application to the Court for alimony" (Cotton, L. J., *ibid.*).

And if, after a decree of judicial separation, the wife is given the custody of the children and the husband refuses to support them, the wife will be held no longer bound by the covenants in the separation deed, and the Divorce Court, being free to disregard it, has power to do what it thinks just in making her an allowance in the shape of alimony, and to take into account whatever circumstances it considers material in arriving at a conclusion as to what is just under the altered position of the parties (*Gandy* v. *Gandy*, 30 Ch. D. 57; *Judkins* v. *Judkins*, (1897) P. 138).

On the other hand, in view of the power given to the Court under sect. 40 of the Indian Divorce Act (22 & 23 Vict. c. 61, s. 5), the Court has the power, upon a dissolution of marriage, to allot the wife permanent maintenance at a higher rate than the allowance which she has covenanted to accept under a deed of separation (*Morrall* v. *Morrall*, 6 P. D. 98; 50 L. J., P. & M. 62).

§ 37.
(b) Upon dissolution of marriage.

In the case last cited, however, the husband had been guilty of incestuous adultery subsequently to the execution of the deed, and even if the wife had merely sued for judicial separation it might well be that such misconduct on his part would have disentitled him to rely upon the deed. But, in a recent case, where the wife, who had obtained a decree of dissolution, petitioned for permanent maintenance, and it appeared that by post-nuptial deeds, made apparently in consideration of the abandonment of former proceedings instituted by her, she was to receive an allowance of 100*l.* a year in the event of her husband's adultery, or cruelty, and that the husband's income was 600*l.* a year, the Court, notwithstanding the deed, ordered permanent maintenance at the rate of 200*l.* a year (*Wilkinson* v. *Wilkinson*, 69 L. T. 459; and see *Bishop* v. *Bishop*, (1897) P. 138; xiii Times L. Reps. 202, where *Gandy* v. *Gandy* is considered and explained).

And, where the marriage is dissolved on account of the wife's misconduct, the Court has the power of setting aside a deed of separation whereby the husband has covenanted to pay an allowance to the wife. In such a case it may grant the wife as permanent maintenance an allowance considerably less than that which she has received under the deed (*Clifford* v. *Clifford*, 9 P. D. 76).

Enforcement of Order for Permanent Maintenance.

Enforcement of order.

An order under sect. 37 of the Indian Divorce Act can be enforced by the imprisonment of the husband, or by the attachment and sale of his property, or by both (sect. 254, Civil Procedure Code, 1882).

As to what property may be so attached and sold, see O'Kinealy's Civil Procedure Code, 1882, notes to sect. 266.

Pensions granted under the Indian Pensions Act, 1871, cannot be assigned, and cannot, therefore, be attached (see *Birch* v. *Birch*, 8 P. D. 163).

The Court has no power to grant an attachment against the husband for non-payment of the arrears of an annuity granted under sect. 32 of the Matrimonial Causes Act, 1857 (*De Lossy* v. *De Lossy*, 15 P. D. 115).

§ 37.

Computation of husband's income.

Husband's Income: how computed.

When there has been a contest as to the amount of alimony *pendente lite*, the Court will not allow the question as to the amount of the husband's income to be re-opened on the application for permanent alimony, unless the income has in the meantime altered (*Franks* v. *Franks*, 31 L. J., P. & M. 25; *Greenwood* v. *Greenwood*, 32 L. J., P. & M. 136; *Bonsor* v. *Bonsor*, (1897) P. 77). And if, upon an application for permanent alimony, either party wishes to show that there has been an alteration of such income since the allotment of alimony *pendente lite*, he or she must file a petition alleging such increase or diminution, as the case may be (*Fisk* v. *Fisk*, 31 L. J., P. & M. 60). But in a subsequent case the Court allowed the husband, upon an application for permanent alimony, to bring the fact of the diminution of his income before the Court by affidavit, although he had filed no petition alleging such diminution (*Davies* v. *Davies*, 32 L. J., P. & M. 152).

In the absence of proof that the husband's income has altered since the application for alimony *pendente lite*, permanent alimony will be allotted upon that which appeared then to be his income, although the wife may since have discovered that his income at that time was greater (*Greenwood* v. *Greenwood*, 32 L. J., P. & M. 136).

Where a wife applied for permanent alimony on a decree of judicial separation by reason of the cruelty of her husband, which the Court stigmatized as gross, and the husband stated on affidavit that, since the allotment of alimony *pendente lite*, he had parted with his business for a yearly payment of 300*l.* and 5 per cent. on the value of the stock-in-trade, warehouse, debts, &c., the Court held that, in allotting alimony, the 300*l.* per annum must be taken as income, and granted the wife permanent alimony at the rate of 150*l.* a year, observing that, if the income subsequently failed, the husband could apply for reduction of the alimony (*Moore* v. *Moore*, 3 S. & T. 606; 34 L. J., P. & M. 146).

In estimating the amount of the husband's income for the purposes of permanent alimony, the same deductions are allowable as in the case of an estimation of such income for the purposes of alimony *pendente lite*.

Voluntary allowance to husband.

The mere fact that the husband's income consists of a voluntary allowance to which he has no legal right does not necessarily preclude the Court from awarding permanent alimony (*Clinton* v. *Clinton*, 1 P. D. 215; *Moss* v. *Moss and*

Bushe, 15 W. R. 532; *Bonsor* v. *Bonsor*, (1897) P. 77; xiii T. L. R. 184). For in such cases injustice to the husband is prevented by the provisions in the Act which allow the maintenance to be reduced or suspended if his means of paying it fail (*Bonsor* v. *Bonsor*, (1897) P. 77).

§ 37.

"**May cause a proper instrument to be executed**":

Execution of proper instrument.

The question whether an allowance to the wife is to continue only *dum casta et sola vixerit* should be left to be decided when the deed of security is settled (*Medley* v. *Medley*, 7 P. D. 122; 51 L. J., P. & M. 74).

Dum casta et sola clause.

Whether or not such a clause should be inserted is a matter for the discretion of the Court; "there is no rule one way or the other, nor ought there to be one; each case ought to depend on its own circumstances"; but, as a general rule, the clause will not be inserted where the wife is the innocent party. The innocence or guilt of the wife is "very material in considering whether the words *dum casta* should be inserted, for although, on the one hand, as forcibly pointed out by Jeune, J., it is unjust to make an allowance cease on marriage and not on illicit intercourse, yet, on the other hand, it is an insult to any woman of spotless character to provide against the contingency of her sinking so low as to render such a provision necessary. This view of the question is quite as important as the other" (Lindley, L. J., *Wood* v. *Wood*, (1891) P. 272; 60 L. J., P. & M. 66).

Nor, where the wife is the innocent party and the conduct of the husband has been bad, will the Court, as a rule, limit the allowance to such time as the wife remains unmarried (*Lister* v. *Lister*, 14 P. D. 175; affirmed in app., 15 P. D. 4; but in an earlier case the Court ordered the insertion of the *dum casta et sola* clause, although the wife was the innocent party (*Sidney* v. *Sidney*, 34 L. J., P. & M. 122).

On the other hand, where the wife is the guilty party, the allowance made to her will, as a rule, be qualified by the insertion of the *dum casta et sola* clause (*Keats* v. *Keats and Montezuma*, 28 L. J., P. & M. 57; *Bent* v. *Bent and Footman*, 30 L. J., P. & M. 175; *Edwards* v. *Edwards*, (1894) P. 33; 63 L. J., P. & M. 62; *Weller* v. *Weller*,* 63 L. T. 263). But even if the

---

* In this case the solicitors for the petitioner and respondent had settled an agreement which was signed by both parties, and contained a clause to the effect that the allowance should continue so long as the respondent should remain chaste and unmarried. Butt, J., expressed disfavour with the *dum casta* clause.

§ 37.

wife is the guilty party the clause will not be inserted if the allowance is but a bare subsistence (*Lander* v. *Lander*, (1891) P. 161).

Monthly or weekly payments.

"**An order on the husband for payment to the wife of such monthly or weekly sums**":

An order for maintenance cannot be made in the alternative for securing a gross or annual sum of money, or else for the payment of monthly or weekly sums by the husband; nor, as the preamble to the Matrimonial Causes Act, 1866 (29 & 30 Vict. c. 32), shows, was it intended that the Court should make an order for payment of monthly or weekly sums in a case in which the husband has property which is abundantly sufficient for securing a gross or annual sum, although such property may be situate abroad (*Medley* v. *Medley*, 7 P. D. 122—C. A.). But it is not only in the case of a poor man that the Court has the power to order monthly or weekly payments; it may exercise this power to order considerable sums to be so paid as permanent maintenance. The real object of the clause is to enable the Court to make orders which can be varied whenever necessary, and is specially applicable to cases in which "the husband has a large capital fairly and reasonably locked up in trade, so that it is not easy to secure upon it a fixed sum without doing that which of course it is most desirable not to do, namely, destroy the very means by which the trade is carried on" (*Jardine* v. *Jardine*, 6 P. D. 213, Full Court).

Power of Court to vary order.

"**Discharge or modify the order or temporarily to suspend the same**":

But the Court has no power, after a decree absolute for dissolution of marriage, to increase the allowance once made; for, as the marriage bond is at an end, there is no reason why the woman's allowance should increase with her late husband's means (*Watkins* v. *Watkins*, (1896) P. 222; 65 L. J., P. & M. 175).

As has been already pointed out, the monthly or weekly sums ordered to be paid to a wife are inalienable by her.

Court may direct payment of alimony to wife or to her trustee.

38. In all cases in which the Court makes any decree or order for alimony, it may direct the same to be paid either to the wife herself, or to any trustee on her behalf to be approved of by the Court, and may

impose any terms or restrictions which to the Court § 38.
seem expedient, and may, from time to time, appoint a
new trustee if it appears to the Court expedient so to do.

Sect. 24 of the Matrimonial Causes Act, 1857, is identical in terms with the above.

"**To be paid either to the wife herself or to any trustee on her behalf**": — Alimony, how payable.

When alimony is by the terms of the order payable to the wife herself, the husband is not bound, at her request, to pay it to her solicitor, but the Court may allow such an order to be amended by making the alimony payable to the wife's solicitor. In such a case it will not allow her the costs of the motion to amend the order (*Parr* v. *Parr and White*, 32 L. J., P. & M. 90). In a case where the order did not state to whom the alimony was payable, but it appeared that the wife and her solicitor had at the same time demanded payment of the husband and he had paid neither, the Court granted an attachment against the husband (*Ladmore* v. *Ladmore*, 32 L. J., P. & M. 157).

The practice of the English Court is not to order alimony to be paid to the wife's solicitor or proctor except upon a written application from the wife, and when it is so paid the solicitor is not entitled to charge for receiving it (*Margetson* v. *Margetson*, 35 L. J., P. & M. 80).

X.—*Settlements.*

39. Whenever the Court pronounces a decree of dissolution of marriage or judicial separation for adultery of the wife, if it is made to appear to the Court that the wife is entitled to any property, the Court may, if it think fit, order such settlement as it thinks reasonable to be made of such property or any part thereof, for the benefit of the husband, or of the children of the marriage, or of both. — Power to order settlement of wife's property for benefit of husband and children.

Any instrument executed pursuant to any order of the Court at the time of or after the pronouncing of a

§ 39.

decree of dissolution of marriage or judicial separation, shall be deemed valid notwithstanding the existence of the disability of coverture at the time of the execution thereof.

Settlement of damages.

The Court may direct that the whole or any part of the damages recovered under section thirty-four shall be settled for the benefit of the children of the marriage, or as a provision for the maintenance of the wife.

Sect. 45 of the Matrimonial Causes Act, 1857 (20 & 21 Vict. c. 85), provides that:—

"In any case in which the Court shall pronounce a sentence of divorce or judicial separation for adultery of the wife, if it shall be made to appear to the Court that the wife is entitled to any property either in possession or reversion, it shall be lawful for the Court, if it shall think proper, to order such settlement as it shall think reasonable to be made of such property or any part thereof, for the benefit of the innocent party, and of the children of the marriage, or either or any of them."

And sect. 6 of the Matrimonial Causes Act, 1860 (23 & 24 Vict. c. 144), provides that:—

"Any instrument executed pursuant to any order of the Court made under the said enactment" [*that is, under sect. 45 of 20 & 21 Vict. c. 85*], "before or after the passing of this Act, at the time of, or after the pronouncing of a final decree of divorce or judicial separation, shall be deemed valid and effectual in the law, notwithstanding the existence of the disability of coverture at the time of the execution thereof."

See Rules of the English Divorce Court, Nos. 95—103, and 204.

Decree of dissolution of marriage.

"**A decree of dissolution of marriage**":

This includes a decree *nisi*, for (a) whenever a decree absolute alone is meant, it is expressly provided that the power given to the Court is to be exercised only when the decree has been made absolute, or, in the case of a decree of a District Court, the decree has been confirmed by the High Court (see sects. 37, 40, 43, 44); (b) the power given to the Court is one that can be exercised as well upon a decree of judicial separation as upon a decree of dissolution; and (c) an instrument executed "*after the pronouncing of a decree of dissolution of marriage* shall be deemed to be valid *notwithstanding the existence of the disability of coverture at the time of the execution thereof.*"

But where property is settled on a wife, by instrument other

SETTLEMENTS.

than the marriage settlement, to her separate use *without power of anticipation*, the Court has no power to make any order for settlement of such property until the wife becomes discovert, *i.e.*, till the decree *nisi* has been made absolute (see *infra*).

§ 39.

"Decree of judicial separation":

It is to be noted that it is only when the decree of judicial separation is made on the ground of the wife's *adultery* that the Court can make an order under this section.

Decree of judicial separation.

"The Court may order such settlement":

Under this section the Court has no power to deal with ante-nuptial or post-nuptial settlements; if, therefore, the wife is entitled to property under such settlements, the Court can inquire into the existence of, and deal with, such property only under sect. 40, that is to say, only after a decree absolute for dissolution of marriage or a decree of nullity of marriage, or, in the case of a District Court, after its decree for dissolution or nullity of marriage has been confirmed by the High Court. The Court cannot, therefore, upon a decree of judicial separation, make any order as to property to which the wife is entitled under a marriage settlement (see *Norris* v. *Norris*, 1 S. & T. 174; 27 L. J., P. & M. 172; *Seatle* v. *Seatle*, 30 L. J., P. & M. 216).

Power of Court to order settlement.

"Wife is entitled to any property":

As has been already observed, in no case can the Court, *under this section*, deal with property to which the wife is entitled under an ante-nuptial or post-nuptial settlement. Such property can only be dealt with under sect. 40. If the property to which the wife is entitled is settled on her, *by instrument other than a marriage settlement*, to her separate use *without power of anticipation*, the Court cannot, upon a decree of judicial separation, make any order for the settlement of such property or any part thereof for the benefit of the husband, or of the children of the marriage, or of both; nor, in a suit for dissolution of marriage, can it make any such order until the wife becomes discovert, that is to say, until after the decree *nisi* has been made absolute (*Michell* v. *Michell*, (1891) P. 208; 60 L. J., P. & M. 46; *Norris* v. *Norris*, 1 S. & T. 174; 27 L. J., P. & M. 172; *Midwinter* v. *Midwinter*, (1892) P. 208).

Wife entitled, under instrument other than marriage settlement, to property without power of anticipation.

But in such a case, although the Court cannot make any order for the settlement of such property until after the decree

§ 39.

absolute, it can, before the decree *nisi* is made absolute, in any case where it is fairly and reasonably apparent that there is a necessity for so doing, direct an inquiry as to what property such wife is entitled to, in order that the Court may be in a position to order a settlement to be made of the wife's property as soon as the final order is pronounced. Before doing so, however, the Court will direct the husband to give security for the costs of the inquiry, in case no final decree should be made. And the settlement should not be ordered by the decree absolute itself, but by a subsequent order, though the latter may be made immediately after the decree absolute has been pronounced (*Midwinter* v. *Midwinter, ubi supra*).

If, however, the wife, in addition to property which she is restrained from anticipating, is entitled to property which she can do what she likes with, the Court, while refraining from dealing with the property subject to the restraint, will compel her to re-settle property which is at her absolute disposal (*Michell* v. *Michell, ubi supra*, explaining *Swift* v. *Swift*, 15 P. D. 118; (1891) P. 129).

Property to which wife is entitled absolutely.

If the wife is possessed of property which is at her absolute disposal, the Court, on pronouncing a decree of dissolution of marriage or of judicial separation on the ground of her adultery, has an absolute discretion to make any order with reference to the settlement of such property for the benefit of the husband, or of the children, or of both.

So, where a wife was entitled to the interest of 4,000*l*. vested in trustees for her life, with a power of appointment amongst her children, and her husband obtained a decree of judicial separation on the ground of her adultery, the Court ordered that the trustees of the wife should pay over a moiety of her income to trustees named by the husband to be applied by them to the maintenance and education of the children of the marriage, but declared that it had no jurisdiction to deal with her power of appointment (*Seatle* v. *Seatle*, 30 L. J., P. & M. 216).

Spes successionis.

But a mere *spes successionis*, or a possibility of income, is not " property " within the meaning of this section.

Where, therefore, the wife, under the marriage settlement of her father, was entitled to a sum of money after his death in the event of his not otherwise disposing of it, the Court held that this possibility of succeeding to her father was not property which could be dealt with under this section (*Stone* v. *Stone and Brownrigg*, 33 L. J., P. & M. 95; cf. *Parsons, In re, Stockley* v. *Parsons*, 45 Ch. D. 51; 59 L. J., Ch. 666).

§ 39.

So, where, under the will of her father, the respondent had a life interest to her separate use in certain property, unless she, being discovert, should do or suffer any act or thing, or any event should happen, whereby the same income or any part thereof should, either voluntarily or involuntarily, be aliened or encumbered, or be receivable otherwise than by herself personally, in which case the trust for her benefit was to be void, and such annual income was to be applied for the benefit of the respondent or her children at the discretion of the trustees, the Court, while ordering a settlement to be made out of the respondent's life income, derived under her father's will, in favour of the husband and his children, refused to extend the order to any moneys the trustees in their discretion might think proper to pay to her in case the substituted trust came into operation by reason of such order, a mere possibility of income not being property in reversion within the meaning of sect. 45 of 20 & 21 Vict. c. 85 (*Milne* v. *Milne and Fowler*, L. R., 2 P. 295).

Property coming to wife after decree *nisi*.

After a decree *nisi* for dissolution of the marriage on the ground of the wife's adultery, the respondent became entitled to a sum of 500*l.*, which was the only property she possessed. The Court refused to order, under the 45th section of 20 & 21 Vict. c. 85, that a part of this sum should be applied to the repayment of costs incurred by the husband in the suit, although she had been guilty of gross misconduct and had increased the costs of the suit by an unfounded counter-charge against the husband, but stated that, if the respondent had been possessed of a considerable sum, it would have compelled her to repay to her husband the costs which he had incurred (*Carstairs* v. *Carstairs, Billson and Dickenson*, 3 S. & T. 538; 33 L. J., P. & M. 170).

"For the benefit of the husband or of the children of the marriage, or of both":

For the benefit of the husband or children, or both.

Under this section the Court can order a settlement to be made for the benefit of the husband or of the children of the marriage, or of both, but it cannot order any part of the property of a guilty wife to be settled on her. It may, however, refuse to make any order as to such property, and so leave it in her possession (*Bacon* v. *Bacon and Bacon*, 29 L. J., P. & M. 125; 2 S. & T. 86).

So, where, on a dissolution of marriage on the ground of the wife's adultery, the husband petitioned that certain jewellery belonging to her should be sold and a settlement made of the proceeds, giving her a life interest in the income arising from

§ 39.

Court will not make allowance to husband variable, or limit it dum solus.

Court will not enter into debtor and creditor account between husband and wife.

the investment of these proceeds, with remainder to himself, and it appeared that his income was substantial and his wife's only 72*l.* a year, the Court refused to order any settlement (*Schofield* v. *Schofield*, 64 L. T. 838).

The Court, in ordering a settlement under sect. 45 of 20 & 21 Vict. c. 85, refused to make the allowance to the husband variable according to the possible fluctuation in the value of the wife's property, or to limit it till such time as he should remain unmarried (*Midwinter* v. *Midwinter*, (1893) P. 93).

In ascertaining the amount of an allowance to be settled by the wife upon the husband, the Court declined to go into a minute debtor and creditor account of the sums spent by the husband or wife on household expenses and the like, but directed that a deduction should be made from the amount of the annual payment to the husband until a loan of 300*l.*, which he had obtained from his wife, was repaid; and also took into consideration the contingency of the husband being able to acquire an income by his own earnings (*Swift* v. *Swift*, (1891) P. 129; 60 L. J., P. & M. 14; see also *Michell* v. *Michell*, (1891) P. 208, in which *Swift* v. *Swift* is explained).

In ordering a settlement under this section, the Court will take into consideration the costs with which the wife will be burdened in defending the suit, for which her husband is not strictly liable (*Bacon* v. *Bacon and Bacon*, 29 L. J., P. & M. 125).

"**Damages recovered under section 34 shall be settled**":
See note to sect. 34, *ante*, pp. 195—199.

Inquiry into existence of ante-nuptial or post-nuptial settlements.

40. The High Court, after a decree absolute for dissolution of marriage, or a decree of nullity of marriage,

and the District Court, after its decree for dissolution of marriage or of nullity of marriage has been confirmed,

may inquire into the existence of ante-nuptial or post-nuptial settlements made on the parties whose marriage is the subject of the decree, and may make such orders, with reference to the application of the whole or a portion of the property settled, whether for the benefit of the husband or the wife, or of the children (if any) of the marriage, or of both children and parents, as to the Court seems fit:

§ 40.

Provided that the Court shall not make any order for the benefit of the parents or either of them at the expense of the children.

The Matrimonial Causes Act, 1859 (22 & 23 Vict. c. 61), s. 5, provides that—

> "The Court after a final decree of nullity of marriage or dissolution of marriage may inquire into the existence of ante-nuptial or post-nuptial settlements made on the parties whose marriage is the subject of the decree, and may make such orders with reference to the application of the whole or a portion of the property settled either for the benefit of the children of the marriage or of their respective parents as to the Court shall seem fit."

The Matrimonial Causes Act, 1878 (41 Vict. c. 19), s. 3, extends the power given by sect. 5 of 22 & 23 Vict. c. 61, and provides that the Court may act under that section notwithstanding that there are no children of the marriage.

See Rules of the English Divorce Court, Nos. 95—103 and 204.

"Inquiry into existence of ante-nuptial or post-nuptial settlements":

A dissolution of marriage does not *per se* create a forfeiture of the interests even of the guilty party under a marriage settlement of the other's property (*Fitzgerald* v. *Chapman*, 1 Ch. D. 563; 45 L. J., Ch. 23; *Burton* v. *Sturgeon*, 2 Ch. D. 318; 45 L. J., Ch. 633).

Dissolution of marriage does not *per se* create forfeiture.

"May inquire":

In order to set the Court in motion, it is necessary to file a separate petition praying for a variation of the marriage settlement (see rule 95 of the English Divorce Court Rules).

Inquiry by Court: only on petition.

Such petition must bear a Court fee stamp of Rs. 20 (Indian Court Fees Act, 1870, 2nd Sch., Art. 20), and must be duly signed and verified by the petitioner or some other competent person (sect. 47, *post*). Ordinarily, such petition should be signed by the petitioner himself or herself; but if it is shown that the petitioner does desire the Court to act under this section,

Court fee stamp.

§ 40.

but that his or her signature cannot be obtained without considerable delay, the Court may allow the petitioner's solicitors to sign the petition (*Ross* v. *Ross*, 7 P. D. 20; 51 L. J., P. & M. 22).

For a form of petition, see the Schedule of Forms, No. 20 (and also *Boynton* v. *Boynton*, 30 L. J., P. & M., at p. 157).

Contents of petition. — The petition should give full information as to the means of the applicant (*Webster* v. *Webster and Mitford*, 32 L. J., P. & M. 29), and the settlement should be brought before the Court upon affidavit (*Horne* v. *Horne*, 30 L. J., P. & M. 200).

When to be filed.

When petition should be filed.—When it is desired to obtain an order varying a settlement, a petition for dissolution of marriage should contain a prayer respecting such settlement, and before the decree *nisi* is pronounced a separate petition for an order as to the application of the settled property should be filed. In order to allow this to be done, the Court will suspend the decree *nisi* (*Porter* v. *Porter*, 30 L. J., P. & M. 112, note).

The petition may, however, be filed at any time before the decree *nisi* is made absolute. And even if the petition is filed after the decree absolute the Court will not refuse to entertain it if the delay is not unreasonable. So, where the petition was filed shortly after the respondent and co-respondent had intermarried, and about four months after the decree had been made absolute, the Court held that, under the circumstances of the case, the delay was not a bar to the petition, especially in view of the fact that the subsequent marriage of the respondent was not with a person ignorant of the facts of the case, but with the co-respondent, "who was cognizant of all the facts, and who knew he was contracting marriage with a person liable to be affected by the order of this Court varying her settlement" (*Benyon* v. *Benyon and O'Callaghan*, 1 P. D. 447; 45 L. J., P. & M. 96; cf. *Marsh* v. *Marsh*, 47 L. J., P. & M. 34; in app. 47 L. J., P. & M. 78).

But, though the petition for variation of marriage settlements should ordinarily be filed before the decree *nisi* is pronounced, the Court has no jurisdiction to make any inquiry or order until after the decree has been made absolute (*Horne* v. *Horne*, 30 L. J., P. & M. 111).

Service of petition.

Service of petition.—Every petition under this section should be served personally on the husband or wife, as the case may be, and on the person or persons who may have any legal or beneficial interest in the property in respect of which the application is made, unless the Court shall direct any other mode of service, or dispense with service of the same on them or either of them (Rule 97 of the English Divorce Court Rules; and see sect. 50, *post*). If, however, the petition for dissolution of marriage contains a prayer for an order under this section and has been served upon the respondent, who has not appeared, notice of the application need not be given. But, if the petition for dissolution contains no such prayer, a copy of the petition for an order under sect. 40, as well as notice of the intended application for an order, should be served upon the respondent who has not appeared in the suit (*Horne* v. *Horne*, 30 L. J., P. & M. 200; *Lawrence* v. *Lawrence*, 32 L. J., P. & M. 124).

§ 40.

Who may apply for an order.—Ordinarily it is the petitioner in the suit who alone can apply, after the final decree, for an order under this section. If, however, the petitioner dies *after the final decree*, and there are children of the marriage which has been dissolved or annulled, the guardian of the children can apply, on their behalf, for an alteration of the terms of the settlement (*Ling* v. *Ling and Croker*, 4 S. & T. 99; 34 L. J., P. & M. 52).

Who can apply for order varying settlements.

Guardian of children.

But if the petitioner has died before the decree *nisi* has been made absolute or confirmed, as the case may be, the suit abates, and the guardian of the children cannot apply to have the decree made absolute or confirmed, so as to enable him to subsequently apply for an order under this section (*Grant* v. *Grant*, 31 L. J., P. & M. 174; cf. *Stanhope* v. *Stanhope*, 11 P. D. 103).

If the guardian of the children happens to be also the executor or administrator of the petitioner, who has died after the final decree, he must apply in his capacity of guardian of the children, and not as executor or administrator of the petitioner (*Smithe* v. *Smithe*, L. R., 1 P. 587).

For sect. 40 was intended for the benefit of living persons, and not for the benefit of the estate of a deceased petitioner. If, therefore, the petitioner has died before any order has been made under the section, and there are no children of the marriage, the Court will refuse to entertain an application by the petitioner's executor for an order to vary a settlement for the benefit of the petitioner's estate. And if, in a marriage settlement, there is an interest in remainder in default of issue, after the death of the parties to the marriage, the persons representing that interest cannot, upon the death of the petitioner, seek to benefit at the

§ 40.

Settlor.

expense of the guilty party by applying for an order under sect. 40 (*Thomson* v. *Thomson*, (1896) P. 263; 65 L. J., P. & M. 65, and, in app., 80).

Nor is the settlor entitled to apply, after the death of the petitioner and in the absence or after the death of any issue of the marriage, to be relieved from the covenants of the settlement: the Court has power to alter the settlement only for the benefit of the husband or wife or of the children, or of both of them, and if the petitioner and the children of the marriage die, the power of the Court is at an end, and the settlor must fulfil such covenants as he has entered into for the benefit of the respondent (*Sykes* v. *Sykes and Smith*, L. R., 2 P. 163; 39 L. J., P. & M. 52).

Guilty wife.

Sect. 40 should be read in connection with sect. 39, and "it would be a gross perversion of the meaning of the legislature if, at the prayer of an adulterous wife, the Court should deprive an innocent husband of any interest he takes under a settlement, even though it be for the benefit of the children of the marriage" (*Thompson* v. *Thompson*, 32 L. J., P. & M. 39).

On the same principle, the Court will refuse, at the prayer of a guilty husband, to deprive an innocent wife of her interest under the settlement.

Trustees of settlement.

The trustees of a marriage settlement can only be heard in support of the settlement; they are not entitled to apply for an order to vary it, nor can they be heard in support of an application to vary it (*Corrance* v. *Corrance*, L. R., 1 P. 495; 45 L. J., P. & M. 44).

Application for permanent maintenance and for variation of settlement.—Upon a dissolution of marriage at her instance, the wife is, apparently, entitled to apply both for permanent maintenance under sect. 37 and for an alteration of the marriage settlement under sect. 40 (*Sowden* v. *Sowden*, 15 W. R. (Eng.) 90).

"Dissolution of marriage or nullity of marriage":

It will be noticed that the Court has no power to deal with settlements after a decree of judicial separation (*Gandy* v. *Gandy*, 7 P. D. 168; 51 L. J., P. & M. 41).

After decree of nullity of marriage.

When a marriage is annulled, and there are no children of the union, the Court will order the property of the parties to be reconveyed to each of them respectively freed from the trusts of the settlement upon the alleged marriage (*A. f. c. M.* v. *M.*, 10 P. D. 178; 54 L. J., P. & M. 31; *Leeds* v. *Leeds*, 57 L. T. 373).

But if there are any children of the union between the parties due provision must be made for them (*Langworthy* v. *Langworthy*, 11 P. D. 85; 55 L. J., P. & M. 33).

§ 40.

"The High Court and the District Court":

The power to act under this section can be exercised only by that High Court or District Court which has pronounced the decree of dissolution or of nullity of marriage. Except so far that orders under sect. 40 are appealable, no Court, other than the Court which pronounced the decree in the suit, can inquire into the existence of settlements or make orders with reference to the application of the settled property. Where, therefore, a marriage had been declared null and void by a decree of the Court of New Zealand, the Court of Divorce in England refused to entertain a petition for variation of the marriage settlement, although both parties desired that the settlement should be varied by the English Court (*Moore f. c. Bull* v. *Bull*, (1891) P. 279; 60 L. J., P. & M. 76).

"After a decree ... may inquire":

While an inquiry is pending under this section the Court will by injunction, if necessary, restrain the husband or wife, as the case may be, from disposing of the settled property (*Watts* v. *Watts*, 24 W. R. (Eng.) 623).

And it will do so even before the order for variation of the settlement has been made (*Noakes* v. *Noakes and Hill*,* 4 P. D. 60; 47 L. J., P. & M. 20).

Injunction to restrain dealing with property pending inquiry.

"Ante-nuptial or post-nuptial settlements":

All deeds, whereby property is settled upon a woman in her character as wife, and to be paid to her while she continues a wife, come within the scope of this section, and the Court has power to deal with them. An ordinary deed of separation, whereby the husband covenants to pay the wife an allowance, is a post-nuptial settlement within the meaning of this section (*Worsley* v. *Worsley and Wignall*, L. R., 1 P. 648; 38 L. J., P. & M. 43).

What are settlements?

Deed of separation.

---

* In *Newton* v. *Newton* (11 P. D. 11) the learned judge, who decided *Noakes* v. *Noakes and Hill*, stated that in that case an order for variation of the settlement had been previously obtained. This appears to be a mistake, for the report (4 P. D. 60) states that the time for obtaining an order for variation of the settlement had not arrived when the application was made for the injunction.

§ 40.

A deed of separation which does not limit the liability of the husband to pay an allowance to the wife only so long as she remains chaste is not rendered void by the subsequent adultery of the wife or by a decree of dissolution of marriage on account of such adultery. In such an event, the husband, if he wishes to be relieved of his liability, must apply, after the decree absolute, for an order under sect. 40. The Court may, then, either deprive the guilty wife of the whole of the income under the deed, or reduce the amount of the allowance, or refuse to interfere at all, according to the circumstances of the case (*Clifford* v. *Clifford*, 9 P. D. 76; 53 L. J., P. & M. 68; *Saunders* v. *Saunders*, 69 L. T. 498).* On the other hand, where the marriage has been dissolved on account of the husband's misconduct, but the wife has covenanted in the deed of separation not to sue for an allowance other than that agreed upon, the Court will not so vary the deed as to give her an increased allowance, unless the misconduct of the husband has been so gross as to altogether disentitle him to rely upon the deed (*Morrall* v. *Morrall*, 6 P. D. 98; *Bishop* v. *Bishop*, (1897) P. 138; cf. *Gandy* v. *Gandy*, 7 P. D. 168—C. A.).

But the mere fact that the petitioner has accepted an allowance from the respondent under a deed of separation will not preclude him or her, after a decree absolute for dissolution of marriage, from applying for an increased provision out of the income of the respondent (*Benyon* v. *Benyon and Callaghan*, 1 P. D. 447). And, if the husband has covenanted to pay his wife an annuity, the Court has power under this section to reduce the amount thereof after a decree absolute has been pronounced in his favour (*Jump* v. *Jump*, 8 P. D. 159).

An absolute assignment by a wife to her husband, during the marriage, of freehold property is not a "settlement" within the meaning of this section (*Chalmers* v. *Chalmers*, 68 L. T. 28).

"Make such orders . . . . as to the Court seems fit":

Discretion of Court.

As expressly provided by this section, the Court is bound not to make any order for the benefit of the husband or wife, or both of them, at the expense of any child or children of the marriage. At the same time, the Court will not, at the instance of the guilty party, deprive the innocent party of his or her interest under the settlement, although to do so might be for the benefit

---

* See also pp. 235—237, *ante.*

of the children (*Thompson* v. *Thompson and Barras*, 32 L. J., P. & M. 39; 2 S. & T. 649).

§ 40.

For the general principle on which the Court acts in varying settlements is to put the innocent party, so far as it is practicable, in the same pecuniary position as he or she was before the marriage was dissolved (*Benyon* v. *Benyon and O'Callaghan*, 1 P. D. 447; *Maudslay* v. *Maudslay*, 2 P. D. 256).

If, therefore, the marriage is dissolved at the instance of the husband, and it is the wife who is possessed of the property, the Court will put the innocent husband in possession of a considerable proportion of the joint income. But if, previously to the institution of the suit for dissolution of marriage, the parties had been living apart under a deed of separation whereby the wife allowed the husband a certain sum *per annum*, and the husband was not in enjoyment of her income beyond such allowance, the Court will merely allot him a sufficient maintenance, having regard to his income and the position of the parties generally. *Primâ facie*, the amount which he has agreed to accept under the deed is a sufficient allowance, but the husband is not thereby precluded from praying for an increased allowance. For "he may have been content with a small portion of the wife's income while she retains the character and position of his wife, and at the same time may reasonably object to an adulterer enjoying her property and the income thereof in her society. It would be of evil example, and morally dangerous, if the wife's pecuniary position could not be altered by reason of her adultery subsequent to her husband's acceptance of an allowance" (*Benyon* v. *Benyon and Callaghan*, *ubi supra*).

Provided that the interests of the children are not adversely affected, the Court has full and absolute discretion to make such order under this section as to the Court seems fit, nor will the Court of Appeal interfere with the exercise of such discretion unless some distinct miscarriage is shown, although, in point of fact, the latter Court might not, if the matter had come before it originally, have made exactly the same order. This discretion must, however, be exercised judicially, and it is the duty of the Court to consider whose fault it is that the marriage has come to an end, not with a view of punishing the guilty party, but for the purpose of seeing what provisions it is reasonable to make (*Wigney* v. *Wigney*, 7 P. D. 177; 51 L. J., P. & M. 60—C. A.).

"In applying this section to the circumstances of any particular case, the first consideration will be this: What is the pecuniary change operated by the wife's criminality? The Court

Consideration for Court.

§ 40.

will look at the probable pecuniary position which the parties and their children would have occupied if the marriage which the settlement contemplated had continued a binding union, and the parties had lived in harmony together upon their joint incomes. If this union has been broken, and the common home abandoned by the criminality of one without fault in the other, it seems just that the innocent party should not, in addition to the grievous wrong done by the breach of the marriage vow, be wholly deprived of means to the scale of which he may have learnt to accommodate his mode of life. Nor, in viewing the matter on the other side, does it seem either just or equitable that funds, which were intended, at the time of the marriage, for the use of both, should be borne off by the guilty party, and perhaps transferred to the hands of the adulterer as the dowry of a second marriage. The interests of society point in the same direction. . . . The relative amounts contributed by each party, the conduct of each, the total amount of their joint income, the relation it bears to the requirements of the parties, and* their respective prospects of increased income, are all elements to be considered" (*March* v. *March and Palumbo*, 36 L. J., P. & M. 28; approved by the full Court at p. 65).

Conduct of both parties to be considered.

Nor is it only the conduct of the respondent that must be considered: regard must also be had to that of the petitioner. For it may happen that, though "the break-up of the married life was caused immediately by the misconduct of the respondent, its stability" may have been "undermined by the withdrawal of the petitioner's affections. It was a subject of fair comment that, but for the extravagance of the petitioner, and the conduct which made her the object of her husband's not unreasonable suspicions, the common fund would have been more than ample." And the Court will further take into consideration the fact that the petitioner has, during the marriage, received a large sum of money, and also the future of the respondent and the available means which would be left to him or her (*Chetwynd* v. *Chetwynd*, 35 L. J., P. & M. 21).

Court will not exercise power for

The power conferred upon the Court by this section will not be exercised by it for any collateral purpose. Where, therefore,

---

* But where the husband (who was the petitioner in the suit) held office in Her Majesty's household, and there was great probability of his promotion, the Court, in acting under this section, refused to take into account such probable promotion and consequent increase of salary (*Tupper* v. *Tupper*, 62 L. T. 665).

after a decree *nisi* had been made on the prayer of the husband for a dissolution of his marriage, the respondent, under cover of an order of the Court for access to her child, took possession of it, and removed it beyond the jurisdiction of the Court, the Court refused to alter the settlement made on the marriage of the parties, so far as related to the property settled on behalf of the respondent, in such a manner and for the express purpose to compel the respondent to submit to the authority of the Court, and to restore the child to the custody of the petitioner (*Symonds* v. *Symonds and Harrison*, L. R., 2 P. 447).

§ 40.

collateral purpose.

Interests of third parties in settled property.—Until a decree has been made for dissolution of marriage, there is no *lis pendens* with reference to the property included in the marriage settlements. Third parties can, therefore, acquire an interest in such property before the decree of dissolution is pronounced, and the Court has power, under this section, to make an order in favour of the interests of such parties, provided they were created before the filing of the petition for variation of the marriage settlement. And, as a rule, the Court is bound to respect the rights of third parties created before the petition for variation of settlements is presented. Where, therefore, a respondent had, before the decree *nisi* for dissolution of his marriage, charged his interest in the settlement with payment of his solicitor's costs of suits, the Court, under the circumstances of the case and with special reference to the facts that the petitioner was in possession of a considerable income altogether independent of her husband, that the husband had no means of his own with which to pay such costs, and that the solicitors had not been guilty of any misconduct, held that the charge was valid, and that the respondent's interests in the settlements could not be extinguished without providing for this charge (*Wigney* v. *Wigney*, 7 P. D. 228; 51 L. J., P. & M. 84).

Interests of third parties.

In the same case, when before the Court of Appeal, it was held that, as the husband was in receipt of about 900*l.* a year from the settled funds, he might reasonably and naturally expect to be able to pay out of that, and out of his wife's independent income of 1,100*l.* a year from the same funds, debts incurred on account of the joint establishment to an amount not exceeding 2,000*l.*, and that, consequently, before his interests under the settlement were extinguished, there must be an inquiry as to the amount of such debts, and that the wife should undertake to pay whatever sum should be found due on the result

§ 40.

Exceptions.

of such inquiry (*Wigney* v. *Wigney*, 7 P. D. 177; 51 L. J., P. & M. 60).

On the other hand, there are exceptional cases where the Court has refused to respect the interests acquired by a third party before the filing of a petition for variation of settlements. For instance, before a petition for this purpose had been filed by the petitioner, who had obtained a decree absolute for dissolution of his marriage, the respondent and co-respondent intermarried. It was held that, if the marriage had been with a stranger ignorant of the facts of the case, the Court might, under such circumstances, have been induced to hold its hand when asked to vary the respondent's interests under the settlement, but inasmuch as the marriage was with the co-respondent, who was cognizant of the facts and knew that he was contracting marriage with a person liable to be affected by an order of the Court varying her settlement, the mere fact that by such marriage the co-respondent had acquired an interest in the respondent's settlement before the petition was filed was no reason for refusing to vary such settlement at the prayer of the petitioner (*Benyon* v. *Benyon and O'Callaghan*, 1 P. D. 447).

Finality of order.

Finality of order.—The Court may make its original order in such a form that the allowance granted shall vary according to circumstances, but once an order has been made it is final, and should not be varied on the ground of a change of circumstances since the date of the order (*Benyon* v. *Benyon*, 15 P. D. 54; 59 L. J., P. & M. 39—C. A.; *Gladstone* v. *Gladstone*, 1 P. D. 442; 45 L. J., P. & M. 82).

At the same time, under special circumstances, the Court will review its order, *e.g.*, if the order as drawn up does not express what the Court intended; but it will not do so in any case without a re-hearing (*Cavendish* v. *Cavendish*, 38 L. J., P. & M. 13).

Whole or portion of the settled property.

"**The whole or a portion of the property settled**":

Where a settled fund is permanently secured by a deed, the legal destination of such fund continues the same until altered by the Court. Accordingly, up to the date of an order, whereby the destination of settled property is effected, it follows the destination mentioned in the deed, and the person who, by the deed, is entitled to the benefit, must obtain it up to that time.

Dividends due and payable before order.

The Court cannot, therefore, alter the destination of dividends due and payable before the date of its order (*Paul* v. *Paul and Farquhar*, L. R., 2 P. 93; 39 L. J., P. & M. 50).

The word "property" here used extends not only to income, but to capital, and the Court has jurisdiction to deal with capital in the same way as the income for the benefit of the husband, wife, and children, and in any case of emergency will not hesitate to do so (*Ponsonby* v. *Ponsonby*, 9 P. D. 122; 53 L. J., P. & M. 112—C. A.).

§ 40.

Capital fund.

An annuity covenanted to be paid in a deed of separation is "property settled" within the meaning of this section (*Jump* v. *Jump*, 8 P. D. 159).

Annuity.

But the Court cannot, under this section, deal with property to which the wife is entitled, under an instrument other than an ante-nuptial or post-nuptial settlement, to her separate use without power of anticipation, or absolutely. Such an instrument is not a settlement within the meaning of this section, and such property can only be dealt with under sect. 39 (see notes thereto).

Wife's power of appointment among the children.—By the marriage settlements, the wife, on account of whose adultery the marriage had been dissolved, had certain interests in her husband's property, and had also a joint power of appointment over the settled property of her husband and herself among the children of the marriage, and a further power of appointment in favour of any husband she might marry after the death of her late husband, and for the children of that marriage. There were two children of the marriage, both of whom were given over to the custody of the husband. The Court ordered that her interest in her husband's property and her power of appointment among the children of the marriage must be extinguished, and that her power of appointment in favour of a future husband and children in respect of her own settled property in possession and reversion, of which half the income was given to the petitioner for himself and the said two children, must not take effect until after the death of her late husband (*Noel* v. *Noel*, 10 P. D. 179; 54 L. J., P. & M. 73).

Wife's power of appointment among children.

In a later case it was argued that an order revoking a wife's power of appointment over a settled fund was not an order "with reference to the application of the whole or any portion of the property settled," within the meaning of this section, and that, therefore, the Court had no power to make such an order. But the Court overruled the objection, and revoked the power (*Bosvile* v. *Bosvile*, 13 P. D. 76; 57 L. J., P. & M. 62; cf. *Evered* v. *Evered*, 43 L. J., P. & M. 86).

§ 40.

Husband's power of appointment.

On the other hand, where the marriage has been dissolved on the ground of the husband's misconduct, and the marriage settlement gave the wife, upon the death of the husband, a power of appointment in favour of a second husband and of the children of a second marriage, the Court, upon the dissolution of the marriage, refused to vary the settlement so as to enable the wife to exercise such power of appointment before the death of her late husband (*Pollard* v. *Pollard*, (1894) P. 172; 63 L. J., P. & M. 174). Nor will the Court, in such a case, necessarily deprive the guilty husband of his power of appointment among the children of the marriage so as to take away from him his power of exercising parental judgment and discrimination with regard to his children (*Maudslay* v. *Maudslay*, 2 P. D. 256; 47 L. J., P. & M. 26).

Wife's power of appointing trustees.

Joint power of appointing trustees.—Whether, when a marriage is dissolved, the Court has power under this section to vary a settlement by depriving a guilty wife of her right to join in the power of appointing fresh trustees, is doubtful.

On the one hand, Lord Penzance was of opinion, though he did not find it necessary to decide the point, that it would be a straining of the language of the statute to say that the power of making orders with reference to the application of the whole or portion of the property settled included the depriving the wife of her right in reference to the appointment of trustees (*Hope* v. *Hope and Erdody*, L. R., 3 P. 226; 44 L. J., P. & M. 31; cf. *Davies* v. *Davies*, 37 L. J., P. & M. 17).

On the other hand, Butt, J., has expressed a contrary opinion, and has stated that the words of the statute are sufficient to give jurisdiction to make such orders (*Oppenheim* v. *Oppenheim and Ricotti*, 9 P. D. 60; 53 L. J., P. & M. 62; cf. *Maudslay* v. *Maudslay*, 2 P. D. 250).

But in both the cases last cited there was no opposition on the part of the respondent, and in a later case, Butt, J., though stating that it was by no means clear that the words of the statute did not give the Court power to deprive the wife of her right to join in the appointment of new trustees, refused, under the circumstances, to exercise it (*Bosvile* v. *Bosvile*, 13 P. D. 76; 57 L. J., P. & M. 62).

But, whether or not the Court has such power, it will not exercise it in any case in which the wife is to retain a substantial interest in the settled fund (*Hope* v. *Hope; Bosvile* v. *Bosvile*, ubi supra; *Tupper* v. *Tupper*, 62 L. T. 665).

Covenant to appoint in favour of the guilty party.—After a final decree in a suit for dissolution of marriage, the Court has authority under this section to relieve an innocent party from a covenant to appoint in favour of the other party who has been guilty of a matrimonial offence (*Benyon* v. *Benyon and O'Callaghan*, 1 P. D. 447; 45 L. J., P. & M. 96).

§ 40.

Variation of settlements: guilty husband.—The Court, in making an order under sect. 40, will act upon the general principles which have been set forth above. As a general rule, when the marriage has been dissolved on account of the husband's misconduct, he will be deprived of all his interest under the settlement in such portion of the settled fund as came from the wife or the wife's family (*Boynton* v. *Boynton*, 30 L. J., P. & M. 156).

Guilty husband.

So, where by ante-nuptial and post-nuptial settlements 724*l*. Consols, the property of the husband, and 700*l*. and some leaseholds, the property of the wife's father, were settled upon the wife for life, and after her death upon the husband for life, and after the death of the survivor upon the children of the marriage, the Court, after a decree absolute for dissolution of the marriage at the suit of the wife, ordered that the trustees of the settlement should deal with the proceeds of the property which came from the wife as if the husband was dead at the date of the decree absolute, but refused to alter the settlement as to the 724*l*. settled by the husband. In this case the Judge Ordinary stated that he had seldom heard of "more savage and unmanly conduct" than that of which the husband had been guilty (*Johnson* v. *Johnson*, 31 L. J., P. & M. 29).

Where, by an ante-nuptial settlement, a share in the *Times* newspaper to which the wife was entitled was assigned to trustees upon trust to pay the income arising therefrom to her for her sole and separate use during her life, and after her death to her husband in case he should survive her, and after the death of the survivor to apply the property for the benefit of the children of the marriage, and it appeared that there were four of such children, that the conduct of the husband had been inexcusable, and that the conduct of the wife had been without reproach, the Court ordered that the settlement should be varied by postponing the interest of the husband, in the event of his surviving the petitioner, till after the interests of all the children (*Horne* v. *Horne*, 30 L. J., P. & M. 182, *note*).

Nor, when the effect of the Court's order is merely to deprive

§ 40.

the guilty husband of his interest in the wife's fortune, and to put the innocent wife into immediate possession of her own income, will the Court impose upon her the condition *dum sola et casta vixerit*, though such condition is perfectly reasonable when the husband is called upon to sacrifice a portion of his own means (*Gladstone* v. *Gladstone*, 1 P. D. 444; 45 L. J., P. & M. 82; *Chetwynd* v. *Chetwynd*, 2 S. & T. 410; 35 L. J., P. & M. 21).

Husband not necessarily deprived of all interest in property settled by wife.

But even if the whole of the settled property came from the wife, the guilty husband will not necessarily be deprived of all interest therein under the settlement. For, " suppose a guilty husband is incapacitated by physical infirmity from earning a livelihood, and has no means of his own, I do not say that no provision can in any case be made for him out of the wife's property " (*Wigney* v. *Wigney*, 7 P. D. 177; 51 L. J., P. & M. 60, *per* Jessel, M. R.). In this case, the whole of the settled fund had been brought in by the wife, and the marriage was dissolved on the ground of the husband's misconduct. The Court ordered that the fund should be held upon the trusts which would be subsisting if the husband were then dead and freed from the ultimate trust in his favour, but certain mortgages which the husband had effected upon his life estate (which, as to part of the fund, was prior, and as to the rest was subsequent, to that of the wife) were permitted to remain a charge on the settled estate, and certain debts, contracted in discharge of household expenses before the separation, were also charged on the same estate.

Property settled by husband.

When the settled fund consists of property that came from the husband or the husband's family, and the marriage is dissolved on the ground of the husband's misconduct, the Court has an absolute discretion as to the amount of income arising therefrom to be given to the wife. It may give her even the whole of such income, or it can, if it thinks fit, hand her over the capital (*Ponsonby* v. *Ponsonby*, 9 P. D. 122; 53 L. J., P. & M. 112—C. A.).

Where the settled property came from the husband's father, and the settlement provided that, in the event of the husband's bankruptcy (he taking a first life interest in the property), the trustees should, as they might think fit, apply the income of the trust funds, or any part thereof, " for the maintenance and personal support of the husband and his then present or any future wife, and child or children and other issue by his then present or any future wife, or any one or more of such objects to the exclusion of the others," and the husband became bankrupt in 1866, and in 1872 the marriage was dissolved upon the wife's petition, the Court subsequently, upon the wife's petition, ordered that, during her life, and so long as she should remain unmarried and the children of the marriage remain under age, the trustee should pay to her the whole of the income of the settled fund, and that as each of the children attained the age of twenty-one, a sum of 20*l.* a year should be paid to such child during the lifetime of the mother (*Marsh* v. *Marsh*, 47 L. J., P. & M. 34; in app., 47 L. J., P. & M. 78).

§ 40.

Variation of Settlements : guilty Wife.

Guilty wife.

(a) *Property brought into settlement by wife.*—On the marriage of the parties, the father of the wife settled property, in the first place, for the benefit of his daughter for life, then for the benefit of her husband, and, on the death of the survivor of them, for the benefit of their children. No property was settled on behalf of the husband. The marriage was subsequently dissolved on the ground of the wife's adultery, and the Court varied the settlement by ordering the whole income of the settled property —about 150*l.* per annum—to be applied during the joint lives of the petitioner and respondent for the benefit of their children, the husband, on the death of the respondent during his lifetime, to enjoy the benefits given him by the settlement (*Paul* v. *Paul and Farquhar*, L. R., 2 P. 93; 39 L. J., P. & M. 50).

Property brought into settlement by wife.

Although the property brought into settlement was the wife's absolute property before the marriage, it is only just and equitable that when the marriage is dissolved by reason of her misconduct, that the husband should not, "in addition to the grievous wrong done by (the wife's) breach of the marriage vow, be wholly deprived of means to the scale of which he may have learnt to accommodate his mode of life. Nor, in viewing the matter on the other side, does it seem just or equitable that funds which were intended, at the time of the marriage, for the use of both, should be borne off by the guilty party, and perhaps transferred to the hands of the adulterer as the dowry of a second marriage. The interests of society point in the same direction. It would be of evil example if this Court were to decide that the entire fortune of a wealthy married woman was to be reckoned as part of the prospects of an adulterer, or the resources of a second home for a guilty woman " (*March* v. *March and Palumbo*, L. R., 1 P. 440; 36 L. J., P. & M. 28).

Where, therefore, by an ante-nuptial settlement, property of

§ 40. the wife, producing an annual income of 909*l*., was settled during the joint lives of husband and wife, to the separate use of the wife, then to the survivor for life, and then for the benefit of the children of the marriage, and other property producing an annual income of 549*l*. was bequeathed to the wife upon the same trusts as those contained in the settlement, the husband on the marriage receiving 3,000*l*., the property of the wife, and having an income of 266*l*., the Court, after a dissolution of the marriage on the ground of the wife's adultery, ordered that, during the joint lives of husband and wife, the trustees of the settlement should pay, first, 200*l*. per annum to the husband for maintenance of the child of the marriage during minority, and after he attained full age to the child; and, secondly, 440*l*. per annum to the husband for his own use (*Ib.*; affirmed on app. 36 L. J.,P. & M. 65).

Nor will the Court, at the instance of an adulterous wife, deprive the innocent husband of his interest under the settlement, though to do so might be for the benefit of the children of the marriage (*Thompson* v. *Thompson and Barras*, 2 S. & T. 649; 32 L. J., P. & M. 39).

Nor where the husband has no sufficient means of his own for the support of himself and the child of the marriage, of whom he has the custody, will the offer of the wife to maintain the child disentitle the husband to an order directing the trustees of the settlement to pay him a certain sum per annum out of the life income of the wife for the maintenance of the child (*Webster* v. *Webster and Mitford*, 32 L. J., P. & M. 29; 3 S. & T. 106). In this case the life income of the wife was 85*l*., and out of this 20*l*. per annum was ordered to be paid for the maintenance of the child.

Where, by a settlement made on the marriage of the parties, certain property of the respondent was settled upon trust (*inter alia*) for the respondent for life, and after her death for the petitioner if he survived her, and, after the death of both, in the event of there being no children of the marriage, for the respondent's next of kin, and there were no children of the marriage, and it appeared that the wife's income under the settlement was 1,050*l*. a year, while the husband possessed an income of about 600*l*. a year, part of which arose from money received from the respondent, the Court varied the trusts of the settlement by ordering the trustees to pay the husband 300*l*. out of the income of the trust moneys during the joint lives of the petitioner and respondent (*Farrington* v. *Farrington and Schooles*, 11 P. D. 84; 55 L. J., P. & M. 69).

(b) *Property brought into settlement by husband.*—By a post-nuptial settlement the petitioner had settled his property on himself for life, and after his death upon his wife for life, and then upon the children of the marriage. The Court, upon an application to vary the settlement after the marriage had been dissolved by reason of the wife's adultery, ordered " that from and after the death of the petitioner the property comprised in the settlement should, in the event of the respondent surviving the petitioner, be applied by the trustee for the benefit of the children of the marriage as if the respondent were then dead" (*Pearce* v. *Pearce and French*, 30 L. J., P. & M. 182).

§ 40.
Guilty wife.
Property settled by husband.

But where the father of the petitioner (the husband) had covenanted to pay 100*l.* per annum to the respondent after the death of the petitioner, and during the joint lives of the petitioner and respondent, or until the respondent should marry again, the Court, while ordering the money covenanted to be paid to be applied for the benefit of the child of the marriage, held that it had no power to deprive the respondent of her interest under the covenant on the death of the child (*Sykes* v. *Sykes and Smith*, L. R., 2 P. 163; 39 L. J., P. & M. 52).

Where the property has been brought into settlement by the petitioner, and the effect of the dissolution of his marriage with the respondent has been to render the rights of the children of a *future* marriage of the petitioner the sole limitation upon his absolute enjoyment of the settled property, there being no living persons whose interests can be prejudiced, and the only persons who, if they come into existence, will be affected being children for whom the petitioner may naturally be expected to provide, the Court will order the settled property to be reconveyed to the petitioner for his own use (*Meredyth* v. *Meredyth and Leigh*, (1895) P. 92; 64 L. J., P. & M. 54; cf. *Wood* v. *Wood*, 14 B. L. R., App. 6).

(c) *Property brought into settlement by husband and by wife.*— The marriage of the parties had been dissolved by reason of the wife's adultery, and there were two children of the marriage who were living with the petitioner. By the marriage settlements the husband's property, which consisted of 10,000*l.* invested on mortgage, and reversionary interests in land yielding about 200*l.* a year, was settled in trust for the husband for life, then for the respondent for life, and afterwards for the children of the marriage as the husband and wife, or the survivor, might appoint, and in default for the children equally, and in default

Property settled by both parties.

§ 40.

of children, for the petitioner and his representatives. The property of the respondent, which consisted of an annuity of 400*l*. payable by her father, and reversionary interests in land yielding about 400*l*. a year, and several sums of money amounting to 26,000*l*., was settled, after a first life interest to her, upon similar trusts to those of the husband's property, except that the ultimate trusts were as she should apppoint, and in default for her next of kin; and it was also provided that if she should survive her husband she should be at liberty, in certain events, to appoint a portion of the income in favour of any husband she might marry after the death of the petitioner, and a certain proportion of the capital for the benefit of the children of such marriage. The incomes of the parties at the time amounted to about 400*l*. a year each. The order of the Court was that (i) half of the respondent's present and reversionary income should be given to the petitioner for himself and the children of the marriage, and (ii) that the interest in her husband's property must be extinguished, and her powers of appointment in favour of a future husband and children must not take effect until after the death of the petitioner. The Court further held that, in varying settlements, the fact that the wife has to pay the costs of the suit should not be taken into consideration in her favour (*Noel* v. *Noel*, 10 P. D. 179; 54 L. J., P. & M. 73).

*Separation deeds.

(d) *Separation deeds, variation of.*—When a marriage is dissolved on the ground of the wife's misconduct, the mere fact that the husband has accepted an allowance from her under a deed of separation, does not preclude him from applying for an increased provision from her income (*Benyon* v. *Benyon and O'Callaghan*, 1 P. D. 447; 45 L. J., P. & M. 96).

So, in the converse case, where a husband has covenanted in a deed of separation to pay his wife an annual allowance, without any *dum casta* clause, and the marriage is afterwards dissolved on the ground of the wife's adultery, the Court may, upon the petitioner's application to vary such deed, reduce the amount of such allowance and make it payable to the respondent only *dum casta et sola vixerit* (*Saunders* v. *Saunders*, 69 L. T. 498; cf. *Worsley* v. *Worsley and Wignall*, L. R., 1 P. 648).

And where by a post-nuptial settlement certain property belonging to the respondent was assigned to trustees in trust, *inter alia*, to pay the interest and annual proceeds thereof to her

---

* See also pp. 235—237, 251, 252, *ante*.

for her separate use, and subsequently a deed of separation was entered into between the parties with the same trustees as those of the settlement, whereby the petitioner covenanted to pay the respondent an annuity for her life, the Court, upon the application of the petitioner after a dissolution of the marriage, ordered that whenever any money should be payable to the respondent under the deed of separation, the trustees should, out of the moneys in their hands payable to the respondent under the post-nuptial settlement, pay and apply a sum equal in amount upon such and the same trusts as would be applicable thereto in case the respondent were dead and had died in the lifetime of the petitioner (*Bullock* v. *Bullock and Strong*, L. R., 2 P. 389; 41 L. J., P. & M. 83).

§ 40.

"**The husband or the wife**":

Husband or wife.

Sect. 5 of the Matrimonial Causes Act, 1859, authorized the Court to make orders "with reference to the application of the whole or a portion of the property settled either for the benefit of the children of the marriage *or of their respective parents.*" The Courts having construed these words to mean that the power so given could be exercised only in cases where there were children of the marriage living at the time (*Thomas* v. *Thomas*, 2 S. & T. 89; *Corrance* v. *Corrance and Lowe*, L. R., 1 P. 495; 37 L. J., P. & M. 44; *Ansdall* v. *Ansdall*, 5 P. D. 138), a later statute (Matrimonial Causes Act, 1878, sect. 3) provided that the power given under the former statute might be exercised notwithstanding that there were no children of the marriage.

"**Provided that the Court shall not make any order at the expense of the children**":

No variation to be made at expense of the children.

The Court in England has always acted upon this principle, and has refused to interfere with the interests of the children under the settlement, even though to do so might possibly be to give the children a larger benefit (see *Crisp* v. *Crisp*, L. R., 2 P. 426; 42 L. J., P. & M. 13; *Forsyth* v. *Forsyth*, (1891) P. 363).

Costs of application to vary settlements.—When, in a suit for dissolution of marriage, the co-respondent has been condemned in costs, he is liable for the costs of the petitioner and respondent incurred in obtaining an alteration of the marriage settlement (*Gill* v. *Gill and Hogg*, 3 S. & T. 354; 33 L. J., P. & M. 43; *Stone* v. *Stone and Brownrigg*, 3 S. & T. 372; 33 L. J., P. & M. 95).

Costs.

In a recent case, on a motion for variation of settlements after

§ 40. a dissolution of marriage on the ground of the wife's adultery, the Court, on the recommendation of the registrar, and with the consent of the guardian *ad litem* of the infant children of the marriage, allowed the costs of all parties to be paid out of the wife's settled funds (*Hamilton* v. *Hamilton*, 68 L. T. 467).

XI.—*Custody of Children.*

Power to make orders as to custody of children in suit for separation.

41. In any suit for obtaining a judicial separation the Court may from time to time, before making its decree, make such interim orders, and may make such provision in the decree as it deems proper with respect to the custody, maintenance and education of the minor children, the marriage of whose parents is the subject of such suit, and may, if it think fit, direct proceedings to be taken for placing such children under the protection of the said Court.

Power to make such orders after decree.

42. The Court, after a decree of judicial separation, may upon application (by petition) for this purpose make, from time to time, all such orders and provision, with respect to the custody, maintenance and education of the minor children, the marriage of whose parents is the subject of the decree, or for placing such children under the protection of the said Court, as might have been made by such decree or by interim orders in case the proceedings for obtaining such decree were still pending.

Power to make orders as to custody of children in suits for dissolution or nullity.

43. In any suit for obtaining a dissolution of marriage or a decree of nullity of marriage instituted in, or removed to, a High Court, the Court may from time to time, before making its decree absolute or its decree (as the case may be), make such interim orders, and may make such provision in the decree absolute or decree,

and in any such suit instituted in a District Court, the Court may from time to time, before its decree is confirmed, make such interim orders, and may make such provision on such confirmation,

as the High Court or District Court (as the case may be) deems proper with respect to the custody, maintenance and education of the minor children, the marriage of whose parents is the subject of the suit;

and may, if it think fit, direct proceedings to be taken for placing such children under the protection of the Court.

44. The High Court after a decree absolute for dissolution of marriage or a decree of nullity of marriage, and the District Court after a decree for dissolution of marriage or of nullity of marriage has been confirmed,

may, upon application by petition for the purpose, make from time to time all such orders and provision, with respect to the custody, maintenance and education of the minor children, the marriage of whose parents was the subject of the decree, or for placing such children under the protection of the said Court, as might have been made by such decree absolute or decree (as the case may be), or by such interim orders as aforesaid.

§§ 41-44.

Power to make such orders after decree or confirmation.

The Matrimonial Causes Act, 1857 (20 & 21 Vict. c. 85), sect. 35, provides that—

> "In any suit or other proceeding for obtaining a judicial separation or a decree of nullity of marriage, and on any petition for dissolving a marriage, the Court may, from time to time, before making its final decree, make such interim orders, and may make such provision in the final decree, as it may deem just and proper with respect to the custody, maintenance, and education of the children, the marriage of whose parents is the subject of such suit or other proceeding, and may, if it shall think fit, direct proper proceedings to be taken for placing such children under the protection of the Court of Chancery."

The Matrimonial Causes Act, 1859 (22 & 23 Vict. c. 61), sect. 4, enables the Court to make, from time to time, similar

§§ 41-44. orders and provision *after* a final decree of judicial separation, nullity of marriage or dissolution of marriage, upon application (by petition) for such purpose.

The Matrimonial Causes Act, 1884 (47 & 48 Vict. c. 68), sect. 6, provides that:—

> "The Court may, at any time before final decree on any application for restitution of conjugal rights, or after final decree if the respondent shall fail to comply therewith, upon application for that purpose, make from time to time all such orders and provisions with respect to the custody, maintenance, and education of the children of the petitioner and respondent as might have been made by interim orders during the pendency of a trial for judicial separation between the same parties."

The Guardianship of Infants Act, 1886 (49 & 50 Vict. c. 27), sect. 7, provides that:—

> "In any case where a decree for judicial separation, or a decree either *nisi* or absolute for divorce, shall be pronounced, the Court pronouncing such decree may thereby declare the parent by reason of whose misconduct such decree is made to be a person unfit to have the custody of the children (if any) of the marriage; and, in such case, the parent so declared to be unfit shall not, upon the death of the other parent, be entitled as of right to the custody or guardianship of such children."

The Matrimonial Causes Act, 1878 (41 Vict. c. 19), sect. 4, provides that:—

> "If a husband shall be convicted summarily or otherwise of an aggravated assault within the meaning of the statute 24th & 25th Victoria, chap. 100, sect. 43, upon his wife, the Court or magistrate before whom he shall be so convicted may, if satisfied that the future safety of the wife is in peril, order that the wife shall be no longer bound to cohabit with her husband; and such order shall have the force in all respects of a decree of judicial separation on the ground of cruelty; and such order may further provide . . . (2) that the legal custody of any children of the marriage under the age of ten years shall, in the discretion of the Court or magistrate, be given to the wife. Provided always, that no order for . . . the custody of the children by the wife shall be made in favour of a wife who shall be proved to have committed adultery, unless such adultery has been condoned; and that any order for . . . the custody of the children may be discharged by the Court or magistrate by whom such order was made upon proof that the wife has, since the making thereof, been guilty of adultery; and provided also, that all orders made under this section shall be subject to appeal to the Probate and Admiralty Division of the High Court of Justice."

"Custody of children":

§§ 41-44.

For the practice of the English Divorce Court in these matters, see Rules Nos. 97—102, 104, 184, 195, and 212.   *Custody of children.*

A party desirous of obtaining an order of the Court as to the custody, maintenance, or education of the minor children should, in all cases, apply by separate petition for that purpose. And it is the more correct procedure not to include a prayer for custody in the original petition (*Ledlie* v. *Ledlie*, I. L. R., xviii Calc. 473). Such petition, *except when made under sect.* 44, must bear a Court fee stamp of Rs. 20 (Court Fees Act, 1870, Second Schedule, Art. 20), and must be served personally on the respondent, unless the Court dispenses with such personal service (sect. 50, *post*).   *Petition.*   *Court fee stamp.*   *Service of petition.*

"Generally speaking, the Court will not act *ex parte*, but the petition must be served, or, in some sufficient form, notice must be given in order to show the respondent what the Court is to be asked to do. On the other hand, it has been held in England that if the notice has been given in an earlier stage of the case, then notice of the petition itself need not be given"; accordingly, if in the original petition the respondent is warned that an application will be made for the custody of the minor children, notice of the subsequent application will be dispensed with (*Ledlie* v. *Ledlie*, I. L. R., xviii Calc. 473, following *Horne* v. *Horne*, 30 L. J., P. & M. 200; *Wilkinson* v. *Wilkinson*, 30 L. J., P. & M. 200 (*n.*)).

And if, after an order has been made for the custody of the children, the other party desires to obtain an order for *access* to them, he or she must apply by petition and not by motion (*Anthony* v. *Anthony*, 30 L. J., P. & M. 208).   *Order for access.*

"Suits for dissolution or nullity of marriage, or for judicial separation":

The power given to the English Divorce Court by the Matrimonial Causes Act, 1884, sect. 6, to make orders, as to the custody, maintenance, and education of the minor children, *in suits for restitution of conjugal rights*, has not been conferred upon the Courts of this country (cf. *Chambers* v. *Chambers*, 39 L. J., P. & M. 56).   *No power to make order in suits for restitution of conjugal rights.*

Nor have the Courts in India been given powers similar to those conferred on the English Court by sect. 7 of the Guardianship of Infants Act, 1886.

§§ 41-44.

"Minor children":

"Minor children."

"Minor children means, in the case of sons of Native fathers, boys who have not completed the age of sixteen years, and in the case of daughters of Native fathers, girls who have not completed the age of thirteen years; in other cases, it means unmarried children who have not completed the age of eighteen years" (sect. 3 (5), *ante*).

Rule in England as to custody, &c. of children.

According to the common law of England, the age at which a child is deemed to have a discretion is fourteen in the case of a boy, and sixteen in the case of a girl (*Reg.* v. *Clarke*, 7 E. & B. 186). After a child has attained the age of discretion, a court of common law will set it free if illegally detained; nor will it force a child against his or her will to remain with his or her father or legal guardian. But the father's common law right to the custody of his child exists until the child attains twenty-one (*In re Agar-Ellis*, 24 Ch. D. 317). And the Court of Chancery, in addition to the co-ordinate jurisdiction over infants which it possesses equally with the courts of common law and enforces by writs of *habeas corpus*, exercises the power of the Crown as *parens patriæ* over infants, and, in the exercise of this jurisdiction, the power of that Court has been much more extensive than that possessed by courts of common law, under a writ of *habeas corpus*, and has frequently been exercised by it in aid of fathers and legal guardians over children who have attained the age of discretion. But the jurisdiction of the Divorce Court, under sect. 35 of the Matrimonial Causes Act, 1857, and sect. 4 of the Matrimonial Causes Act, 1859, is far greater than that exercised by any Court previously existing. "Nothing can be wider than the discretion and power conferred upon the Divorce Court by these two sections. It can order parents to maintain and educate their children at their own expense, which no Court could do before; and if it were not for the decisions* to which I am about to refer, I should have thought that the power to order payment of a proper sum for the maintenance and education of the children under twenty-one of persons who had been divorced or judicially separated too clear for reasonable doubt"

---

* The decisions referred to are to the effect that the Divorce Court had no jurisdiction to make orders for the custody, maintenance or education of children who had completed the age of sixteen (*Ryder* v. *Ryder*, 2 S. & T. 225; *Webster* v. *Webster*, 31 L. J., P. & M. 184; *Mallinson* v. *Mallinson*, L. R., 1 P. 221; 35 L. J., P. & M. 84; *Blandford* v. *Blandford*, (1892) P. 148).

(Lindley, L.J., *Thomasset* v. *Thomasset*, (1894) P. 295; 63 L. J., §§ 41-44.
P. & M. 140). In this case the Court of Appeal, overruling the
decisions referred to by the Lord Justice, held that the Divorce
Court in England has power to make orders respecting the
custody, maintenance, and education of children during the
whole period of their infancy — that is, till they attain the
age of twenty-one. The Lords Justices, however, expressly
stated that, except under very special circumstances, a child
who has attained years of discretion cannot properly be ordered
into the custody of either parent against such child's own wishes.
But, "subject to such unwillingness on the part of the child,
I can entertain no doubt that the parent is entitled to the
custody of his child as against anybody detaining the child
against its will up to the age of twenty-one" (Lopes, L.J.,
ibid.).

The power of the Courts of this country to make orders for
the custody, maintenance, and education of "minor children"
is expressly limited by the definition of the term "minor children" in sect. 3 (5) of the Indian Divorce Act. But, though
the Court has jurisdiction to give a parent the custody of every
such child as comes within that definition, there is no power in
the Court to compel a child who has, according to the personal
law to which such child is subject, attained the years of discretion, to remain in such custody contrary to his or her own
wishes.

Intervention of third parties.—Upon any question regarding Intervention
the custody, maintenance, or education of the children, the of third
marriage of whose parents is the subject of the suit, persons parties.
who are not parties to the suit have been permitted to intervene and plead on behalf of such children, when they have been
able to show that they are entitled to do so. "It was the
obvious intention of the legislature that the Court should have
the power to make such orders as it might think necessary for
the benefit of the children themselves; and it could not properly
exercise that most useful power if it were to decline altogether
to hear what third persons had to say on the matter. It might
be that a worthless father and mother having been divorced
might marry again, and neither of them might be willing to
have the care of the children. It would be a great misfortune
if this Court were to abdicate the power given to it by these
sections, by holding that no third persons could intervene for
the benefit of the children" (*Chetwynd* v. *Chetwynd*, 34 L. J.,
P. & M. 130; L. R., 1 P. 39).

§§ 41-44. Thus, even after a final decree of judicial separation, the grandfather of the children was allowed to intervene on their behalf to question the propriety of the continuance of the order, which had been made in favour of the petitioner, for the custody of the children (*Goodrich* v. *Goodrich*, L. R., 3 P. 134).

But in a later case, Butt, J., held that sect. 4 of the Matrimonial Causes Act, 1859, refers only to an application to be made by one of the parents, and that, upon the death of the parent who was entitled under a decree of judicial separation to the custody of the child, it was not competent to a third party to apply for the custody of such child (*Davis* v. *Davis*, 14 P. D. 162).

And, in any case, if a third party is allowed to intervene for such purpose, he does so at the peril of being condemned in costs if the intervention proves unsuccessful (*March* v. *March*, L. R., 1 P. 437).

Interim Orders under Sections 41 and 43.

Interim orders under sects. 41, 43.

Until the final decree in the suit, the Court can only make an interim order as to the custody, maintenance or education of the minor children (cf. *Cubley* v. *Cubley*, 30 L. J., P. & M. 161).

Nor can the District Court make a final order, under sect. 43, till after the confirmation of its decree. Where, therefore, the decree of the District Court for dissolution of marriage contained a passage to the effect that "the Court further awards the petitioner the custody of the children," the Chief Court of the Punjab held that such an order should not have been contained in the decree for dissolution. After such decree has been confirmed, but not till then, the Court may make such provision as it thinks proper for this purpose under sect. 43 (*Burroughs* v. *Burroughs*, No. 62, *Punjab Record*, 1887).

Primâ facie right of father to custody of child.

At common law a father has a legal right to the custody of his child, whether male or female, from its birth until it attains the age of twenty-one (*In re Agar Ellis*, 24 Ch. D. 317; *Thomasset* v. *Thomasset*, (1894) P. 295; 63 L. J., P. & M. 140).

Accordingly, in making interim orders as to the custody, maintenance and education of a minor child, the Court, though it has under the Act a very wide discretion to adhere to or depart from the common law rule, will not deprive the father of his right even in the case of an infant of very tender age, unless good cause is shown (*Cartledge* v. *Cartledge*, 2 S. & T. 567; 31 L. J., P. & M. 85; *Spratt* v. *Spratt*, 1 S. & T. 215).

The fact that the mother's health is seriously affected by the separation from her child is such good cause, and in such an event the Court will give her the custody of the child *pendente lite*, even though she is accused of adultery (*Barnes* v. *Barnes*, L. R., 1 P. 463). In this case the Court made the order the more readily because the child was at the time living with a stranger and not with its father.

§§ 41-44. *Interim orders.*

In making an interim order for the custody of the child the Court will also take into consideration the conduct of the applicant. Pending a suit by the husband for dissolution of his marriage on the ground of his wife's adultery, the wife improperly obtained possession of the infant child of the marriage, who was then living with its father. The father took it away again from the mother, whereupon the latter, after she had failed to recover it by violence, applied to the Court for an interim order for its custody, but the Court refused to grant the application on account of her improper proceedings (*Allen* v. *Allen and D'Arcy*, 29 L. J., P. & M. 166).

Both parties must be before the Court before an interim order can be made (*Stacey* v. *Stacey*, 29 L. J., P. & M. 63).

Both parties to be before Court.

Applications for interim orders for the custody of a child should be kept distinct from the main question in the suit. But the Court, at the hearing of a cause, will not entertain an application for custody of children if it is founded on evidence which would not be admissible in the cause. If, however, at the hearing, the facts proved would warrant such an order, *e.g.*, if the respondent's adultery is proved, the Court may direct that the petitioner have the custody of the children until further orders (*Wallace* v. *Wallace*, 32 L. J., P. & M. 34).

Application to be kept distinct from main question in suit.

Access to child pending suit.—The Court has power to order that the party who has not the custody of the child shall have access to it *pendente lite* (*Thompson* v. *Thompson*, 2 S. & T. 402; 31 L. J., P. & M. 213).

Access to child pending suit.

The Court has, however, a discretion in the matter of granting such parent access to the child pending suit, and in the exercise of that discretion the paramount consideration for the Court is the interests of the child itself. Where, therefore, it appeared that the visits of the mother to the child, who was in a very weak state of health, might retard its recovery, the Court refused to make an order for access pending suit in her favour, although there was reason to apprehend that the separation from her child would affect the mother's health (*Phillip* v. *Phillip*, 41 L. J., P. & M. 89).

R.   T

§§ 41-44. When the mother is the respondent in the suit and the child is in the custody of the father, the Court will act on the presumption that the respondent is innocent, and will ordinarily allow her access pending suit, provided that the Court is satisfied that her motive is natural love and affection for the child, and that she has no indirect object in view (*Codrington* v. *Codrington and Anderson*, 3 S. & T. 496; 10 L. T. 387).

But when once the adultery of the mother has been sufficiently established the Court will refuse to treat an application by her for custody of the child on the same principles as an *interim* order, although the final decree has not been pronounced (*Shewell* v. *Shewell and Fox*, 20 L. T. 404; but cf. *Goodrich* v. *Goodrich*, 19 L. T. 611).

Costs of wife's unsuccessful application. The costs of a wife's unsuccessful motion for access to the children pending suit will not be allowed her (*Hepworth* v. *Hepworth*, 30 L. J., P. & M. 253).

Orders on or after final decree. "**Orders as to custody, &c., of minor children on or after final decree**":

The Court has no power, upon the *dismissal* of a petition for judicial separation or for dissolution or nullity of marriage, to make orders with reference to the custody, maintenance or education of the minor children (*Seddon* v. *Seddon*, 2 S. & T. 640; 31 L. J., P. & M. 101). Sect. 42 contemplates that, after a decree has been made, the intervention of the Court shall be sought by petition, and it is the more correct procedure not to include a prayer for the custody in the original petition (*Ledlie* v. *Ledlie*, I. L. R., xviii Calc. 473).

Discretion of Court. But, if the petition is granted, the Court has the very widest discretion, under the provisions of the Divorce Act, to weigh the comparative advantages or disadvantages of giving the custody of all, or any, of the children to the one parent or the other, and no general rule for the guidance of the Court can be laid down (*Symington* v. *Symington*, L. R., 2 H. L. (Sc.) 415; *Suggate* v. *Suggate*, 29 L. J., P. & M. 167).

The jurisdiction as to the custody, maintenance and education of minor children conferred upon the Divorce Court is far greater than that exercised by any Court previously existing, and nothing can be wider than the discretion so conferred. It overrides both the common law rules and the Chancery rules as to the custody of children, and the judge is not bound to follow any of those rules, though he will have regard to them in exercising his discretion; but he will be mainly guided by the particular circumstances of the case before him (*Thomasset* v. *Thomasset*, (1894) P. 295; 63 L. J., P. & M. 140; *Handley* v. *Handley*, (1891) P. 124, per Lindley, L. J.—C. A.; cf. *Goad* v. *Goad*, No. 69 *Punjab Record*, 1870). §§ 41-44.

Nor will the Court of Appeal overrule the discretion of the lower Court except under very special circumstances (*Handley* v. *Handley, ubi supra*).

But, although no general rule can be laid down for the guidance of the Court, and the discretion given to the Court must be exercised according to the circumstances of each case, there are certain general principles upon which the Court ordinarily acts. These are as follows:— *General principles.*

(a) "*The first duty of the Court is to consider what is for the benefit of the children,—that should be the paramount consideration with the Court*" (Sir R. Phillimore, *D'Alton* v. *D'Alton*, 4 P. D. at p. 91). *1st. Interests of minor children.*

Accordingly, if such a course appears to be more conducive to the future welfare of the children, the Court may refuse to give the custody of them to the innocent parent, and may hand them over into the charge of some third person or even of the guilty parent.

Thus, where the wife, after a decree of judicial separation had been made in her favour, applied for the custody of the children for the avowed purpose of bringing them up in a religion different from that of their father and from that in which they had been brought up during the cohabitation of their parents, the Court held that it was not in the interest of the children that they should have their course of education interrupted and their religion altered, and that it was desirable in the same interest that the children should not be troubled with their parents' dissensions, nor be made the depositary of their parents' grievances, the one against the other. Their custody was, therefore, given to a third person, in whose establishment they were at the time being educated, but with full access on the part of both parents (*D'Alton* v. *D'Alton*, 4 P. D. 87; aff. on app. at p. 90).

Nor will the Court necessarily deprive a guilty father of the custody of his *minor sons* when it appears to be for their benefit that they should remain in his charge. *Distinction between minor sons and minor daughters.*

But it is a different matter with regard to the *minor daughters*, to the custody of whom the mother, against whom nothing has been proved, is the person naturally entitled under ordinary

§§ 41-44. circumstances (*Symington* v. *Symington*, L. R., 2 H. L. (Sc.) 415).

But, even in the case of minor sons, a father who continues to live in adultery is presumably not a person who should be entrusted with their custody, and, if the continuance of the adultery be proved, their custody, as well as that of the minor daughters, may be given to the mother, provision being made for access on the part of the father to the sons (*Hyde* v. *Hyde*, 29 L. J., P. & M. 150).

2nd. *Primâ facie* right of innocent parent.

(b) *Provided that the interests of the minor children are not likely to be thereby affected, the innocent parent has a* primâ facie *right to their custody* (*Martin* v. *Martin*, 29 L. J., P. & M. 106).

"With regard to the rights of the petitioner, the principle which guides the Court is, that the innocent party shall suffer as little as possible from the dissolution of the marriage, and be preserved, as far as the Court can do so, in the same position in which she was while the marriage continued—*first*, by giving her a sufficient pecuniary allowance for her support, and, *secondly*, by providing that she should not be deprived of the society of her children unnecessarily. As it has been put by one of my predecessors, 'the wife ought not to be obliged to buy the relief to which she is entitled owing to her husband's misconduct, at the price of being deprived of the society of her children'" (Hannen, J., *D'Alton* v. *D'Alton*, 4 P. D. at p. 88).

Accordingly, a wife, who succeeds in her suit against her husband, will, in general, be given the custody of the minor children (*Boynton* v. *Boynton*, 30 L. J., P. & M. 156; 2 S. & T. 275; *Suggate* v. *Suggate*, 29 L. J., P. & M. 167; *Marsh* v. *Marsh*, 28 L. J., P. & M. 13; 1 S. & T. 312; *Macleod* v. *Macleod*, 6 B. L. R. 318; *Goad* v. *Goad*, 69 *Punjab Record*, 1870).

Where, however, there are both minor sons and minor daughters, the father will not necessarily be deprived of the custody of the former, if it appears that he is no longer living in adultery and has always treated his children kindly (*Martin* v. *Martin*, 29 L. J., P. & M. 106; *Symington* v. *Symington*, L. R., 2 H. L. (Sc.) 415).

Innocent wife not to be deprived of her right simply because she

When the custody of the children has been given to the wife, whose conduct has been wholly blameless and who has done nothing to forfeit her natural right to have possession of the children, she will not be deprived of their society and custody merely because she is subsequently compelled to pray the Court to order the respondent to pay her a sum or sums of money for the past and future maintenance of the children. In such a case the Court will order the respondent to contribute in a moderate extent to their maintenance, even if his father or sister is quite prepared at his or her own cost to provide for them, if placed in his or her custody (*Milford* v. *Milford*, L. R., 1 P. 715).

§§ 41-44.

is compelled to ask for allowance.

The right of an innocent wife to the custody of her child is based on the principle that she should not unnecessarily be deprived of the solace which she derives from the society of the child. If, therefore, the society of the child can afford her no solace,—if, for instance, it is an idiot,—the Court will not give her the custody of it, no matter how blameless her conduct has been (*Cooke* v. *Cooke*, 3 S. & T. 248; 32 L. J., P. & M. 180).

When the custody of the children is given to the mother, the Court will not interfere with the relations of the children with their father to any greater extent than is inevitable from their remaining in the custody of their mother. It will not, therefore, deprive him of the power of exercising parental judgment and discrimination with regard to his children by extinguishing his power of appointment amongst them (*Maudslay* v. *Maudslay*, L. R., 2 P. 256).

But guilty father will not be deprived of all control.

(c) *Ordinarily, the Court will refuse to give the custody of the minor children to the guilty party, whether husband or wife* (*Hyde* v. *Hyde*, 29 L. J., P. & M. 150; *Marsh* v. *Marsh*, 1 S. & T. 312; 28 L. J., P. & M. 13; *Suggate* v. *Suggate*, 1 S. & T. 489; 29 L. J., P. & M. 167; *Milford* v. *Milford*, L. R., 1 P. 715; 38 L. J., P. & M. 63; *Bent* v. *Bent and Footman*, 2 S. & T. 292; 30 L. J., P. & M. 175; *Clout* v. *Clout and Helbone*, 2 S. & T. 391; 30 L. J., P. & M. 176; *Kelly* v. *Kelly and Saunders*, 5 B. L. R. 71; *Goad* v. *Goad*, No. 69 Punjab Record, 1870).

3rd. Court will not give custody to guilty party.

Exceptional cases.—Where the guilty party is the father and it is shown that he has discontinued his adultery and is living a respectable life, and that he has always treated his children with kindness, the Court, while placing the minor daughters in the custody of their mother, may allow the minor sons to remain with their father (*Symington* v. *Symington*, L. R., 2 H. L. (Sc.) 415; *Martin* v. *Martin*, 29 L. J., P. & M. 106).

Exceptions.

But, in the case of a guilty wife, the circumstances will have to be very exceptional before the Court will give her the custody

§§ 41-44. of the minor children. Possibly it may do so when the child is of a very tender age, is at the time living with someone other than its father, and the health of the mother or the child is being seriously affected by the separation (*Barnes* v. *Barnes and Beaumont*, L. R., 1 P. 463).

4th. If neither parent fit to have custody.

(d) *If neither the father nor the mother is a fit and proper person to have the custody of the minor children, the Court will, in the interests of the children, place them in the custody of some fit and proper third person* (*Chetwynd* v. *Chetwynd*, 35 L. J., P. & M. 21; *D'Alton* v. *D'Alton*, 4 P. D. 87).

Where a decree for dissolution of marriage had been made in favour of the husband, who was away in India, the Court decreed the custody of the minor children to the petitioner or his agent, with a view that, in the absence of their father, their grandfather should have charge of them (*Ling* v. *Ling and Prior*, 13 L. T. 683).

Where, after a decree of judicial separation, the children have been placed in the custody of one of the parents, and such parent subsequently dies, the Court has no jurisdiction to grant an application by a third party for their custody, sect. 4 of the Matrimonial Causes Act, 1859 (corresponding to sects. 42 and 44 of the Indian Divorce Act), referring only to applications to be made by one or other of the parents, and not to applications by strangers (*Davis* v. *Davis*, 14 P. D. 162; 58 L. J., P. & M. 88).

5th. Subsequent variation of order.

(e) If the parent, in whose custody the minor children have been placed, is subsequently proved to be leading a life which renders it unfit that the custody of the children should continue with him or her, the Court will rescind its order and give the custody of them to the other parent if proved to be leading a respectable life, or to some other proper person (*Marsh* v. *Marsh and Palumbo*, L. R., 1 P. 437; *Witt* v. *Witt*, (1891) P. 163; 60 L. J., P. & M. 63).

But the Court looks with disfavour on an attempt to get up a charge of adultery against the person, to whose charge the children have been entrusted, by tracking him or her about from place to place with the view to obtain a rescission or variation of the order as to the custody of the children (*Marsh* v. *Marsh and Palumbo, ubi supra*).

Enforcement of order.

Enforcement of order.—Sect. 55 provides that "all orders and decrees made by the Court in any suit or proceeding under this Act shall be . . . enforced in the like manner as the decrees and orders of the Court made in the exercise of its original civil §§ 41-44. jurisdiction are enforced." An order of the Court as to the custody, maintenance, or education of, or for access to, the minor children, will, therefore, be enforced in the manner provided by the Civil Procedure Code for execution of decrees (Chapter XIX of the Code).

A person who refuses or fails to comply with an order directing him or her to hand over the children to the custody of another person, or to allow such other person access to them, is guilty of contempt of Court. And, independently of the Civil Procedure Code, a High Court has a jurisdiction to punish for contempt of Court which it has inherited from the old Supreme Court, and in virtue of which it may, if it think fit, keep a person guilty of contempt imprisoned for a longer period than the six months referred to in sect. 342 of the Code. For " sect. 342 applies only to those cases where parties have been imprisoned under process of execution in satisfaction of a decree, and does not apply at all to cases of imprisonment " (under an order of a High Court) " for contempt of Court " (*Martin* v. *Lawrence*, I. L. R., iv Calc. 655).

As a general rule, there must be personal service of the order upon the respondent before proceedings can be taken for non-compliance therewith. But " there are exceptions to that rule. If it were proved, for instance, that the person was actually in Court when the order was made, service would be unnecessary in order to obtain process for contempt, and personal service is also dispensed with if it is shown that the reason why there has been no personal service is that the person to be served has evaded service " (Cotton, L. J., *Hyde* v. *Hyde*, 13 P. D. at pp. 171, 172; cf. *Allen* v. *Allen*, 10 P. D. 187).

Order after final decree that guilty parent shall have access to children.—As a general rule, the Court, when it gives the custody of the children to the parent in whose favour a decree of judicial separation or dissolution of marriage has been made, will not order that the other party shall have access to them. The Court has, however, a very wide discretion in such matters, and has occasionally exercised it in favour of the guilty party. Thus, an order for access to the children was made in favour of the father, although he was proved to be continuing his adulterous connexion (*Hyde* v. *Hyde*, 29 L. J., P. & M. 150).

But the Court will not exercise such discretion in favour of an adulteress except under very exceptional circumstances (*Handley*

Access to children after final decree.

§§ 41-44. v. *Handley*, (1891) P. 124; *Bent* v. *Bent and Footman*, 2 S. & T. 392; 30 L. J., P. & M. 175; *Clout* v. *Clout and Helbone*, 30 L. J., P. & M. 176; *Kelly* v. *Kelly and Saunders*, 5 B. L. R. 71).

But, in the case of a judicial separation on the ground of cruelty or desertion, which affected merely the other party to the suit and not the children, the party guilty of such offence would probably not be denied access to the children if the latter were handed over to the custody of the petitioner.

Maintenance of children.

"**Order for maintenance of children**":

Under sect. 39, "whenever the Court pronounces a decree of dissolution of marriage or judicial separation for adultery of the wife, if it is made to appear to the Court that the wife is entitled to any property, the Court may, if it think fit, order such settlement as it thinks reasonable to be made of such property, or any part thereof, for the benefit of the husband, or of the children of the marriage, or of both." And under sect. 40, after a final decree of dissolution or nullity of marriage, the Court "may inquire into the existence of ante-nuptial or post-nuptial settlements made on the parties whose marriage is the subject of the decree, and may make such orders with reference to the application of the whole or a portion of the property settled, whether for the benefit of the husband or the wife, or of the children (if any) of the marriage, or of both children and parents, as to the Court seems fit: provided that the Court shall not make any order for the benefit of the parents or either of them at the expense of the children."

Under Chapter XI. of the Act, the Court has no jurisdiction, when ordering a provision to be made for the children, to order also that the party who is to make such provision shall secure payment thereof (*Hunt* v. *Hunt*, 8 P. D. 161).

Decree of nullity: provision for children.

Decree of nullity: provision for children of the union.—Under sects. 43 and 44, the Court has jurisdiction to order provision to be made for the children of a marriage which it has annulled. "The section" (sect. 35 of the Matrimonial Causes Act, 1859) "refers to the children 'not of the marriage,' but 'the marriage of whose parents is the subject of such suit or other proceedings.' The section includes sentences of nullity of marriage, and must, therefore, in my judgment, be considered as enacting that, in cases where there is no valid marriage, the children of the union may be provided for" (Cotton, L. J., *Langworthy* v. *Langworthy*, 11 P. D. at p. 89).

XII.—*Procedure.*

45. Subject to the provisions herein contained, all proceedings under this Act between party and party shall be regulated by the Code of Civil Procedure. *Code of Civil Procedure to apply.*

Except as is otherwise expressly provided in the Act, all matters of procedure in suits or proceedings under the Indian Divorce Act are to be regulated by the Code of Civil Procedure. Thus, any question as to the time within which a respondent may file an answer to a petition is to be decided not by the Rules of the English Divorce Court, but by the provisions of the Code dealing with written statements. Where, therefore, in a suit for dissolution of marriage on account of the wife's adultery, the co-respondent did not file his written statement until four days before the hearing, and did not give notice of it until the day before the hearing, the Court held that the written statement, having been filed before the first hearing, was in time (*Abbott* v. *Abbott and Crump*, 4 B. L. R., O. C. 51).

But by sect. 7 of the Indian Divorce Act the Court is enabled to follow the rules and practice of the English Divorce Court in all matters which are not expressly dealt with either in the Act itself or in the Code. Thus, the Court has adopted Rule 158 of the English Rules, and ordered a husband to give security for his wife's costs (*Mayhew* v. *Mayhew*, I. L. R., xix Bomb. 293).

46. The forms set forth in the schedule to this Act, with such variation as the circumstances of each case require, may be used for the respective purposes mentioned in such schedule. *Forms of petitions and statements.*

"Forms": *Forms in schedule.*
But "these forms were not intended to be literally followed, but merely to serve as general examples" (Sir C. Cresswell, *Evans* v. *Evans*, 1 S. & T. 78).

47. Every petition under this Act for a decree of dissolution of marriage, or of nullity of marriage, or of judicial separation, . . . shall . . . state that there is *Petition to state absence of collusion.*

§ 47.

not any collusion or connivance between the petitioner and the other party to the marriage.

Statements to be verified.

The statements contained in every petition under this Act shall be verified by the petitioner or some other competent person in manner required by law for the verification of plaints, and may at the hearing be referred to as evidence.

The Matrimonial Causes Act, 1857 (20 & 21 Vict. c. 85), s. 41, provides that—

> "Every person seeking a decree of nullity of marriage, or a decree of judicial separation, or a dissolution of marriage, or decree in a suit of jactitation of marriage, shall, together with the petition or other application for the same, file an affidavit verifying the same so far as he or she is able to do so, and stating that there is not any collusion or connivance between the deponent and the other party to the marriage."

See Rules 2, 3, 175, of the English Divorce Court Rules.

Stamp.

Stamp.

Under this section as originally enacted, every petition for a decree of dissolution or nullity of marriage, or of judicial separation, or of reversal of judicial separation, or for restitution of conjugal rights, or for damages, had to bear a stamp of five rupees. But by the Court Fees Act, 1870, 2nd Sched., Art. 20, every petition under the Indian Divorce Act, except a petition under sect. 44 thereof, which is specially exempted, must bear a Court fee stamp of Rs. 20.

Collusion or connivance.

"**Collusion or connivance**":

As to "collusion," see note to sect. 13, *ante*, and as to "connivance," see note to sect. 12, *ante*.

Verification

"**Shall be verified**":

In England the petitioner has to file an affidavit in support of his or her petition (see Rule 2).

The law for the verification of plaints is contained in sects. 51 and 52 of the Civil Procedure Code of 1882. And by sect. 115 of the Code written statements filed by the respondent must be verified in the manner provided for the verification of plaints.

In all cases the person verifying a petition or a written statement should state shortly what paragraphs he verifies of his own knowledge, and what paragraphs he believes to be true from the observation of others (*In re Upendro Lall Bose*, I. L. R., ix Calc. 675).

§ 47.

If the petitioner or respondent is unable from * absence or other good cause to sign the petition or written statement, it may be signed by any person duly authorized by him in this behalf (sect. 51, Civil Procedure Code).

If the verification is signed by a person other than the petitioner or respondent, the Court must be satisfied that the person verifying is acquainted with the facts (*Kastolino* v. *Rustomji*, I. L. R., iv Bomb. 468).

"**May at the hearing be referred to as evidence**":

Petition may be referred to as evidence.

In England the affidavit filed in support of a petition cannot be taken as evidence at the hearing, and the petitioner must prove his or her case *aliunde* (*Deane* v. *Deane*, 1 S. & T. 90).

48. When the husband or wife is a lunatic or idiot, any suit under this Act (other than a suit for restitution of conjugal rights) may be brought on his or her behalf by the committee or other person entitled to his or her custody.

Suits on behalf of lunatics.

See Rule 196 of the English Divorce Court Rules.

"**Husband or wife is a lunatic or idiot**":

Petitioner lunatic or idiot.

It is to be noticed that this section only provides for the case of a lunatic or idiot petitioner. But by sect. 463 of the Civil Procedure Code, 1882, provision is made for the due representation of either party, provided that he or she has been formally adjudged to be of unsound mind. It is doubtful whether when one of the parties is obviously of unsound mind, but has not been formally adjudged to be so, the Court can allow a self-constituted next friend to sue, or appoint a guardian *ad litem* to defend, on his or her behalf (see *Venkatramana* v. *Timappa*, I. L. R., xvi Bomb. 132, where it was held that the Court could

---

* But it must be remembered that, by sect. 2 of the Indian Divorce Act, the petitioner in any suit under the Act must be *resident* in British India at the time of presenting the petition.

§ 48. do so, and, for the contrary view, *Tukaram* v. *Vithal*, I. L. R., xiii Bomb. 656; *Jonnagadlu* v. *Thatiparthi*, I. L. R., vi Mad. 380; *Muhammad Kalu* v. *Saigulla*, No. 90 *Punjab Record*, 1887; *Kanwal Ram* v. *Bhawani Ram*, No. 13 *Punjab Record*, 1896).

By Rule 196 of the English Divorce Court Rules, "a committee duly appointed of a person *found by inquisition* to be of unsound mind may take out a citation or prosecute a suit on behalf of such person as a petitioner, or enter an appearance, intervene or proceed with the defence on behalf of such person as a respondent; but if no committee should have been appointed, application is to be made to one of the registrars, who will assign a guardian to the person of unsound mind for the purpose of prosecuting, intervening in, or defending the suit on his or her behalf; provided that, if the opposite party is already before the Court when the application for the assignment of a guardian is made, he or she shall be served with notice by summons of such application."

The Court of Appeal has held that an order ought not to be made under this rule assigning a guardian *ad litem* to a person as regards whose alleged unsoundness of mind there is a substantial and *bonâ fide* dispute, and, further, expressed a doubt whether the rule applied where the person had not been found lunatic by inquisition (*Fry* v. *Fry*, 15 P. D. 50; s. c., *Routh* v. *Fry*, 59 L. J., P. & M. 43).

In England it was formerly held that, though the committee of a lunatic might sue on his or her behalf for a judicial separation (*Woodgate* v. *Taylor*, 2 S. & T. 512), a committee could not sue on behalf of such person for dissolution of marriage (*Mordaunt* v. *Mordaunt*, L. R., 2 P. 109; 39 L. J., P. & M. 6). But it is now settled that a committee can sue either for a dissolution of marriage (*Baker* v. *Baker*, 6 P. D. 12; 49 L. J., P. & M. 83), or for nullity of marriage (*Hancock* v. *Peatty*, L. R., 1 P. 335).

It was also held formerly that a suit for dissolution of marriage could not proceed against a respondent who was of unsound mind, and that in such a case proceedings must be stayed (*Bawden* v. *Bawden*, 31 L. J., P. & M. 34; 2 S. & T. 417). This case has, however, been overruled by the decision of the House of Lords in *Mordaunt* v. *Moncrieffe* (L. R., 2 H. L. (Sc.) 374; 43 L. J., P. & M. 49), in which it was held that the lunacy of the respondent is no ground for staying proceedings in a suit for dissolution of marriage.

As to how far the insanity of the respondent is a ground of

defence in a suit for dissolution of marriage on the ground of his or her adultery, see note to sect. 10, *ante*.

§ 48.

49. Where the petitioner is a minor, he or she shall sue by his or her next friend to be approved by the Court; and no petition presented by a minor under this Act shall be filed until the next friend has undertaken in writing to be answerable for costs.

Such undertaking shall be filed in Court, and the next friend shall thereupon be liable in the same manner and to the same extent as if he were a plaintiff in an ordinary suit.

Suits by minors.

See Rules 105—108 of the English Divorce Court Rules.

"**Where petitioner is a minor**":

Minors.

As nothing in the Indian Majority Act (IX of 1875) affects the capacity of any person to act in the matters of marriage or divorce (sect. 2 (a)), the age of minority will depend upon the *personal* law of the class to which the party belongs. It has been held that the minority of English subjects not domiciled in British India continues till the attainment of twenty-one years (*Rohilkand and Kumaon Bank* v. *Row*, I. L. R., vii All. 490).

Minor Petitioner.

(a) Petitioner.

Chapter XXXI of the Civil Procedure Code, 1882, deals with the subject of suits by, and against, minors.

"Every suit by a minor shall be instituted *in his name* by an adult person, who in such suit shall be called the next friend of the minor, and may be ordered to pay any costs in the suit as if he were the plaintiff.

"If a minor has a guardian appointed or declared by an authority competent in this behalf, a suit shall not be instituted on behalf of the minor by any person other than such guardian, except with the leave of the Court granted after notice to such guardian, and after hearing any objections which he may desire to make with respect to the institution of the suit, and the Court shall not grant such leave unless it is of opinion that it is for the welfare of the minor that the person proposing to institute

§ 49.

the suit in the name of the minor should be permitted to do so" (sect. 440, Civil Procedure Code).

A father is entitled (at least in England) to institute a suit for the nullity of his minor child's marriage in his own right; if, therefore, such suit is brought by the father, the petition must show on the face of it whether the suit is instituted in the father's own right or by him as next friend (*Wells* v. *Cottam*, 3 S. & T. 364; 33 L. J., P. & M. 41).

Undertaking by next friend as to costs.

Undertaking as to costs.—This must bear a Court fee stamp of 8 annas (see Court Fee Act, 1870, 2nd Sch., No. 7).

Ordinarily the next friend is liable for costs only in his representative capacity, and, if he is made personally liable, the fact should be expressly stated in the decree (see *Kumal Chunder* v. *Surbessur Das*, 21 W. R. 298; *Omrao Singh* v. *Prem Singh*, 24 W. R. 264).

As a rule the next friend will be allowed his costs out of the minor's estate for any proceeding instituted for the minor's benefit, even though unsuccessful, provided that he has acted *bonâ fide*, but not otherwise (*Kenrick* v. *Wood*, L. R., 9 Eq. 333; *Dera Kabai* v. *Jefferson*, I. L. R., x Bomb. 248).

Minor suing without next friend.

Petition filed by minor himself or without next friend.—If a petition be filed by or on behalf of a minor without a next friend the respondent may apply to have it taken off the file, with costs to be paid by the person by whom it was presented. Notice of such application shall be given to such person by the respondent; and the Court, after hearing his objections, if any, may make such order in the matter as it thinks fit (sect. 442, Civil Procedure Code).

This section only refers to a case where, on the face of the petition, it appears that it was filed by a person who was a minor, and it does not contemplate any inquiry into the question of minority (*Beni Ram* v. *Ram Lall*, I. L. R., xiii Calc. 189). In a case where a petition is presented by a person professing to be an adult, and the respondent objects to the suit on the ground that the petitioner is not an adult but a minor, the proper procedure, it seems, is for the Court to raise an issue on the point, and, if it finds the respondent's allegation correct, to suspend all proceedings and to allow sufficient time to the minor to enable him to have himself properly represented in the suit by a next friend (*ibid.*).

This section does not give authority to a Court to make the

minor's estate liable for costs (*Aminchund* v. *Collector of Sholapur*, **§ 49.**
I. L. R., xiii Bomb. 234).

Who may be next friend of minor.—Any person being of Who may act
sound mind and full age may act as next friend of a minor, as next friend.
provided his interest is not adverse to that of such minor, and
he is not the defendant in the suit (sect. 445, Civil Procedure
Code).

Of course, under sect. 440, if a minor has a duly appointed
or declared guardian, that person shall, as an ordinary rule, act
as his next friend.

A married woman may be appointed as next friend (*Asirun
Bibi* v. *Shariss Mundle*, I. L. R., xvii Calc. 488).

Removal of next friend.—If the interest of the next friend of a Removal of
minor is adverse to that of such minor, or if he is so connected next friend.
with a defendant whose interest is adverse to that of the minor
as to make it unlikely that the minor's interests will be properly
protected by him, or if he does not do his duty, or, pending the
suit, ceases to reside in British India, or for any other sufficient
cause, application may be made on behalf of the minor or by a
defendant for his removal; and the Court (if satisfied of the
sufficiency of the cause assigned) may order the next friend to
be removed accordingly. If the next friend is not a guardian
appointed or declared by an authority competent in this behalf,
and an application is made by a guardian so appointed or
declared who desires himself to be appointed in the place of the
next friend, the Court shall remove the next friend, unless it
considers, for reasons to be recorded by it, that the guardian
ought not to be appointed the next friend of the minor (sect. 446,
Civil Procedure Code).

Retirement of next friend.—Unless otherwise ordered by the Retirement of
Court, a next friend shall not retire at his own request without next friend.
first procuring a fit person to be put in his place and giving
security for the costs already incurred. The application for the
appointment of a new next friend shall be supported by affidavit
showing the fitness of the person proposed, and also that he has
no interest adverse to the minor (sect. 447, Civil Procedure
Code).

On the death or removal of a next friend, further proceedings
shall be stayed until the appointment of a next friend in his
place (sect. 448, Civil Procedure Code). If the pleader of the

§ 49.

Petitioner attaining majority.

Compromise of suit.

minor omits, within reasonable time, to take steps to get a new next friend appointed, any person interested in the minor or the matter at issue may apply to the Court for the appointment of one, and the Court may appoint such person as it thinks fit (sect. 449, Civil Procedure Code).

Attainment of majority by petitioner.—A minor petitioner on coming of age is entitled to elect whether he will proceed with the suit (sect. 450, Civil Procedure Code). But the cases must be rare indeed, and exceedingly exceptional, in which a suit under the Indian Divorce Act is instituted otherwise than with the full concurrence of the minor. If such a suit be instituted, it cannot be doubted that it would be forthwith dismissed on the minor's representation that it was brought without his concurrence, and he would not have to wait till his majority to disown such suit.

But, if the minor elects to proceed with the suit, he must apply for an order discharging the next friend and for leave to proceed in his own name. The title of the suit or application shall in such case be corrected so as to read thenceforth thus :— " A. B., late a minor, by C. D., his next friend, but now of full age " (sect. 451, Civil Procedure Code). Such application may be made *ex parte*, and it must be proved by affidavit that the late minor has attained his full age (sect. 453, Civil Procedure Code).

As there may be cases in which a petitioner on coming of age elects to abandon the suit, it is sufficient to point out that he or she is entitled to do so; in such a case an application must be made to dismiss the suit on repayment of the costs incurred by the respondent, or which may have been paid by the next friend (sect. 452, Civil Procedure Code). If the minor on attaining his majority can prove to the satisfaction of the Court that a suit instituted in his name by a next friend was unreasonable or improper, he may apply to have the suit dismissed. Notice of such application must be served on all the parties concerned; and the Court, upon being satisfied of such unreasonableness or impropriety, may grant the application, and order the next friend to pay the costs of all the parties in respect of the application and of anything done in the suit (sect. 455, Civil Procedure Code).

Compromise of suit.—No next friend can, without the leave of the Court, enter into any agreement or compromise on behalf of a minor with reference to the suit in which he acts as next friend. Any such agreement or compromise entered into without the leave of the Court is voidable as against all parties other than the minor (sect. 462, Civil Procedure Code). It is hardly necessary to state that a Court is not likely to allow a suit under the Indian Divorce Act to be compromised contrary to the wishes of the petitioner. If it takes place without the leave of the Court, the minor can apply to the Court to set it aside.

§ 49.

Minor respondent or co-respondent.—Sect. 49 of the Divorce Act makes no provision for the case of a minor respondent or co-respondent. But sect. 443 of the Civil Procedure Code enacts that, "where the defendant to a suit is a minor, the Court, on being satisfied of the fact of his minority, shall appoint a proper person to be guardian for the suit for such minor, to put in the defence for such minor, and generally to act on his behalf in the conduct of the case. Where an authority competent in this behalf has appointed or declared a guardian or guardians of the person or property, or both, of the minor, the Court shall appoint him or one of them, as the case may be, to be guardian for the suit under this section, unless it considers, for reasons to be recorded by it, that some other person ought to be so appointed."

(b) Respondent.

No order appointing a guardian *ad litem* for an infant defendant, on the application of the plaintiff, should be made *ex parte*, and no such order should be made until the Court is satisfied that the infant has been duly served, and there has been an opportunity for making an application on behalf of the infant (*Suresh Chunder* v. *Tugert Chunder*, I. L. R., xiv Calc. 204—F. B). "An order for the appointment of a guardian for the suit may be obtained upon application in the name and on behalf of the minor or by the plaintiff. Such application must be supported by an affidavit verifying the fact that the proposed guardian has no interest in the matters in question in the suit adverse to that of the minor, and that he is a fit person to be so appointed. When there is no other person fit and willing to act as guardian for the suit, the Court may appoint any of its officers to be such guardian: Provided that he has no interest adverse to that of the minor" (sect. 456, Civil Procedure Code). A married woman may not be appointed guardian *ad litem* (sect. 457, Civil Procedure Code).

A guardian *ad litem* may be removed by the Court for neglect of duty or other sufficient cause, and he may be ordered to pay such costs as may have been occasioned to any party by his

§ 49.

breach of duty (sect. 458, Civil Procedure Code). But unless his appointment is revoked by the Court, or he dies pending the suit, he continues to be guardian *ad litem* until the end of the litigation (*Jowala* v. *Pirhbu*, I. L. R., xiv All. 35).

A new guardian must be appointed by the Court in place of a guardian who has died pending the suit, or has been removed by the Court (sect. 459, Civil Procedure Code).

By sect. 444 of the Civil Procedure Code, it is provided that "every order made in a suit or on any application before the Court, in or by which a minor is in any way concerned or affected, without such minor being represented by a next friend or guardian for the suit, as the case may be, may be discharged, and if the pleader of the party at whose instance such order was obtained knew, or might reasonably have known, the fact of such minority, with costs to be paid by such pleader."

The effect of this section is that no order by which a minor may in any way be concerned or affected can legally be made without him being represented by a next friend or guardian for the suit (*Aminchand* v. *Collector of Sholapur*, I. L. R., xiii Bomb. 234).

Practice in England.

The practice of the English Divorce Court with regard to the representation of minors will be found in Rules 105 to 108 of the Rules and Regulations. It will be noticed that under Rule 108 it is not necessary for a minor co-respondent to elect a guardian or to have a guardian assigned to him for the purpose of conducting his defence. But in view of the wide terms of sect. 444, Civil Procedure Code, it is submitted that a co-respondent who is a minor must in suits under the Indian Divorce Act be represented by a guardian *ad litem*. Moreover a co-respondent is a "defendant," and sect. 443 of the Code is as applicable to him as to a respondent.

(c) Co-respondent.

Service of petition.

50. Every petition under this Act shall be served on the party to be affected thereby, either within or without British India, in such manner as the High Court by general or special order from time to time directs:

Provided that the Court may dispense with such service altogether in case it seems necessary or expedient so to do.

PROCEDURE.

§ 50.

The Matrimonial Causes Act, 1857 (20 & 21 Vict. c. 85), s. 42, provides that—

> "Every such petition shall be served on the party to be affected thereby, either within or without Her Majesty's dominions, in such manner as the Court shall by any general or special order from time to time direct, and for that purpose the Court shall have all the powers conferred by any statute on the Court of Chancery: Provided always, that the said Court may dispense with such service altogether in case it shall seem necessary or expedient so to do."

And see Rules 10—18 of the English Divorce Court Rules.

"**Service of petition**":

See Appendix (E.), "Practice," "Petition, service of," pp. 347—349.

Service of petition.

51. The witnesses in all proceedings before the Court, where their attendance can be had, shall be examined orally, and any party may offer himself or herself as a witness, and shall be examined, and may be cross-examined and re-examined, like any other witness: Provided that the parties shall be at liberty to verify their respective cases in whole or in part by affidavit, but so that the deponent in every such affidavit shall, on the application of the opposite party, or by direction of the Court, be subject to be cross-examined by or on behalf of the opposite party orally, and after such cross-examination may be re-examined orally as aforesaid by or on behalf of the party by whom such affidavit was filed.

Mode of taking evidence.

The Matrimonial Causes Act, 1857 (20 & 21 Vict. c. 85), s. 46, provides that—

> "Subject to such rules and regulations as may be established as herein provided, the witnesses in all proceedings before the Court where their attendance can be had shall be sworn and examined orally in open Court: Provided that parties, except as hereinbefore provided, shall be at liberty to verify their respective cases in whole or in part by affidavit, but so that the deponent in every such affidavit shall, on the application of the opposite party or by direction of the Court, be subject to be cross-examined by or on behalf of the opposite party orally in open Court, and after

§ 51.

such cross-examination may be re-examined orally in open Court as aforesaid by or on behalf of the party by whom such affidavit was filed."

See also Rules 51—55 and 188 of the English Divorce Court Rules, and the Matrimonial Causes Act, 1857, sect. 43, and the Evidence Act, 1869 (32 & 33 Vict. c. 68), s. 3 (set out in the notes to this section, *infra*).

Parties to suit, when compellable witnesses:
(a) Husband or wife.

" **Any party** ":

"In all civil proceedings the parties to the suit, and the husband or wife of any party to the suit, shall be competent witnesses" (sect. 120, Indian Evidence Act, 1872).

But in suits or proceedings under the Indian Divorce Act a husband or a wife, though a *competent*, is not a *compellable*, witness, *except* (a) when he or she "offers" himself or herself as a witness, *or* verifies his or her case in whole or in part by affidavit, in either of which cases he or she can be compelled to give evidence as to any matter relevant to the issue, and is not to be excused from answering any relevant question (sect. 51, Indian Divorce Act, and sect. 132, Indian Evidence Act, 1872); or (b) where *the wife* has presented a petition *for dissolution of marriage* on the ground of her husband's adultery and cruelty, or adultery and desertion without reasonable excuse, in which case the husband and wife may be compelled to give evidence of, or relating to, *such cruelty and desertion*. But in this case the evidence which they may be compelled to give is strictly limited to evidence of or relating to the alleged cruelty or desertion, and neither of them is bound to give evidence of or relating to the alleged adultery (sect. 52, Indian Divorce Act).

(b) Co-respondent.

A co-respondent is "a party" to the suit, and may, if he chooses, "offer" himself as a witness. But unless he does so offer himself, or unless he verifies his case in whole or in part by affidavit (sect. 51, Indian Divorce Act), he cannot be compelled to give evidence in the suit.

"Offer himself or herself as a witness."

" **Offer himself or herself as a witness** ":

A party does not "offer" himself or herself as a witness who, having been summoned by the opposite party, gives evidence, not voluntarily, but in obedience to the direction of the Court. So where, in a suit for dissolution of marriage, the co-respondent, who had been summoned as a witness by the petitioner, did not object to being sworn or to answering questions until he was asked whether he had had sexual intercourse with the respondent, when he asked the Court whether he was bound to answer the question, and when told that he was bound, answered it in the affirmative, it was held that he had not, under the circumstances, offered himself as a witness within the meaning of sect. 51 of the Indian Divorce Act, and that his evidence must, therefore, be regarded as being struck out of the record (*De Bretton* v. *De Bretton and Holme*, I. L. R., iv All. 49).

§ 51.

In this case the Court did not explain to the co-respondent before he was sworn that he was under no compulsion to give evidence in the suit, and he was evidently under the impression that he was bound, in obedience to the summons, to come forward as a witness. Had it been explained to him before he was sworn that it was optional with him to give or withhold his evidence, and had he thereafter allowed himself to be sworn as a witness, he might well have been considered as having "offered" himself as a witness, and none the less so because he had originally appeared in Court in obedience to the summons.

Practice in England.—Previous to the Matrimonial Causes Act, 1857, neither a husband nor a wife was a competent witness in a matrimonial suit, but by sect. 43 of that Act it was provided that "the Court may, if it shall think fit, order the attendance of *the petitioner*, and may examine him or her, or permit him or her to be examined or cross-examined on oath on the hearing of any petition, but no such petitioner shall be bound to answer any question tending to show that he or she has been guilty of adultery." Subsequently (Matrimonial Causes Act, 1859, s. 6) it was provided that "on any petition presented by a wife praying that her marriage may be dissolved by reason of her husband having been guilty of adultery coupled with cruelty, or of adultery coupled with desertion, the husband and wife respectively shall be competent and compellable to give evidence of or relating to such cruelty or desertion." And sect. 3 of the Evidence Act, 1869 (32 & 33 Vict. c. 68), enacts that "the parties to any proceeding instituted in consequence of adultery, and the husbands and wives of such parties, shall be competent to give evidence in such proceedings: *provided* that no witness in any proceeding, whether a party to the suit or not, shall be liable to be asked or bound to answer any question tending to show that he or she has been guilty of adultery, *unless* such witness shall have already given evidence in the same proceeding in disproof of his or her alleged adultery."

Practice in England.

Under the proviso to the section last quoted it has been held

§ 51.

that a party to a cause who is produced as a witness on his own behalf, and in his examination-in-chief denies the truth of some of the charges of adultery contained in the pleadings, and is asked no question as to the other charges of adultery, is liable to be asked and bound to answer questions in cross-examination respecting all the charges contained in the pleadings (*Brown* v. *Brown and Paget*, L. R., 3 P. 198; but cf. *Babbage* v. *Babbage and Manning*, L. R., 2 P. 222).

Verification of case by affidavit.*

"**Parties shall be at liberty to verify their cases in whole or in part by affidavit**":

A party to a suit for dissolution of marriage is not entitled as of right to give evidence by affidavit, and where a petitioner "offers" himself or herself as a witness he or she should be examined orally and in the presence of the Court trying the petition (*Skinner* v. *Skinner*, No. 13, *Punjab Record*, 1891).

In England a party can prove his or her case, in whole or in part, by affidavit only under the directions of the Court, and in practice such direction is rarely given. But while "the Court is never again likely to allow a case to be proved *wholly* by affidavits, it may now be taken that the Court will allow a case to be *completed* by evidence supplied on affidavit, if the justice of the case allows it and there is no reason to suspect collusion" (Browne on Divorce, 5th ed. by Powles, pp. 398, 399). And in the note to *March* v. *March* (28 L. J., P. & M. 30) it is stated that "numerous applications have been made to the Court to allow petitions for dissolution of marriage to be proved by affidavit, which have uniformly been refused except in the above case, in *Ling* v. *Ling and Croker* (27 L. J., P. & M. 58), and in *Armitage* v. *Armitage and Macdonald* (*ibid.* 50), in which cases there had been a sentence of divorce *a mensâ et thoro*, and the petitioner had recovered substantial damages in an action for *crim. con.*" And in one of the cases quoted in the note, in which such applications had been made and rejected, the Judge Ordinary observed, "I cannot consent to so serious a matter as dissolution of marriage being tried on affidavits. The consent of the other side is an additional reason for refusing the application, as it is of the utmost importance to guard against anything like collusion between the parties."

Cases where petition partly proved by affidavits.

The cases, however, are not few in which a petitioner has been permitted to prove his or her case *in part* by affidavit.

---

* As regards affidavits generally, see Chap. XVI (sects. 194—197) of the Civil Procedure Code, 1882.

In an undefended suit for dissolution of marriage the Court allowed the petitioner to prove the *factum* of his marriage by affidavits on the ground that the ceremony had taken place in Scotland, and all the witnesses who could prove it resided there (*McKechnie* v. *McKechnie*, 1 S. & T. 550; 28 L. J., P. & M. 31).

§ 51.
Suits for dissolution of marriage.

In a case where bigamy was charged, the Court, while expressing its unwillingness to dispense with oral evidence in a suit for dissolution of marriage, consented to allow the bigamy to be proved by affidavit upon an affidavit being filed to the effect that there had been a conviction, and that the witnesses who could prove it resided at a distance, and oral evidence would be expensive (*Macartney* v. *Macartney*, L. R., 1 P. 259; 36 L. J., P. & M. 38; cf. *March* v. *March*, 2 S. & T. 49; 28 L. J., P. & M. 30).

Where the respondent was proved to have gone through a ceremony of marriage with a woman in America, the Court held that the mere proof that the ceremony had been performed was insufficient to satisfy the words "bigamy with adultery" in sect. 27 of the Matrimonial Causes Act, 1857, and that there must be substantive evidence of the adultery. But under the special circumstances of the case the Court allowed proof of the adultery to be completed by affidavit (*Ellam* v. *Ellam*, 58 L. J., P. & M. 56).

In a suit by the wife for dissolution of marriage, which was undefended, the Court allowed the petitioner to prove the bigamy, adultery and identity of her husband at the hearing by affidavit, the witnesses being resident in America and the expense of a commission being beyond the wife's means (*Burslem* v. *Burslem*, 67 L. T. 719).

Where the petitioner was in permanent employ abroad, and the wife's adultery was committed during his absence, the Court allowed the domicil, marriage, cohabitation and separation to be proved at the trial by affidavit (*Ex parte Hobson*, 70 L. T. 816).

In a suit for nullity of marriage on the ground of the respondent's physical incapacity, the Court, with the respondent's consent, allowed the petitioner (the woman) to give her evidence on affidavit (*B. f. c. C.* v. *C.*, 32 L. J., P. & M. 135).

Suits for nullity of marriage.

In a suit for restitution of conjugal rights, where no answer was filed, the Court allowed the petitioner to prove the marriage and the circumstances under which she was separate from her husband by affidavit (*Ford* v. *Ford*, 36 L. J., P. & M. 86).

Suit for restitution of conjugal rights.

§ 51. "Opposite party":

Opposite party, right of cross-examination.

In no case can the evidence of one party be received as evidence against another party in the same litigation, unless the latter has had an opportunity of testing its truthfulness by cross-examination. The evidence, therefore, of a respondent, whom the co-respondent is not permitted to cross-examine, is not admissible as against such co-respondent. And (*semble*) the right of cross-examination exists between a respondent and co-respondent, and if cross-examination is permitted the evidence of either party is admissible against the other (*Allen* v. *Allen and Ball*, (1894) P. 248; 63 L. J., P. & M. 120, doubting *Glennie* v. *Glennie*, 3 S. & T. 109—C. A.).

Competence of husband and wife to give evidence as to cruelty or desertion.

52. On any petition presented by a wife, praying that her marriage may be dissolved by reason of her husband having been guilty of adultery coupled with cruelty, or of adultery coupled with desertion without reasonable excuse, the husband and wife respectively shall be competent and compellable to give evidence of or relating to such cruelty or desertion.

The Matrimonial Causes Act, 1859 (22 & 23 Vict. c. 61), s. 6, is identical in terms with sect. 52 of the Indian Divorce Act.

Husband and wife, evidence of.

"Competent and compellable to give evidence":

See the notes to the previous section (pp. 292, 293).

It has been held under this section that a petitioner and a respondent who are examined upon an issue of cruelty or desertion may be cross-examined upon issues of their own adultery and of each other's adultery (*Boardman* v. *Boardman*, L. R., 1 P. 233; but see *Fisher* v. *Fisher*, 30 L. J., P. & M. 24, where it was held that a wife who, in a suit by her for dissolution of marriage on the ground of adultery and cruelty, gives evidence in support of the charge of cruelty, cannot in cross-examination be asked questions tending to show that she has been guilty of adultery).

Of course, if, in a suit by the wife for dissolution of marriage, the petitioner or respondent "*offers*" herself or himself as a witness, within the meaning of sect. 51 of the Indian Divorce Act, she or he will not be excused from answering any question tending to show that she or he has been guilty of adultery (see notes to sect. 51, *ante;* and cf. *Kelly* v. *Kelly and Saunders,* 3 B. L. R., App. 6).

§ 52.

53. The whole or any part of any proceeding under this Act may be heard, if the Court thinks fit, with closed doors.

Power to close doors.

"**With closed doors**":

Hearing *in camerâ.*

The power hereby conferred on the Courts in British India is much more extensive than that possessed by the English Court. The latter Court, by virtue of sect. 22 of the Matrimonial Causes Act, 1857, is enabled in all suits and proceedings other than in proceedings to dissolve a marriage, to follow the practice of the Ecclesiastical Courts, and as those Courts usually heard a suit for nullity *in camerâ*, the English Divorce Court can also, if it thinks fit, hear such a suit with closed doors. But it has been held that the Court has no power to hear a suit for dissolution of marriage otherwise than in open Court, even though the parties consent to the hearing being *in camerâ* (*A.* v. *A.*, L. R., 3 P. at p. 231; *C.* v. *C.*, L. R., 1 P. 640). But every other suit which the Ecclesiastical Courts might have heard in private may still, if the Court thinks fit, be heard *in camerâ* (*A.* v. *A.*, *ubi supra*, where a suit for restitution of conjugal rights was ordered to be so heard).

"**If the Court thinks fit**":

When suit will be heard *in camerâ.*

As a general rule the Court will hear a case *in camerâ* when the evidence is likely to be of a revolting character, and it is desirable in the interests of public decency that the hearing should be private. But it does not necessarily follow that, " when charges of unnatural practices are made, the investigation of them will be of such a character as to require the exclusion of the public, for in Courts of justice we cannot be over fastidious in such matters, and, disagreeable as it may be to inquire into the truth of such charges, it must be done if circumstances require it, whether few or many persons are present" (Hannen, J., *A.* v. *A.*, *ubi supra*).

54. The Court may from time to time adjourn the

Power to adjourn.

§ 54.

hearing of any petition under this Act, and may require further evidence thereon if it sees fit so to do.

The Matrimonial Causes Act, 1857 (20 & 21 Vict. c. 85), sect. 44, is in similar terms.

Adjournment. "**Adjourn the hearing**":

"The Court may, if sufficient cause be shown, at any stage of the suit, grant time to the parties, or to any of them, and may, from time to time, adjourn the hearing of the suit.

"In all such cases the Court shall fix a day for the further hearing of the suit, and may make such order as it thinks fit with respect to the costs occasioned by the adjournment: Provided that, when the hearing of the evidence has once begun, the hearing of the suit shall be continued from day to day until all the witnesses in attendance have been examined, unless the Court finds the adjournment of the hearing to be necessary for reasons to be recorded by the judge with his own hand" (Civil Procedure Code, 1882, sect. 156).

"If, on any day to which the hearing of the suit is adjourned, the parties or any of them fail to appear, the Court may proceed to dispose of the suit in one of the modes directed in that behalf by Chapter VII, or make such other order as it thinks fit" (Civil Procedure Code, 1882, sect. 157).

"If any party to a suit to whom time has been granted fails to produce his evidence, or to cause the attendance of his witnesses, or to perform any other act necessary to the further progress of the suit, for which time has been allowed, the Court may, notwithstanding such default, proceed to decide the suit forthwith" (Civil Procedure Code, 1882, sect. 158).

In England an adjournment is generally granted when any of the parties is taken by "surprise," that is to say, when one party wishes to give evidence of matters of which the opposite party has not had reasonable notice. Thus, where a petition contains merely a general allegation of cruelty, evidence of an act of actual violence is not admissible. But in such a case the Court will allow the petition to be amended, and, if the respondent desires it, will grant an adjournment to enable the charge to be met (*Brook* v. *Brook*, 12 P. D. 19; 56 L. J., P. & M. 108).

So, where in a suit for dissolution of marriage by the husband, in which the respondent did not appear, the co-respondent, who, in his answer, had merely denied the adultery with which he was charged, put a question to the petitioner tending to charge the latter with adultery, the Court disallowed the question, but adjourned the hearing in order to give the co-respondent an opportunity of pleading the charge in question and other matters in answer, reserving the question of costs until the conclusion of the suit (*Plumer* v. *Plumer and Bygrave*, 29 L. J., P. & M. 63).

§ 54.

And where a petition contains a general charge of adultery, of which particulars are ordered and delivered, but the petitioner desires to give evidence of other acts of adultery not included in such particulars, notice of them should be given to the other side a reasonable time before the hearing; otherwise the hearing will be adjourned (*Bancroft* v. *Bancroft and Rumney*, 3 S. & T. 610; 34 L. J., P. & M. 31).

If one of the parties intends to apply for an adjournment of the hearing in order to amend his or her pleadings so as to include fresh charges, reasonable notice of such application must be given to the other side, otherwise the application will be refused (*Hepworth* v. *Hepworth*, 2 S. & T. 514; 30 L. J., P. & M. 198).

The Court will itself adjourn the hearing when it requires further evidence on any point. So, where in a suit by the wife for dissolution of marriage, on the ground of her husband's adultery, cruelty and desertion, a doubt arose as to whether the parties had not voluntarily separated, the Court adjourned the hearing to have further evidence produced (*Ward* v. *Ward*, 1 S. & T. 185).

If, after an adjournment has once been granted to the petitioner, he desires to amend his petition by adding a fresh charge, his application will be refused if it appears that he knew of such charge before the original petition was drawn (*Banister* v. *Banister and Davis*, 29 L. J., P. & M. 53). But in a case which, after the hearing had been adjourned, part heard, the respondent was allowed to file an answer to the petition on showing that she had been prevented from doing so previously by the contrivance of the petitioner, who had told her that if she resisted the suit she would be left destitute (*Alexander* v. *Alexander and Amos*, 29 L. J., P. & M. 56).

Where, in a suit by the husband for dissolution of marriage, the guilt of the respondent had been conclusively proved, and, in fact, practically admitted by her, the Court refused to stay proceedings to enable her to examine witnesses in India and Australia in order to prove condonation on the part of the husband (*Campbell* v. *Campbell*, 3 Jur., N. S. 845).

§ 54.

Two years, desertion not complete at time of suit.

In a recent case, where the wife sued for dissolution of marriage on the ground of her husband's adultery and desertion, and the adultery was proved, but the evidence of desertion fell short of the required period of two years by several months, the Court allowed the hearing to be adjourned, and twelve months afterwards, the respondent not having returned to cohabitation, the petitioner filed a supplemental petition charging desertion, on proof of which the Court granted a decree nisi (*Wood* v. *Wood*, 13 P. D. 22; 57 L. J., P. & M. 48).

But in a later case the Court held that under such circumstances the proper course was either for the petitioner to withdraw the petition altogether and sue again *de novo* when the cause of action was complete, or for the Court, if the petitioner preferred it, to grant a judicial separation on the ground of adultery, and for the petitioner, when the two years' desertion was complete, to sue for a decree of dissolution of marriage based upon the former decree of judicial separation coupled with desertion for the full statutory period (*Lapington* v. *Lapington*, 14 P. D. 21; 58 L. J., P. & M. 25).

In a suit by the wife for dissolution of marriage on the ground of her husband's adultery and cruelty, the Court was satisfied with the evidence of adultery but not with that of cruelty, and adjourned the hearing for further evidence. Subsequently to the adjournment, an allegation was added to the petition, by leave of the Court, charging the respondent, who did not appear, with bigamy. The amended petition was reserved on the respondent, and when the case came on for hearing the petitioner's counsel stated that he intended to produce evidence of the bigamy only. The Court held that this could not be done except by suing *de novo* (*Walker* v. *Walker*, 31 L. J., P. & M. 117).

Enforcement of and appeals from orders and decrees

55. All decrees and orders made by the Court in any suit or proceeding under this Act shall be enforced and may be appealed from, in the like manner as the decrees and orders of the Court made in the exercise of its original civil jurisdiction are enforced and may be appealed from, under the laws, rules, and orders for the time being in force :

Provided that there shall be no appeal from a decree

of a district judge for dissolution of marriage or of nullity of marriage : nor from the order of the High Court confirming or refusing to confirm such decree :

§ 55.

Provided also that there shall be no appeal on the subject of costs only.

No appeal as to costs.

The Matrimonial Causes Act, 1857 (20 & 21 Vict. c. 85), sect. 52, provides that—
"All decrees and orders to be made by the Court in any suit, proceeding, or petition to be instituted under authority of this Act shall be enforced and put in execution in the same manner or the like manner as the judgments, orders and decrees of the High Court of Chancery may now be enforced and put in execution."

As to appeals in England, see the Supreme Court of Judicature Act, 1881 (44 & 45 Vict. c. 68), sects. 9 and 10.

As regards costs, the Matrimonial Causes Act, 1857, sect. 51, provides that—
"The Court, on the hearing of any suit, proceeding, or petition under this Act, and the House of Lords on the hearing of any appeal under this Act, may make such order as to costs as to such Court or House respectively may seem just : provided always that there shall be no appeal on the subject of costs only."

For the rules of the English Divorce Court dealing with the subject of costs, see rules Nos. 151—157 (taxing bills of costs), 158, 159 (wife's costs), 177—179, 199—201.

"**Shall be enforced**" :

Decrees and orders under the Indian Divorce Act are enforced in the manner provided by the Civil Procedure Code, 1882, for the execution of decrees.

Enforcement of orders and decrees.

"**May be appealed from**" :

Appeals:

Court fee.—Every memorandum of appeal under this section must bear a Court fee stamp of Rs. 20 (Court Fees Act, 1870, 2nd Sch., Art. 20).

(a) Court fee stamp.

Appeals from decrees of district judges in Oudh.—Although the High Court at Allahabad is for certain purposes* the High

---

* *E.g.*, for the purposes of withdrawing the suit before decision from the Court of the district judge, of advising on a reference the

§ 55.   Court for Oudh under the Indian Divorce Act, appeals from the district judges of Oudh do not lie to that High Court (*Percy* v. *Percy*, I. L. R., xviii All. 375, disapproving *Morgan* v. *Morgan*, I. L. R., iv All. 306). In this case the High Court, while refraining from deciding to what Court such appeals do lie, pointed out the difficulty which would arise if the Court of the Judicial Commissioners of Oudh accepted and entertained an appeal from a district judge of Oudh, and made a decree of dissolution of marriage. This difficulty is as to whether a decree *nisi* made on appeal can be confirmed by the Court of such Judicial Commissioner, he not being a High Court for the purposes of the Indian Divorce Act. "It might be that the decree of the Judicial Commissioner could never be confirmed. Their Lordships of the Privy Council are not a High Court for the purposes of Act IV of 1869, and the decree of the Judicial Commissioner's Court, if one is made on appeal in this case, would not be the decree of a district judge, and consequently would not be capable of confirmation by this Court under sect. 17. It appears to us that speedy legislation is necessary to remove the difficulties which we have pointed out, which in our opinion are obviously caused by an oversight on the part of the gentlemen who drafted Act IV of 1869" (*Percy* v. *Percy*, at p. 379).

Appeal by respondent.

On an appeal by a respondent on the ground that the Court ought not to have held that adultery on her part had been established, the co-respondent cannot be heard in opposition to the appeal (*Kelly* v. *Kelly and Saunders*, 5 B. L. R. 71).

Award of damages by District Court.

Although a co-respondent does not appeal against the award of damages by the District Court, the High Court, when moved to confirm the decree, can also deal with that part of it awarding damages (*Kyte* v. *Kyte and Cooke*, I. L. R., xx Bomb. 362).

Evidence not in existence at date of decree appealed against.

At the hearing of an appeal from a decree dismissing a petition, the appellant produced certain letters, written after the appeal was filed, by the respondent and one M. to each other, which showed a criminal intimacy existing between them. The Court held that these letters were admissible in evidence,

---

district judge on a question of law arising in the suit, and of confirming the decrees of dissolution or nullity of marriage passed by district judges (*Percy* v. *Percy*, *ubi supra*). The ground of this distinction is, that in the above matters jurisdiction is made to depend on the original *criminal* jurisdiction in cases of European British subjects (sect. 3 of the Act), whereas the jurisdiction in appeal is made to depend on the original *civil* jurisdiction (sect. 55 of the Act).

and that having been brought to the Court's notice by appellant's counsel, the Court was bound in the interests of justice to require their production in order to enable it to decide the appeal on its real merits (*Morgan* v. *Morgan*, I. L. R., iv All. 306).

§ 55.

When the period of limitation for filing an appeal has expired during vacation, a party to the suit has the right, under sect. 5 of the Limitation Act, 1877, to have the appeal admitted on the day the Court re-opens, and the prothonotary of the High Court has power to receive and file a memorandum of appeal on that day. In such a case, in order to save the right of appeal to the appellant, the appeal may be admitted without requiring security (*King* v. *King*, I. L. R., vi Bomb. 487).

Limitation.

"**Provided there shall be no appeal**":

This does not mean that there is no appeal to Her Majesty in Council from an order of a High Court confirming or refusing to confirm the decree of a District Court; an appeal of such a kind does lie (see sect. 56, *infra*, and *Hay* v. *Gordon*, 18 W. R. 480; 10 B. L. R., P. C. 301, where the order of a High Court confirming the decree of a District Court for dissolution of marriage was reversed as against the co-respondent).

Appeal from order of High Court confirming, &c. decree of District Court.

"**The subject of costs**":

Costs.

The only express provisions on the subject of costs in the Indian Divorce Act are those contained in sects. 16, 35 and 55, but there can be no doubt that it was not intended by the Legislature to deprive the Court of their ordinary discretionary power in the matter of costs. At the same time it is curious that the first part of sect. 51 of the Matrimonial Causes Act, 1857, which corresponds to part of sect. 55 of the Indian Divorce Act and gives the Courts in England a general power over costs, is omitted from the Indian Divorce Act. This omission may, possibly, have been due to an oversight on the part of the draftsman, and, in any case, the Courts are (it is submitted) entitled, in virtue of sect. 45 of the Act, to exercise the power over costs given to them by the Civil Procedure Code, 1882.

On the subject of costs in general, see Appendix (F.), "Costs."

56. Any person may appeal to Her Majesty in Council from any decree (other than a decree *nisi*) or order under this Act of a High Court made on appeal or otherwise,

Appeal to Queen in Council.

THE INDIAN DIVORCE ACT.

§ 56.

and from any decree (other than a decree *nisi*) or order made in the exercise of original jurisdiction by judges of a High Court or of any Division Court from which an appeal shall not lie to the High Court,

when the High Court declares that the case is a fit one for appeal to Her Majesty in Council.

Appeal to Privy Council.

"**Appeal to Her Majesty in Council**":

As to appeals to the Privy Council in general, see Chap. XLV of the Civil Procedure Code, 1882.

The limitation on the right to appeal to the Privy Council laid down in this section cannot affect the prerogative right of the Privy Council to admit an appeal in cases other than those in which the High Court declares that the case is a fit one for appeal to Her Majesty in Council. The Privy Council can always grant special leave to appeal to it; "practically, however, it is found that the Privy Council will respect the limitation imposed by the local Legislature on appeal, when such limitations are reasonable" (Speech of Sir H. Maine, Gazette of India, 6th March, 1869, p. 297; cf. *Rahimbay* v. *Turner*, I. L. R., xv Bomb. 155).

Findings of lower Courts.

"Their lordships are not unmindful that they have, on more than one occasion, laid it down as a general rule, subject to possible exceptions, that they would not reverse the concurrent findings of two Courts on a question of fact. But they consider that the circumstances of this case are of so peculiar a character as to take it out of the scope of that general rule. They are dealing with a jurisdiction of an important and delicate character, new to the Courts of India" (*Hay* v. *Gordon*, 18 W. R. 480; 10 B. L. R., P. C. 301).

XIII.—*Remarriage.*

Liberty to parties to marry again.

57. When six months after the date of an order of a High Court confirming the decree for a dissolution of marriage made by a district judge have expired,

or when six months after the date of any decree of a High Court dissolving a marriage have expired,

and no appeal has been presented against such § 57.
decree to the High Court in its appellate jurisdiction,

or when any such appeal has been dismissed,

or when in the result of any such appeal any marriage is declared to be dissolved,

but not sooner, it shall be lawful for the respective parties to the marriage to marry again, as if the prior marriage had been dissolved by death:

Provided that no appeal to Her Majesty in Council has been presented against any such order or decree.

When such appeal has been dismissed, or when in the result thereof the marriage is declared to be dissolved, but not sooner, it shall be lawful for the respective parties to the marriage to marry again as if the prior marriage had been dissolved by death.

The Matrimonial Causes Act, 1857 (20 & 21 Vict. c. 85), s. 57, provides that—

> "When the time hereby limited for appealing against any decree dissolving a marriage shall have expired, and no appeal shall have been presented against such decree, or when any such appeal shall have been dismissed, or when in the result of any appeal any marriage shall be declared to be dissolved, but not sooner, it shall be lawful for the respective parties thereto to marry again, as if the prior marriage had been dissolved by death: Provided always, that no clergyman in holy orders of the United Church of England and Ireland shall be compelled to solemnize the marriage of any person whose former marriage may have been dissolved on the ground of his or her adultery, or shall be liable to any suit, penalty, or censure for solemnizing or refusing to solemnize the marriage of any such person."

The above section is to be read and construed with reference to the time for appealing as varied by the Matrimonial Causes Act, 1868, and in cases where under that Act there is no right of appeal the parties respectively shall be at liberty to marry again at any time after the pronouncing of the decree absolute (Matrimonial Causes Act, 1868 (31 & 32 Vict. c. 77), s. 4).

"**Remarriage**":   Remarriage.

Any marriage by one of the parties, in the lifetime of the

§ 57.

other party, before the expiration of the periods here specified, or before the time for appealing against the decree of dissolution has expired, is absolutely null and void (*Chichester* v. *Mure f. c. Chichester*, 32 L. J., P. & M. 146; 3 S. & T. 223; *Rogers, otherwise Briscoe, f. c. Halmshaw* v. *Halmshaw*, 3 S. & T. 509; 33 L. J., P. & M. 141).

Decree of High Court dissolving marriage.

"**Decree of High Court dissolving a marriage**":

This means the decree absolute, and not the decree *nisi*. A marriage, therefore, by one of the parties, the other party living, within six months of the decree absolute of a High Court, is null and void; and the prohibition contained in this section against the marriage of either party within such period is an integral part of the proceeding, and a condition which must be fulfilled before the parties can contract a fresh marriage, nor can the parties evade the prohibition by obtaining a domicil in another country (*Warter* v. *Warter*, 15 P. D. 152; 59 L. J., P. & M. 87).

Can the parties intermarry again?

"**As if such prior marriage had been dissolved by death**":

Though from the above words it would appear that the parties cannot again intermarry, there can be no doubt that a remarriage between them is legally valid (see *Fendall, otherwise Goldsmid* v. *Goldsmid*, 2 P. D. 263; 46 L. J., P. & M. 70).

But children born of such remarriage are not entitled to the benefit of a settlement made on the former marriage upon the children of the parties (*Bond* v. *Taylor*, 31 L. J., P. & M. 784).

English clergyman not compelled to solemnize marriages of persons divorced for adultery.

58. No clergyman in Holy Orders of the Church of England shall be compelled to solemnize the marriage of any person whose former marriage has been dissolved on the ground of his or her adultery, or shall be liable to any suit, penalty, or censure for solemnizing or refusing to solemnize the marriage of any such person.

(*This section is as amended by Act XII of* 1873.)

See sect. 57 of the Matrimonial Causes Act, 1857 (20 & 21 Vict. c. 85), quoted under sect. 57, *ante*.

Marriage of divorced person.

"**On the ground of his or her adultery**":

It is only the marriage of that party whose former marriage

has been dissolved on the ground of his or her adultery that a clergyman is not bound to solemnize: he is not excused from solemnizing a second marriage of the innocent party. And, in any case, there is nothing to prevent the guilty party from having his or her second marriage solemnized before a marriage registrar, under Act XV of 1872.

59. When any minister of any church or chapel of the said church refuses to perform such marriage service between any persons who, but for such refusal, would be entitled to have the same service performed in such church or chapel, such minister shall permit any other minister in Holy Orders of the said church, entitled to officiate within the diocese in which such church or chapel is situate, to perform such marriage service in such church or chapel.

English minister refusing to perform ceremony to permit use of his church.

(*Sect. 59 is as amended by Act XII of* 1873.)
The Matrimonial Causes Act, 1857 (20 & 21 Vict. c. 85), sect. 58, is in similar terms.

XIV.—*Miscellaneous.*

60. Every decree for judicial separation or order to protect property, obtained by a wife under this Act, shall, until reversed or discharged, be deemed valid, so far as necessary, for the protection of any person dealing with the wife.

Decree for separation or protection order to be valid as to persons dealing with wife before reversal.

No reversal, discharge or variation of such decree or order shall affect any rights or remedies which any person would otherwise have had in respect of any contracts or acts of the wife entered into or done between the dates of such decree or order, and of the reversal, discharge or variation thereof.

All persons who in reliance on any such decree or order make any payment to, or permit any transfer or

Indemnity of persons making pay-

§ 60.
ment to wife
without notice
of reversal of
decree or
protection
order.

act to be made or done by, the wife who has obtained the same shall, notwithstanding such decree or order may then have been reversed, discharged or varied, or the separation of the wife from her husband may have ceased, or at some time since the making of the decree or order been discontinued, be protected and indemnified as if, at the time of such payment, transfer or other act, such decree or order were valid and still subsisting without variation, and the separation had not ceased or been discontinued.

unless, at the time of the payment, transfer or other act, such persons had notice of the reversal, discharge or variation of the decree or order or of the cessation or discontinuance of the separation.

See sect. 26, *ante,* and sect. 23 of the Matrimonial Causes Act, 1857 (20 & 21 Vict. c. 85). Sect. 8 of the Matrimonial Causes Act, 1858 (21 & 22 Vict. c. 108), is as follows :—

"In every case in which a wife shall, under this Act, or under the said Act of the 20th and 21st Vict. c. 85, have obtained an order to protect her earnings or property, or a decree for judicial separation, such order or decree shall, until reversed or discharged, so far as necessary for the protection of any person or corporation who shall deal with the wife, be deemed valid and effectual; and no discharge, variation or reversal of such order or decree shall prejudice or affect any rights or remedies which any person would have had in case the same had not been so reversed, varied or discharged in respect of any debts, contracts or acts of the wife incurred, entered into, or done between the times of the making such order or decree and of the discharge, variation or reversal thereof; and property of or to which the wife is possessed or entitled for an estate in remainder or in reversion at the date of the desertion or decree (as the case may be) shall be deemed to be included in the protection given by the order or decree."

Sect. 10 of the said Act is as follows :—

"All persons and corporations who shall, in reliance on any such order or decree as aforesaid, make any payment to or permit any transfer or act to be made or done by the wife who has obtained the same, shall, notwithstanding such order or decree may then have been discharged, reversed or varied, or the separation of the wife from her husband may have ceased, or at some time since the making of the order or decree been discontinued, be protected and indemnified in the same way in all respects as if, at the time of such payment, transfer or other act, such order or decree were valid and still subsisting without variation in full force and effect, and the separation of the wife from her husband had not ceased or been discontinued, unless at the time of such payment, transfer or other act such persons or corporations had notice of the discharge, reversal or variation of such order or decree, or the cessation or discontinuance of such separation."

§ 60.

61. After this Act comes into operation, no person competent to present a petition under sections two and ten shall maintain a suit for criminal conversation with his wife.

Bar of suit for criminal conversation.

The Matrimonial Causes Act, 1857 (20 & 21 Vict. c. 85), sect. 59, provides that—
  "After this Act shall have come into operation, no action shall be maintainable in England for criminal conversation."

"Criminal conversation":

Action for criminal conversation.

Although no person competent to present a petition under sects. 2 and 10 of this Act can maintain a suit for criminal conversation with his wife, it is still open to a husband to present a petition under sect. 34, merely claiming damages from an adulterer. But, if such adultery has been condoned, no damages in respect thereof can be claimed (*Bernstein* v. *Bernstein*, (1893) P. 292; 63 L. J., P. & M. 3).

It is to be remembered that adultery with a person who is, and whom the adulterer knows or has reason to believe to be, the wife of another man without the consent or connivance of that man, is a criminal offence under sect. 497 of the Indian Penal Code, and is punishable with imprisonment of either description for a term which may extend to five years, or with fine, or with both. But it is only on the complaint of the husband or of the person having the care of the wife on his behalf that such offence is cognizable.

62. The High Court shall make such rules under this Act as it may from time to time consider expedient, and may from time to time alter and add to the same:
  Provided that such rules, alterations and additions

Power to make rules.

§ 62. are consistent with the provisions of this Act and the Code of Civil Procedure.

All such rules, alterations and additions shall be published in the local official Gazette.

Sect. 53 of the Matrimonial Causes Act, 1857 (20 & 21 Vict. c. 85), provides that—

> "The Court shall make such rules and regulations concerning the practice and procedure under this Act as it may from time to time consider expedient, and shall have full power from time to time to revoke or alter the same."

Sect. 54 of the said Act provides that :—

> "The Court shall have full power to fix and regulate from time to time the fees payable upon all proceedings before it, all which fees shall be received, paid, and applied as herein directed; provided always that the said Court may make such rules and regulations as it may deem necessary and expedient for enabling persons to sue in the said Court *in formâ pauperis.*"

By sect. 18 of 38 & 39 Vict. c. 77, the President for the time being of the Probate, Divorce and Admiralty Division of the High Court is empowered to exercise the authority conferred on the Court by sect. 53 of 20 & 21 Vict. c. 85.

The Rules of the English Divorce Court are printed as Appendix (G.).

Rules. **"Rules" :**

The author has been informed by the Registrars of the High Courts of Calcutta, Bombay, Madras, and Allahabad that no rules have been issued by their respective Courts under the provisions of this section.

[SCHEDULE.

*SCHEDULE OF FORMS.

No. 1.—*Petition by Husband for a Dissolution of Marriage, with Damages against Co-respondent by reason of Adultery.*

(See sections 10 and 34.)

In the (High) Court of .
   To the Honorable Mr. Justice
   [*or* To the Judge of   ].
            The   day of   , 189 .
            The petition of *A. B.*, of   .

SHEWETH,

1. That your petitioner was, on the   day of   , one thousand eight hundred and   , lawfully married to *C. B.*, then *C. D.*, spinster, at   (*a*).

2. That from his said marriage, your petitioner lived and cohabited with his said wife at   and at   , in   , and lastly at   , in   , and that your petitioner and his said wife have had issue of their said marriage *five* children, of whom *two* sons only survive, aged respectively *twelve* and *fourteen* years.

3. That during the *three* years immediately preceding the   day of   , one thousand eight hundred and   , *X. Y.* was constantly, with few exceptions, residing in the house of your petitioner at   , and that, on divers occasions, during the said period, the dates of which are unknown to your petitioner, the said *C. B.*, in your petitioner's said house, committed adultery with the said *X. Y.*

4. That no collusion or connivance exists between me

---

* See sect. 46.

Schedule. and my said wife for the purpose of obtaining a dissolution of our said marriage, or for any other purpose.

Your petitioner, therefore, prays that this (Honorable) Court will decree a dissolution of the said marriage, and that the said X. Y. do pay the sum of Rs. 5,000 as damages by reason of his having committed adultery with your petitioner's said wife, such damages to be paid to your petitioner, or otherwise paid or applied as to this (Honorable) Court seems fit.

(Signed)   A. B. (b).

Form of Verification.

I, A. B., the petitioner named in the above petition, do declare that what is stated therein is true to the best of my information and belief.

(a) If the marriage was solemnized out of India, the adultery must be shown to have been committed in India.

(b) The petition must be signed by the petitioner.

No. 2.—*Respondent's Statement in answer to No. 1.*

In the Court of   , the   day of   .

Between A. B., petitioner,
C. B., respondent, and
X. Y., co-respondent.

C. B., the respondent, by D. E. her attorney [or vakíl], in answer to the petition of A. B. says that she denies that she has on divers or any occasions committed adultery with X. Y., as alleged in the third paragraph of the said petition.

Wherefore the respondent prays that this (Honorable) Court will reject the said petition.

(Signed)   C. B.

SCHEDULE OF FORMS. 313

Schedule.

No. 3.—*Co-respondent's Statement in answer to No. 1.*

In the (High) Court of .
   The   day of   .
            Between *A. B.*, petitioner,
                C. B., respondent, and
                X. Y., co-respondent.

X. Y., the co-respondent, in answer to the petition filed in this cause, saith that he denies that he committed adultery with the said *C. B.* as alleged in the said petition.

> Wherefore the said *X. Y.* prays that this (Honorable) Court will reject the prayer of the said petitioner and order him to pay the costs of and incident to the said petition.
>
> (Signed)   X. Y.

No. 4.—*Petition for Decree of Nullity of Marriage.*
(See section 18.)

In the (High) Court of .
   To the Honorable Mr. Justice
   [*or* To the Judge of   ].
            The   day of   , 186 .
   The petition of *A. B.* falsely called *A. D.*,

SHEWETH,

1. That on the   day of   , one thousand eight hundred and   , your petitioner, then a spinster, eighteen years of age, was married in fact, though not in law, to *C. D.*, then a bachelor of about thirty years of age, at [*some place in India*].

2. That from the said   day of   , one thousand eight hundred and   , until the month of   , one thousand eight hundred and   , your petitioner lived and cohabited with the said *C. D.*, at divers places, and particularly at   aforesaid.

3. That the said *C. D.* has never consummated the said pretended marriage by carnal copulation.

Schedule.

4. That at the time of the celebration of your petitioner's said pretended marriage, the said *C. D.* was, by reason of his impotency or malformation, legally incompetent to enter into the contract of marriage.

5. That there is no collusion or connivance between her and the said *C. D.* with respect to the subject of this suit.

Your petitioner therefore prays that this (Honorable) Court will declare that the said marriage is null and void.

(Signed)   *A. B.*

Form of Verification : see No. 1.

No. 5.—*Petition by Wife for Judicial Separation on the Ground of her Husband's Adultery.*

(See section 22.)

In the (High) Court of   .
   To the Honorable Mr. Justice
   [*or* To the Judge of   ].
            The   day of   , 186 .

The petition of *C. B.*, of   , the wife of *A. B.*

SHEWETH,

1. That on the   day of   , one thousand eight hundred and *sixty-*   your petitioner, then *C. D.*, was lawfully married to *A. B.*, at the Church of   , in the   .

2. That after her said marriage, your petitioner cohabited with the said *A. B.* at   and at   , and that your petitioner and her said husband have issue living of their said marriage, *three* children, to wit, &c., &c.   (*a*).

3. That on divers occasions in or about the months of *August, September* and *October*, one thousand eight hundred and *sixty-*   , the said *A. B.*, at   aforesaid, committed adultery with *E. F.*, who was then living in the service of the said *A. B.* and your petitioner at their said residence   aforesaid.

SCHEDULE OF FORMS. 315

Schedule.

4. That on divers occasions in the months of *October, November* and *December*, one thousand eight hundred and *sixty-* , the said *A. B.* at aforesaid, committed adultery with *G. H.*, who was then living in the service of the said *A. B.* and your petitioner at their said residence aforesaid.

5. That no collusion or connivance exists between your petitioner and the said *A. B.* with respect to the subject of the present suit.

> Your petitioner therefore prays that this (Honorable) Court will decree a judicial separation to your petitioner from her said husband by reason of his aforesaid adultery.
> (Signed) *C. B.* (*b*).

Form of Verification: see No. 1.

(*a*) State the respective ages of the children.
(*b*) The petition must be signed by the petitioner.

No. 6.—*Statement in answer to No. 5.*

In the (High) Court of .
B. against *B.*
The day of .

The respondent, *A. B.*, by *W. Y.*, his attorney [*or* vakíl], saith,—

1. That he denies that he committed adultery with *E. F.*, as in the third paragraph of the petition alleged.
2. That the petitioner condoned the said adultery with *E. F.*, if any.
3. That he denies that he committed adultery with *G. H.*, as in the fourth paragraph of the petition alleged.
4. That the petitioner condoned the said adultery with *G. H.*, if any.

> Wherefore this respondent prays that this (Honorable) Court will reject the prayer of the said petition.
> (Signed) *A. B.*

Schedule.

No. 7.—*Statement in reply to No. 6.*

In the (High) Court of .

B. against B.

The   day of   .

The petitioner, *C. B.*, by her attorney [*or* vakíl], says—

1. That she denies that she condoned the said adultery of the respondent with *E. F.* as in the second paragraph of the statement in answer alleged.

2. That even if she had condoned the said adultery, the same has been revived by the subsequent adultery of the respondent with *G. H.* as set forth in the fourth paragraph of the petition.

(Signed)   *C. B.*

No. 8.—*Petition for a Judicial Separation by reason of Cruelty.*

(See section 22.)

In the (High) Court of   .

To the Honorable Mr. Justice
[*or* To the Judge of   ].

The   day of   , 186 .

The petition of *A. B.* (wife of *C. B.*) of   .

SHEWETH,

1. That on the   day of   , one thousand eight hundred and   , your petitioner, then *A. D.*, spinster, was lawfully married to *C. B.*, at   .

2. That from her said marriage, your petitioner lived and cohabited with her said husband at   until the   day of   , one thousand eight hundred and   , when your petitioner separated from her said husband as hereinafter more particularly mentioned, and that your petitioner and her said husband have had no issue of their said marriage.

3. That from and shortly after your petitioner's said marriage, the said *C. B.* habitually conducted himself towards your petitioner with great harshness and cruelty,

frequently abusing her in the coarsest and most insulting language, and beating her with his fists, with a cane, or with some other weapon.

4. That on an evening in or about the month of   , one thousand eight hundred and   , the said *C. B.* in the highway and opposite to the house in which your petitioner and the said *C. B.* were then residing at   aforesaid, endeavoured to knock your petitioner down, and was only prevented from so doing by the interference of *F. D.*, your petitioner's brother.

5. That subsequently on the same evening, the said *C. B.* in his said house at   aforesaid, struck your petitioner with his clenched fist a violent blow on her face.

6. That on one Friday night in the month of   , one thousand eight hundred and   , the said *C. B.*, in   , without provocation, threw a knife at your petitioner, thereby inflicting a severe wound on her right hand.

7. That on the afternoon of the   day of   , one thousand eight hundred and   , your petitioner, by reason of the great and continued cruelty practised towards her by her said husband, with assistance withdrew from the house of her said husband to the house of her father at   : that from and after the said   day of   , one thousand eight hundred and   , your petitioner hath lived separate and apart from her said husband, and hath never returned to his house or to cohabitation with him.

8. That there is no collusion or connivance between your petitioner and her said husband with respect to the subject of the present suit.

> Your petitioner therefore prays that this (Honorable) Court will decree a judicial separation between your petitioner and the said *C. B.*, and also order that the said *C. B.* do pay the costs of and incident to these proceedings.
>
> (Signed)   *A. B.*

Form of Verification: see No. 1.

Schedule.

No. 9.—*Statement in answer to No. 8.*

In the (High) Court of .
The day of .
Between *A. B.*, petitioner, and
C. B., respondent.

C. B., the respondent, in answer to the petition filed in this cause by *W. J.* his attorney [or vakíl], saith that he denies that he has been guilty of cruelty towards the said *A. B.*, as alleged in the said petition.

(Signed) *C. B.*

No. 10.—*Petition for Reversal of Decree of Separation.*
(See section 24.)

In the (High) Court of .
To the Honorable Mr. Justice
[*or* To the Judge of].
The day of , 186 .
The petition of *A. B.*, of .

SHEWETH,

1. That your petitioner was on the day of lawfully married to .

2. That on the day of , this (Honorable) Court, at the petition of , pronounced a decree affecting the petitioner to the effect following, to wit,—

[*Here set out the decree.*]

3. That such decree was obtained in the absence of your petitioner, who was then residing at .

[*State facts tending to show that the petitioner did not know of the proceedings; and, further, that had he known he might have offered a sufficient defence.*]

or

That there was reasonable ground for your petitioner leaving his said wife, for that his said wife

[*Here state any legal grounds justifying the petitioner's separation from his wife.*]

Your petitioner therefore prays that this (Honorable) Court will reverse the said decree.

(Signed) *A. B.*

Form of Verification: see No. 1.

SCHEDULE OF FORMS.

Schedule.

No. 11.—*Petition for Protection Order.*

(See section 27.)

In the (High) Court of .
   To the Honorable Mr. Justice
   [*or* To the Judge of   ].
         The   day of   , 186 .

The petition of *C. B.*, of   ,
the wife of *A. B.*

SHEWETH,

That on the   day of   she was lawfully married to *A. B.*, at   .

That she lived and cohabited with the said *A. B.* for   years at   , and also at   , and hath had   children, issue of her said marriage, of whom   are now living with the applicant, and wholly dependent upon her earnings.

That on or about   , the said *A. B.*, without any reasonable cause, deserted the applicant, and hath ever since remained separate and apart from her.

That since the desertion of her said husband, the applicant hath maintained herself by her own industry [*or* on her own property, *as the case may be*], and hath thereby and otherwise acquired certain property consisting of [*here state generally the nature of the property*].

        Wherefore she prays an order for the protection of her earnings and property acquired since the said   day of   , from the said *A. B.*, and from all creditors and persons claiming under him.

        (Signed)   *C. B.*

Schedule.

No. 12.—*Petition for Alimony pending the Suit.*

(See section 36.)

In the (High) Court of .

      B. against *B.*

To the Honorable Mr. Justice
[*or* To the Judge of].
      The day of , 186 .

The petition of *C. B.*, the lawful wife of *A. B.*

SHEWETH,

1. That the said *A. B.* has for some years carried on the business of , at , and from such business derives the nett annual income of from Rs. 4,000 to 5,000.

2. That the said *A. B.* is possessed of plate, furniture, linen and other effects at his said house, aforesaid, all of which he acquired in right of your petitioner as his wife, or purchased with money he acquired through her, of the value of Rs. 10,000.

3. That the said *A. B.* is entitled, under the will of his father, subject to the life interest of his mother therein, to property of the value of Rs. 5,000 or some other considerable amount (*a*).

    Your petitioner therefore prays that this (Honorable) Court will decree such sum or sums of money by way of alimony, pending the suit, as to this (Honorable) Court may seem meet.

        (Signed) *C. B.*

Form of Verification: see No. 1.

(*a*) The petitioner should state her husband's income as accurately as possible.

SCHEDULE OF FORMS.

Schedule.

No. 13.—*Statement in answer to No. 12.*

In the (High) Court of .
            B. against B.
        A. B. of   , the above-named respondent, in answer to the petition for alimony, pending the suit, of C. B., says—

1. In answer to the first paragraph of the said petition, I say that I have for the last *three* years carried on the business of   , at   , and that, from such business, I have derived a nett annual income of Rs. 900, but less than Rs. 1,000.

2. In answer to the second paragraph of the said petition, I say that I am possessed of plate, furniture, linen and other chattels and effects at my said house   aforesaid, of the value of Rs. 7,000, but as I verily believe of no larger value. And I say that a portion of the said plate, furniture, and other chattels and effects of the value of Rs. 1,500, belonged to my said wife before our marriage, but the remaining portions thereof I have since purchased with my own moneys. And I say that, save as hereinbefore set forth, I am not possessed of the plate and other effects as alleged in the said paragraph in the said petition, and that I did not acquire the same as in the said petition also mentioned.

3. I admit that I am entitled under the will of my father, subject to the life interest of my mother therein, to property of the value of Rs. 5,000, that is to say, I shall be entitled under my said father's will, upon the death of my mother, to a legacy of Rs. 7,000, out of which I shall have to pay to my father's executors the sum of Rs. 2,000, the amount of a debt owing by me to his estate, and upon which debt I am now paying interest at the rate of five per cent. per annum.

4. And, in further answer to the said petition, I say that I have no income whatever, except that derived from my aforesaid business, that such income, since my said wife left me, which she did on the   day of   last, has been considerably diminished, and that such diminution is

Schedule. likely to continue. And I say that out of my said income I have to pay the annual sum of Rs. 100 for such interest as aforesaid to my late father's executors, and also to support myself and my two eldest children.

5. And, in further answer to the said petition, I say that, when my wife left my dwelling-house on the day of   last, she took with her, and has ever since withheld and still withholds from me, plate, watches and other effects in the second paragraph of this my answer mentioned, of the value of, as I verily believe, Rs. 800 at the least; and I also say that, within five days of her departure from my house as aforesaid, my said wife received bills due to me from certain lodgers of mine, amounting in the aggregate to Rs.   , and that she has ever since withheld and still withholds from me the same sum.

(Signed)   *A. B.*

No. 14.—*Undertaking by Minor's Next Friend to be answerable for Respondent's Costs.*

(See section 49.)

In the (High) Court of   .

I, the undersigned *A. B.*, of   being the next friend of *C. D.* who is a minor, and who is desirous of filing a petition in this Court, under the Indian Divorce Act, against *D. D.* of   , hereby undertake to be responsible for the costs of the said *D. D.* in such suit, and that, if the said *C. D.* fail to pay to the said *D. D.*, when and in such manner as the Court shall order, all such costs of such suit as the Court shall direct him [*or* her] to pay to the said *D. D.*, I will forthwith pay the same to the proper officer of this Court.

Dated this   day of   , 186 .

(Signed)   *A. B.*

APPENDIX (A).
MARRIAGE.

* " **Marriage, Validity of** " :   Marriage, validity of.

As has been already stated (see notes to sect. 19, *ante*), the *essentialia* of a marriage depend for their validity upon the law of the parties' domicil.

The validity of a marriage as regards its *formalities* depends, on the other hand, upon the law of the country in which the marriage was solemnized. Therefore, "although *the forms* of celebrating the foreign marriage may be different from those required by the law of the country of domicil, the marriage may be good everywhere" (Lord Campbell, *Brook* v. *Brook*, 9 H. L. Ca. 193).

Conversely, if as regards its formalities, a marriage is invalid by the *lex loci celebrationis*, it is invalid (subject to the exception to be mentioned) by the law of every other country, even though it was solemnized in accordance with the forms required by the *lex domicilii* of the parties. Thus, a marriage solemnized at Antwerp between two English persons in the British church by a Protestant clergyman, appointed by the English Government, but without performance of the ceremonies required by Belgian law, was held to be invalid as contrary to the *lex loci* (*Kent* v. *Burgess*, 11 Sim. 361; 5 Jur. 166).

But it is, of course, competent to the legislature of any country to enact that, *for the purposes of its own municipal law*, marriages between its subjects shall be valid though not celebrated in due accordance with formalities prescribed by the law of the country where solemnized, *e.g.*, the statute 4 Geo. IV. c. 91, which renders valid, for the purposes of municipal law, marriages between British subjects celebrated abroad, otherwise than in accordance with the forms prescribed by the *lex loci*, in the chapel or house of a British ambassador, or in a British factory.

---

* By the term "marriage" is meant "a marriage in Christendom," *i.e.*, the voluntary union for life of one man with one woman to the exclusion of all others, and a union which is not repugnant to the principles of Christianity. In no case will the Courts of a country recognize as a valid marriage a union which the law of that country regards as incest (*Fenton* v. *Livingstone*, 3 Macq., H. L. Ca. 497; 5 Jur., N. S. 1183).

App. (A).

Celebration of marriage—
(a) of Christians;

"**Marriage, celebration of**":

(a) Marriages in India between persons one or both of whom is or are a Christian or Christians, are governed by the provisions of the Indian Christian Marriage Act (XV of 1872). By sect. 4 of that Act, any such marriage solemnized otherwise than in accordance with the provisions of sect. 5 shall be void.

Sect. 5 of the Act enacts that: "Marriages may be solemnized in India—

"(i) by any person who has received episcopal ordination, provided that the marriage be solemnized according to the rules, rites, ceremonies, and customs of the church of which he is a minister;

"(ii) by any clergyman of the Church of Scotland, provided that such marriage be solemnized according to the rules, rites, ceremonies, and customs of the Church of Scotland;

"(iii) by any minister of religion licensed under this Act to solemnize marriages;

"(iv) by, or in the presence of, a marriage registrar appointed under this Act;

"(v) by any person licensed under this Act to grant certificates of marriage between native Christians."

It is further provided by sect. 77 of the Act that "whenever a marriage has been solemnized in accordance with the provisions of sects. 4 and 5, it shall not be void merely on account of any irregularity in respect of any of the following matters, namely:

"(i) Any statement made in regard to the dwelling of the persons married, or to the consent of any person whose consent is required by law;

"(ii) The notice of the marriage;

"(iii) The certificate or translation thereof;

"(iv) The time and place at which the marriage has been solemnized;

"(v) The registration of the marriage."

It may be a question whether sect. 77 was intended to be exhaustive, that is to say, whether irregularities other than those therein specified would have the effect of rendering a marriage invalid. Would, *e.g.*, a marriage celebrated by a marriage registrar otherwise than in the presence of the two witnesses required by sect. 51 of the Act be invalid? In England, no doubt, it has been held that the statute 4 Geo. IV. c. 76 (sect. 28), which requires that two witnesses should be present at a marriage and sign the marriage register, is merely directory, and that non-compliance with such directions is no ground for annulling a marriage (*Wing* v. *Taylor*, 30 L. J., P. & M. 258). But the English statute under which the case cited was decided makes no mention of irregularities which shall not render a marriage invalid. However this may be, it is clear that the Courts of this country cannot entertain a suit of a matrimonial nature otherwise than as provided by the Indian Divorce Act, and have, therefore, no jurisdiction to grant a decree of nullity on the ground that the marriage is invalid for reasons other than those specified in sect. 19 of the Act (*Gasper* v. *Gonsalves*, 13 B. L. R. 109). App. (A).

Although a marriage which has been duly solemnized in accordance with the provisions of sects. 4 and 5 is not void merely because of any irregularity in respect of the notice of the marriage, it may well be that a notice in a wholly false name, given fraudulently and with intent to deceive the other party to the marriage, cannot amount to a notice at all, and may possibly entitle the party so deceived to pray for a decree of nullity on the ground that his or her consent to such alleged marriage was obtained by fraud (see sect. 19 of the Indian Divorce Act, and cf. *Holmes* v. *Simmons*, L. R., 1 P. 523 ; 37 L. J., P. & M. 58).

(b) The provisions of the Indian Divorce Act apply to marriages contracted under Act III of 1872, which was enacted for the purpose of providing a form of marriage for persons, neither of whom professes the Christian, Jewish, Hindu, Muhammadan, Parsi, Buddhist, Sikh, or Jaina religion. (b) under Act III of 1872.

By sect. 2 of that Act, marriages may be celebrated between such persons upon the following conditions :—
(i) Neither party must, at the time of the marriage, have a husband or wife living ;
(ii) The man must have completed his age of eighteen years, and the woman her age of fourteen years, according to the Gregorian calendar ;
(iii) Each party must, if he or she has not completed the age of twenty-one years, have obtained the consent of his or her father or guardian to the marriage ;
(iv) The parties must not be related to each other in any degree of consanguinity or affinity which would, according to any law to which either of them is subject, render a marriage between them illegal.
"1st Proviso.—No such law or custom, other than one relating to consanguinity or affinity, shall prevent them from marrying.
"2nd Proviso.—No law or custom as to consanguinity shall prevent them from marrying unless a relationship can be traced between the parties through some common ancestor who stands to each of them in a nearer relationship than that of great-great-grandfather, or great-great-grandmother, or unless one of the parties is the lineal ancestor, or the brother or sister of some lineal ancestor of the other."

By sect. 17 any marriage contracted under the Act may be declared null and void or dissolved in the manner provided, and for the causes mentioned in the Indian Divorce Act, *or* on the ground that it contravenes some one or more of the conditions prescribed in clauses (1), (2), (3), or (4) of sect. 2 of the Act. Accordingly, a marriage contracted between parties of whom one is under the age of twenty-one years, may be declared null and void on the ground that the consent of the father or guardian of such party was not previously obtained to the marriage. The absence of such consent in the case of marriages contracted under the Indian Christian Marriage Act, 1872, amounts merely to an irregularity which does not affect the validity of a marriage otherwise duly celebrated (see sect. 77 of Act XV of 1872). And in England the marriage of a minor by licence, without the consent required by 4 Geo. IV. c. 76, sect. 16, is valid, the statute being directory only (*Reg.* v. *Birmingham*, 2 M. & R. 230 ; 8 B. & C. 29 ; and see 6 & 7 Will. IV. c. 85, sect. 25).

As the various grounds on which a marriage contracted under the Act may be declared null or dissolved are expressly specified in sect. 17, it may be inferred that any other irregularity or informality would not render valid, a marriage, otherwise valid, liable to be declared null. Thus, the provisions in the Act relating to the presence of three witnesses and to the form of declaration to be made at the ceremony by the parties, would probably be held to be merely directory (cf. *Wing* v. *Taylor*, 30 L. J., P. & M. 258). This is on the general principle that, in interpreting statutes relating to marriage, the Court will not hold a nullity to be created by mere prohibitory words unless such nullity is expressly declared in the Act (*Catterall* v. *Sweetman*, 1 Robert. 317).

<small>Marriage Acts— Prohibitory words, how construed.</small>

<small>"*Omnia præsumuntur rite esse acta.*"</small>

And it is a presumption of law that, when a marriage is shown to have been solemnized, the ceremony was duly celebrated with all requisite formalities (*Reg.* v. *Mainwaring*, 26 L. J., P. & M. 10).

Therefore, when a man and woman intend to become husband and wife, and a ceremony of marriage is performed between them by a clergyman competent to perform a valid marriage, the presumption in favour of everything necessary to give validity to such marriage is one of exceptional strength, and, unless rebutted by evidence strong, distinct, satisfactory and conclusive, must prevail (*Lopez* v. *Lopez*, I. L. R., xii Calc. 706, following *Piers* v. *Piers*, 2 H. L. Ca. 331).

<small>Proof of marriage.</small>

"Marriage—Proof of" :

As regards marriages contracted under Act XV of 1872 (the Indian Christian Marriage Act), sect. 80 of that Act enacts that "every certified copy, purporting to be signed by an officer entrusted under this Act with the custody of any marriage register or certificate or duplicate required to be kept or delivered under this Act, shall be received as evidence of the marriage purporting to be so entered or of the facts purporting to be so certified therein without further proof of such register or certificate or duplicate, or of any entry therein, respectively, or of such copy."

As regards the marriages of native Christians, solemnized under Part VI of the said Act, sect. 61 provides that "when, in respect of any marriage solemnized under this Part, the conditions prescribed in sect. 60 have been fulfilled, the person licensed as aforesaid, in whose presence the said declaration has been made, shall, on the application of either party to such marriage, and on the payment of a fee of four annas, grant a certificate of the marriage. The certificate shall be signed by such licensed person, and shall be received in any suit touching

MARRIAGE. 327

the validity of such marriage as conclusive proof of its having **App. (A).**
been performed."

As to marriages contracted under Act III of 1872, sect. 13 of that Act provides that "when a marriage has been solemnized, the registrar shall enter a certificate thereof in a book to be kept by him for that purpose, and to be called 'the Marriage Certificate Book under Act III of 1872,' in the form given in the third schedule to this Act, and such certificate shall be signed by the parties to the marriage and the three witnesses."

Sect. 14 further provides that "the said Marriage Certificate Book shall at all reasonable times be open for inspection, and shall be admissible as evidence of the truth of the statements therein contained. Certified extracts therefrom shall, on application, be given by the registrar on the payment to him by the applicant of a fee to be fixed by the local government for each such extract."

Sect. 79 of the Indian Evidence Act, 1872, provides that "the Court shall presume every document purporting to be a certificate, certified copy, or other document which is by law declared to be admissible as evidence of any particular fact, and which purports to be duly certified by any officer in British India, or by any officer in any native state in alliance with Her Majesty, who is duly authorized thereto by the Governor-General in Council, to be genuine: Provided that such document is substantially in the form and purports to be executed in the manner directed by law in that behalf. The Court shall also presume that any officer, by whom any such document purports to be signed or certified, held, when he signed it, the official character which he claims in such paper."

In the case of a marriage solemnized in India, the usual mode of proving it for the purposes of a suit under the Indian Divorce Act, is for the petitioner to file a certified copy of the marriage certificate with the petition, and at the hearing to testify that he or she was married to the respondent at the time and place mentioned in such certified copy.

A marriage solemnized out of India is ordinarily proved by the production of such documentary evidence as there may be concerning it, and the evidence of the petitioner. Thus, a marriage solemnized in India was allowed by the English Divorce Court to be proved by the production from the India Office of a register kept in the custody of the Secretary of State, and by a copy of the entry signed by the Under-Secretary of State and sealed with the seal of the Secretary of State, the parties themselves also swearing to the marriage (*Regan* v. *Regan*, 67 L. T. 720; and see sect. 78 (6) of the Indian Evidence Act, 1872).

But in order to prove a marriage, a certificate of marriage or a certified copy thereof is not absolutely essential, and an alleged marriage may (at least in England) be proved in various ways; the testimony of either party to the marriage, being a competent witness, that the parties are husband and wife, or of any person who was present at the ceremony and can swear that it was performed; evidence of cohabitation of the parties as man and wife;

App. (A).

Indian Evidence Act, s. 50.

the admission of the marriage by the party against whom it is to be proved, are all legal evidence of marriage, though whether in any particular case the evidence adduced is *sufficient* to prove the marriage is a question of fact to be decided upon the circumstances of the case (see *Patrickson* v. *Patrickson*, L. R., 1 P. 86; 35 L. J., P. & M. 48; *Rooker* v. *Rooker*, 33 L. J., P. & M. 42).

In India there is a conflict of judicial opinion as to what evidence is necessary to prove a marriage for the purposes of proceedings under the Indian Divorce Act. Sect. 50 of the Indian Evidence Act enacts that "opinion expressed by conduct," as to the existence of the relationship of one person to another, of any person who as a member of that family or otherwise has special means of knowledge on the subject, is a relevant fact : " provided that such opinion shall not be sufficient to prove a marriage in proceedings under the Indian Divorce Act, or in prosecutions under sects. 494, 495, 497, or 498 of the Indian Penal Code." This proviso has been construed as meaning that in the proceedings therein specified, "a marriage must be proved strictly in the regular way," that is, apparently, that a marriage ceremony must be proved (*Empress* v. *Pitamber Singh*, I. L. R., v Calc. 566; *Empress* v. *Arshed Ali*, 13 C. L. R. 125; *Empress* v. *Kallu*, I. L. R., v All. 233; *Rathnammal* v. *Manikkan*, I. L. R., xvi Mad. 455; No. 40, *Punjab Record*, 1882, crim. judgments).

In the cases cited it was held that the evidence of one or both of the parties to an alleged marriage to the effect that such parties were husband and wife was insufficient *in law* to prove such marriage. On the other hand, it has been held that such evidence is not insufficient *in point of law*—apart from the question of its sufficiency or insufficiency *in point of fact*—to prove a marriage for the purposes of proceedings specified in the proviso to sect. 50 (*Queen-Empress v. *Subbarayan*, I. L. R., ix Mad. 9).

With all due deference to the learned judges who decided the cases first cited, it does not seem to necessarily follow from the negative provision that a marriage cannot be proved by opinion *only*, that in the specified proceedings marriage must be proved in a particular way. As pointed out in a recent judgment by the late senior judge of the Chief Court of the Punjab, the logical inference from such negative provision is only that in the specified proceedings marriage must be proved otherwise than by evidence of opinion only. " It appears to us," adds the learned judge, " that the English law and the Indian law of evidence are substantially the same " (that is, as regards proof of marriage), " and that in the former, as in the latter, the only definite and settled rule is that in certain matrimonial and criminal proceedings marriage must be more strictly proved than in other proceedings, and, when marriage is alleged, it must be proved that the parties were *actually* married, and not

---

* This decision may, perhaps, be now considered as overruled by the F. B. decision of the same High Court in *Rathnammal* v. *Manikkan*, I. L. R., xvi Mad. 455.

merely *reputed* to be married. It must be remembered that **App. (A).**
marriage is an equivocal expression denoting in our language
equally the conjugal relation and the ceremony by which it is
commenced, and there are English cases which show that the
marriage relation may be proved, otherwise than by opinion or
repute, in the absence of proof of any ceremony" (*Wadhawa* v.
Fatteh Muhammad, No. 5 *Punjab Record*, 1894, Crim. Judgments). And, in a very recent case, the High Court of Bombay
held that the District Court had jurisdiction, under sect. 2 of the
Indian Divorce Act, to make a decree of dissolution of marriage
upon proof of the commission of the adultery in India, and was
under no obligation to take evidence as to the place of the
marriage of the parties, the learned Chief Justice (Sargent, C. J.)
remarking, in the course of the argument, that in suits for
dissolution of marriage "strict proof of marriage is not necessary.
The mere fact that people apply to a Court for divorce raises a
presumption of marriage" (*Kyte* v. *Kyte and Cooke*, I. L. R.,
xx Bomb. 362; see, too, *Rooker* v. *Rooker and Newton*, 33 L. J.,
P. & M. 42, where the Judge Ordinary observed that "it was
hardly credible that persons should apply for a dissolution of
marriage which had never taken place").

In a suit for dissolution of marriage by reason of the cruelty *Marriage*
and adultery of the respondent, the Court held that the first proved by
charge and the marriage of the parties were sufficiently estab- previous
lished by the production of a previous decree for judicial decree of
separation on account of cruelty, and by proof of the identity of judicial
the parties (*Ledlie* v. *Ledlie*, I. L. R., xxii Calc. 544). separation.

Appendix (B).

IDENTITY OF PARTIES.

Identity of parties to suit.

(a) "**Proof that the petitioner and respondent are husband and wife or vice versa**":

In all cases clear proof must be given that the petitioner and respondent are the same persons as those who went through a form of marriage on a certain occasion. The marriage register, or a certificate of marriage, or a duly certified copy thereof, is proof that a marriage was celebrated between A. and B., but further evidence must be given in proof of the identity of the petitioner and respondent with A. and B. Such proof may consist of (i) the direct evidence of a witness who was present at the ceremony and can identify the parties thereto; (ii) evidence that the signatures in the original register are those of the petitioner and respondent. For this purpose it is not necessary to produce the original register if a witness can state that he has seen it and that the signatures therein are those of the parties (*Sayer* v. *Glossop*, 2 C. & K. 694; 2 Ex. 409). But a certified copy of the register must be put in evidence in such a case; (iii) by photographs. These must first be proved to be photographs of the petitioner and the respondent, and must then be proved by someone who was present at the ceremony to be likenesses of the man and woman who went through the ceremony of marriage at the time when, according to the register, such ceremony was celebrated; and (iv) *possibly*, by the admissions of the petitioner and respondent to the effect that they are the same persons as those whose marriage is recorded in the register. It is doubtful, however, whether this would be regarded as sufficient proof of identity, and in any case the evidence of the petitioner alone is insufficient, unless corroborated, to prove the identity of the respondent (cf. *Harris* v. *Harris and Milton*, L. R., 2 P. 77; 39 L. J., P. & M. 86).

Identity of party referred to in evidence.

.(b) "**Identity of the party referred to in evidence**":

As a general rule the identity of the party with the person referred to in evidence must be clearly proved by direct evidence. The witness should be shown the party, and must then testify that he or she is the same person as that to whom his evidence refers. *It is only under very exceptional circumstances that the*

IDENTITY OF PARTIES.

Court will accept as sufficient an identification by photograph only (*Frith* v. *Frith,* (1896) P. 74).

Nor is an identification by the petitioner alone sufficient. Where, therefore, a cohabitation between the respondent and co-respondent was proved by the keeper of the lodging-house in which they had lived, but the only evidence of the respondent's identity was that of the petitioner himself, who had seen her at the house, the Court refused to grant a decree upon such evidence without some corroboration (*Harris* v. *Harris and Milton,* L. R., 2 P. 77; 39 L. J., P. & M. 86).

But upon the trial of an issue of adultery raised by the Queen's Proctor intervening to show cause against a decree *nisi* being made absolute, the Court does not require such strict proof of the identity of the person charged with adultery as upon the trial of such an issue in a suit between husband and wife. Where, therefore, after evidence had been given that a man passing under the name of the petitioner lived in the house mentioned in the Queen's Proctor's plea, and there committed adultery at the time and with the person specified in the plea, and that the same man afterwards took lodgings in a certain place, where he gave a card on which were names corresponding with the names of the petitioner, the Court held that there was a strong inference that the man referred to was the petitioner, that a *primâ facie* case of identity had been established, and that, full notice of the charge having been given to the petitioner, he was bound to produce evidence to rebut it, or else his petition would be dismissed (*Hulse* v. *Hulse and Tavernor,* L. R., 2 P. 357; 41 L. J., P. & M. 19). The reason for this distinction is that in a suit between husband and wife every possible precaution is necessary in order to guard against collusion, whereas, in the case of an intervenor showing cause against a decree *nisi* being made absolute, there is no reason to doubt that the petitioner will contest the matter and refute the evidence if possible.

App. (B).

In cases of intervention.

Appendix (C).

*PROOF OF ADULTERY.

Proof of adultery.

"It is not necessary for me to state much at large the rules of evidence which this Court holds upon subjects of this nature, or the principles upon which those rules are constructed: they are principles so consonant to reason, and to the exigencies of justice, and so often called for by the cases which occur in these Courts, that it is on all accounts sufficient to advert to them briefly. It is a fundamental rule that it is not necessary to prove the direct fact of adultery; because, if it were otherwise, there is not one case in a hundred in which that proof would be attainable; it is very rarely indeed that the parties are surprised in the direct fact of adultery. In every case, almost, the fact is inferred from circumstances that lead to it by fair inference as a necessary conclusion; and unless this were the case, and unless this were so held, no protection whatever could be given to marital rights. What are the circumstances which lead to such a conclusion cannot be laid down universally, though many of them, of a more obvious nature, and of more frequent occurrence, are to be found in the ancient books. At the same time, it is impossible to indicate them universally, because they may be infinitely diversified by the situation and character of the parties, by the state of general manners, and by many other incidental circumstances, apparently slight and delicate in themselves, but which may have most important bearings in decisions upon the particular case. The only general rule that can be laid down upon the subject is, that the circumstances must be such as would lead the guarded discretion of a reasonable and just man to the conclusion: for it is not to lead a rash and intemperate judgment, upon appearances that are equally capable of two interpretations; neither is it to be a matter of artificial reasoning, judging upon such things differently from what would strike the careful and cautious consideration of a discreet man. The facts are not of a technical nature; they are facts determinable upon common grounds of reason, and Courts of Justice would wander very much from their proper office of giving protection to the rights of mankind if they let

---

* As to pleading adultery, see Appendix (E), "Petition," p. 343.

themselves loose to subtilties and remote and artificial reasonings upon such subjects. Upon such subjects the rational and legal interpretation must be the same. It is the consequence of this rule that it is not necessary to prove a fact of adultery in time and place; circumstances need not be so specially proved, as to produce the conclusion that the fact of adultery was committed at that particular hour or in that particular room; general cohabitation has been deemed enough" (Lord Stowell, *Loveden* v. *Loveden*, 2 Hagg. Con. Rep. 2; *Kelly* v. *Kelly and Saunders*, 5 B. L. R. 71).

App. (C).

"To lay down any general rule, to attempt to define what circumstances would be sufficient and what insufficient upon which to infer the fact of adultery, is impossible. Each case must depend upon its own particular circumstances. It would be impracticable to enumerate the infinite variety of circumstantial evidentiary facts, which of necessity are as various as the modifications and combinations of events in actual life. A jury, in a case like the present, ought to exercise their judgment with caution, applying their knowledge of the world and of human nature to all the circumstances relied on in proof of adultery, and then determine whether these circumstances are capable of any other reasonable solution than that of the guilt of the party sought to be implicated" (Lopes, L.J., *Allen* v. *Allen*, (1894) P. at p. 252—C. A.).

"**Guilty affection and opportunity**":

The Court may, however, presume adultery when it is satisfied that a guilty attachment subsisted between the parties, and that opportunities occurred when a guilty intercourse might with ordinary facilities have taken place (*Grant* v. *Grant*, 2 Curt. 57; *Williams* v. *Williams*, 1 Hagg. Cons. 299; *Davidson* v. *Davidson*, 2 Jur., N. S. 547; *Adley* v. *Adley and Campion*, No. 70 *Punjab Record*, 1873).

Guilty attachment and opportunities.

"**Admission of guilt by respondent**":

"No doubt the admissions of a wife, unsupported by corroborative proof, should be received with the utmost circumspection and caution. Not only is the danger of collusion to be guarded against, but other sinister motives which might lead to the making of such admissions if, though unsupported, they could effect their purpose, are sufficient to render it the duty of the Court to proceed with the utmost caution in giving effect to statements of this kind; the more so as it must always be borne in mind that the co-respondent, though not in a legal point of view interested in the result, inasmuch as from the absence of evidence available as against him he is entitled to an acquittal, has yet, socially and morally, the deepest interest in the result. Nevertheless, if, after looking at the evidence with all the distrust and vigilance with which it ought to be regarded, the Court should come to the conclusion, first, that the evidence is trustworthy; secondly, that it amounts to a clear, distinct, and unequivocal admission of adultery, we have no hesitation in

Admission by the respondent.

saying that the Court ought to act upon such evidence, and afford to the injured party the redress sought for" (*Cockburn, C.J., Robinson v. Robinson and Lane*, 29 L. J., P. & M. at p. 191; cf. *Williams v. Williams*, L. R., 1 P. 29; 35 L. J., P. & M. 8). And entries in a private diary kept by the wife, detailing acts of adultery committed by her with the co-respondent, are evidence against her as an admission, though not as against the co-respondent (*Robinson v. Robinson and Lane*).

But an admission of adultery by the respondent is evidence merely as against herself, and is not evidence as against the co-respondent with whom she alleges that she committed adultery (*Robinson v. Robinson and Lane*, ubi supra; *Jinkings v. Jinkings*, L. R., 1 P. 330; *Gordon v. Gordon and Hay*, 58 Punjab Record, 1870; in app. 18 W. R. 480; 10 B. L. R., P. C. 301).

Evidence of respondent.

Nor in a suit for dissolution of marriage is the evidence of the respondent admissible against the co-respondent, if the Court refuses to allow the co-respondent to cross-examine her upon it. *Semble*, a right of cross-examination exists between a respondent and a co-respondent, and if cross-examination is permitted, the evidence of either party is admissible against the other (*Allen v. Allen and Bell*, (1894) P. 248; 63 L. J., P. & M. 120—C. A.).

In a case where counsel for the co-respondent stated that he was instructed to admit the adultery, of which the only evidence was the admission of the respondent, the Court acted upon the admission, and made a decree for dissolution of the marriage (*Le Marchant v. Le Marchant and Radcliffe*, 45 L. J., P. & M. 43).

Visiting brothel.

"**Presumption from visiting brothel**":

The fact of a married man or woman going to a brothel, with a full knowledge of the character of the house, raises a strong presumption as against him or her of the commission of adultery, and such presumption can only be rebutted by the very best and clearest evidence (*Astley v. Astley*, 1 Hagg. Eccl. 1720).

So, where a married man, an apothecary, went to a brothel for the purpose, as he alleged, of dressing for a calico-ball, he being aware of the character of the house, it was held by the Chief Court of the Punjab that his visit to the house raised a violent presumption of adultery which could be rebutted only by the very strongest evidence (*McCulloch v. McCulloch*, No. 84 Punjab Record, 1875).

Birth of bastard.

"**Birth of a bastard**":

If it is clearly and conclusively proved that the husband had not, or could not have had, access to his wife before the birth of the child at such time as for him to be the father of it, the birth of the child is necessarily proof positive of adultery on the part of the wife (*Richardson v. Richardson*, 1 Hagg. Eccl. 11).

It must, however, be remembered that a child born of a married woman is presumed to be legitimate, and that this presumption is exceedingly strong and can be rebutted only by evidence of the clearest and most satisfactory kind. Indeed, so strong is the presumption that "even if it were proved to demonstration that, at the time when the husband was sleeping with his wife, she was carrying on an adulterous intercourse with some other man, so that it would be possible that the child should be the child of either the husband or the paramour, still the presumption is that it is the child of the husband" (*Bosville* v. *Att.-Gen.*, 12 P. D. at p. 179).

App. (C).

Sect. 112 of the Indian Evidence Act, 1872, enacts that "the fact that any person was born during the continuance of a valid marriage between his mother and any man, or within 280 days after its dissolution, the mother remaining unmarried, shall be *conclusive proof* that he is the legitimate son of that man, *unless it can be shown that the parties to the marriage had no access to each other* * at any time when he could have been begotten.*"

To rebut the presumption of legitimacy it is not necessary to prove that access was physically impossible, but the evidence must preponderate to convince the Court that access did not take place at a time and under circumstances which would enable the husband to be the father of the child (*Atchley* v. *Sprigg*, 33 L. J., Ch. 345; *Gurney* v. *Gurney*, 32 L. J., Ch. 456).

"**Venereal disease**":

Venereal disease.

The existence of venereal disease cannot be relied upon as *proof* of adultery. It may, under certain circumstances, amount to *primâ facie* evidence of that offence, but its existence is consistent with the adultery of the husband, with the adultery of the wife, and with accidental communication of the disease; and in any case, to establish adultery on the part of a husband, it is not sufficient to prove that the wife is infected with a venereal disease. No matter how free from suspicion she may be, it must also be shown that the husband himself was suffering at the same time from the disease† (*Collett* v. *Collett*, 1 Curt. 678; *Popkin* v. *Popkin*, 1 Hagg. 267, note).

---

* The normal period of gestation is from 270 to 275 days, but it may extend to much longer—according to some authorities, to 323 days. The longest period that has been proved is, according to Lyon (Medical Jurisprudence, p. 343), 296 days.

† Statements made by a patient to his medical adviser are not privileged under the Indian Evidence Act, 1872 (Field's Law of Evidence, 5th ed., p. 582). A doctor may, therefore, be asked, and is bound to answer, any question relevant to the matter in issue, *e.g.*, as to the symptoms of the illness upon which he advised his patient, or as to communications made to him by the patient as to how or where he contracted a venereal disease. The rule is, apparently, the same in England (*R.* v. *Kingston*, 20 How. St. Tr. 573; *Gilham's Case*, 1 Moo. C. C. 186; but see *Witt* v. *Witt and Klindworth*, 32 L. J., P. & M. 179, where letters written by a patient to a medical man were held to be inadmissible in evidence).

"Evidence of prostitute":

Evidence of prostitute.

The evidence of a prostitute in support of a charge of adultery against a man is, though admissible, entitled to very little weight, and will not, as a general rule, be regarded as sufficient proof of such adultery, unless it is corroborated (see *Ginger* v. *Ginger*, 35 L. J., P. & M. 9).

Res judicata.

"Decree in another suit":

The adultery of the respondent cannot be proved by the production of a decree in another suit in which he was co-respondent (*Ruck* v. *Ruck*, (1896) P. 152).

Nor is the conviction or acquittal of the husband in a criminal court sufficient to prove or disprove a charge of incestuous adultery, bigamy, or rape. Thus, where a man had been tried and acquitted in a criminal court of a charge of incestuous adultery committed with his own child, the Court held that such acquittal did not debar it, in a suit against him for dissolution of marriage, from allowing evidence to be given to prove that it had actually taken place (*Virgo* v. *Virgo*, 69 L. T. 460; cf. *March* v. *March*, 28 L. J., P. & M. 30).

Proof of adultery when pleaded as defence to suit.

"Adultery of petitioner pleaded by way of defence to suit":

Where the petitioner's adultery is pleaded by way of defence to a matrimonial suit, the same strictness of proof is required to establish it as if it had been alleged in a petition as the foundation of a suit (*Sopwith* v. *Sopwith*, 30 L. J., P. & M. 131).

Acts of adultery not charged in petition.

"Evidence of acts of adultery not pleaded in petition":

As a general rule, evidence of acts of adultery other than those charged in the petition is inadmissible (*Keats* v. *Keats and Montezuma*, 26 L. J., P. & M. 169, note). Nor can proof of adultery committed subsequently to the date of the petition sustain the suit, but evidence of such adultery is admissible for the purpose of showing the character and quality of previous acts of familiarity (*Boddy* v. *Boddy and Grover*, 30 L. J., P. & M. 23).

APPENDIX (D).

RES JUDICATA—ESTOPPEL.

"The existence of any judgment, order or decree which by law prevents any Court from taking cognizance of a suit or holding a trial is a relevant fact when the question is whether such Court ought to take cognizance of such suit or to hold such trial" (Indian Evidence Act, 1872, s. 40). *Res judicata.*

"No Court shall try any suit or issue in which the matter directly and substantially in issue has been directly and substantially in issue in a former suit between the same parties in a Court of jurisdiction competent to try such subsequent suit or the suit in which such issue has been subsequently raised, and has been heard and finally decided by such Court.

"*Explanation* I.—The matter above referred to must in the former suit have been alleged by one party, and either denied or admitted, expressly or impliedly, by the other.

"*Explanation* II.—Any matter which might and ought to have been made ground of defence or attack in such former suit shall be deemed to have been a matter directly and substantially in issue in such suit.

"*Explanation* III.—Any relief claimed in the plaint, which is not expressly granted by the decree, shall, for the purpose of this section, be deemed to have been refused.

"*Explanation* IV.—A decision is final within the meaning of this section when it is such as the Court making it could not alter (except on review) on the application of either party, or reconsider of its own motion. A decision liable to appeal may be final within the meaning of this section until the appeal is made.

* * * * * *

"*Explanation* VI.—Where a foreign judgment is relied on, the production of the judgment duly authenticated is presumptive evidence that the Court which made it had competent jurisdiction, unless the contrary appear on the record; but such presumption may be removed by proving the want of jurisdiction" (Civil Procedure Code, 1882, s. 13).

The principles of estoppel or *res judicata* as laid down in the above section are applicable to matrimonial suits (*Sopwith* v. *Sopwith*, 2 S. & T. 160; 30 L. J., P. & M. 131).

But, as an exception to the general rule, a petitioner, whose petition for dissolution of marriage has been dismissed by the District Court, may nevertheless present a similar petition to the High Court (Indian Divorce Act, s. 13). Exception to rule of *res judicata*.

APPENDIX (D).

App. (D).

The following brief remarks on the subject of *res judicata*, as applicable to matrimonial suits, may prove useful:—

Identity of matter in issue.

I.—**The matter directly and substantially in issue in the second suit to be res judicata must have been directly and substantially in issue in the former suit, and must have been heard and finally decided in the former suit.**

Where, in a suit for dissolution of marriage, the petitioner established his wife's adultery, but his petition was dismissed on the ground that he had himself been proved guilty of adultery, it was held, in a suit subsequently instituted by him, that the judgment in the former suit was conclusive proof of his guilt (*Conradi* v. *Conradi, Worrall and Way,* L. R., 1 P. 514; 37 L. J., P. & M. 55; cf. *Lisbey* v. *Lisbey,* No. 6 *Punjab Record,* 1888).

So where a wife, in a suit for judicial separation, alleged certain acts of cruelty on the part of her husband, but the Court found that they were not proved and dismissed her petition, it was held that she could not set up the same charges of cruelty, coupled with adultery, in a subsequent suit by her for dissolution of marriage (*Finney* v. *Finney,* L. R., 1 P. 483; 37 L. J., P. & M. 43).

Conversely, in a suit by the wife for dissolution of marriage on the ground of her husband's adultery and cruelty, the charge of cruelty was held established on the production of a decree for judicial separation, previously pronounced in her favour, on the ground of the respondent's cruelty (*Bland* v. *Bland,* L. R., 1 P. 237; 35 L. J., P. & M. 104; followed in *Ledlie* v. *Ledlie,* I. L. R., xxii Calc. 544).

A verdict of cruelty and adultery against the husband upon a wife's petition, followed by a decree *nisi*, which is afterwards rescinded on grounds *dehors* the verdict and wholly unconnected therewith, is conclusive evidence of the husband's guilt in a subsequent suit between the same parties, where the husband seeks similar relief against the wife (*Butler* v. *Butler* (No. 2), 63 L. J., P. & M. 1).

But in such a case as that last mentioned the husband may, in the subsequent suit, show that there were surrounding circumstances which may induce the Court not to withhold the relief which he asks (*Butler* v. *Butler* (No. 1), (1893) P. 185; 62 L. J., P. & M. 105).

* If a petition by a husband for dissolution of marriage on the ground of his wife's adultery with A. is dismissed, he is not, of course, estopped from subsequently instituting another suit on the ground of her adultery with B., of which he had no know-

---

* If, however, at the time of the former suit he knew of the adultery with B., the second suit would probably be held to be barred under Explanation II. to sect. 13, Civil Procedure Code.

ledge at the time of the former suit (*Yeatman* v. *Yeatman and* App. (D). *Rummal*, 21 L. T. 401).

And in order to be *res judicata*, the matter must have been heard and *finally decided*. If, therefore, a petitioner is allowed to withdraw his suit, he is not debarred from relying on the same acts in support of a subsequent petition (*Hall* v. *Hall*, 48 L. J., P. & M. 57).

II.—The former suit must have been between the same parties.

Identity of parties.

Therefore the adultery of a respondent cannot be proved by the production of a decree in a previous suit in which he was a co-respondent (*Ruck* v. *Ruck*, (1896) P. 152). In such a case the finding in the former suit, that the respondent had committed adultery with the wife of another person, is not *res judicata* in a suit subsequently instituted against him by his own wife.

"The effect of a decree in a suit for a divorce *à vinculo matrimonii* is to cause the relationship of husband and wife to cease. It is conclusive upon all persons that the parties have been divorced, and that the parties are no longer husband and wife; *but it is not conclusive, nor even* primâ facie *evidence, against strangers that the cause for which the decree was pronounced existed.* For instance, if a divorce between A. and B. were granted upon the ground of the adultery of B. with C., it would be conclusive as to the divorce, but it would not be even *primâ facie* evidence against C. that he was guilty of adultery with B., unless he were a party to the suit" (Sir Barnes Peacocke, *Kanhya Lal* v. *Radha Charan*, 7 W. R. 339). The words, "*unless he were a party to the suit*," cannot (it is submitted) have been intended to mean that, if he were a party to the suit, the decree would be proof of his guilt in a suit subsequently instituted against him by his own wife, but merely that, for the purposes of the suit between A. and B., C. would be bound by the verdict against him in that suit.

III.—The Court which decided the former suit must have been one competent to decide the subsequent suit.

Court must have been competent to decide subsequent suit.

It is, therefore, a general rule that a judgment in a criminal case cannot be received in a civil action to establish the truth of the facts upon which it was given.

Thus, where it appeared that the respondent had been tried and acquitted in a criminal Court of a charge of incestuous adultery with his own daughter, aged thirteen, the Divorce Court, in a suit subsequently instituted by the wife for dissolution of marriage on the ground of the said incestuous adultery, allowed evidence to be given to prove that the offence had in fact been committed, and finding this as a fact, pronounced a decree *nisi* for dissolution of the marriage (*Virgo* v. *Virgo*, 69 L. T. 460).

So, where bigamy or rape is charged, it must be proved, and

App. (D). it is not enough merely to prove a conviction in a criminal Court for bigamy or rape (*March* v. *March*, 28 L. J., P. & M. 30).

Judgment of foreign Court. Jurisdiction of foreign Court depends on international law.

IV.—**The judgment of a *foreign Court will operate as a bar to a subsequent suit in India, if the foreign Court had jurisdiction to decide the former suit.**

(a) As regards foreign judgments, the competency of the jurisdiction of the Court which passed judgment has to be decided by international law, and not by municipal law. If, therefore, the Court had jurisdiction by international law, its judgment is none the less binding because by its own rules, or according to its own municipal law, it had no jurisdiction in the suit (*Vanquelin* v. *Bonsard*, 15 C. B., N. S. 341; Foote's Private International Law, 1878, p. 445; Rattigan's Private International Law, 1895, pp. 232, 233).

"The foreign decree may be perfectly valid and unimpeachable within the territorial jurisdiction of the judge who pronounced it. It may there fix the legal *status* of persons, and conclude the right and title to property; but it may still not be such a sentence as by the comity of nations (that is, by the general principles of jurisprudence which are recognized by the Christian States of Europe) has an extra-territorial effect and authority. The first essential of a foreign decree is that it should be pronounced by a Court of competent jurisdiction between persons who are *bonâ fide* subjects to that jurisdiction. . . . . No nation can be required to admit that its domiciled subjects may lawfully resort to another country for the purpose of evading the laws under which they live. When they return to the country of their domicil, bringing back with them a foreign judgment so obtained, the tribunals of the domicil are entitled, or even *bound*, to reject such judgment as having no extra-territorial force or validity. They are entitled to reject it if it be pronounced by a tribunal not having competent jurisdiction; and they are bound to reject it if it be an invasion of their own laws and polity" (Lord Westbury, *Shaw* v. *Gould*, L. R., 3 H. L. Ca. at p. 80).

Foreign Courts: when of competent jurisdiction.

(b) For the purposes of international law, and in order to have extra-territorial force and validity—

(i) A decree of dissolution of marriage can be made only by the Courts of the domicil of the parties.

(ii) In matrimonial suits other than those involving the disruption or annulment of the marriage tie, a Court is competent, according to international law, to make decrees in all cases where the parties are resident within the territorial limits of such Court's jurisdiction, or where

---

* "Foreign Court" means a Court situate beyond the limits of British, and not having authority in British India, nor established by the Governor-General in Council (Civil Procedure Code, 1882, s. 2).

the defendant, though not so resident, has voluntarily appeared and submitted to the Court's jurisdiction.

App. (D).

(iii) A decree of nullity of marriage can be made only by the Courts of the country where the marriage was celebrated.

(c) A "judgment *in rem*" of a foreign Court can be impeached on three grounds only, viz., (i) want of jurisdiction; (ii) fraud; or (iii) collusion (Indian Evidence Act, 1872, s. 44).

Grounds upon which foreign judgments may be impeached.

A "judgment *in personam*" of a foreign Court can be impeached on any of the following grounds, viz., (i) want of jurisdiction; (ii) fraud; (iii) collusion (Indian Evidence Act, 1872, s. 44); nor will such a judgment operate as a bar to a suit in British India (i) if it has not been given on the merits of the case; (ii) if it appears on the face of the proceedings to be founded on an incorrect view of international law, or of any law in force in British India; (iii) if it is, in the opinion of the Court before which it is produced, contrary to natural justice; (iv) if it has been obtained by fraud; or (v) if it sustains a claim founded on a breach of any law in force in British India (Civil Procedure Code, 1882, s. 14, "which obviously is intended to apply merely to 'judgments *in personam*'"; Broughton's Estoppel by Matter of Record, p. 108).

As regards matrimonial suits, a judgment is *in rem* if it is the final judgment of a competent Court, and confers or takes away from any person any legal character, or declares any person to be entitled to any such character (see sect. 41, Indian Evidence Act, 1872). A final judgment dissolving a marriage or declaring a marriage null and void is, therefore, a judgment *in rem*.

Judgment *in rem*.

A judgment in a matrimonial suit which does not alter the *status* of the parties to a marriage (*e.g.*, a judgment in a suit for judicial separation), is a judgment *in personam*.

Judgment *in personam*.

A foreign judgment *in rem* or *in personam* can be impeached on the ground that it was obtained by fraud or collusion. But this does not mean an allegation of fraud which might have been raised as a defence in the foreign Court upon the facts which were then before it. "To impeach a foreign judgment on such grounds as that would be to allow a plea which ought to have been pleaded in the action on which the judgment was founded" (Foote's Private International Law, 1878, p. 472).

Fraud; collusion.

APPENDIX (E).

NOTES ON PLEADINGS AND PRACTICE.

Civil Procedure Code to apply.

Sect. 45 of the Indian Divorce Act provides that, "subject to the provisions herein contained, all proceedings under this Act between party and party shall be regulated by the Code of Civil Procedure."

In matters, however, for which no provision is made either in the Indian Divorce Act or in the Civil Procedure Code, sect. 7 of the Act would appear to be sufficient authority for the application of the rules and practice of the English Divorce Court. For instance, the Indian Courts have adopted the English rule, which compels a husband to pay into the registry, or give security for, a sum sufficient to meet his wife's probable costs of suit (see Appendix (F), "Costs").

The following brief notes on certain important points may prove useful :—

Petitions.

(a) **Petitions:**

(i) Court fee stamp.

Every petition under the Indian Divorce Act, except a petition under sect. 44 of the Act, which is altogether exempted, must bear a Court fee stamp of Rs. 20 (Indian Court Fees Act, 1870, 2nd Sched., Art. 20).

(ii) Verification.

The statements contained in every petition under the Act must be verified by the petitioner or some other competent person in manner required by law for the verification of plaints, and may at the hearing be referred to as evidence (Indian Divorce Act, s. 47).

Sects. 51 and 52 of the Civil Procedure Code, 1882, deal with the verification of plaints. In every case the person who verifies should state shortly what paragraphs he verifies of his own knowledge, and what paragraphs he believes to be true from the observations of others (*In re Upendro Bose*, I. L. R., ix Calc. 675).

(iii) Absence of collusion or connivance.

Every petition for a decree of dissolution of marriage, or of nullity of marriage, or of judicial separation, must state that there is not any collusion or connivance between the petitioner and the other party to the marriage (Indian Divorce Act, s. 47).

(iv) Contents of petition.

The rule laid down in sect. 10 of the Act, that every petition for dissolution of marriage shall state as distinctly as the nature of the case permits the facts on which the claim to have the marriage dissolved is founded, applies equally to petitions for nullity of marriage and judicial separation. But all pleadings should be as short as is consistent with alleging a legal ground for the prayer (*Suggate* v. *Suggate*, 28 L. J., P. & M. 7).

App. (E).

(b) **Pleading adultery in petition or by way of counter-charge:**

Pleading adultery.

The general rule is that adultery must in all cases be alleged in distinct and unequivocal terms. Thus, a paragraph to the effect that the respondent (the wife) lived in Preston for twelve months, and during that time resided in and frequented houses of ill-fame; led a very loose and disorderly life; was on several occasions dragged by the police out of necessaries, where she was found in company with men, and was once during that period committed for fourteen days to the house of correction as a disorderly person, was held not to allege adultery with sufficient distinctness (*Ambler* v. *Ambler and Houghton*, 32 L. J., P. & M. 6). Nor is it sufficient to state that the petitioner "is informed and believes" that the respondent has committed adultery (*Spilsbury* v. *Spilsbury*, 3 S. & T. 210; 32 L. J., P. & M. 126).

Nor, again, is it sufficient to state that "the respondent and co-respondent are living and cohabiting together" (*Forman* v. *Forman and Davis*, 32 L. J., P. & M. 80).

But an allegation that the co-respondent lived in the same house with petitioner and his wife for two years, and that the adultery was committed on divers occasions during that period, was held to give sufficient information to the respondent (*Smith* v. *Smith and Liddard*, 29 L. J., P. & M. 62).

A mere allegation that the respondent has committed adultery is insufficient; particulars should be given as to the person with whom, and place and time at which such adultery was committed (*Wyndham* v. *Wyndham and Giuglimi*, 32 L. J., P. & M. 89; *Porter* v. *Porter and Tuggard*, 3 S. & T. 796; 33 L. J., P. & M. 207).

So, where a petition stated that the petitioner's wife had "committed adultery with Jonathan Farrow at Mundham," the Court ordered it to be amended "by stating something more tangible. Mundham is very vague. It should be stated where in Mundham the adultery was committed. The time should also be more precisely stated" (*Wodehouse* v. *Wodehouse and Farrow*, 32 L. J., P. & M., note).

Where a petition alleged that on divers occasions since a specified date, the respondent had accompanied the co-respondent to divers places in Bristol and its neighbourhood unknown to the petitioner, and had committed adultery with the co-respondent, the Court ordered that particulars of this charge should be given, or that the petitioner should file an affidavit that he was unable to give such particulars. "In numerous cases where there is a general intercourse between a married woman and a man, it is impossible to fix the precise date or place of any act of adultery; but if that is the petitioner's case, he can have no difficulty in so stating" (*Higgs* v. *Higgs and Hopkins*, 32 L. J., P. & M. 64).

A petition alleged that between certain specified dates, while respondent was living at a certain hotel in the Isle of Wight, the co-respondent had frequently visited her, and that they had frequently driven out together without the knowledge of the petitioner, and had been absent several hours, and on divers occasions had committed adultery at places unknown to the petitioner; and that between other specified dates the respondent and co-respondent had resided in the same hotel in the Isle of Wight, and had frequently driven out together without the knowledge of the petitioner, and on divers occasions had committed adultery at places unknown to the petitioner; and similar allegations were made as to their conduct between other specified dates in London. The Court held that sufficient information was given in the petition as to the sort of charges the respondent had to meet (*Foster* v. *Foster and Thomas*, 32 L. J., P. & M. 64, note).

A paragraph in a petition to the effect that at various times between the month of October, 1857, and the month of May, 1862, the respondent had committed adultery with the co-respondent at Macao, in the Empire of China, Bath, in the county of Somerset, and at divers other specified places, was ordered to be amended by setting out the charges with more particularity (*King* v. *King and Dent*, 32 L. J., P. & M. 64, note).

A respondent in her answer counter-charged as follows:— *Third paragraph*, that at divers times in the year 1862, and particularly in and about the month of July in that year, the petitioner at a house, No. 8, Chapter Road, Walworth, committed adultery with one Mrs. Swift; *fourth paragraph*, that during the years 1860, 1861, and 1862, the petitioner had cohabited and habitually committed adultery with one Mrs. Creed at No. 8, Grove Place, Camberwell, and that in or about the month of June, 1861, the said Mrs. Creed gave birth to an illegitimate child, the issue of her adulterous intercourse with the petitioner; *fifth paragraph*, that at divers times during the years 1861 and 1862 the petitioner had at divers brothels in and about the neighbourhood of the London Road, Walworth, and Newington, all in the county of Surrey, committed adultery with divers prostitutes whose names were unknown to the respondent. The Court ordered that, as to the *third* paragraph, particulars should be given; as to the latter part of the *fourth* paragraph, that it was irrelevant and should be struck out; as to the *fifth* paragraph, that it was too vague, and must be amended by stating with more particularity where the said brothels were, and the occasions on which adultery was committed (*Wells* v. *Wells and Hammerston*, 32 L. J., P. & M. 65, note).

So, a paragraph in a petition to the effect that "on divers occasions since the 12th day of May, 1850" (the date of the marriage), "the respondent had committed adultery," was held to be too vague, and particulars were ordered to be given of such adultery (*Lidstone* v. *Lidstone and Edmonds*, 32 L. J., P. & M. 66, note).

NOTES ON PLEADINGS AND PRACTICE.

In this country the proper procedure, if either party's pleading is too vague, is for the Court to act either under sect. 112, Civil Procedure Code, and call for a further written statement, or under sect. 146, and at the first hearing examine the parties as to their pleadings, and ascertain upon what material propositions they are at variance, and thereupon frame and record issues on which the right decision of the case appears to the Court to depend. Defects of pleadings should not be anticipated or supplied by framing interrogatories (*Ali Kadar* v. *Gobind Dass*, I. L. R., xvii Calc. 840).

App. (E).

Procedure when pleading is vague.

Although the adultery must be alleged distinctly and particulars given, *evidence* of such adultery must not be pleaded. Thus, a paragraph alleging that the respondent (the husband) had had two illegitimate children, the issue of an adulterous intercourse, born on specified dates, was ordered to be struck out (*Martin* v. *Martin*, 29 L. J., P. & M. 80; cf. *Wells* v. *Wells and Hammerston*, 32 L. J., P. & M. 65, note).

Evidence not to be pleaded.

Nor should ante-nuptial incontinence be pleaded, although it and the adultery charged are alleged to have been committed with one and the same person (*Fitzgerald* v. *Fitzgerald*, 32 L. J., P. & M. 12; *Mawford* v. *Mawford*, 14 W. R. (Eng.) 516).

If adultery is committed by the respondent subsequently to the date of the petition, the better course is to file a supplemental petition in respect thereof. When the preliminary proceedings are completed the two petitions will be consolidated and heard together (*Borham* v. *Borham and Brown*, L. R., 2 P. 193; 40 L. J., P. & M. 86).

Adultery subsequent to date of petition.

(c) **Pleading cruelty:**

Pleading cruelty.

Cruelty is a matter specially within the knowledge of the party complaining of it, and it is, therefore, only right that every species of cruelty, in respect of which it is intended to give evidence, should be expressly pleaded. If it is not, the Court will not, as a general rule, allow the issue to be raised or evidence given of it (*Austin* v. *Austin*, 41 L. J., P. & M. 8; *Kelly* v. *Kelly and Saunders*, 3 B. L. R., App. 6).

But the Courts in England will admit evidence of violent demeanour and language which, though not pleaded, leads up to and makes probable acts of violence pleaded (*Jewall* v. *Jewall*, 2 S. & T. 573; *Squires* v. *Squires*, 3 S. & T. 541). Such evidence would be inadmissible under sect. 52 of the Indian Evidence Act (see below).

And in a case in which the wife was aware of the facts to be charged as cruelty before filing her petition, but kept them back from motives of delicacy, the Court allowed the petition to be amended, and ordered that the respondent should be served with a copy of the amended petition (*Rowley* v. *Rowley*, 1 S. & T. 487; 29 L. J., P. & M. 15). But the Court will have to be satisfied that the fresh charge is not trumped up and brought merely for the purpose of vexation.

When there is only a general allegation of cruelty in the petition, evidence is inadmissible to prove a specific act of violence. If, however, such evidence is offered, the Court may adjourn the hearing in order to allow particulars of the act of cruelty to be furnished to the respondent, and may allow the petition to be amended (*Brook* v. *Brook*, 12 P. D. 19; 56 L. J., P. & M. 108).

If the pleading of either party contains merely a vague allegation of cruelty, the Courts of this country will either demand a further written statement from such party (sect. 112, Civil Procedure Code), or will examine him or her upon such pleading, and thereafter frame and record such issues as will enable it to come to a right decision in the case (sect. 146, Civil Procedure Code). The Court has also power, at any time before passing a decree, to amend the issues or to frame additional issues on such terms as it thinks fit, and all such amendments or additional issues as may be necessary for determining the controversy between the parties shall be so made or framed. Moreover, at any time before passing its decree, the Court may strike out any issues that appear to it to be wrongly framed or introduced (Civil Procedure Code, sect. 149).

Cruelty is *nomen generale*, and it is impossible to say what a petitioner may mean by "acts of cruelty." It should appear on the face of the petition that the respondent has been guilty of acts which, if proved, would constitute "legal cruelty" (*Goldney* v. *Goldney*, 32 L. J., P. & M. 13).

But it is not necessary that each paragraph of the petition should allege an independent act of cruelty sufficient in itself to warrant a decree. An allegation that the respondent used foul oaths is admissible as tending to show the temper and habits of the person charged with cruelty (*Leete* v. *Leete*, 31 L. J., P. & M. 121). Sect. 52 of the Indian Evidence Act, 1872, would, however, appear to preclude such evidence, for " in civil cases the fact that the character of any person is such as to render probable or improbable any conduct imputed to him is irrelevant, except in so far as such character appears from facts otherwise relevant."

It is not necessary to specify the precise date of the commission of each act of cruelty charged (*Suggate* v. *Suggate*, 1 S. & T. 489; 28 L. J., P. & M. 7).

Acts of cruelty to the children should not be mixed up with acts of cruelty to the wife, unless the cruelty to the children was committed in the presence of the wife, so as to amount to constructive cruelty to her (*Suggate* v. *Suggate*, 28 L. J., P. & M. 46).

An allegation of an act which, if proved, would obviously not amount to legal cruelty, will be ordered to be struck out, but it is not the practice of the Court to strike out a pleading where a reasonable doubt exists as to the legal effect of the allegation therein contained, and where such legal effect can be properly discussed after all the facts have been elicited in evidence at the trial (*Russell* v. *Russell*, 71 L. T. 268).

(d) **Pleading desertion:**

Where desertion is charged, it should be pleaded that the abandonment was against the wish of the party charging it, and was without reasonable excuse. The date of the commencement of such desertion should also be specified. Some statements of the circumstances of such desertion may be necessary, but, as in all pleadings, mere evidence should not be pleaded (*Pyne* v. *Pyne*, 1 S. & T. 80).

App. (E).

(e) Claim for damages against adulterer:

When damages are claimed against an alleged adulterer, the petition should specify the amount claimed (*Spedding* v. *Spedding and Smith*, 31 L. J., P. & M. 96).

Claim for damages.

(f) Petition for reversal of decree of judicial separation:

In a petition for reversal of a decree of judicial separation, it is not sufficient to allege merely the non-appearance of the petitioner; the cause of his non-appearance, and circumstances tending to show that the decree was wrong on the merits, should also be stated (*Phillips* v. *Phillips*, L. R., 1 P. 169; 35 L. J., P. & M. 70).

Petition for reversal of decree of judicial separation.

Service of petition:

"Every petition under this Act shall be served on the party to be affected thereby, either within or without British India, in such manner as the High Court by general or special order from time to time directs: Provided that the Court may dispense with such service altogether in case it seems necessary or expedient so to do" (Indian Divorce Act, s. 50).

For the practice of the English Divorce Court, see the Rules of the English Court of Divorce, Nos. 8—18.

Chapter VI of the Civil Procedure Code, 1882, deals generally with the subject of the issue and service of summons.

The general rule is that personal service upon the party to be affected should only be dispensed with when every reasonable effort has been made to trace him or her without success (*Appleyard* v. *Appleyard*, L. R., 3 P. 257; *Rebertest* v. *Rebertest*, No. 68 *Punjab Record*, 1870).

The mere fact that such person is absent abroad is not sufficient ground for dispensing with personal service; there must be some attempt to serve him or her personally (*Sudlow* v. *Sudlow*, 28 L. J., P. & M. 4).

Nor is the undertaking by the solicitor of such person to accept service sufficient, unless the Court has dispensed with personal service (*De Niceville* v. *De Niceville*, 37 L. J., P. & M. 43; *Milne* v. *Milne*, 4 S. & T. 143; 34 L. J., P. & M. 143).

But "where the Court is satisfied that there is reason to believe that the defendant is keeping out of the way for the purpose of avoiding the service, or that for any other reason the summons cannot be served in the ordinary way, the Court shall order the summons to be served by affixing a copy thereof in some conspicuous place in the Court-house and also upon some conspicuous part of the house, if any, in which the defendant is known to have last resided, or in such other

Service of petition.

manner as the Court thinks fit" (Civil Procedure Code, 1882, s. 82).

An application to the Court to allow substituted service of the petition should be supported by an affidavit on the part of the petitioner himself, an affidavit on the part of his solicitor not being sufficient (*Williams* v. *Williams and Pocock*, (1896) P. 153).

Substituted service will not, as a rule, be allowed when there is someone who knows the address of the party to be affected, and has undertaken to forward the petition to such party (*Robotham* v. *Robotham*, 1 S. & T. 73; 27 L. J., P. & M. 33; *Chandler* v. *Chandler*, 27 L. J., P. & M. 35).

Where the Court has dispensed with personal service, substituted service shall be effected in such manner as the Court directs.

The usual mode is, in England, to insert advertisements in the newspapers, the citation only, and not the petition, being advertised (*Jolly* v. *Jolly and Peckover*, 1 S. & T. 219; *Elsley* v. *Elsley*, 32 L. J., P. & M. 145).

If the address of the person to be affected is known, but there are difficulties about serving him or her personally, the Court may allow the petition to be served by registered letter. But the service will not be considered sufficient unless the Court is satisfied that the letter was actually received (*Cox* v. *Cox*, 61 L. T. 698; *Trubner* v. *Trubner*, 15 P. D. 24; 59 L. J., P. & M. 56).

Service of amended petition:

When a petition is allowed to be amended, the general rule is that it must, after amendment, be re-served on the party to be affected, though such re-service may, possibly, be dispensed with if such party has already put in an appearance (*Wallace* v. *Wallace*, 32 L. J., P. & M. 42; *Love* v. *Love*, 32 L. J., P. & M. 134; *Charter* v. *Charter*, 58 L. J., P. & M. 44).

Where the name of the co-respondent was misspelt in the citation, and the co-respondent did not appear, the Court ordered a fresh citation to be extracted (*Cotton* v. *Cotton and Kinnis*, 4 S. & T. 275; 32 L. J., P. & M. 133).

So, where the Christian names of the respondent were wrongly given in the petition, with a copy of which he had been served, the petition was allowed to be amended subsequently, but it was ordered that the amended petition should be re-served on the respondent, he not having appeared (*Kisch* v. *Kisch*, 33 L. J., P. & M. 115).

In some cases the amended petition has been ordered to be re-served, even when the party to be affected has put in an appearance. Thus, where a wife was permitted to alter her suit for judicial separation into one for dissolution of marriage by adding a charge of adultery, of which she had no previous knowledge, the respondent having appeared, the Court dispensed with a fresh citation, but ordered the amended petition to be served on the respondent (*Cartlidge* v. *Cartlidge*, 4 S. & T. 249; 31 L. J., P. & M. 135; cf. *Rowley* v. *Rowley*, 1 S. & T. 487; 29 L. J., P. & M. 15, where the wife had been allowed to add a

NOTES ON PLEADINGS AND PRACTICE. 349

charge of cruelty to her petition for dissolution of marriage on the ground of adultery and desertion).
When a person is allowed by the Court to be cited by advertisement, the citation alone, and not the petition, is advertised. If, therefore, the petition is subsequently amended, it need not be advertised (*Smith* v. *Smith*, 3 S. & T. 216; 32 L. J., P. & M. 145).

App. (E).

Service of petition dispensed with altogether:

It is only in very exceptional cases that service of a petition will be altogether dispensed with.

A respondent who had been served with a copy of a petition for dissolution of marriage, praying also for an order as to the settled property, did not put in an appearance, and the Court held that no notice need be given him of the subsequent application under sect. 6 of 23 & 24 Vict. c. 144 (*Horne* v. *Horne*, 30 L. J., P. & M. 200).

A petition for a decree of judicial separation by a wife contained a statement in the body thereof to the effect that the petitioner was desirous of having the custody of the children of the marriage, but contained no prayer to that effect. The respondent appeared, and filed an answer to the petition in which he expressly noticed that portion of it which referred to the children. Pending the hearing an application was made by the petitioner for custody of the children *pendente lite*, which was opposed by the respondent and refused. After decree for judicial separation, the respondent not appearing at the hearing, an application was made by the petitioner under sect. 42 of the Indian Divorce Act for custody of the children, but no notice of the application was given to the respondent. The Court held that it was unnecessary under the circumstances to give further notice of the application (*Ledlie* v. *Ledlie*, I. L. R., xviii Calc. 473; cf. *Wilkinson* v. *Wilkinson*, 30 L. J., P. & M. 200, note).

Service altogether dispensed with.

Withdrawal of petition:

"If, at any time after the institution of the suit, the Court is satisfied on the application of the plaintiff (a) that the suit must fail by reason of some formal defect, or (b) that there are sufficient grounds for permitting him to withdraw from the suit or to abandon part of his claim, with liberty to bring a fresh suit for the subject-matter of the suit or in respect of the part so abandoned, the Court may grant such permission on such terms as to costs or otherwise as it thinks fit.

"If the plaintiff withdraw from the suit, or abandon part of his claim, without such permission, he shall be liable for such costs as the Court may award, and shall be precluded from bringing a fresh suit for the same matter or in respect of the same part" (Civil Procedure Code, 1882, s. 373).

But "nothing in this chapter"—*i.e.*, Ch. XXII—"shall apply to any application or other proceeding in any suit subsequent to the decree.

"*Explanation.*—An application to the Appellate Court pending

Withdrawal of petition.

an appeal is not an application subsequent to the decree appealed from within the meaning of this section" (Civil Procedure Code, 1882, s. 375A).

Nor is the decree *nisi* in a suit a "decree" within the meaning of sect. 1 of the Civil Procedure Code (*King* v. *King*, I. L. R., vi Bomb. 416). An application subsequent to a decree *nisi* would not, therefore, be an application "subsequent to the decree" within the meaning of sect. 375A of the Code.

After intervention.

But where a person has intervened to show cause against a decree *nisi* being made absolute, the Court will not allow the petition to be withdrawn, on the ground that it is not competent to the party, after that intervention, to seek to defeat the object of the proceeding taken under the authority of the Legislature for the purpose of evading the consequences of his or her misconduct by withdrawing the petition (*Gray* v. *Gray*, 30 L. J., P. & M. 119; in app. 2 S. & T. 266).

A petition by a husband for dissolution of marriage on the ground of his wife's adultery will not be allowed to be withdrawn after the respondent has appeared, unless she consents or has had notice of the application (*Lutwyche* v. *Lutwyche*, 28 L. J., P. & M. 56).

Amendment of petition,

Amendment of petition:

The object of pleading is to let the opposite side know, as far as is possible, the case that will be set up (*Green* v. *Green*, 33 L. J., P. & M. 83). If a petition does not give the opposite side reasonably full information as to the petitioner's case, or if it is vague, or does not state correctly and without prolixity the facts upon which the claim is founded, it may be returned for amendment under sect. 53 of the Civil Procedure Code. Or the Court may demand a further written statement from the petitioner under sect. 112 of the Code, or examine the petitioner upon the petition and act under sect. 146 of the Code.

by adding new charge.

As a general rule, a petitioner will not be allowed to amend the petition by the addition of a charge, unless the facts upon which the charge is founded were not within the petitioner's knowledge before the petition was filed (*Cartlidge* v. *Cartlidge*, 31 L. J., P. & M. 135; *Walker* v. *Walker*, 30 L. J., P. & M. 214; *Bannister* v. *Bannister and Davis*, 29 L. J., P. & M. 53).

The principle, however, upon which such amendments should be allowed is that justice between the parties may be done, and the Court, if satisfied that the charge, which it is desired to add, is not trumped up and brought for the purpose of vexation, may allow it to be pleaded, and frame such additional issue on it as it thinks fit (see sect. 149, Civil Procedure Code).

So, where a wife filed affidavits to the effect that until the hearing she was ignorant that certain acts on the part of her husband amounted to legal cruelty, the Court allowed the petition, which was originally for dissolution of marriage by reason of the respondent's adultery and desertion, to be amended by the addition of a charge of cruelty (*Parkinson* v. *Parkinson*, L. R., 2 P. 27; 39 L. J., P. & M. 21).

And in another case the wife was allowed to add a charge of

cruelty founded on facts of which she had knowledge previously to the filing of the petition, but which she had refrained from setting out in her petition from motives of delicacy (*Rowley* v. *Rowley*, 29 L. J., P. & M. 15).

If it is desired to add a charge of adultery on facts which have occurred since the filing of the petition, the better course is to file a supplemental petition and pray the Court to consolidate the two at the hearing. For "the 20 & 21 Vict. c. 85, s. 27, says it shall be lawful for a husband to present a petition praying his marriage may be dissolved on the ground that his wife has *since the celebration thereof* been guilty of adultery, and the 30th section says that if in any case the Court, on the evidence in relation to any such petition, shall not be satisfied that the *alleged* adultery has been committed, it shall dismiss the petition. I think, therefore, that acts of adultery subsequent to the date of the petition cannot properly be taken into consideration at the hearing of the petition itself, and that if a judgment for dissolution be founded on such subsequent acts, the whole proceedings would be held by a Court of Appeal to be erroneous. I am willing, however, if the petitioner desires it, to allow the amendment to be made, or he may file a new petition. If he determines to commence a new proceeding, the question of costs will be reserved; and I will take care that the respondent and co-respondent are not prejudiced in that respect" (*Borham* v. *Borham and Brown*, L. R., 2 P. 193; 40 L. J., P. & M. 6). In the case cited, leave was subsequently given to the petitioner to file a supplemental petition setting out the acts of adultery alleged to have been committed subsequently to the filing of the original petition, and to the respondent and co-respondent to file answers thereto, on the understanding that the two petitions should be consolidated at the hearing.

And where at the hearing the petitioner fails to prove desertion for the full period of two years, relief in respect of such desertion can only be obtained by filing a fresh petition when the full period has elapsed (*Lapington* v. *Lapington*, 14 P. D. 21; 58 L. J., P. & M. 26). In an earlier case, under similar circumstances, the Court adjourned the hearing until the period was completed, and allowed a supplemental petition to be then filed in respect of such desertion (*Wood* v. *Wood*, 13 P. D. 22).

App. (E).

Desertion for two years not complete at date of hearing.

If no injustice can arise to the opposite side and the Court sees no objection, a petition for dissolution of marriage may be converted into one for judicial separation, even if the facts proved would warrant a decree for dissolution. For "the Court is always better pleased to grant a decree for judicial separation than for dissolution, and will not dissolve a marriage against the petitioner's wishes" (*Dent* v. *Dent*, 4 S. & T. 105; 34 L. J., P. & M. 118; *Mycock* v. *Mycock*, L. R., 2 P. 98; 39 L. J., P. & M. 56; *Duplany* v. *Duplany*, (1892) P. 53).

Petition for dissolution converted into one for judicial separation.

And it is competent for the Court to grant the petitioner a decree for judicial separation, although the petition prays only for a decree of dissolution of marriage, if the facts proved will entitle the petitioner to the former, but not to the latter decree (*Smith* v. *Smith*, 1 S. & T. 359; 28 L. J., P. & M. 27).

APPENDIX (E).

Changing suit for judicial separation into one for dissolution.

The Court has also granted an application by a wife that a petition for judicial separation, filed by her, might be dismissed, and that she might substitute for it a petition for dissolution of marriage upon the terms of her paying the costs (*Lewis* v. *Lewis*, 29 L. J., P. & M. 123).

The Court has also allowed a petitioner, in a case in which both parties were before the Court, to amend her petition by adding a charge of adultery, of which she had no previous knowledge, and to pray for a dissolution of marriage instead of for judicial separation, without issuing a fresh citation, but ordered the amended petition to be re-served on the respondent (*Cartlidge* v. *Cartlidge*, 4 S. & T. 249; 31 L. J., P. & M. 135).

Adding claim for damages against co-respondent.

A petitioner has also been allowed, upon payment of costs, to amend his petition for dissolution of marriage by adding a prayer for damages against the co-respondent (*Bartlett* v. *Bartlett and Balmanno*, 34 L. J., P. & M. 64).

Appearance of parties.

Appearance of parties at hearing:

Chapter VII of the Civil Procedure Code, 1882, deals with the appearance of the parties and the consequence of non-appearance. As to the effect of appearance upon the question of jurisdiction, see note to sect. 4, *ante*. Speaking generally, nothing can give a Court jurisdiction which it does not inherently possess; but if the want of jurisdiction does not arise from incapacity on the part of the Court to entertain the suit or proceeding—if it is merely that the Court has no jurisdiction over the person of one of the parties—the appearance of such party, except under protest, will be taken as an admission of, and submission to, the jurisdiction of the Court.

If neither party appears.

"If on the day fixed for the defendant to appear and answer, or on any subsequent day to which the hearing of the suit is adjourned, neither party appears, the suit shall be dismissed, unless the judge, for reasons to be recorded under his hand, otherwise directs" (Civil Procedure Code, s. 98).

But in such a case the petitioner may, subject to the law of limitation, bring a fresh suit, or, if within thirty days from the order dismissing the suit, he satisfies the Court that there was sufficient excuse for his non-appearance, the Court shall pass an order to set aside the dismissal and appoint a day for proceeding with the suit (*Ib.*, s. 99).

If respondent fails to appear.

If on the day appointed the plaintiff (petitioner) appears, and the defendant (respondent or co-respondent) does not appear, and it is proved that the summons has been duly served upon such defendant and in sufficient time to enable him to appear and answer on the day fixed in the summons, the Court may proceed *ex parte* against such defendant (*Ib.*, s. 100).

If an *ex parte* decree is passed against a defendant, the latter can apply under sect. 108 of the Code to have such decree set aside for any of the reasons therein specified. But a decree *nisi* is not a "decree" within the definition of a decree given in sect. 1 of the Code, and, consequently, an *ex parte* decree *nisi* cannot be set aside under sect. 108. The defendant must, if he wishes to have such decree *nisi* reversed, apply, within the time prescribed by the Limitation Act, 1877, for a review of judgment under sect. 623, Civil Procedure Code (*King* v. *King*, I. L. R., vi Bomb. 416).

Nor can a respondent, against whom a decree *nisi* has been passed *ex parte*, intervene, under sect. 16 of the Indian Divorce Act, to show cause against the decree being made absolute. But where a respondent attempted to intervene in this manner, and based his application on affidavits which alleged, *inter alia*, collusion on the part of the petitioner, the Court refused the application, but ordered the affidavits to be filed and notice to be given to the petitioner to the effect that the decree would not be made absolute until the matters set forth in the affidavits had been cleared up (*Stephen* v. *Stephen*, I. L. R., xvii Calc. 570).

"If the Court has adjourned the hearing of the suit *ex parte*, and the defendant, at or before such hearing, appears and assigns good cause for his previous non-appearance, he may, upon such terms as the Court directs as to costs or otherwise, be heard in answer to the suit, as if he had appeared on the day fixed for his appearance" (Civil Procedure Code, s. 101).

"If the defendant appears and the plaintiff does not appear, the Court shall dismiss the suit, unless the defendant admits the claim, or part thereof, in which case the Court shall pass a decree against the defendant upon such admission, and, where part only of the claim has been admitted, shall dismiss the suit so far as it relates to the remainder" (*Ibid.*, s. 102).

<small>App. (E).</small>

<small>If petitioner fails to appear.</small>

It is hardly necessary, however, to remark that the Court would certainly not grant a decree for dissolution or nullity of marriage, or for judicial separation, in the absence of the petitioner, simply upon the admissions of the respondent.

"When a suit is wholly or partially dismissed under sect. 102, the plaintiff shall be precluded from bringing a fresh suit in respect of the same cause of action. But he may apply for an order to set the dismissal aside, and if it be proved that he was prevented by any sufficient cause from appearing when the suit was called on for hearing, the Court shall set aside the dismissal upon such terms as to costs or otherwise as it thinks fit, and shall appoint a day for proceeding with the suit.

"No order shall be made under this section unless the plaintiff has served the defendant with notice in writing of his intention" (*Ibid.*, s. 103).

In England, the rule is, that if the petitioner does not appear on the day appointed for the hearing, the respondent is entitled to have the petition dismissed (*Desmarest* v. *Desmarest*, 31 L. J., P. & M. 34).

But, before the Court will order the petition to be dismissed, it must be satisfied that the petitioner has no intention of going on with the proceedings; otherwise it will issue a rule for the petitioner to show cause why the petition should not be dismissed (*Curtis* v. *Curtis*, 38 L. J., P. & M. 9; *Round* v. *Round*, 20 L. T. 87).

APPENDIX (E).

App. (E).
Answer.

Written statement in answer to petition:

Under the provisions of the Civil Procedure Code, 1882 (Chap. VIII), a defendant in an ordinary civil suit is not bound to file a written answer to the plaint, unless specially required to do so by the Court (see sects. 110, 112).

There can, however, be no doubt that in suits under the Indian Divorce Act the Court will invariably require a written statement from a respondent or a co-respondent who appears in such suit.

The time within which a written statement, which the respondent or co-respondent desires to tender, must be filed is that prescribed by the provisions of the Civil Procedure Code, and not that fixed by the English rules (*Abbott* v. *Abbott and Crump*, 4 B. L. R., O. C. 51).

"If any party from whom a written statement is so required" —*i.e.*, under sect. 112—"fails to present the same within the time fixed by the Court, the Court may pass a decree against him, or make such order in relation to the suit as it thinks fit" (Civil Procedure Code, s. 113).

In suits for dissolution or nullity of marriage, the Court is not likely to grant a decree against the *respondent*, simply because he or she has not so presented the required written statement. Possibly the order it would pass in such an event would be one founded on the practice of the English Court in such cases. Rule 50 of the English Rules provides that "either of the respondents in the cause, after entering an appearance, without filing an answer to the petition in the principal cause, may be heard in respect of any question as to costs, and a respondent, who is husband or wife of the petitioner, may be heard also in respect to any question as to custody of children, but a respondent who may be so heard is not at liberty to bring in affidavits touching matters in issue in the principal cause, and no such affidavits can be read or made use of as evidence in the cause." The only objection to a rule of this kind is that it might shut out valuable evidence. If, for instance, the respondent in default is not at liberty to give evidence in the principal cause, there is considerable likelihood of the Court giving a decree to a petitioner who, upon the excluded evidence, might have been proved guilty of collusion or connivance or misconduct disentitling him or her to relief.

Frame of written statements.

"Written statements shall be as brief as the nature of the case admits, and shall not be argumentative, but shall be confined as much as possible to a simple narrative of the facts which the party by whom, or on whose behalf, the written statement is made, believes to be material to the case, and which he either admits or believes he will be able to prove. Every such statement shall be divided into paragraphs numbered consecutively, and each paragraph containing as nearly as may be a separate allegation" (Civil Procedure Code, s. 114).

In ordinary civil suits the rule is that a written statement is not in the nature of a pleading, and should not be written after inspecting that of the other party, nor by way of rejoinder to it (see *Judub Ram* v. *Ram Luchun*, 5 W. R. 56). This rule, how-

NOTES ON PLEADINGS AND PRACTICE.

over, cannot apply to a respondent or co-respondent's written **App. (E).**
statement by way of answer to a petition (see sect. 46, Indian
Divorce Act, and the Forms given in the Schedule to the Act).
   An answer is intended to be a substantial statement of the
respondent or co-respondent's case; it should be as brief as the
circumstances admit, and should not contain anything in the
shape of evidence (*Gaston* v. *Gaston*, 13 L. T. 412).
   Every written statement must be signed and verified in the **Verification.**
manner provided for signing and verifying plaints, and cannot
be received until it is so signed and verified (Civil Procedure
Code, s. 115).
   "If it appears to the Court that any written statement, **Amendment,**
whether called for by the Court or spontaneously tendered, is **&c. of written**
argumentative or prolix, or contains matter irrelevant to the **statement.**
suit, the Court may amend it then and there, or may, by an
order to be endorsed thereon, reject the same, or return it to the
party by whom it was made for amendment within a time to be
fixed by the Court, imposing such terms as to costs or otherwise as the Court thinks fit. When any amendment is made
under this section, the judge shall attest it by his signature.
   "When a statement has been rejected under this section,
the party making it shall not present another unless it be expressly called for or allowed by the Court" (Civil Procedure
Code, s. 116).
   Under the Civil Procedure Code interrogatories should not
be framed for the purpose of supplying defects of pleading. If
a written statement in answer to a petition is vague or prolix,
or contains irrelevant matter, it should either be amended
under sect. 116 of the Code, or rejected and another written
statement called for under sect. 112. Or, if the Court prefers,
the Court may, under sect. 146, examine the parties upon their
pleadings, ascertain what facts they are at variance upon, and
thereupon frame and record such issues as the Court thinks fit
(cf. *Ali Kadir* v. *Gobind Das*, I. L. R., xvii Calc. 840).
   The English practice is for the petitioner to apply by summons
in chambers for particulars of charges set up in an answer, if
such charges are not set out with sufficient particularity (*Higgs*
v. *Higgs and Hopkins*, 11 W. R. (Eng.) 154; see English Rules,
Nos. 38, 181—184).
   As a general rule, the respondent or co-respondent in a suit **What may**
under the Divorce Act is entitled to plead every matter which **be pleaded in**
is material for the consideration of the Court in adjudicating **answer.**
upon the petition before it (*Allen* v. *Allen and D'Arcy*, 28 L. J.,
P. & M. 81).
   And "in any suit instituted for dissolution of marriage, if
the respondent opposes the relief sought, on the ground, in case
of such a suit instituted by a husband, of his adultery, cruelty,
or desertion without reasonable excuse, or in case of such a suit
instituted by a wife, on the ground of her adultery* and cruelty,

---

* *Quære*, whether "and" here should be "or." Possibly, what is
intended is, that a husband is not at liberty to oppose his wife's suit
for dissolution of marriage merely on the ground of her cruelty. But,

the Court may, in such suit, give to the respondent, on his or her application, the same relief to which he or she would have been entitled in case he or she had presented a petition seeking such relief, and the respondent shall be competent to give evidence of or relating to such cruelty or desertion" (Indian Divorce Act, s. 15).

Under this section the respondent may plead the cruelty of the petitioner as a ground for refusing him or her the relief sought, though cruelty on the part of the petitioner was held by the Ecclesiastical Courts to be no bar to a suit for dissolution on the ground of adultery (see *Tuthill* v. *Tuthill*, 31 L. J., P. & M. 214).

Evidence should never be pleaded.
Anything in the shape of *evidence* ought not to be pleaded (*Gaston* v. *Gaston*, 13 L. T. 412).

Ante-nuptial incontinence.
Ante-nuptial incontinence on the part of the petitioner should not be pleaded, even though it and the adultery counter-charged against petitioner are alleged to have been committed with the same person (*Mawford* v. *Mawford*, 14 W. R. (Eng.) 516).

Impediment to marital intercourse.
In answer to his wife's suit for dissolution of marriage, the husband is not entitled to plead an impediment to marital intercourse supervening after marriage in consequence of the disease of the wife (*M.* v. *M.*, 31 L. J., P. & M. 168), nor is a plea that she wilfully withdrew from his bed and refused him marital rights admissible (*Rowe* v. *Rowe*, 4 S. & T. 162; 34 L. J., P. & M. 111).

Refusal to render marital rights.

Desertion.
As is clear from sect. 15 of the Indian Divorce Act, a wife may plead, in answer to her husband's suit for dissolution of marriage, desertion without reasonable excuse on his part. And such desertion, if proved, will be a bar to his suit (*Yeatman* v. *Yeatman and Rummell*, L. R., 2 P. 187; 39 L. J., P. & M. 77). It may, possibly, act as a bar to his suit for judicial separation on the ground of her adultery (*Lempriere* v. *Lempriere*, L. R., 1 P. 569). For if "chastity be the duty of the wife, protection is no less the duty of the husband."

But desertion on the part of the wife is no bar to her suit for judicial separation (*Duplany* v. *Duplany*, (1892) P. 53; 66 L. T. 267). It is, however, a ground upon which the Court may refuse, under sect. 11 of the Indian Divorce Act, to grant her a decree for dissolution of marriage. Accordingly, the husband would seem entitled to plead such desertion on her part, and oppose the relief sought on that ground, though he might not be entitled to apply, under sect. 15, for such relief in respect thereof as he would have been entitled to in case he had presented a petition praying for such relief.

Deed of separation.
An ordinary deed of separation is no bar to a suit under the Indian Divorce Act. But a covenant not to sue for dissolution of marriage or for nullity of marriage on the ground of impotence, or for judicial separation (*and, possibly, also a covenant

---

surely, he is entitled to plead her cruelty, or desertion without reasonable excuse, as a ground for a decree of judicial separation in his favour if her petition is dismissed. As a bar to her suit for dissolution her adultery would, *per se*, be sufficient.

* As to suits for restitution of conjugal rights, see note to sect. 33.

not to sue for restitution of conjugal rights), is a bar to any suit subsequently instituted for the purpose of obtaining the relief which the petitioner has covenanted not to sue for (*Besant* v. *Wood*, 12 Ch. D. 605; *Spering* v. *Spering*, 32 L. J., P. & M. 116; *Tress* v. *Tress*, 12 P. D. 128; 56 L. J., P. & M. 93; *Moore* v. *Moore*, 12 P. D. 193; 56 L. J., P. & M. 104; *Brown* v. *Brown and Shelton*, L. R., 3 P. 202; 43 L. J., P. & M. 47; *Parkinson* v. *Parkinson*, L. R., 2 P. 35; 39 L. J., P. & M. 14; *Marshall* v. *Marshall*, 5 P. D. 19; *Clark* v. *Clark*, 10 P. D. 188; 54 L. J., P. & M. 57; *Aldridge* v. *Aldridge*, 13 P. D. 210; 58 L. J., P. & M. 8).

App. (E).

Any misconduct on the part of a petitioner in a suit for dissolution of marriage which may have conduced to the respondent's adultery is a ground upon which the Court may refuse to grant the petitioner a decree, and may, therefore, be pleaded by way of answer to such suit. Thus, in a suit by the husband for dissolution of marriage, the wife was allowed to plead acts of undue familiarity on the part of the petitioner with a certain lady, on the ground that, if the acts alleged were proved, it was not impossible that the Court might come to the conclusion that the petitioner had by his acts conduced to the adultery on the part of the wife (*Cox* v. *Cox*, 70 L. T. 200—C. A.).

Misconduct on part of petitioner not amounting to matrimonial offence.

In answer to a charge of "desertion," the respondent may plead that the separation was by mutual consent, and, of course, may set out facts showing that there was reasonable cause for the alleged desertion. But such facts should be stated succinctly (*Hill* v. *Hill*, 33 L. J., P. & M. 187).

Answer to charge of desertion.

A plea that the husband has made the wife a reasonable allowance is irrelevant, and is no answer to her charge of desertion (*Yeatman* v. *Yeatman*, L. R., 1 P. 489; 37 L. J., P. & M. 37).

But to such a charge the husband may plead a *bonâ fide* offer by him, before the elapse of the full statutory period of two years, to resume cohabitation (*Lodge* v. *Lodge*, 15 P. D. 159; 59 L. J., P. & M. 84; *French-Brewster* v. *French-Brewster*, 62 L. T. 609).

In answer to a suit for restitution of conjugal rights, anything may be pleaded which would be a good ground for a suit for judicial separation or for a decree of nullity of marriage (Indian Divorce Act, s. 33).

Answer to suit for restitution of conjugal rights.

In a suit for restitution of conjugal rights, it is not admissible to plead the petitioner's incontinence before marriage with a view of showing that her child, born after marriage, is not the child of the respondent (*Mason* v. *Mason*, 61 L. T. 304; and generally, as to what may or may not be pleaded in answer to a petition for restitution of conjugal rights, see note to sect. 33, *ante*).

To a charge of cruelty an answer alleging that the use of force was necessary and justified by the conduct of the petitioner is bad; the nature of the petitioner's conduct should be stated, but particulars of time and place need not be given (*Shaw* v. *Shaw*, 2 S. & T. 515; 31 L. J., P. & M. 35).

Answer to charge of cruelty.

But the Court in another case refused to strike out a plea by the respondent (the husband) that the petitioner had habitually

APPENDIX (E).

App. (E).

treated him with insolence and neglect, set his orders at defiance, and for two years wilfully absented herself from his residence. The Court considered that the plea was properly introduced as explanatory of the violent conduct imputed to the respondent (*Hughes* v. *Hughes*, L. R., 1 P. 219; 35 L. J., P. & M. 94).

Answer to suit for nullity of marriage.

In suits for nullity of marriage the only relevant issue is, marriage or no marriage; accordingly, it is not open to the respondent to plead, in answer to the suit, adultery, cruelty, desertion or the like on the part of the petitioner (see *Humphreys* v. *Williams f. c. Humphreys*, 29 L. J., P. & M. 62; *Taverner f. c. Ditchford* v. *Ditchford*, 33 L. J., P. & M. 105).

Counter-charges.

The rule that charges in the petition should be set out with particularity sufficient to enable the respondent to prepare to meet such charges, applies equally to counter-charges in an answer.

Doubt as to legal effect of plea.

No plea will be ordered to be struck out where a reasonable doubt exists as to the legal effect of the allegations therein contained, and where such legal effect can properly be discussed after all the facts have been elicited at the trial (*Russell* v. *Russell*, 71 L. T. 268).

Interrogatories and discovery.

Interrogatories and discovery of documents:

These subjects are dealt with in Chapter X of the Civil Procedure Code, and it is not necessary to refer to them in detail.

The Calcutta High Court has held that *interrogatories* should not be framed to anticipate or supply defects of pleadings, or to ascertain the case of the other side. If the pleading of either party is vague, the Court may call for a further written statement under sect. 112 of the Civil Procedure Code, or may frame and record issues under sect. 146 of the Code until the case raised by the pleadings is recorded with sufficient clearness (*Ali Kadir* v. *Gobind Das*, I. L. R., xvii Calc. 840).

The respondent is entitled to have brought into Court letters written by her to the petitioner while the facts to which they speak were fresh in her memory. If the petitioner has none, he should make an affidavit to that effect. Should any letters be brought into Court, the Court will look into them, and decide which of them the respondent is entitled to inspect as being material to the case (*Gordon* v. *Gordon*, 3 B. L. R., O. C. 100; cf. *Shaw* v. *Shaw*, 2 S. & T. 642; 31 L. J., P. & M. 95).

So, at the instance of the co-respondent, the petitioner was ordered to bring into the registry letters written by the respondent to him, or to file an affidavit that he had no such letters, or that they contained no such matters as suggested by the affidavit in support of the summons (*Pollard* v. *Pollard and Hemming*, 3 S. & T. 613).

When discovery should not be required.

But discovery ought not to be required from the parties in a divorce suit for the purpose of proving adultery. " If there is reason to believe that a party has documents relating to matters in question in the cause, *other than his or her adultery*, it would be quite right to require an affidavit as to such documents; but if there is reason to believe that the affidavit is required only for the purpose of discovering documents tending to prove adultery by the person required to make the affidavit, no order for such affidavit ought to be made" (Lindley, L. J., *Redfern* v. *Redfern*, (1891) P. 139; 60 L. J., P. & M. 9— C. A.). The reason for this is, that "it is one of the inveterate principles of English law that a party cannot be compelled to discover that which, if answered, would tend to subject him to any punishment, penalty, forfeiture or ecclesiastical censure" (Bowen, L. J., *ibid.*). But this rule does not apply in this country, for no witness is excused from answering a relevant question upon the ground that it may tend to expose him to penalty or forfeiture of any kind (sect. 132, Indian Evidence Act, 1872).

App. (E).

The hearing of the suit:

The procedure laid down in Chap. XV of the Civil Procedure Code, 1882, for the hearing of ordinary civil suits, is equally applicable to suits and proceedings under the Indian Divorce Act.

Hearing of suit.

In ordinary civil suits "the plaintiff has the right to begin unless where the defendant admits the facts alleged by the plaintiff and contends that either in point of law or on some additional facts alleged by the defendant, the plaintiff is not entitled to any part of the relief which he seeks, in which case the defendant has the right to begin" (Civil Procedure Code, 1882, s. 179, explanation).

Right to begin.

The same rule applies in suits for dissolution of marriage. Thus, where the respondent in her answer has not traversed the adultery alleged in the petition, but has set up counter-charges of adultery, cruelty and misconduct, upon which counter-charges issue has been joined, it is for the respondent to begin (*Bacon* v. *Bacon and Bacon*, 2 S. & T. 53; 29 L. J., P. & M. 61).

But if the adultery charged in the petition is traversed, the petitioner has the right to begin, although the respondent alleges nullity of marriage by reason of the petitioner's incurable impotence (*Serrel* v. *Serrel and Bamford*, 2 S. & T. 422; 31 L. J., P. & M. 55).

* In a suit for restitution of conjugal rights, it is incumbent on the petitioner to first prove the marriage, and this, too, though the respondent may have admitted it.

Accordingly, the petitioner has the right to begin even when the substantive issue is upon the respondent (*Burroughs* v. *Burroughs*, 2 S. & T. 544; 31 L. J., P. & M. 56).

"Where there are several issues, the burden of proving some of which lies on the other party, the party beginning may, at his option, either produce his evidence on these issues or reserve it by way of answer to the evidence produced by the other party. In the latter case the party beginning may produce evidence on

---

* If, however, the case is being tried by a *jury*, the respondent will have the right to begin if the substantive issue is upon him or her (*Cherry* v. *Cherry*, 1 S. & T. 319; 28 L. J., P. & M. 36).

APPENDIX (E).

App. (E). those issues after the other party has produced all his evidence, and the other party may then reply specially on the evidence so produced by the party beginning; but the party beginning will then be entitled to reply generally on the whole case" (Civil Procedure Code, 1882, s. 180).

The practice in England is very similar. Thus, where, in answer to a petition by a husband for dissolution of marriage on the ground of his wife's adultery, the respondent counter-charged adultery on the part of the petitioner, it was held that the petitioner might, as part of the case opened by him, give his own evidence and call his witnesses in answer to the respondent's charge, or that he might, in the alternative, reserve his answer to the charge until the respondent's witnesses in support of it had been examined; but that he was not entitled to divide his case by giving his own evidence in the opening, and afterwards calling his witnesses in reply to the respondent's charge (*Jackman* v. *Jackman*, 14 P. D. 62; 68 L. J., P. & M. 72).

Evidence of the parties.

Examination and cross-examination of the parties:

Any party to a suit under the Indian Divorce Act may "offer" himself or herself as a witness, and shall be examined and may be cross-examined and re-examined like any other witness (sect. 51, Indian Divorce Act). In other words, any party to such a suit is a *competent* witness, but is only a *compellable* witness under the circumstances specified in the note to sect. 51 of the Act. But once a party has voluntarily appeared as a witness, he or she is not excused from answering any question as to any matter relevant to the issue in any suit, or in any civil or criminal proceeding, upon the ground that the answer to such question will criminate, or may tend, directly or indirectly, to criminate him or her, or that it will expose, or tend, directly or indirectly, to expose him or her to penalty or forfeiture of any kind (sect. 132, Indian Evidence Act, 1872).

A co-respondent's counsel is not entitled to cross-examine a witness upon such part of his evidence as is not evidence against the co-respondent. He cannot, therefore, cross-examine a witness who speaks to a confession made by the respondent (*Pearman* v. *Pearman and Burgess*, 29 L. J., P. & M. 54).

The evidence of one party cannot be received as evidence against another party in the same litigation unless the latter has had an opportunity of testing it by cross-examination. Consequently, in a divorce suit the evidence of the respondent is not admissible against the co-respondent if the Court refuses to allow the latter to cross-examine upon it. But, *semble*, a right of cross-examination exists between a respondent and a co-respondent, and if cross-examination is permitted, the evidence of either party is admissible against the other (*Allen* v. *Allen and Bell*, (1894) P. 248; 63 L. J., P. & M. 120—C. A.).

According to the English practice, a co-respondent from whom damages are claimed cannot, if he has appeared and filed no answer, cross-examine the petitioner's witnesses at the hearing or address the jury upon the question of damages. But where the damages have been assessed and the decree has been pronounced, he is entitled to recall any of the witnesses and cross-examine them upon the question of costs (*Lyne* v. *Lyne and Blackney*, L. R., 1 P. 508; 37 L. J., P. & M. 9).

App. (E).

Where the Queen's Proctor intervenes and alleges collusion and adultery on the part of the petitioner, he is entitled to cross-examine all the witnesses called by the petitioner and the respondent, and also the petitioner and respondent themselves (provided that the latter have "offered" themselves as witnesses at the hearing of the suit) (*Boardman* v. *Boardman*, L. R., 1 P. 233).

APPENDIX (F).

COSTS.

Provisions in Indian Divorce Act as to costs.

The only provisions of the Indian Divorce Act which deal with the subject of costs are those contained in (a) *sect.* 16— "The High Court may order the costs of counsel and witnesses and otherwise arising from such cause being shown, to be paid by the parties or such one or more of them as it thinks fit, including a wife if she have separate property"; (b) *sect.* 35— "Whenever in any petition presented by a husband the alleged adulterer has been made a co-respondent and the adultery has been established, the Court may order the co-respondent to pay the whole or any part of the costs of the proceedings: Provided that the co-respondent shall not be ordered to pay the petitioner's costs (1) if the respondent was at the time of the adultery living apart from her husband and leading the life of a prostitute, or (2) if the co-respondent had not at the time of the adultery reason to believe the respondent to be a married woman. Whenever any application is made under sect. 17, the Court, if it thinks that the applicant had no grounds or no sufficient grounds for intervening, may order him to pay the whole or any part of the costs occasioned by the application"; (c) *sect.* 55—"Provided also, that there shall be no appeal on the subject of costs only"; and (d) *sect.* 49.

Discretion of Court in matter of costs.

There can, however, be no doubt that the Court has, in addition to the powers given it by sects. 16 and 35, full power over the payment of costs, either under sect. 7 of the Act, which would confer upon it * the powers of the English Court, or under Chapter XVIII of the Civil Procedure Code, 1882 (see sect. 45 of the Indian Divorce Act).

For the exercise of the wide discretion which the Court possesses in the matter of costs no general rules can be laid down, and in each case the Court, in making an order as to the payment of the costs of any proceeding under the Act, will regard the circumstances of the particular case. At the same time this discretion is a judicial discretion, to be exercised in

---

* See Rules 151—158, 177—179, 199—201, 216—218 of the English Divorce Court Rules, and sect. 51 of the Matrimonial Causes Act, 1857 (20 & 21 Vict. c. 85).

accordance with judicial principles. Such general principles may be summarized as follows:— App. (F).

Costs incurred by wife pending suit:

As a general rule a wife, whether she be the petitioner or the respondent, is entitled to have her costs up to, and of and incidental to, the hearing taxed de die in diem, *and the husband may be ordered to pay into Court a sum sufficient to cover such costs or to give security for the same. If the sum be paid into Court, the costs of the wife are taxed and paid out of such sum* de die in diem *to her or to her attorney.*

Wife's costs *pendente lite.*
General rule.

AUTHORITIES—*Weber* v. *Weber and Pyne*, 1 S. & T. 219; 28 L. J., P. & M. 11.
Natall v. *Natall*, I. L. R., ix Mad. 12.
Mayhew v. *Mayhew*, I. L. R., xix Bomb. 293.
Kelly v. *Kelly and Saunders*, 3 B. L. R., App. 4.
Broadhead v. *Broadhead*, 5 B. L. R., App. 9.
Rule 158, English Divorce Court Rules.

The rule applies to suits for nullity of marriage as well as to other matrimonial suits.

AUTHORITY—*Bird* v. *Bird*, 1 Lee, 209.

The fact that the wife is, at the time when the husband presents his petition, living in adultery with the co-respondent, or is separated from her husband under such circumstances that she does not pledge his credit, is not a ground for refusing her her costs *pendente lite*, though alimony *pendente lite* might be refused under such circumstances.

AUTHORITY—*Gordon* v. *Gordon*, 3 B. L. R., App. 13.

But she is entitled to such costs only up to the time when her guilt is proved; and after her adultery has once been established she is not, as an ordinary rule, entitled to costs, though the case may, in a sense, be still said to be pending.

AUTHORITY—*Whitmore* v. *Whitmore*, 35 L. J., P. & M. 51.

To the general rule, as above stated, there are *certain exceptions:*—

(a) *A wife, who has sufficient separate property of her own, should be left to pay her own costs.*

Exceptions to rule:
(a) Wife possessed of separate property.

AUTHORITIES—*Wells* v. *Wells and Cottam*, 33 L. J., P. & M. 72.
Milne v. *Milne*, L. R., 2 P. 202; 40 L. J., P. & M. 13.
Natall v. *Natall*, I. L. R., ix Mad. 12.
Thomson v. *Thomson*, I. L. R., xiv Calc. 580.
Mayhew v. *Mayhew*, I. L. R., xix Bomb. 293.
Rule 158, English Divorce Court Rules.

At the same time the mere fact that the wife has separate property sufficient to pay her own costs is not *per se* enough to

App. (F). *Wife's costs pendente lite.*	take the case out of the general rule. Before the Court concludes not to order the husband to secure the wife's costs, it should take into consideration the relative incomes of the husband and wife, " for the means of the wife to defend the action must in some measure depend upon what is necessary for her maintenance, and the wife of a man with 4,000*l.* a year is entitled to spend more on her maintenance than the wife of a poorer man." AUTHORITY—*Allen* v. *Allen,* (1894) P. 134, Davey, L. J.—C. A.
(b) Wife in receipt of ample allowance from husband.	(b) *A wife, who is in receipt of an ample allowance from her husband or from his estate, is not, as a rule, entitled to have her costs* pendente lite *paid by him.* AUTHORITY—*Woodgate* v. *Taylor,* 30 L. J., P. & M. 197, note.
(c) Husband and wife subject to sect. 4 of Act X of 1865.	(c) *If the husband and wife are subject to the provisions of sect. 4 of the Indian Succession Act,* 1865, *the husband will not be ordered to secure the wife's costs* (?). AUTHORITIES—*Proby* v. *Proby,* I. L. R., v Calc. 357. *Thomson* v. *Thomson,* I. L. R., xiv Calc. 580. *Thomas* v. *Thomas,* I. L. R., 23 Calc. 913. *Young* v. *Young,* I. L. R., 23 Calc. 916, note.

The reason for this exception is stated by the learned judges who decided *Proby* v. *Proby* (Pontifex and Wilson, JJ.) to be that " the principle upon which the Divorce Court in England acts in requiring the husband in a suit for judicial separation to provide for his wife's costs is based upon the absolute right which the law formerly gave the husband upon marriage to the whole of his wife's personal estate and to the income of her real estate, leaving her destitute of all means to conduct her case; *but this state of the law has been completely altered in India by sect. 4 of the Indian Succession Act, which prevents any person from acquiring or losing rights in respect of property by marriage."

But in *Broadhead* v. *Broadhead* (5 B. L. R., App. 9), although the husband raised the objection that he and his wife were subject to sect. 4 of the Indian Succession Act, Phear, J. made the usual order that the husband should deposit a sum sufficient to secure the wife's costs, she being the respondent in the suit and having no separate property of her own. And in *Young* v. *Young, ubi supra,* Pigot, J., while holding that he was bound by *Proby* v. *Proby,* remarked that " were the matter not concluded by authority, I should give effect to another consideration not referred to, that, inasmuch as the wife, in discharge of her duties as mistress of the household, is wholly occupied, it is impossible for her to acquire any property, and I should have

---

* Cf. Cotton, L.J. (*Otway* v. *Otway,* 13 P. D. at p. 156): "If a case comes before us where a married woman has been married after the Act of 1882, it will be a very serious question for consideration how far we ought to follow the old rule, or what decision we ought to give."

thought that consideration might fairly be used to influence the Court in determining whether in cases such as these the wife might not be entitled to obtain the necessary costs from her husband apart from any question of right to her property."

App. (F).
Wife's costs pendente lite.

Nor has the decision in *Proby* v. *Proby* commended itself to the Madras High Court (*Natall* v. *Natall*, I. L. R., ix Mad. 12), or to the Bombay High Court (*Mayhew* v. *Mayhew*, I. L. R., xix Bomb. 293). In the last-mentioned case the husband and wife were subject to sect. 4 of the Indian Succession Act, but Farren, J., refused on that ground alone to depart from the general rule. "It does not appear to me," observed the learned judge, "that those provisions affect the rule as to costs which ought to be applied to the case. The rule has always been that an order as to costs pending the hearing ought not to be made against the husband if the wife is possessed of means (technically styled separate property) sufficient to enable her to pay her own costs in the first instance, the reason for the continuance of the rule, whatever may have been its origin, being that 'it is not considered just either that a wife should be left without the means of putting her case fairly before the Court,* or that a practitioner should run the risk of losing the proper remuneration for his labours if he take up a case which he honestly believes to be genuine, but which may, after all, turn out to be unfounded' (Browne and Powles on Divorce, 5th ed., p. 342). It is a rule of public policy. . . . Too much stress seems to me to have been placed on the origin of the rule in *Proby* v. *Proby*, and too little upon the real reason for its continuance." In support of his views the learned judge referred to the recent case of *Allen* v. *Allen*, (1894) P. 134, where it was held by the Court of Appeal in England that "the relative incomes of husband and wife may, under Rule 158, be taken into account by the judge when exercising his discretion as to whether he will allow the wife her costs already incurred *pendente lite*, and he is not bound to refuse the application because the wife has separate property the amount of which is much more than sufficient for the payment of her costs."

(d) *The wife's costs when taxed de die in diem are generally payable to the wife or her attorney out of the fund in Court; but if the Court has reason to suspect that the suit has been instituted mala fide, it will order the sum deposited to be retained in the registry to abide the event of the hearing.*
AUTHORITY—*Rogers* v. *Rogers*, 4 S. & T. 82; 34 L. J., P. & M. 87.

(d) Sum deposited will not be paid to wife if her suit is *mala fide*.

---

* As to this see *Taylor* v. *Hailstone* (52 L. J., Q. B. 101), where it was held that the costs of a solicitor employed by a married woman to institute proceedings on her behalf against her husband, to obtain a judicial separation, can only be recovered against the husband when the necessity for such proceedings has been made out in point of fact, and that the mere fact that such solicitor had reasonable grounds for believing, upon information obtained, that proceedings ought to be taken, is not sufficient to render the husband liable for costs incurred in obtaining such information, unless it appears to the Court that there was any necessity for such proceedings.

App. (F). Wife's costs pendente lite. (e) Suit for nullity instituted by husband's parent.	(e) *In a suit for nullity of marriage instituted by the father of a minor husband, in such father's own interest, the minor and his de facto wife being made co-defendants, the wife's costs will not be taxed either against the petitioner or the minor husband, unless the circumstances of the case appear to the Court to warrant the usual order being made against the husband, that is, unless her costs have been made necessary by her husband's conduct.* AUTHORITY—*Wells* v. *Cottam f. c. Wells*, 3 S. & T. 593; 34 L. J., P. & M. 12. But under the Indian Divorce Act it is not (apparently) open to the parent of either party to a marriage to sue for a decree of nullity of such marriage otherwise than in the interests of the husband or wife (see note to sect. 18).
Suit by lunatic husband's committee.	*Suit by lunatic husband's committee.*—Where the husband is a lunatic, and a suit is brought on his behalf by his committee, or other person entitled to his custody, such committee or other person must give the usual security for the wife's costs. AUTHORITY—*Smith* v. *Morris*, 3 Ad. 67.
Suit by next friend of minor husband.	*Suit by next friend of minor husband.*—When a minor husband sues by his next friend, the latter must file an undertaking in writing to be answerable for the costs of the proceeding (sect. 49, *ante*), and must also either deposit, or give security for, a sum sufficient to meet the wife's costs of the hearing. AUTHORITY—*Beavan* v. *Beavan*, 2 S. & T. 652; 31 L. J., P. & M. 166.
Failure to comply with order to give security for wife's costs. (a) Husband petitioner.	(a) The general rule is that where the husband is the petitioner, and has failed to comply with an order to deposit or give security for a sum sufficient to cover his wife's costs, all proceedings in the suit will be stayed on the application of the wife until such sum is deposited or secured; but the Court will not grant an attachment against the petitioner. AUTHORITIES—*Keats* v. *Keats and Montezuma*, 28 L. J., P. & M. 138, note. *Keane* v. *Keane*, L. R., 3 P. 52; 42 L. J., P. & M. 12. *Hepworth* v. *Hepworth*, 2 S. & T. 414; 31 L. J., P. & M. 18. *Clarke* v. *Clarke*, (1891) P. 278; 60 L. J., P. & M. 97. Nor does the subsequent bankruptcy of the husband cancel or vacate an order to secure such costs, and, the bankruptcy notwithstanding, the Court will refuse to allow the husband's petition to be heard until the wife has been put into a position to defend herself. AUTHORITY—*Morris* v. *Morris*, 15 L. T. 545. But, if it be proved to the satisfaction of the Court that the petitioner is a man of next to no means, and is unable to pay into Court the sum certified by the registrar as the wife's

probable costs of suit, the Court will refuse to stay the proceedings upon the application of the respondent.

App. (F).
Wife's costs pendente lite.

AUTHORITIES—*Walker* v. *Walker*, 1 Curt. 560.
Thomson v. *Thomson*, I. L. R., xiv Calc. 580.

Nor is the fact that the petitioner has failed to pay the costs of a previous unsuccessful suit by him for dissolution of marriage any ground for staying proceedings in a subsequent suit for dissolution by reason of fresh adultery.

AUTHORITY—*Yeatman* v. *Yeatman and Rummell*, 39 L. J., P. & M. 37.

(b) Where the husband is the respondent and has failed to comply with an order to deposit, or give security for, a sum sufficient to cover his wife's costs, the order can be enforced against him in the manner provided by the Code of Civil Procedure for the execution of a money decree.

(b) Husband respondent.

AUTHORITY—Civil Procedure Code, 1882, s. 220.

A respondent who refuses or fails to comply with such an order is guilty of contempt of Court, and is liable to attachment for such disobedience, such default not being "default in payment of a sum of money" within the meaning of sect. 4 of the Debtors Act, 1869 (32 & 33 Vict. c. 62).

AUTHORITY—*Bates* v. *Bates*, 14 P. D. 17—C. A.

The inability of the respondent, through poverty, to pay or give security for his wife's costs is not *per se* a ground for refusing to make such an order against him, but the Court will, probably, decline to grant an attachment against him if he fails to comply with the order.

AUTHORITIES—*Ward* v. *Ward*, 1 S. & T. 484; 29 L. J., P. & M. 17.
Contra—*Hepworth* v. *Hepworth*, 2 S. & T. 414; 31 L. J., P. & M. 18.

Dismissal or withdrawal of suit before hearing.—A petition by a wife, who resumes cohabitation with the respondent before the hearing, will be dismissed on the latter's application, but only on condition that he pays all taxed costs; and, in such a case, the respondent's application will be ordered to stand over until the wife's attorney has had an opportunity of taxing his costs and enforcing them against the respondent.

Dismissal or withdrawal of suit before hearing.

AUTHORITIES—*Cooper* v. *Cooper*, 3 S. & T. 392; 33 L. J., P. & M. 71.
Dixon v. *Dixon*, L. R., 2 P. 253; 40 L. J., P. & M. 38.
P. v. *P.*, 9 B. L. R., App. 6.

Nor will a husband be allowed to withdraw his petition before the hearing except upon payment of his wife's taxed costs.

AUTHORITY—*Pearce* v. *Pearce*, 30 L. J., P. & M. 182.

Where notice was given by the husband's solicitor to the solicitors of the wife and co-respondent that the petitioner had abandoned the petition, the Court, on motion by the respondent

APPENDIX (F).

App. (F).
Wife's costs pendente lite.

and co-respondent, supported by an affidavit of service of motion on the petitioner's solicitor, dismissed the petition, and condemned the petitioner in costs.

AUTHORITY—*Symons* v. *Symons and Pike*, 2 S. & T. 435; 31 L. J., P. & M. 84.

Interlocutory motions, applications, &c.

If the Court grants an application by the husband alone, or by the husband and wife jointly, for the issue of a commission to examine witnesses, the husband will be ordered to advance the wife a sum to enable her to defray the expenses of the commission.

AUTHORITIES—*Hood* v. *Hood*, 2 S. & T. 112, note.
Baily v. *Baily and De la Rocca*, 2 S. & T. 112; 30 L. J., P. & M. 47.

The following costs will not, as a rule, be taxed against the husband:—

(i) Of an application by the wife for further time to answer to the petition; (ii) of a motion for the husband to attend and be examined on the wife's petition for alimony after he has answered on oath thereto, if the result of his examination is to establish the truth of his answer; (iii) of an unsuccessful opposition by the wife to a motion for further particulars of the charges in her petition for dissolution of marriage; (iv) of appearing on a motion if such appearance is unnecessary, though she may have received notice to appear from the other side.

AUTHORITIES—*Harding* v. *Harding and Lance*, 2 S. & T. 549; 31 L. J., P. & M. 76.
Hepworth v. *Hepworth*, 30 L. J., P. & M. 253.
Frebout v. *Frebout and Penney*, 30 L. J., P. & M. 214.

Costs incurred previous to institution of suit.

An order having been made, during the progress of a suit by the wife for judicial separation, that her costs should be taxed against the husband, the registrar disallowed all charges incurred previously to the commencement of the suit, as also charges by her solicitor for attendance upon her father, which was alleged to have been rendered necessary by reason of her illness. The Court held that this taxation was right, inasmuch as charges incurred previous to the commencement of the proceedings and for the attendance of a proctor, except on his client personally, could not be allowed.

AUTHORITY—*Dickens* v. *Dickens*, 2 S. & T. 103; 28 L. J., P. & M. 94.

Costs of wife after decree.

Costs payable to wife after decree:

"The judgment shall direct by whom the costs of each party are to be paid, whether by himself or by any other party to the suit, and whether in whole or in what part or proportion" (Civil Procedure Code, 1882, s. 219).

"The Court shall have full power to give and apportion costs of every application and suit in any manner it thinks fit, and the fact that the Court has no jurisdiction to try the case is no bar to the exercise of such power: Provided that if the Court directs that the costs of any application or suit shall not follow the event, the Court shall state its reasons in writing. Every order relating to costs made under this code and not forming part of a decree may be executed as if it were a decree for money" (Civil Procedure Code, 1882, s. 220).

In every case the decree must direct by whom and in what proportion the costs should be paid; an omission to do so is not a mere clerical error, and must be rectified by review.

AUTHORITY—*Ram Sahoy* v. *Rookhoo*, 15 W. R. 414.

App. (F).
Costs of wife after decree.

Where the wife is the petitioner and is successful in her suit, her husband will, as a matter of course, be ordered to pay her costs.

AUTHORITIES—*Peacock* v. *Peacock*, 27 L. J., P. & M. 71.
Dixon v. *Dixon*, 28 L. J., P. & M. 96.
Kaye v. *Kaye*, 4 S. & T. 239.

Where wife succeeds in her suit.

Nor does the fact that she sued *in formâ pauperis* disentitle her to her costs against her husband.

AUTHORITY—*Afford* v. *Afford*, 2 S. & T. 387; 30 L. J., P. & M. 174.

Where the wife is the respondent, but has established a good defence in law to her husband's petition, she will be entitled to have her costs taxed against him, even though she may have omitted to take the precaution of having a sum of money deposited in Court, or security given, to meet the costs of the hearing.

Wife establishing good defence to husband's suit.

AUTHORITIES—*Ellyatt* v. *Ellyatt and Hulse*, 3 S. & T. 504; 33 L. J., P. & M. 137.
Burroughs v. *Burroughs*, 31 L. J., P. & M. 124.

A wife, who is respondent in a suit, will be entitled to all costs, though they may exceed the amount deposited in Court, if her husband's suit is dismissed on account of his own marital misconduct, even though her own adultery has been established.

AUTHORITY—*Starkey* v. *Starkey and Irwin*, 30 L. J., P. & M. 118.

The costs of the wife, when payable by the husband, are not limited to the amount paid into Court, or secured by the husband for that purpose.

Costs not limited to amount paid into registry.

AUTHORITIES—*Chetwynd* v. *Chetwynd*, 4 S. & T. 108; 34 L. J., P. & M. 65.
Starkey v. *Starkey and Irwin*, 30 L. J., P. & M. 118.
Robertson v. *Robertson and Favagrossa*, 6 P. D. 119; 51 L. J., P. & M. 5—C. A.
Otway v. *Otway*, 13 P. D. 141; 57 L. J., P. & M. 81—C. A.

The amount deposited in Court by the husband is primarily liable to the payment of his wife's taxed costs, although the co-respondent may have been condemned in all the costs, including

Amount in deposit primarily liable.

R.   B B

Appendix (F).

App. (F).
Costs of wife after decree.

those of the wife, and the husband may be unable to obtain them from him.

AUTHORITY—*Evans* v. *Evans and Robinson*, 1 S. & T. 328; 28 L. J., P. & M. 136.

Application for balance of wife's costs.

Application for balance of the wife's costs, over and above the amount deposited in the registry, should be made on summons, and not on motion.

AUTHORITY—*Cooke* v. *Cooke and Allen*, 3 S. & T. 603; 34 L. J., P. & M. 15.

Wife partly successful in her suit,

Where the wife is partly successful in her suit, but fails to prove all the charges pleaded by her against her husband, the registrar in taxing her costs should satisfy himself whether her attorney had, or had not, reasonable grounds for bringing the several matters pleaded before the Court. If he had, he will be allowed all proper costs of attempting to prove such matters, though the decision of the Court on some of them may be against the wife.

AUTHORITY—*Allen* v. *Allen and D'Arcy*, 2 S. & T. 107; 30 L. J., P. & M. 9.

or in establishing her counter-charges.

If the wife succeeds in establishing her counter-charges against the petitioner, she will be entitled to all her costs of proving such counter-charges.

AUTHORITIES—*Chaldecott* v. *Chaldecott and Cartwright*, 29 L. T. 699.
Otway v. *Otway*, 13 P. D. 141; 57 L. J., P. & M. 81—C. A.

Wife successful in suit: subsequent intervention.

A wife who has obtained a decree *nisi* with costs is entitled to enforce payment of those costs from the husband notwithstanding the intervention of the Queen's Proctor before the decree is made absolute.

AUTHORITY—*Gladstone* v. *Gladstone*, L. R., 3 P. 260; 44 L. J., P. & M. 46.

Even if the wife is proved guilty of adultery on such intervention she will be entitled to the costs directed to be paid to her by the decree *nisi*.

AUTHORITY—*Whitmore* v. *Whitmore*, L. R., 1 P. 96; 35 L. J., P. & M. 52.

In a recent case, however, Butt, J., held that where a decree *nisi* is rescinded, after intervention by the Queen's Proctor, on the ground that it was obtained by collusion to which the wife's solicitors were parties, that part of the decree which ordered the husband to pay the wife's costs was rescinded with it, and that, consequently, the wife was not entitled to an order that certain money paid into the registry by her husband should be paid out to her or her solicitors.

AUTHORITY—**Butler* v. *Butler*, 15 P. D. 32; 59 L. J., P. & M. 30.

---

* In an earlier stage of this case, Butt, J., held that, when the Queen's Proctor had intervened and charged the wife with adultery and collusion, the wife was not entitled to have the money in the registry paid out until the decree *nisi* had been made absolute (*Butler* v. *Butler*, 14 P. D. 160; 58 L. J., P. & M. 71).

A wife is not entitled to security from her husband for her costs incidental to an intervention of the Queen's Proctor. **App. (F).** *Costs of wife after decree.*

AUTHORITIES—*Gladstone* v. *Gladstone*, L. R., 3 P. 260; 44 L. J., P. & M. 46.
Butler v. *Butler*, 15 P. D. 32; 59 L. J., P. & M. 30.

A wife who is possessed of separate property may be ordered to pay the costs of an intervention under sect. 16 of the Indian Divorce Act. *Wife unsuccessful in her suit or her defence.*

Rule 159 of the English Divorce Court Rules provides that "when on the hearing or trial of a cause the decision of the Judge Ordinary or the verdict of the jury is against the wife, no costs of the wife of and incidental to such hearing shall be allowed as against the husband, except such as shall be applied for, and ordered to be allowed by the Judge Ordinary, at the time of such hearing or trial."

But this rule is not absolutely imperative, and the Court may dispense with it and entertain an application for the wife's costs subsequently to the hearing, provided that there are special circumstances in the wife's favour.

AUTHORITY—*Conradi* v. *Conradi and Flashman*, L. R., 1 P. 63; 35 L. J., P. & M. 49.

Sects. 219 and 220 of the Civil Procedure Code, 1882, provide that (i) the judgment must direct by whom the costs of each party are to be paid, and whether in whole or in part, and (ii) if the Court directs that costs of an application or suit shall not follow the event, the Court shall state its reasons in writing.

It has been held that the omission to state by whom the costs are to be paid, and whether in whole or in part, is not a mere clerical error, and can be rectified only upon a review of judgment.

AUTHORITY—*Ram Sahoy* v. *Rookhoo*, 15 W. R. 414.

As a general rule, the husband will be ordered to pay the wife's costs, even though she has either failed in a suit instituted by her against him, or has failed to prove her counter-charges, or has been proved guilty of the charges preferred against her by her husband. And the husband's liability extends not merely to the estimated costs for which he has already given security, but to all costs actually incurred by the wife. *General rule.*

AUTHORITIES—*Flower* v. *Flower*, L. R., 3 P. 132; 42 L. J., P. & M. 45.
Jones v. *Jones*, L. R., 2 P. 333; 41 L. J., P. & M. 21, 53.
Robertson v. *Robertson and Favagrossa*, 6 P. D. 119; 51 L. J., P. & M. 5.
Otway v. *Otway*, 13 P. D. 141.
Hall v. *Hall*, (1891) P. 302; 60 L. J., P. & M. 73.
T. v. *D. f. c. T.*, L. R., 1 P. 127.

The reasons given for this rule are as follows: "If the question of costs were a question solely between husband and wife, it would be reasonable that a husband who had successfully *Reasons for rule.*

App. (F).
Costs of wife after decree.

rebutted a charge brought against him by his wife should not be obliged to pay her costs. But unfortunately in the vast majority of cases the wife has no means of her own. She has to find an attorney to take up her case for her, and if she could not obtain from her husband the means of employing him she would be powerless, and however good a cause she might have for taking proceedings, she would be unable to enforce her rights. Therefore it is necessary to take into consideration the position of the attorney, and provision is made for his payment by enabling the wife to call upon the husband to give security for the costs of the hearing to the amount that may be fixed by the registrar. That course was taken in this case, and the amount of security was fixed at 60*l*.; and the wife's attorney undertook the litigation on her behalf, in the anticipation that he would be allowed his costs out of that sum for which security had been given. By not allowing the costs, the Court would be depriving the attorney of that which he looked to, and had a right to look to, as his security in conducting the litigation on the wife's behalf. It is plain that the Court is not absolutely bound to give the wife her costs, but it would only be justified in refusing them in cases when it appeared that the attorney had done something wrong, or that he had instituted proceedings without reasonable ground, that is, when he had the means of seeing, before instituting the suit, that it was one which ought not to be instituted. When such a case arises, I will disallow the wife's costs, and thus cause the punishment to fall on the attorney. . . . It would be in the highest degree prejudicial to the interests of the women who are litigants in this Court to cast upon the attorneys whom they consult the dangerous responsibility of coming to a conclusion in doubtful cases as to what is likely to be the finding of the Court upon the facts submitted to them. If I were to disallow these costs I should say in effect that the wife's attorney ought to have come to the conclusion that the charge of cruelty could not be made out. But the attorney ought not, I think, to be compelled to stake his chance of remuneration upon his judgment upon such a question" (Hannen, J., *Flower* v. *Flower*, *ubi supra*).

The rule is also explained by Jessel, M. R.: "Now on principle it is plain that the whole foundation of the rule depends on the liability of the husband to pay the necessary and fair costs of the wife's defence. I take it that that rule is founded on the old English law, which gave the whole personal property of the wife to the husband, and gave him also the income of her real estate; so that, in the absence of a settlement (which, as we all know, is a comparatively modern introduction), she was absolutely penniless, and, therefore, the Ecclesiastical Court not only provided for the costs of her defence, but also gave her alimony *pendente lite* so as to provide for her maintenance. Of course the husband may say 'it is a hardship on me to have to pay the costs of my wife's false defence to a charge of adultery, or the costs of a false countercharge against myself of adultery or cruelty.' No doubt it is a hardship, but what would the wife have to say in answer? Suppose the wife had brought him 10,000*l*., or

20,000*l.*, or 50,000*l.*, would not she have a right to say, 'You have taken all my property from me, and am I to be left defenceless and not able to meet your false charge of adultery?' Of course it is manifest that there must be money provided for the wife to defend herself, and who is to take up the defence? Only a solicitor, who must look for payment, not to the wife, who has nothing, but to the husband; and, therefore, it was quite right to secure him that payment by getting money paid into Court, and finally by payment of the proper costs incurred when the suit was heard. Now, as was observed by the learned judge in the case of *Flower* v. *Flower*, it is not the solicitor's fault if the wife is wrong. If he himself conducts the litigation properly, if he fairly investigates the charges and sees a reasonable foundation for a defence, he is not to lose his costs and the fair remuneration for his labour, because he is not successful. No solicitor would engage in the practice of the profession on the terms of not getting paid whenever he was unsuccessful; and, therefore, unless he himself has been guilty of misconduct, there is no reason for depriving him of his costs. It appears to me, therefore, that where the defence is fairly and reasonably conducted, the solicitor ought to be paid in full his costs, that is, his costs properly incurred. . . . . I have given what I believe to be the true view of the origin of the liability of the husband; but I am not oblivious to the nobler view, if I may so express it, held in the House of Lords, that no gentleman, indeed, no man of right feeling, would wish that his wife should not have the means of fairly investigating and fairly defending herself against so odious a charge as that of adultery. Really, if there had not been, as I do believe there is, the common and pecuniary reason for fixing the husband with costs, I think that that reason ought to be sufficient to all right-minded men" (*Robertson* v. *Robertson*, *ubi supra*).

App. (F).
Costs of wife after decree.

To the general rule as above laid down, there are two exceptions.

Exceptions to general rule:

(a) If the wife's solicitor is guilty of misconduct,—"if he either knowingly promotes a case which it must be clear to anybody has no foundation at all, so that he is countenancing improper litigation, or if he takes steps which are merely oppressive or obviously unnecessary, or if he crowds a case with absurd evidence, all these are reasons why, if he so misconducts himself, the costs of the wife should be disallowed either in whole or in part" (per Gorell Barnes, J., *Ash* v. *Ash*, (1893) P. 222; 62 L. J., P. & M. 97; *Wilson* v. *Wilson*, L. R., 2 P. 435; 41 L. J., P. & M. 74; *Hough* v. *Hough*, 71 L. T. 703).

(a) Misconduct of solicitor.

(b) A wife, who is possessed of sufficient separate property of her own, is not entitled to burden the husband with the costs of a suit in which she has been unsuccessful, even though security for her costs may have been given by him; and she may be ordered to pay the costs of an intervention under sect. 16 of the Indian Divorce Act.

(b) Wife possessed of sufficient separate property.

AUTHORITIES—*Heal* v. *Heal*, L. R., 1 P. 300; 36 L. J., P. & M. 62.
Sect. 16, Indian Divorce Act.

App. (F).
Costs of wife after decree.

In such a case, she may herself be condemned in costs.
AUTHORITIES—*Milne* v. *Milne and Fowler*, L. R., 2 P. 202;
40 L. J., P. & M. 13.
Miller v. *Miller*, L. R., 2 P. 13.
Millward v. *Millward*, 57 L. T. 569.
**M. f. c. C.* v. *C.*, L. R., 2 P. 414; 41 L. J., P. & M. 37.

The question for the Court is not whether at the time the wife committed the wrongful act she had or had not any separate estate, but only what is just at the time when it has to arrive at a decision; if the Court finds that at that time there is property of the guilty wife upon which an order for costs, if made, can operate, the guilty wife, like any other unsuccessful litigant, will be condemned in costs.
AUTHORITY—*Hyde* v. *Hyde*, 59 L. T. 523.

But if the separate property of the wife's is small in amount, no order for costs will be made against her which would deprive her of the means of subsistence.
AUTHORITY—*Carstairs* v. *Carstairs*, 33 L. J., P. & M. 170.

Notice to wife.

And the Court will refuse to entertain an application to condemn a wife in costs, if she has not appeared to defend the suit, until she has had notice of the application.
AUTHORITY—*Field* v. *Field*, 13 P. D. 23.

Taxation of wife's costs.

Taxation of wife's costs.—The general principles of taxing costs against a husband in matrimonial suits are the same as in other causes.
AUTHORITY—*Suggate* v. *Suggate*, 1 S. & T. 497.

In England such costs are taxed as between party and party.
AUTHORITY—*Allen* v. *Allen and D'Arcy*, 2 S. & T. 107; 30 L. J., P. & M. 9.

In India they are taxed, as a general rule, as between attorney and client.
AUTHORITIES—*Kelly* v. *Kelly and Saunders*, 3 B. L. R., App. 6.
Natall v. *Natall*, I. L. R., ix Mad. 12.

The taxation of costs is in the discretion of the registrar, and the Court will not interfere with his discretion in respect of particular items allowed or disallowed, unless it can be shown that the taxation proceeded on an erroneous principle.
AUTHORITY—*Cooke* v. *Cooke*, 3 S. & T. 374; 33 L. J., P. & M. 79.

The proper mode of reviewing a taxation of costs is by moving for a rule to show cause why the taxation should not be reviewed, and not by an act on petition.
AUTHORITY—*Dickens* v. *Dickens*, 28 L. J., P. & M. 94.

---

* An unsuccessful suit by the wife for nullity of marriage.

The number of witnesses whose expenses will be allowed is a question for the discretion of the registrar, who should allow the expenses only of such of them as there was reasonable ground for calling; he should also allow the reasonable expenses of journeys and inquiries taken and instituted for the purpose of procuring information.

App. (F).
Taxation of costs against husband.

AUTHORITY—*Allen* v. *Allen and D'Arcy,* 2 S. & T. 107; 30 L. J., P. & M. 9.

Term refresher fees, and the fee of counsel for advising on the sufficiency of an answer which is special, and not a mere traverse of the allegations in the wife's petition will ordinarily be allowed.

AUTHORITIES—*Stoate* v. *Stoate,* 30 L. J., P. & M. 214.
Hepworth v. *Hepworth,* 30 L. J., P. & M. 253.

A wife, who is respondent in a suit for dissolution of marriage, will not be allowed the costs of a motion for leave to show cause why a decree *nisi* should not be made absolute, even though she may have received notice from the other side to appear.

AUTHORITIES—*Dickens* v. *Dickens,* 28 L. J., P. & M. 94.
Stoate v. *Stoate,* 2 S. & T. 384.

Where, after a decree of judicial separation in favour of the husband, the wife, without making a personal application to the husband, applied for and obtained an order for access to the children, the Court refused to allow the costs of such motion to be taxed against the husband, on the ground that the wife ought to have personally applied to the husband in the matter before applying to the Court, and none the less so because, previously to the decree, the latter had refused such an application on her part.

AUTHORITY—*Bacon* v. *Bacon,* L. R., 1 P. 167.

The solicitor of a wife who had obtained a decree absolute for dissolution of marriage, had his costs in the suit taxed as between party and party in the Divorce Court. He subsequently sued the husband for (i) costs incurred before, but incidental to, the institution of the suit; (ii) extra costs in the suit as between solicitor and client, which had been disallowed on the taxation; and (iii) extra costs, as between solicitor and client, of rectifying the wife's marriage settlement after decree *nisi.* The Court of Appeal held that the wife could pledge her husband's credit for, and the solicitor was entitled to recover, such of the above-mentioned costs as had been reasonably incurred.

AUTHORITY—*Ottaway* v. *Hamilton,* 3 C. P. D. 393; 47 L. J., C. P. 725.

A wife, who appeals against the decision of the Court dismissing her petition, is entitled to security from her husband for the costs of appeal.

Wife's costs on appeal.

AUTHORITIES—*Jones* v. *Jones,* L. R., 2 P. 333; 41 L. J., P. & M. 53.
Fowle v. *Fowle,* I. L. R., iv Calc. 260.

No provision should be made for the costs of a wife on her appeal from a decision by which she has been found guilty of adultery; but where she merely defends herself against an appeal on the part of her husband, although her adultery prevents her from pledging the credit of her husband, or her getting any alimony or allowance from him, yet it does not prevent her from requiring her husband to provide for the costs reasonably incurred in bringing her case against his appeal before the Court.

AUTHORITY—*Otway* v. *Otway*, 13 P. D. at pp. 153—156.

A wife will not be allowed the costs of an unsuccessful appeal on her part against an interlocutory order.

AUTHORITY—*Thompson* v. *Thompson and Sturmfalls*, 2 S. & T. 402; 31 L. J., P. & M. 213.

Wife's costs on intervention.—It is not the practice of the Court to order the husband to give security, or pay a sum of money, for his wife's costs incidental to an intervention of the Queen's Proctor.

AUTHORITIES—*Gladstone* v. *Gladstone*, L. R., 3 P. 260.
   Butler v. *Butler*, 15 P. D. 32; 59 L. J., P. & M. 30.

Co-respondent, when condemned in costs:

"Whenever, in any petition presented by a husband, the alleged adulterer has been made a co-respondent and the adultery has been established, the Court may order the co-respondent to pay the whole or any part of the costs of the proceedings.

Provided that the co-respondent shall not be ordered to pay the petitioner's costs: (i) if the respondent was at the time of the adultery living apart from her husband and leading the life of a prostitute, or (ii) if the co-respondent had not at the time of the adultery reason to believe the respondent to be a married woman" (sect. 35, Indian Divorce Act).

As a general rule, a co-respondent, whose adultery with a woman whom he has reason to believe to be a married woman has been established, will be condemned in the costs of the suit, even though the petitioner does not expressly pray for costs in his petition.

AUTHORITIES—*Evans* v. *Evans and Robinson*, 28 L. J., P. & M. 136.
   Finlay v. *Finlay and Radall*, 30 L. J., P. & M. 104.
   Goldsmith v. *Goldsmith and others*, 31 L. J., P. & M. 163.

Nor does the fact that the petitioner claims damages against the co-respondent debar the Court from making such order as to costs as it deems fit.

AUTHORITY—*West* v. *West and Parker*, L. R., 2 P. 196; 40 L. J., P. & M. 11.

Even if the adultery be not established as against the co-respondent, he will not be allowed his costs if it is proved that he acted so imprudently with a woman whom he knew, or had reason to believe, to be a married woman, as to justify a reasonable suspicion in the mind of the petitioner that adultery had been committed; in such a case he will neither be allowed nor condemned in costs.

App. (F).
Costs against co-respondent.

Co-respondent guilty of imprudence with married woman.

AUTHORITIES—*Robinson* v. *Robinson and Gamble*, 32 L. J., P. & M. 210.
Winscom v. *Winscom and Plowden*, 33 L. J., P. & M. 45.
Carstairs v. *Carstairs and Dickens*, 33 L. J., P. & M. 170.
West v. *West and Parker*, L. R., 2 P. 196; 40 L. J., P. & M. 11.

A co-respondent, whose adultery has been established, is not liable to be condemned in the petitioner's costs:—

Co-respondent not liable to pay costs in certain cases.

(a) *If the respondent was at the time of the adultery living apart from her husband and leading the life of a prostitute.*

(a) Respondent living apart from husband as prostitute.

Where the respondent was living, not a life of promiscuous intercourse with all who sought her, but living with separate persons in succession, and professed to be able to attribute her respective children to a father, she was held not to be leading a life of prostitution within the meaning of the Indian Divorce Act (*Roe* v. *Roe*, 3 B. L. R., App. 9).

Moreover, a co-respondent will not be ordered to pay the petitioner's costs in a case where the wife's conduct has been profligate, and that to the knowledge of the petitioner, before the adultery was committed between her and the co-respondent.

AUTHORITIES—*Manton* v. *Manton and Stevens*, 4 S. & T. 159; 34 L. J., P. & M. 121.
Nelson v. *Nelson and Howson*, L. R., 1 P. 510.

Where a wife, who had been a prostitute before marriage, left her husband in Australia against his will, and on arriving in England commenced an adulterous intercourse with the co-respondent, with whom she had had an immoral intercourse before her marriage, and the co-respondent did not discover that she was a married woman until a week after the intimacy had commenced, but thereafter still continued to cohabit with her, because (as he alleged) she received no support from her husband, and would otherwise have been driven back to prostitution, the Court refused to condemn the petitioner in costs, although the petitioner had done his best to prevent his wife leaving Australia and was unable to make her an allowance while living apart from him.

AUTHORITY—*Learmouth* v. *Learmouth*, 59 L. J., P. & M. 14.

If a husband allows his wife to lead a life of prostitution, the co-respondent will assuredly not be ordered to pay costs, even though at the time of the adultery the wife was living with her husband. On the contrary, the petitioner's conduct in such a

App. (F).
Costs against co-respondent.

case would amount to connivance, and he would probably be ordered to pay the costs of the respondent and co-respondent.

AUTHORITY—*Adams* v. *Adams and Colter*, L. R., 1 P. 333; 36 L. J., P. & M. 62.

(b) Ignorance of fact that respondent was married.

(b) *If the co-respondent had not at the time of adultery reason to believe the respondent to be a married woman.*

The petitioner must prove that at the time of the adultery the co-respondent knew, or had reason to believe, that the respondent was a married woman.

AUTHORITY—*Boddington* v. *Boddington and Nossiter*, 27 L. J., P. & M. 53.

If at the time when his connection with the respondent commenced, the co-respondent had no reason to believe her to be married, he will not be condemned in costs.

AUTHORITIES—*Priske* v. *Priske and Goldby*, 29 L. J., P. & M. 195.
Learmouth v. *Learmouth*, 59 L. J., P. & M. 14.
Howe v. *Howe*, 15 W. R. (Eng.) 498.

But even if it is proved that, at the time of the adultery, the co-respondent knew that the respondent was a married woman, it does not necessarily follow that he will be condemned in costs, for the conduct of the petitioner and respondent must be considered as well as that of the co-respondent.

AUTHORITY—*Codrington* v. *Codrington and Anderson*, 4 S. & T. 63; 34 L. J., P. & M. 60.

The usual course is to grant costs against a co-respondent when his conduct has made the suit necessary; he will not, therefore, be condemned in costs when his adultery has been connived at, or condoned, by the petitioner. In such a case the petitioner may be ordered to pay the co-respondent's costs.

AUTHORITIES—*Norris* v. *Norris and Lawson*, 4 S. & T. 237; 30 L. J., P. & M. 111.
Adams v. *Adams and Colter*, L. R., 1 P. 233; 36 L. J., P. & M. 62.
Bernstein v. *Bernstein*, (1893) P. 292; 63 L. J., P. & M. 3.

But mere remissness of conduct on the part of the petitioner towards his wife will not necessarily deprive him of his right to costs against the co-respondent.

AUTHORITY—*Badcock* v. *Badcock*, 1 S. & T. 188.

A co-respondent, whose adultery with the respondent has been established, is not as a matter of course relieved from the payment of costs of that issue merely because the petition has been dismissed.

AUTHORITIES—*Bremner* v. *Bremner and Brett*, 33 L. J., P. & M. 202.
*Long v. *Long and Johnson*, 15 P. D. 218.

---

* In this case the Court came to the conclusion that the adultery had not been established against the respondent on the ground that

If, however, the petition is dismissed on the ground of the petitioner's own gross misconduct, *e.g.*, if he has been proved guilty of incestuous adultery, or of connivance at his wife's adultery, the petitioner may be ordered to pay the costs of the respondent and co-respondent, although the adultery between the latter has been established.

App. (F).
Costs against co-respondent.

AUTHORITIES—*Goode* v. *Goode and Hansom*, 30 L. J., P. & M. 105.
Seddon v. *Seddon and Doyle*, 2 S. & T. 640; 30 L. J., P. & M. 101.
Conradi v. *Conradi and Flashman*, L. R., 1 P. 63; 35 L. J., P. & M. 49.

Costs payable by co-respondent.—When a co-respondent has been condemned in costs, he will, as a general rule, be ordered to pay all the costs of the proceedings, as well those of the respondent as those of the petitioner.

Costs payable by co-respondent.

AUTHORITY—*Evans* v. *Evans and Robinson*, 1 S. & T. 328; 28 L. J., P. & M. 136.

In such a case the respondent is liable to pay the following costs:—

(a) Costs of the petitioner and respondent in obtaining an alteration of their marriage settlement; and of proceedings to obtain alimony.
AUTHORITY—*Gill* v. *Gill and Hogg*, 33 L. J., P. & M. 43; 10 L. T. 137.

(b) Costs of the petitioner and the trustees of a marriage settlement incidental to a petition to vary the settlement.
AUTHORITY—*Smithe* v. *Smithe*, L. R., 1 P. 592.

But if part of an application to vary a marriage settlement fails, and the costs of that part can be separated from the other costs, the former ought not to be thrown on the co-respondent.
AUTHORITY—*Stone* v. *Stone and Brownrigg*, 10 L. T. 140.

(c) Costs of and incidental to proceedings before the registrar for the apportionment and settlement of damages that may have been awarded.
AUTHORITY—*Irwin* v. *Irwin*, 59 L. J., P. & M. 53.

(d) Where the petition is dismissed, but the adultery between the co-respondent and respondent has been established, and the co-respondent has been condemned in the costs of that issue, he will be liable for all the expenses incidental to the filing and prosecution of the petition so far as they relate to such adultery.
AUTHORITIES—*Bremner* v. *Bremner and Brett*, 33 L. J., P. & M. 202.
Baker v. *Baker and Grigg*, 36 L. J., P. & M. 119.

---

she had been forced to it by the co-respondent, and dismissed the petition, but gave judgment against the co-respondent for damages with costs.

App. (F).
Costs against co-respondent.

But the rule that a successful plaintiff suing *in formâ pauperis* in an action tried before a judge and jury is entitled upon taxation, as against the defendant, only to costs out of pocket, applies equally to the case of a pauper petitioner in the Divorce Division as against a co-respondent.

AUTHORITY—*Richardson* v. *Richardson and Plowman*, (1895) P. 346; 64 L. J., P. & M. 119—C. A.

Costs against co-respondent: subsequent intervention.

Co-respondent condemned in costs: subsequent intervention.—When a co-respondent has been condemned in costs, but the decree *nisi* is subsequently set aside on the intervention of a third party, who proves misconduct on the part of the petitioner, that part of the decree which condemns the co-respondent in costs will also be reversed.

AUTHORITIES—*Ravenscroft* v. *Ravenscroft*, L. R., 2 P. 376; 41 L. J., P. & M. 28.
Hechler v. *Hechler*, 58 L. J., P. & M. 27.

But where the decree *nisi* is rescinded on the ground of the petitioner's adultery subsequent to the date of the decree, that part of the decree which condemns the co-respondent in costs will not be reversed.

AUTHORITY—*Hulse* v. *Hulse and Tavernor*, L. R., 2 P. 357; 41 L. J., P. & M. 19.

Costs arising from intervention.—Sect. 16 of the Indian Divorce Act provides that, when cause is shown why a decree should not be made absolute, "the High Court may order the costs of counsel and witnesses, and otherwise, arising from such cause being shown, to be paid by the parties or such one or more of them as it thinks fit, including a wife if she have separate property."

Where the Queen's Proctor intervened, after a decree *nisi* for dissolution of marriage in favour of the husband, and proved collusion and conspiracy between the petitioner and co-respondent, who was cited but did not appear, the Court condemned the co-respondent in the costs of the intervention.

AUTHORITY—*Taplen* v. *Taplen and Cowen*, (1891) P. 283; 60 L. J., P. & M. 88.

*In an earlier case, however, Butt, J., held that he had no power to condemn a co-respondent, who had not been dismissed

---

* In *Taplen* v. *Taplen*, Collins, J., distinguished *Blackhall* v. *Blackhall* on the ground that in that case the co-respondent had not been made a party to the intervention, whereas in the case before him the co-respondent had been cited as a party, though in point of fact he had not appeared. Apparently, however, Butt, J., based his decision on the ground that the co-respondent (whether cited or not) had no right to *appear* on the intervention, and should not, therefore, be condemned in the costs arising therefrom.

from the suit, in the costs of an unsuccessful intervention. "Whether," observed the learned judge, "the proceedings which ensue on the appearance of the Queen's Proctor are proceedings in the case or not, the co-respondent never does appear in them. I infer from the fact that a co-respondent never has been a party to a Queen's Proctor's intervention that he has not the right to appear. That being so, I think it would be unjust to condemn him in the costs of a proceeding over which he has, and can have, no control" (*Blackhall* v. *Blackhall and Clarke*, 13 P. D. 94; 57 L. J., P. & M. 60).

App. (F).
Costs against co-respondent.

Co-respondent, when allowed costs:

When the husband's petition is dismissed, or allowed to be withdrawn, as against the co-respondent, on the ground that there is no evidence against him, the petitioner will ordinarily have to pay the co-respondent's costs.

AUTHORITY—*Smith* v. *Smith and Millett*, 33 L. J., P. & M. 11.

If, however, the adultery between the co-respondent and respondent has been established, the dismissal of the petitioner's suit does not necessarily entitle the co-respondent to costs from the petitioner, unless the suit is dismissed on the ground that the adultery in question had been condoned, or connived at, by the petitioner.

AUTHORITIES—*Forster* v. *Forster and Berridge*, 3 S. & T. 144.
Bremner v. *Bremner and Brett*, 33 L. J., P. & M. 102.
Goode v. *Goode and Hansom*, 30 L. J., P. & M. 105.
Seddon v. *Seddon and Doyle*, 31 L. J., P. & M. 101.
Adams v. *Adams and Colter*, L. R., 1 P. 333; 36 L. J., P. & M. 62.
Bernstein v. *Bernstein*, (1893) P. 292; 63 L. J., P. & M. 3.

But if the petition is dismissed on the ground that the petitioner has been proved by the co-respondent to have been guilty of incestuous adultery, the co-respondent will be entitled to be paid the costs of that issue, though, if his own adultery with the respondent has also been established, he may be liable for the costs of proving the respondent's adultery with him.

AUTHORITY—*Conradi* v. *Conradi and Flashman*, L. R., 1 P. 63; 35 L. J., P. & M. 49.

And even if the petition is dismissed as against the co-respondent on the ground that the charge of adultery has not been established against him, he may nevertheless be ordered to pay his own costs if he has acted so imprudently with a woman, whom he had reason to believe to be a married woman, as to

Co-respondent, when allowed costs.

App. (F.)
Co-respondent, when allowed costs.

raise a reasonable suspicion of adultery in the mind of the petitioner.

AUTHORITIES—*Carstairs* v. *Carstairs and Dickenson*, 3 S. & T. 538.
Robinson v. *Robinson and Gamble*, 32 L. J., P. & M. 210.
Winscom v. *Winscom and Plowden*, 3 S. & T. 380; 33 L. J., P. & M. 45.

Costs of intervenors.

Costs of intervenors:

When any person intervenes to show cause why a decree *nisi* made by a High Court should not be made absolute, " the High Court may order the costs of counsel and witnesses and otherwise arising from such cause being shown to be paid by the parties, or such one or more of them as it thinks fit, including a wife if she have separate property" (sect. 16, Indian Divorce Act).

And " whenever any application is made under sect. 17, the Court, if it thinks that the applicant had no grounds for intervening, may order him to pay the whole or any part of the costs occasioned by the application" (sect. 35, *ibid.*).

As to whether the Court can condemn a co-respondent to pay the costs of an intervention under sect. 16, see *Blackhall* v. *Blackhall*, and *Taplen* v. *Taplen*, *ante*, p. 380.

Reading sect. 16 and sect. 35 of the Indian Divorce Act together, the results would appear to be as follows:—

(a) If a person shows cause why a decree *nisi* made by a High Court should not be made absolute, the High Court may order the costs arising from such intervention to be paid either by the petitioner,* or (possibly) by the respondent, or (possibly) by the co-respondent (sect. 16).

(b) Possibly, the costs of an intervention under sect. 17 may be ordered to be paid by the petitioner,* or the respondent or the co-respondent (sects. 219, 220, Civil Procedure Code, 1882).

(c) A person *who intervenes under sect.* 17, may be ordered to pay the whole or any part of the costs occasioned by such intervention (sect. 35).

(d) It is very doubtful whether a person *who intervenes under sect.* 16 can be ordered to pay any part of the costs occasioned by such intervention, for (i) there is no express provision in the Indian Divorce Act conferring upon the Court a power similar to that conferred upon it by the

---

* Inasmuch, however, as neither the respondent nor the co-respondent seem to have the right to appear on an intervention, it would hardly be just to condemn them in the costs of a proceeding over which they can have no control (see *Blackhall* v. *Blackhall;* but cf. *Taplen* v. *Taplen*, *ante*, p. 380). A co-respondent is not "a party" to an intervention simply because he was a party in the original suit (*Crawford* v. *Crawford and Dilke*, 34 W. R. (Eng.) 677).

last clause of sect. 35, and the maxim "*expressio unius exclusio alterius*" may apply; (ii) under the penultimate clause of sect. 7 of the Matrimonial Causes Act, 1860 (which corresponds with the clause in question of sect. 16 of the Indian Act, but applies only to intervention by the Queen's Proctor), it has been held that the Court has no power to condemn that officer in the costs of an unsuccessful intervention (*Wilson* v. *Wilson*, L. R., 1 P. 180; 14 L. T. 674). It was also held (previously to the enactment of the *Matrimonial Causes Act, 1878, s. 2) that a private intervenor could not be condemned in the costs of his intervention (*Bowen* v. *Bowen*, 3 S. & T. 530; 33 L. J., P. & M. 129; *Vivian* v. *Vivian and Waterford*, L. R., 2 P. 100; 39 L. J., P. & M. 54).

App. (F).
Costs of intervenors.

---

* This section provides that "when the Queen's Proctor or any other person shall intervene or show cause against a decree *nisi* in any suit or proceeding for divorce or for nullity of marriage, the Court may make such order as to the costs of the Queen's Proctor, or of any other person who shall intervene or show cause as aforesaid, or of all and every party or parties thereto, occasioned by such intervention or showing cause as aforesaid, as may seem just; and the Queen's Proctor, any other person as aforesaid, and such party or parties, shall be entitled to recover such costs in like manner as in other cases," &c.

APPENDIX (G).

RULES AND REGULATIONS OF THE ENGLISH COURT OF DIVORCE

MADE UNDER THE PROVISIONS OF

20 & 21 Vict. c. 85.	32 & 33 Vict. c. 62.
23 & 24 Vict. c. 144.	38 & 39 Vict. c. 77.

RULES AND REGULATIONS, 26TH DECEMBER, 1865.

All rules and regulations heretofore made and issued for Her Majesty's Court for Divorce and Matrimonial Causes shall be revoked on and after the 11th day of January, 1866, except so far as concerns any matters or things done in accordance with them prior to the said day.

The following rules and regulations shall take effect in Her Majesty's Court for Divorce and Matrimonial Causes on and after the 11th day of January, 1866.

Petition.

1. Proceedings before the Court for Divorce and Matrimonial Causes shall be commenced by filing a petition.—A form of petition is given in the Appendix, No. 1.

2. Every petition shall be accompanied by an affidavit made by the petitioner, verifying the facts of which he or she has personal cognizance, and deposing as to belief in the truth of the other facts alleged in the petition, and such affidavits shall be filed with the petition.

See also Rule 175.

3. In cases where the petitioner is seeking a decree of nullity of marriage, or of judicial separation, or of dissolution of marriage, or a decree in a suit of jactitation of marriage, the petitioner's affidavit, filed with his or her petition, shall further state that no collusion or connivance exists between the petitioner and the other party to the marriage or alleged marriage.

Co-respondents.

4. Upon a husband filing a petition for dissolution of marriage on the ground of adultery the alleged adulterers shall be made co-respondents in the cause, unless the Judge Ordinary shall otherwise direct.

RULES, ETC. OF THE ENGLISH COURT OF DIVORCE.

5. Application for such direction is to be made to the Judge Ordinary on motion founded on affidavit. **App. (G).**

6. If the names of the alleged adulterers or either of them should be unknown to the petitioner at the time of filing his petition, the same must be supplied as soon as known, and application must be made forthwith to one of the registrars to amend the petition by inserting such name therein, and the registrar to whom the application is made shall give his directions as to such amendment, and such further directions as he may think fit as to service of the amended petition.

7. The term "respondent" where the same is hereinafter used shall include all co-respondents so far as the same is applicable to them.

Citation.

8. Every petitioner who files a petition and affidavit shall forthwith extract a citation, under seal of the Court, for service on each respondent in the cause.—A form of citation is given in the Appendix, No. 2.

9. Every citation shall be written or printed on parchment, and the party extracting the same, or his or her proctor, solicitor, or attorney, shall take it, together with a præcipe, to the registry, and there deposit the præcipe and get the citation signed and sealed.—A form of præcipe is given in the Appendix, No. 3. The address given in the præcipe must be within three miles of the General Post Office.

Service.

10. Citations are to be served personally when that can be done.

11. Service of a citation shall be effected by personally delivering a true copy of the citation to the party cited, and producing the original, if required.

12. To every person served with a citation shall be delivered, together with the copy of the citation, a certified copy of the petition, under seal of the Court.

13. In cases where personal service cannot be effected, application may be made by motion to the Judge Ordinary, or to the registrars in his absence, to substitute some other mode of service.

14. After service has been effected, the citation, with a certificate of service indorsed thereon, shall be forthwith returned into and filed in the registry.—The form of certificate of service is given in the Appendix, No. 4.

15. When it is ordered that a citation shall be advertised, the newspapers containing the advertisements are to be filed in the registry with the citation.

16. The above rules, so far as they relate to the service of citations, are to apply to the service of all other instruments requiring personal service.

17. Before a petitioner can proceed, after having extracted a citation, an appearance must have been entered by or on behalf of the respondents, or it must be shown by affidavit,

filed in the registry, that they have been duly cited, and have not appeared.

18. An affidavit of service of a citation must be substantially in the form given in the Appendix, No. 5, and the citation referred to in the affidavit must be annexed to such affidavit, and marked by the person before whom the same is sworn.

Appearance.

19. All appearances to citations are to be entered in the registry in a book provided for that purpose.—The form of entry of appearance is given in the Appendix, No. 6.

20. An appearance may be entered at any time before a proceeding has been taken in default, or afterwards, as hereinafter directed, or by leave of the Judge Ordinary, or of the registrars in his absence, to be applied for by motion founded on affidavit.

See also Rule 185.

21. Every entry of an appearance shall be accompanied by an address, within three miles of the General Post Office.

22. If a party cited wishes to raise any question as to the jurisdiction of the Court, he or she must enter an appearance under protest, and within eight days file in the registry his or her act on petition in extension of such protest, and on the same day deliver a copy thereof to the petitioner. After the entry of an absolute appearance to the citation a party cited cannot raise any objection as to jurisdiction.

See Rules from 56 to 61 as to proceedings on act on petition.

Interveners.

23. Application for leave to intervene in any cause must be made to the Judge Ordinary by motion, supported by affidavit.

24. Every party intervening must join in the proceedings at the stage in which he finds them, unless it is otherwise ordered by the Judge Ordinary.

Suits in formâ Pauperis.

25. Any person desirous of prosecuting a suit *in formâ pauperis* is to lay a case before counsel, and obtain an opinion that he or she has reasonable grounds for proceeding.

26. No person shall be admitted to prosecute a suit *in formâ pauperis* without the order of the Judge Ordinary; and to obtain such order the case laid before counsel and his opinion thereon, with an affidavit of the party or of his or her proctor, solicitor, or attorney, that the said case contains a full and true statement of all the material facts, to the best of his or her knowledge and belief, and an affidavit of the party applying as to his or her income or means of living, and that he or she is not worth 25*l.*, after payment of his or her just debts, save and except his or her wearing apparel, shall be produced at the time such application is made.

See also Rules 208 to 211.

27. Where a husband admitted to sue as a pauper neglects to proceed in a cause, he may be called upon by summons to show

cause why he should not pay costs, though he has not been dispaupered, and why all further proceedings should not be stayed until such costs be paid.

Answer.

28. Each respondent who has entered an appearance may within twenty-one days after service of citation on him or her file in the registry an answer to the petition.—A form of answer is given in the Appendix, No. 7.
See also Rule 186.

29. Each respondent shall on the day he or she files an answer, deliver a copy thereof to the petitioner, or to his or her proctor, solicitor, or attorney.

30. Every answer which contains matter other than a simple denial of the facts stated in the petition, shall be accompanied by an affidavit made by the respondent, verifying such other or additional matter, so far as he or she has personal cognizance thereof and deposing as to his or her belief in the truth of the rest of such other or additional matter, and such affidavit shall be filed with the answer.

31. In cases involving a decree of nullity of marriage or of judicial separation, or of dissolution of marriage, or a decree in a suit of jactitation of marriage, the respondent who is husband or wife of the petitioner shall, in the affidavit filed with the answer, further state that there is not any collusion or connivance between the deponent and the petitioner.

Further Pleadings.

32. Within fourteen days from the filing and delivery of the answer the petitioner may file a reply thereto, and the same period shall be allowed for filing any further pleading by way of rejoinder, or any subsequent pleading.

33. A copy of every reply and subsequent pleading shall on the day the same is filed be delivered to the opposite parties, or to their proctor, solicitor, or attorney.

General Rules as to Pleadings.

34. Either party desiring to alter or amend any pleading must apply by motion to the Court for permission to do so, unless the alteration or amendment be merely verbal, or in the nature of a clerical error, in which case it may be made by order of the Judge Ordinary, or of one of the registrars in his absence, obtained on summons.
See also Rules 181 to 184 and Rule 187.

35. When a petition, answer, or other pleading has been ordered to be altered or amended, the time for filing and delivering a copy of the next pleading shall be reckoned from the time of the order having been complied with.

36. A copy of every pleading showing the alterations and amendments made therein shall be delivered to the opposite parties on the day such alterations and amendments are made in the pleadings filed in the registry; and the opposite parties,

App. (G). if they have already pleaded in answer thereto, shall be at liberty to amend such answer within four days, or such further time as may be allowed for the purpose.

37. If either party in the cause fail to file or deliver a copy of the answer, reply, or other pleading, or to alter or amend the same, or to deliver a copy of any altered or amended pleading, within the time allowed for the purpose, the party to whom the copy of such answer, reply, or other pleading, or altered or amended pleading, ought to have been delivered, shall not be bound to receive it, and such answer, reply, or other pleading shall not be filed, or be treated or considered as having been filed, or be altered or amended, unless by order of the Judge Ordinary, or of one of the registrars, to be obtained on summons. The expense of obtaining such order shall fall on the party applying for it, unless the Judge Ordinary or registrar shall otherwise direct.

38. Applications for further particulars of matters pleaded are to be made to the Judge Ordinary, or to one of the registrars in his absence, by summons, and not by motion.

See also Rules 181 to 184.

Service of Pleadings, &c.

39. It shall be sufficient to leave all pleadings and other instruments, personal service of which is not expressly required by these rules and regulations, at the respective addresses furnished by or on behalf of the several parties to the cause.

See also Rule 114.

Mode of Trial.

40. When the pleadings on being concluded have raised any questions of fact, the petitioner, within fourteen days from the filing of the last pleading, or at the expiration of that time, on the next day appointed for hearing motions in this Court, or in case the petitioner should fail to do so at such time, either of the respondents on whose behalf such questions have been raised, may apply to the Judge Ordinary by motion to direct the truth of such questions of fact to be tried by a special or common jury.

See also Rule 205.

Questions of Fact for the Jury.

41. Whenever the Judge Ordinary directs the issues of fact in a cause to be tried by a jury, the questions of fact raised by the pleadings are to be briefly stated in writing by the petitioner, and settled by one of the registrars.—A form is given in the Appendix, No. 8.

42. Should the petitioner fail to prepare and deposit the questions for settlement in the registry within fourteen days after the Judge Ordinary has directed the mode of trial, either of the respondents on whose behalf such questions have been raised shall be at liberty to do so.

43. After the questions have been settled by the registrar, the

RULES, ETC. OF THE ENGLISH COURT OF DIVORCE.

App. (G).

party who has deposited the same shall deliver a copy thereof as settled to each of the other parties to be heard on the trial of the cause, and either of such parties shall be at liberty to apply to the Judge Ordinary, by summons within eight days, or at the expiration of that time on the next day appointed for hearing summonses in this Court, to alter or amend the same, and his decision shall be final.

Setting down the Cause for Trial or Hearing.

44. In cases to be tried by a jury, the petitioner, after the expiration of eight days from the delivery of copies of the questions for the jury to the opposite parties, or from alteration or amendment of the same, in pursuance of the order of the Judge Ordinary, shall file such questions as finally settled in the registry, and at the same time set down the cause as ready for trial, and on the same day give notice of his having done so to each party for whom an appearance has been entered.

See also Rule 206.

45. In cases to be heard without a jury, the petitioner shall, after obtaining directions as to the mode of hearing, set the cause down for hearing, and on the same day give notice of his having done so to each party in the cause for whom an appearance has been entered.

See also Rules 205 and 206.

46. If the petitioner fail to file the questions for the jury, or to set down the cause for trial or hearing, or to give due notice thereof, for the space of one month, after directions have been given as to the mode in which the cause shall be tried or heard, either of the respondents entitled to be heard at such trial or hearing may file the questions for the jury, and set the cause down for trial or hearing, and shall on the same day give notice of his having done so to the petitioner, and to each of the other parties to the cause for whom an appearance has been entered.

47. A copy of every notice of the cause being set down for trial or hearing shall be filed in the registry, and the cause shall come on in its turn, unless the Judge Ordinary shall otherwise direct.

Trial or Hearing.

48. No cause shall be called on for trial or hearing until after the expiration of ten days from the day when the same has been set down for trial or hearing, and notice thereof has been given, save with consent of all parties to the suit.

49. The registrar shall enter in the Court Book the finding of the jury and the decree of the Court, and shall sign the same.

50. Either of the respondents in the cause, after entering an appearance, without filing an answer to the petition in the principal cause, may be heard in respect of any question as to costs, and a respondent, who is husband or wife of the petitioner, may be heard also in respect to any question as to custody of children, but a respondent who may be so heard is not at liberty

App. (G). to bring in affidavits touching matters in issue in the principal cause, and no such affidavits can be read or made use of as evidence in the cause.

Evidence taken by Affidavit.

51. When the Judge Ordinary has directed that all or any of the facts set forth in the pleadings be proved by affidavits, such affidavits shall be filed in the registry within eight days from the time when such direction was given, unless the Judge Ordinary shall otherwise direct.

See also Rule 188.

52. Counter-affidavits as to any facts to be proved by affidavit may be filed within eight days from the filing of the affidavits which they are intended to answer.

53. Copies of all such affidavits and counter-affidavits shall on the day the same are filed be delivered to the other parties to be heard on the trial or hearing of the cause, or to their proctors, solicitors, or attorneys.

54. Affidavits in reply to such counter-affidavits cannot be filed without permission of the Judge Ordinary or of the registrars in his absence.

55. Application for an order for the attendance of a deponent for the purpose of being cross-examined in open Court shall be made to the Judge Ordinary, on summons.

Proceedings by Petition.

56. Any party to a cause who has entered an appearance may apply on summons to the Judge Ordinary, or in his absence to the registrars, to be heard on his petition touching any collateral question which may arise in a suit.

57. The party to whom leave has been given to be heard on his petition shall within eight days file his act on petition in the registry, and on the same day deliver a copy thereof to such parties in the cause as are required to answer thereto.

58. Each party to whom a copy of an act on petition is delivered shall within eight days after receiving the same file his or her answer thereto in the registry, and on the same day deliver a copy thereof to the opposite party, and the same course shall be pursued with respect to the reply, rejoinder, &c., until the act on petition is concluded.

59. A form of act on petition, answer, and conclusion is given in the Appendix, No. 9.

60. Each party to the act on petition shall within eight days from that on which the last statement in answer is filed, file in the registry such affidavits and other proofs as may be necessary in support of their several averments.

61. After the time for filing affidavits and proofs has expired, the party filing the act on petition is to set down the petition for hearing in the same manner as a cause; and in the event of his failing to do so within a month any party who has filed an answer thereto may set the same down for hearing, and the petition will be heard in its turn with other causes to be heard by the Judge Ordinary without a jury.

New Trial and Hearing.

62. An application to the Judge Ordinary for a new trial of issues of fact tried by a jury, or for a re-hearing of a cause, may be made by motion within fourteen days from the day on which the issues were tried or the cause was heard, if the Judge Ordinary be then sitting to hear motions, if not, on the first day appointed for hearing motions in this Court after the expiration of the fourteen days.

Petition for reversal of Decree of Judicial Separation.

63. A petition to the Court for the reversal of a decree of judicial separation must set out the grounds on which the petitioner relies.—A form of such petition is given in the Appendix, No. 10.

64. Before such a petition can be filed, an appearance on behalf of the party praying for a reversal of the decree of judicial separation must be entered in the cause in which the decree has been pronounced.

65. A certified copy of such a petition, under seal of the Court, shall be delivered personally to the party in the cause in whose favour the decree has been made, who may within fourteen days file an answer thereto in the registry, and shall on the day on which the answer is filed deliver a copy thereof to the other party in the cause, or to his or her proctor, solicitor, or attorney.

66. All subsequent pleadings and proceedings arising from such petition and answer shall be filed and carried on in the same manner as before directed in respect of an original petition for judicial separation, and answer thereto, so far as such directions are applicable.

Demurrer.

67. All demurrers are to be set down for hearing in the same manner as causes, and will come on in their turn with other causes to be heard by the Judge Ordinary without a jury, unless the Judge Ordinary shall direct otherwise.

Intervention of the Queen's Proctor.

68. The Queen's Proctor shall, within fourteen days after he has obtained leave to intervene in any cause, enter an appearance and plead to the petition; and on the day he files his plea in the registry shall deliver a copy thereof to the petitioner, or to his proctor, solicitor, or attorney.

69. All subsequent pleadings and proceedings in respect to the Queen's Proctor's intervention in a cause shall be filed and carried on in the same manner as before directed in respect of the pleadings and proceedings of the original parties to the cause.

See also Rule 202.

Appendix (G).

Showing Cause against a Decree.

70. Any person wishing to show cause against making absolute a decree *nisi* for dissolution of a marriage shall enter an appearance in the cause in which such decree *nisi* has been pronounced.

71. Every such person shall at the time of entering an appearance, or within four days thereafter, file affidavits setting forth the facts upon which he relies.

72. Upon the same day on which such person files his affidavits he shall deliver a copy of the same to the party in the cause in whose favour the decree *nisi* has been pronounced.

73. The party in the cause in whose favour the decree *nisi* has been pronounced may, within eight days after delivery of the affidavits, file affidavits in answer, and shall, upon the day such affidavits are filed, deliver a copy thereof to the person showing cause against the decree being made absolute.

74. The person showing cause against the decree *nisi* being made absolute may within eight days file affidavits in reply, and shall upon the same day deliver copies thereof to the party supporting the decree *nisi*.

75. No affidavits are to be filed in rejoinder to the affidavits in reply without permission of the Judge Ordinary or of one of the registrars in his absence.

76. The questions raised on such affidavits shall be argued in such manner and at such time as the Judge Ordinary may on application by motion direct; and if he thinks fit to direct any controverted questions of fact to be tried by a jury, the same shall be settled and tried in the same manner and subject to the same rules as any other issue tried in this Court.

Rules 70 to 76 not applicable to the Queen's Proctor. *See* Rule 202.

Appeals to the full Court.

77. An appeal to the full Court from a decision of the Judge Ordinary must be asserted in writing and the instrument of appeal filed in the registry within the time allowed by law for appealing from such decision; and on the same day on which the appeal is filed, notice thereof, and a copy of the appeal, shall be delivered to each respondent in the appeal, or to his or her proctor, solicitor, or attorney.—A form of instrument of appeal is given in the Appendix, No. 11.

78. The appellant within ten days after filing his instrument of appeal, or within such further time as may be allowed by the Judge Ordinary, or by the registrars in his absence, shall file in the registry his case in support of the appeal in triplicate, and on the same day deliver a copy thereof to each respondent in the appeal, or to his proctor, solicitor, or attorney, who, within ten days from the time of such filing and delivery or from such further time as may be allowed for the purpose by the Judge Ordinary, or the registrars in his absence, shall be at liberty to file in the registry a case against the appeal, also in triplicate,

and the respondent shall on the same day deliver a copy thereof to the appellant, or to his proctor, solicitor, or attorney.

79. After the expiration of ten days from the time when the respondent has filed his case, or, if he has filed none, from the time allowed him for the purpose, the appeal shall stand for hearing at the next sittings of the full Court, and will be called on in its turn, unless otherwise directed.

Decree absolute.

80. All applications to make absolute a decree *nisi* for dissolution of a marriage must be made to the Court by motion. In support of such applications it must be shown by affidavit filed with the case for motion that search has been made in the proper books at the registry up to within two days of the affidavit being filed, and that at such time no person had obtained leave to intervene in the cause, and that no appearance had been entered nor any affidavits filed on behalf of any person wishing to show cause against the decree *nisi* being made absolute; and in case leave to intervene had been obtained, or appearance entered, or affidavits filed on behalf of any such person, it must be shown by affidavit what proceedings, if any, had been taken thereon, but it shall not be necessary to file a copy of the decree *nisi*.— A form of affidavit is given in the Appendix, No. 12.

See also Rules 194 and 207.

Alimony.

81. The wife, being the petitioner in a cause, may file her petition for alimony pending suit at any time after the citation has been duly served on the husband, or after order made by the Judge Ordinary to dispense with such service, provided the factum of marriage between the parties is established by affidavit previously filed.

82. The wife, being the respondent in a cause, after having entered an appearance, may also file her petition for alimony pending suit.

83. A form of petition for alimony is given in the Appendix, No. 13.

84. The husband shall, within eight days after the filing and delivery of a petition for alimony, file his answer thereto upon oath.

85. The husband, being respondent in the cause, must enter an appearance before he can file an answer to a petition for alimony.

86. The wife, if not satisfied with the husband's answer, may object to the same as insufficient, and apply to the Judge Ordinary on motion to order him to give a further and fuller answer, or to order his attendance on the hearing of the petition for the purpose of being examined thereon.

See also Rule 189.

87. In case the answer of the husband alleges that the wife has property of her own, she may (within eight days) file a reply on oath to that allegation; but the husband is not at

liberty to file a rejoinder to such reply without permission of the Judge Ordinary, or of one of the registrars in his absence.

88. A copy of every petition for alimony, answer and reply, must be delivered to the opposite party, or to his or her proctor, solicitor, or attorney, on the day the same is filed.

89. After the husband has filed his answer to the petition for alimony (subject to any order as to costs), or, if no answer is filed, at the expiration of the time allowed for filing an answer, the wife may proceed to examine witnesses in support of her petition, and apply by motion for an allotment of alimony pending suit, notice of the motion, and of the intention to examine witnesses, being given to the husband, or to his proctor, solicitor, or attorney, four days previously to the motion being heard and the witnesses examined, unless the Judge Ordinary shall dispense with such notice.

See also Rules 191 and 192.

90. No affidavits can be read or made use of as evidence in support of or in opposition to the averments contained in a petition for alimony, or in an answer to such a petition, or in a reply, except such as may be required by the Judge Ordinary or by one of the registrars.

91. A wife who has obtained a final decree of judicial separation in her favour, and has previously thereto filed her petition for alimony pending suit, on such decree being affirmed on appeal to the full Court, or after the expiration of the time for appealing against the decree, if no appeal be then pending, may apply to the Judge Ordinary by motion for an allotment of permanent alimony; provided that she shall, eight days at least before making such application, give notice thereof to the husband, or to his proctor, solicitor, or attorney.

See also Rule 190.

92. A wife may at any time after alimony has been allotted to her, whether alimony pending suit or permanent alimony, file her petition for an increase of the alimony allotted by reason of the increased faculties of the husband, or the husband may file a petition for a diminution of the alimony allotted by reason of reduced faculties; and the course of proceeding in such cases shall be the same as required by these rules and regulations in respect of the original petition for alimony, and the allotment thereof, so far as the same are applicable.

93. Permanent alimony shall, unless otherwise ordered, commence and be computed from the date of the final decree of the Judge Ordinary, or of the full Court on appeal, as the case may be.

94. Alimony, pending suit, and also permanent alimony, shall be paid to the wife, or to some person or persons to be nominated in writing by her, and approved of by the Court, as trustee or trustees on her behalf.

Maintenance and Settlements.

95. Applications to the Court to exercise the authority given by sects. 32 and 45 of 20 & 21 Vict. c. 85, and by sect. 5 of the 22 & 23 Vict. c. 61, are to be made in a separate petition,

RULES, ETC. OF THE ENGLISH COURT OF DIVORCE. 395

which must, unless by leave of the judge, be filed as soon as by App. (G).
the said statutes such applications can be made, or within one
month thereafter.

96. In cases of application for maintenance under sect. 32 of the 20 & 21 Vict. c. 85, such petition may be filed as soon as a decree *nisi* has been pronounced, but not before.

97. A certified copy of such petition, under seal of the Court, shall be personally served on the husband or wife (as the case may be), and on the person or persons who may have any legal or beneficial interest in the property in respect of which the application is made, unless the Judge Ordinary on motion shall direct any other mode of service, or dispense with service of the same on them or either of them.

98. The husband or wife (as the case may be), and the other person or persons (if any) who are served with such petition, within fourteen days after service, may file his, her, or their answer on oath to the said petition, and shall on the same day deliver a copy thereof to the opposite party, or to his proctor, solicitor, or attorney.

99. Any person served with the petition, not being a party to the principal cause, must enter an appearance before he or she can file an answer thereto.

100. Within fourteen days from the filing the answer, the opposite party may file a reply thereto, and the same period shall be allowed for filing any further pleading by way of rejoinder.

101. Such pleadings, when completed, shall in the first instance be referred to one of the registrars, who shall investigate the averments therein contained, in the presence of the parties, their proctors, solicitors, or attorneys, and who for that purpose shall be at liberty to require the production of any documents referred to in such pleadings, or to call for any affidavits, and shall report in writing to the Court the result of his investigation, and any special circumstances to be taken into consideration with reference to the prayer of the petition.

See also Rule 204.

102. The report of the registrar shall be filed in the registry by the husband or wife on whose behalf the petition has been filed, who shall give notice thereof to the other parties heard by the registrar; and either of the parties, within fourteen days after such notice has been given, if the Judge Ordinary be then sitting to hear motions, otherwise on the first day appointed for motions after the expiration of fourteen days, may be heard by the Judge Ordinary on motion in objection to the registrar's report, or may apply on motion for a decree or order to confirm the same, and to carry out the prayer of the petition.

103. The costs of a wife of and arising from the said petition or answer shall not be allowed on taxation of costs against the husband before the final decree in the principal cause, without direction of the Judge Ordinary.

Custody of and Access to Children.

104. Before the trial or hearing of a cause a husband or wife

App. (G). who are parties to it may apply for an order with respect to the custody, maintenance, or education of or for access to children, issue of their marriage, to the Judge Ordinary, by motion founded on affidavit.

See also Rule 212.

Guardians to Minors.

105. A minor above the age of seven years may elect any one or more of his or her next of kin, or next friends, as guardian, for the purpose of proceeding on his or her behalf as petitioner, respondent, or intervener in a cause.—The form of an instrument of election is given in the Appendix, No. 14.

106. The necessary instrument of election must be filed in the registry before the guardian elected can be permitted to extract a citation or to enter an appearance on behalf of the minor.

107. When a minor shall elect some person or persons other than his or her next of kin, as guardian for the purposes of a suit, or when an infant (under the age of seven years) becomes a party to a suit, application, founded on affidavit, is to be made to one of the registrars, who will assign a guardian to the minor or infant for such suit.

108. It shall not be necessary for a minor who, as an alleged adulterer, is made a co-respondent in a suit, to elect a guardian or to have a guardian assigned to him for the purpose of conducting his defence.

Subpœnas.

109. Every subpœna shall be written or printed on parchment, and may include the names of any number of witnesses. The party issuing the same, or his or her proctor, solicitor, or attorney, shall take it, together with a præcipe, to the registry, and there get it signed and sealed, and there deposit the præcipe.—Forms of Subpœna, Nos. 15 and 17, and Forms of Præcipe, Nos. 16 and 18, are given in the Appendix.

See also Rule 180.

Writs of Attachment and other Writs.

110. Applications for writs of attachment, and also for writs of *fieri facias* and of sequestration, must be made to the Judge Ordinary by motion in Court.

See also Rules 179 and 203.

111. Such writs, when ordered to issue, are to be prepared by the party at whose instance the order has been obtained, and taken to the registry, with an office copy of the order, and, when approved and signed by one of the registrars, shall be sealed with the seal of the Court, and it shall not be necessary for the Judge Ordinary or for other judges of the Court to sign such writs.

112. Any person in custody under a writ of attachment may apply for his or her discharge to the Judge Ordinary if the Court be then sitting; if not, then to one of the registrars, who for good cause shown shall have power to order such discharge.

RULES, ETC. OF THE ENGLISH COURT OF DIVORCE.   397

App. (G).

Notices.

113. All notices required by these rules and regulations, or by the practice of the Court shall be in writing, and signed by the party, or by his or her proctor, solicitor, or attorney.

Service of Notices, &c.

114. It shall be sufficient to leave all notices and copies of pleadings and other instruments which by these rules and regulations are required to be given or delivered to the opposite parties in the cause, or to their proctors, solicitors, or attorneys, and personal service of which is not expressly required at the address furnished as aforesaid by the petitioner and respondent respectively.
   See *also* Rule 39.

115. When it is necessary to give notice of any motion to be made to the Court, such notice shall be served on the opposite parties who have entered an appearance four clear days previously to the hearing of such motion, and a copy of the notice so served shall be filed in the registry with the case for motion, but no proof of the service of the notice will be required, unless by direction of the Judge Ordinary.

116. If an order be obtained on motion without due notice to the opposite parties, such order will be rescinded on the application of the parties upon whom the notice should have been served; and the expense of and arising from the rescinding of such order shall fall on the party who obtained it, unless the Judge Ordinary shall otherwise direct.

117. When it is necessary to serve personally any order or decree of the Court, the original order or decree, or an office copy thereof, under seal of the Court, must be produced to the party served, and annexed to the affidavit of service marked as an exhibit by the Commissioner or other person before whom the affidavit is sworn.

Office Copies, Extracts, &c.

118. The registrars of the Principal Registry of the Court of Probate are to have the custody of all pleadings and other documents now or hereafter to be brought in or filed, and of all entries of orders and decrees made in any matter or suit depending in the Court for Divorce and Matrimonial Causes; and all rules and orders, and fees payable in respect of searches for and inspection or copies of and extracts from and attendance with books and documents in the registry of the Court of Probate, shall extend to such pleadings and other documents brought in or filed, and all entries of orders and decrees made in the Court for Divorce and Matrimonial Causes, save that the length of copies and extracts shall in all cases be computed at the rate of seventy-two words per folio.

119. Office copies or extracts furnished from the registry of the Court of Probate will not be collated with the originals from which the same are copied, unless specially required. Every

App. (G).

copy so required to be examined shall be certified under the hand of one of the principal registrars of the Court of Probate to be an examined copy.

120. The seal of the Court will not be affixed to any copy which is not certified to be an examined copy.

Time fixed by these Rules.

121. The Judge Ordinary shall in every case in which a time is fixed by these rules and regulations for the performance of any act, or for any proceeding in default, have power to extend the same to such time and with such qualifications and restrictions and on such terms as to him may seem fit.

122. To prevent the time limited for the performance of any act, or for any proceeding in default, from expiring before application can be made to the Judge Ordinary for an extension thereof, any one of the registrars may, upon reasonable cause being shown, extend the time, provided that such time shall in no case be extended beyond the day upon which the Judge Ordinary shall next sit in Chambers.

See also Rules 181 to 184.

123. The time fixed by these rules and regulations for the performance of any act, or for any proceeding in a cause, shall in all cases be exclusive of Sundays, Christmas Day, and Good Friday.

Protection Orders.

124. Applications on the part of a wife deserted by her husband for an order to protect her earnings and property, acquired since the commencement of such desertion, shall be made in writing to the Judge Ordinary in Chambers, and supported by affidavit.—A form of application is given in the Appendix, No. 19.

See also Rule 197.

125. Applications for the discharge of any order made to protect the earnings and property of a wife are to be made to the Judge Ordinary by motion, and supported by affidavit. Notice of such motion, and copies of any affidavit or other document to be read or used in support thereof, must be personally served on the wife eight clear days before the motion is heard.

Bond not required.

126. On a decree of judicial separation being pronounced, it shall not be necessary for either party to enter into a bond conditioned against marrying again.

Change of Proctor, Solicitor, or Attorney.

127. A party may obtain an order to change his or her proctor, solicitor, or attorney upon application by summons to the Judge Ordinary, or to the registrars in his absence.

See also Rules 181 to 184.

128. In case the former proctor, solicitor, or attorney neglects to file his bill of costs for taxation at the time required by the

RULES, ETC. OF THE ENGLISH COURT OF DIVORCE.   399

order served upon him, the party may, with the sanction and App. (G).
by order of the Judge Ordinary or of the registrars, proceed in
the cause by the new proctor, solicitor, or attorney, without
previous payment of such costs.

Order for the immediate Examination of a Witness.

129. Application for an order for the immediate examination
of a witness who is within the jurisdiction of the Court is to be
made to the Judge Ordinary, or to the registrars in his absence,
by summons, or if on behalf of a petitioner proceeding in default
of appearance of the parties cited in the cause without summons
before one of the registrars, who will direct the order to issue,
or refer the application to the Judge Ordinary, as he may
think fit.

See also Rules 181 to 184.

130. Such witness shall be examined *vivâ voce*, unless otherwise directed, before a person to be agreed upon by the parties
in the cause, or to be nominated by the Judge Ordinary or by
the registrars to whom the application for the order is made.

131. The parties entitled to cross-examine the witness to be
examined under such an order shall have four clear days notice
of the time and place appointed for the examination, unless the
Judge Ordinary or the registrars to whom the application is
made for the order shall direct a shorter notice to be given.

Commissions and Requisitions for Examination of Witnesses.

132. Application for a commission or requisition to examine
witnesses who are out of the jurisdiction of the Court is to be
made by summons, or if on behalf of a petitioner proceeding in
default of appearance without summons, before one of the registrars, who will order such commission or requisition to issue, or
refer the application to the Judge Ordinary, as he may think fit.

133. A commission or requisition for examination of witnesses
may be addressed to any person to be nominated and agreed
upon by the parties in the cause, and approved of by the registrar, or for want of agreement to be nominated by the registrar
to whom the application is made.

134. The commission or requisition is to be drawn up and
prepared by the party applying for the same, and a copy thereof
shall be delivered to the parties entitled to cross-examine the
witnesses to be examined thereunder two clear days before such
commission or requisition shall issue, under seal of the Court,
and they or either of them may apply to one of the registrars
by summons to alter or amend the commission or requisition,
or to insert any special provision therein, and the registrar shall
make an order on such application, or refer the matter to the
Judge Ordinary.—A form of a commission and requisition is
given in the Appendix, No. 20.

135. Any of the parties to the cause may apply to one of the
registrars by summons for leave to join in a commission or
requisition, and to examine witnesses thereunder; and the
registrar to whom the application is made may direct the

necessary alterations to be made in the commission or requisition for that purpose, and settle the same, or refer the application to the Judge Ordinary.

136. After the issuing of a summons to show cause why a party to the cause should not have leave to join in a commission or requisition, such commission or requisition shall not issue under seal without the direction of one of the registrars.

137. In case a husband or wife shall apply for and obtain an order or a commission or requisition for the examination of witnesses, the wife shall be at liberty, without any special order for that purpose, to apply by summons to one of the registrars to ascertain and report to the Court what is a sufficient sum of money to be paid or secured to the wife to cover her expenses in attending at the examination of such witnesses in pursuance of such order, or in virtue of such commission or requisition, and such sum of money shall be paid or secured before such order or such commission or requisition shall issue from the registry, unless the Judge Ordinary or one of the registrars in his absence shall otherwise direct.

See also Rule 198.

Affidavits.

138. Every affidavit is to be drawn in the first person, and the addition and true place of abode of every deponent is to be inserted therein.

139. In every affidavit made by two or more persons, the names of the several persons making it are to be written in the jurat.

140. No affidavit will be admitted in any matter depending in the Court for Divorce and Matrimonial Causes in which any material part is written on an erasure, or in the jurat of which there is any interlineation or erasure, or in which there is any interlineation the extent of which at the time when the affidavit was sworn is not clearly shown by the initials of the registrar, commissioner, or other authority before whom it was sworn.

141. Where an affidavit is made by any person who is blind, or who, from his or her signature or otherwise, appears to be illiterate, the registrar, commissioner, or other authority before whom such affidavit is made is to state in the jurat that the affidavit was read in the presence of the party making the same, and that such party seemed perfectly to understand the same, and also made his or her mark, or wrote his or her signature thereto, in the presence of the registrar, commissioner, or other authority before whom the affidavit was made.

142. No affidavit is to be deemed sufficient which has been sworn before the party on whose behalf the same is offered, or before his or her proctor, solicitor, or attorney, or before a partner or clerk of his or her proctor, solicitor, or attorney.

143. Proctors, solicitors, and attorneys, and their clerks respectively, if acting for any other proctor, solicitor, or attorney, shall be subject to the rules and regulations in respect of taking affidavits which are applicable to those in whose stead they are acting.

RULES, ETC. OF THE ENGLISH COURT OF DIVORCE.

App. (G).

144. No affidavit can be read or used unless the proper stamps to denote the fees payable on filing the same are delivered with such affidavit.

145. Where a special time is fixed for filing affidavits, no affidavit filed after that time shall be used unless by leave of the Judge Ordinary.

146. The above rules and regulations in respect to affidavits shall, so far as the same are applicable, be observed in respect to affirmations and declarations to be read or used in the Court for Divorce and Matrimonial Causes.

Cases for Motion.

147. Cases for motion are to set forth the style and object of, and the names and descriptions of the parties to, the cause or proceeding before the Court; the proceedings already had in the cause, and the dates of the same; the prayer of the party on whose behalf the motion is made, and briefly, the circumstances on which it is founded.

148. If the cases tendered are deficient in any of the above particulars, the same shall not be received in the registry without permission of one of the registrars.

149. On depositing the case in the registry, and giving notice of the motion, the affidavits in support of the motion, and all original documents referred to in such affidavits, or to be referred to by counsel on the hearing of the motion, must be also left in the registry; or in case such affidavits or documents have been already filed or deposited in the registry, the same must be searched for, looked up, and deposited with the proper clerk, in order to their being sent with the case to the Judge Ordinary.

150. Copies of any affidavit or documents to be read or used in support of a motion are to be delivered to the opposite parties to the suit who are entitled to be heard in opposition thereto.

Taxing Bills of Costs.

151. All bills of costs are referred to the registrars of the principal registry of the Court of Probate for taxation, and may be taxed by them, without any special order for that purpose. Such bills are to be filed in the registry.

See also Rule 177.

152. Notice of the time appointed for taxation will be forwarded to the party filing the bill, at the address furnished by such party.

153. The party who has obtained an appointment to tax a bill of costs shall give the other party or parties to be heard on the taxation thereof at least one clear day's notice of such appointment, and shall at or before the same time deliver to him or them a copy of the bill to be taxed.

154. When an appointment has been made by a registrar of the Court of Probate for taxing any bill of costs, and any

parties to be heard on the taxation do not attend at the time appointed, the registrar may nevertheless proceed to tax the bill after the expiration of a quarter of an hour, upon being satisfied by affidavit that the parties not in attendance had due notice of the time appointed.

155. The bill of costs of any proctor, solicitor, or attorney will be taxed on his application as against his client, after sufficient notice given to the person or persons liable for the payment thereof, or on the application of such person or persons, after sufficient notice given to the practitioner.

156. The fees payable on the taxation of any bill of costs shall be paid by the party on whose application the bill is taxed, and shall be allowed as part of such bill; but if more than one sixth of the amount of any bill of costs taxed as between practitioner and client is disallowed on the taxation thereof, no costs incurred in such taxation shall be allowed as part of such bill.

See also Rule 200.

157. If an order for payment of costs is required, the same may be obtained by summons, on the amount of such costs being certified by the registrar.

See also Rules 178, 179 and 201.

Wife's Costs.—As amended 14th July 1875.

158. After directions given as to the mode of hearing or trial of a cause, or in an earlier stage of a cause by order of the Judge Ordinary, or of the registrars, to be obtained on summons, a wife who is petitioner, or has entered an appearance as respondent in a cause, may file her bill or bills of costs for taxation as against her husband, and the registrar to whom such bills of costs are referred for taxation shall, when directions as to the mode of hearing or trial have been given, ascertain what is a sufficient sum of money to be paid into the registry, or what is a sufficient security to be given by the husband to cover the costs of the wife of and incidental to the hearing of the cause; and shall thereupon issue an order upon the husband to pay or secure the said sum within a time to be fixed by the registrar; provided that in case the husband should by reason of his wife having separate property, or for other reasons, dispute her right to recover any costs pending suit against him, the registrar may suspend the order to pay the wife's taxed costs, or to pay or secure the sum ascertained to be sufficient to cover her costs of and incidental to the hearing of the cause, for such length of time as shall seem to him necessary to enable the husband to obtain the decision of the Court as to his liability.

159. When on the hearing or trial of a cause the decision of the Judge Ordinary or the verdict of the jury is against the wife, no costs of the wife of and incidental to such hearing or trial shall be allowed as against the husband, except such as shall be applied for, and ordered to be allowed by the Judge Ordinary, at the time of such hearing or trial.

See also Rule 201.

RULES, ETC. OF THE ENGLISH COURT OF DIVORCE.

Summonses.

App. (G).

160. A summons may be taken out by any person in any matter or suit depending in the Court for Divorce and Matrimonial Causes, provided there is no rule or practice requiring a different mode of proceeding.

161. The name of the cause or matter, and of the agent taking out the summons, is to be entered in the summons book, and a true copy of the summons is to be served on the party summoned one clear day at least before the summons is returnable, and before 7 o'clock p.m. On Saturdays the copy of the summons is to be served before 2 o'clock p.m.

162. On the day and at the hour named in the summons the party taking out the same is to present himself with the original summons at the judge's chambers, or elsewhere appointed for hearing the same.

163. Both parties will be heard by the Judge Ordinary, who will make such order as he may think fit, and a minute of such order will be made by one of the registrars in the summons book.

See also Rules 181 to 184.

164. If the party summoned do not appear after the lapse of half an hour from the time named in the summons, the party taking out the summons shall be at liberty to go before the Judge Ordinary, who will thereupon make such order as he may think fit.

165. An attendance on behalf of the party summoned for the space of half an hour, if the party taking out the summons do not during such time appear, will be deemed sufficient, and bar the party taking out the summons from the right to go before the Judge Ordinary on that occasion.

166. If a formal order is desired, the same may be had on the application of either party, and for that purpose the original summons, or the copy served on the party summoned, must be filed in the registry. An order will thereupon be drawn up, and delivered to the person filing such summons or copy.

167. If a summons is brought to the registry, with consent to an order indorsed thereon, signed by the party summoned, or by his proctor, solicitor, or attorney, an order will be drawn up without the necessity of going before the Judge Ordinary; provided that the order sought is in the opinion of the registrar one which, under the circumstances, would be made by the Judge Ordinary.

168. The same rules and regulations shall, so far as applicable, be observed in respect to summonses which may be heard and disposed of by the registrars.

Payment of Money out of Court.

169. Persons applying for payment of money out of Court are to bring into the registry a notice in writing setting forth the day on which the money applied for was paid into the registry, the minute entered in the Court books on receiving the same, the date and particulars of the order for payment to the applicant. In case the money applied for be in payment of costs,

the notice must also set forth the date of filing the bill for taxation, and of the registrar's certificate.

170. The above notice must be deposited in the registry two clear days at least before the money is paid out, and is, in that interval, to be examined by one of the clerks of the registry with the original entries in the Court books, and the bills of costs referred to in it, and certified by such clerk to be correct.

171. When the Court is not sitting, payment of money out of Court will be made only on such day or days of the week as may be fixed by the registrars, notice whereof will be given in the registry.

Registries and Officers.

172. The registry of the Court for Divorce and Matrimonial Causes, and the clerks employed therein, shall be subject to and under the control of the registrars of the Principal Registry of the Court of Probate.

173. The record keepers, the sealer, and other officers of the Principal Registry of the Court of Probate, shall discharge the same or similar duties in the Court for Divorce and Matrimonial Causes, and in the registry thereof, as they discharge in the Court of Probate and the Principal Registry thereof.

Proceedings under "The Legitimacy Declaration Act, 1858."

174. The above rules and regulations so far as the same may be applicable, shall extend to applications and proceedings under "The Legitimacy Declaration Act, 1858."

ADDITIONAL RULES—30TH JANUARY, 1869.

Restitution of Conjugal Rights.

175. The affidavit filed with the petition, as required by Rule 2, shall further state sufficient facts to satisfy one of the registrars that a written demand for cohabitation and restitution of conjugal rights has been made by the petitioner upon the party to be cited, and that after a reasonable opportunity for compliance therewith, such cohabitation and restitution of conjugal rights have been withheld.

176. At any time after the commencement of proceedings for restitution of conjugal rights the respondent may apply by summons to the judge, or to the registrars in his absence, for an order to stay the proceedings in the cause by reason that he or she is willing to resume or to return to cohabitation with the petitioner.

As to Costs.

177. In all cases in which the Court at the hearing of a cause condemns any party to the suit in costs, the proctor, solicitor, or attorney of the party to whom such costs are to be paid may

RULES, ETC. OF THE ENGLISH COURT OF DIVORCE. . 405

forthwith file his bill of costs in the registry, and obtain an **App. (G).**
appointment for the taxation, provided that such taxation shall
not take place before the time allowed for moving for a new
trial or re-hearing shall have expired; or, in case a rule *nisi*
should have been granted, until the rule is disposed of, unless
the Judge Ordinary shall, for cause shown, direct a more speedy
taxation.

178. Upon the registrar's certificate of costs being signed, he
shall at once issue an order of the Court for payment of the
amount within seven days.

See also Rules from 151 to 158, and 201.

179. This order shall be served on the proctor, solicitor, or
attorney of the party liable, [or if it is desired to enforce the
order by attachment, on the party himself,] and if the costs be
not paid within the seven days a writ of *fieri facias* or writ of
sequestration shall be issued as of course in the registry, upon
an affidavit of service of the order and nonpayment.

See also Rules 110, 111, and 203.

As to Subpœnas.

180. The issuing of fresh subpœnas in each term shall be
abolished, and it shall not be necessary to serve more than one
subpœna upon any witness.

DEBTORS ACT, 1869.

ADDITIONAL RULE—15TH FEBRUARY, 1870.

180A. In pursuance of "The Debtors Act, 1869," it is ordered
that, on and after this date, the following rules shall be in force
for regulating the practice under and carrying into effect the
first part of the said "Debtors Act, 1869."

1. All applications to commit to prison under sect. 5 shall,
in the first instance, be made by summons before the Judge
Ordinary, which shall specify the date and other particulars of
the order for nonpayment of which the application is made,
together with the amount due, and be indorsed with the name
and place of abode or office of business of the proctor or attorney
actually suing out the summons, and in case such attorney shall
not be an attorney of this Court, then also with the name and
place of abode or office of business of the attorney in whose name
such summons shall be taken out, and when the attorney
actually suing out such summons shall sue out the same as
agent for an attorney in the country, the name and place of
abode of such attorney in the country shall also be indorsed
upon the said summons, and in case no attorney shall be employed to issue the summons then it shall be endorsed with a
memorandum expressing that the same has been sued out by
the petitioner or respondent or co-respondent in person, as the
case may be, mentioning the city, town, or parish, and also the

name of the hamlet, street, and number of the house of such petitioner's, respondent's, or co-respondent's residence, if any such there be.

2. The service of the summons, whenever it may be practicable, shall be personal; but if it appear to the Judge Ordinary that reasonable efforts have been made to effect personal service, and either that the summons has come to the knowledge of the debtor, or that he wilfully evades service, an order may be made as if personal service had been effected upon such terms as to the Judge Ordinary may seem fit.

3. Proof of the means of the debtor shall, whenever practicable, be given by affidavit; but if it appear to the Judge Ordinary either before or at the hearing that a *vivâ voce* examination, either of the debtor or of any other person, or the production of any document, is necessary or expedient, an order may be made commanding the attendance of any such person before the Judge Ordinary at a time and place to be therein mentioned for the purpose of being examined on oath touching the matter in question (or and) for the production of any such document, subject to such terms and conditions as to the Judge Ordinary may seem fit. The disobedience to any such order shall be deemed a contempt of Court, and punishable accordingly.

4. The order of committal (which may be in the Form A. in the Appendix, or to the like effect) shall before delivery to the sheriff be indorsed with the particulars required by Rule 1 of these Rules. Concurrent orders may be issued for execution in different counties. The sheriff shall be entitled to the same fees in respect thereof as are now payable upon a *ca. sa.*

5. Upon payment of the sum or sums mentioned in the order (including the sheriff's fees in like manner as upon a *ca. sa.*) the debtor shall be entitled to a certificate in the Form B. in the Appendix, or to the like effect, signed by the proctor or attorney in the cause, of the petitioner, respondent, or co-respondent, as the case may be, or signed by the petitioner, respondent, or co-respondent, as the case may be, and attested by an attorney or justice of the peace.

6. The sheriff or other officer named in an order of committal shall within two days after the arrest indorse on the order the true date of such arrest.

Additional and Amended Rules—23rd February, 1875.

181. All summonses heretofore heard by the registrars of the Principal Registry of the Court of Probate in the absence of the Judge Ordinary shall hereafter be heard before one or more of the registrars at the Principal Registry of that Court during the period appointed for the sittings of the Court at Westminster, as well as in the judge's absence.

182. All rules and regulations in respect to summonses now

RULES, ETC. OF THE ENGLISH COURT OF DIVORCE.

heard before the Judge Ordinary in chambers at Westminster shall, so far as the same are applicable, be observed in respect of the summonses heard before one or more of the registrars at the principal registry.

App. (G).

See Rules from 160 to 168.

183. The registrar before whom the summons is heard will direct such order to issue as he shall think fit, or refer the matter at once to the Judge Ordinary.

184. Any person heard on the summons objecting to the order so issued under the direction of the registrars may, subject to any order as to costs, apply to the Judge Ordinary on summons to rescind or vary the same.

ADDITIONAL RULES.—14TH JULY, 1875.

Appearance.

185. Application for leave to enter an appearance after a proceeding has been taken in default heretofore made to the Judge Ordinary on motion in pursuance of Rule 20 shall hereafter be made by summons before one of the registrars.

See also Rule 20.

Answer.

186. In case the time allowed for entry of appearance to a citation should be more than eight days after service thereof, a respondent who has entered an appearance may, within fourteen days from the expiration of the time allowed for the entry of appearance, file in the registry an answer to the petition.

See also Rule 28.

General Rule as to Pleadings.

187. Either of the parties before the Court desiring to alter or amend a pleading may apply by summons to one of the registrars for an order for that purpose.

See also Rule 34.

Evidence taken by Affidavit.

188. In an undefended cause when directions have been given that all or any of the facts set forth in the petition be proved by affidavits, such affidavits may be filed in the registry at any time up to ten clear days before the cause is heard.

See also Rule 51.

Alimony.

189. Application for an order for a further and fuller answer to a petition for alimony, heretofore made to the Judge Ordinary on motion in pursuance of Rule 86, shall hereafter be made by summons before one of the registrars.

See Rule 86.

190. A wife who has obtained a final decree of judicial separation, on such decree being affirmed on appeal, or after the expiration of the time for appealing against the decree if no appeal be then pending, may apply to the Court by petition for an allotment of permanent alimony, though no alimony shall have been allotted to her pending suit, and the Rules from 84 to 88, both inclusive, of the rules and regulations for this Court, bearing date 26th December, 1865, relating to petitions for alimony pending suit as varied by these and other additional rules and regulations shall, so far as the same are applicable, be observed in respect to the proceedings upon such petitions for permanent alimony.

See also Rules 84 to 88, and 91 and 92.

191. All applications for an allotment of alimony pending suit, and for an allotment of permanent alimony heretofore made to the Court by motion in pursuance of Rules 89 and 91, shall hereafter be referred to one of the registrars at the principal registry, who shall investigate the averments in the petition for alimony, answer, and reply, in the presence of the parties, their proctors, solicitors, or attorneys, and who, if he think fit, shall be at liberty to require the attendance of the husband for the purpose of being examined or cross-examined, and to take the oral evidence of witnesses, and to require the production of any documents or to call for affidavits, and shall direct such order to issue as he shall think fit, or refer the application, or any question arising out of it, to the Judge Ordinary for his decision.

See Rules 89 and 91.

192. Any person heard on the reference as to alimony before one of the registrars, objecting to the order issued under his direction, may (subject to any order as to costs) apply to the Judge Ordinary on summons to rescind or vary the same.

Dismissal of Petition.

193. When an order has been made for the dismissal of a petition on payment of costs, the cause will not be removed from the list of causes in the Court books without an order of one of the registrars, to obtain which it must be shown to his satisfaction the costs have been paid.

Decree Absolute.

194. In case application by motion to make absolute a decree *nisi* for the dissolution of a marriage should from any cause be deferred beyond six days from the time when the affidavit required by Rule 80 is filed with the case for motion, it must be shown by further affidavit that search has been made in the proper books up to within six clear days of the motion for decree absolute being heard, and that at such time no person had obtained leave to intervene, and that no appearance had been entered nor any affidavits filed on behalf of any person wishing to show cause against the decree *nisi* being made absolute; and in case leave to intervene had been obtained, or appearance entered or affidavits filed on behalf of any such person, it must

RULES, ETC. OF THE ENGLISH COURT OF DIVORCE. 409

also be shown by such further affidavit what proceedings, if **App. (G)**. any, have been taken thereon.
See also Rules 80 and 207.

Custody, Maintenance, and Education of Children.

195. Rules from 97 to 102, both inclusive, of the rules and regulations for this Court, bearing date 26th December, 1865, shall, so far as the same are applicable, be observed in respect to applications by petition, after a final decree in a cause for orders and provision with respect to the custody, maintenance, and education of children, the marriage of whose parents was the subject of the decree under the authority given to the Court by 22 & 23 Vict. c. 61, s. 4.
See Rules 97 to 102.

Persons of Unsound Mind.

196. A committee duly appointed of a person found by inquisition to be of unsound mind may take out a citation and prosecute a suit on behalf of such person as a petitioner, or enter an appearance, intervene, or proceed with the defence on behalf of such person as a respondent; but if no committee should have been appointed, application is to be made to one of the registrars, who will assign a guardian to the person of unsound mind, for the purpose of prosecuting, intervening in, or defending the suit on his or her behalf; provided that if the opposite party is already before the Court when the application for the assignment of a guardian is made he or she shall be served with notice by summons of such application.

Protection Orders.

197. In the affidavit in support of an application on the part of a wife deserted by her husband for an order to protect her earnings and property acquired since the commencement of such desertion, the applicant must state whether she has any knowledge of the residence of her husband, and if he is known to be residing within the jurisdiction of the Court, he must be served personally with a summons to show cause why such order should not be made.
See also Rule 124.

Commission and Requisitions for Examination of Witnesses.

198. The registrar to whom a commission or requisition for examination of witnesses is referred for settlement, on application on behalf of the wife, may proceed at once and without summons to ascertain what is a sufficient sum of money to be paid or secured to her to cover her expenses in attending at the examination of such witnesses, and shall thereupon issue an order upon the husband to pay or secure the said sum within a time to be fixed in such order.
See also Rule 137.

Appendix (G).

Costs.

199. The bond taken to secure the costs of a wife of and incidental to the hearing of a cause shall be filed in the registry of the Court of Probate, and shall not be delivered out or be sued upon without the order of the Court.

200. If more than one sixth of the amount of any bill of costs taxed as between practitioner and client is disallowed on taxation thereof, the party on whose application the bill is taxed shall be at liberty to deduct the costs incurred by him in the taxation from the amount of the bill as taxed, if so much remains due, otherwise the same shall be paid by the practitioner to the person on whose application the bill is taxed.

See also Rule 156.

201. The order for payment of costs of suit in which a respondent or co-respondent has been condemned by a decree *nisi* shall, if applied for before the decree *nisi* is made absolute, direct the payment thereof into the registry of the Court of Probate, and such costs shall not be paid out of the said registry to the party entitled to receive them under the decree *nisi* until the decree absolute has been obtained; but a wife who is unsuccessful in a cause, and who at the hearing of the cause has, in pursuance of Rule 159, obtained an order of the Judge Ordinary that her costs of and incidental to the hearing or trial of the cause shall be allowed against her husband to the extent of the sum paid or secured by him to cover such costs, may nevertheless proceed at once to obtain payment of such costs after allowance thereof on taxation.

See also Rules 157, 178, and 179.

Additional Rules.—17th April, 1877.

Showing Cause against a Decree Nisi.

202. When the Queen's Proctor desires to show cause against making absolute a decree *nisi* for dissolution or nullity of marriage, he shall enter an appearance in the cause in which such decree *nisi* has been pronounced, and shall within fourteen days after entering appearance file his plea in the registry, setting forth the grounds upon which he desires to show cause as aforesaid, and on the day he files his plea in the registry, shall deliver a copy thereof to the person in whose favour such decree has been pronounced, or to his or her solicitor, and all subsequent pleadings and proceedings in respect to such plea shall be filed and carried on in the same manner as directed by the existing Rules and Regulations Nos. 68 and 69, in regard to the plea of the Queen's Proctor, filed after obtaining leave to intervene in a cause, and the existing Rules and Regulations from No. 70 to No. 76, both inclusive, shall no longer be applicable to the Queen's Proctor on his showing cause as aforesaid, save as far as regards any proceedings already commenced in pursuance of the said Rules and Regulations.

See Rules 68 and 69.

RULES, ETC. OF THE ENGLISH COURT OF DIVORCE.

Writs of Fieri Facias and other Writs.   App. (G).

203. In default of payment of any sum of money at the time appointed by any order of the Court for the payment thereof, a writ of *fieri facias* or writ of sequestration or writ of *elegit* shall be issued as of course in the registry upon an affidavit of service of the order and nonpayment.

See also Rules 110, 111, and 179.

Maintenance and Settlements.

204. The registrar to whom pleadings are referred for investigation under Rule 101 shall, if he thinks fit, be at liberty to require the attendance of the husband or wife for the purpose of being examined or cross-examined, and to take the oral evidence of witnesses in the same manner as on a reference for an allotment of alimony.

See Rule 101.

ADDITIONAL AND AMENDED RULES.—JULY, 1880.

Mode of Hearing or Trial.

205. It shall not be necessary in any case to apply to the Court by motion for directions as to the mode of hearing or trial of a cause. When the pleadings are concluded the parties to a cause may proceed in all respects as though upon the day of filing the last pleading a special direction had been given by the Court as to the mode of hearing or trial to the effect following:

1st. In cases in which damages are not claimed that the cause be heard by oral evidence before the Court itself, without a jury.

2nd. In cases in which damages are claimed that the cause be tried before the Court with a common jury.

And any party to a cause may apply by summons for a direction that the cause may be heard or tried otherwise than is hereby provided.

See Rules 40 and 45.

206. Before a cause is set down for hearing or trial the pleadings and proceedings in the cause shall be referred to one of the registrars, who shall certify that the same are correct and in order, and the registrar to whom the same are referred shall cause any irregularity in such pleadings or proceedings to be corrected, or refer any question arising therefrom to the Court for its direction; any party to the cause objecting to such direction of the registrar may (subject to any order as to costs) apply to the Court on summons to rescind or vary the same.

Decree Absolute.

207. Application to make absolute a decree *nisi* for dissolution or nullity of a marriage need not hereafter be made to the Court by motion as directed by Rules 80 and 194, but it shall be a sufficient compliance with the said rules to file in the registry,

with the affidavit or affidavits therein required, a notice in writing setting forth that application is made for such decree absolute, which will thereupon be pronounced in open Court at a time appointed for that purpose.

See Rules 80 and 194.

Suits in Formâ Pauperis.

208. Applications for leave to prosecute or defend a suit *in formâ pauperis* may hereafter be made to one of the registrars, who will make such order thereon as he may see fit or refer the application to the Court.

209. The affidavit required by Rule 26, if application is made by a wife to prosecute a suit against her husband *in formâ pauperis*, shall state to the best of her knowledge and belief the amount of income or means of living of her husband.

See also Rules 25 and 26.

210. When a husband has been admitted to prosecute a suit against his wife *in formâ pauperis*, the wife may apply for an order that she be at liberty to proceed with her defence *in formâ pauperis* on production of an affidavit that she has no separate property exceeding 25*l*. in value after payment of her just debts.

211. When a wife has been permitted to prosecute a suit against her husband *in formâ pauperis*, the husband may apply for leave to proceed with his defence *in formâ pauperis* on production of an affidavit as to his income or means of living, and showing that besides his wearing apparel he is not worth 25*l*. after payment of his just debts.

Access to Children.

212. Application on behalf of a husband or wife, parties to a cause, for access to the children of their marriage may hereafter be made by summons before one of the registrars, who shall direct such order to issue as he thinks fit, subject to appeal to the Court by either party dissatisfied with the order as authorised by Rule 184.

See also Rules 104 and 184.

The Greek Marriages Act, 1884.

213. In pursuance of the provisions of the Act of Parliament 47 & 48 Vict. c. 20, s. 1, whereby it was enacted that any petition to the Probate and Matrimonial Division of Her Majesty's High Court of Justice under the said Act should be accompanied by such affidavit verifying the same as the said Court might from time to time direct:

Now, I, the Right Honourable Sir James Hannen, Knight, the President of the said Division, do hereby direct that the affidavits verifying a petition under the said Act shall be in the form and to the effect required by Rule 2 of the Rules and Regulations for Her Majesty's Court for Divorce and Matrimonial Causes, bearing date 26th December, 1865.

(*Signed*) JAMES HANNEN.

Dated 6th August, 1884.

APPENDIX.

Forms *which are to be followed as nearly as the circumstances of each case will allow.*

No. 1.—*Petition.*

In the High Court of Justice.
    Probate, Divorce, and Admiralty Division.
        (Divorce.)
    To the Right Honourable the President of the said Division.
                The   day of   , 18 .

The petition of *A. B.*, of   , showeth,—

1. That your petitioner was on the   day of   , 18 , lawfully married to *C. B.*, then *C. D.* [spinster *or* widow] at the *parish church of*, &c.
    [*Here state where the marriage took place.*]
2. That after his said marriage your petitioner lived and cohabited with his said wife at   and at   , and that your petitioner and his said wife have had issue of their said marriage   children; to wit:
    [*Here state the names and ages of the children issue of the marriage.*]
3. That on the   day of   , 18 , and on other days between that day and   , the said *C. B.*, at   in the county of   , committed adultery with *R. S.*:
4. That in and during the months of January, February, and March, 18 , the said *R. S.* frequently visited the said *C. D.* at   , and on divers of such occasions committed adultery with the said *C. D.*

Your petitioner therefore humbly prays,—
    That your Lordship will be pleased to decree:
        [*Here set out the relief sought.*]
    And that your petitioner may have such further and other relief in the premises as to your Lordship may seem meet.
                [*Petitioner's Signature.*]

No. 2.—Citation.

In the High Court of Justice.
    Probate, Divorce, and Admiralty Division.
        (Divorce.)

VICTORIA, by the grace of God, of the United Kingdom of Great Britain and Ireland Queen, Defender of the Faith.

                To C. B., of   in the county of   .

WHEREAS A. B., of, &c., claiming to have been lawfully married to   has filed   petition against   in the Divorce Registry of our said Court, praying   wherein alleges that you have been guilty of adultery [*or* have been guilty of cruelty towards   the said   *or as the case may be*]: NOW THIS IS TO COMMAND YOU, that within eight days after service hereof on you, inclusive of the day of such service, you do appear in our said Court then and there to make answer to the said petition, a copy whereof, sealed with the seal of our said Court, is herewith served upon you. AND TAKE NOTICE, that in default of your so doing, our said Court will proceed to hear the said charge [*or* charges] proved in due course of law, and to pronounce sentence therein, your absence notwithstanding. And take further notice, that for the purpose aforesaid you are to attend in person, or by your solicitor, at the Divorce Registry of our said Court at Somerset House, Strand, in the county of Middlesex, and there to enter an appearance in a book provided for that purpose, without which you will not be allowed to address the Court, either in person or by counsel, at any stage of the proceedings in the cause.

    Dated at London the   day of   18 , and in the year of our reign.

                                  (L.S.)
                (Signed)   X. Y., Registrar.

No. 3.—*Præcipe for Citation.*

In the High Court of Justice.
    Probate, Divorce, and Admiralty Division.
        (Divorce.)

    Citation for A. B., of   , against C. B., of   , to appear in a suit for   by reason of   .

            (Signed)   A. B. in person,
                          or
                      C. D., solicitor, for the said A. B.

[*Here insert the address required within three miles of the General Post Office.*]

RULES, ETC. OF THE ENGLISH COURT OF DIVORCE.

No. 4.—*Certificate of Service.* App. (G).

This citation was duly served by the undersigned *G. H.* on the within-named *C. B.* of   at   on the   day of   18 .

(Signed)   *G. H.*

No. 5.—*Affidavit of Service of Citation.*

In the High Court of Justice.
    Probate, Divorce, and Admiralty Division.
        (Divorce.)
            A. B. against *C. B.* and *E. F.*

I, *C. D.* of, &c., make oath and say,—
    That the citation, bearing date the   day of   18   issued under seal of this Court against *C. B.* the respondent [*or R. S.* the co-respondent] in this cause, and now hereunto annexed, marked with the letter A, was duly served by me on the said *C. B.* (*or R. S.*) at   in the county of, &c., by showing to h   the original under seal, and by leaving with h   a true copy thereof, on the   day of   18 . And I further make oath and say that I did at the same time and place deliver to the said *C. B.* (*or R. S.*) personally a certified copy, under seal of this Court, of the petition filed in this cause.

Sworn at, &c. on the   day ⎫
   of   18 . Before me ⎬

No. 6.—*Entry of an Appearance.*

In the High Court of Justice.
    Probate, Divorce, and Admiralty Division.
        (Divorce.)

A. B., petitioner, ⎫ The respondent *C. B.* [*or* the co-respon-
    against   ⎬ dent *R. S.*] appears in person [*or C. D.*,
C. B., respondent, ⎬ the solicitor for *C. B.* the respondent
    and   ⎬ (*or R. S.* the co-respondent), appears for
R. S., co-respondent. ⎭ the said respondent *or* co-respondent].

[*Here insert the address required within three miles of the General Post Office.*]

Entered this   day of   18 .

No. 7.—*Answer.*

In the High Court of Justice.
    Probate, Divorce, and Admiralty Division.
        (Divorce.)
                    The   day of   18 .
                A. B. v. *C. B.*

The respondent *C. B.*, by *C. D.* her solicitor [*or* in person], in answer to the petition filed in this cause, saith,—

1. That she denies that she committed adultery with *R. S.* as set forth in the said petition:

2. Respondent further saith, that on the   day of 18   , and on other days between that day and   , the said *A. B.*, at   in the county of   , committed adultery with *K. L.*

    [*In like manner respondent is to state connivance, condonation, or other matters relied on as a ground for dismissing the petition.*]

Wherefore this respondent humbly prays,—
    That your Lordship will be pleased to reject the prayer of the said petition, and decree, &c.

No. 8.—*Questions of Fact for the Jury.*

In the High Court of Justice.
    Probate, Divorce, and Admiralty Division.
        (Divorce.)
            A. B. against *C. B.* and *R. S.*

Questions for the Jury.

1. Whether *C. B.*, the respondent, committed adultery with *R. S.*, the co-respondent.
2. Whether *A. B.*, the petitioner, has condoned the adultery (if any) committed by *C. B.*, the respondent.
3. Whether *A. B.*, the petitioner, has been guilty of cruelty towards *C. B.*, the respondent.
    [*Here set forth in the same form all the questions at issue between the parties.*]
4. What amount of damages should be paid by *R. S.*, the co-respondent, in respect of the adultery (if any) by him committed.

RULES, ETC. OF THE ENGLISH COURT OF DIVORCE. 417

No. 9.—*Act on Petition.* App. (G).

In the High Court of Justice.
    Probate, Divorce, and Admiralty Division.
        (Divorce.)
            A. B. against C. B. and R. S.
On the   day of   18 .

A. B., the petitioner [*or* C. D., the solicitor of A. B. the petitioner], alleged that   [*Here state briefly the facts and circumstances upon which the petition is founded.*]

Wherefore the said A. B., or C. D., referring to the affidavits and proofs to be by him exhibited in verification of what he so alleged, prayed that
    [*Here set forth the prayer of the petitioner.*]
                      (Signed)   A. B.
                                   or
                                   C. D.

Answer.

In the High Court of Justice.
    Probate, Divorce, and Admiralty Division.
        (Divorce.)
            A. B. against C. B. and R. S.
On the   day of   18 .

C. B., the respondent [*or* G. H., the solicitor of C. B. the respondent], in answer to the allegations in the act on petition, bearing date the   day of   18 of A. B., admitted [*or* denied*]* that
    [*Here set forth any allegations admitted or denied.*]
And he alleged that
    [*Here state any facts or circumstances in explanation or in answer.*]

Wherefore the said C. B., G. H., referring to the affidavits and proofs to be by her exhibited in verification of what she so alleged, prayed
    [*Here state the prayer of respondent.*]
                      (Signed)   C. B.
                                   or
                                   G. H.

Conclusion.

            A. B. against C. B. and R. S.
On the   day of   18 .

A. B., the petitioner [*or* C. D., the solicitor for A. B. the petitioner], in reply to the allegations of C. B. [*or* G. H.] in her answer, bearing date   denied the same in great part to be true or relevant. Wherefore he alleged and prayed as before.
                      (Signed)   A. B.
                                   or
                                   C. D.

No. 10.—*Petition for Reversal of Decree.*

In the High Court of Justice.
 Probate, Divorce, and Admiralty Division.
  (Divorce.)
To the Right Honourable the President of the said Division.
      The day of 18 .
The petition of A. B., of , showeth,—
1. That your petitioner was on the day of 18 lawfully married to C. B., then C. D. spinster [or widow], at the parish of, &c.
 [*Here state where the marriage took place.*]
2. That on the day of your Lordship, by your final decree, pronounced in a cause then depending in this Court, entitled C. B. against A. B., decreed as follows; to wit:
 [*Here set out the decree.*]
3. That the aforesaid decree was obtained in the absence of your petitioner, who was then residing at .
 [*State facts tending to show that the petitioner did not know of the proceedings; and further, that had he known of them he might have offered a sufficient defence.*]
      or
That there was reasonable ground for your petitioner leaving his said wife, for that his said wife
 [*Here state any legal grounds justifying the petitioner's separation from his wife.*]

Your petitioner therefore humbly prays,—
That your Lordship will be pleased to reverse the said decree.

No. 11.—*Appeal.*

I, A. B., the petitioner [or C. D., the solicitor of A. B., the petitioner], in a suit lately depending in the Probate, Divorce, and Admiralty Division of the High Court of Justice, entitled A. B. against C. D. and R. S., do hereby, in due time and place, complain of and appeal against a certain order or decree made in the said cause by the Right Honourable the President of the said Division on the day of 18 , whereby, amongst other things, the said President did order and decree [*here set forth the whole of the decree, or such part of it as may be appealed against*].

        (Signed) A. B.
          or
          C. D.

This instrument of appeal was lodged in the Divorce Registry of the Probate, Divorce, and Admiralty Division of the High Court of Justice this day of 188 .
To be signed by a clerk in the registry.

RULES, ETC. OF THE ENGLISH COURT OF DIVORCE. 419

No. 12.—*Affidavit in support of Application for Decree Absolute.*   App. (G).

In the High Court of Justice.
    Probate, Divorce, and Admiralty Division.
      (Divorce.)
            A. B. against C. B. and R. S.

I, C. D. of, &c., solicitor for A. B. the petitioner in this cause, make oath and say, that on the   day of   18 , I carefully searched the books kept in the divorce registry of this Court for the purpose of entering appearances, from and including the   day of   18 , the day of the date of the decree *nisi* made in this cause, to the   day of   18 , and that during such period no appearance has been entered in the said books by Her Majesty's Procurator General, or by or on behalf of any other person or persons whomsoever. And I further make oath and say, that I have also carefully searched the books kept in the said registry for entering the minutes of proceedings had in this cause from and including the said   day of   18 , to the   day of   18 , and that no leave has been obtained by Her Majesty's Procurator General, or by any other person or persons whomsoever, to intervene in this cause, and that no affidavit or affidavits, instruments, or other documents whatsoever, have been filed in this cause by Her Majesty's Procurator General or any other persons whomsoever during such period, or at any other period during the dependence of this cause, in opposition to the said decree *nisi* being made absolute.

Sworn at, &c., on the   day }
    of   18 . Before me }

No. 13.—*Petition for Alimony.*

To the Right Honourable the President of the Probate, Divorce, and Admiralty Division of the High Court of Justice.
         A. B. against C. B. and R. S.
The   day of   188 .
The petition of C. B., the lawful wife of A. B., showeth,—
1. That the said A. B. does now carry on and has for many years past carried on the business of a   at   , and from such business he derives the net annual income of £   :
2. That the said A. B. is now or lately was possessed of or entitled to   proprietary shares of the   Railway Company, amounting in value to £   , and yielding a clear annual dividend of £   :

E E 2

App. (G).

3. That the said *A. B.* is possessed of certain stock-in-trade in his said business of a   of the value of £   .
   [*In same manner state particulars of any other property which the husband may possess.*]

Your petitioner therefore humbly prays,—
That your Lordship will be pleased to decree her such sum or sums of money by way of alimony *pendente lite* [*or* permanent alimony] as to your Lordship shall seem meet.

No. 14.—*Election of a Guardian.*

By a petitioner.

Whereas a suit is about to be instituted in the Probate, Divorce, and Admiralty Division of our High Court of Justice on behalf of *A. B.* against *C. B.* (the wife of the said *A. B.*) and *R. S.* And whereas the said *A. B.* is now a minor of the age of   years and upwards, but under the age of twenty-one years, and therefore by law incapable of acting in his own name.

Now I the said *A. B.* do hereby make choice and elect *G. H.*, my natural and lawful father and next of kin, to be my curator or guardian for the purpose of instituting the said suit, and for the purpose of carrying on and prosecuting the same until a final decree shall be given and pronounced therein, or until I shall attain the age of twenty-one years, and I hereby appoint *C. D.*, of, &c., my solicitor to file or cause to be filed this my election for me in the divorce registry of the said Division.

In witness whereof I have hereunto set my hand and seal this   day of   in the year 18   .

(Signed)   *A. B.*   (L.S.)

Signed, sealed, and delivered by the within-named *A. B.* in the presence of   .
    One attesting witness.

By a respondent.

Whereas a citation bearing date the   day of   18   has issued under seal of the High Court of Justice, Probate, Divorce, and Admiralty Division, at the instance of *A. B.*, claiming to have been lawfully married to *C. B.*, citing the said *C. B.* to appear in the said Court, and then and there to make answer to a certain petition of the said *A. B.* filed in the divorce registry of the said Court. And whereas the said *C. B.* is now a minor of the age of   years and upwards, but under the age of twenty-one years, and therefore by law incapable of acting in her own name.

Now I the said *C. B.* do hereby make choice of and elect *G. H.*, my natural and lawful father and next of kin, to be my curator or guardian for the purpose of entering an appearance for me and on my behalf in the said Court, and for the purpose of making answer for me to the said petition, and of defending me in the said cause, and to abide for me in judgment until a final decree shall be given and pronounced therein, or until I shall attain the age of twenty-one years, and I hereby appoint, &c.

App. (G).

FORMS OF SUBPŒNAS IN ADDITIONAL RULES DATED 30TH JANUARY, 1869.

No. 15.—*Subpœna ad testificandum.*

VICTORIA, by the grace of God, of the United Kingdom of Great Britain and Ireland Queen, Defender of the Faith, to [*names of all witnesses included in the subpœna to be inserted*], greeting. We command you and every of you to be and appear in your proper persons before the Right Honourable Sir James Hannen, Knight, the President of the Probate, Divorce, and Admiralty Division of our High Court of Justice at Westminster, in our county of Middlesex, on   the   day of   18 , by half past ten of the clock in the forenoon of the same day, and so from day to day whenever the said Division of our said Court is sitting, until the cause or proceeding is heard, to testify the truth, according to your knowledge, in a certain cause now in our said Court before our said judge depending between *A. B.*, petitioner, and *C. B.*, respondent, and *R. S.*, co-respondent, on the part of the petitioner, *or* respondent, *or* co-respondent [*or as the case may be*], and on the aforesaid day, between the parties aforesaid to be heard. And this you or any of you shall by no means omit, under the penalty of each of you of 100*l.* Witness the Right Honourable Sir James Hannen, Knight, at our High Court of Justice, the   day of   18   in the   year of our reign.

(Signed)   *X. Y.*, registrar.

Subpœna issued by
  solicitor for the   .

N.B.—Notice will be given to you of the day on which your attendance will be required.

APPENDIX (G).

No. 16.—*Præcipe for Subpœna ad testificandum.*

In the High Court of Justice.
    Probate, Divorce, and Admiralty Division.
        (Divorce.)

Subpœna for [*insert witnesses' names*], to testify between *A. B.*, petitioner, *C. B.*, respondent, and *R. S.*, co-respondent, on the part of the petitioner [*or* respondent *or* co-respondent].

(Signed) $\left\{ \begin{array}{c} \underline{A.\ B.} \\ \underline{C.\ B.} \\ \underline{R.\ S.} \end{array} \right\}$ *or* { *P. A.*, petitioner's [*or* respondent's *or* co-respondent's] solicitor.

No. 17.—*Subpœna duces tecum.*

VICTORIA, by the grace of God of the United Kingdom of Great Britain and Ireland Queen, Defender of the Faith, to [*names of all parties included in the subpœna to be inserted*], greeting. We command you and every of you to be and appear in your proper persons before the Right Honourable Sir James Hannen, Knight, President of the Probate, Divorce, and Admiralty Division of our High Court of Justice at Westminster, in our county of Middlesex, on   the   day of   18   , by eleven of the clock in the forenoon of the same day, and so from day to day whenever the said division of our said Court is sitting until the cause or proceeding is heard, and also that you bring with you, and produce at the time and place aforesaid [*here describe shortly the deeds, letters, papers, &c. required to be produced*], then and there to testify and show all and singular those things which you or either of you know, or the said deed or instrument doth import, of and concerning a certain cause or proceeding now in the said Court before our said judge, depending between *A. B.*, petitioner, and *C. D.*, respondent, and *R. S.*, co-respondent, on the part of the petitioner [*or* the respondent *or* co-respondent, *as the case may be*], and on the aforesaid day between the parties aforesaid to be heard. And this you or any of you shall by no means omit under the penalty of each of you of 100*l*. Witness, The Right Honourable Sir James Hannen, Knight, President of the Probate, Divorce, and Admiralty Division of our High Court of Justice, the   day of   18   , in the   year of our reign.

                              (Signed)   *X. Y.*, Registrar.

Subpœna issued by   solicitor for the   .

N.B.—Notice will be given to you of the day on which your attendance will be required.

App. (G).

No. 18.—*Præcipe for Subpœna duces tecum.*

In the High Court of Justice.
    Probate, Divorce, and Admiralty Division.
       (Divorce.)

Subpœna for   to testify and produce, &c. between *A. B.*, petitioner, *C. D.*, respondent, and *R. S.*, co-respondent, on the part of the petitioner [*or* respondent *or* co-respondent].

(Signed) $\left\{\begin{array}{c}\underline{A.\ B.}\\ \underline{C.\ B.}\\ \underline{R.\ S.}\end{array}\right\}$ *or* $\left\{\begin{array}{l}P.\ A.,\text{ petitioner's [}or\text{ respondent's}\\ or\text{ co-respondent's] solicitor.}\end{array}\right.$

No. 19.—*Application for a Protection Order.*

To the Right Honourable the President of the Probate, Divorce, and Admiralty Division of the High Court of Justice.

The application of *C. B.*, of   , the lawful wife of *A. B.*, showeth,—

That on the   day of   she was lawfully married to *A. B.* at   :

That she lived and cohabited with the said *A. B.* for   years at   , and also at   , and hath had   children, issue of her said marriage, of whom   are now living with the applicant, and wholly dependent upon her earnings:

That on or about   the said *A. B.*, without any reasonable cause, deserted the applicant, and hath ever since remained separate and apart from her:

That since the desertion of her said husband the applicant hath maintained herself by her own industry, and hath thereby and otherwise acquired certain property [*or* hath become possessed of certain property], consisting of [*here state generally the nature of the property*].

Wherefore the said *C. B.* prays an order for the protection of her earnings and property acquired since the said   day of   , from the said *A. B.*, and from all creditors and persons claiming under him.

                              (Signed)   *C. B.*

No. 20.—*Commission or Requisition for Examination of Witnesses.*

In the High Court of Justice.
   Probate, Divorce, and Admiralty Division.
            (Divorce.)

VICTORIA, by the grace of God of the United Kingdom of Great Britain and Ireland Queen, Defender of the Faith, to [*here set forth the name and proper description of the Commissioner*], greeting. Whereas a certain cause is now depending in the Probate, Divorce, and Admiralty Division of our High Court of Justice between *A. B.*, petitioner, and *C. B.*, respondent, and *R. S.*, co-respondent, wherein the said *A. B.* has filed his petition praying for a dissolution of his marriage with the said *C. B.* [*or otherwise as in the prayer of the petition*]. And whereas by an order made in the said cause on the   day of   18 , on the application of the said *A. B.* it was ordered that a commission [*or* requisition] should issue under seal of our said Court for the examination of [*here insert name and address of one of the persons to be examined*] and others as witnesses to be produced on the part of the said *A. B.*, the petitioner, in support of his said petition (saving all just exceptions). Now know ye that we do by virtue of this commission [*or* requisition] to you directed, authorize [*or* request] you within thirty days after the receipt of this commission [*or* requisition] at a certain time and place to be by you appointed for that purpose with power of adjournment to such other time and place as to you shall seem convenient to cause the said witnesses to come before you and to administer to the said witnesses respectively an oath truly to answer such questions as shall be put to them touching the matters set forth in the said petition (a true and authentic copy whereof sealed with the seal of our said Court is hereunto annexed), and such oath being administered we do hereby authorize [*or* request] and empower you to take the examination of the said witnesses touching the matters set forth in the said petition, and to reduce the said examination or cause the same to be reduced into writing. And that for the purpose aforesaid you do assume to yourself some notary public or other lawful scribe as and for your actuary in that behalf if to you it should seem meet and convenient so to do. And the said examination being so taken and reduced into writing as aforesaid, and subscribed by you, we do require [*or* request] you forthwith to transmit the said examination, closely sealed up, to the divorce registry of our said Court at Somerset House, Strand, in the county of Middlesex, together with these presents. And we do hereby give you full power and authority to do all such acts, matters, and things as may be necessary, lawful, and expedient for the due execution of this our commission [*or* requisition].

Dated at London the   day of   in the year of our Lord one thousand eight hundred and   , and in the   year of our reign.

                              (Signed)   *X. Y.*, Registrar.

App. (G).

No. 21.—*Bond for securing Wife's Costs in Amended Rules dated 14th July, 1875.*

KNOW all men by these presents, that we, A. B. of, &c., G. H. of, &c., and K. L. of, &c., are held and firmly bound unto X. Y. of   , the proctor or solicitor for   , of   , in the penal sum of   pounds of good and lawful money of Great Britain, to be paid to the said X. Y., and for which payment to be well and truly made we bind ourselves and each of us for the whole, our heirs, executors, or administrators, firmly by these presents. Sealed with our seals.

Dated the   day of   in the year of our Lord 18 .

Whereas a certain cause is now depending in the Probate, Divorce, and Admiralty Division of the High Court of Justice between the said A. B., petitioner of the one part, and the said C. D., respondent, and R. S., co-respondent, of the other part. And whereas by an order made in the said cause, it was ordered that the said A. B., the petitioner [or the said C. D., the respondent], should within   days from the service thereof pay or cause to be paid into the divorce registry of the said Division the sum of   pounds to cover the costs of the said respondent [or petitioner] of and incidental to the hearing of the said cause or file in the said registry a bond under the hand and seal of the said A. B., and of two sufficient sureties in the penal sum of   pounds, conditioned for the payment of such costs of the said C. D., as shall be certified to be due and payable by the said A. B., not exceeding the sum of   pounds as security for the costs aforesaid. Now the condition of this obligation is such that if the above-bounden A. B., his heirs, executors, or administrators, shall well and truly pay or cause to be paid to the above-named X. Y., his heirs, executors, administrators, or assigns, the full sum of   of good and lawful money of Great Britain, or the lawful costs of the said C. D., the respondent [or petitioner], of and incidental to the hearing and trial of this cause to the extent of   pounds, then this obligation is to be void and of none effect, otherwise to remain in full force and virtue.

Sealed and delivered by the said   A. B.   (L.S.)
A. B., G. H., and K. L., in the   G. H.   (L.S.)
presence of   .   K. L.   (L.S.)
  One attesting witness.

Forms A. and B. annexed to Additional Rule, 15th February, 1870.

A.

Upon hearing, &c. [*christian and surname of the debtor and party claiming*] I do order, That the said *A. B.* be for default of payment of the debt hereinafter mentioned committed to prison for the term of   weeks from the date of his arrest, including the day of such date, or until he shall pay £   , being the amount of [*here state the particulars of the debt or liability*], and which the said *A. B.* was on the   day of   ordered by the Court for Divorce and Matrimonial Causes to pay to the said   [*or*, into the registry of the said Court], together with £   for costs of this order, and sheriff's fees for the execution thereof, and I order that the sheriff of   do take the said *A. B.* for the purpose aforesaid, if he shall be found within his bailiwick.

Dated, &c.

B.

I certify, That *A. B.*, now in the gaol of   upon an order of the Judge Ordinary of Her Majesty's Court for Divorce and Matrimonial Causes, at the suit of *C. D.* for non-payment of a debt of   has satisfied the said debt, together with the costs mentioned in the said order.

Dated, &c.
          E. F., of, &c.,
      Proctor *or* Attorney for the said *C. D.*,
           or
         C. D., of, &c.

Witness to the signature of *C. D.*,
   G. H., his Attorney,
     or
  I. K., Justice of the Peace for

INDEX.

ABANDONMENT. See *Desertion*.

ABATEMENT OF SUIT,
    death of petitioner or respondent, 38, 113.
    decree *nisi* does not terminate suit, 112.
    reconciliation of parties, 120, 121, 126.

ABSENCE,
    of respondent from India at time of suit, 6, 7.
    decree of judicial separation obtained during absence of husband or wife may be reversed, 164, 165, 347.
    of either party at hearing, 352, 353.

ABSOLUTE, DECREE. See *Decree Absolute*.

ABSOLUTE, MAKING DECREE NISI,
    when decree *nisi* to be made absolute, 110, 113, 114.
    who may apply, 114.
    application to be supported by affidavit, 114.
    notice to respondent, 115.
    application to be made within reasonable time, 111, 115.

ACCESS TO CHILDREN,
    pending suit, 273, 274.
    after decree, 279, 280.

"ACCESSORY TO THE ADULTERY,"
    meaning of, 73.
    adultery brought about by petitioner's agent, 73, 74, 106, 107.

ACTION, RIGHT OF,
    to wife when judicially separated, 161.
    to wife having protection order, 171.

ADJOURNMENT OF PROCEEDINGS, power of Court to adjourn proceedings, 297—300.

ADMISSIONS,
    decree of dissolution should not be made merely on parties,' 91.
    of adultery by wife, evidence only against herself, 333, 334.

ADULTERER,
   alleged adulterer should be made co-respondent, 68—73.
   counter-charge of adultery, right of alleged adulterer to intervene, 70, 108.
   claim of damages against, 187—199.
   petition to be served upon alleged, 187.
   when liable for costs of proceedings, 199, 376—381.
   when allowed costs despite his adultery, 381.

ADULTERESS, no provision in act for making alleged adulteress co-respondent, 68, 69.

ADULTERY,
   as ground for dissolution of marriage, 35.
   incestuous, 19, 23.
   bigamy with, 19, 23.
   committed by petitioner, disentitles to relief, 93, 94, 153, 184.
   condonation of petitioner's, 95, 153.
   committed by petitioner in ignorance of fact or law, 96, 97.
   committed by wife under compulsion, 97.
   isolated act, long since condoned, 98, 99.
   condonation of. See *Condonation*.
   of respondent brought about by petitioner's agent, 106, 107.
   committed by petitioner after decree *nisi*, 119.
   petitioner accessory to, or conniving at respondent's, 73—78.
   petitioner's, no bar to relief in suits for nullity, 135.
   as ground for judicial separation, 150.
   permanent maintenance for wife guilty of, 217, 231.
   wife guilty of, entitled to alimony *pendente lite*, 204.
   party guilty of, will not ordinarily be given custody of children, 277.
   damages against adulterer in respect of, 187 *et seq.*
   wife's power of Court to order settlement of her property, 241—246.
   wife guilty of, not necessarily deprived of her costs, 371—374.
   evidence of, 332—336.
   pleading, 343—345.

AFFIDAVITS,
   on motion to dispense with making adulterer co-respondent, 70, 71.
   when parties may verify their case by, 91, 92, 291, 294, 295.
   application to make decree *nisi* absolute to be supported by, 114.
   petition by deserted wife for protection order to be supported by, 168.
   by wife as to husband's means for purposes of alimony *pendente lite*, 211.

AFFINITY,
   what is, 19, 139.
   not constituted by mere carnal intercourse without marriage, 139.

AFFINITY—*continued.*
  affinity within prohibited degrees is ground for decree of nullity, 128.

AGE,
  no rule as to age of petitioner constituting bar to suit for nullity by reason of impotency, 130.
  of majority, for purposes of Chap. XI. of Act, 19, 23.
  　　　　　　　 for purposes of suing or being sued under Divorce Act, 285.

AGENTS,
  collusion between parties' agents, 88.
  respondent's adultery brought about by petitioner's agents, 73, 74, 106, 107.

ALIMONY, PENDING SUIT,
  when wife may apply for, 200.
  in suits for nullity, 201.
  in suits for dissolution of marriage, 201.
  in suits for judicial separation, 202.
  in suits for restitution of conjugal rights, 175, 202.
  payable from date of service of citation till final decree, 203.
  pending appeal, 203.
  pending application for review of judgment, 203, 204.
  wife to be considered innocent, 204.
  protection order does not disentitle wife to, 173, 200.
  wife supported by co-respondent, 205, 206.
  wife undergoing sentence of imprisonment, 205.
  plea by husband as to jurisdiction of Court, 32, 205.
  considerations for Court when allotting, 205.
  wife having independent means, 206.
  wife's means derived from co-respondent, 206.
  when both parties nearly penniless, 206.
  conduct of wife as affecting her right to, 206.
  wife receiving allowance from husband, 207.
  husband's average nett income, 207, 208.
  husband should state his *gross* income, 207.
  all valuable property to be taken into consideration, 208.
  mortgaged property, 208.
  deductions claimable by husband, 208, 209.
  expenses of maintaining children, 209.
  joint income of husband and wife, 209.
  increase or reduction of amount allotted, 209, 210.
  husband excused from paying, instances, 210, 211.
  husband's income derived from voluntary allowance, 211.
  practice of Court as regards, 211, 212.
  affidavit by wife as to husband's income, 211.
  right of wife to subpœna husband, 212.
  injunction to restrain husband dissipating his property, 212.
  arrears of alimony not provable in bankruptcy, 213.
  wife's promise to forego right to, 213.
  when co-respondent is liable for costs of proceedings to obtain, 213.

ALIMONY, PERMANENT,
    power of Court to order, 213—241.
    how payable, 213.
    order for, when to be made, 215—217.
    after decree of judicial separation, 217, 218.
    husband not complying with order to pay after decree of judicial separation, 162.
    no power to order, after decree for restitution of conjugal rights, 217.
    order of district judge, when to be made, 218.
    how secured, 218, 219.
    charging order on husband's property, 219.
    injunction to restrain husband from dissipating his property, 220.
    various forms of, 220, 221.
    when alienable by wife and when inalienable, 221—223.
    bankruptcy of husband, effect of, 223.
    considerations for Court when allotting, 223—228.
    power to order gross or annual sum to be secured exerciseable once and for all, 228.
    instances, 228—231.
    provision for guilty wife, 231—235.
    allowance under deed of separation, effect of, as regards, 235—237.
    enforcement of order for, 237.
    husband's income, how computed, 238.
    husband's income consisting of voluntary allowance, 238, 239.
    execution of proper instrument, 239.
    dum casta et sola clause, 239, 240.
    monthly or weekly payments, 240.
    power of Court to vary order for such payments, 240.
    such allowance is inalienable by wife, 240.
    Court may direct payment to be made to wife or her trustee, 240, 241.

"ALLEGED ADULTERER." See *Adulterer*.

ALLOWANCE,
    wife in receipt of allowance from husband, alimony pending suit, 207.
    effect of, as regards permanent alimony, 235—237.
    making wife an allowance is no compliance with decree for restitution of conjugal rights, 176.
    making wife an allowance is no answer to charge of desertion, 58, 357.

AMENDMENT OF PLEADINGS,
    of petition, 350—352.
    of answer, 355.
    service of amended petition, 348.

"ANNUAL OR GROSS SUM,"
    power of Court to order husband to secure to wife, 213.
    how secured, 218, 219.
    is alienable by wife in certain cases only, 221, 222, 223.

INDEX. 431

ANSWER,
  generally, 354—358.
  when to be filed, 354.
  effect of not filing, 354.
  frame of, 354, 355.
  must be duly verified, 355.
  amendment of, 355.
  what may be pleaded in answer, 355.
  evidence not to be pleaded, 356.
  nor ante-nuptial incontinence, 356.
  nor impediment to marital intercourse supervening after marriage, 356.
  desertion on part of petitioner, 356.
  covenant not to sue when pleadable in bar, 356, 357.
  misconduct of petitioner not amounting to matrimonial offence, 357.
  answer to charge of desertion, 357.
  to suit for restitution of conjugal rights, 357.
  to charge of cruelty, 357.
  to suit for nullity of marriage, 358.
  counter-charges in, 358.
  doubt as to legal effect of plea in, 358.

ANTE-NUPTIAL INCONTINENCE is not pleadable, 39, 345, 356.

APOSTACY OF HUSBAND,
  gives jurisdiction to Court to entertain suit for dissolution, 2, 15, 16.
  is not *per se* sufficient ground for dissolving marriage, 15, 35, 39.

APPEAL,
  from orders and decrees, 300—304.
  no appeal in certain cases, 300, 301, 303.
  Court fee on memorandum of, 301.
  from decrees of district judges in Oudh, 301, 302.
  co-respondent cannot oppose appeal by respondent, 302.
  power of High Court to deal with decree of district judge, 302.
  evidence not in existence at date of decree appealed from, 302, 303.
  limitation, 303.
  no appeal merely as to costs,
  to her Majesty in Council, 303, 304.
  when wife is entitled to security for costs of appeal, 375, 376.
  alimony pending appeal, 203.

APPEARANCE OF PARTIES,
  regulated by Code of Civil Procedure, 352.
  absolute appearance admits jurisdiction, 4.
  failure of respondent to appear, 352, 353.
  of petitioner, 353.
  decree passed *in absentem*, 6, 7.

APPOINTMENT, POWER OF, when Court will vary or deprive guilty party of power, 257, 258.

ARREARS OF ALIMONY,
not provable in husband's bankruptcy, 213.
promise by wife to release, 213.
decree *nisi* will not be made absolute in favour of husband when there are, 113.

ASSESSMENT OF DAMAGES. See *Damages*.

ATHEISTS AND INFIDELS cannot claim relief under Act except in certain cases, 2, 3.

BASTARD, BIRTH OF, how far proof of adultery, 334, 335.

BESTIALITY, dissolution of marriage on ground of, 35, 41.

BIGAMY,
must be proved, criminal conviction not sufficient, 24.
how established, 24, 141—143.

" BIGAMY WITH ADULTERY,"
defined, 19, 23.
adultery not inferred from mere charge of bigamy, 24.

BOND, to secure permanent alimony, 218, 219.

" BRITISH SUBJECTS," British subjects resident in native states, applicability of Act to, 2.

BROTHEL, VISITING, how far presumptive proof of adultery, 334.

CHILDREN,
minor, defined, 19, 23, 270.
custody, maintenance and education of. See *Custody of Children*.
settlement of guilty wife's property for benefit of, 241—246.
variation of marriage settlements, not to be at expense of, 247, 265.
damages applied for benefit of, 196, 197.
provision for children of annulled marriage, 148—150.

" CHRISTIAN MARRIAGE," meaning of, 3, 4, 5.

CHRISTIAN RELIGION,
petitioner must profess, 2, 3.
perversion from, consequences of, 15, 16, 39.

CIVIL PROCEDURE CODE, proceedings to be regulated by, 281.

CLERGYMAN,
  not bound to solemnize marriages of persons divorced for adultery, 346.
  but must permit use of his church, 307.

CLOSED DOORS, proceedings may be heard with, 297.

COHABITATION,
  condonation not perfect without, 78, 79.
  condonation on part of wife not necessarily presumed from continuance of, 79, 80.
  rule of triennial, in suits for nullity *causa impotentiæ*, 131.
  withdrawal from, when amounting to desertion. See *Desertion*.
  resumption of, effect of, 154, 181.

COLLUSION,
  meaning of, 86.
  petition for dissolution or nullity of marriage, or for judicial separation, must state absence of, 281, 282.
  Court must satisfy itself of absence of collusion before decreeing dissolution of marriage, 73.
  dismissal of petition by reason of, 85 *et seq.*
  what amounts to, 86—89.
  between agents of parties, 88.
  expression of wish for divorce does not constitute, 88.
  subsequent to decree *nisi*, 88.
  must be in pending suit, 89.
  as ground for intervention, 117—120, 125, 127.
  in suit for nullity of marriage, where marriage is null and void, 127.

COMMISSION, to examine witnesses, costs of, 368.

COMMISSIONER of division to be "district judge," 18.

COMMITTEE OF LUNATIC may institute proceedings on behalf of charge, 283, 284.

COMPENSATIO CRIMINUM,
  doctrine of, 94, 95.
  in suits for restitution of conjugal rights, 185, 186.

COMPROMISE,
  of suit for dissolution, 37.
  of suit for judicial separation, 155.
  of suit for restitution of conjugal rights, 180—182.
  of suit for nullity of marriage *causa impotentiæ*, 129.

CONCURRENT JURISDICTION of High Court and district Court to entertain suits, 26.

CONDONATION,
  Court to be satisfied of absence of, before decreeing dissolution, 73.
  is a question of fact and not of law, 78.

CONDONATION—*continued.*
  meaning of, 78.
  of adultery, 78.
  of other offences, 79.
  on part of wife, 79.
  offence condoned may be revived by subsequent misconduct, 80, 81.
  is conditional, 81.
  agreement not to sue in respect of condoned offence, 81.
  pending suit or after decree *nisi*, 82.
  Court will take notice of, though not pleaded, 82.
  limited to particular offence condoned, 82.
  claim for damages after, 83.
  suit by party whose own adultery has been condoned, 83, 95.

CONFIRMATION OF DECREE,
  of district judge for dissolution of marriage, 124—127.
  of district judge for nullity of marriage, 147.

CONJUGAL RIGHTS, SUIT FOR RESTITUTION OF. See *Restitution of Conjugal Rights.*

CONNIVANCE,
  Court to be satisfied of absence of, before decreeing dissolution, 73.
  petition for dissolution or nullity or judicial separation to state absence of, 281, 282.
  what amounts to, 74, 75.
  presumption is against, 74, 76.
  delay in suing may be construed as, 77.
  operates as permanent bar to suit for dissolution, 77, 78.

CONSANGUINITY as ground for decree of nullity, 128, 135—139.

CONSENT necessary to contract of marriage, 144, 147.

CONSTRUCTIVE CRUELTY, doctrine of, 51, 52.

CONTRACT OF MARRIAGE. See *Marriage.*

CONVICTION OR ACQUITTAL IN CRIMINAL COURT, no proof in Divorce Court, 40, 339, 340.

CO-RESPONDENT,
  alleged adulterer to be made, 68—73.
  death of, pending suit, 38.
  right of, to cross-examine respondent, 296, 334, 360.
  cannot oppose appeal by respondent, 302.
  when liable for costs, 199, 376—381.
  when not liable, 199, 377—379.
  for what costs liable, 379, 380, 381.
  cannot intervene, 117.
  no provision for making alleged adulteress, 68, 69.

COSTS,
    of intervention proceedings in High Court, 110.
    when co-respondent may be ordered to pay, 199, 376—381.
    of intervention in suit in District Court, 199.
    no appeal merely as regards, 301, 303.
    next friend of minor must give undertaking as to, 285.
    discretion of Court, 362.
    wife's pending suit, 363—368.
    husband must give security for wife's, 363.
    when husband may be excused, 363—366.
    committee of lunatic husband must give security for wife's, 366.
    non-compliance with order to give security for wife's, 366, 367.
    dismissal or withdrawal of suit before hearing, 367.
    of interlocutory motions, 368.
    incurred previous to institution of suit, 368.
    wife's, after decree, 368—376.
    judgment and decree to direct, by whom payable, 368, 369.
    when wife successful in suit, 369.
    husband's liability not limited to amount of security, 369.
    amount deposited primarily liable, 369.
    wife partly successful in suit, 370.
    wife not entitled to security for costs of intervention, 371.
    wife unsuccessful in suit or defence, 371—373, 374.
    wife may in certain cases be ordered to pay costs of intervention, 371.
    taxation of wife's costs, 374, 375.
    when wife entitled to security for costs of appeal, 375, 376.
    when co-respondent liable for, 199, 376—381.
    for what costs co-respondent is liable, 379, 380.
    co-respondent condemned in, subsequent intervention, 380, 381.
    when co-respondent allowed costs, 381.
    intervenor's, when allowed or disallowed, 382, 383.

COUNTER-CHARGE,
    Court bound to inquire into, against petitioner, 73, 84.
    relief to respondent upon proof of, 107, 108.
    alleged adulterer allowed to intervene on, 108.
    of adultery, cruelty or desertion not permissible in suit for nullity, 110, 358.
    costs of wife's unfounded, 371, 373.
    what may be pleaded by way of, 355—358.

"COURT," defined, 19.

COVENANT,
    not to sue, when a bar to suit for dissolution, 37, 54, 356.
    when bar to suit for judicial separation, 155, 356.
    when bar to suit for restitution of conjugal rights, 180—182.
    not to sue for an increased allowance, 235—237, 252.
    to appoint in favour of guilty party, 259.

CRIMINAL CONVERSATION, action for, abolished, 309.

CRIMINAL COURT, conviction or acquittal in, no proof in divorce proceedings, 40, 339, 340.

CROSS-EXAMINATION,
    of husband and wife in suit by wife for dissolution, 296, 297.
    right of, as between respondent and co-respondent, 296, 334, 360.

CRUELTY,
    with adultery on part of husband, entitles wife to dissolution of marriage, 35.
    what amounts to legal, 41—54.
    charge of unnatural offence or of immorality, 44, 45.
    acts evincing lack of self-control, 45.
    single act of violence, 45.
    neglect of wife and adultery with servants, 47.
    threats, 47.
    spitting in wife's face, 48.
    communication of disease, 48, 49.
    drunkenness, 49.
    violence by lunatic, 50.
    undue familiarities with servants, 51.
    constructive, doctrine of, 51, 52.
    on part of wife, 51—53.
    is a question of fact, 53.
    condoned, may be revived, 53, 54.
        unless wife has covenanted not to sue in respect thereof, 54.
    judicial separation on account of husband's, effect of husband's subsequent adultery, 54.
    on part of petitioner generally disentitles to relief, 90, 101, 102, 153.
    when wife may sue for judicial separation by reason of husband's, 150.
    pleading acts of, 345, 346, 357.
    not pleadable as answer to suit for nullity of marriage, 358.
    on part of petitioner in suit for restitution of conjugal rights, 179, 186.

CUSTODY, EDUCATION, AND MAINTENANCE OF MINOR CHILDREN,
    power of Court to make interim orders as to, 266—268, 272—274.
    Court must be moved by separate petition, 269.
    Court fee on petition, 269.
    service of petition, 269.
    access to children pending suit, 269, 273, 274.
    no power to make orders as to, in suits for restitution of conjugal rights, 269.
    "minor children," defined, 19, 270, 271.
    intervention of third parties as to, 271, 272.
    interim orders, 272—274.
    primâ facie right of father, 272.

CUSTODY, &c. OF MINOR CHILDREN—*continued.*
 both parties must be before the Court, 273.
 application for, to be kept distinct from main question, 273.
 order as to, on or after final decree, 266—268, 274—280.
 Court has no power to make order as to, on dismissal of suit, 274.
 wide discretion of Court, 274, 275.
 general principles upon which Court acts, 275.
 primary consideration for Court, 275.
 distinction between minor sons and minor daughters, 275, 276.
 primâ facie right of innocent party, 276, 277.
 guilty father will not be deprived of all control, 277.
 guilty party will not as a rule be given custody of children, 277.
 when neither parent is fit to have custody, 278.
 subsequent variation of order as to, 278.
 enforcement of order as to, 278, 279.
 access to children after final decree, 279, 280.
 maintenance of minor children, 280.
 children of annulled marriage, 280.

CUTANEOUS DISEASE,
 communication of, when cruelty, 48, 49.
 as proof of adultery, 335.

DAMAGES,
 husband may claim, from adulterer, 187, 188.
 must be ascertained by Court, 187.
 but petition must specify amount, 188, 347.
 Court fee on petition, 188.
 awarded by District Court, power of High Court to deal with, 189.
 cannot be claimed in respect of condoned adultery, 189.
 petition limited to claim for, to be served on wife as well, 187, 189.
 absolute bars to claim for, 190.
 pleas in mitigation of, 190.
 nominal damages, 191.
 measure of damages, 191—194.
 husband's conduct to be considered, 192.
 means of co-respondent immaterial, 193.
 husband and wife living apart under a deed of separation, 193.
 non-appearance of alleged adulterer, 194.
 bankruptcy of alleged adulterer, 194.
 assignee of, right to intervene in suit, 195.
 apportionment of, 195—199.
 order for settlement of, may be made part of decree *nisi* or after decree absolute, 196.
 adding claim for, to prayer for dissolution, 352.

DEAF AND DUMB PERSON, can contract valid marriage, 141, 147.

DEATH OF PARTIES,
 of petitioner before decree absolute terminates suit for all purposes, 38, 113, 249.
 of respondent, effect of, 38.
 of co-respondent, 38.
 of wife who has obtained protection order or been judicially separated, 161, 173.

DECREE,
 of dissolution, 2, 90, 92.
 of dissolution by High Court to be decree *nisi* in first instance, 110.
 of dissolution by District Court must be confirmed by High Court, 124.
 of nullity of marriage, 2, 127.
  grounds for, 128.
  by District Court must be confirmed by High Court, 147.
 of judicial separation, 150, 152.
  reversal of, 164.
 for restitution of conjugal rights, 173.
  satisfaction of, 176.
  enforcement of, 177.
 enforcement of, and appeals from, 300—304.

DECREE ABSOLUTE,
 effect of, 122, 123.
 as regards third parties, 123, 124.
 permanent alimony may be allotted after, 215.
 variation of settlements after, 246, *et seq.*

DECREE NISI,
 decree of dissolution by High Court to be, in first instance, 110, 112.
 does not terminate suit, 112.
 is not a decree within meaning of Civil Procedure Code, s. 1 ...112.
 is appealable, 113.
 when to be made absolute, 113,
 death of petitioner or respondent after, 38, 113.
 who may apply to make absolute, 114.
 application to be supported by affidavits, 114, 115.
 notice of application to respondent or co-respondent, 115.
 when application should be made, 115.
 intervention after. See *Intervention.*

DEDUCTIONS, claimable by husband upon petition by wife for alimony, 208, 209, 238.

DEED OF SEPARATION.
 valid only if it contemplates immediate separation, 180.
 desertion impossible while parties voluntarily separated under, 61.

DEED OF SEPARATION—*continued*.
　failure to fulfil terms of, 61, 62.
　never acted upon, 62, 156.
　fraudulently obtained, 62.
　avoided by resumption of cohabitation, 63, 181.
　will not bar suit for judicial separation, 156, 356.
　　　unless it contains covenant not to sue, 155, 156, 356.
　covenant not to sue will not debar respondent from pleading petitioner's misconduct by way of answer to suit, 157.
　how far an answer to suit for restitution of conjugal rights, 180—182.
　covenant not to sue in respect of future misconduct, 157, 158, 356.
　husband and wife living apart under, effect of, upon damages awardable, 193.
　covenant not to apply for increased maintenance, 235—237, 252.
　is a post-nuptial settlement within meaning of s. 40...251, 252.

DEFINITIONS,
　"Christian Marriage," 4.
　"Domicil," 13.
　"High Court," 17, 18.
　"District Judge," 18, 19.
　"District Court," 19.
　"Court," 19.
　"Minor Children," 19.
　"Incestuous Adultery," 19.
　"Bigamy with Adultery," 19.
　"Marriage with another woman," 19.
　"Desertion," 20.
　"Property," 20.
　"Cruelty," 41.

DEGREES, PROHIBITED, marriage of persons within, 128, 135—139.

DELAY,
　unreasonable, as bar to suit for dissolution, 99—101.
　as bar to suit for nullity *propter impotentiam*, 133—135.
　as bar to suit for judicial separation, 154.
　as bar to suit for restitution of conjugal rights, 183.
　in applying for permanent alimony, 216.

DEMAND FOR COHABITATION, written, before institution of suit for restitution, 174.

DESERTION,
　defined, 20.
　coupled with adultery, ground for dissolution in suit by wife, 35.
　in suit for dissolution, must have been for two years or upwards, 35, 54.

DESERTION—*continued.*
 bonâ fide offer by husband to resume cohabitation before expiry of two years, 55, 63.
 implies abandonment, 20, 55.
 must be against actively expressed wish of other party, 55.
 separation due to husband's misconduct, 56, 57.
 separation due to wife's conduct, 57.
 facts constituting, vary, 58.
 absence on business, 58, 66.
 husband making wife an allowance, 58.
 must be a withdrawal from existing cohabitation, 59.
 separation may become, though not so at first, 60, 61.
 voluntary separation under separation deed, 61, 62.
 separation must be voluntary to constitute, 63, 64, 66.
 imprisonment of husband, 64.
 separation must have been without reasonable excuse, 65.
 what is, and what is not, reasonable cause, 65, 66, 67.
 on part of petitioner may disentitle to decree of dissolution, 90, 102, 103.
 on part of wife, no positive bar to her suit for dissolution, 109, 356.
 is a ground for judicial separation, 150.
 on part of petitioner, how far a bar to relief in suit for judicial separation, 154.
 gives wife a right to apply for protection order, 165, 169.
 how to be pleaded, 346.
 charge of, answer to, 357.

DISCOVERY, should not be required from parties to prove adultery, 358, 359.

DISCRETION OF COURT,
 in granting or refusing decree for dissolution, 93.
 when petitioner has been guilty of adultery, 83, 93—99.
  or of unreasonable delay, 99—101.
  or of cruelty, 101, 102.
  or of desertion, 102, 103.
  or of neglect or misconduct, 103, 104—107.
 in fixing time for making decree nisi absolute, 113, 114.
 in granting or refusing decree for judicial separation, 153—158.
 in suits for restitution of conjugal rights, 175, 180, 182.
 in assessing damages, 191.
 in the settlement of damages, 196.
 in allotting permanent alimony, 223 *et seq.*
 as to insertion of *dum casta* clause, 239.
 as to settlement of guilty wife's property for benefit of husband and children, 241 *et seq.*
 as to variation of settlements, 252 *et seq.*
 as to custody of minor children, 272—280.
 as to dispensing with service of petition, 290, 347—349.
 as to adjourning proceedings, 297.

DISEASE. See *Cutaneous Disease.*

INDEX. 441

DISMISSAL OF PETITION,
   for dissolution of marriage, 85, 90—107.
   by district Court does not bar petition to High Court, 85.
   for judicial separation, 152—158.
   for restitution of conjugal rights, 177—187.
   Court has no power to make orders as to custody of children upon, 274.
   of wife, costs, 367, 371.
   co-respondent not necessarily granted costs upon, 378, 379, 381.

DISSOLUTION OF MARRIAGE,
   jurisdiction of Court to decree, 2—16.
   when husband may petition for, 35.
   when wife may petition for, 35.
   alleged adulterer to be made co-respondent in suit for, 68.
   Court to be satisfied of absence of collusion in suit for, 73.
   dismissal of petition for, 85.
   power of Court to pronounce decree of, 90, 91, 93, 107.
   relief to respondent in case of opposition to suit for, 107.
   decree of, by High Court to be *nisi* in first instance, 110, 112, 113.
   decree of, by District Court to be confirmed by High Court, 124.
   petition for, contents of, 25, 67, 68.
           Court fee upon, 37.
   decree of judicial separation in suit for, 39, 92.
   Court not bound to decree, against wish of petitioner, 92, 93.
   decree absolute, effect of, 122, 123.
   does not *per se* create forfeiture under settlements, 247.

DISTRICT COURT,
   defined, 19, 22.
   matrimonial jurisdiction of, 25—28.
   to act on principles of English Divorce Court, 33.
   removal of suit from, 34.
   reference of questions to High Court by, 34.
   petitions for dissolution to, 35.
   dismissal of petition for dissolution by, 85, 89.
   confirmation of decree for dissolution of, 124, 125.
   intervention during progress of suit for dissolution, 125.
   petition for nullity to, 127.
   confirmation of decree of nullity of, 147.
   petition for judicial separation to, 152.
   reversal of decree for judicial separation by, 164.
   petition for protection order to, 165.
   discharge of protection order by, 171.
   petition for restitution of conjugal rights to, 173.
   to ascertain damages, 187.
   may order alimony, 200, 213.
   may order settlement of guilty wife's property, 241.
   may inquire into settlements, 246.
   may make orders as to custody, &c. of minor children, 266, 267.
   enforcement of, and appeals from, decrees of, 300, 301, 302.

442   INDEX.

"DISTRICT JUDGE,"
    defined, 18.
        See *District Court*.

DIVORCED PERSON,
    condition of, 122.
    right of divorced wife to retain marriage name, 122.
    re-marriage of, 304—307.

DOMICIL,
    only test of jurisdiction in suits for dissolution, 7.
    definition of, 13.
    distinct from nationality, 13.
    of origin, 13.
    of choice, 13, 14.
    of married woman, 15.
    capacity to contract valid marriage depends on parties', 135.

DRUNKENNESS,
    not *per se* legal cruelty, 49, 52, 53.
    on part of wife does not justify desertion by husband, 53, 65.

DUM CASTA ET SOLA CLAUSE, insertion of, in instrument securing wife an allowance, 289.

DURESS, power of High Court to annul marriage obtained by, 128.

ENFORCEMENT OF DECREES AND ORDERS,
    decree for restitution of conjugal rights, 177.
    generally, 300—304.

ENGLISH COURT OF DIVORCE,
    Court to act on principles of, 33.
    rules and regulations of, 384 *et seq.*

ENGLISH MARRIAGE, jurisdiction of foreign Court to dissolve, 8.

ESTOPPEL, *res judicata* in matrimonial suits, 37, 337—341.

EUROPEAN BRITISH SUBJECT defined, 20, 302.

EVIDENCE,
    of acquisition of new domicil, 14, 15.
    of bigamy with adultery, 23, 24.
    of respondent's ante-nuptial incontinence inadmissible, 39.
    of criminal conviction for offence, 40.
    of sodomy, 41.
    when Court not satisfied on the, petition to be dismissed, 85.
    when Court is satisfied on the, 90, 152.
    decree for dissolution not to be made without recording, 91.
    respondent competent to give, as to petitioner's cruelty or desertion, 108, 109.
    power of High Court to require additional, 110, 124.
    of respondent's impotency in suits for nullity, 129, 131, 132, 133.

EVIDENCE—*continued.*
    of insanity of one of the parties, 140, 141.
    of marriage in suit for restitution of conjugal rights, 175.
    what is admissible, in suits for restitution of conjugal rights, 177—187.
    of character, 190, 346.
    mode of taking, 291.
    when the parties may be compelled to give, 292, 293.
    verification of case by affidavits, 291, 294—295.
    cross-examination of respondent by co-respondent, 296.
    of husband and wife in suits by wife for dissolution, 296.
    of marriage, 326—329.
    of identification, 330, 331.
    of adultery, 332—336.
    estoppel and *res judicata,* 337—341.
    not to be pleaded, 345, 356.
    of cruelty, 345.
    examination and cross-examination of parties, 296, 360, 361.

EXAMINATION AND CROSS-EXAMINATION of parties, 296, 360, 361.

EXCUSE,
    for delay in suing. See *Delay.*
    for desertion, 65—67.
    for petitioner's own adultery, 96—98.

EXECUTION OF DECREE OR ORDER stayed pending reference to High Court, 34.

EXTENT OF ACT, 2.

FACE, spitting in wife's, 48.

FAMILIARITIES, UNDUE,
    with female servants not *per se* cruelty to wife, 51.
    wife permitting, 66.
    falling short of adultery revive condoned adultery, 80, 81.

FATHER,
    child's domicil at birth is that of the, 13.
    age of minority of child of native, 19.
    primâ facie right of, to custody of child, 23, 266—280.

FORCE,
    physical or moral, when legal cruelty, 47.
    jurisdiction of High Court to annul marriage obtained by, 128.
    marriage obtained by, void not merely voidable, 143, 144.

FOREIGN COURT,
    jurisdiction of, to dissolve marriage, 8—10.
    judgment and decree of, how far *res judicata,* 340, 341.

INDEX.

Formâ Pauperis,
husband suing in, for restitution, 182.
wife suing in, costs payable by husband, 369.
costs of husband's suing in, 380.

Forms,
of petitions, statements, &c., 311—322.
prescribed by rules of English Divorce Court, 413—426.
intended merely as examples, 281.
of decrees for restitution of conjugal rights, 176.

Fraud,
deed of separation obtained by, 62.
jurisdiction of High Court to annul marriage obtained by, 128.
marriage obtained by, void and not merely voidable, 143, 144.

Gross or Annual Sum,
power of Court to award as permanent alimony, 213.
how secured, 219.
when alienable, 221—223.

Guardian
of children, application to vary settlement by, 249.
of lunatic, suits by, 283—285.
of minor, suit by, 285—290.

Guilty Party,
not entitled to apply to make decree *nisi* absolute, 114.
not entitled to intervene, 117.
wife, settlement of her property in favour of husband and children, 241—246.
wife, permanent provision for, 231.
not entitled to apply for variation of settlements, 250.
interests of, in marriage settlements, 259—265.
not entitled ordinarily to custody of children, 277—279.
wife, costs of, 371—374.

Hearing Case in Camerâ, 297.

High Court,
defined, 17, 18.
jurisdiction of, 25.
to act on principles of English Divorce Court, 33.
extraordinary jurisdiction of, 33, 34.
reference to, 34.
petitions to, 35, 85, 127, 152, 165, 173, 187.
decree for dissolution to be *nisi*, 110.
intervention proceedings in, 110.
may make decree absolute, or reverse decree *nisi*, or require further evidence, 110.
discretion as to costs of intervention, 110.

INDEX. 445

HIGH COURT—*continued.*
    may dismiss suit in default of application to make decree *nisi* absolute, 111.
    to confirm decrees of dissolution by district judges, 124.
    may direct further inquiry before confirming decree, 124.
    during suit in district Court intervenor may apply to, for removal of suit, 125.
    may remove suits from district Court or direct district judge to take steps, 125.
    jurisdiction of, to make decree of nullity on ground of force or fraud not affected by sect. 19...128.
    to confirm decree of nullity by district Court, 147.
    power of, to order permanent alimony, 213.
    may inquire into existence of settlements, 246.
    power of, to make orders as to custody of children, 266, 267.
    may direct manner of service of petitions, 290.
    no appeal from order of, confirming or refusing to confirm decree, 301, 303.
    appeal to Privy Council from order of, 303, 304.
    power of, to make rules, 309.

HUSBAND AND WIFE, when competent and compellable witnesses, 292, 293, 296.

HUSBAND,
    apostacy of, gives Court jurisdiction in suits for dissolution, 2, 15, 16.
    domicil of, 6, 7, 11, 15.
    primâ facie right of, to custody of children, 23.
    when may petition for dissolution of marriage, 35.
    when wife may petition for dissolution against, 35.
    apostacy of, and marriage with another woman, 39.
    must make alleged adulterer co-respondent, 68.
    connivance on part of, 74, 75.
    condonation of offence by, 78, 79.
    collusion by, 86—89.
    relief to wife in suit for dissolution by, 107.
    relief to, in suit by wife for dissolution, 107—109.
    not entitled to decree absolute until arrears of alimony are paid, 113.
    when may sue for nullity of marriage, 127, 128.
    when may obtain decree of judicial separation, 150—158.
    loses all interest in property of wife after decree of judicial separation, 158, 161.
    when liable for necessaries supplied to wife after decree of judicial separation, 162.
    when may petition for reversal of decree of separation, 164.
    wife deserted by, may apply for protection order, 165.
    may apply for discharge of protection order, 171.
    effect of protection order as regards the, 171.
    may apply for restitution of conjugal rights, 173—187.
    may claim damages from adulterer, 187—199.
    alimony *pendente lite* payable by, 200—213.
    permanent alimony payable by, 213—240.

HUSBAND—*continued.*
    settlement of guilty wife's property for benefit of children and husband, 241—246.
    rights of, as to custody of minor children, 266—280.
    suit on behalf of, or against, lunatic, 283, 284.
                          minor, 285—290.
    when competent or compellable witness, 291—293, 296.
    liability for wife's costs, 363—376.
    liability of co-respondent for costs of, 376—382.

IDENTIFICATION OF PARTIES, 330, 331, 339.

IDIOT,
    nullity of marriage on ground that either party was an, at time of marriage, 128.
    custody of child who is an, 277.
    suit by, or against, 283.

IGNORANCE OF FACT, adultery committed by petitioner in, 96.

IGNORANCE OF LAW,
    adultery committed by petitioner in, 96.
    as excuse for delay in suing, 100.

IMPOTENCY of either party to marriage, ground for nullity, 128—135.

IMPRISONMENT,
    husband undergoing, may yet be guilty of desertion, 63, 64.
    wife undergoing, entitled to alimony *pendente lite*, 205.

IN CAMERÂ, proceedings may be heard, 297.

INCESTUOUS ADULTERY,
    defined, 19, 23, 139.
    as ground for dissolution of marriage, 35, 40.
    condoned, may be revived by subsequent adultery, 81.

INCOME OF HUSBAND, computation of, for purposes of allotting alimony, 207—209, 238.

INCONTINENCE, ANTE-NUPTIAL, not pleadable, 39, 345, 356.

INFORMALITY of marriage, Court cannot decree nullity on ground of, 129, 187, 324.

INJUNCTION,
    to restrain husband from dissipating his property, 212, 220.
    to restrain husband or wife from disposing of property pending inquiry under sect. 40...251.

INSANITY,
    of respondent in suit for dissolution, 38, 39.
    cruelty committed under influence of, 50.
    of party at time of marriage as ground for decree of nullity, 128, 139—141.

INSANITY—*continued.*
    children of marriage annulled on ground of, 148.
    of petitioner, in suit for restitution of conjugal rights, 183.
    of husband or wife, 283, 284.

INSPECTION, when allowed, 358, 359.

INSPECTORS, MEDICAL, appointment of, in suits for nullity *causâ impotentiæ*, 132, 133.

INTEMPERANCE,
    does not *per se* amount to legal cruelty, 49, 52, 53.
    on part of wife does not justify desertion by husband, 65.

INTERCOURSE, MARITAL,
    wilful refusal of, may justify separation, 66.
    may be ground for decree of nullity, 133.

INTERIM ORDERS,
    as to alimony, 200—213.
    as to custody of children, 266, 272—274.

INTERROGATORIES, and discovery of documents, 358.

INTERVENTION,
    in suits for dissolution of marriage in High Court, 110, 116.
    permissible at any time before decree *nisi* is made absolute, 116.
    who may intervene, 116, 117.
    grounds of, 117—121.
    "material facts not being brought before the Court," 118—120.
    reconciliation of parties after decree *nisi*, 120, 121, 126.
    evidence of adultery pleaded by intervenor, 121, 331.
    prevents withdrawal of petition, 121.
    admissions by, or non-appearance of, petitioner upon, 122.
    in suits for dissolution in District Court, 125, 126.
    not permissible in suit for nullity, 127, 147, 148.
    power of Court to order intervenor to pay costs, 199, 382, 383.
    when co-respondent will be ordered to pay costs of, 380, 382.
    effect of, as regards order in decree *nisi* to pay costs, 370.
    wife not entitled to security for costs incidental to, 371.
    of third parties, upon questions as to custody of children, 271, 272.

INTESTACY,
    of wife judicially separated, 161.
    of wife who had obtained protection order, 173.

JACTITATION OF MARRIAGE, Courts have no power to entertain suit in respect of, 25.

JOINT,
    income of husband and wife in question of alimony, 205, 209, 223.
    power of appointment, variation of, 257, 258.
    separated wife may join in exercise of joint power, 162.

JUDICIAL SEPARATION,
    when decreed in suits for dissolution, 39, 151, 351.
    grounds for, 150.
    at prayer of respondent in suit for restitution of conjugal rights, 151.
    application for, to be made by petition, 152.
    bars to relief, 152—158.
        (a) petitioner's adultery, 153.
        (b) petitioner's cruelty, 153.
        (c) petitioner's desertion, 154.
        (d) petitioner's delay in suing, 154.
        (e) petitioner's misconduct or neglect, 155.
        (f) petitioner's covenant not to sue, 155.
        (g) *res judicata*, 158.
    position of wife after decree of, 158—163.
    reversal of decree of, 164, 165.
    husband may claim damages in suit for, 187.
    in suit for, adulterer may be ordered to pay costs, 199.
    wife entitled to alimony pending suit for, 200.
    when wife entitled to permanent alimony after decree of, 217, 218.
    permanent alimony inalienable when granted after decree of, 221.
    wife in receipt of allowance under deed of separation applying for increase of maintenance after decree of, 235, 236.
    power of Court to order settlement of guilty wife's property after decree of, 241.
    power of Court to inquire into, and vary, settlements after decree of, 246.
    power of Court to make orders as to custody of children in suits for, 266.
    petition for, to state absence of collusion and to be verified, 281, 282.
    suit for, on behalf of lunatic or minor, 283—290.
    service of petition for, 290, 347—349.
    enforcement of, and appeal from decree of, 300—304.
    decree for, effect of, as regards persons dealing with wife, 307, 308.
    prayer for dissolution substituted for prayer for, 352.

JURISDICTION,
    to grant any relief under Act, 2, 3—7, 25.
    to decree dissolution of marriage, 2, 7—16, 26, 36.
    to decree nullity of marriage, 2, 17.
    party estopped from denying, 12, 13.
    Courts have no jurisdiction to make decrees of legitimacy or to entertain suits in respect of jactitation of marriage, 25.
    objections to, 31, 32.
    Court not debarred from granting alimony pending suit by reason of objection to, 32.
    facts giving Court, to appear on face of record, 27.
    extraordinary, of High Court, 33.
    of High Court to annul marriage on ground of force or fraud, 128, 143.

LEAVE TO APPEAL to Privy Council, 303, 304.

LEGITIMACY,
Courts have no jurisdiction to make decrees of, 25.
as regards children of annulled marriage, 148, 149.

LEX LOCI CELEBRATIONIS, importance of, as regards formalities of marriage, 323.

LIS,
decree *nisi* does not terminate, 112.
no *lis pendens* before decree *nisi* as regards settlements, 255.
suit for restitution of conjugal rights pending suit for dissolution, &c., 183.

LOLLEY'S CASE, what was actually decided in, 8.

LUMP SUM, when decreed as permanent alimony, alienability of, 221—223.

LUNACY. See *Insanity*.

MAINTENANCE OF CHILDREN,
damages recovered ordered to be settled for, 195.
by wife, no ground for allotting increased alimony, 224.
by husband, as regards amount of alimony *pendente lite* to wife, 209.
guilty wife's property may be settled for, 241.
variation of settlements to provide for, 246, 265.
custody, maintenance and education of children, 266—280.

MAINTENANCE OF WIFE. See *Alimony*.
does not alter character of desertion, 58, 65.
no sufficient compliance with decree for restitution, 176.

MAKING DECREE NISI ABSOLUTE, 113—115.

MARRIAGE,
"in Christendom," meaning of, 3—6.
English, dissolubility of, 8.
with another woman, 19, 24, 35.
bigamous, how proved, 23.
not dissolved until decree absolute, 112.
capacity to contract valid, depends on *lex domicilii*, 135.
jactitation of, suit in respect of, 25.
must be proved before Court can decree restitution of conjugal rights, 175.
validity of, 135—139, 323—326.
proof of, 326—329.
presumption in favour of, 128, 326.

MARRIAGE, DISSOLUTION OF. See *Dissolution of Marriage*.

MARRIAGE-NAME, right of divorced wife to retain, 122.

MARRIAGE, NULLITY OF. See *Nullity of Marriage*.

MARRIAGE SETTLEMENTS. See *Settlements.*

MARRIED WOMEN'S PROPERTY ACT (INDIA) OF 1874...159.

"MATERIAL FACTS NOT BROUGHT TO KNOWLEDGE OF COURT," 118—120.

"MATRIMONIAL HOME," 9.

MEANS,
    of husband, in questions as to amount of alimony *pendente lite*, 206, 210.
    wife having sufficient, of her own, alimony *pendente lite*, 206.
    of co-respondent, not to be considered in assessing damages, 193.

MEDICAL INSPECTORS. See *Inspectors, Medical.*

MINOR,
    age of majority, 285.
    suits by or against, 285—290.

"MINOR CHILDREN,"
    defined, 19, 23, 270.
    custody, maintenance and education of, 266—280.

MISCONDUCT,
    of petitioner, as bar to suit for dissolution, 90, 103—107, 357.
    of petitioner, no bar to suit for nullity, 358.
    of petitioner, as bar to suit for judicial separation, 155.
    of petitioner, as bar to suit for restitution of conjugal rights, 178—180.
    of wife, as disentitling to alimony, 205, 206, 231—234.
    of husband, as disentitling him to rely on deed of separation, 236, 237.
    of husband, as disentitling him to costs, 378, 379.
    of wife's solicitor, costs, 373.

MONTHLY OR WEEKLY PAYMENTS,
    as permanent provision for wife, 213.
    nature of, 221, 222, 240.

MOTHER, when given custody of children. See *Custody of Children.*

NAME, MARRIAGE, right of divorced wife to retain, 122.

NATIVE FATHER, age of majority of children of, 19.

NECESSARIES, supplied to wife judicially separated, 162, 163.

NEGLECT,
    neglect of wife does not constitute legal cruelty, 47.
    on part of petitioner may act as bar to decree of dissolution, 90, 103—106.
    on part of petitioner may act as bar to decree of judicial separation, 155.

INDEX. 451

NEW TRIAL, no provision for, in Indian law, 28.

NEXT FRIEND may sue on behalf of minor, 285—289.

NON-REGULATION PROVINCES,
"High Court," for, 17, 18.
"District Court" for, 18, 19.

NOTICE,
of application to make decree *nisi* absolute, 115.
liability of husband seizing wife's property after notice of protection order, 171.
of application to vary settlements, 248, 249.
of application for custody of children, 269, 349.
decree for separation or protection to be valid as to persons dealing with wife without notice of reversal, 307, 308.

NULLITY OF MARRIAGE,
jurisdiction to decree, 2, 17, 128.
respondent may not plead petitioner's adultery, &c., 110, 127, 358.
who may sue for, 127.
collusion between parties, 127, 281.
Court fee on petition for, 127.
ceremony of marriage must be proved in suit for, 128.
grounds for, 128, 129.
decree for, in England is decree *nisi* at first, 128.
Court cannot entertain suit for, otherwise than as provided by Act, 128.
on ground of impotency, 129—135.
impotency of petitioner, 129.
marriage only voidable, not void, 129.
suit for, on ground of impotency, can be compromised, 129.
age of parties, 130.
what constitutes impotency, 130.
impotency *quoad hunc vel hanc,* 131.
burden of proof, 131.
triennial cohabitation, 131.
evidence of impotency, 132, 133.
presumption of impotency, 133.
delay in suing suggestive of insincerity, 133, 134.
marriage within prohibited degrees, 135—139.
capacity to contract valid marriage, 135.
consanguinity or affinity, 139.
lunacy or idiocy of party to marriage, 139—141.
person subject to delusions, 140.
burden of proof, 140.
supervening lunacy, 140.
marriage of deaf and dumb person, 141.
suit by committee of lunatic, 141.
marriage of person already married, 141—143.
bigamy, 141, 142.
burden of proof, 142.
re-marriage of divorced person before expiry of appointed time, 142, 143.

G G 2

452 INDEX.

NULLITY OF MARRIAGE—*continued.*
    fraud or force as affecting marriage, 143—147.
    deceit as to position and means, 147.
    mistake, 147.
    decree of, by district judge, to be confirmed, 147, 148.
    no provision for intervention in suits for, 148.
    children of annulled marriage, 148—150, 251, 280.
    alimony *pendente lite* in suit for, 201.
    variation of settlements upon decree of, 246, 250, 251.
    orders as to custody, &c. of children in suits for, 266—280.
    husband to give security for wife's costs in suit for, 363.

OFFER to return to cohabitation before expiry of two years' desertion, 55, 57, 63.

"OMNIA PRÆSUMUNTUR RITE ESSE ACTA," presumption in favour of marriage, 128, 326.

ORDERS,
    enforcement of, and appeals from, 300—304.
    See *Alimony; Custody of Children; Protection Order; Settlements.*

ORIGIN, DOMICIL OF. See *Domicil.*

PANJAB,
    "High Court," for, 17, 18.
    "District judge," in, 20.

PARTICULARS, order for further, 355, 358.

PARTIES,
    domicil of, as affecting jurisdiction, 6—16.
    death of one of the, 38, 113.
    collusion between, 85—89, 120, 125.
    both guilty of adultery, 83, 93—99, 153, 184—186.
    costs of intervention may be ordered to be paid by, 110.
    reconciliation of, after decree *nisi*, 120, 121, 126.
    effect of decree absolute as regards the, 122—124.
    to suit for nullity of marriage, 127.
    to marriage within prohibited degrees, 128, 135—139.
    adulterer liable for costs when made party to suit, 199.
    to petition for variation of settlements, 248, 249.
    intervention of third, on application for custody of children, 271, 272.
    lunacy or idiocy of either of the, 283, 284.
    minority of either of the, 285—290.
    when competent or compellable witnesses, 291—297, 360, 361.
    re-marriage of the, after divorce, 304—307.
    evidence of, as to marriage, 327, 328.

INDEX. 453

PARTIES—*continued*.
    identity of, 330, 331, 339.
    appearance of, at hearing, 352, 353.
    costs as between the, 362—383,
    co-respondent not "a party" to an intervention, 382.

PAUPER,
    suit for restitution by husband who is a, 182.
    petitioner, costs of, 369, 380.
    husband excused from payment of alimony pending suit, 206.
    payment of monthly or weekly sums not confined to, 240.
    security for wife's costs from, 367.

PENDENTE LITE, ALIMONY. See *Alimony pending Suit*.

PERMANENT ALIMONY. See *Alimony, Permanent*.

PERSONAL REPRESENTATIVE, of petitioner not entitled to apply to make decree *nisi* absolute, 113.

PERSONAL SERVICE, of petition, 347—349.

PETITION,
    petitioner must profess Christianity and reside in India at time of presenting, 2.
    for dissolution of marriage, 35.
    alleged adulterer to be made co-respondent to, 68.
    Court to be satisfied of absence of collusion, 73.
    dismissal of, 85.
    petitioner may present similar, to High Court, 85.
    intervention prevents withdrawal of, 121.
    for nullity of marriage, 127.
    for judicial separation, 150, 152.
    for reversal of decree of separation, 164, 347.
    for protection order, 165.
    for restitution of conjugal rights, 173.
    for damages, 187, 347.
    for alimony pendente lite, 200.
    for permanent alimony, 215.
    for variation of settlements, 247.
    for custody of children, 269.
    to be verified and to state absence of collusion or connivance, 281, 282.
    service of, 290, 347—349.
    adjournment of hearing of, 297.
    evidence of adultery not pleaded in, 336.
    pleadings, 342—346.
    withdrawal of, 121, 349, 350.
    amendment of, 350—352.

PETITIONER,
    must profess Christianity and reside in India at time of presenting petition, 2.
    lunatic or idiot or minor, 36, 283—288.

PETITIONER—*continued.*
    death of, 38.
    connivance or collusion on part of, 73, 74.
    guilty of adultery, 83, 93—99, 119, 135, 153, 184—186, 336.
    counter-charge against, 84.
    guilty of delay in suing, 99—101, 133—135, 154, 183, 216.
    guilty of cruelty, 90, 101, 102, 153, 179, 186, 358.
    guilty of desertion, 90, 102, 103, 109, 154, 356.
    guilty of wilful neglect or misconduct, 90, 103—107, 155, 178—180, 205, 206, 358.
    agent of, bringing about respondent's adultery, 106, 107.
    condonation by, 78—83.
    impotency of, 129.
    covenant by, not to sue, 155, 180.
    appearance of, 352, 353.
    admissions by, or non-appearance of, upon intervention, 122.

PHOTOGRAPH, identification by, 330, 331.

PLEADINGS,
    to state facts succinctly, 342.
    pleading adultery, 343—345.
        cruelty, 345, 346.
        desertion, 346, 347.
    answer to petition, 354—358.
        for alimony, 207—209.
    amendment of, 350—352, 358.

POLYGAMOUS UNION not marriage for purposes of Act, 4, 5.

POST-NUPTIAL SETTLEMENT, deed of separation is a, for purposes of sect. 40...251.

POWER OF APPOINTMENT, when Court will vary, or deprive guilty party of, 257—259.

PRACTICE, notes on matters relating to, 342—361.

PRESUMPTION,
    is against connivance, 74.
        condonation, 78, 79.
    in favour of validity of marriage, 128, 326.

PRINCIPAL responsible for acts of agent, 73, 74, 88, 106, 107.

PRIVY COUNCIL, appeal to, 303, 304.

PROCEDURE, CODE OF CIVIL, to regulate proceedings under Act, 281.

PROHIBITED DEGREES of consanguinity or affinity, 135—139.

PROPERTY,
    defined, 20, 161.
    injunction to restrain husband dissipating, 212, 220, 251.
    order protecting property of wife, 165—173.

PROPERTY—*continued.*
   of wife acquired after judicial separation, 158—161.
   of husband, computation of, for purposes of alimony, 207—210, 238.
   power of Court to order settlement of guilty wife's, 241—246.
   wife possessed of separate, costs, 363, 373, 374.

PROSTITUTE,
   wife living as, husband excused from making adulterer co-respondent, 68—71.
   adulterer not liable for costs when wife leading life of, 199.
   evidence of, 336.

PROTECTION ORDER,
   when deserted wife may apply for, 165.
   Court fee on petition, 168.
   affidavit in support of petition for, 168.
   petition to be served on husband, 168.
   desertion need not have been for two years, 169.
   property covered by order, 169.
   order to be in general terms, 170.
   discharge or variation of order, 171.
   application for discharge may be made at any time, 171.
   liability of husband seizing wife's property after notice of, 171.
   wife's legal position during continuance of, 171.
   has retrospective effect, 172.
   continuing liability of husband after, 172, 173.
   death of wife intestate after, 173.
   reversal of, as regards persons dealing with wife, 307, 308.

QUEEN'S PROCTOR, no corresponding official in India, 93.

QUOAD HUNC VEL HANC, impotency, 131.

RAPE,
   is ground for dissolution on wife's petition, 40.
   proof of conviction for, not sufficient, 40.

REASONABLE CAUSE, for leaving wife, 65—67.

RECONCILIATION OF PARTIES, after decree *nisi*, 120, 121, 126.

REDUCTION OF ALIMONY, power of Court to reduce amount of alimony *pendente lite*, 209.

REFERENCE TO HIGH COURT, by district Court, 34.

REFUSAL OF MARITAL RIGHTS,
   may excuse husband's desertion, 66.
   may raise presumption of impotency, 133.

REGULATION PROVINCES,
  High Court in, 17.
  District Court in, 18.

RELIEF,
  bargaining away right to, 62, 155, 156, 180, 182, 356.
  to respondent in suits for dissolution, 107—110.

REMARRIAGE,
  of persons after divorce, 142, 143, 304—306.
  can divorced persons intermarry again, 306.
  clergyman not bound to solemnize marriage of guilty party, 306, 307.

REMOVAL OF SUITS, power of High Court to order, 33, 34, 125.

REPLY. See *Answer*.

RESIDENCE,
  petitioner must have, in India, 2, 6—12.
  meaning of term, 21, 22.
  fact of, should be set out in judgment, 22.
  of husband and wife within jurisdiction of Court, 18, 19.

RES JUDICATA, in matrimonial suits, 336—341.

RESPONDENT,
  death of, 38.
  insanity of, 38, 39, 283.
  leading life of prostitute, 68, 71, 199.
  minority of, 289, 290.
  relief to, in suits for dissolution, 107—110.
  impotency of, in suits for nullity, 129.
  decree against, *in absentem*, 6, 7.
  may not intervene, 117.
  cannot apply to make decree *nisi* absolute, 114.

RESTITUTION OF CONJUGAL RIGHTS,
  Court cannot decree in suit for dissolution, 109.
  application for, when to be made, 173.
  Court fee on petition, 174.
  previous written demand for cohabitation, 174.
  marriage must first be proved, 175.
  alimony pending suit for, 175.
  motives of petitioner, 175.
  after decree for, husband respondent must take initiative, 176.
  allowance to wife not sufficient compliance with decree for, 176.
  form of decree, 176.
  satisfaction of decree, 176, 177.
  answer to suit for, 177, 356.
  what may be pleaded by way of answer to suit for, 177—187, 356.
  respondent may plead that separation was for good cause, 178.
  covenant not to sue for, 180—182.

INDEX. 457

RESTITUTION OF CONJUGAL RIGHTS—*continued.*
    poverty of husband petitioner, 182.
    husband's change of religion, 182.
    delay in suing for, 183.
    insanity of petitioner, 183.
    petition for, pending suit by respondent, 183, 184.
    right to begin, 184.
    doctrine of *compensatio criminis*, 185, 186.
    petitioner guilty of cruelty or desertion, 186.
    marriage null and void, 187.

RESTRAINT UPON ANTICIPATION, decree of judicial separation removes, 160, 161.

RETURN,
    bonâ fide offer by husband to resume cohabitation after separation, 55, 63.
    wife willing to, but under reasonable conditions, 57.

REVERSAL OF DECREE,
    of judicial separation, 164, 165, 347.
    of protection, 171.
    effect of reversal as to persons dealing with wife, 307, 308.

REVIEW OF JUDGMENT, 28—31.

REVIVAL of condoned offence, 80—81.

RULES,
    power of High Court to make, 309, 310.
    of English Divorce Court, 384—426.

SCHEDULE OF FORMS, 311—322.

SECURITY FOR COSTS. See *Costs.*

SEPARATE PROPERTY,
    wife possessed of, costs, 363, 373, 374.
    acquired by wife after judicial separation, 158—161.
    of wife, covered by protection order, 165—173.

SEPARATION DEED. See *Deed of Separation.*

SERVICE OF PETITION, 290, 291, 347—349.

SETTLEMENTS, MARRIAGE,
    of guilty wife's property for benefit of husband or children, 241, 242.
    no power under sect. 39 to deal with marriage settlements, 243.
    wife entitled to property without power of anticipation, 243, 244.
    spes successionis not property, 244, 245.
    property acquired by wife after decree *nisi*, 245.
    Court will not make allowance to husband variable, 246.
        nor enter into accounts between husband and wife, 246.

R.   H H

SETTLEMENTS, MARRIAGE—*continued.*
 when Court may inquire into existence of settlements, 246—266.
 dissolution of marriage does not entail forfeiture under, 247.
 inquiry made by Court only on petition, 247.
 Court fee on petition, 247.
 contents of petition, 248.
 when petition to be filed, 248.
 service of petition, 248.
 who may apply, 249, 250.
 variation of, after judicial separation or decree of nullity, 250.
 injunction to restrain dealing with property pending inquiry, 251.
 what are marriage settlements, 251.
 discretion of Court in dealing with, 252, 253.
 considerations for Court, 253—256.
 conduct of parties to be considered, 254.
 no variation of, for collateral purpose, 254.
 interests of third parties in, 255, 256.
 finality of order, 256.
 dividends due before order made, 256.
 property includes capital as well as income, 257.
 annuity under deed of separation, 257.
 wife's power of appointment among children, 257.
 husband's power of appointment, 258.
 power of appointing new trustees, 258.
 variation of, guilty husband, 259—261.
 guilty wife, 261—264.
 variation of deeds of separation, 264, 265.
 no variation at expense of children, 265.
 costs of application to vary, 265.

SODOMY or bestiality, ground for dissolution on wife's petition, 35, 41.

SPITTING IN WIFE'S FACE, legal cruelty or not, 48.

STATUS, question of divorce is incident of, 9.

STAY OF PROCEEDINGS,
 on husband's failure to give security for costs, 366, 367.
 as regards alimony, 216.

SUBSTITUTED SERVICE, when Court will allow, 347.

SUCCESSION ACT (INDIA), 165, 167, 168, 364.

SUIT,
 abatement of, 38, 113.
 compromise of, 37, 129.
 decree *nisi* does not terminate, 112.
 withdrawal of, 121, 349, 350.
 dismissal of, 85.

SUPREME COURT, enforcement of decrees made by, 32.

TAXATION OF COSTS of wife, 374, 375.

THIRD PARTIES, intervention as to custody of children, 271, 272.

THREATS,
do not amount to legal cruelty, 47, 48.
adultery of wife due to husband's, 97.
marriage obtained by, 144—147.

TRIENNIAL COHABITATION, in suits for nullity *causa impotentiæ*,
rule as to, 130, 131.

TRUSTEES, power of appointing new, 258.

TWO YEARS, statutory period for desertion, 35, 54, 150.

UNDERTAKING AS TO COSTS by next friend of minor, 285, 286.

UNDUE DELAY may suggest want of sincerity or connivance,
99, 100, 132—135, 154.

VALIDITY OF MARRIAGE,
as to *essentialia*, 135—139.
as to formalities, 323.

VARIATION OF SETTLEMENTS. See *Settlements*.

VENEREAL DISEASE,
communication of, when legal cruelty, 48, 49.
as proof of adultery, 335.

VERIFICATION of petitions, 281—283.

VEXATIOUS SUITS BY WIFE, ground for allotting her less than
usual amount of alimony *pendente lite*, 206.

VOIDABLE MARRIAGE,
on ground of impotency, 129.
as to fraud or duress, 143, 144.

WAGES, husband in receipt of weekly, only, alimony *pendente
lite*, 211.

WANT OF MEANS, as excuse for delay in suing, 100.

WEEKLY OR MONTHLY PAYMENTS,
power of Court to order, as provision for wife, 213, 214, 240.
inalienability of, 220—223.

WIFE,
domicil of, 15.
property of, 20, 158—161, 165—173.
when may apply for dissolution of marriage, 35.

WIFE—*continued.*
    ante-nuptial incontinence of, 39, 345—356.
    uncorroborated evidence of, as to sodomy, 41.
    cruelty on part of, 51, 52.
    misconduct on part of, may excuse husband's desertion, 37, 66, 67.
    entitled to husband's society and protection, 58.
    connivance on part of, 75.
    condonation by, 79.
    adultery by, due to husband's compulsion, 97.
    may apply for nullity of marriage, 127, 128.
            for judicial separation, 150, 152.
    after judicial separation, to be deemed *feme sole*, 158—163.
    when deserted, may apply for protection order, 165—173.
    may apply for restitution of conjugal rights, 163—187.
    petition for damages against adulterer to be served on, 187.
    alimony *pendente lite*, 200—213.
    permanent alimony, 213—241.
    property of guilty, may be settled on husband and children, 241—246.
    variation of settlements as regards a, 246—266.
    rights of, as to custody of children, 266—280.
    lunatic or idiot, suit by or against, 283—285.
    minor, suit by or against, 285—290.
    when competent or compellable witness, 291—297, 360, 361.
    as to persons dealing with, after judicial separation or protection order, 307, 308.
    costs of, or against, 362—376.

WITHDRAWAL OF PETITION,
    intervention prevents, 121.
    when permissible, 349, 350.

www.ingramcontent.com/pod-product-compliance
Lightning Source LLC
Chambersburg PA
CBHW051851300426
44117CB00006B/344